Egerton Ryerson, J. George Hodgins

The story of my life

Egerton Ryerson, J. George Hodgins

The story of my life

ISBN/EAN: 9783742858429

Manufactured in Europe, USA, Canada, Australia, Japa

Cover: Foto ©ninafisch / pixelio.de

Manufactured and distributed by brebook publishing software (www.brebook.com)

Egerton Ryerson, J. George Hodgins

The story of my life

"THE STORY OF MY LIFE."

BY THE LATE

REV. EGERTON RYERSON, D.D., LLD.,

(BEING REMINISCENCES OF SIXTY YEARS' PUBLIC SERVICE IN CANADA.)

PREPARED UNDER THE SUPERVISION OF HIS LITERARY TRUSTEES:
THE REV. S. S. NELLES, D.D., LL.D., THE REV. JOHN POTTS, D.D., AND J. GEORGE HODGINS, ESQ., LL.D.

EDITED BY

J. GEORGE HODGINS, Esq., LL.D.

" His life was gentle ; and the elements
So mix't in him, that Nature might stand up,
And say to all the world, This was a Man !"
—SHAKESPEARE. *Julius Cæsar*, Act v., sc. 5.

Justum et tenacem propositi virum
Non civium ardor prava jubentium,
Non vultus instantis tyranni
Mente quatit solida—
—HORACE. *Odes*, iii. 3.

WITH PORTRAIT AND ENGRAVINGS.

TORONTO:
WILLIAM BRIGGS, 78 AND 80 KING STREET EAST.
1884.

CONTENTS.

	PAGE
PREFACE	ix
ESTIMATE OF REV. DR. RYERSON'S CHARACTER AND LABOURS	17

CHAPTER I.—1803-1825.
Sketch of Early Life.. 28

CHAPTER II.—1824-1825.
Extracts from Dr. Ryerson's Diary of 1824 and 1825 32

CHAPTER III.—1825-1826.
First Year of Ministry and First Controversy........................ 47

CHAPTER IV.—1826-1827.
Missionary to the River Credit Indians.............................. 58

CHAPTER V.—1826-1827.
Diary of Labours among Indians 64

CHAPTER VI.—1827-1828.
Labours and Trials.—Civil Rights Controversy....................... 80

CHAPTER VII.—1828-1829.
Ryanite Schism.—M. E. Church of Canada organized................... 87

CHAPTER VIII.—1829-1832.
Establishment of the *Christian Guardian.*—Church Claims resisted...... 93

CHAPTER IX.—1831-1832.
Methodist Affairs in Upper Canada.—Proposed Union with the British Conference 107

CHAPTER X.—1833.
Union between the British and Canadian Conferences................. 114

CHAPTER XI.—1833-1834.
"Impressions of England" and their effects......................... 121

CHAPTER XII.—1834.
Events following the Union.—Division and Strife.................... 141

CHAPTER XIII.—1834-1835.
Second Retirement from the *Guardian* Editorship................... 144

CHAPTER XIV.—1835–1836.
Second Mission to England.—Upper Canada Academy 152

CHAPTER XV.—1835–1836.
The "Grievance" Report; Its Object and Failure 155

CHAPTER XVI.—1836–1837.
Dr. Ryerson's Diary of his Second Mission to England 158

CHAPTER XVII.—1836.
Publication of the Hume and Roebuck Letters 167

CHAPTER XVIII.—1836–1837.
Important Events transpiring in England 170

CHAPTER XIX.—1837–1839.
Return to Canada.—The Chapel Property Cases 172

CHAPTER XX.—1837.
The Coming Crisis.—Rebellion of 1837 175

CHAPTER XXI.—1837–1838.
Sir F. B. Head and the Upper Canada Academy 179

CHAPTER XXII.—1838.
Victims of the Rebellion.—State of the Country 182

CHAPTER XXIII.—1795–1861.
Sketch of Mr. William Lyon Mackenzie 185

CHAPTER XXIV.—1838.
Defence of the Hon. Marshall Spring Bidwell 188

CHAPTER XXV.—1838.
Return to the Editorship of the *Guardian* 199

CHAPTER XXVI.—1838–1840.
Enemies and Friends Within and Without............................... 205

CHAPTER XXVII.—1778–1867.
The Honourable and Right Reverend Bishop Strachan.................... 213

CHAPTER XXVIII.—1791–1836.
The Clergy Reserves and Rectories Questions........................... 218

CHAPTER XXIX.—1838.
The Clergy Reserve Controversy Renewed 225

CHAPTER XXX.—1838–1839.
The Ruling Party and the Reserves.—"Divide et Impera."................ 236

CHAPTER XXXI.—1839.
Strategy in the Clergy Reserve Controversy............................. 245

CHAPTER XXXII.—1839.
Sir G. Arthur's Partisanship.—State of the Province..................... 250

CONTENTS.

CHAPTER XXXIII.—1838-1840.
The New Era.—Lord Durham and Lord Sydenham 257

CHAPTER XXXIV.—1840.
Proposal to leave Canada.—Dr. Ryerson's Visit to England 269

CHAPTER XXXV.—1840-1841.
Last Pastoral Charge.—Lord Sydenham's Death 282

CHAPTER XXXVI.—1841.
Dr. Ryerson's Attitude toward the Church of England 291

CHAPTER XXXVII.—1841-1842.
Victoria College.—Hon. W. H. Draper.—Sir Charles Bagot 301

CHAPTER XXXVIII.—1843.
Episode in the case of Hon. Marshall S. Bidwell 308

CHAPTER XXXIX.—1844.
Events preceding the Defence of Lord Metcalfe 312

CHAPTER XL.—1844.
Preliminary Correspondence on the Metcalfe Crisis 319

CHAPTER XLI.—1844.
Sir Charles Metcalfe Defended against his Councillors 328

CHAPTER XLII.—1844-1845
After the Contest.—Reaction and Reconstruction 337

CHAPTER XLIII.—1841-1844.
Dr. Ryerson appointed Superintendent of Education 342

CHAPTER XLIV.—1844-1846.
Dr. Ryerson's First Educational Tour in Europe 352

CHAPTER XLV.—1844-1857.
Episode in Dr. Ryerson's European Travels.—Pope Pius IX 365

CHAPTER XLVI.—1844-1876.
Ontario School System.—Retirement of Dr. Ryerson 368

CHAPTER XLVII.—1845-1846.
Illness and Final Retirement of Lord Metcalfe 375

CHAPTER XLVIII.—1843-1844.
Clergy Reserve Question Re-Opened.—Disappointments 378

CHAPTER XLIX.—1846-1848.
Re-Union of the British and Canadian Conferences 383

CHAPTER L.—1846-1853.
Miscellaneous Events and Incidents of 1846-1853 410

CHAPTER LI.—1849.
The Bible in the Ontario Public Schools 423

CONTENTS.

CHAPTER LII.—1850–1853.
The Clergy Reserve Question Transferred to Canada...................... 433

CHAPTER LIII.—1851.
Personal Episode in the Clergy Reserve Question........................ 454

CHAPTER LIV.—1854–1855.
Resignation on the Class-Meeting Question.—Discussion.................. 470

CHAPTER LV.—1855.
Dr. Ryerson resumes his Position in the Conference..................... 491

CHAPTER LVI.—1855–1856.
Personal Episode in the Class-Meeting Discussion....................... 499

CHAPTER LVII.—1855–1856.
Dr. Ryerson's Third Educational Tour in Europe........................ 514

CHAPTER LVIII.—1859–1862.
Denominational Colleges and the University Controversy................. 518

CHAPTER LIX.—1861–1866.
Personal Incidents.—Dr. Ryerson's Visits to Norfolk County............. 534

CHAPTER LX.—1867.
Last Educational Visit to Europe.—Rev. Dr. Punshon.................... 539

CHAPTER LXI.—1867.
Dr. Ryerson's Address on the New Dominion of Canada 547

CHAPTER LXII.—1868–1869.
Correspondence with Hon. Geo. Brown—Dr. Punshon 554

CHAPTER LXIII.—1870–1875.
Miscellaneous Closing Events and Correspondence........................ 559

CHAPTER LXIV.—1875–1876.
Correspondence with Rev. J. Ryerson, Dr. Punshon, etc.................. 573

CHAPTER LXV.—1877–1882.
Closing Years of Dr. Ryerson's Life Labours 585

CHAPTER LXVI.—1882.
The Funeral Ceremonies 593

Tributes to Dr. Ryerson's Memory and Estimates of his Character and Work. 598

LIST OF ILLUSTRATIONS.

	PAGE
PORTRAIT OF REV. DR. RYERSON	Frontispiece.
INDIAN VILLAGE AT RIVER CREDIT, IN 1837	59
JOHN JONES' HOUSE AT THE CREDIT, WHERE DR. RYERSON RESIDED	65
OLD CREDIT MISSION, 1837	78
OLD ADELAIDE STREET METHODIST CHURCH	283
VICTORIA COLLEGE, COBOURG	302
ONTARIO EDUCATIONAL DEPARTMENT AND NORMAL SCHOOL	421, 422
EDUCATIONAL EXHIBIT AT PHILADELPHIA	584, 585
METROPOLITAN CHURCH	564
DR. RYERSON'S RESIDENCE IN TORONTO	587

PREFATORY NOTE.

TWELVE months ago, I began to collect the necessary material for the completion of "THE STORY OF MY LIFE," which my venerated and beloved friend, Dr. Ryerson, had only left in partial outline. These materials, in the shape of letters, papers, and documents, were fortunately most abundant. The difficulty that I experienced was to select from such a miscellaneous collection a sufficient quantity of suitable matter, which I could afterwards arrange and group into appropriate chapters. This was not easily done, so as to form a connected record of the life and labours of a singularly gifted man, whose name was intimately connected with every public question which was discussed, and every prominent event which took place in Upper Canada from 1825 to 1875-78.

Public men of the present day looked upon Dr. Ryerson practically as one of their own contemporaries—noted for his zeal and energy in the successful management of a great Public Department, and as the founder of a system of Popular Education which, in his hands, became the pride and glory of Canadians, and was to those beyond the Dominion, an ideal system—the leading features of which they would gladly see incorporated in their own. In this estimate of Dr. Ryerson's labours they were quite correct. And in their appreciation of the statesmanlike qualities of mind, which devised and developed such a system in the midst of difficulties which would have appalled less resolute hearts, they were equally correct.

But, after all, how immeasurably does this partial view of his character and labours fall short of a true estimate of that character and of those labours!

As a matter of fact, Dr. Ryerson's great struggle for the civil and religious freedom which we now enjoy, was almost over when he assumed the position of Chief Director of our Educational System. No one can read the record of his labours from 1825 to 1845, as detailed in the following pages, without being impressed with the fact that, had he done no more for his native country than that which is therein recorded, he would have accomplished a great work, and have earned the gratitude of his fellow-countrymen.

It was my good fortune to enjoy Dr. Ryerson's warm, personal friendship since 1841. It has also been my distinguished privilege to be associated with him in the accomplishment of his great educational work since 1844. I have been able, therefore, to turn my own personal knowledge of most of the events outlined in this volume to account in its preparation In regard to what transpired before 1841, I have frequently heard many narratives in varied forms from Dr. Ryerson's lips.

My own intimate relations with Dr. Ryerson, and the character of our close personal friendship are sufficiently indicated in hi private letters to me, published in various parts of the book, but especially in Chapter liii. And yet they fail to convey the depth and sincerity of his personal attachment, and the feeling of entire trust and confidence which existed between us.

I am glad to say that I was not alone in this respect. Dr. Ryerson had the faculty, so rare in official life, of attaching his assistants and subordinates of every grade to himself personally. He always had a pleasant word for them, and made them feel that their interests were safe in his hands. They therefore respected and trusted him fully, and he never failed to acknowledge their fidelity and devotion in the public service.

I had, for some time before he ceased to be the Head of the Education Department, looked forward with pain and anxiety to that inevitable event. Pain, that he and I were at length to be separated in the carrying forward of the great work o. our lives, in which it had been my pride and pleasure to be his principal assistant. Anxiety at what, from my knowledge of him, I feared would be the effect of release from the work on fully accomplishing which he had so earnestly set his heart. Nor were my fears groundless. To a man o. his application and ardent temperament, the feeling that his work was done sensibly affected him. He lost a good deal of his elasticity, and during the last few years of his life, very perceptibly failed.

The day on which he took official leave of the Department was indeed a memorable one. As he bade farewell to each of his assistants in the office, he and they were deeply moved. He could not, however, bring himself to utter a word to me at our official parting, but as soon as he reached home he wrote to me the following tender and loving note :—

171 VICTORIA STREET, TORONTO,
MONDAY EVENING, FEBRUARY 21ST, 1876.

MY DEAR HODGINS,—I felt too deeply to-day when parting with you in the Office to be able to say a word. I was quite overcome with the thought of severing our official connection, which has existed between us for thirty-two years, during the whole of which time, without interruption, we have laboured as one mind and heart in two bodies, and I believe with a single eye to promote the best interests of our country, irrespective of religious sect or political party—to devise, develop, and mature a system of instruction which embraces and provides for every child in the land a good education; good teachers to teach; good inspectors to oversee the Schools; good maps, globes, and text-books; good books to read; and every provision whereby Municipal Councils and Trustees can provide suitable accomodation, teachers, and facilities for imparting education and knowledge to the rising generation of the land.

While I devoted the year 1845 to visiting educating countries and investigating their system of instruction, in order to devise one for our country, you devoted the same time in Dublin in mastering, under the special auspices of the Board of Education there, the several different branches of their Education Office, in administering the system of National Education in Ireland, so that in the details of our Education Office here, as well as in our general school system, we have been enabled to build up the most extensive establishment in the country, leaving nothing, as far as I know, to be devised in the completeness of its arrangements, and in the good character and efficiency of its officers. Whatever credit or satisfaction may attach to the accomplishment of this work, I feel that you are entitled to share equally with myself. Could I have believed that I might have been of any service to you, or to others with whom I have laboured so cordially, or that I could have advanced the school system, I would not have voluntarily retired from office. But all circumstances considered, and entering within a few days upon my 74th year, I have felt that this was the time for me to commit to other hands the reins of the government of the public school system, and labour during the last hours of my day and life, in a more retired sphere.

But my heart is, and ever will be, with you in its sympathies and prayers, and neither you nor yours will more truly rejoice in your success and happiness, than

Your old life-long Friend
And Fellow-labourer,
E. RYERSON.

Dr. Ryerson was confessedly a man of great intellectual resources. Those who read what he has written on the question—perilous to any writer in the early days of the history of this Province—of equal civil and religious rights for the people of Upper Canada, will be impressed with the fact that he had thoroughly mastered the great principles of civil and religious liberty, and expounded them not only with courage, but with clearness and force. His papers on the clergy reserve question, and the rights of the Canadian Parliament in the matter, were statesmanlike and exhaustive.

His exposition of a proposed system of education for his native country was both philosophical and eminently practical. As a Christian Minister, he was possessed of rare gifts, both in the pulpit and on the platform; while his warm sympathies and his deep religious experience, made him not only a "son of consolation," but a beloved and welcome visitor in the homes of the sorrowing and the afflicted. Among his brethren he exercised great personal influence; and in the counsels of the Conference he occupied a trusted and foremost place.

Thus we see that Dr. Ryerson's character was a many-sided one; while his talents were remarkably versatile. He was an able writer on public affairs; a noted Wesleyan Minister, and a successful and skilful leader among his brethren. But his fame in the future will mainly rest upon the fact that he was a distinguished Canadian Educationist, and the Founder of a great system of Public Education for Upper Canada. What makes this widely conceded excellence in his case the more marked, was the fact that the soil on which he had to labour was unprepared, and the social condition of the country was unpropitious. English ideas of schools for the poor, supported by subscriptions and voluntary offerings, prevailed in Upper Canada; free schools were unknown; the very principle on which they rest—that is, that the rateable property of the country is responsible for the education of the youth of the land—was denounced as communistic, and an invasion of the rights of property; while "compulsory education"—the proper and necessary complement of free schools—was equally denounced as the essence of "Prussian despotism," and an impertinent and unjustifiable interference with "the rights of British subjects."

It was a reasonable boast at the time that only systems of popular education, based upon the principle of free schools, were possible in the republican American States, where the wide diffusion of education was regarded as a prime necessity for the stability and success of republican institutions, and, therefore, was fostered with unceasing care. It was the theme on which the popular orator loved to dilate to a people on whose sympathies with the subject he could always confidently reckon. The practical mind of Dr. Ryerson, however, at once saw that the American idea of free schools was the true one. He moreover perceived that by giving his countrymen facilities for freely discussing the question among the ratepayers once a year, they would educate themselves into the idea, without any interference from the State. These facilities were provided in 1850; and for twenty-one years the question of free-schools *versus* rate-bill schools (fees, &c.) was discussed every January in from 3,000 to 5,000 school sections, until free schools became voluntarily the rule, and rate-bill schools the exception. In 1871, by common consent, the free school principle was incorporated into our school system by the Legislature, and has ever since been the universal practice. In the adoption of this principle, and in the successful administration of the Education Department, Dr. Ryerson at length demonstrated that a popular (or, as it had been held in the United States, the democratic) system of public schools was admirably adapted to our monarchial institutions. In point of fact, leading American educationists have often pointed out that the Canadian system of public education was more efficient in all of its details and more practically successful in its results, than was the ordinary American school system in any one of the States of the Union. Thus it is that the fame of Dr. Ryerson as a successful founder of our educational system, rests upon a solid basis. What has been done by him will not be undone; and the ground gone over by him will not require to be traversed again. In the "STORY OF MY LIFE," not much has been said upon the subject with which Dr. Ryerson's name has been most associated. It was distinctively the period of his public life, and its record will be found in the official literature of his Department. The personal reminiscences left by him are scanty, and of themselves would present an utterly inadequate picture of his educational work. Such a history may one day be written as would do it justice, but I feel that in such a work as the present it is better not to attempt a task, the proper performance of which would make demands upon the space and time at my disposal that could not be easily met.

There was one *rôle* in which Dr. Ryerson pre-eminently excelled—that of a controversialist. There was nothing spasmodic in his method of controversy, although there might be in the times and occasions of his indulging in it. He was a well-read man and an accurate thinker. His habit, when he meditated a descent upon a foe, was to thoroughly master the subject in dispute; to collect and arrange his materials, and then calmly and deliberately study the whole subject—especially the weak points in his adversary's case, and the strong points of his own. His habits of study in early life contributed to his after success in this matter. He was an indefatigable student; and so thoroughly did he in early life ground himself in English subjects— grammar, logic, rhetoric—and the classics, and that, too, under the most adverse circumstances, that, in his subsequent active career as a writer and controversialist, he evinced a power and readiness with his tongue and pen, that often astonished those who were unacquainted with the laborious thoroughness of his previous mental preparation.

It was marvellous with what wonderful effect he used the material at hand. Like a skilful general defending a position—and his study was always to act on the defensive—he masked his batteries, and was careful not to exhaust his ammunition in the first encounter. He never offered battle without having a sufficient force in reserve to overwhelm his opponent. He never exposed a weak point, nor espoused a worthless cause. He always fought for great principles, which to him were sacred, and he defended them to the utmost of his ability, when they were attacked. In such cases, Dr. Ryerson was careful not to rush into print until he had fully mastered the subject in dispute. This statement may be questioned, and apparent examples to the contrary adduced; but the writer knows better, for he knows the facts. In most cases Dr. Ryerson scented the battle from afar. Many a skirmish was improvised, and many a battle was privately fought out before the Chief advanced to repel an attack, or to fire the first shot in defence of his position.

A word as to the character of this work. It may be objected that I have dealt largely with subjects of no practical interest now—with dead issues, and with controversies for great principles, which, although important, acrimonious, and spirited at the time, have long since lost their interest. Let such critics reflect that the "Story" of such a "Life" as that of Dr. Ryerson cannot be told without a statement of the toils and difficulties which he encountered, and the triumphs which he achieved? For this reason I have written as I have done, recounting them as briefly as the subjects would permit.

In the preparation of this work I am indebted to the co-operation of my co-trustees the Rev. Dr. Potts and Rev. Dr. Nelles, whose long and intimate acquaintance with Dr. Ryerson (quite apart from their acknowledged ability) rendered their counsels of great value.

And now my filial task is done,—imperfectly, very imperfectly. I admit. While engaged in the latter part of the work a deep dark shadow fell—suddenly fell—upon my peaceful, happy home. This great sorrow has almost paralyzed my energies, and has rendered it very difficult for me to concentrate my thoughts on the loving task which twelve months ago I had so cheerfully begun. Under these circumstances, I can but crave the indulgence of the readers of these memorial pages of my revered and honoured Friend, the Rev. Dr. Ryerson—the foremost Canadian of his time.

TORONTO, 17th May, 1883.

On the accompanying page, I give a *fac-simile* of the well-known hand-writing of Dr. Ryerson, one of the many notes which I received from him.

ESTIMATE
OF THE REV. DR. RYERSON'S CHARACTER AND LABOURS.

By the Rev. William Ormiston, D.D., LL.D.

NEW YORK, Oct. 6th, 1882.

My Dear Dr. Hodgins,—It affords me the sincerest pleasure, tinged with sadness, to record, at your request, the strong feelings of devoted personal affection which I long cherished for our mutual *father* and friend, Rev. Dr. Ryerson; and the high estimate, which, during an intimacy of nearly forty years, I had been led to form of his lofty intellectual endowments, his great moral worth, and his pervading spiritual power. He was very dear to me while he lived, and now his memory is to me a precious, peculiar treasure.

In the autumn of 1843, I went to Victoria College, doubting much whether I was prepared to matriculate as a freshman. Though my attainments in some of the subjects prescribed for examination were far in advance of the requirements, in other subjects, I knew I was sadly deficient. On the evening of my arrival, while my mind was burdened with the importance of the step I had taken, and by no means free from anxiety about the issue, Dr. Ryerson, at that time Principal of the College, visited me in my room. I shall never forget that interview. He took me by the hand; and few men could express as much by a mere hand-shake as he. It was a welcome, an encouragement, an inspiration, and an earnest of future fellowship and friendship. It lessened the timid awe I naturally felt towards one in such an elevated position,—I had never before seen a Principal of a College,—it dissipated all boyish awkwardness, and awakened filial confidence. He spoke of Scotland, my native land, and of her noble sons, distinguished in every branch of philosophy and literature; specially of the number, the diligence, the frugality, self-denial, and success of her college students. In this way, he soon led me to tell him of my parentage, past life and efforts, present hopes and aspirations. His manner was so gracious and paternal—his sympathy so quick and genuine—his counsel so ready and cheering—his assurances so grateful and inspiriting, that not only was my heart *his* from that hour, but my future career seemed brighter and more certain than it had ever appeared before.

Many times in after years, have I been instructed, and guided, and delighted with his conversation, always replete with interest and information; but that first interview I can never forget: it is as fresh and clear to me to-day as it was on the morning after it took place. It has exerted a profound, enduring, moulding influence on my whole life. For what, under God, I am, and have been enabled to achieve, I owe more to that noble, unselfish, kind-hearted man than to any one else.

Dr. Ryerson was, at that time, in the prime of a magnificent manhood. His well-developed, finely-proportioned, firmly-knit frame; his broad, lofty brow; his keen, penetrating eye, and his genial, benignant face, all proclaimed him every inch a man. His mental powers vigorous and well-disciplined, his attainments in literature varied and extensive, his experience extended and diversified, his fame as a preacher of great pathos and power widely-spread, his claims as a doughty, dauntless champion of the rights of the people to civil and religious liberty generally acknowledged, his powers of expression marvellous in readiness, richness, and beauty, his manners affable and winning, his presence magnetic and impressive,—he stood in the eye of the youthful, ardent, aspiring student, a tower of strength, a centre of healthy, helpful influences—a man to be admired and honoured, loved and feared, imitated and followed. And I may add that frequent intercourse for nearly forty years, and close official relations for more than ten, only deepened and confirmed the impressions first made. A more familiar acquaintance with his domestic, social, and religious life, a more thorough knowledge of his mind and heart, constantly increased my appreciation of his worth, my esteem for his character, and my affection for his person.

Not a few misunderstood, undervalued, or misrepresented his public conduct, but it will be found that those who knew him best, loved him most, and that many who were constrained to differ from him, in his management of public affairs, did full justice to the purity and generosity of his motives, to the nobility, loftiness, and ultimate success of his aims, and to the disinterestedness and value of his varied and manifold labours for the country, and for the Church of Christ.

As a *teacher*, he was earnest and efficient, eloquent and inspiring, but he expected and exacted rather too much work from the average student. His own ready and affluent mind sympathized keenly with the apt, bright scholar, to whom his praise was warmly given, but he scarcely made sufficient allowance for the dullness or lack of previous preparation which failed to keep pace with him in his long and rapid strides; hence his censures were occasionally severe. His methods of examination furnished the very best kind of mental discipline, fitted alike to cultivate the memory and to strengthen the judgment. All the students revered him, but the best of the class appreciated him most. His counsels were faithful and judicious; his admonitions paternal and discriminating; his rebukes seldom administered, but scathingly severe. No student ever left his presence, without resolving to do better, to aim higher, and to win his approval.

His acceptance of the office of Chief Superintendent of Education, while offering to him the sphere of his life's work, and giving to the country the very service it needed—*the man for the place*—was a severe trial to the still struggling College, and a bitter disappointment to some young, ambitious hearts.

Into this new arena he entered with a resolute determination to succeed, and he spared no pains, effort, or sacrifice to fit himself thoroughly for the onerous duties of the office to which he had been appointed. Of its nature, importance, and far-reaching results, he had a distinct, vivid perception, and clearly realized and fully felt the responsibilities it imposed. He steadfastly prosecuted his work with a firm, inflexible will, unrelaxing tenacity of purpose, an amazing fertility of expedient, an exhaustless amount of information, a most wonderful skill in adaptation, a matchless ability in unfolding and vindicating his plans, a rare adroitness in meeting and removing difficulties —great moderation in success, and indomitable perseverance under discouragement, calm patience when misapprehended, unflinching courage when opposed,—until he achieved the consummation of his wishes, the establishment of a system of public education second to none in its efficiency and adaptation to the condition and circumstances of the people. The system is a noble monument to the singleness of purpose, the unwavering devotion, the tireless energy, the eminent ability, and the administrative powers of Dr. Ryerson, and it will render his name a familiar word for many generations in Canadian schools and homes; and place him high in the list of the great men of other lands, distinguished in the same field of labour. His entire administration of the Department of Public Instruction was patient and prudent, vigorous and vigilant, sagacious and successful.

He repeatedly visited Europe, not for mere recreation or personal advantage, but for the advancement of the interests of religion and education in the Province. During these tours, there were opened to him the most extended fields of observation and enquiry, from which he gathered ample stores of information which he speedily rendered available for the perfecting, as far as practicable, the entire system of Public Instruction.

A prominent figure in Canadian history for three score years, actively and ceaselessly engaged in almost every department of patriotic and philanthropic, Christian and literary, enterprise, Dr. Ryerson was a strong tower in support or defence of every good cause, and no such cause failed to secure the powerful aid of his advocacy by voice and pen. His was truly a catholic and charitable spirit. Nothing human was alien to him. A friend of all good men, he enjoyed the confidence and esteem of all, even of those whose opinions or policy on public questions he felt constrained to refute or oppose. He commanded the respect, and secured the friendship of men of every rank, and creed, and party. None could better appreciate his ability and magnanimity than those who encountered him as an opponent, or were compelled to acknowledge him as victor. His convictions were strong, his principles firm, his purposes resolute, and he could, and did maintain them, with chivalrous daring, against any and every assault.

In the heat of controversy, while repelling unworthy insinuations, his indignation was sometimes roused, and his language not unfrequently was fervid, and forcible, and scathingly severe, but seldom, if ever, personally rancorous or bitter. When violently or vilely assailed his sensitive nature keenly felt the wound, but though he carried many a scar, he bore no malice.

His intellectual powers, of a high order, admirably balanced, and invigorated by long and severe discipline, found their expression in word and work, by pulpit, press, and platform, in the achievements of self-denying, indefatigable industry, and in wise and lofty statesmanship.

His moral nature was elevated and pure. He was generous, sympathetic, benevolent, faithful, trusting, and trustworthy. He rejoiced sincerely in the weal, and deeply felt the woes of others, and his ready hand obeyed the dictates of his loving, liberal heart.

His religious life was marked by humility, consistency, and cheerfulness. The simplicity of his faith in advanced life was childlike, and sublime. His trust in God never faltered, and, at the end of his course, his hopes of eternal life, through Jesus Christ our Lord, were radiant and triumphant.

Dr. Ryerson was truly a great man, endowed with grand qualities of mind and heart, which he consecrated to high and holy aims; and though, in early life, and in his public career, beset with many difficulties, he heroically achieved for himself, among his own people, a most enviable renown. His work and his worth universally appreciated, his influence widely acknowledged, his services highly valued, his name a household word throughout the Dominion, and his memory a legacy and an inspiration to future generations.

And while Canada owes more to him than any other of her sons, his fame is not confined to the land of his birth, which he loved so well, and served so faithfully, but in Britain and in the United States of America his name is well known, and is classed with their own deserving worthies.

Whatever judgment may be formed of some parts of his eventful and distinguished career as a public man, there can be but one opinion as to the eminent and valuable services he has rendered to his country, as a laborious, celebrated pioneer preacher, an able ecclesiastical leader, a valiant and veteran advocate of civil and religious liberty—as the founder and administrator of a system of public education second to that of no other land—as the President and life-long patron of Victoria University, *whose oldest living alumnus* will hold his memory dear to life's close, when severed friends will be reunited; and whose successive classes will revere as the first President and firm friend of their Alma Mater, as the promoter of popular education, the ally of all teachers, and an example to all young men.

I lay this simple wreath on the memorial of one, whom I found able and helpful as *a teacher* in my youth—wise and prudent as *an adviser* in after life—generous and considerate as *a superior officer*—tender and true as a *friend*. He loved me, and was beloved by me. He doubtless had his faults, but I cannot recall them; and very few, I venture to think, will ever seek to mention them. The green turf which rests on his grave covers them. His memory will live as one of the purest, kindest, best of men. A patriot, a scholar, a Christian—the servant of God, the friend of man.

"Amicum perdere est damnorum maximum."

Yours, very faithfully, in bonds of truest friendship,

W. ORMISTON.

To J. George Hodgins, Esq., LL.D., Toronto

THE STORY OF MY LIFE.

CHAPTER I.
1803–1825.
Sketch of Early Life.

I HAVE several times been importuned to furnish a sketch of my life for books of biography of public men, published both in Canada and the United States; but I have uniformly declined, assigning as a reason a wish to have nothing of the kind published during my lifetime. Finding, however, that some circumstances connected with my early history have been misapprehended and misrepresented by adversaries, and that my friends are anxious that I should furnish some information on the subject, and being now in the seventieth year of my age, I sit down in this my Long Point Island Cottage, retired from the busy world, to give some account of my early life, on this blessed Sabbath day, indebted to the God of the Sabbath for all that I am,—morally, intellectually, and as a public man, as well as for all my hopes of a future life.

I was born on the 24th of March, 1803, in the Township of Charlotteville, near the Village of Vittoria, in the then London District, now the County of Norfolk. My Father had been an officer in the British Army during the American Revolution, being a volunteer in the Prince of Wales' Regiment of New Jersey, of which place he was a native. His forefathers were from Holland, and his more remote ancestors were from Denmark.

At the close of the American Revolutionary War, he, with many others of the same class, went to New Brunswick, where he married my Mother, whose maiden name was Stickney, a descendant of one of the early Massachusetts Puritan settlers.

Near the close of the last century my Father, with his family, followed an elder brother to Canada,* where he drew some 2,500 acres of land from the Government, for his services in the army, besides his pension. My Father settled on 600 acres of land lying about half-way between the present Village of Vittoria and Port Ryerse, where my uncle Samuel settled, and where he built the first mill in the County of Norfolk.

On the organization of the London District in 1800, for legal purposes, my uncle was the Lieutenant of the County, issuing commissions in his own name to militia officers; he was also Chairman of the Quarter Sessions. My Father was appointed High Sheriff in 1800, but held the office only six years, when he resigned it in behalf of the late Colonel John Bostwick (then a surveyor), who subsequently married my eldest sister, and who owned what is now Port Stanley, and was at one time a Member of Parliament for the County of Middlesex.

My Father devoted himself exclusively to agriculture, and I learned to do all kinds of farm-work. The district grammar-school was then kept within half-a-mile of my Father's residence, by Mr. James Mitchell (afterwards Judge Mitchell), an excellent classical scholar; he came from Scotland with the late Rt. Rev. Dr. Strachan, first Bishop of Toronto. Mr. Mitchell married my youngest sister. He treated me with much kindness. When I recited to him my lessons in English grammar he often said that he had never studied the English grammar himself, that he wrote and spoke English by the Latin grammar. At the age of fourteen I had the opportunity of attending a course of instruction in the English language given by two professors, the one an Englishman, and the other an American, who taught nothing but English grammar. They professed in one course of instruction, by lectures, to enable a diligent pupil to parse any sentence in the English language. I was sent to attend these lectures, the only boarding abroad for school instruction I ever enjoyed. My previous knowledge of the *letter* of the grammar was of great service to me, and gave me an advantage over other pupils, so that before the end of the course I was generally called up to give visitors an illustration of the success of the system, which was certainly the most effective I have ever since witnessed, having charts, etc., to illustrate the agreement and government of words.

This whole course of instruction by two able men, who did

---

* My father's eldest brother Samuel was known as Samuel Ryerse, in consequence of the manner in which his name was spelled in his Army Commission which he held; but the original family name was Ryerson.

nothing but teach grammar from one week's end to another had to me all the attraction of a charm and a new discovery. It gratified both curiosity and ambition, and I pursued it with absorbing interest, until I had gone through Murray's two volumes of "Expositions and Exercises," Lord Kames' "Elements of Criticism," and Blair's "Lectures on Rhetoric," of which I still have the notes which I then made. The same professors obtained sufficient encouragement to give a second course of instruction and lectures at Vittoria, and one of them becoming ill, the other solicited my Father to allow me to assist him, as it would be useful to me, while it would enable him to fulfil his engagements. Thus, before I was sixteen, I was inducted as a teacher, by lecturing on my native language. This course of instruction, and exercises in English, have proved of the greatest advantage to me, not less in enabling me to study foreign languages than in using my own.

But that to which I am principally indebted for any studious habits, mental energy, or even capacity or decision of character, is religious instruction, poured into my mind in my childhood by a Mother's counsels, and infused into my heart by a Mother's prayers and tears. When very small, under six years of age, having done something naughty, my Mother took me into her bedroom, told me how bad and wicked what I had done was, and what pain it caused her, kneeled down, clasped me to her bosom, and prayed for me. Her tears, falling upon my head, seemed to penetrate to my very heart. This was my first religious impression, and was never effaced. Though thoughtless, and full of playful mischief, I never afterwards knowingly grieved my Mother, or gave her other than respectful and kind words.

At the close of the American War, in 1815, when I was twelve years of age, my three elder brothers, George, William, and John, became deeply religious, and I imbibed the same spirit. My consciousness of guilt and sinfulness was humbling, oppressive, and distressing; and my experience of relief, after lengthened fastings, watchings, and prayers, was clear, refreshing, and joyous. In the end I simply trusted in Christ, and looked to Him for a present salvation; and, as I looked up in my bed, the light appeared to my mind, and, as I thought, to my bodily eye also, in the form of One, white-robed, who approached the bedside with a smile, and with more of the expression of the countenance of Titian's Christ than of any person whom I have ever seen. I turned, rose to my knees, bowed my head, and covered my face, rejoiced with trembling, saying to a brother who was lying beside me, that the Saviour was now near us. The change within was more marked than anything without and, perhaps, the inward change may have suggested what appeared an outward manifestation. I henceforth had new views, new feelings, new joys, and new strength. I truly delighted in the law of the Lord, after the inward man, and—

"Jesus, all the day long, was my joy and my song."

From that time I became a diligent student, and new quickness and strength seemed to be imparted to my understanding and memory. While working on the farm I did more than ordinary day's work, that it might show how industrious, instead of lazy, as some said, religion made a person. I studied between three and six o'clock in the morning, carried a book in my pocket during the day to improve odd moments by reading or learning, and then reviewed my studies of the day aloud while walking out in the evening.

To the Methodist way of religion my Father was, at that time, extremely opposed, and refused me every facility for acquiring knowledge while I continued to go amongst them. I did not, however, formally join them, in order to avoid his extreme displeasure. A kind friend offered to give me any book that I would commit to memory, and submit to his examination of the same. In this way I obtained my first Latin grammar, "Watts on the Mind," and "Watts' Logic."

My eldest brother, George, after the war, went to Union College, U. S., where he finished his collegiate studies. He was a fellow-student with the late Dr. Wayland, and afterwards succeeded my brother-in-law as Master of the London District Grammar School. His counsels, examinations, and ever kind assistance were a great encouragement and of immense service to me; and though he and I have since differed in religious opinions, no other than most affectionate brotherly feeling has ever existed between us to this day.*

When I had attained the age of eighteen, the Methodist minister in charge of the circuit which embraced our neighbourhood, thought it not compatible with the rules of the Church to allow, as had been done for several years, the privileges of a member without my becoming one. I then gave in my name for membership. Information of this was soon communicated to my Father, who, in the course of a few days, said to me: "Egerton, I understand you have joined the Methodists; you must either leave them or leave my house." He said no more, and I well knew that the decree was final; but I had formed

---

* This brother of Dr. Ryerson's passed quietly away on the 19th of December, 1882, aged 92. Dr. Ryerson died on the 19th of February of the same year, aged 79. Their father, Col. Ryerson, died at the age of 94.—J. G. H.

my decision in view of all possible consequences, and I had the aid of a Mother's prayers, and a Mother's tenderness, and a conscious Divine strength according to my need. The next day I left home and became usher in the London District Grammar School, applying myself to my new work with much diligence and earnestness, so that I soon succeeded in gaining the good-will of parents and pupils, and they were quite satisfied with my services,—leaving the head master to his favourite pursuits of gardening and building!

During two years I was thus teacher and student, advancing considerably in classical studies. I took great delight in "Locke on the Human Understanding," Paley's "Moral and Political Philosophy," and "Blackstone's Commentaries," especially the sections of the latter on the Prerogatives of the Crown, the Rights of the Subject, and the Province of Parliament.

As my Father complained that the Methodists had robbed him of his son, and of the fruits of that son's labours, I wished to remove that ground of complaint as far as possible by hiring an English farm-labourer, then just arrived in Canada, in my place, and paid him out of the proceeds of my own labour for two years. But although the farmer was the best hired man my Father had ever had, the result of his farm-productions during these two years did not equal those of the two years that I had been the chief labourer on the farm, and my Father came to me one day uttering the single sentence, 'Egerton, you must come home," and then walked away. My first promptings would have led me to say, "Father, you have expelled me from your house for being a Methodist; I am so still. I have employed a man for you in my place for two years, during which time I have been a student and a teacher, and unaccustomed to work on a farm, I cannot now resume it." But I had left home for the honour of religion, and I thought the honour of religion would be promoted by my returning home, and showing still that the religion so much spoken against would enable me to leave the school for the plough and the harvest-field, as it had enabled me to leave home without knowing at the moment whether I should be a teacher or a farm-labourer.

I relinquished my engagement as teacher within a few days, engaging again on the farm with such determination and purpose that I ploughed every acre of ground for the season, cradled every stalk of wheat, rye, and oats, and mowed every spear of grass, pitched the whole, first on a waggon, and then from the waggon on the hay-mow or stack. While the neighbours were astonished at the possibility of one man doing so much work, I neither felt fatigue nor depression, for "the joy of the Lord was my strength," both of body and mind, and I made nearly, if not quite, as much progress in my studies as I had done while teaching school. My Father then became changed in regard both to myself and the religion I professed, desiring me to remain at home; but, having been enabled to maintain a good conscience in the sight of God, and a good report before men, in regard to my filial duty during my minority, I felt that my life's work lay in another direction. I had refused, indeed, the advice of senior Methodist ministers to enter into the ministerial work, feeling myself as yet unqualified for it, and still doubting whether I should ever engage in it, or in another profession.

I felt a strong desire to pursue further my classical studies, and determined, with the kind counsel and aid of my eldest brother, to proceed to Hamilton, and place myself for a year under the tuition of a man of high reputation both as a scholar and a teacher, the late John Law, Esq., then head master of the Gore District Grammar School. I applied myself with such ardour, and prepared such an amount of work in both Latin and Greek, that Mr. Law said it was impossible for him to give the time and hear me read all that I had prepared, and that he would, therefore, examine me on the translation and construction of the more difficult passages, remarking more than once that it was impossible for any human mind to sustain long the strain that I was imposing upon mine. In the course of some six months his apprehensions were realized, as I was seized with a brain fever, and on partially recovering took cold, which resulted in inflammation of the lungs by which I was so reduced that my physician, the late Dr. James Graham, of Norfolk, pronounced my case hopeless, and my death was hourly expected.

In that extremity, while I felt even a desire to depart and be with Christ, I was oppressed with the consciousness that I should have yielded to the counsels of the chief ministers of my Church, as I could have made nearly as much progress in my classical studies, and at the same time been doing some good to the souls of men, instead of refusing to speak in public as I had done. I then and there vowed that if I should be restored to life and health, I would not follow my own counsels, but would yield to the openings and calls which might be made in the Church by its chief ministers. That very moment the cloud was removed; the light of the glory of God shone into my mind and heart with a splendour and power that I had never before experienced. My Mother, entering the room a few moments after, exclaimed: "Egerton, your countenance is changed, you are getting better!" My bodily recovery was rapid; but the recovery of my mind from the shock which it had experienced was slower, and for some weeks I could not even read, much less study. While thus recovering, I exercised myself as I best could in writing down my meditations.

My Father so earnestly solicited me to return, that he offered me a deed of his farm if I would do so and live with him; but I declined acceding to his request under any circumstances, expressing my conviction that even could I do so, I thought it unwise and wrong for any parent to place himself in a position of dependence upon any of his children for support, so long as he could avoid doing so. One day, entering my room and seeing a manuscript lying on the bed, he asked me what I had been writing, and wished me to read it. I had written a meditation on part of the last verse of the 73rd Psalm: "it is good for me to draw near to God." When I read to him what I had written my Father rose with a sigh, remarking: "Egerton, I don't think you will ever return home again," and he never afterwards mooted the subject, except in a general way.

On recovering, I returned to Hamilton and resumed my studies; shortly after which I went on a Saturday to a quarterly meeting, held about twelve miles from Hamilton, at "The Fifty," a neighborhood two or three miles west of Grimsby, where I expected to meet my brother William, who was one of the ministers on the circuit, which was then called the Niagara Circuit—embracing the whole Niagara Peninsula, from five miles east of Hamilton, and across to the west of Fort Erie. But my brother did not attend, and I learned that he had been laid aside from his ministerial work by bleeding of the lungs. Between love-feast and preaching on Sunday morning, the presiding elder, the Rev. Thomas Madden, the late Hugh Willson, and the late Smith Griffin (grandfather of the Rev. W. S. Griffin), circuit stewards, called me aside and asked if I had any engagements that would prevent me from coming on the circuit to supply the place of my brother William, who might be unable to resume his work for, perhaps, a year or more.

I felt that the vows of God were upon me, and I was for some moments speechless from emotion. On recovering, I said I had no engagements beyond my own plans and purposes; but I was yet weak in body from severe illness, and I had no means for anything else than pursuing my studies, for which aid had been provided.

One of the stewards replied that he would give me a horse, and the other that he would provide me with a saddle and bridle. I then felt that I had no choice but to fulfill the vow which I had made, on what was supposed to my deathbed. I returned to Hamilton, settled with my instructor and for my lodgings, and made my first attempt at preaching at or near Beamsville, on Easter Sunday, 1825, in the morning, from the 5th verse of the 126th Psalm: "They that sow in tears shall reap in joy;" and in the afternoon at "The Fifty," on "The Resurrection of Christ."—Acts ii. 24.

TORONTO, Nov. 11th, 1880.

Such was the sketch of my life which I wrote on Sabbath in my Long Point Island Cottage, on the 24th of March, 1873, the 70th anniversary of my birthday. I know not that I can add anything to the foregoing story of my early life that would be worth writing or reading.

[In his cottage at Long Point, on his seventy-fifth birthday, Dr. Ryerson wrote the following paper, which Dr. Potts read on the occasion of his funeral discourse. It will be read with profoundest interest, as one of the noblest of those Christian experiences which are the rich heritage of the Church.—J. G. H.]

LONG POINT ISLAND COTTAGE, March 24th, 1878.

I am this day seventy-five years of age, and this day fifty-three years ago, after resisting many solicitations to enter the ministry, and after long and painful struggles, I decided to devote my life and all to the ministry of the Methodist Church.

The predominant feeling of my heart is that of gratitude and humiliation; gratitude for God's unbounded mercy, patience, and compassion, in the bestowment of almost uninterrupted health, and innumerable personal, domestic, and social blessings for more than fifty years of a public life of great labour and many dangers; and humiliation under a deep-felt consciousness of personal unfaithfulness, of many defects, errors, and neglects in public duties. Many tell me that I have been useful to the Church and the country; but my own consciousness tells me that I have learned little, experienced little, done little in comparison of what I might and ought to have known and done. By the grace of God I am spared; by His grace I am what I am; all my trust for salvation is in the efficacy of Jesus' atoning blood. I know whom I have trusted, and " am persuaded that He is able to keep that which I have committed unto Him against that day." I have no melancholy feelings or fears. The joy of the Lord is my strength. I feel that I am now on the bright side of seventy-five. As the evening twilight of my earthly life advances, my spiritual sun shines with increased splendour. This has been my experience for the last year. With an increased sense of my own sinfulness, unworthiness, and helplessness, I have an increased sense of the blessedness of pardon, the indwelling of the Comforter, and the communion of saints.

Here, on bended knees, I give myself, and all I have and am, afresh to Him whom I have endeavoured to serve, but very imperfectly, for more than threescore years. All helpless, myself, I most humbly and devoutly pray that Divine strength may be perfected in my weakness, and that my last days on earth may be my best days—best days of implicit faith and unreserved consecration, best days of simple scriptural ministrations and public usefulness, best days of change from glory to glory, and of becoming meet for the inheritance of the saints in light, until my Lord shall dismiss me from the service of warfare and the weariness of toil to the glories of victory and the repose of rest.

E. RYERSON.

CHAPTER II.

1824—1825.

EXTRACTS FROM MY DIARY OF 1824 AND 1825.

THE foregoing sketch of my early life may be properly followed by extracts from my diary; pourtraying my mental and spiritual exercises and labours during a few months before and after I commenced the work of an itinerant Methodist Preacher.

The extracts are as follow, and are very brief in comparison to the entire diary, which extends over eight years from 1824, to 1832, after which time I ceased to write a daily diary, and wrote in a journal the principal occurrences and doings in which I was concerned.*

Hamilton, August 12th, 1824.—I arrived here the day after I left home. Mr. John Law (with whom I am to study) received me with all the affection and kindness of a sincere and disinterested friend. Even, without expecting it, he told me that his library was at my service; that he did not wish me to join any class, but to read by myself, that he might pay every attention, and give me every assistance in his power. Indeed he answered my highest expectation. I am stopping with Mr. John Aikman. He is one of the most respectable men in this vicinity. I shall be altogether retired. At the Court of Assize, the Chief-Justice and the Attorney-General will stop here, which will make a very agreeable change for a few days. To pursue my studies with indefatigable industry, and ardent zeal, will be my set purpose, so that I may never have to mourn the loss of my precious time.

Aug. 16th.—This day I commenced my studies by reading Latin and Greek with Mr. Law. I began the duties of the day in imploring the assistance of God; for without Him I cannot do anything. God has been pleased to open my understanding, to enlighten my mind, and to show me the necessity and blessedness of an unreserved and habitual devotion to his heavenly will. I have heard Bishop Hedding preach, also Rev. Nathan Bangs. I am resolved to improve my time more diligently, and to give myself wholly to God. Oh, may his long-suffering mercy bear with me, his wisdom guide, his power support and defend me, and may his mercy bring me off triumphant in the dying day!

Aug. 17th.—I have been reading Virgil's Georgics. I find them very diffi-

---

* These voluminous diaries and journals are full of detail, chiefly of Dr. Ryerson's religious experience. They are rich in illustration of the severe mental and spiritual disciplinary process—self-imposed—through which he passed during these eventful years of his earlier life. They are singularly severe in their personal reflections upon his religious shortcomings, and want of watchfulness. They are tinged with an asceticism which largely characterized the religious experience of many of the early Methodist preachers of Mr. Wesley's time—an asceticism which strongly marked the Methodist biography and writings, which were almost the only religious reading accessible to the devoted Methodist pioneers of this country,—J. G. H.

cult, and have only read seventy lines. In my spiritual concerns I have been greatly blessed; and felt more anxiously concerned for my soul's salvation, have prayed more than usual, and experienced a firmer confidence in the blessed promises of the Gospel. I have enjoyed sweet intercourse with my Saviour, my soul resting on his divine word, with a prayerful acquiescence in his dispensations. But alas! what evil have I done, how much time have I lost, how many idle words have I spoken; how should these considerations lead me to watch my thoughts, to husband my time with judgment, and govern my tongue as with a bridle! Oh, Lord bless me and prosper me in all my ways and labours, and keep me to thyself!

Aug. 18th.—The Lord has abundantly blessed me this day both in my spiritual and classical pursuits. I have been able to pursue my studies with facility, and have felt his Holy Spirit graciously enlightening my mind, showing me the necessity of separating myself from the world, and being given up entirely to his service.

Aug. 19th.—I have this day proved that, with every temptation, the Lord makes a way for my escape. I have enjoyed much peace. Oh, Lord, help me to improve my precious time, so as to overcome the assaults and escape the snares of the adversary!

Aug. 20th.—In all the vicissitudes of life, how clearly is the mysterious providence and superintending care of Jehovah manifested! how strikingly can I observe the divine interposition of my heavenly Father, and how sensibly do I realize his benevolence, kindness, and mercy in the whole moral and blessed economy of his equitable and infinitely wise government! On no object do I cast my eyes without observing an affecting instance of a benevolent and overruling power; and, while in mental contemplations my mind is absorbed, my admiration rises still higher to the exalted purposes and designs of Almighty God. I behold in the soul noble faculties, superior powers of imagination, and capacious desires, unfilled by anything terrestrial, and wishes unsatisfied by the widest grasp of human ambition. What is this but immortality? Oh, that my soul may feed on food immortal!

Another week is gone, eternally gone! What account can I give to my Almighty Judge for my conduct and opportunities? Has my improvement kept pace with the panting steeds of unretarded time? Must I give an account of every idle word, thought, and deed? Oh, merciful God! if the most righteous, devoted, and holy scarcely are saved, where shall I appear? How do my vain thoughts, and unprofitable conversation, swell heaven's register? Where is my watchfulness? Where are my humility, purity, and hatred of sin? Where is my zeal? Alas! alas! they are things unpractised, unfelt, almost unknown to me. How little do I share in the toils, the labours, or the sorrows of the righteous, and consequently how little do I participate in their confidence, their joys, their heavenly prospects? Oh, may these awful considerations drive me closer to God, and incite to a more diligent improvement of my precious time, so that I may bear the mark of a real follower of Christ!

Aug. 22nd—Sabbath.—When I arose this morning I endeavoured to dedicate myself afresh to God in prayer, with a full determination to improve the day to his glory, and to spend it in his service. Accordingly, I spent the morning in prayer, reading, and meditation; but when I came to mingle with the worldly-minded, my devotions and meditations were dampened and distracted, my thoughts unprofitable and vain. I attended a Methodist Class-meeting where I felt myself forcibly convinced of my shortcomings. Sure I am that unless I am more vigilant, zealous, and watchful, I shall never reach the Paradise of God. I must be willing to bear reproach for Christ's sake, confess him before men, or I never can be owned by him in the presence of his Father, and the holy angels.

Merciful God! forbid that I should barter away my heavenly inheritance for a transient gleam of momentary joy, and the empty round of worldly pleasure:

"Help me to watch and pray,
And on thyself rely,
Assured if I my trust betray,
I shall forever die."

Aug. 23*rd.*—I have been abundantly prospered in my studies to-day; and have been enabled to maintain an outward conformity in my conduct. But alas! how blind to my own interest, to deprive myself of the highest blessings and exalted honours the Almighty has to bestow. Oh, Lord! help me henceforth to be wise unto salvation. May I be sober and watch unto prayer! Amen.

Aug. 24*th.*—Through the mercy of God I have been enabled in a good degree to overcome my besetments, and have this day maintained more consistency in conversation and conduct. Still I feel too much deterred by the fear of man, and thirst too ardently for the honours of the world. Merciful God! give me more grace, wisdom, and strength, that I may triumphantly overcome and escape to heaven at last!

I shall finish the first book of the Georgics to-day, which is the seventh day since I commenced them. I expect to finish them in four weeks from this time. My mind improves, and I feel much encouraged. My labour is uniform and constant, from the dawn of day till near eleven at night. I have not a moment to play on the flute.

Aug. 25*th.*—There is nothing like implicit trust in the Almighty for assistance, protection, and assurance! His past dispensations and dealings with me leave not the least suspicion of his inviolable veracity, and his efficacious promises cheer the sadness, calm the fears of every soul that practically reposes in and seeks after him. The truth of this, blessed be God, I have in some measure experienced to-day. Help me, O Lord, with increasing grace to attain still more sublime enjoyments and triumphant prospects!

Aug. 26*th.*—I feel a growing indifference to worldly pleasures, and increasing love to God, to holiness, and heaven. Entire confidence in a superintending Providence heals the wounded heart of even the disconsolate widow, and gives the oil of joy for sorrow, and the garment of praise for the spirit of heaviness.

Aug. 27*th.*—This day I attended a funeral; those connected with it were very ignorant; how strikingly this showed to me the advantages of a good education. God forbid that I should idle away my golden moments. Help me to choose the better part, and honour God in all things!

Aug. 28*th.*—The labours of another week are ended; during it I have enjoyed much of the presence of God; surely the religion of Christ dazzles all the magnificence of human glory; were I only to regard the happiness of this life, I would embrace its doctrines, practice its laws, and exert my influence for its extension.

Aug. 29*th—Sabbath.*—The blessings of the Lord have abundantly surrounded me this day, and my heart has been enlarged.

Aug. 30*th.*—In observing my actions and words this day, I find I have done many things that are culpable; and yet, blessed be God, his goodness to me is profuse. Help me to watch and pray that I enter not into temptation.

Aug. 31*st.*—How many youths around me do I see trifling away the greatest part of their time, and profaning their Maker's name? My soul magnifies His name that I have decided to be on the Lord's side; how many evils have I escaped; how many blessings obtained; what praise enjoyed, through the influence of this religion. To God be all the glory!

September 1st.—In no subject can we employ our thoughts more profitably than on the atonement of Christ, and justification through his merits. With wonder we gaze on the love of Deity; with profound awe we behold a God descending from heaven to earth. Unbounded love! Unmeasured grace! And while in deep silence his death wraps all nature; while his yielding breath rends the temple and shakes earth's deep foundations; may my redeemed soul in silent rapture tune her grateful song aloft; and fired by this blood-bought theme, may I mend my pace towards my heavenly inheritance!

I generally close up the labours of the day by writing a short essay or theme on some religious subject. In doing this I have two objects in view: the improvement of my mind and heart. And what could be more appropriate than to close the day by reflection upon God, and heaven, and time, and eternity? No private employment, except that of prayer, have I found more pleasing and profitable than this. Youth is the seed-time of the life that now is, as well as of that which is to come. Youthful piety is the germ of true honour, lawful prosperity, and everlasting blessedness. One day of humble, devotional piety in youth will add more to our happiness at the last end of life than a year of repentance and humiliation in old age. I have no intention of entering the ministry, and yet I prefer religious topics. To-day I have chosen the atonement of our Lord, and have written a few thoughts on it.

Sept 2nd.—Implicit trust in a superintending Providence is a constant source of comfort and support to me.

Sept. 3rd.—God has blessed me to-day in my studies. I have also felt the efficacy of Divine aid. Help me still, most merciful God!

Sept. 4th.—In the course of the past week I have experienced various feelings, especially with respect to the dealings of Divine Providence with me; but in all I have had this consolation, that whatever happens, "the will of the Lord be done." It is my duty to perform and obey.

Sept. 5th.—This morning I attended church and heard a sermon on Ezekiel xviii. 27. When we consider the importance of repentance, its connection with our eternal happiness, surely every feeling heart, and ministers especially, should exhibit with burning zeal the conditions of salvation, the slavery of vice, the heinousness of sin, the vanity of human glory, and the uncertainty of life.

Sept. 6th.—When I laid aside my studies to commit my evening thoughts to paper, my mind wandered on various subjects, until much time was lost; the best antidote against this is, not to put off to the next moment what can be done in this. We should be firm and decided in all our pursuits, and whatever our minds "find to do, do it with all our might."

Sept. 7th.—The mutual dependence of men cements society, and their social intercourse communicates pleasure. If we are called to endure the pains and inconveniences of poverty, possessing this we forget all; and in the pleasant walks of wealth, it adds to every elegance a charm. Friendship associated with religion, elevates all the ties of Christian love and mutual pleasure.

Sept. 8th.—I have found myself too much mingled with the common crowd, and like others, too indifferent to the subject of all others the chief.

Sept. 9th.—We "cannot serve God and Mammon." May I be firm in my attachment to the Saviour, remembering that "godliness has the promise of the life that now is, and of that which is to come."

Sept. 12th.—I heard a practical sermon on making our "calling and election sure," which closed with these words, "He that calleth upon the name of the Lord shall be saved." I felt condemned on account of my negligence, and resolved, by God's help, to gain victory over my tendency to inconsistencies of life and conduct.

Sept. 14th.—I observe men embarked on the stream of time, and carried forward with irresistible force to that universal port which shall receive the whole human family. Amongst this passing crowd, how few are there who reflect upon the design and end of their voyage; surfeited with pleasure, involved in life's busy concerns, the future, with its awful realities, is forgotten and time, not eternity, is placed in the foreground.

Sept. 15th.—In a letter to my brother George, to-day, I said:—It would be superfluous for me to tell you that the letter I received from you gave me unspeakable pleasure. Your fears with respect to my injuring my health are groundless, for I must confess I don't possess half that application and burning zeal in these all-important pursuits that I ought to have. For who can estimate the value of a liberal education? Who can sufficiently prize that in which all the powers of the human mind can expand to their utmost and astonishing extent? What industry can outstretch the worth of that knowledge, by which we can travel back to the remotest ages, and live the lives of all antiquity? Nay, who can set bounds to the value of those attainments, by which we can, as it were, fly from world to world, and gaze on all the glories of creation; by which we can glide down the stream of time, and penetrate the unorganized regions of uncreated futurity? My heart burns while I write. Although literature presents the highest objects of ambition to the most refined mind, yet I consider health, in comparison with other temporal enjoyments, the most bountiful, and highest gift of heaven.

I have read three books of the Georgics, and three odes of Horace, but this last week I have read scarcely any, as I have had a great deal of company, and there has been no school. But I commence again to-day with all my might. The Attorney-General stops at Mr. Aikman's during Court. I find him very agreeable. He conversed with me more than an hour last night, in the most sociable, open manner possible.

Sept. 16th.—There is nothing of greater importance than to commence early to form our characters and regulate our conduct. Observation daily proves that man's condition in this world is generally the result of his own conduct. When we come to maturity, we perceive there is a right and a wrong in the actions of men; many who possess the same hereditary advantages, are not equally prosperous in life; some by virtuous conduct rise to respectability, honour, and happiness; while others by mean and vicious actions, forfeit the advantages of their birth, and sink into ignominy and disgrace. How necessary that in early life useful habits should be formed, and turbulent passions restrained, so that when manhood and old age come, the mind be not enervated by the follies and vices of youth, but, supported and strengthened by the Divine Being, be enabled to say, "O God, thou hast taught me from my youth, and now when I am old and grey-headed, O God, thou wilt not forsake me!"

Sept. 21st.—I have just parted with an old and faithful friend, who has left for another kingdom. How often has he kindly reproved me, and how oft have we gone to the house of God together! We may never meet again on earth, but what a mercy to have a good hope of meeting in the better land!

Sept. 23rd.—When I reflect on the millions of the human family who know nothing of Christ, my soul feels intensely for their deliverance. What a vast uncultivated field in my own country for ministers to employ their whole time and talents in exalting a crucified Saviour. Has God designed this sacred task for me? If it be Thy will, may all obstacles be removed, my heart be sanctified and my hands made pure.

Sept. 26th.—I have been much oppressed with a man-fearing spirit, but what have I to fear if God be for me? Oh, Lord, enable me to become a bold witness for Jesus Christ!

Sept. 28th.—In all the various walks of life, I find obstructions and labours, surrounded with foes, powerful as well as subtle; although I have all the promises of the Gospel to comfort and support me, yet find exertion on my own part absolutely necessary. When heaven proclaims victory, it is only that which succeeds labour. I consider it a divine requisition that my whole course of conduct, both in political and social life, should be governed by the infallible precepts of revelation; hypocrisy is inexcusable, even in the most trifling circumstances.

Sept. 29th.—I find difficulties to overcome in my literary pursuits, I had never anticipated; and it is only by the most indefatigable labour I can succeed. I am much oppressed by the labours of this day. I need Divine aid in this as well as in spiritual pursuits.

Sept. 30th.—I have been enabled to study with considerable facility. Prayer I find the most profitable employment, practice the best instructor, and thanksgiving the sweetest recreation. May this be my experience every day!

October, 2nd.—I am another week nearer my eternal destiny! Am I nearer heaven, and better prepared for death than at its commencement? Do I view sin with greater abhorence? Are my views of the Deity more enlarged? Is it my meat and drink to do his holy will? Oh, my God, how much otherwise!

From the 3rd to the 9th Oct.—During this period the afflicting hand of God has been upon me; thank God, when distressed with bodily pain, I have felt a firm assurance of Divine favour, so that all fear of death has been taken away. My soul is too unholy to meet a holy God, and mingle with the society of the blest. Oh, God, save me from the deceitfulness of my own heart!

Oct. 10th, Sabbath.—I am rapidly recovering health and strength. The Lord is my refuge and comfort. Surrounded by temptations, the applause of men is often too fascinating, and my treacherous heart dresses things in false colours. But, bless God, in his goodness and mercy he recalls my wandering steps, and invites me to dwell in safety under the shadow of his wing.

Oct. 11th.—No graces are of more importance than patience and perseverance. They give consistency and dignity to character. We may possess the most sparkling talents and the most interesting qualities, but without these graces, the former lose their lustre, and the latter their charms. In religion their influence is more important, as they form the character, by enabling us to surmount difficulties and remove obstacles. I am far from thinking them constitutional virtues, with a little additional cultivation, but I consider them the gift of heaven, less common than is generally imagined, though sometimes faintly counterfeited. They differ from natural or moral excellence in this being the proper and consistent exercise of those virtues.

Oct. 12th.—It is two weeks to-day since I first wrote home. A week ago I received a kind letter from my brother George, but was too ill with fever to read it, or to write in reply until to-day. I said : " I feel truly thankful to you for the tender concern and warm interest which you express in your letter. Tell my dear Mother that I share with her her afflictions, and that I am daily more forcibly convinced that every earthly comfort and advantage is transient and unsatisfactory, that this is not our home, but that our highest happiness amidst these fluctuating scenes, is to insure the favour and protection of him who alone can raise us above afflictions and calamities."

November 20th.—More than a month has elapsed since I recorded my religious feelings and enjoyments on paper. During this period, I have sometimes realized all the pleasures of health; at other times, borne down with pain and sickness, the spirit would be cast down. At such seasons of depression, religion would come in as my only comfort, and with the

Psalmist I would exclaim, "Hope thou in God, for I shall yet praise him who is the light of my countenance, and my God." Thus I find from blessed experience, that in every state and condition, union and intercourse with God brings true peace, joy, trust, and praise. If there be any honour, here it is. If there be any wealth, this is it. "I would rather be a door-keeper in the house of my God than dwell in the tents of wickedness." O Lord, give me more of the mind of Christ !

Nov. 25th.—In entering on the field of life, I find my mind much perplexed with the variety of objects presented to my view. The comforts and tranquility of domestic happiness attract my attention, and excite warm desires in my heart. Am I not to taste the pleasures which two hearts reciprocally united in one, mutually communicate ? or must I give up the home of domestic enjoyment to the calls of duty, and the salvation of men ? Has heaven designed that I should spend my days in seeking the lost sheep of the House of Israel ? May divine wisdom direct me, and suffer me not to follow the dictates of my own will !

Nov. 26th.—By taking a retrospective view of what is past, we learn to ask more wisely in the time to come. The cool dictates of reason, assisted by that inward monitor, conscience, placed within the breast of every individual, strongly condemns every deviation from propriety, justice, or morality. By mingling with society we learn human nature, and the scenes of public resort afford us a field for useful observation, yet retirement is the place to acquire the most important knowledge—*the knowledge of ourselves.* What would it avail us to dive into the mysteries of science, or entertain the world with new discoveries, to acquaint ourselves with the principles of morality, or learn the whole catalogue of Christian doctrines, if we are unacquainted with our own hearts, and strangers to the business of self-government ?

February 12th, 1825.—During the long period since I last penned my religious meditations, my feelings, hopes, and prospects have been extremely varied. While I was promising myself health and many temporal pleasures, God saw fit to show me the uncertainty of earthly things, and the necessity and wisdom of submission to his will, by the rod of affliction. During my sickness I have derived much pleasure and profit from the visits of pious friends, so that I have felt it is good to be afflicted.*

Feb. 13th.—I am resolved, by God's assisting grace, to keep the following resolutions :—(1) Endeavour to fix my first waking thoughts on God ; (2) By rising early to attend to my devotions, and reading the Scriptures ; (3) By praying oftener each day, and maintaining a more devotional frame of mind ; (4) By being more circumspect in my conduct and conversation ; (5) By improving my time more diligently in reading useful books, and study ; (6) By watching over my thoughts, and keeping my desires within proper bounds ; (7) By examining myself more closely by the scripture rule; (8) By leaving myself and all that concerns me to God's disposal ; (9) By reviewing every evening the actions of the day, and especially every Sabbath, examining wherein I have come short, or have kept God's precepts.

Feb. 16th.—I have lately been closely employed in reading Bishop Burnet's History of the Reformation. How sad to reflect on the cruelties that were then practised against the professors of true religion ! What a reason for thankfulness that the sway of papal authority can no longer inflict papal obligations on the consciences of men ! But after careful research into this highly authentic history, I find but few vestiges of that apostolic purity which churchmen so boastfully attribute to that memorable period of Chris-

---

* In a previous and subsequent chapter Dr. Ryerson refers more particularly to this illness (pp. 28, 39, and elsewhere). It was a turning point in his life, and decided him to enter the ministry on his twenty-second birthday.—J. G. H.

tian history. Great allowance, is, however, to be made when we consider that they were just emerging out of the superstitions of popery. That doctrines, discipline, and ceremonies, cannot be established without the royal assent, even when they are approved both by ecclesiastical and legislative authority, is a practice so different from anything that the Primitive Church authorizes, it seems to me to originate from quite a different source; that a whole nation should be bound in their religious opinions by a single individual, savours so much of popery, I think it may properly be called its offspring. Pretentions to regal supremacy in church affairs were never made till a late period, although this interference of papal authority in matters entirely spiritual, does not annul any ecclesiastical power, or prove its doctrines to be corrupt, or its ordinations illegal. It may be justly ranked among the invasions of modern corruption.

Feb. 17th.—Since I drew up, four days since, several resolutions for amendment, I bless God I have reason to believe I have made some improvement. I have applied myself more closely to study, prayed oftener, and governed my thoughts with more rigour.

Feb. 27th.—I am now emerging into life, surrounded by blessings and opportunities for usefulness and improvement; but, alas! where is my gratitude, my love to God, my zeal for his cause, and for the salvation of those who are ignorant of the great truths of the Gospel? If, O God, thou hast designed this awfully important work for me, qualify me for it; increase and enlarge my desires for the salvation of immortal souls!

March 15th.—This day I have recommenced my studies with Mr. John Law, at Hamilton. How necessary that I should be very careful in my conduct for the credit of religion and Methodism!

March 24th.—I have this day finished twenty-two years of my life. I have decided this day to travel in the Methodist Connexion and preach Jesus to the lost sons of men. Oh, the awful importance of this work! How utterly unfit I am for the undertaking! How little wisdom, experience, and, above all, grace do I possess for the labours of the ministry! Blessed Jesus, fountain of wisdom, God of power, I give myself to thee, and to the Church, to do with me according to thy will. Instruct and sanctify me, that whether I live, it may be to the Lord, and when I die it may be to the Lord!

April 3rd.—Easter Sunday.—I this day commenced my ministerial labours. Bless the Lord, he has given me a heart to feel. He hears my prayer. Oh, my soul, hang all thy hopes upon the Lord! Forbid I should seek the praise of men, but may I seek their good and God's glory.

In the morning I endeavoured to speak from Ps. cxxvi. 5, and in the evening from Acts ii. 24—a subject suitable for the day; bless the Lord, I felt something of the power of my Saviour's resurrection resting on my soul.

April 8th.—The Lord being my helper, my little knowledge and feeble talents shall be unreservedly devoted to his service. I do not yet regret giving up my worldly pursuits for the welfare of souls. I want Christ to be all in all.

April 10th.—Sabbath.—I endeavoured this morning to show the abundant provisions, the efficacy, and the triumphs of the Gospel from Isaiah xxv. 6, 7, 8, and in the afternoon I described the righteous man and his end from Prov. xiv. 32. I felt much of the presence of the Lord, and I do bless the Lord he has converted one soul in this place to-day. I feel encouraged to go on.

April 13th.—I have been depressed in spirit on account of having no abode for domestic retirement, and becoming exposed to all the besetments of public life.

April 15th.—So bowed down with temptation to-day, I almost resolved to return to my native place. But, in God's strength, I will try to do my best during the time I have engaged to supply my brother William's place.

April 16th.—In reading Rollin's account of the conquest of Babylon, I conceive more exalted ideas of the truth of the Word of God, whose predictions were so exactly fulfilled in the destruction of that city.

April 17th.—Sabbath.—My labours this day have been excessive, having delivered three discourses. In the morning my mind was dull and heavy, in the afternoon warm and pathetic, in the evening clear and fertile. I feel encouraged to continue on.

April 23rd.—I feel nothing but condemnation in reviewing the actions of the past week. Would it not be better for me to return home until I gain better government over myself. Oh, Lord, I throw myself upon thy mercy! "Take not thy Holy Spirit from me! Restore unto me the joy of thy salvation!"

April 25th and 26th.—And thus I go on, depressed and refreshed; almost discouraged because of the way, and then cheered by the kind and fatherly conversation of Rev. Thomas Madden.

April 29th.—In travelling to-day a tree fell across the road four or five rods before me, and another not far behind, but I escaped unhurt. My heart glowed with gratitude; I felt that the Lord was indeed my protector. But whilst so narrowly escaping myself, two persons, a woman and her son, who were travelling a short distance behind me, were suddenly killed by the falling of a tree, and thus in an instant hurried into eternity.

May 4th.—I watched to-day a large concourse of people assembled to witness horse-racing. I stood at a distance that I might observe an illustration of human nature. Curiosity and excitement were depicted in every countenance. What is to become of this thoughtless multitude? Is there no mercy for them? Surely there is. Why will they not be saved? Because they will not come to Him.

May 5th.—During the day I preached once, to a listening but wicked assembly. In the afternoon I heard my brother William. I was affected by the force of his reasoning, and the power of his eloquence. I hope the Lord will help me to imitate his piety and zeal.

May 7th.—A camp-meeting was commenced this afternoon on Yonge Street, near the town of York. Rev. Thomas Madden preached from, "Lord help me!" Every countenance indicated interest, and every heart appeared willing to receive the word. In the evening a pious, aged man spoke (Mr. D. Y.) His discourse was full of God. Several were converted and made very happy.

May 8th.—The people rose at 5 a.m. After prayers and breakfast, there was a prayer meeting, during which God was especially present. At 8 a.m. I preached from Hosea xiii. 3. This was followed by two exhortations; then Rev. Rowley Heyland preached from, "Buy the truth, and sell it not." About two o'clock the people were again assembled to hear the Rev. James Richardson (formerly a lieutenant in the British Navy) from the words, "Be ye reconciled to God." His style was plain but unadorned, his reasoning clear, and his arguments forcible. The services concluded with the celebration of the Lord's Supper. About three hundred communicated, sixty-two professed to have obtained the pardon of their sins, and forty-two gave their names as desirous of becoming members of the Methodist Society. After this, a concluding address was delivered by the Rev. Wm. Ryerson, in which he gave particular directions to the Methodists as subjects under the civil constitution, as members of the Church of Christ, as parents, as children, as individuals. He animadverted on the groundless and disingenuous aspersions that had been thrown out through the press against Methodism, on account of the suspected loyalty of its constitutional principles. He warmly insisted on a vigorous observance, support, and respect for the Civil Government, both from the beneficence of its laws and the equity of its administration, as well as from the authority of God. The concluding ceremony was the most affecting I ever witnessed, especially in the affection which the people showed for their ministers.

May 12th.—I have this day ridden nearly thirty miles, preached three times, and met two classes. I felt very much fatigued, yet the Lord has given me " strength equal to my day."

May 19th.—I have been much blessed in the society of pious friends. A part of the week I felt very sick, but was greatly comforted by the conversation and affectionate treatment of my kindest friend, Mrs. Smith. Since I commenced labouring for my Master I have found fathers and mothers, brothers and sisters, all ready to supply my every want.

May 24th.—A Camp-meeting commenced at Mount Pleasant. The presence of both Mississauga and Mohawk Indians added greatly to the interest of the meeting. Peter Jones addressed his people in their own tongue; although I did not understand, I was much affected by his fervency and pathos. He spoke in English in a manner that astonished all present.

Another Indian Chief addressed his brethren in the Mohawk tongue. I could not understand a word of it, but was carried away with his pathos and energy. These Indians thanked the white people for sending them the Gospel. He said that upwards of sixty Indians had been converted, and could testify that God had power to forgive sin. He, *i. e.*, a young Chippewa said that the most earnest desire and prayer of the Christian Indians was that God would drive the horrid whiskey from their nation. It was truly affecting to see this young man arise and testify in the presence of God and this large assembly, that " he had the witness in his own soul, that God for Christ's sake had forgiven all his sins." The congregation was much moved, and prayers and praises were heard in every part of the assembly. At the close of the exercises, on the following day, the Mohawk Chief said, " They considered that they belonged to the Methodist Church, as they had done all for them."

May 29th.—For many days I have been cast down by a weight of care. My Father is exceedingly anxious that I should return home, and remain with him during his lifetime. A position in the Church of England has presented itself, and other advantageous attractions with regard to this world, offer themselves.* It makes my heart bleed to see the anxiety of my parents. But is it duty? If they were in want I would return to them without hesitation, but when I consider they have everything necessary, can it be my duty to gratify them at the expense of the cause of God? Surely if a man may leave father and mother to join himself to a wife, how much more reasonable *to leave all* to join himself to the Christian ministry. My parents are dear to me, but my duty to God is dearer still. One thing do I desire, that I may live in the House of the Lord for ever !

And shall I leave a Church through whose faithful instructions I have been brought to know God, for any advantages that the entrance to another might afford me? No, far be it from me ; as I received the Lord Jesus, so I will walk in him. Earthly distinctions will be but short ; but the favour of God will last forever. Besides, is it a sacrifice to do my duty ? Is it not rather a cause of gratitude that I know my duty, and am allowed to perform it ? My heart is united with the Methodists, my soul is one with theirs ; my labours are acceptable, and they are anxious that I should continue with them. I believe in their Articles, I approve of their Constitution, and I believe them to be of the Church of Christ.

* Dr. Ryerson refers in another chapter to the overtures which were made to him at this time to enter the ministry of the Church of England.—J. G. H.

Saltfleet, May 30*th*.—[Amongst Dr. Ryerson's papers I find the two following letters. The first addressed from Saltfleet, on this day, to his brother George; the second to his Mother on the following day.—J. G. H.]

[To his brother, Rev. George Ryerson, he said : I suppose your first inquiry is to know my spiritual condition and prospects. As to my religious enjoyments, I think that I have reason to believe I am daily blessed with the divine presence to enlighten, to instruct, and to assist me in my researches and meditations, and in the other arduous duties I have to discharge. Never did I so sensibly feel the importance of the work in which I am now engaged, as I have these few days past. I feel that I am altogether inadequate to it; but God has in a very special manner, at different times, been my wisdom and strength. I do not feel sorry that I have commenced travelling as a preacher. I think I feel more deeply the worth of souls at heart. I feel willing to spend my all, and be spent in the cause of God, if I may become the unworthy instrument in doing some good to the souls of men. The greatest assistance I receive in my public labours, is that which results from a firm dependence on God for light, life, and power. When I forget this I am visited with that barrenness of mind, and hardness of heart which are always the companions of those who live at a distance from God. In discharging every public duty, my prayer to God is, to renew my commission afresh, and give me wisdom and energy, and I do not find him slack concerning his promise. I am striving to pursue my studies with unabating ardour. My general practice is to retire at ten o'clock, or before, and rise at five. When I am travelling, I strive to converse no more than is necessary and useful, endeavouring at all times to keep in mind the remark of Dr. Clarke, that a preacher's whole business is to save souls, and that that preacher is the most useful who is the most in his closet. On my leisure days I read from ten to twenty verses of Greek a day, besides reading history, the Scriptures, and the best works on practical divinity, among which Chalmers' has decidedly the preference in my mind, both for piety and depth of thought. These two last studies employ the greatest part of my time. My preaching is altogether original. I endeavour to collect as many ideas from every source as I can; but I do not copy the expression of any one. For I do detest seeing blooming flowers in dead men's hands. I think it my duty, and I try to get a general knowledge, and view of any subject that I discuss before-hand; but not unfrequently I have tried to preach with only a few minutes previous reflection. Remember me to my dear Mother, and give her this letter to read, and tell her that I will write soon.]

Saltfleet, May 31st.—[To his Mother he writes: My dear Mother, I am thankful to say that I am well, and am trying in a weak way to serve the Lord, and persuading as many others to do so as I can. I feel that I am almost destitute of every necessary qualification for so important a work. The Lord has blessed me in a very special manner at many different times. Our prospects are very favourable in some places. Our congregations are generally large, and still increasing. We have twenty-four appointments in four weeks. I have formed some very useful and pious acquaintances since I left home. The Lord seems to be with me, and renders my feeble efforts acceptable in general. My acquaintance seems to be sought by all classes, and I try to improve such advantages in spreading, by my example and conversation, the blessed religion of Christ among all ranks. I have many temptations to contend with, and many trials to weigh me down at times. Some of these arise from a sense of the injustice which I have done to important subjects, on account of my ignorance, which drives me to a throne of grace, and a closer application to my studies. My situation is truly a state of trial, and none but God could support and direct me. And I do feel the comforting and refreshing influence of his divine power at times very sensibly. I am determined, by his assistance, never to rest contented until he not only becomes my wisdom, but my sanctification, and my full redemption. And blessed be the Lord, my dear Mother, I do feel a hope, and a confidence that the same divine power and goodness which supports and comforts you in your ill state of health, and which gives you victory over your trials, and consolation in your distress, will conduct me, too, through this stormy maze, and we shall yet have the blessedness of meeting at our Father's table in Heaven. And God being my helper, my dear Mother, when you have gone home to rest with God, I am determined to pursue the same path, which you have strewn with prayers, with tears, and living faith, until I reach the same blessed port. I hope that you will pray that the Lord would help and save me forever! If I had no other inducement to serve God, and walk in the path of religion, but your comfort, I would try and devote my life to it while I live; but when Heaven's transcendant glory beams forth in prospective view, my soul burns to possess the kingdom, and my heart is enlarged for the salvation of others. I wish you would get George to write immediately, and let me know the state of your mind, and your opinion about my returning home, also his own opinion on that subject.—J. G. H.]

July 2nd.—This week has been a season of trial. I have left my Father's house once more, and arrived on my Circuit.

July 3rd—Sabbath.—I have preached twice to-day in Niagara for the first time; felt very embarrassed, but my trust was in God, and my prayer to Him for assistance.

July 4th.—This evening I have been distressed in mind on account of leaving my parents. My heart melts within me when I think of my Father's faltering voice, when lying on his bed he said, "Good-bye, Egerton," and reached forth his trembling hand, saying by his countenance that he never expected to see his son a resident in his house again. He laid himself back in his bed in apparent despair, no more to enjoy the society of the child he loved. Oh, my God! is it not too much for humanity? Nature sinks beneath the weight. It is only God that can sustain. May I endure manfully to the end!

July 6th and 7th.—I have been much interested in reading Dr. Coke's discourses, also Wesley's sermons on "The Kingdom of God."

July 9th.—I have crossed the river to the United States to-day for the first time. The manners of the people are not pleasant to me.

July 10th—Sabbath.—The Lord has greatly blessed me this day. I have preached three times. My heart overflowed with love for immortal souls. Many wept, and God's people seemed stirred up to engage afresh in His service. In the evening, I preached to very a wicked congregation, from Matt. xvi. 24. My mind was clear, particularly in argument, but they seemed to be unaffected.

July 14th.—I have been afflicted with illness, but the Lord has comforted me. Again had to mourn over light conversation, still I think I have gained some victory. I am determined to watch and pray until I obtain a triumph over this trying besetment.

July 17th.—I felt so ill this morning that I could not attend my appointment, but recovered so as to preach feebly in the afternoon. The Word seemed to rest with power on the people.

July 21st.—For several days I have been much interested in reading Fletcher's "Portrait of St. Paul." When I compare my actions and feelings with the standard there laid down, I blush on account of my ignorance in the duties and labours connected with my calling. Did the ministers of the Gospel obtain and possess a deeper communion with God? Did they cultivate primitive piety in their lives, and Gospel simplicity in their preaching, surely the power of darkness could not stand before them! How many learned discourses are entirely lost in the wisdom of words, whereas plain and simple sermons, delivered with power and demonstration of the Spirit, have been attended with astonishing success.

July 27th.—I have been considerably agitated in my mind for the last two days, having lost my horse. The fatigue in searching for her has been considerable. Thank God she is found!

July 31st—Sabbath.—Greatly blessed in attending a Quarterly meeting in Hamilton; also in hearing an interesting account of the Indians receiving their presents at York. Peter Jones had written to Col. Givens to enquire just what time they must be there, stating that as many of them had become Christianized and industrious, they did not want to lose time. The Colonel was surprised at the news, and replied, giving the necessary information. Peter Jones' letter was shown to Rev. Dr. Strachan and His Excellency the Governor. It excited great curiosity. When the Indians arrived, the Colonel had, as usual, brought liquor to treat them, but as Peter Jones informed him the Christian Indians would not drink, he very wisely said "the others should not have it either," and sent it back. How the Lord honours those who honour Him. Rev. Dr. Strachan and several ladies and gentlemen assembled to see the distribution of presents. The Christian Indians were requested to separate from the others, that they might read and sing. The company was much pleased, and Dr. Strachan prayed with them. On the following Sabbath, the Dr. visited the Credit settlement, and attended one of the meetings which was addressed by Peter Jones. Dr. Strachan proposed their coming under the superintendence of the Church of England; but after holding a council, they declined, deciding to remain under the direction of the Methodists. May the Lord greatly prosper his work amongst them, preserve them from every delusive snare, and may their happy souls be kept blameless unto the day of Jesus Christ!

August 1st.—This day I have been admitted into the Methodist Connexion, licensed as a Local Preacher, and recommended to the Annual Conference to be received on trial. How awful the responsibility! How dreadful my condition if I violate my charge or deal deceitfully with souls! Oh, God, assist me to declare Thy whole counsel! and help me to instruct by example as well as precept. How swiftly am I gliding down time's rapid stream! I am daily reminded of the uncertainty and shortness of life. I went to-day to visit a friend, and (as usual) smilingly came to the door, when behold! all was mourning and sorrow! An infant son had just taken its everlasting flight to the arms of Jesus. He was a fine boy, active and promising, but he had suddenly gone to return no more! The father's philosophy forsakes him now; parental feeling has uncontrolled sway. I recommended religion as the only sufficient support and comfort. I touched on the mysterious government of God; that truly "Clouds and darkness are round about him," yet "righteousness and judgment are the habitation of his throne." I pointed out the happiness of the beloved babe, which should lead us to devote our all to His service, that we might eventually share in the unspeakable blessedness to which the lovely infant is now raised.

Aug. 10th.—My soul rejoices at the news I have heard from home, that my eldest brother (George) has resolved to join the Methodists, and become a missionary among the Indians. How encouraging and comforting the thought that four of us are now united in the same Church, and pursue the same glorious calling. My Father has become reconciled, and my Mother is willing to part with her sons for the sake of the Church of Christ.

Aug. 14th—Sabbath.—Never did I feel my pride more mortified in the discharge of public duty. I was desirous of delivering a discourse, in Niagara, which would meet the approbation of all, after carefully adjusting the subject, by the assistance of a variety of authors; but through fatigue (having rode twelve miles), and embarrassment, I was scarcely able to finish. My heart felt hard and my mind barren, conscience reproached me that I had not acted with a single eye to the glory of God. In the afternoon, I threw myself on the mercy of God; my tongue was loosened and my heart warmed. Surely, "They that trust in the Lord shall not be confounded."

Aug. 17th.—This morning a lady died with whom I had considerable conversation on the subject of Methodism, and on the propriety of her daughters joining the society contrary to her wish. She appeared to be satisfied with my account of the principles and nature of Methodism, but did not like to acknowledge the propriety of her daughters' proceedings, although her judgment seemed convinced as I adverted to the principles of her own church. I am informed that yesterday she said, "The girls are right and I am wrong." How comforting this must be to her daughters, who have entirely overcome her opposition by their kindness, affection, and gospel simplicity.

Aug. 22nd.—Yesterday I delivered a discourse on the subject of Missions, for the purpose of forming a Missionary Society in this place (Niagara).

September 3rd, 1825.—I took tea this afternoon at Youngstown, U.S., for the first time.

Sept. 6th.—Had the pleasure of meeting my brother to-day, whom I have not seen for a year. How comforting to meet with those who are not only near by the ties of nature, but much more by the changing power of divine grace.

Sept. 9th.—Have been greatly benefitted to-day by hearing Bishop Hedding preach from Rev. iii. 5.

Sept. 16th.—I bless God for what mine eyes hath seen, and mine ears have heard to-day, being the first anniversary of the Canadian Missionary Society. The Hon. John Willson, M.P.P., was requested to take the chair. Several Indians, who had been brought to a knowledge of the truth, through the efforts of this Society, were present and spoke. How delightful to see the warlike Mohawk, and the degraded Mississauga, exchanging the heathen war-whoop for the sublime praise of the God of love! This is the commencement of greater things which the Lord will do for the aboriginies of Canada.

Sept. 23rd.—I have this day received my appointment for York and Yonge street. Never did I feel more sensibly the necessity of Divine help. Help me, O God, to go forth in Thy strength, and contend manfully under the banner of Christ! **Amen.**

CHAPTER III.

1825—1826.

FIRST YEAR OF MY MINISTRY AND FIRST CONTROVERSY.

MY first appointment after my admission on trial was to the (what was then called the York and Yonge Street Circuit), which then embraced the Town of York (now the City of Toronto) Weston, the Townships of Vaughan, King, West Gwillimbury, North Gwillimbury, East Gwillimbury, Whitchurch, Markham, Pickering, Scarboro', and York, over which we travelled, and preached from twenty-five to thirty-five sermons in four weeks, preaching generally three times on Sabbath and attending three class meetings, besides preaching and attending class meetings on week days. The roads were (if in any place they could be called roads) bad beyond description; could only be travelled on horse-back, and on foot; the labours hard, and the accommodations of the most primitive kind; but we were received as angels of God by the people, our ministrations being almost the only supply of religious instruction to them; and nothing they valued more than to have the preacher partake of their humble and best hospitality.

It was during the latter part of this the first year of my itinerant ministry (April and May, 1826) that I was drawn and forced into the controversy on the Clergy Reserves and equal civil and religious rights and privileges among all religious persuasions in Upper Canada.* There had been some controversy between the leaders of the Churches of England and Scotland on their comparative standing as established churches in Upper Canada. In my earliest years, I had read and studied Blackstone's Commentaries on the laws of England, especially the rights of the Crown, and Parliament and Subject, Paley's Moral and Political Philosophy; and when I read and observed the character of the policy, and state of things in Canada, I felt that it was not according to the principles of British liberty, or of the British Constitution; but I had not the slightest idea of writing anything on the subject.

At this juncture, (April, 1826,) a publication appeared, entitled "Sermon Preached and Published by the Venerable Archdeacon of York, in May, 1826, on the Death of the Late Bishop of

---

* A fuller reference to this subject will be found in Chapters vi. and viii.—H.

Quebec," containing a sketch of the rise and progress of the Church of England in these provinces, and an appeal on behalf of that Church to the British Government and Parliament. In stating the obstacles which impeded the progress of the Church of England in Upper Canada, the memorable Author of the able discourse attacked the character of the religious persuasions not connected with the Church of England, especially the Methodists, whose ministers were represented as American in their origin and feelings, ignorant, forsaking their proper employments to preach what they did not understand, and which, from their pride, they disdained to learn; and were spreading disaffection to the civil and religious institutions of Great Britain. In this sermon, not only was the status of the Church of England claimed as the Established Church of the Empire, and exclusively entitled to the Clergy Reserves, or one seventh of the lands of Upper Canada, but an appeal was made to the Imperial Government and Parliament for a grant of £300,000 per annum, to enable the Church of England in Upper Canada, to maintain the loyalty of Upper Canada to England. And these statements and appeals were made ten years after the close of the war of 1812–1815, by the United States against Britain, with the express view of conquering Canada and annexing it to the United States; and during which war both Methodist preachers and people were conspicuous for their loyalty and zeal in defence of the country.

The Methodists in York (now Toronto) at that time (1826) numbered about fifty persons, young and old; the two preachers arranged to meet once in four weeks on their return from their country tours, when a social meeting of the leading members of the society was held for conversation, consultation, and prayer. One of the members of this company obtained and brought to the meeting a copy of the Archdeacon's sermon, and read the parts of it which related to the attacks upon the Methodists, and the proposed method of exterminating them. The reading of those extracts produced a thrilling sensation of indignation and alarm, and all agreed that something must be written and done to defend the character and rights of Methodists and others assailed, against such attacks and such a policy. The voice of the meeting pointed to me to undertake this work. I was then designated as "The Boy Preacher," from my youthful appearance, and as the youngest minister in the Church. I objected on account of my youth and incompetence; but my objections were overruled, when I proposed as a compromise, that during our next country tour the Superintendent of the Circuit (Rev. James Richardson), and myself should each write on the subject, and from what we should both write, something might be compiled to meet the case. This was agreed to, and at our next social monthly meeting in the town, inquiry was made as to what had been written in defence of the Methodists and others, against the attacks and policy of the Archdeacon of York. It was found that the Superintendent of the Circuit had written nothing; and on my being questioned, I said I had endeavoured to obey the instructions of my senior brethren. It was then insisted that I must read what I had written. I at length yielded, and read my answer to the attacks made on us. The reading of my paper was attended with alternate laughter and tears on the part of those present, all of whom insisted that it should be printed, I objecting that I had never written anything for the press, and was not competent to such a task, and advanced to throw my manuscript into the fire, when one of the elder members caught me by the arms, and another wrenched the manuscript out of my hands, saying he would take it to the printer. Finding my efforts vain to recover it, I said if it were restored I would not destroy it but rewrite it and return it to the brethren to do what they pleased with it. I did so. Two of the senior brethren took the manuscript to the printer, and its publication produced a sensation scarcely less violent and general than a Fenian invasion. It is said that before every house in Toronto might be seen groups reading and discussing the paper on the evening of its publication in June; and the excitement spread throughout the country. It was the first defiant defence of the Methodists, and of the equal and civil rights of all religious persuasions; the first protest and argument on legal and British constitutional grounds, against the erection of a dominant church establishment supported by the state in Upper Canada.

It was the Loyalists of America, and their descendants, in Upper Canada who first lifted up the voice of remonstrance against ecclesiastical despotism in the province, and unfurled the flag of equal religious rights and liberty for all religious persuasions.

The sermon of the Archdeacon of York was the third formal attack made by the Church of England clergy upon the characters of their unoffending Methodist brethren and those of other religious persuasions; but no defence of the assailed parties had as yet been written. In a subsquent discussion on another topic, referring to this matter, I said :

"Up to this time not a word had been written respecting the clergy of the Church of England, or the Clergy Reserve question, by any minister or member of the Methodist Church. At that time the Methodists had no law to secure a foot of land, on which to build parsonages, Chapels, and in which to bury their dead ; their ministers were not allowed to solemnize matrimony; and some of them had been the objects of cruel and illegal persecution on the part of magistrates and others in authority. And now they were the butt of unprovoked and unfounded aspersions from two heads of Episcopal Clergy, while pursuing the 'noiseless tenor of their way,' through trackless forests and bridgeless rivers and streams, to preach among the scattered inhabitants the unsearchable riches of Christ."*

The Review, in defence of the Methodists and others against such gratuitous and unjust imputations, consisted of about thirty octavo pages, appeared over the signature of "A Methodist Preacher;" it was commenced near Newmarket, in a cottage owned by the late Mr. Elias Smith, whose wife was a sister of the Lounts—a woman of great excellence. It was written piecemeal in the humble residences of the early settlers, in the course of eight days, during which time I rode on horseback nearly a hundred miles and preached seven sermons. On its publication I pursued my country tour of preaching, &c., little conscious of the storm that was brewing; but on my return to town, at the end of two weeks, I received newspapers containing four replies to my *Review*—three of them written by clergymen, and one by a scholarly layman of the Church of England. In those replies to the then unknown author of the *Review*, I was assailed by all sorts of contemptuous and criminating epithets—all denying that the author of such a publication could be "a Methodist Preacher,"—but was "an American," "a rebel," "a traitor,"—and that the *Review* was the "prodigious effort of a party."

My agitation was extreme; finding myself, against my own intention and will, in the very tempest of a discussion for which I felt myself poorly prepared, I had little appetite or sleep. At length roused to a sense of my position, I felt that I must either flee or fight. I decided upon the latter, strengthened by the consciousness that my principles were those of the British Constitution and in defence of British rights. I devoted a day to fasting and prayer, and then went at my adversaries in good earnest. In less than four years after the commencement of this controversy, laws were passed authorising the different religious denominations to hold land for churches, parsonages, and burying grounds, and their Ministers to solemnize matrimony; while the Legislative Assembly passed, by large majorities, resolutions, and addresses to the Crown against the exclusive pretensions of the Church of England to the Clergy Reserves and being the exclusive established Church of Upper Canada, though the Clergy Reserve question itself continued to be discussed, and was not finally settled until more than ten years afterwards.

* Letters to the Hon. W. H. Draper on "*The Clergy Reserve Question; as a Matter of History, a Question of Law, and a Subject of Legislation.*" Toronto, 1839, pp. 11, 12.

Several months after the commencement of this controversy I paid my first annual visit to my parents, and for the first two days the burden of my Father's conversation was this controversy which was agitating the country. At length, while walking in the orchard, my Father turned short, and in a stern tone, said, "Egerton, they say that you are the author of these papers which are convulsing the whole country. I want to know whether you are or not?" I was compelled to acknowledge that I was the writer of these papers, when my Father lifted up his hands, in an agony of feeling, and exclaimed, "My God! we are all ruined!"

The state of my own mind and the character of my labours during this first year of my ministry, may be inferred from the following brief extracts from my diary:—

October 4th,—I have this evening arrived on my Circuit at York. I feel the change to be awfully important, and entirely inadequate to give proper instruction to so intelligent a people. The Lord give me his assisting grace. I am resolved to devote my time, my heart, my all, to God without reserve. I do feel determined, by God's assistance, to rise early, spend no more time than is absolutely necessary, pray oftener, and more fervently, to be modest and solemn in the discharge of my public duties—to improve every leisure moment by reading or meditation, and to depend upon the assistance of Almighty God for the performance of every duty. Oh, Lord, assist an ignorant youth to declare thy great salvation!

Oct. 9th.—Commenced my labours this day. In the morning, the Lord was very near to help me, giving me a tongue to speak, and a heart to feel. But in the evening, after I got through my introduction, recollection failed and my mind was entirely blank. For nearly five minutes I could scarcely speak a word; after this my thoughts returned. This seemed to be the hand of God, to show me my entire weakness.

Oct. 16th—Sabbath.—Oh, God, water the efforts of this day with thy grace! If I am the means of persuading only one soul to embrace the Lord Jesus, I shall be amply rewarded. "Paul planted, Apollos watered, but God gave the increase." 1 Cor. iii. 6.

Oct. 20th.—Once more, my Saviour, I renew my covenant and give myself away; 'tis all that I can do.

Oct. 27th.—For several days past the Lord has been very gracious to my soul, and has greatly helped me in declaring His glorious counsels. But to-day, my heart felt very hard while preaching to a company of graceless sinners. It was in a tavern, and I doubt the propriety of preaching in such places.

Oct. 31st.—I am one month nearer my end; am I so much nearer God and heaven? There are many precious hours I can give no favourable account of. Had I been more faithful, I might have led some poor wanderer into the way of truth. Oh, God, enter not into judgment with me! Spare the barren fig-tree a little longer.

November 4th—Friday (Fast Day.)—One reason why my labours are not more blessed, is because I feel and know so little of spiritual things myself. There is too much of self about me.

"When, gracious Lord, when shall it be,
That I shall find my all in Thee;
The fulness of Thy promise prove,
The seal of Thine eternal love."

Nov. 6th.—I felt greatly blessed while addressing a large Sabbath-school of more than a hundred scholars.

Nov. 7th.—[On this day, the following letter was written from York by Dr. Ryerson to his Father. He said: On leaving the old home lately, I promised to write to you, my dear Father, and let you know how I am getting on. I arrived here a few days after I left home. I have received a letter from brother William, who told me that his prospects are encouraging. I received a letter also from brother John. He reached Perth about a fortnight after he left home, and was cordially received by all classes. He preached the Sabbath after he got there to large and respectable congregations. He was very much pleased with his appointment, and his prospects are very favourable. On the first evening of his preaching, one professed to experience justification by faith, and several were deeply convicted. He thinks, from several circumstances, that his appointment is of God. I am very well pleased with my appointment. I travel with a person who is deeply pious, a true and disinterested friend, and a very respectable preacher. I travel about two hundred miles in four weeks, and preach twenty-five times, besides funerals. I spend two Sabbaths in York, and two in the country. Our prospects on the circuit are encouraging. In York we have most flattering prospects. We have some increase almost every week. Our morning congregations fill the chapel, which was never the case before; and in the evening the chapel will not contain but little more than three-quarters of the people. Last evening several members of Parliament were present. I never addressed so large an audience before, and I never was so assisted from heaven in preaching as at this place. I have spent the last two Sabbaths in York, and I go to-day into the country. I was requested yesterday to address the Union Sunday-school, which contains about 150 or 200 children. It was a public examination of the School. I never heard children recite so correctly, and so perfectly before, as they did. There was quite a large congregation present, as it was designed to make a contribution for the support of the School. I first addressed a short discourse to the children, and then addressed the assembly. It was the most precious season that I ever experienced. It is, my dear Father, the most delightful employment I ever engaged in, to proclaim the name of Jesus to lost sinners. I feel more firmly attached to the cause than ever. The Lord has comforted, blessed, and prospered me beyond my expectations. I am resolved to devote all that I have and am, to his service. Get George to write shortly all the news of the day. Remember me to my dear Mother.—H.]

[After writing to his Father, he wrote on the same day to his brother George, as follows :—

I have just heard the Governor's Speech to the two Houses of the Legislature. In the latter part of his address he hinted at a certain communication, which, by the permission of His Majesty, he would make by Message, to remove apprehensions that affected the civil rights of a very considerable part of the community. As to my religious enjoyments, I think that Christ has been more precious to me than ever. When I came into this Circuit, I began to fast and pray more than ever I had done before, and the Lord has greatly blessed me. I have scarcely had a barren time in preaching. I feel more strongly attached to the cause than ever. While the Lord will help, I am resolved to go forward. Rev. James Richardson is a man of good sense, and deep piety, and a very acceptable and useful preacher.—H.]

Nov. 10th.—Travelled twenty-two miles and preached twice. My views of Scripture of late have been obscure; I can recall the truths to my mind, but they don't make that impression they have hitherto done. Is this change of feeling inherent, or the effect of neglect of duty, and want of watchfulness? I will examine this point more fully. I know it is my privilege to enjoy peace with God, but whether it be my privilege at all times to possess equal feeling, I am not certain.

Nov. 23rd.—I think Mr. Wesley's advice indispensably necessary, "to rise as soon as we wake." I am resolved to be more punctual in rising for the time to come.

Nov. 29th.—How painful does my experience prove the truth of the Apostle, that "when 1 would do good evil is present with me." I have thought sometimes it would be impossible to forget God, or to be lukewarm in His cause ; but alas ! I am prone to evil continually.

December 14th.—The Lord has greatly delivered my soul from the burden of guilt and fear with which I have been so painfully bowed down for several days past ; and, blessed be the name of the Lord, He begins to revive His work on the circuit. Five more have been added to the Church this week. Glory to God for His mercy and love !

Dec. 30th.—A part of the day I spent in the Legislature. The first three months of last year I was in bad health, confined to my bed part of the time. The last nine months I have spent in trying to seek the lost sheep of the house of Israel.

York, January 1st, 1826.—How faithful is the Saviour to that promise, "Lo, I am with thee, even to the end of the world." Though weak in body I have had to preach three times a day, and travel many miles. Jesus has been very precious to my soul.

February 3rd.—I have travelled to-day in an Irish settlement, and preached twice to them. My life is a scene of toil and pain, I am far from well, and far from parents and relatives. While others enjoy all the advantages of domestic life, I am doomed to deny myself. Oh, my soul, behold the example the Saviour has set. "He had not where to lay his head." Is the servant above his Lord?

Feb. 11th.— For several days I have been visiting my friends. I think they are improving in religious knowledge. What an unspeakable blessing to see them showing a desire to walk in the narrow way that leads to life eternal.

Feb. 18th.—I have just returned to my Circuit. This is the first time I ever dropped appointments for the gratification of seeing my friends. It has taught me the lesson, that labouring in the vineyard of the Lord is more blessed than any personal gratification.

Feb. 28th.—This month presents the most mournful portrait I have ever beheld in retrospect of my past time since I began to travel. Since I visited my friends everything has gone against me. The season of recreation was not improved as it ought to have been ; I lost the unction of the Holy One, and returned to my Circuit depressed in mind. Shall I sink down in despair ? No, I will return unto the Lord. He has smitten, He will heal. I will go to the fountain open for sin and uncleanness. I will renew my covenant, and offer my poor all to him once more.

March 23rd.—This day closes my twenty-third year and the first of my ministry. How mysterious was the providence which induced me to enter the itinerant ministry. It was the Lord's doing, and it is marvellous in my eyes. Since I have devoted myself to Him in a perpetual covenant, how great has been His paternal care over me. I have felt the rod of affliction, but, He has sanctified it. I have been assailed by temptation, but He has delivered me. I have been caressed and flattered, but the Lord, in great mercy, has saved me from the dangerous rocks of vanity and pride. My soul has at times been overspread with clouds and darkness, but the "Sun of Righteousness has again risen" with brightness on his wings. I have oft been cast down, but blessed be the Lord who has given me the "oil of joy for mourning, and the garment of praise for the spirit of heaviness." My mind at times has been filled with doubts and fears, and I have been tempted to say, " I have cleansed my heart in vain, and washed my hands in innocency," but the Lord has saved my feet from slipping, and established my goings upon a firm foundation. He has put a new song into my mouth, and enabled me to say, "What time I am afraid I will trust in Thee."

April 17th.—This day, for the first time, I have declared to the aborigines of the country that "Jesus is precious to those who believe." My heart rejoiced in God, who is claiming the heathen for His inheritance.

April 19th.—[On this day Dr. Ryerson wrote from Saltfleet to his Mother. He said :—

As you, my dear Mother, were always anxious about my health, I write to-day to assure you that since I left home it has been extremely good. I think I am making some small progress in those attainments which are only acquired by prayer, and holy devotedness to God. I find the work I have undertaken is an all-important one. I have many things to learn, and many things to unlearn. I have had some severe trials, and some mortifying scenes. At other times I have been unspeakably blessed, and I have been greatly encouraged at some favourable prospects. Several times my views have been greatly enlarged, and my mind enlightend, while, with a warm and full heart, I have been trying to address a large and much affected congregation. It is not my endeavour to shine, or to please, but to speak to the heart and the conscience. And with a view to this, I have aimed at the root of injurious prejudices, and notions that I have found prevalent in different places. I find, by experience, that a firm reliance on the power and grace of Christ is everything. I hope that you, my dear Mother, will pray for me that the Lord will give me grace, power, and wisdom to do my whole duty.

I am very sorry to hear of your ill-health. I hope and pray that the Father of all mercies will continue to support, comfort, and deliver you, in the midst of your afflictions and sorrows. Blessed be the Lord, dear Mother, the day is not far distant when you can rest your weary spirit in the arms of Jesus; and should I survive you, while you are pursuing the blessed, triumphant theme of redeeming love, in strains the most exalted, I will endeavour in my feeble way to follow you to the same blessed kingdom.

Brother William received a letter from John last week. His health is very bad. His excessive labour has overcome him. He has forty appointments in four weeks. He is now stationed in Kingston.—H.]

April 25*th*.—For several days past I have been altogether engaged in writing a controversial pamphlet, and have attended little to the duty of self-examination.

April 28*th*.—I have been much blessed in reading the Journal of John Nelson. When I compare the unwearied labours, and severe sufferings of that brave soldier of the Cross, with my little efforts and sufferings, I blush for my lukewarmness, and am ashamed of my fearfulness.

May 10*th*.—[In these early days, the Methodist ministers had but little time for study before commencing their ministerial labours, and, as Dr. Ryerson often told me, they had to resort to many expedients to secure the necessary time for reading and study. This had often to be done on horseback. Dr. Ryerson's eldest brother, George, who had attended Union College, N.Y., turned his advantages in this respect to a good account. He sought to stimulate his younger brothers to devote every spare moment to suitable preparation for their work. In reply to a letter on this subject, from Rev. George Ryerson to his brother William, he said:—

I thank you for your kind advice respecting composition, and shall endeavour to follow it, although my necessary duties leave but very little time for literary improvement. Since I saw you, I have been principally engaged in Biblical studies which I find both profitable and interesting. I am now engaged in reading the Bible through in course with Dr. Adam Clarke's notes, also Paley's books. I received a letter from brother John a few days since. He had received a number into the Society, and there were a number more who appeared to be seriously awakened. Elder Madden, who was at York last week, says that Egerton is well, and that the cause of religion is prospering in York, and on the Yonge Street Circuit. We have had but very little increase in Niagara since I saw you, although our congregation is very large and attentive.—H.]

May 18*th.*—[In writing to-day to his brother George, Dr. Ryerson mentioned that he and Elder Case had visited the Credit Indians. Elder Case, he said, had come up to get Mrs. Wm. Kerr (*née* Brant) to correct the translation of one of the Gospels, and some hymns, in order to have them printed. He also wished Peter Jones to go down and preach to the Indians on the Bay of Quinte (Tyendinaga). It was there, he said, that the work of religion had begun to spread among them. About twelve had experienced religion, and others are under awakening. They do not, he said, understand enough English to receive religious instruction in that language; and, therefore, he wished Peter Jones to go down for two or three weeks.

In this letter Dr. Ryerson said: I think the cause of religion is prospering in different parts of the Circuit. Upwards of thirty have been added to us in this town (York) since Conference, and our present prospects are equally encouraging. My colleague is a man who is wholly devoted to the work of saving souls. I hope that God will give us an abundant harvest.

I am employing all my leisure time in the prosecution of my studies. I also practice composition. I am reading Rollin's Ancient History, Greek, and miscellaneous works. Are Father, and Mother, and all the family well? How are their minds disposed towards God and heaven?

We have formed a Missionary Society in this place. I think we shall collect $40 or $50. I hope that period is not remote when the whole colony will be brought into a state of salvation!—H.]

June 7*th.*—My mind has been much afflicted with care and anxiety, for some days, on account of the controversy in which I am engaged. I feel it to be the cause of God; and I am resolved to follow truth and the Holy Scriptures in whatever channel they will lead me. Oh, Lord, I commend my feeble efforts to thy blessings! Grant me wisdom from above; and take the cause into thy own hands, for thy name's sake!

June 25*th.*—I have spent some days in visiting my friends, and also attending a Camp-meeting. The weather has been very unfavourable; but the showers that watered the earth are now past, and showers of Divine blessing are descending. The song of praise is ascending, and sinners are crying for mercy. Oh, Lord, carry on the glorious work!

July 7*th.*—The enemy gained victory over me to-day, by tempting me to neglect Class for other employments. But I was defeated. Company coming in, I was hindered from doing what I desired. Conscience condemned, and darkness and distress followed. Oh, Lord, henceforth help me *to do my duty!*

July 9*th.—Sabbath.*—I was called this evening to a drunken, dying man. He was entirely ignorant both of his bodily and spiritual danger. What a scene! An immortal soul just plunging into hell, and yet hoping for heaven! How awful is the state of one whom God gives over to believe a lie! His life is ended, his family destitute, and his soul lost!

July 19*th.*—Surely nothing can afford more pleasure to an enquiring mind bent on historical researches, than the perusal of documents relating to the ancient chosen people of God. That a people who could, according to their legitimate records, number more than eight hundred thousand fighting men, should slip from the records of men, hide themselves from human observation, and inhabit limits beyond geographical research, is a phenomenon unprecedented in the world's history; and that they should remain in this state more than two thousand years, among the vast discoveries which travellers have made, is still more surprising. Such is the wonderful government of Him whose ways are past finding out. I trust the day is not far distant when the lost will be found, and the dead be alive!

July 26th.—For several days I have been holding meetings and conferences with the Indians. Their hearts are open to receive instruction, and their hands extended to receive the bread of life. If the Lord will open the way, I will try to acquire a knowledge of their language. My soul longs to bring them to the Word of Truth.

July 30th—A day or two since I had the pleasure of seeing a brother whose ecclesiastical duties have separated us for nearly a year. How many tender recollections of God's care and merciful dealings, since our last meeting rushed upon our minds. But while enabled to rejoice together, we were called upon to mourn the loss of one brother, taken away to the world of spirits.

August 17th.—Scarcely a day passes without beholding new openings to extend my ministerial labours. To-day, in an affecting manner, I witnessed the hands of suffering humanity stretched forth to receive the word of life. More than five hundred aborigines of the country were assembled in one place. In a moral point of view, they may be said to be "sitting in the valley of the shadow of death." "The day star from on high" has not yet dawned upon them. Alas! are they to perish for lack of knowledge? Can not the dry bones live? Oh, thou who art able to raise up children unto Abraham! speak the word, devise the means, and these long lost prodigals shall return to their father's house! I noticed activity, both in body and mind, superior skill in curious workmanship; genius flashed in their countenances; and yet shall these noble powers be bound fast in the cruel chains of ignorance, and these immortal spirits go from a rayless night to midnight tomb? Oh, Thou Light of the World, shine upon them! One of their nation whom God has plucked as a brand from the burning, attempted to explain the Christian religion to them. They listened and bowed assent, saying "ha, ha." Oh, Lord, if Thou wilt qualify me and send me to dispense to them the Bread of Life, I will throw myself upon Thy mercy, and submit to Thy will.

August 20th.—Amongst all the authors with whom I am acquainted, who treat on Church Government, the Rev. Dr. Campbell is the most clear and satisfactory. With a great deal of talent, penetration, and research, he exhibits the Church in all her various forms, till her power made empires tremble, and her riches bid defiance to poverty. His excellent lectures have enlarged my mind on the subject of ecclesiastical polity, and rendered my feelings more liberal. I am convinced that form of government is best which most secures order and union in society.

August 20th—Sabbath.—To-day closes my ministerial labours at York, where I have been stationed for two years. Many precious seasons have I enjoyed; and, blessed be the Lord, He has set His seal to my labours, and I think I can call God to witness that I have not failed in my feeble way to declare the whole counsel of God. Oh, Lord, seal it with Thy Spirit's power!

CHAPTER IV.

1826—1827.

MISSIONARY TO THE RIVER CREDIT INDIANS.

AT the Conference of 1826, I was appointed Missionary to the Indians at the Credit, but was required to continue the second year as preacher, two Sundays out of four, in the Town of York, of which my elder brother, William, was superintendent, including in his charge several other townships. He was aided by a colleague, who preached in the country, but not in the town.

The Chippewa tribe of Indians had a tract of land on the Credit River, on which the Government proposed to build a village of some twenty or thirty cottages, with the intention of building a church for them and inducing them to join the Church of England, upon the pretext that the Methodist preachers were Yankees. As my Father had been a British officer, and fought seven years during the American Rebellion for the unity of the Empire, was the first High Sheriff in the London District (having been appointed in 1808); and had, with his sons, fought in defence of the country in the war of the United States with Great Britain, in 1812-1815, and my father's elder brother having been the organizer of the Militia and Courts of the London District, the name Ryerson became a sort of synonym for loyalist throughout the official circles of the province; and my appointment, therefore, as the first stationed Missionary among the Indians, and from thence to other tribes, was a veritable and standing proof that the imputation of disloyalty against the Methodist Missionaries was groundless.

When I commenced my labours among these poor Credit Indians (about two hundred in number) they had not entered into the cottages which the Government had built for them on the high ground, but still lived in their bark-covered wigwams on the flats beside the bank of the River Credit. One of them, made larger than the others, was used for a place of worship. In one of these bark-covered and brush-enclosed wigwams, I ate and slept for some weeks; my bed consisting of a plank, a mat, and a blanket, and a blanket also for my covering; yet I was never more comfortable and happy :—God, the Lord, was the strength of my heart, and—

"Jesus, all the day long, was my joy and my song."

Maintaining my dignity as a minister, I showed the Indians that I could work and live as they worked and lived.

Having learned that it was intended by the advisers of the Lieutenant-Governor, on the completion of the cottages, to erect an Episcopal Church of England for the absorption of the Indian

INDIAN VILLAGE AT THE RIVER CREDIT IN 1827—WINTER.

converts from the Methodists into that Church, I resolved to be before them, and called the Indians together on the Monday morning after the first Sunday's worship with them, and using the head of a barrel for a desk, commenced a subscription among them to build a house for the double purpose of the worship of God and the teaching of their children. Never did the Israelites, when assembled and called upon by King David, (as recorded in the 29th chapter of the first book of Chronicles) to subscribe for the erection of the Temple, respond with more cordiality and liberality, in proportion to their means, than did these converted children of the forest come forward and present their humble offerings for the erection of a house in which to worship God, and teach their children. The squaws came forward to subscribe from shillings to dollars, the proceeds of what they might earn and sell in baskets, mats, moccasins, &c., and the men subscribed with corresponding heartiness and liberality of the salmon that they should catch—which were then abundant in the river, and which, I think, sold for about twelve and a half cents each.

On the same day, a plan of the house was prepared, and I engaged on my own individual responsibility, a carpenter-mason, by the name of Priestman (who had been employed by the Government to build the Indian cottages), to build and finish the house for the double purpose of worship and school, and then mounted my horse and visited my old friends in York, on Yonge Street, Hamilton, and Niagara Circuits, and begged money to pay for all, and at the end of six weeks the house was built and paid for, while our "swell" friends of the Government and of the Church of England were consulting and talking about the matter. It was thus that the Church-standing of these Indian converts was maintained, and they were enabled to walk in the Lord Jesus as they had found Him.

My labours this season were very varied and severe. I had to travel to York (eighteen miles) on horseback, often through very bad roads, and preach two Sundays out of four (my second year in town). After having collected the means necessary to build the house of worship and school-house, I showed the Indians how to enclose and make gates for their gardens, having some knowledge and skill in mechanics.*

Between daylight and sunrise, I called out four of the Indians in succession, and showed them how, and worked with them, to clear and fence in, and plow and plant their first wheat and corn fields. In the afternoon, I called out the school-boys to go with me, and cut and pile, and burn the underbrush in and around the village. The little fellows worked with great glee, as long as I worked with them, but soon began to play when I left them.

In addition to my other work, I had to maintain a heavy

* When about fourteen years of age, an abridged "Life of Benjamin Franklin" fell into my hands, and I read it with great eagerness. I was especially attracted by the account of his mechanical education and of its uses to him in after years, during and after the American Revolution, when he became Statesman, Ambassador, and Philosopher. My father was then building a new house, and I prevailed on him to let me work with the carpenter for six months. I did so, agreeing to pay the old carpenter a York shilling a day for teaching me. During that time, I learned to plane boards, shingle, and clapboard the house, make window frames and log floors. The little knowledge and skill I then acquired, was of great service when I was labouring among the Indians, as well as my early training as a farmer. I became head carpenter, head farmer, as well as missionary, among these interesting people, during the first year of their civilized life.

controversy with several clergymen of the Church of England on Apostolic Ordination and Succession, and the equal civil rights and privileges of different religious denominations.*

A few months after my appointment to the Credit Indian Mission, the Government made the annual distribution of presents to the Georgian Bay and Lake Simcoe Indians—all of whom were assembled at the Holland Landing, on the banks of the Holland River, at the southwest extremity of Lake Simcoe. They consisted chiefly of the Snake tribe, the Yellowhead tribe (Yellowhead was the head Chief), and the John Aissance tribe. Peter Jones and I, with John Sunday, had visited this tribe at Newmarket, the year before, and preached to them and held meetings with them, when they embraced the Christian religion, and remained true and faithful. Peter Jones and myself attended the great annual meeting of the Indians, and opened the Gospel Mission among them. In my first address, which was interpreted by Peter Jones, I explained to the assembled Indians the cause of their poverty, misery, and wretchedness, as resulting from their having offended the Great Being who created them, but who still loved them so much as to send His Son to save them, and to give them new hearts, that they might forsake their bad ways, be sober and industrious; not quarrel, but love one another, &c. I contrasted the superiority of the religion we brought to them over that of those who used images. This gave great offence to the French Roman Catholic Indian traders, who said they would kill me, and beat Peter Jones. On hearing this, Col. Givens, the Chief Indian Superintendent, called them together and told them that the Missionary Ryerson's father was a good man for the King, and had fought for him in two wars—in the last of which his sons had fought with him—and that if they hurt one of these sons, they would offend their great father the King; that Peter Jones' father had surveyed Government lands on which many of the Indians lived. This representative of the Government, a man of noble feelings and generous impulses, threw over us the shield of Royal protection.

After the issuing of the goods to the Indians, Peter Jones remained with the Huron and Georgian Bay Indians, and preached to them with great power; while I went on board a schooner, with the Yellowhead Indians, for the Narrows, on the northern shore of Lake Simcoe, near Orillia, where the Indians owned Yellowhead (now Chief) Island, and which I examined with a view of selecting a place for worship, and for establishing a school. A Mission-school was established on this island. It was afterwards removed by Rev. S. (now Dr.) Rose and others

* See note on p. 85; also Chapters vi. and viii.—H.

to the mainland at Orillia, and was faithfully taught by the late William Law (1827) and by the Rev. S. Rose (1831).

An amusing incident occurred during this little voyage on the schooner, which was managed by the French traders who had threatened my life two days before. The wind was light, and the sailors amused themselves with music—one of them playing on a fife. He was attempting to play a tune which he had not properly learned. I was walking the deck, and told him to give me the fife, when I played the tune. The Frenchmen gathered around my feet, and looked with astonishment and delight. From that hour they were my warm friends, and offered to paddle me in their canoes among the islands and along the shore wherever I wished to go.

By the advice of some of my brethren, I called on the Lieutenant-Governor, Sir Peregrine Maitland, after I arrived in Toronto, for the purpose of giving him a general account of the progress of the Christian religion amongst the Indian tribes I said to him:—

"The object I have in view is the amelioration of the condition of the Indians in this Province. The importance of this, both to the happiness of the Indian tribes, and the honour of the govenment under which they live, has been deeply felt by the parent state, so forcibly that a church was built and the Protestant religion introduced amongst the Six-Nations at the Grand River, about the beginning of the century. This effort of Christian benevolence has been so far successful as to induce some hundreds of them to receive the ordinances of the Christian religion. But the Chippewa tribes have hitherto been overlooked, till about four years ago, when the Methodists introduced the Christian religion amongst them.

In a short time about one hundred embraced the religion of Christ, exhibiting every mark of a sound conversion. Their number soon increased, and a whole tribe of Mississaugas renounced their former superstitions and vices, and became sober, quiet Christians. They then felt anxious to become domesticated; their desire being favourably regarded, a village was established at the Credit, and houses built for them.

They have this season planted about forty acres of corn and potatoes, which promise an abundant harvest. About forty children attend the common school, nearly twenty can write intelligibly, and read the Holy Scriptures and the English Reader.

At Belleville a change especially interesting has been effected. The work was commenced there about two years ago, and now in their whole tribe, numbering about two hundred, there is not one drunkard! They are also becoming domesticated and are building a village on one of their islands in the Bay of Quinte, which they had squandered away in their drunken revels, but which is now repurchased for them by some benevolent individuals. A Day and Sunday School are established in which upwards of fifty children are taught.

From the Belleville Indians the Gospel spread to the tribes which inhabit the country adjacent to Rice Lake. Here also may be seen a wonderful display of the "power of God unto Salvation to every one that believeth." In less than a year, the whole of this body, whose census is 300, renounced their idolatrous ceremonies and destructive habits, for the principles, laws and blessings of that kingdom which is righteousness, peace, and joy in the

Holy Ghost." They are all, save a few, converted and changed in their hearts and lives, and earnestly desire a settled life.

The uniform language of all, so soon as they embrace the Christian religion is, "Let us have houses, that we may live together in one place, learn to till the ground, hear the word of the Great Spirit, and have our children taught to read the good book." Another field of Christian labour is already ripe amongst the Lake Simcoe Indians, who number about 600 souls. About two months ago an opportunity opened for introducing the Christian religion to them, and such was their readiness to hear and believe the words of salvation, that more than 100 have already professed the Christian faith, and are entirely reformed. A school is established in which forty are taught by a young man named William Law, lately from England.

This extensive reformation, has been effected and continued, by means, which, to all human appearance, are altogether inadequate to the accomplishment of such a work. A school at the Grand River containing thirty scholars, one at the Credit forty, another at Belleville upwards of thirty, and one lately established at Lake Simcoe containing forty, and the missionaries who have been employed amongst the Indians, together with the boarding of a number of Indian boys, have only amounted to a little more than £150 per annum. It is of the last importance to perpetuate and extend the impressions which have already been made on the minds of these Indians. The schools and religious instruction must be continued ; and the Gospel must be sent to tribes still in a heathen state. But in doing this our energies are weakened, and the progress of Christian labour much impeded by serious difficulties which it is in the power of the government to remove. These obstacles are principally confined to the Lake Simcoe Indians, the most serious of which is occasioned by the traders, who are Roman Catholic Frenchmen, employed to accompany the Indians in their hunting for the purpose of procuring their furs, and who are violently opposed to the reformation of the Indians. These traders are about eighty in number, and have long been accustomed to defraud and abuse the Indians in the most inhuman manner ; they have even laid violent hands on some of the converted Indians, and tried to pour whiskey down their throats ; but, thank God, have failed, the Indians successfully resisted them. To shake the faith of some, and deter others from reforming, they have threatened to strip them naked in the winter, when they were at a distance of 100 miles from the white settlement, and there leave them to freeze to death.

Col. Givens, when he was up issuing their presents about a month ago, threatened the traders severely if they disturbed the Indians in their devotions, or did any violence to their teachers. He also suggested the idea of your Excellency issuing a proclamation to prevent any further abuses. Sir Peregrine replied :

"When the Legislature meets, I shall see if something can be done to relieve them more effectively, but I do not think that I can do anything by the way of proclamation. If, upon deliberation, I find that I can do something for them, I shall certainly do it." I observed : The civil authority would be an ample security, while the Indians are among the white inhabitants ; but these abuses are practised when they are one or two hundred miles from the white settlements. The traders follow them to their hunting grounds, get them intoxicated, and then get their furs for one fourth of their value, nay, sometimes take them by force. These Frenchmen are able-bodied men, and have abused the Indians so much they are afraid of them ; and, therefore, have not courage, if they had strength to defend themselves. Under these circumstances your Excellency will perceive the Indians have no means of obtaining justice, and from their remote situation the power of civil authority is merely nominal in regard to them. His Excellency observed, " I am very much obliged to you for this information ; I shall do all in my power for them,"

CHAPTER V.

1826–1827.

DIARY OF MY LABOURS AMONG THE INDIANS.

THE following extracts from my diary contain a detailed account of my mental and spiritual exercises and labours at this time, as well as many interesting particulars respecting the Indians, not mentioned in the foregoing chapter:—

Credit, September 16th, 1826.—I have now arrived at my charge among the Indians. I feel an inexpressible joy in taking up my abode amongst them. I must now acquire a new language, to teach a new people.

Sept. 17th.—This day I commenced my labours amongst my Indian brethren. My heart feels one with them, as they seemed to be tenderly alive to their eternal interests. May I possess every necessary gift to suffer labour, and teach the truth as it is in Jesus.

Sept. 23rd.—Greatly distressed to-night on account of a sad circumstance. Three or four of the Indians have been intoxicated; and one of them, in a fit of anguish, shot himself! This was caused by a wicked white man, who persuaded them to drink cider in which he mixed whiskey. [See letter below.]

Sept. 24th.—Sabbath.—I tried to improve the mournful circumstance that occurred yesterday, as the Indians seemed much affected on account of the awful death of their brother.

Sept. 25th.—We have resolved upon building a house, which is to answer the double purpose of a school-house, and a place for divine worship. In less than an hour these poor Indians subscribed one hundred dollars, forty of which was paid at once. What a contrast, a short time ago they would sell the last thing they had for whiskey; now they economize to save something to build a Temple for the true God!

Sept. 26th.—To-day I buried two Indians, one the man who committed suicide, the other a new-born babe.

Oct. 8th.—For many days I have been employed in an unpleasant controversy, for our civil and religious rights, which has taken much of my time and attention.

Oct. 9th.—One of my brethren has been suddenly called from his labours, to his eternal home. Alas! my beloved Edward Hyland is no more. He entered the field after me, but he has gone before me!

Oct. 14th.—I have been employed the whole week in raising subscriptions for the Indian Church; we have now enough subscribed.

Oct. 19th—[In a letter, to-day, to his brother George, who wished to hear something about the Indian work, Dr. Ryerson said: I have to attend to various things previous to settling myself permanently at the Credit. I preached there to the Indians the two succeeding Sabbaths after I left home, and have been employed since that time in building a chapel for them at the Credit. The Indians in general, appear to be steadfast in their religious profession. They are faithful in their religious duties, and exemplary in their lives. One unhappy circumstance occurred there. [See entry in Diary of 23rd September.] I preached a solemn discourse on the subject of guarding against temptation and intemperance

John Jones' House at the Credit, where Dr. Ryerson resided.

the same day, illustrating it throughout by this lamentable example. The Indians appeared to be much affected; and, I think, through the mercy of God, it has, and will prove a salutary warning to them. The Indians were very spirited in building their chapel. They made up more than a hundred dollars towards it, and are willing to do more, if necessary. By going in different parts of the country, I have got about enough subscribed and paid to finish it. I have now permanently resided at the Credit Mission not quite a fortnight. I board with John Jones; have a bed-room, but no fire-place, except what is used by the family. I can speak a little Mississauga, and understand it pretty well. As to my enjoyments in religion, I have lately had the severest conflicts I ever experienced; but at times the rich consolations of religion have flowed sweetly to my heart and God has abundantly blessed me, especially in my pulpit ministrations. It is the language of my heart to my blessed Saviour, Thy will, not mine, be done. Our prospects in little York are favourable. The chapel is enlarged, and the congregation greatly increased, some having lately joined.—H.]

Nov. 9th.—This evening in visiting a sick Indian man, I endeavoured, through an interpreter, to explain to him the causes of our afflictions, the sympathy of Jesus, and the use of them to Christians. We afterwards had prayer, many flocked into the room. The sick man was filled with peace in believing, insomuch that he clapped his hands for joy.

Nov. 26th.—Sabbath.—This has been an important day. We opened our Indian Chapel by holding a love-feast, and celebrating the Lord's supper. The Indians with much solemnity and feeling expressed what God had done for them. Rev. Wm. Case addressed them. In the evening he gave them most important instruction, as to domestic economy and Christian duties. After this a short time was spent in teaching them the Ten Commandments, the Indian speaker repeating them audibly sentence by sentence, which was responded to by the whole congregation. At the close, eight persons, seven adults and one infant were baptized. Three years ago they were without suitable clothes, home, morality, or God. Now they are decently clothed, sheltered from the storm by comfortable dwellings, and many of them rejoicing in the hope of a glorious immortality.

Nov. 29th.—Last evening, in addressing a few of the Indians, who were collected on account of the death of one of them, (John Muskrat) I felt a degree of light spring up in my mind. This Indian was converted about a year ago, and has ever since maintained a godly walk and holy conversation. Thus missionary labour has not been in vain. This is the third that has left an encouraging testimony behind of a glorious resurrection.

Nov. 30th.—I have this day divided the Indian society into classes, selected a leader for each, from the most pious and intelligent. I meet these leaders once a week separately, to instruct them in their duty.

Dec. 7th—I have been often quite unwell, owing to change of living, being out at night; my fare, as to food *is very plain*, but wholesome, and I generally lie on boards with one or two blankets intervening.*

Dec. 8th.—I am feeling encouraged in the prosecution of the Indian language, and in the spirit of my mission. There is a tenderness in the disposition of many of the Indians, especially of the women, which endears them to the admirers of natural excellence. One of them kindly presented me with a handsome basket, which is designed to keep my books in. This afternoon I collected about a dozen of the boys, to go with me to the woods, in order to cut and carry wood for the chapel. Their exertions and activity were astonishing.

Dec. 16th.—I have this week been trying to procure for the Indians the exclusive right of their salmon fishery, which I trust will be granted by the Legislature.† I have attended one of their Councils, when everything was conducted in the most orderly manner. After all the business was adjusted, they wished to give me an Indian name. The old Chief arose, and approached the table where I was sitting, and in his own tongue addressed me in the following manner: " Brother, as we are brothers, we will give you a name.

---

*My home was mostly at John Jones', brother of Peter Jones; sometimes at Wm. Herkimer's, a noble Indian convert, with a noble little wife.

† See page 78.

My departed brother was named Cheehock; thou shalt be called Cheehock."* I returned him thanks in his own tongue, and so became initiated among them.

Dec. 22nd.—My brother John, writing from Grimsby, thus acknowledges the kind advice of brother George: I thank you for your kind advice, and I can assure you I have felt of late, more than ever, the importance of preaching Christ, and Christ alone. It is my aim and constant prayer to live in that way, so that I can always adopt the language of the Apostle, Romans xiv. 7, 8. I wish you to write as often as convenient. Any advice or instruction that you may have at any time to give, will be thankfully received.

January 4th, 1827.—After the absence of more than a week, I again return to my Indians, who welcome me with the tenderest marks of kindness. Watch-night on New Year's Eve was a season of great rejoicing among them. About 12 o'clock, while their speaker was addressing them, the glory of the Lord filled the house, and about twenty fell to the floor. They all expressed a determination to commence the New Year with fresh zeal. My soul was abundantly blessed at the commencement of the year, while speaking at the close of the Watchnight services in York.

My engagement in controversial writing savours too much of dry historical criticism to be spiritual, and often causes leanness of soul; but it seems to be necessary in the present state of matters in this Colony, and it is the opinion of my most judicious friends, that I should continue it till it comes to a successful termination.

Jan. 10th.—[Having received a letter of enquiry from his brother George, Dr. Ryerson replied at this date, and said :—

I have been unwell for nearly two months with a continuance of violent colds, occasioned by frequent changes from a cold house and a thinly-clad bed at the Credit, to warm rooms in York. My indisposition of body has generally induced a depression of spirits, which has often unfitted me for a proper discharge of duties, or proficiency in study. However, in the midst of bodily indisposition, the blessings of the Holy Spirit have been at times abundantly poured into my soul, insomuch that I could glory in tribulation, and rejoice that I am counted worthy to labour and suffer among the most unprofitable and worthless of the labourers in my Saviour's vineyard. The Indians are firm in their Christian profession, and some of them are making considerable improvement in the knowledge of doctrine and duties of religion, and of things in general. They are affectionate and tractable.

I am very unpleasantly situated at the Credit, during the cold weather, as there are nearly a dozen in the family, and only one fire-place. I have lived at different houses among the Indians, and thereby learned some of their wants, and the

---

* *Cheehock,* "A bird on the wing," referring to my going about constantly among them.

proper remedies for them. Having no place for retirement, and living in the midst of bustle and noise, I have forgotten a good deal of my Greek and Latin, and have made but little progress in other things. My desire and aim is, to live solely for the glory of God and the good of men.

By the advice of Mr. M. S. Bidwell and others, I am induced to continue the Strachan controversy, till it is brought to a favourable termination. I shall be heartily glad when it is concluded.—H.]

Jan. 16th.—One of the Indians (Wm. Sunegoo) has been tempted to drink. I visited him as soon as he returned to the village. I entreated him to tell me the whole truth, which he did. After showing him his sin and ingratitude to God and his friends, he wept aloud, almost despairing of mercy. I pointed him to the Saviour of penitent sinners. He fell on his knees, and we spent some time in prayer. After evening service he confessed his sin publicly, asked forgiveness of his brethren, and promised in the strength of God to be more watchful. Thus have we restored our brother in the spirit of meekness.

Jan. 26th.—Last Sunday we held our quarterly meeting at York. About thirty of the Indian brethren were present; their cleanliness, modesty, and devout piety were the subject of general admiration.

Feb. 4th.—To-day I preached to the Indians. Peter Jacobs, an intelligent youth of 18, interpreted, and afterwards spake with all the simplicity and eloquence of nature.

A scene never to be forgotten was witnessed by me in visiting an Indian woman this evening; after months of severe suffering, she sweetly yielded up the ghost in the triumphs of faith. She embraced the Christian religion about eight months ago, and was baptized by Rev. T. Madden. Notwithstanding her many infirmities, she went to the house of God as long as her emaciated frame, with the assistance of friends, could be supported. A few days previous to her decease, she gave (to use her own words) "her whole heart into the hands of Jesus, and felt no more sorry now, but wanted to be with Jesus." While addressing a number assembled in her room, who were weeping around her bed, her happy spirit took its triumphant flight to the arms of the Saviour she loved so much.

How would the hearts of a Wesley and Fletcher burst forth in rapture, could they have seen their spiritual posterity gathering the wandering tribes of the American forest into the fold of Christ, and heard the wigwam of the dying Indian resound with the praises of Jehovah!

Feb. 10th.—A blessed quarterly meeting—Elder Case preached in the morning, and my brother George in the evening. The singing was delightful, and the white people present were extremely interested. At the close a collection of $26.75 was taken up, principally from the Indians! Peter Jacobs was one of the speakers.

Feb. 16th.—The importance of fostering our school among the Indians, and of encouraging the teacher in this discouraging and very difficult task, cannot be overestimated. Rev. Wm. Case, thinking that I had some aptitude for teaching, wrote me a day or two ago, as follows :—

Do you think the multitude of care, and burden of the school does sometimes mar the patience of the teacher? If so, you would do well to kindly offer to assist him occasionally, when he is present, and so by example, as well as by occasional kind remarks, help him to correct any inadvertencies of taste. I know the burden of a teacher in a large school, and a perpetual sameness in the same employment, especially in this business, is a tiresome task. I consider this school of vast importance, on several accounts, and especially considering the hopes to be entertained of several interesting youths there.

Feb. 27th.—I have written from fifteen to sixteen hours to-day in vindicating the cause of dissenters against the anathemas of high churchmen.

March 5th, 1827.—To-day I am on my way to see my parents. My Father is becoming serious, and my younger brother Edwy has joined the Methodist Society. I thank God for this blessed change.

York, March 8th.—[As an interesting bit of personal history, decriptive of Dr. Ryerson's manner of life among the Credit Indians, I give the following extract from a letter written by Rev. William to Rev. George Ryerson. William says :—

I visited Egerton's Mission at the Credit last week, and was highly delighted to see the improvement they are making both in religious knowledge and industry. I preached to them while there, and had a large meeting and an interesting time. The next morning we visited their schools. They have about forty pupils on the list, but there were only thirty present. The rest were absent, making sugar. I am very certain I never saw the same order and attention to study in any school before. Their progress in spelling, reading, and writing is astonishing, but especially in writing, which certainly exceeds anything I ever saw. They are getting quite forward with their work. When I was there they were fencing the lots in the village in a very neat, substantial manner. On my arrival at the Mission I found Egerton, about half a mile from the village, stripped to the shirt and pantaloons, clearing land with between twelve and twenty of the little Indian boys, who were all engaged in chopping and picking up the brush. It was an interesting sight. Indeed he told me that he spent an hour or more every morning and evening in this way, for the benefit of his own health, and the improvement of the Indian children. He is almost worshipped by his people, and I believe, under God, will be a great blessing to them.—H.]

March 14th.—After several pleasant days absence I return again to my Indian brethren. Have been much profited by reading the lives of Cranmer, Latimer. Burnet, Watts, Doddridge, and especially that of Philip Skelton, an Irish Prelate. The piety, knowledge, love, zeal, and unbounded charity, are almost beyond credit, except on the principle that he that is *spiritual*, can do all things.

March 19th.—An Indian who has lately come to this place, and has embraced the religion of Christ, came to Peter Jones, and asked him, what he should do with his implements of witchcraft, whether throw them in the fire, or river, as he did not want anything more to do with them. What a proof of his sincerity! Nothing but Christianity can make them renounce witchcraft, and many of them are afraid of it long after their conversion.

March 20th.—Busy to-day selecting suitable places for planting, and employed the school boys in clearing some land for pasture.

Macrh 24th.—I am this day twenty-four years old. During the past year my principal attention has been called to controversial labours. If the Lord will, may this cup pass by in my future life.

March 25th—Sabbath.—This day is the second anniversary of my ministerial labours. My soul has been refreshed, my tongue loosened, and my heart warmed.

April 1st, 1827—Sabbath.—In speaking to my Indian brethren, the word seemed deeply to affect their hearts.

April 2nd.—In meeting Class this evening, I spoke for the first time in Indian. My mind was much affected. The Indians broke forth in exclamations of joy to hear a white man talk about God and religion in their own tongue.

April 6th.—My dear brother William and Dr. T. D. Morrison have spent a night here, and greatly refreshed me by their converse.

April 9th.—Another lesson of mortality in the death of Brother John Jones' only child. I have been trying to comfort the parents, who seem to bear their trial with Christian fortitude

York, April 15th.—[In a letter to his brother George at this date, Dr. Ryerson thus speaks of the work under his care:—

We are all well, and are blessed in our labours at this place, and at the Credit. I think the Indians are growing in knowledge and in grace. They are getting on pretty well with their spring work. But in some respects they are Indians, though they have become Christians.

I came from Long Point with a full determination to live wholly for God and His Church. Through the blessing of God I have received greater manifestations of grace than I had felt before during the year. I have lately read "*Law's Serious Call to a Devout and Holy Life,*" which has been very beneficial to me. My greatest grief of late is, that my love to God and His people is not more humble, more fervent, and more importunate. O could I feel as Jesus felt when he said, "My meat and drink is to do the will of him that sent me." How much more happy and useful I would be! I pray that I may.

John and Peter Jones seem to thirst after holiness, and are growing in grace. The Society in this place (York) appears to be increasing in grace and in number. I was abundantly assisted by heavenly aid to-day, while preaching. The congregation seemed to be deeply affected this evening. I hope the word has not gone forth in vain. The Sunday-schools are prospering in this place. I proposed the new method of increasing the Sunday-schools, by giving a reward ticket to every scholar who would procure another that had not attended any other school. In two Sabbaths between twenty and thirty new scholars were procured in one school.—H.]

April 16th.—The last part of last week I was powerfully assailed by the devil, and became greatly dejected. Alas! I fear I was more disturbed on account of my own reputation than for the cause of Jesus. While preaching on Sabbath evening, heavenly light broke in on my soul, and all was peace.

I am now among the dear objects of my care. My heart leaped for joy as

I came in sight of the village, and received such a hearty welcome. Much refreshed with meeting them in Class, and particularly in private conversation with Peter Jones, about the dispensations of God towards us in the increase of our graces and gifts. We had about thirty boys out at work this evening clearing land. They are very apt in learning to work.

April 18th.—I was impressed to-day with the fact that the untutored Indian can display all the noble feelings of gratitude, love, and benevolence. An Indian, who has lately come to this place and embraced the Christian religion, has ever since shown great attachment to me. He has, without my knowledge, watered, fed, and taken care of my horse, saying he lived closer to the stable than I did. Yesterday I got out of hay, and could not get any till this afternoon. When I came to the stable I found grass in the manger; the Indian was there, and had just fed him. I said I was very glad, for he must be very hungry, but the Indian replied, "No, he not very hungry. I took him down where grass grow, and let him eat plenty." Oh, God, thought I, do such principles dwell in the people whom the white man despises? Is not this as noble and pure as it is simple? Though the circumstance is small in itself, it involves a moral principle to which many mighty men are strangers. He gave the widow's mite. Enfeebled by sickness, he exposed himself; touched by compassion, he relieved the sufferer. A few weeks ago, a heathen from the forest, he now performs an act that might make many Christians blush. How many professing Christians consider it a condescension to attend upon the servant of Christ and his beast, but this wild man of the woods esteems it a privilege to wash His disciple's feet. "Many that are first shall be last, and the last shall be first."

April 25th.—Last Sunday, four Indians came from Lake Simcoe, over fifty miles, to hear the words of eternal life, while many professors will scarcely go a mile. Does not this fulfil prophecy, "Many shall come from the east, and the west, and sit down in the kingdom of God, while the children of the kingdom are thrust out?" Last summer they heard Peter Jones, at Lake Simcoe, tell the story of the Saviour's love. They then determined to renounce ardent spirits, and pray to the Great Spirit. With this little preparation, they had been enabled to totter along in the path of morality from that time till now. The old man (Wm. Snake) seems under deep convictions, weeps much, and expresses much sorrow for his former bad doings. They have gone back, determined to get as many of their tribe as possible to return by the first of June. Surely this is "hungering and thirsting after righteousness."

April 29th—Sabbath.—In our Class-meetings, one of the Indian Leaders expressed himself thus:—" I am happy to-day. It is not with my life alone I love Jesus, but I love Him right here (pressing his hand upon his heart.) If I did not serve Him, what would I tell Him when He came? Would I tell Him a lie? No, my brothers, I will tell Him no story. I will serve Him with my whole heart. When I hear any of my brothers or my sisters praying in the daytime alone,* it makes my heart feel so glad. The tears run out o' my two eyes, I feel so happy. I love Jesus more and more. Pray for me, that I may hold on to the end; and when Jesus comes, I may go with Him and all of you up to heaven." Another one said, "Three of us have been two or three days in the bush, but we prayed, three poor souls of us, three times a day, and Jesus did make our souls so happy.

April 30th.—According to announcement, we assembled in the Chapel to examine into the cases of several who had acted disorderly. We were compelled to expel two from the Society. Many were deeply affected, and groans, and sighs might be heard in the different parts of the house. After a long

---

* They often retire to the woods for private prayer, and sometimes their souls are so blessed, they praise God aloud, and can be heard at a considerable distance.

and wise address from the old Chief, Joseph Sawyer, I said, "We must turn them out of the Society. What do you think about sending them away from the village? Tell us." Several spoke, and it was at last decided, by holding up the right hand, that they must go. I then said, "I am sorry to hear one or two have been drinking." I asked one if this was true. He confessed that he drank some beer, being coaxed by a white man. He felt very sorry, as he wished to be a good Christian. I then reproved with considerable severity, and showed him it was as bad to get drunk on cider or beer as whiskey. The devil often cheats us in this way, but we are exhorted not to "touch, taste, or handle" the accursed thing. This talk was explained to them in Indian by Peter Jones, and their opinions requested. Several spoke, but Brother William Herkimer, with a pathos that affected us all, said, "Brothers, the white man can't pour it down your throat, if you will not drink. When white man ask me to drink, I tell him, 'I am a Christian, I love Jesus,' and they go right away and look ashamed." He then concluded with a most pathetic prayer: "Oh, Jesus, let us poor, weak creatures be faithful, and serve Thee as long as we live." Having adjusted these matters, I next observed, "Our God has given us another commandment which was, 'To keep holy the Sabbath day.' Now, brothers, if a man gave you six dollars, and kept only one for himself, would you not think it very bad to rob him of that one? Oh, yes, you will say. Well the Lord has done more for us. He has given us our lives, our clothes, our health, nay, everything we have, and six days too, to do all our work in; but He has kept out one day for Himself. Let us not rob God of this day, but let us keep it holy. I am sorry to hear that one of you went to York on Sunday." I turned to the guilty Indian, and told him I wanted him to tell us why he had done so. He stated he had got out of provisions, and he was afraid the wind would rise on Monday, and unthinkingly he started on Sunday afternoon. He promised to do so no more. I then spoke a few words from Gal. vi. 1, and Peter Jones closed with an affecting exhortation and prayer.

May 2nd.—Yesterday I was almost in despair, and I was really devising means to relinquish my present work; when in the height of agitation I took down a package of tracts, and providentially (surely not by chance) cast my eyes upon one entitled, "Disobedience Punished, Repented of, and Pardoned." This was no other than the history of Jonah; and was made the means of reviving my expiring faith, and showing me how God alone could give me victory over myself. I cried to Him like Jonah, and He delivered me out of my distress.

May 3rd.—To-day I have felt peace with God and good will towards men. Several Indian women have arrived from Scugog Lake. They report that the Indians there have all stood firm, daily meeting for prayer to the Great Spirit, and that there has only been one case of intoxication since Peter Jones was there last autumn. This unhappy circumstance was caused by one (Carr) an old Methodist back-slider (a fit emissary of the devil), who took his barrel of whiskey, in order to trade with the Indians. He tried in vain to persuade them to taste, till at length he made some of the whiskey into bitters, which he called medicine, and prevailed on one unwary man to take for his health. This he repeated several times, till at length the poor fellow got to relish it, and becoming overpowered he fell into the water! The Indians immediately assembled for prayer, and through the mercy of God, he is now restored to his former steadfastness. They then ordered Carr to take his whiskey away, or they would destroy it. He took it on the ice, on the lake, no doubt hoping that it would tempt some of them to drink. But in this the devil was disappointed, the ice thawed, and the barrel floated on the water. What an instance of human depravity, does this man's conduct exhibit, and what a picture of the power of Divine grace is seen in the

SCHOOL AND COUNCIL HOUSE. CHURCH. PETER JONES' STUDY.
OLD CREDIT MISSION. *(From a sketch by Mrs. E. Carey.)*

inflexible firmness of the Indians! May we not sing in the language of Paradise Regained—

> "The tempter foiled
> In all his wiles, defeated, and repuls'd,
> And Eden raised in the waste wilderness."

The Indian woman who related the above, gave another proof of the amiable and benevolent character of her race, especially when sanctified by grace. In token of their esteem for Peter Jones, who had been the means of opening their eyes to immortality and eternal life, they brought him several pounds of maple sugar, which one of them presented in a wooden bowl. No doubt this sugar, which they had carried sixty miles, was nearly their all. Is not this a feeling of gratitude and love to the disciple for the master's sake? Oh! that I may learn lessons of simplicity and contentment from these children of the forest, for they are taught of God only. Oh! that I may have Mary's lot in time and in eternity.

May 6th—Sunday.—A number of white people being present this morning I addressed them on the subject of the barren fig-tree. In the evening we had a precious time; the Indians were enraptured, and we all, as it were, with one heart, dedicated ourselves afresh to God. In the class meeting we all wept tears of joy and holy triumph. Several of them said, "Jesus is the best master I ever served." "I love Jesus better than anything else."

May 8th.—I witnessed an affecting instance of how pleasant a thing it is for brethren to dwell together in unity, in the departure of two Indians who had paid us a few days' visit from Belleville. Nearly the whole village, according to Apostolic custom, collected to bid them farewell in John Crane's house, when an Indian arose (in the absence of the chief) inviting any of the Belleville Indians who might like to come and settle amongst them. Others rose and spoke on Christian love, pointing them forward to that period when they should meet to part no more. How does the spirit of primitive Christianity lead to the adoption of the same customs which were practised by the first followers of our Lord, when the multitudes of them that believed were of one heart and soul. We then sang a few verses and all knelt down, commending our dear brothers to the care of Him who never leaves nor forsakes his children. After this one of the Indians from Belleville delivered a pathetic parting address; they then all shook hands, exhorting one another to cleave to Jesus. This Indian appeared to me to be one of the most heavenly minded men I ever saw, not an able speaker but with a peculiar nervousness in his words, spoken with energy and pathos that deeply affected us all.

May 13th—Sunday.—I spent the last week in assisting the Indians in their agricultural pursuits. They are teachable, willing, and apt to learn. This constant change of employment debars me from literary and theological improvement, and leaves me less qualified to expound Scripture to refined assemblies. Thus I am perplexed to know what is best for me to do. The Lord direct me in this momentous matter!

May 14th.—The temporal and spiritual interests of the Indians bring upon me much care, and weigh me down. I experienced some comfort in the class meeting. Spoke in Indian, and for the first time repeated the Lord's prayer in Chippewa. Many of my dear brethren praised the Lord.

June 9th—Sabbath.—This day we held quarterly meeting at York—about twenty Indians present. I am informed that some of the Indians on Lake Simcoe are hungering for the bread of life, and that twelve of them were at worship at Newmarket, and expressed a desire to become Christians. Sixteen Indian children attend a Sabbath-school established there whose parents encamp near, for that purpose. Several of these children learnt the alphabet in four hours. This awakening arose through four of the Rice Lake Indians influenced by the divine love, traversing in their canoe the back lakes to tell their benighted brethren about Jesus, and exhorting them to become Christians.

June 7th.—The first quarterly conference ever held amongst Indians in British America was held to-day. After deliberating on several subjects, that of sending some of their pious and experienced men on a missionary tour to Lake Simcoe, and the Thames was proposed for consideration. Four of them soon volunteered their services. Their hearts seemed fired at the thought of carrying the news of salvation to their benighted brethren. At their own suggestion $12 was soon taken up to help pay expenses.

June 10th.—About fifty converted Indians from Rice Lake, Scugog Lake, Mud Lake, and the Credit, assembled in York to-day for the purpose of worshipping God. The Rice Lake Indians have come to see the Governor about building them a village, and deduct the money due them from the lands their fathers have ceded to the British Government, and likewise for getting boundaries of their hunting-grounds established. The other Indians have come for the purpose of attending the approaching camp-meeting, as they have never had but three days' instruction from Peter Jones last autumn. As soon as any of them experience the love of Jesus in their own souls, they begin to feel for others, and, like the ancient Christians, go wherever they can preaching the Lord Jesus. Here is a whole tribe converted to God, with the external aid of only three days' instruction, except what they communicate to one another, and who for six months have proved the reality of their Christian experience by blameless and holy lives. Surely "this is the Lord's doing, and marvellous in our eyes."

Elder Case told me that on his way from Cobourg to York, he saw an Indian sitting by the road-side, he asked him where his brothers and sisters were, he replied, encamped in the woods. Elder Case told him to call them, as he wanted to talk some good words to them. They soon came together to hear the *me-ko-to-wik*, or black coat man. They pitched a little Bethel of logs, about breast high, over-topped with bushes, for the purpose of worshipping *Keshamunedo* (God.) After kneeling down to implore God's blessing, they took their seats. As soon as Elder Case commenced to speak, their hearts seemed to melt like wax. So much for the Scugog and Mud Lake Indians. The Rice Lake Indians appear to be more intelligent, and are the handsomest company of men I have seen. Potash, their chief, is very majestic in appearance, possesses a commanding voice, and speaks with great animation.

June 12th.—My brother William, who came from Newmarket yesterday, informs me that he preached to more than fifty of these bewildered enquirers after truth on Sunday—none of them could interpret, but some could understand English, and they told others what the good man said. An Indian woman came to a little white boy, holding out her book (as most of them have bought books) and said, "boy, boy," showing great anxiety that the boy would teach her, but the little fellow was afraid, and slipped off. Then a little Indian boy about his age, held out his book that he might teach him, the white boy complied, and by the time he had showed him three or four letters, he was unable to contain his grateful feelings, clasped the white boy round his neck, and began to hug and kiss him.

June 15th.—A camp-meeting commenced this afternoon on Yonge street, about twelve miles from York. A large number of white people have assembled, and about seventy-five Indians. About a dozen of these embraced Christianity about six months ago, the rest are heathens from the forest. How interesting a sight that they should travel forty miles to hear about the Great Spirit, and what he would have them do. As soon as they arrived they commenced building their tents. Our Saviour said to His disciples, "Go ye into all the world, &c.," but we here see heathens coming to the disciples of Jesus and asking for the Gospel. The services were commenced by Rev. James Richardson, followed by the Rev. Thaddeus Osgood, who is a great lover of Sunday-schools, Peter Jones interpreted, when they were directed to Jesus, who came to save the Indian as well as the white man, they were melted to tears.

June 16th.—Rev. D. Yeomans preached this morning, also the Rev. Thaddeus Osgood, first to the children, then to the Indians, which was interpreted by Peter Jones. A lame boy, fourteen years old, seemed to have his whole soul broken under the hammer of the word. The Ten Commandments were recited in their own tongue, and they repeated them sentence by sentence. It was a very impressive exercise, giving great solemnity to the sacred decalogue.

June 17th, Sunday.—The first sermon this morning was delivered by Rev. John Ryerson, on the sufferings of Christ, followed by Rev. James Richardson. By this time the concourse of people was immense—when the Rev. William Ryerson preached from Gen. vii. 1, a most able and affecting discourse, interpreted by Peter Jones, who afterwards addressed the white people, telling of the former degradation of his people, their present happy condition, the feeble instruments God had made use of to accomplish this glorious work; he thanked the white people for their kindness, and earnestly entreated them to pray on, that the good work might go on and prosper—he concluded by saying, "My dear brethren, if you go forward the work will prosper, till the missionary from the western tribes, shall meet with the missionary from the east, and both will shake hands together."

June 18th.—About mid-day the Camp-meeting was brought to a close, it was very solemn and refreshing, three hundred and thirteen whites partook of the Communion, and about forty Indians. Thirty-five Indians, men, women, and children were baptized; with others it was deferred till further instructed.

July 3rd.—Peter Jones has just returned from Lake Simcoe, bringing a glorious account of the steadfastness and exceeding joy of the Indians there. Thirty more are added to their number; a school is established, taught by Bro. Wm. Law, in a temporary building, put up by themselves. The traders are showing great opposition, threatening to beat the Indians and burn their camps if they will attend the meetings; their craft is in danger. They that trust in the Lord need not fear.

July 5th.—Rev. Wm. Ryerson, under this date, writes from Lake Simcoe: If Yellowhead, the Head Chief, embraces religion, his influence will counteract the opposition of the traders, which is very strong. I think if Peter Jones can come and remain with them awhile, as soon as possible, they will embrace Christianity.

July 15th.—Peter Jones and I arrived at Lake Simcoe this evening, for the purpose of being present during the distribution of Indian goods. The change in their appearance since a year ago is most striking. The traders are still very hostile.

July 16th.—In the morning I gave the Indians a long talk. I showed them the superiority of the Christian religion over that of those who worshipped images. At this remark, the French traders present looked very angry, muttering, but making no disturbance. Peter Jones then spoke at length, answering and correcting statements the traders had made. Colonel Givens soon arrived and the meeting closed.

July 17th.—Collected the Indians again, and preached from Matt. xi. 28. Peter Jones expounded the Lord's Prayer. The Frenchmen were much displeased at his remarks on the subject of forgiving sins. They afterwards tried to force some of the Christians to drink, but failed. The Lord have mercy on these wicked men, and open their eyes before it is too late! When the presents were to be given out, the men were seated by themselves, and also the women; the boys and girls according to their ages. The chiefs then requested all who were Christians, or wished to be, to sit together, and about 150 rose and did so. The difference in their countenances, as well as their appearance and manners, was most marked. They looked healthy, clean, and happy, whereas many of the others were almost naked; some with bruised heads, and black faces, and almost burnt up with liquor. When the distribution of presents ended, an Indian Council was held at Phelps' Inn, at which I was invited to be present. Chief Yellowhead spoke first, saying "The desire of his heart was that their Great Father would grant them a place where they might all settle down together. His people wished to throw away their bad ways, and worship the Great Spirit." Many others spoke, particularly requesting the Indian Agent to do what he could to quiet the rage of the French traders. We have reason to thank God for the kind friendly influence the Indian agents exert, especially in closing the mouths of the traders. Oh, Lord, I will praise Thee!

July 20th.—I left the Holland Landing this morning for the purpose of visiting the islands north-east of Lake Simcoe, to ascertain their desirability for a settlement. I find the situation very pleasant. The chief has a comfortable house containing four rooms, with everything decent and convenient. This island contains about four hundred acres of beautiful basswood, beech, and maple. The chief told me that the Mohawks once had a village there, probably a century ago; as there is a navigable creek running to the mouth of the river, there was every attraction for a convenient settlement. The chief also offers any one who will come and teach the children, two rooms in his house for that purpose, and the Indians will support him. Such is the field of philanthropic and Christian labour in this place, and which demand most vigorous cultivation.

July 22nd.—I assembled the Indians this morning, and gave them my parting advice; after which the Chief (Wahwahsinno) spoke with great power. He is the most interesting, intelligent Indian I ever saw. He warned them to beware of the evil spirit which was lurking around them on every side; to be honest and cheat nobody; not to get drunk, but buy food and clothing for their children. You know, he said, how our fathers, grandfathers, and great-grandfathers have been killed by liquor—now, don't do as they have done. We are thankful to our Great Father, over the waters, for the clothes he has given us, and to our good brother for the good things he has taught us. We then embraced each other and bade farewell.

July 23rd.—Arrived again at the Narrows, and found the Indians firmly established in the faith. I have now spent eight days among these long-neglected and injured people, and happy are my eyes that have seen these glorious things.

[The missionary efforts of these times were in Upper Canada chiefly directed toward the Indians. Of this abundant evidence is given in the preceding pages. That these efforts were also put forth by the Church of England, may be gathered from the fact that at a public meeting held in York, on the 29th of October, 1830, a Society was formed, under the presidency of the Bishop of Quebec, "for the converting and civilizing of the Indians of Upper Canada." In his address, on that occasion, the Bishop stated that the Rev. G. Archbold, with true missionary zeal, had resided among the Indians on the north side of Lake Huron during the greater part of the summer, and at his departure had left them in care of Mr. James W. Cameron. Mr. Cameron was, in 1832 succeeded by Mr. (now Archdeacon) McMurray at Sault Ste. Marie. Funds for the support of this Indian Mission were collected in England, by the Bishop in 1831, and also by Rev. A. N. (subsequently Bishop) Bethune. The scope of this Society was soon enlarged to "Propagating the Gospel among Destitute Settlers." The missionaries employed in 1831 were Rev. J. O'Brian (St. Clair), Rev. Salteen Givens (Bay of Quinte), and Mr. James W. Cameron (La Cloche, Saulte Ste. Marie, etc.)

That this interest was not confined to spiritual matters is evident from many letters and other references to the domestic and material improvement in the condition of the Indians, which I find in Dr. Ryerson's papers. I select the following, which touch upon many different matters relating to the temporal and spiritual interests of the Indians :—

In a letter written by Rev. William Case, from Hallowell, to Dr. Ryerson, he thus speaks of the success of a school established by the Conference among the Indians. He says:

> Last evening (10th March) was exhibited the improvement of the Indian School, at Grape Island, one boy, whose time at school amounted to but about six months, read well in the Testament. Several new tunes were well sung and had a fine effect. The whole performance was excellent. More than twenty names were given in to furnish provisions for the children of the school. These exhibitions have a good effect. It animates the children and the teachers, and affords a most gratifying opportunity to the friends of the Missions to witness that their benevolence is not in vain.—H.]

[Shortly after this letter was written, Elder Case went to New York, to solicit aid on behalf of the Indian Schools. He was accompanied by John Sunday and one or two other Indians. Writing from there, on the 19th April, to Dr. Ryerson, then at Cobourg, he says:

> We have attended meetings frequently, and visited a great number of schools and other institutions, both literary and religious. This has a fine effect on our Indian brethren. The aid we are obtaining will assist us for the improvement of our Indian Schools. We have an especial view to the Indians of Rice Lake. Please look well to the school there, and to the comfort of the teacher. The Indians should be encouraged to cultivate their islands. The most that we can do is to keep them at school, &c., and instruct them in their worldly concerns.
> The managers of the Missionary Society in New York, as well as in Philadelphia, are very friendly. In case we shall be set off as a Conference, they will continue to afford us assistance in the Mission cause. You will judge something of the feeling of the people here, when I inform you that a neice of the unfortunate Miss McCrae, who was killed by the Indians in the revolutionary war, has given us $10 towards the Indian schools, and two sets of very fine diaper cloths for the communion table. We shall bring with us an Indian book, containing the decalogue, the creed, hymns, and our Lord's Sermon on the Mount. This will stimulate our schools, as well as afford instruction to the Indian converts. I wish you to encourage the Indian sisters to make a quantity of fancy trinkets, we could sell them to advantage here. They should be well made. We have been introduced to Mr. Francis

Hall, of the New York *Spectator*, and about forty ladies, who are engaged in preparing bedding, clothing, &c., for our missions and schools. We gave them a short address on the happy effects of the gospel on the mind and condition of Indian female converts. John Sunday's address to them in Indian was responded to with sobs through the room. Brother Baugs addressed those present on behalf of the Indians exhorting them to diligence and faithfulness. He said that we would always find in the Christian females true encouragement and aid."—H.]

[Elder Case was anxious to re-open the school for Indian girls at Grape Island. In writing from the Credit, he says:

"When we gave up the female school it was designed to revive it, and we had in view to employ one of the Miss Rolphs. If she can be obtained we shall be much gratified. We wish everything done that can be done to bring forward the children in every necessary improvement, especially at the most important stations, and the Credit is one of the most important. Can you afford any assistance to Peter Jacobs? We are very solicitous to see some talent in composition among some of our most promising scholars.

We are authorised by the Dorcas Society, of New York, to draw for $20 to purchase a cow for the use of the mission family at the Credit, and you are at liberty to get one now, or defer it till the Spring. As probably the $20 will purchase a cow, and pay for her keeping through the winter.

Our way this far has been prosperous. I never saw the pulse of Missionary ardour beat higher. Tickets of admission at the anniversaries might be sold by hundreds for a dollar each. But they were distributed gratis. The collection at the female anniversary was $217, and a handful of gold rings (about 20). The superintendent is truly missionary; rejoicing in the plan of our aiding them in the conversion of the Indians on this side of the lines. Bros. Doxtadors and Hess' visit is well received, and a good work commenced at the Oneida."—H.]

[In a letter written to Dr. Ryerson, by the Rev. James Richardson, on the 2nd Oct., 1829, referring to the privilege granted to the Indians of taking salmon (as mentioned on p. 66), he said:

As I came home, I stopped at James Gages', and found that he was much displeased with the Indians for holding their fish so high. He says his son could obtain them for less than 1/3d. currency (25c.). Some of them were not worth half that. He remarked that Wm. Kerr and others expressed great dissatisfaction with the Indians for taking advantage of the privilege granted to them, and also for haughtiness in their manner of dealing with their old friends. I am afraid that unless they be moderate and civil, a prejudice will be excited against them, which may prove detrimental to the missionary cause. The respectable part of the inhabitants would be pleased to have the Indians supported in this privilege, if they could purchase fish of them at a moderate price.—H.]

[Elder Case, who was greatly interested in the success of the Indian Schools, and who—with a view to demonstrate the usefulness of the schools—proposed to take two of the Credit Indian boys to the Missionary Meetings in January, 1830, says:—

I should be glad to have something interesting at the York Anniversary. Perhaps we may have a couple of promising boys from this Station. Henry Steinheur will accompany me to Lake Simcoe, and perhaps Allen Salt* will come up as far as York. They are both fine boys, and excellent singers.]

* These Indian boys subsequently became noted for their piety and missionary zeal on behalf of their red brethren.—H.

[A providential opening having occurred for getting the Scriptures translated into the Indian language, Rev. Wm. Ryerson, in a letter to Dr. Ryerson, dated York, 24th February, 1830, says :—

I lately received a letter from the Rev. Mr. West, one of the agents for the British and Foreign Bible Society, expressing the anxiety he felt that the Scriptures should be translated into the Chippewa language. He said that if proper application were made, he would take great pleasure in laying it before the Committee of the Parent Society, and use his influence to obtain any assistance that might be wanted. Viewing this as a providential opening, I think that steps should be taken to have the translation made. From your residence among the Indians, and knowledge of their manners and customs, and your acquaintance with those natives that are the best advanced in religious knowledge and experience, do you not think that the Joneses are the best qualified to translate the Scriptures ?—H.]

NOTE.—[The reply was in the affirmative, and Peter Jones was entrusted by the U. C. Bible Society with the work.*—H.]

April 7th, 1829.—[Writing to Dr. Ryerson, from Philadelphia, at this date, Elder Case says :

There is a fine feeling here in favour of the Canada Church and the Mission cause. Peter Jones and J. Hess are in New York overlooking the printing of the gospels, etc. We hope to bring back with us the Gospel of Mark, with other portions contained in the Book of Common Prayer. The Spelling-book and a Hymn book in Mohawk, and a Hymn-book in Chippewa They are all in the press, and will be ready by 5th May, when we leave to return.—H.]

* An unexpected delay occurred in getting the translation made by Rev. Peter Jones printed, as explained in a letter from Rev. George Ryerson to Dr. Ryerson, dated Bristol, August 6th, 1831. He says :—
Peter Jones, after his return from London, experienced several weeks' delay in getting his translation prepared for the press, in consequence of a letter from the Committee on the Translations of the U. C. Bible Society—Drs. Harris, Baldwin, and Wenham—stating that the translation was imperfect. He had, in consequence, to go over the whole translation with Mr. Greenfield, the Editor of the Bible Society Translations. Mr Greenfield is a very clever man, and has an extensive knowledge of languages. He very soon acquired the idiom of the Chippewa language so that he became better able to judge of the faithfulness of the translation. Mr. Greenfield went cheerfully through every sentence with Mr. Jones, and made some unimportant alterations, expressed himself much pleased with the translation, and thinks it the most literal of any published by the Bible Society. It is now passing through the press, and will soon be sent to Canada.

CHAPTER VI.

1827–1828.

LABOURS AND TRIALS—CIVIL RIGHTS CONTROVERSY.

AT the Conference of 1827 I was appointed to the Cobourg Circuit, extending from Bowmanville village to the Trent, including Port Hope, Cobourg, Haldimand, Colborne, Brighton, and the whole country south of Rice Lake, with the townships of Seymour and Murray. On this extensive and labourious Circuit I am not aware that I missed a single appointment, notwithstanding my controversial engagements* and visits to the Indians of Rice Lake and Mud Lake. I largely composed on horseback sermons and replies to my ecclesiastical adversaries. My diary of those days gives the following particulars:—

Hope, Newcastle District, Sept. 23rd, 1827.—I have now commenced my ministerial labours amongst strangers. Religion is at a low ebb among the people; but there are some who still hold fast their integrity, and are "asking the way to Zion with their faces thitherwards." I have preached twice to-day and been greatly assisted from above.

Sept. 25th.—I have laboured with much heaviness to-day. I spent part of the day in visiting the Rice Lake Indians. They seem very healthy, and are happy in the Lord. We have selected a place for building a school house. With gratitude and joy they offer to assist in the building.

Sept. 30th.—Another month gone! I review the past with mingled feelings of gratitude and regret.

October 2nd.—Yesterday and to-day I have laboured under severe affliction of mind. I am as one tempest driven, without pilot, chart, or compass.

Oct. 4th.—This evening at the prayer-meeting, how delightful was it to hear two children pour out their melting supplications at the throne of grace. "Out of the mouths of babes and sucklings thou hast perfected praise."

Oct. 9th.—I began my labours last Sunday, weak and sick, but my strength increased with my labour, and I was stronger in body and happier in soul at night than in the morning.

Oct. 10th.—I have now finished my first journey round the circuit. My health has not been good. Two persons have joined the society to-night, and several more in class expressed a determination never to rest till they found peace with God through Jesus Christ.

Oct. 17th.—I have been employed in controversial writing, and sorely tempted to desist from preaching.

Oct. 20th.—I have been greatly interested and strengthened in reading the "Life of Dr. Coke." The trials with which he was assailed, and the spirit in which he encountered them, afforded encouragement to me. His meeting

---

* The first of these controversial engagements extended from the spring of 1826 until the spring of 1827; the second from the spring of 1828 until near midsummer of the same year.—H.

with the venerable Asbury, in the Church built in the vast forest, is one of the most affecting scenes I ever read.

Oct. 21st.—To-day we held our first quarterly meeting on the circuit, and, bless the Lord, it was a reviving time.

Oct. 27th.—[Archdeacon's Strachan's Ecclesiastical Chart had so excited the righteous indignation of Elder Case, that he wrote to Dr. Ryerson, at this date, from Cobourg, in regard to it. I insert his letter, as it expresses (though in strong language) the general feeling of those outside of the Church of England in regard to this Chart.* He said:—

Notice the providence which has brought to light the misstatements of the Ecclesiastical Chart. This is one instance out of many in which false representations have gone Home in regard to the character of the people and the state of religion.

As such a spirit of intolerance is altogether averse to the mild spirit of the gospel, so it is also a most dangerous and daring assumption of power over the rights of conscience. Against this high-handed and domineering spirit, God himself has ever set his face. Let the Doctor be reminded of the case of Haman and the despised dissenting Jew, who refused to bow down to the courtiers of the king. The Doctor's wrath is kindled against those whom he calls "dissenters," and who refuse to submit to his Church rule. We have said, "whom the Doctor calls 'dissenters.'" I aver that the term is not at all applicable to the religious denominations in this country. From what Church have they dissented? Indeed most of the first inhabitants of this country never belonged to the Church of England at all. They were from the first attached to the denominations. Some to the Presbyterian, some to the Baptist, some to the Methodist, and only a small portion to the Church of England. Nor had they any apprehensions, while supporting the rights of the Crown, that an ecclesiastical establishment of ministers of whom they have never heard, was to be imposed, upon them, as a reward for their loyalty! Indeed, they had the faith of the Government pledged, that they should enjoy the rights of conscience. And in view of this was the charter of the Province formed, to secure liberty of conscience and freedom of thought. The blow at a loyal portion of Her Majesty's subjects was aimed at them in the dark, 4,000 miles away, and without an opportunity of defending themselves. An act so ungenerous, and in a manner so impious too, cannot be endured. We must defend ourselves against the unjust slanders of the Doctor.—H.]

* The nature and purpose of this Chart are fully explained and discussed by Dr. Ryerson in his "Epochs of Canadian Methodism," pp. 165-220."—H.

Nov. 19th.—I have been blessed with more comfort this evening in preaching from Matt. xxii. 11-13, to a congregation composed principally of drunkards and swearers. My heart was warmed, my tongue loosened, and my understanding enlarged.

Nov. 20th.—I have been to the Rice Lake Mission: found them still growing in grace. The children are clean—many of them handsome. The school teacher is happy in his work.

Dec. 12th.—My mind has been greatly afflicted this evening in settling a difference between two brethren.

Dec. 25th.—Last night we had a service in this place (Presque Isle) to celebrate the incarnation of our blessed Saviour. Seven souls professed to experience the pardoning love of Christ. Many who came mourning went home rejoicing.

January 1st, 1828.—I am now brought to the close of another year, and the commencement of a new era of existence. The first part of the year I spent principally amongst the Indians, and have reason to believe the Lord blest my labours amongst those needy and loving people, but my own soul was oft in heaviness. The latter part of the year I have been on a Circuit, and have found my enjoyments and improvement increased. The Societies are growing in piety, my bodily wants have been all supplied, and I have experienced the fulfilment of the promise, If ye forsake father and mother, the Lord will take thee up. May I ever rest on it!

Jan. 2nd.—[The following letter was written at this date to Dr. Ryerson by his Mother. She says:—

My not writing to you, I understand from your letter to Father, has given you much uneasiness; but I can assure you I have felt much concerned about it myself, for fear that you should entertain the thought of its proceeding from unkindness or neglect: but let the feelings of affection of a Mother suffice and answer it all. Be convinced that her happiness depends upon your welfare, and that her daily prayers will ever be offered up to the throne of grace in yours and the rest of her children's behalf. O that the Lord may keep you humble and faithful, looking unto him for grace and strength to enable you to work in His blessed cause, to proclaim the glad tidings of salvation through a dear Redeemer to lost and perishing souls! This is a great comfort to me, and more than I deserve. None other compensates for all my trials and afflictions here, as that God, of His goodness, should have inclined the hearts of many of my dear children to seek His face and to testify to the ways of God being the ways of pleasantness and peace. At so much goodness my soul doth bless and praise my God and Redeemer. My dear boy, you must not forget to pray for your poor unworthy Mother, that she may be daily renewed in the inner man, and so kept by the grace of God, as to be able to endure unto the end, and at last to be received among those that are made perfect, to praise Him that hath redeemed us for ever and ever. Your kind and anxious enquiries about home, I shall endeavour to answer. Your dear Father has returned, and is as well as usual, but still suffers much at times. Your heavenly Father has been pleased to lay His hand of affliction once more upon your sister, Mrs. Mitchell, by taking away her youngest boy in November last. Edwy, I am happy to say, appears to persevere in serving God, which, with the blessing of God, may he continue to do. Your brother George has left for England. He desires that all your letters be sent to him in England, which contain anything interesting about the Indians, or of the work of religion. The state of religion in this part, I think, is rather on the rise, that is to say, they attend better to public worship, and receive their preacher in a more friendly manner than before. Write as often as you can to let us know how you are, and how the work of religion is progressing.—H.]

Jan. 3rd.—I have this day visited the Indians at Rice Lake : all prosperity here. I have been much refreshed this evening in meeting my beloved brother and fellow-labourer in the Gospel, Peter Jones. These pleasing interviews bring to mind many refreshing seasons we have enjoyed together, when seeking the lost sheep of the house of Israel. This year thus far, has been attended with peculiar trials; my health has not been good; I have had conflicts without, and fears within.

Jan. 30th.— Visited a poor woman to-day in the last stage of consumption, she gives evidence that her peace is made with God. I find it a heavy cross to visit the sick. Help me, Lord, to search out the mourner, bind up broken hearts, and comfort the sorrowful.

February 22nd.—[A Central Committee at York having, of behalf of the various non-Episcopal denominations, deputed Rev. George Ryerson to proceed to England to present petitions to the Imperial Parliament against the claims of the Church of England in this Province,* the Rev. William Ryerson was requested to write to his brother George on the subject. In his letter he gave the following explanation of the sources of information from which Archdeacon Strachan's Ecclesiastical Chart was compiled. He said :—

It may be proper to apprise you that the Church of England has been making an enquiry into the religious state of the Province, the result of which they have sent home to the Imperial Parliament. And in order to swell their numbers as much as possible, they have sent persons through almost every part of the Province, who, when they come into a house, enquire of the head of the family as to what Church he belongs. If he says, to the Methodist, or any other body of dissenters, they next enquire if their children belong to the same Church. If they say no, they set the children as members of the Church of England ! If they say that neither themselves nor their children belong to any particular Church, they set them all down as

* See " Epochs of Canadian Methodism," p. 222.

members of the Church of England! So that should they make a parade of their numbers you can tell how they got them.

The Report of the Society for the Promotion of Christian Knowledge, for 1821, gives the number of communicants in the Church of England here as between 4,000 and 5,000. In the Chart, the Methodist communicants only have been returned, which is about 9,000. The number of those who call themselves Methodists, is, at least, four times that number, or 36,000. This is the way in which almost all the other bodies estimate their numbers, the Baptists excepted.

Cobourg, Feb. 27th.—Dr. Ryerson's youngest brother, Edwy, who remained at home, wrote from there on the 20th, in regard to his Father's health and religious life. He says:—

I think there is no doubt but that he will, in a short time be able, with the care and the mercy of Almighty God, to enjoy himself again at the family altar. He says that, by the grace of God, the remainder of his days shall be devoted to the service of God. He feels that he has acceptance with God; that God condescends to receive him—blessed be God! My dear Egerton, although we have had great difficulties and many trials to contend with, yet the Lord has stood by us, and by His goodness and mercy He has kept us from sinking under them, by pointing out ways and means for our escape, and He has brought our aged Father to the knowledge of Jesus Christ, our Lord. Oh, my dear brother, let us praise the name of God forever, who hath dealt so bountifully with us. Mother is much better than when you were here. Father and Mother send their love to you. May the Lord give you good speed, and crown your labours with success in the saving of souls.

April 3rd.—With a view to throw an incidental light upon the personal influence which prompted Dr. Ryerson to controvert certain statements made by Archdeacon Strachan,* I quote a letter which Dr. Ryerson's brother William wrote to him from York, on the 1st, as follows:—

I send you a pamphlet containing Dr. Strachan's defence before the Legislative Council. If I had time I would write a

---

* "Letters from the Reverend Egerton Ryerson to the Honourable and Reverend Dr. Strachan. Published originally in the *Upper Canada Herald*, Kingston, U.C., 1828. Pp. 42—In his "advertisement" or preface, Dr. Ryerson illustrates the pressing nature of his engagements at the time when he was engaged in the controversy with Archdeacon Strachan. He also referred to the unusual difficulties with which he had to contend in writing these "Letters" to the Archdeacon. Of many important and most forcible arguments against establishments, especially those derived from the Holy Scriptures, the author has not availed himself, nor has he referred to so many historical authorities as might have been adduced, * * * as he has had to travel nearly two hundred miles, and preach from twenty to thirty sermons a month." (See note on p. 80 and also Chapter viii.—H.

reply, at least to a part of it. I think you had better write a full answer to it. You will perceive that the Doctor's defence consists in telling what he told certain gentlemen in England and what they told him. The misstatements and contradictions with which he has been charged, he has not noticed. Such as that "the Church is rapidly increasing, and spreading over the whole country, and that the tendency of the population is towards the Church of England, and that the instructions of dissenters are rendering people hostile to our institutions, civil and religious." He says: "It is said I have offended the Methodists." Who told him so? I presume it must have been his own conscience. If you write a full answer would it not be better to do it in the form of letters, addressed to the doctor, and signed by your real name? Write in a candid, mild, and kindly style, and it will have a much more powerful effect upon the mind of the public. Do not cramp yourself, but write fully, seriously, and effectually.

Dr. Ryerson's reflections upon the peculiar difficulties of his itinerant life at this time are recorded in his diary, under date of April 13th, as follows:—

No situation of life is without its inconveniences; but, perhaps, the Methodist itinerant Preacher is more exposed to privations than most others. His home is everywhere, and amongst persons of every description; and if he needs retirement or books, where can he find a retreat to hide himself, or a secret place where he can, like Jacob, wrestle till the dawn of day? He is a target to be shot at by every one; his weaknesses and failings tried every way; and, after his youth, his health, his life, his all are spent, he too often dies an enfeebled and impoverished man. But, bless the Lord, all does not end here. We have "a building of God, eternal in the heavens;" and we have a home "where the wicked cease from troubling, and the weary are at rest."

Dr. Ryerson resumes his diary on the 9th of May. He says:

My time has of late been much taken up with provincial affairs. I have felt a hardness towards those who I think are injuring the interests of the country, and with whom it has fallen to my lot to be much engaged in controversy. Necessity seems at present to be laid upon me, from which I cannot free myself.

May 10th—Sunday.—To-day I delivered a discourse on Missions. I had intended much, this being a favourite topic with me, but I made out nothing, and I felt truly humbled.

Aug. 1st.—For months past I have been greatly tried. My controversial labours have occupied too much of my time and attention. I thank God, the day of deliverance seems to be dawning. The invisible hand of the infinitely wise Being is clearly at work, and I have no doubt the result will be to His glory.

Dr. Ryerson then continues the narrative of his life. He says:—

A change in my domestic and public life now commenced,

which involved my marriage, and my appointment to the Hamilton and Ancaster Circuits. In my diary I say :—

Aug. 24th.—I soon expect to alter my situation in life. What an important step! How much depends upon it in respect to my comfort, my literary and religious improvement, and my usefulness in the Church? I have kept up a correspondence with a lady since and before I was an itinerant preacher; but postponed marriage since I became a minister, thinking that I should be more useful as a single man. My ministerial friends all advise me now to marry, as every obstacle seems moved out of the way and I have now travelled three years.

Ancaster, Oct. 31st.—I have passed through a variety of scenes since I last noted the dealings of the Lord with me. On the 10th of September, 1828, I entered into the married state with Miss Hannah Aikman, of Hamilton. Through the tender mercy of God, I have got a companion who, I believe, will be truly a help-meet to me, in spiritual as well as temporal things.*

The Hamilton and Ancaster Circuit reached from Stoney Creek, east of Hamilton, to within five miles of Brantford, including the township of Glandford; thence including the Jersey settlement, Dundas Street, and Nelson, to ten miles north of Dundas Street, embracing Trafalgar, the mountain beyond the town of Milton, Credit, and back to Stoney Creek.

The death of the Rev. Wm. Slater, my colleague and Superintendent, about the middle of the year, was a great loss and affliction to me, as I had to take his place. Brother Slater had been the colleague of my brother John for two years, and he was now mine for the second year. He was a true Englishman, a true friend, and a faithful and cheerful minister.

About the middle of this year (1828) were held the Ryan Conventions at Copetown, in West Flamboro', and Picton, Prince Edward District, of which I have given an account in " The Epochs of Canadian Methodism," pp. 247-269.

* This union was of comparatively short duration. Mrs. Ryerson died on the 31st of January, 1832, at the early age of 28. (See the latter part of Chapter ix.)

CHAPTER VII.

1828–1829.

RYANITE SCHISM—M. E. CHURCH OF CANADA ORGANIZED.

THERE is a break in Dr. Ryerson's "Story" at this point; no record of any of the events of his life, from August, 1828, to September, 1829, was found among the MSS. left by him. The Editor, therefore, avails himself of the numerous letters preserved by the venerable author, from which he is enabled to continue a narrative, at least in part, of the principal events in his then active life.—H.

Hamilton, 6th Nov.—Writing at this date, from Cobourg, to Dr. Ryerson, on the expediency of petitioning the Legislature to give the Methodist Ministry the right to perform the marriage ceremony amongst their own people, Elder Case, says:—

Should not the petition include all "dissenters," and the prayer be for authority to perform the marriage rite for members of our congregations? I would rather not have any law in our favour, but that which gives the privilege to the Calvinists. If the Church of England is not the established religion of this province (and who believes it is?) "dissenters" at least, have an equal right with the Church. If numbers and priority are to determine the right, the "dissenters" have a superior right, for they were first here, and they are more numerous. We cannot but feel a pious indignation at the idea, that all should not enjoy the same privilege, in regard to marriage; and can this be the fact when one denomination, in any sense whatever, has a control over the marriage ceremony of another denomination?

The Ryanite Schism, which commenced in 1824, is fully described by Dr. Ryerson in his "Epochs of Canadian Methodism," pp. 247-269. In a letter from his brother John, dated River Thames, January 28th, 1824, the strife caused by this schism is thus referred to. Mr. Ryerson also describes the state of the Societies in the London District during this crisis. He said:—

I am happy to hear that Mr. Ryan's plans are defeated, and that the measures you have adopted to frustrate his machinations against Elder Case, have proved successful. I hope you will continue to assist and support Elder Case, especially in this affair, and on many other accounts he is deserving of much esteem; his disinterested exertions in behalf of the Missionary interest in Canada, are deserving of the highest praise.

The work is prospering in the different parts of this District. Niagara and Ancaster Circuits are rising. There is a good work in Oxford, on the Long Point Circuit, as also on the London and Westminster Circuits. The Indian Mission, on the Grand River, is progressing finely. At the Salt Springs, about thirty have been added to the Society, amomg whom are some of the most respectable chiefs of the Mohawk and Tuscarora nations. Visiting them, from wigwam to wigwam, they in general appear to be thankful.—H.]

The Ryanite controversy turned chiefly on the refusal at first of the American General Conference to separate the Canada work from its jurisdiction. Rev. John Ryerson, in a letter from Pittsburg, Pa., dated May, 1828, gave Dr. Ryerson the particulars of the reversal of that decision. He says:—

A Committee of five persons has been appointed on the Canada Question. Dr. Bangs is the chairman. The Committee reported last Thursday pointedly against the separation; declaring it, in their opinion, to be unconstitutional. Dr. Bangs brought the report before the Conference, and made a long speech against the separation. William and myself replied to him pointedly, and at length, and were supported by the Rev. Drs. Fisk and Luckey. Dr. Bangs was supported by Rev. Messrs. Henings, Lindsey, and others. The matter was debated with astonishing ability and deep-felt interest on both sides, for two days, when the question being put, there were 105 in favour of the separation, and 43 against—a majority on our side of 62. Our kind friends were much delighted, and highly gratified at our singular and remarkable triumph; and those who opposed us, met us with a great deal of respect and affection. You will, doubtless, be surprised on hearing of Dr. Bangs' opposing us as he has done, but you are not more surprised and astonished than we were; and we had no knowledge of his opposition to the separation until the morning of the debate, when he got up and commenced his speech in Conference. But, blessed be God for ever, amidst the painful and trying scenes through which we have passed in the Conference business, the God of David has stood by us, and has given us a decided victory.

Nov. 22nd.—Elder Case, in a letter from Cobourg, gives a detailed account of the efforts put forth by Rev. Henry Ryan to foment discord among the societies. He says:

As in the west so in the east, Elder Ryan had induced several members to attend as delegates at his convention in Hallowell. At Matilda, George Brouse; at Kingston, Bro. Burchel and Henry Benson have been elected to go. Mr. Case then urges that a circular be issued to the societies setting forth "that the Conference, so far as they have had evidence, has laboured in every instance to do justice to Mr. Ryan, and even to afford him greater lenity, on account of former standing, than, perhaps the discipline of the Church would justify.

In a subsequent letter, dated Prescott, 27th November, Elder Case thus describes the proceedings of Mr. Ryan. He says:

On my way down, I spent a few hours at Kingston, one day at Brockville, and one here. I have learned all the circumstances of Mr. Ryan's proceedings. At one place he would declare in the most positive manner that he would " head no division," that he " would even be the first to oppose any such work," he " would esteem it the happiest day in his life if, by their assistance, he could regain his standing in the Church," and that " the measures which he was now professing would prevent a division." But when he thought he had gained the confidence of his listeners, and they had entered fully into his views, he would throw off his disguise, and openly declare, as he did at Matilda, " Now, we will pull down the tyrannical spirit of the Conference. There will, there must be a split," &c. Brother, there is one very material obstacle in the way of effecting a "split," in our societies, and raising a "fog" of any considerable duration, *i. e.*, the authors of this work may, by their strong and positive statements, make a people mad for a " division." But, when there is a sense of religion in the mind, they will become good natured—they can't be kept mad long. Our people in these parts are becoming quite good natured, and now perceive their arch friend has made a fool of them.

To show how deeply the Ryanite schism had affected the Societies, and how widely the agitation had spread, we give a few extracts from a letter written from London (U.C.), to Dr. Ryerson, by his brother John, dated 2nd January. He says :—

The day I left you I rode to Oxford (52 miles), and after preaching, I gave an explanation of Ryan's case, an hour and a half long. My dear brother, this is a desperate struggle. I am using every possible exertion to defeat Ryan. I go from house to house to see the friends I don't see at the meetings. Could you not go to Burford and see Mr. Matthews, as he has a great deal of influence in Burford and the Governor's Road? Egerton, by all means, try and go, even if you have to neglect appointments. Though I know it is hard for you, I am sure the approbation of your conscience, and the approbation of the Church, will afford you an ample reward. It will also be necessary for you to keep a look out about Ancaster. Write to

Rev. James Richardson, and tell him to look out, and also write to Rev. S. Belton, and Rev. A. Green. Don't fail to go to Burford and, if you can, to Long Point also, and hold public meetings on the subject.*

Nov. 26*th.*—At the Conference held this year (1828), at Switzer's Chapel, Ernestown, Bishop Hedding presiding, resolutions were adopted organizing the Canada Conference into an "independent Methodist Episcopal Church in Canada." Subsequently, Rev. Wilbur Fisk, A.M., Principal of the Wilbraham Academy, U.S., was elected General Superintendent, or Bishop, of the newly organized Church. Dr. Ryerson was deputed to convey the announcement of this election to Mr. Fisk, which he did on this day, as follows :—

The Canada Conference of the M.E. Church have taken the liberty of nominating you for our General Superintendent, agreeably to the resolutions of the General Conference. I take the liberty, and have the pleasure of observing that the nomination was warm and unanimous ; and I hope and pray, that while our wants excite your compassion, our measures, in this respect, will meet your cordial approbation and receive your pious compliance. Although writing to a person whom I have never seen, yet the pleasure and profit I have derived in perusing your successful apologies in favour of the pure Gospel of Christ against the invasions of modern libertinism, remind me that I am not writing to an entire stranger ; and your able and affectionate appeal to the late General Conference in behalf of Canada—of which my brothers gave a most interesting account —emboldens me to speak to you "as a man speaketh with his friend." Rev. Dr. Fisk's reply to this letter is as follows :—

The deep solicitude I have felt, to weigh the subject well, to watch the openings of divine providence, and decide in the best light, have induced me to deliberate until this time [April]. All my deliberations upon this subject have resulted in a confirmation of my earliest impressions in relation to it—that it will not be prudent for me to accept of the affectionate and flattering invitation of the Canada Conference. I feel, however, the influence of contrary emotions. My high sense of the honour you have done me, is enhanced by the consideration that "the nomination was unanimous and warm." I highly appreciate, and cordially reciprocate those warm and concurrent expressions of confidence and affection. The information I have of the character of the Conference, joined with my personal acquaintance with some of its members, convinces me, that whoever

* Rev. Henry Ryan was born 1776, entered the ministry in 1800, and died at his residence, in Gainsborough, on the 2nd September, 1833, aged 57 years.—H.

superintends the Canada Church, will have a charge that will cheer his heart, and hold up his hands in his official labours. Equally encouraging and inviting, are the growing prospects of your country and your Church, and especially of your missionary stations. These to a man of missionary enterprise, who loves to bear the banner of the cross, and push its victories more and more upon the territories of darkness and sin, are motives of high and almost irresistible influence. And they have so affected my mind, that although my local attachments to the land of my fathers, and for that branch of the Church where I was, and have been nutured, are strong; although my aged parents lean upon me to support their trembling steps, as they descend to the tomb; although I might justly fear the influence of your climate upon an infirm constitution; yet these considerations, strengthened as they are by a consciousness of my own inability, and by the almost unanimous dissuasives of my friends, would hardly of themselves have induced me to decline your invitation, were it not that I am connected with a literary institution that promises much advantage to the Church and to the public, but which, as yet, will require close and unremitting attention and care on my part for some time to come, to give it that direction and permanency which will secure its usefulness.*

Nov. 28th, 1828.—Mr. H. C. Thompson, of Kingston, who had charge of the re-printing in pamphlet form of Dr. Ryerson's recent letters on Archdeacon Strachan's sermon, writes to him to say :—It lingers in the press, merely for the want of workmen, who cannot be procured in this place.† He adds :—The

---

* The post-office endorsement on this letter was as follows :—Paid to Lewistown, N.Y., 25c. postage; ferryage to Niagara, 2d.; from Niagara to Hamilton, 4½d.; total, 36 cents postage, for what in 1882 costs only one-twelfth of that amount.—H.

† The title of this pamphlet (in possession of the Editor) is: Claims of Churchmen and Dissenters of Upper Canada brought to the test in a Controversy between several Members of the Church of England and a Methodist Preacher. Kingston, 1828. pp. 232. (See note on page 80, and also Chapter viii.)

Rev. Dr. Green, in his *Life and Times*, thus speaks of the effect of the publication of these letters upon Rev. Franklin Metcalf and himself:—The sermon was ably reviewed in the columns of the *Colonial Advocate*, in a communication over the signature of "A Methodist Preacher." Mr. Metcalf and I took the paper into a field, where we sat down on the grass to read. As we read, we admired; and as we admired, we rejoiced; then thanked God, and speculated as to its author, little suspecting that it was a young man who had been received on trial at the late Conference (1825). We read again, and then devoutly thanked God for having put it into the heart of some one to defend the Church publicly against such mischievous statements, and give the world the benefit of the facts of the case. The "Reviewer" proved to be Mr. Egerton Ryerson, then on the Yonge Street Circuit. This

changes which have recently taken place in the two provinces cannot fail to gratify every lover of his country, though the party in power will no doubt hang their heads in sullen silence. I am highly pleased with the Methodist Ministers' Address to the Governor, and the reply thereto,—Strachanism must seek a more congenial climate.

March 19th, 1829.—Dr. Ryerson had, at this time, met with an accident, but his life was providentially spared. Elder Case, writing from New York, at this date, speaking of it, says:

Thank the Lord that your life was preserved. The enemies of our Zion would have triumphed in your death. May God preserve you to see the opponents of religious liberty, and the abettors of faction frustrated in all their selfish designs and hair-brained hopes!

I have seen a letter from the Rev. Richard Reece, dated London, 19th January, to Mr. Francis Hall, of the New York *Commercial Advertiser* and the *Spectator*, in which he says:

I am of opinion that the English Conference can do very little good in Upper Canada. Had our preachers been continued they might have raised the standard of primitive English Methodism, which would have had extensive and beneficial influence upon the work in that province, but having ceded by convention the whole of it to your Church, I hope we shall not interfere to disturb the people. They must, as you say, struggle for a while, and your bishops must visit them, and ordain their ministers, till they can do without them. He speaks of being highly gratified at the conversion of the Indians in Canada.

was the commencement of the war for religious liberty. pp. 83, 84. (See also page 143 of Dr. Ryerson's "Epochs of Canadian Methodism.")—H.

For specimens of Dr. Ryerson's controversial style in this his first encounter, see the extracts which he has given from the pamphlet itself on pages 146—140, etc., of "Epochs of Canadian Methodism."—H

CHAPTER VIII.

1829–1832.

ESTABLISHMENT OF THE "CHRISTIAN GUARDIAN—" CHURCH CLAIMS RESISTED.

DR. RYERSON takes up the Story of his Life at the period of the Conference of 1829. He says that ;—
At this Conference it was determined to establish the *Christian Guardian* newspaper. The Conference elected me as Editor, with instructions to go to New York to procure the types and apparatus necessary for its establishment.* In this I was greatly assisted by the late Rev. Dr. Bangs, and the Rev. Mr. Collard, of the New York Methodist Book Concern.

The hardships and difficulties of establishing and conducting the *Christian Guardian* for the first year, without a clerk, in the midst of our poverty, can hardly be realized and need not be detailed. The first number was issued on the 22nd November, 1829. The list of subscribers at the commencement was less than 500. Three years afterwards (in 1832), when the first Editor was appointed as the representative of the Canadian Conference to England, the subscription list was reported as nearly 3,000.

The characteristics of the *Christian Guardian* during these three eventful years (it being then regarded as the leading newspaper of Upper Canada) were defence of Methodist institutions and character, civil rights, temperance principles, educational progress, and missionary operations. It was during this period that the Methodist and other denominations obtained the right to hold land for places of worship, and for the burial

---

* The following is a copy of the document under the authority of which Dr. Ryerson was deputed to go to New York to procure presses and types for the proposed *Christian Guardian* newspaper :—

This is to certify that the Bearer, Rev. Egerton Ryerson, is appointed agent for procuring a printing establishment for the Canada Conference, and is hereby commended to the Christian confidence of all on whom he may have occasion to call for advice and assistance for the above purpose.

(Signed) WILLIAM CASE, *Superintendent.*
JAMES RICHARDSON, *Secretary.*

Ancaster, Upper Canada,
Sept. 4th, 1829.

of their dead, and the right of their ministers to solemnize matrimony, as also their rights to equal civil and religious liberty, against a dominant church establishment in Upper Canada, as I have detailed in the "Epochs of Canadian Methodism," pp. 129-246.

The foregoing is the only reference to this period of his life which Dr. Ryerson has left. I have, therefore, availed myself of his letters and papers to continue the narrative.

June—August, 1830.—With a view to correct the misstatements made in regard to the Methodists in Canada, and to set forth their just rights, Dr. Ryerson devoted a considerable space in the *Christian Guardian* of the 26th June, and 3rd, 10th, 24th, and 31st July, and 14th August, 1830, to a concise history of that body in this country, in which he maintained its right to the privileges proposed to be granted to it under the Religious Societies Relief Bill of that time.* He pointed out, as he expressed it, that—

His Majesty's Royal assent would have been given to that bill had it not unfortunately fallen in company with some ruthless vagrant (in the shape of a secret communication from our enemies in Canada) who had slandered, abused, and tomahawked it at the foot of the throne.

Oct. 11th.—Being desirous of availing himself of his brother George's educational advantages and ability in his editorial labours, Dr. Ryerson, under this date, wrote to him in his new charge at the Grand River. He said:—

I am glad to hear that you enjoy peace of mind, and feel an increasing attachment to your charge. It is more than I do as Editor. I am scarcely free from interruption long enough to settle my mind on any one thing, and sometimes I am almost distracted. On questions of right and liberty, as well as on other subjects, I am resolved to pursue a most decided course. Your retired situation will afford you a good opportunity for writing useful articles on various subjects. I hope you will write often and freely.

Nov. 1st.—Another reason, which apparently prompted Dr Ryerson to appeal to his brother George for editorial help, was the fear that the increasing efforts of the influential leaders of the Church of England to secure a recognition of her claims to be an established church in Upper Canada might be crowned with success. He, therefore, at this date wrote to him again on the subject, and said:—

The posture of affairs in England appears, upon the whole,

---

* These seven papers, taken together, were the first attempt to put into a connected form the history of the Methodist Church in Canada, down to 1830.—H.

more favourable to reform than in Upper Canada. We are resolved to double our diligence; to have general petitions in favour of the abolition of every kind of religious domination, circulated throughout the Province, addressed to the Provincial and Imperial Parliaments, and take up the whole question—decidedly, fully, and warmly. We must be up and doing while it is called to-day. It is the right time. There is a new and Whig Parliament in England, and I am sure our own House of Assembly dare not deny the petitions of the people on this subject.

NATURE OF THE STRUGGLE FOR RELIGIOUS EQUALITY.

During this and many succeeding years the chief efforts of Dr. Ryerson and those who acted with him were directed, as intimated before, against the efforts put forth to establish a "dominant church" in Upper Canada. A brief *resumé* of the question will put the reader in possession of the facts of the case :—

The late Bishop Strachan, in his speech delivered in the Legislative Council, March 6th, 1828, devoted several pages of that speech (as printed) to prove that "the Church of England is by law the Established Church of this Province." This statement in some form he put forth in every discussion on the subject.

The grounds upon which this claim was founded were also fully stated by Rev. Wm Betteridge, B.D. (of Woodstock), who was sent to England to represent the claims of the Church of England in this controversy. These claims he put forward in his "Brief History of the Church in Upper Canada," published in England in 1838. He rests those claims upon what he considers to have been the intention of the Imperial Parliament in passing the Clergy Reserve sections of the Act (31 Geo III., c. 31) in 1791, and also on the "King's Instructions" to the Lieutenant-Governor of Upper Canada in 1818. He further contended that the "Extinction of the Tithes Act," passed by the Upper Canada Legislature in 1823, inferentially recognized the dominancy of the Church of England in Canada as a Church of the Empire. Beyond this alleged inferential right to be an Established Church in Upper Canada, none in reality existed. It was, therefore, to prevent this inference,—which was insisted upon as perfectly clear and irresistible,—from receiving Imperial or Provincial recognition as an admitted or legal fact, that the persistent efforts of Dr. Ryerson and others were unceasingly directed during all of those years.

Few in the present day can realize the magnitude of the task thus undertaken. Nor do we sufficiently estimate the significance of the issues involved in that contest—a contest waged for the recognition of equal denominational rights and the supremacy of religious liberty. All of these questions are now happily settled "upon the best and surest foundation." But it might have been far otherwise had not such men as Dr. Ryerson stepped into the breach at a critical time in our early history; and if the battle had not been fought and won before the distasteful yoke of an "establishment" had been imposed upon this young country, and burdensome vested interests been thereby created, which it would have taken years of serious and protracted strife to extinguish.

As the fruits of that protracted struggle for religious equality have been long quietly enjoyed in this province, there is a disposition in many quarters to undervalue the importance of the contest itself, and even to question the propriety of reviving the recollection of such early conflicts. In so far as we may adopt such views we must necessarily fail to do justice to the heroism and self-sacrifice of those who, like Dr. Ryerson, encountered the prolonged and determined opposition, as well as the contemptuous scorn of the dominant party while battling for the rights which he and others ultimately secured for us. Those amongst us who would seek to depreciate the importance of that struggle for civil and religious freedom, must fail also to realize the importance of the real issues of that contest.

To those who have given any attention to this subject, it is well known that the maintenance of the views put forth by Dr. Ryerson in this controversy involved personal odium and the certainty of social ostracism. It also involved, what is often more fatal to a man's courage and constancy, the sneer and the personal animosity, as well as ridicule, of a powerful party whose right to supremacy is questioned, and whose monopoly of what is common property is in danger of being destroyed. Although Dr. Ryerson was a gentleman by birth, and the son of a British officer and U. E. Loyalist, yet the fact that, as one of the "despised sect" of Methodists, he dared to question the right of "the Church" to superiority over the "Sectaries," subjected him to a system of petty and bitter persecution which few men of less nerve and fortitude could have borne. As it was, there were times when the tender sensibilities of his noble nature were so deeply wounded by this injustice, and the scorn and contumely of his opponents, that were it not that his intrepid courage was of the finest type, and without the alloy of rancour or bravado in it, it would have failed him. But he never flinched. And when the odds seemed to be most against him, he would, with humble dependence upon Divine help, put forth even greater effort; and, with his courage thus reanimated, would unexpectedly turn the flank of his enemy; or, by concentrating all his forces on the vulnerable points of his adversary's case, completely neutralize the force of his attack.

It must not be understood from this that Dr. Ryerson cherished any personal animosity to the Church of England as a Divine and Spiritual power in the land. Far from it. In his first "campaign" against the Venerable Archdeacon of York (Dr. Strachan), he took care to point out the difference between the principles maintained by the aggressors in that contest and the principles of the Church itself. He said :—

> Whatever remarks the Doctor's discourse may require me to make, I wish it to be distinctly understood that I mean no reflection on the doctrines, liturgy, or discipline of the Church of which he has the honour to be a minister. Be assured I mean no such thing. I firmly believe in her doctrines, I admire her liturgy, and I heartily rejoice in the success of those principles which are therein contained, and it is for the prosperity of the truths which they unfold that I shall ever pray and contend. And, with respect to Church government, I heartily adopt the sentiments of the pious and the learned Bishop Burnet, that "that form of Church government is the best which is most suitable to the customs and circumstances of the people among whom it is established."*

Such was Dr. Ryerson's tribute to the Church of England in 1826. His disclaimer of personal hostility to that Church (near the close of the protracted denominational contest in regard to the Clergy Reserves), will be found in an interesting personal correspondence, in a subsequent part of this book, with John Kent, Esq., Editor of *The Church* newspaper in 1841-2.

With a view to enable Canadians of the present day more clearly to understand the pressing nature of the difficulties with which Dr. Ryerson had to contend, almost single-handed, fifty years ago, I shall briefly enumerate the principal ones:—

1. The whole of the official community of those days, which had grown up as a united and powerful class, were bound together by more than official ties, and hence, as a "family compact," they were enabled to act together as one man. This class, with few exceptions, were members of the Church of England. They regarded her—apart from her inimitable liturgy and scriptural standards of faith—with the respect and love which her historical prestige and assured status naturally inspired them. They maintained, without question, the traditional right of the Church of England to supremacy everywhere in the Empire. They, therefore, instinctively repelled all attempts to deprive that Church of what they believed to be her inalienable right to dominancy in this Province.

2. Those who had the courage, and who ventured to oppose the Church claims put forth by the clerical and other leaders of

* "Claims of Churchmen and Dissenters," &c., 1826, p. 27. (See p. 80.)

the dominant party of that time, were sure to be singled out for personal attack. They were also made to feel the chilling effects of social exclusiveness. The cry against them was that of ignorance, irreverence, irreligion, republicanism, disloyalty, etc. These charges were repeated in every form; and that, too, by a section both of the official and religious press, a portion of which was edited with singular ability; a press which prided itself on its intelligence, its unquestioned churchmanship and exalted respect for sacred things, its firm devotion to the principle of "Church and State"—the maintenance of which was held to be the only safeguard for society, if not its invincible bulwark. An illustration of the profession of this exclusive loyalty is given by Dr. Ryerson in these pages. He mentions the fact that the plea to the British Government put forth by the leaders of the dominant party, as a reason why the Church of England in this Province should be made supreme and be subsidized, was that she might then be enabled " to preserve the principles of loyalty to England from being overwhelmed and destroyed" by the "Yankee Methodists," as represented by the Ryersons and their friends!

3. The two branches of the Legislature were divided on this subject. The House of Assembly represented the popular side, as advocated by Dr. Ryerson and other denominational leaders. The Legislative Council (of which the Ven. Archdeacon Strachan was an influential member,) maintained the clerical views so ably put forth by this reverend leader on the other side.

4. Except by personal visits to England—where grievances could alone be fully redressed in those days—little hope was entertained by the non-Episcopal party that their side of the question would (if stated through official channels), be fairly or fully represented. Even were their case presented through these channels, they were not sure but that (as strikingly and quaintly put by Dr. Ryerson, on page 94).

In company with some ruthless vagrant—in the shape of a secret communication from enemies in Canada—it would be slandered, abused, and tomahawked at the foot of the throne.

As an illustration also of the spirit of the Chief Executive in Upper Canada in dealing with the questions in dispute, I quote the following extract from the reply of Sir John Colborne to an address from the Methodist Conference in 1831.* He said:

Your dislike to any church establishment, or to the particular form of Christianity which is denominated the Church of England, may be the

* For various reasons (apparently prudential at the time) this reply was never published in the *Christian Guardian*, as were other replies of the Governor.—H.

natural consequence of the constant success of your own efficacious and organized system. The small number of our Church* is to be regretted, as well as that the organization of its ministry is not adapted to supply the present wants of the dispersed population in this new country; but you will readily admit that the sober-minded of the province are disgusted with the accounts of the disgraceful dissensions of the Episcopal Methodist Church and its separatists, recriminating memorials, and the warfare of one Church with another. The utility of an Establishment depends entirely on the piety, assiduity, and devoted zeal of its ministers, and on their abstaining from a secular interference which may involve them in political disputes.

The labours of the clergy of established churches in defence of moral and religious truth will always be remembered by you, who have access to their writings, and benefit by them in common with other Christian Societies. You will allow, I have no doubt, on reflection that it would indeed be imprudent to admit the right of societies to dictate, on account of their present numerical strength, in what way the lands set apart as a provision for the clergy shall be disposed of.

The system of [University] Education which has produced the best and ablest men in the United Kingdom will not be abandoned here to suit the limited views of the leaders of Societies who, perhaps, have neither experience nor judgment to appreciate the value or advantages of a liberal education....

Such was the spirit in which the Governor in those days replied to the respectful address of a large and influential body of Christians. He even went further in another part of his reply, and referred to "the absurd advice offered by your missionaries to the Indians, and their officious interference."† Such language

* This expression, "our Church," illustrates the fact which I have indicated in first paragraph on page 97.

† This charge, preferred by such high authority, was taken up boldly by the Methodist authorities. Rev. James (afterwards Bishop) Richardson, Presiding Elder, was commissioned to inquire into its truthfulness. He made an exhaustive report, proving the entire incorrectness of the statement, and that the whole difficulty arose from the persistent efforts of a Mr. Alley (an employé of the Indian Department) to promote his own interest at the expense of that of the Indians, and to remove out of the way the only obstacle to the accomplishment of his purpose—the Methodist Missionary. Dr. Ryerson having pointed out these facts in the *Guardian*, Capt. Anderson, Superintendent of Indian affairs at Coldwater, questioned his conclusion "that the advice given to the Indians was both prudent and loudly called for, and perfectly respectful to His Excellency." Dr. Ryerson then examined the whole of the evidence in the case, and (See *Guardian*, vol. iii., p. 76) came to the following conclusion :—1. That sometimes the local agents of the Indian Department are men who have availed themselves of the most public occasions to procure ardent spirits, and entice the Indians to drunkenness, and other acts of immorality; being apparently aware that with the introduction of virtue and knowledge among these people will be the departure of gain which arises from abuse, fraud, and debauchery. 2. That these agents are not always men who respect the Sabbath. 3. That the Missionary's "absurd advice" was in effect that the Indians should apply to their Great Father to remove such agents from among them. 4. That their "craft being endangered," the agents and parties concerned, "with studied design, sought to injure the missionary in the estimation of His Excellency, and to destroy all harmony in their operations, in order, if possible, to compel the Missionary to abandon the Mission Station." The effect of this controversy was very salutary. His Excellency, having reconsidered the case, "gave merited reproof and suitable instructions to the officers of the Indian Department in regard to their treatment of the Methodist Missionary." Dr. Ryerson adds :—We had no trouble thereafter on the subject.

from the lips of Her Majesty's Representative, if at all possible in these days, would provoke a burst of indignation from those to whom it might be addressed, but it had to be endured fifty years ago, when to question the prerogative of the Crown, or the policy of the Executive, was taken as *prima facie* evidence of disloyalty, and republicanism.

5. Into the discussion of the claims of the Church of England in Upper Canada, two questions entered, which were important factors in the case. Both sides thoroughly understood the significance of either question as an issue in the discussion; and both sides were, therefore, equally on the alert—the one to maintain the affirmative, and the other the negative, side of these questions. The first was the claim that it was the inherent right of the Church of England to be an established church in every part of the empire, and, therefore, in Upper Canada. Both sides knew that the admission of such a claim, would be to admit the exclusive right of that Church to the Clergy Reserves as her heritage. It was argued, as an unquestionable fact, that the exclusive right of the Church of England in Upper Canada to such reserves must have been uppermost in the mind of the royal donor of these lands, when the grant was first made. The second point was, that the admission of this inherent right of the Church of England to be an established church in Upper Canada, would extinguish the right of each one of the nonconformist bodies to the status of a Church. It can well be understood that in a contest which involved vital questions like these (that is, of the exclusive endowment of one Church, and its consequent superior status as a dominant Church), the struggle would be a protracted and bitter one. And so it proved to be. But justice and right at length prevailed. A portion of the Reserves was impartially distributed, on a common basis among the denominations which desired to share in them, and the long-contested claims of the Church of England to the exclusive status of an established church were at length emphatically repudiated by the Legislature; and, in 1854, the last semblance of a union between Church and State vanished from our Statute Book.*—J. G. H.]

* Another disturbing element entered subsequently into this controversy. And this was especially embarrassing to Dr. Ryerson, as it proceeded from ministers in the same ecclesiastical fold as himself. I refer to the adverse views on church establishments, put forth by members of the British Conference in this country and especially in England (to which reference is made subsequently in this book). Dr. Ryerson was, as a matter of course, taunted with maintaining opinions which had been expressly repudiated by his Methodist "superiors" in England. He had, therefore, to wage a double warfare. He was assailed from within as well as from without. Besides, he had to bear the charge of putting forth heretical views in church politics, even from a Methodist standpoint. He, however, triumphed over both parties—those within as well as those without. And his victory over the former was the

Dec. 18th, 1830.—In the *Guardian* of this day, Dr. Ryerson published a petition to the Imperial Parliament, prepared by a large Committee, of which he was a member, and of which Dr. W. W. Baldwin was Chairman. In that petition the writer referred to the historical fact, that, had the inhabitants of this Province been dependent upon the Church of England or of Scotland for religious instruction, they would have remained destitute of it for some years, and also that the pioneer non-Episcopal ministers were not dissenters, because of the priority of their existence and labours in Upper Canada. The petition, having pointed out that there were only five Episcopal clergy in Canada during the war of 1812, and that only one Presbyterian minister was settled in the Province in 1818, declared that:

> The ministers of several other denominations accompanied the first influx of emigration into Upper Canada, (1783-1790,) and have shared the hardships, privations, and sufferings incident to missionaries in a new country. And it is through their unwearied labours, that the mass of the population have been mainly supplied with religious instruction. They, therefore, do not stand in the relation of Dissenters from either the Church of England or of Scotland, but are the ministers of distinct and independent Churches, who had numerous congregations in various parts of the Province, before the ministerial labours of any ecclesiastical establishment were, to any considerable extent, known or felt.

Jan. 20th, 1831.—As an evidence that the views put forth by Dr. Ryerson, in the *Guardian*, against an established Church in Upper Canada, were acceptable outside of his own denomination, I give the following letter, addressed to him at this date from Perth, by the Rev. Wm. Bell, Presbyterian :

> Though differing from you in many particulars, yet in some we agree. Your endeavours to advance the cause of civil and religious liberty have generally met my approbation. Some of your writings that I have seen discover both good sense and Christian feeling. The liberality, too, you have discovered, both in regard to myself and in regard of my brethren, has not escaped my observation. Be not discouraged by the malice of the enemies of religion. Your *Guardian* I have seldom seen, but from this time I intend to take it regularly. Consider me one of your "constant readers." The matters in which we differ are nothing in comparison of those in which we agree.

Feb. 9th.—Some members of the Church of England in the Province evinced a good deal of hostility to the Methodists of this period, chiefly from the fact that they had been connected with the Methodist Episcopal Church in the United States, and that the Canada Conference had formed one of the Annual Conferences of that Church, presided over by an American Bishop.

more easily won, as the views of the "British Methodists," on this question were almost unanimously repudiated by the Methodists of Canada. See "Epochs of Canadian Methodism," pp. 330-353.—H.

As an evidence of this hostility, Dr. Ryerson stated in the *Guardian* of this date, that Donald Bethune, Esq., and others, of Kingston, had petitioned the House of Assembly :—

To prohibit any exercise of the functions of a priest, or exhorter, or elder of any denomination in the Province except by British subjects ; 2nd, to prevent any religious society connected with any foreign religious body to assemble in Conference; 3rd, to prevent the raising of money by any religious person or body for objects which are not strictly British, etc.

The Legislature appointed a Committee on the subject, and Dr. Ryerson, as representing the Methodists, Rev. Mr Harris the Presbyterians, and Rev. Mr. Stewart the Baptists, were summoned to attend this Committee with a view to give evidence on the subject. This Dr. Ryerson did at length, (as did also these gentlemen). Dr. Ryerson traced the history of the Methodist body in Canada, and showed that, three years before this time, the Canada Conference had taken steps to sever its connection with the American General Conference, and had done so in a friendly manner.*

The petition was aimed at the Methodists, as they alone answered the description of the parties referred to by the petitioners. The petition was also a covert re-statement of the often disproved charge of disloyalty, etc., on the part of the Methodists. The House very properly came to the conclusion—

"That it was inconsistent with the benign and tolerant principles of the British Constitution to restrain by penal enactment any denomination of Christians, whether subjects or foreigners," etc.

This, however, was a sample of the favourite mode of attack, and the system of persecution to which the early Methodists were exposed in this Province. At the same session of Parliament in 1831, the Marriage Bill, which had been before the House each year for six successive years, was finally passed. This Bill gave to the Methodists and to other non-Episcopal ministers the right for the first time to solemnize matrimony in Upper Canada.

Feb. 19th.—Sir John Colborne, the Lieutenant-Governor, having nominated an Episcopal chaplain to the House of Assembly, the question, "Is the Church of England an established church in Upper Canada?" was again debated in the House of Assembly and discussed in the newspapers. With a view to a calm, dispassionate, and historical refutation of the claims set up by the Episcopal Church on the subject, Dr. Ryerson reprinted in the *Guardian* of this day, the sixth of a series of letters which he had addressed from Cobourg to Archdeacon Strachan, in May and June, 1828. It covered the whole ground in dispute.†

---

* See pages 63, 64 of the *Christian Guardian* for 1831; also page 90, *ante*.
† See *Christian Guardian* of Feb. 19th, 1831, and also the pamphlet con-

Nov. 6th, 1832.—Archdeacon Strachan, in his sermon, preached at the visitation of the Bishop of Quebec at York, on the 5th of September, speaking of the Methodists, said that he would—

Speak of them with praise, notwithstanding their departure from the Apostolic ordinance, and the hostility long manifested against us by some of their leading members.

In reply to this statement, Dr. Ryerson wrote from St. Catharines to the Editor of the *Guardian.* He pointed out that :—

It was not until after Archdeacon Strachan's sermon on the death of the former Bishop of Quebec was published, in 1826, that a single word was written, and then to refute his slanders. In that sermon, when accounting for the few who attend the Church of England, the Archdeacon said that their attendance discouraged the minister, and that—

His influence is frequently broken or injured by numbers of uneducated, itinerant preachers, who, leaving their steady employment, betake themselves to preaching the Gospel from idleness, or a zeal without knowledge . . . and to teach what they do not know, and which from their pride they disdain to learn.*

Again, in May, 1827, Archdeacon Strachan sent an " Ecclesiastical Chart " to the Colonial Office, and in the letter accompanying it stated that :—

The Methodist teachers are subject to the orders of the United States of America, and it is manifest that the Colonial Government neither has, nor can have any other control over them, or prevent them from gradually rendering a large portion of the population, by their influence and instructions, hostile to our institutions, civil and religious, than by increasing the number of the Established Clergy.

Who then [Dr Ryerson asked] was the author of contention ? Who was the aggressor ? Who provoked hostilities ? The slanders in the Chart were published in Canada, and in England, by Dr. Strachan before a single effort was made by a member of any denomination to counteract his hostile measures, or a single word was said on the subject.

Nov. 19th, 1834.—In connection with this subject I insert here the following reply (containing several historical facts) to a singularly pretentious letter which Dr. Ryerson had inserted in the *Guardian* of this date, denouncing the opposition of a certain " sect called Methodists " to the claims of the Church of England as an established church in the Colony. The reply was inserted in order to afford strangers and new settlers in taining the whole of this series of eight letters, entitled : "Letters from the Reverend Egerton Ryerson to the Honourable and Reverend Doctor Strachan, published originally in the *Upper Canada Herald;* Kingston, 1828," pp. 42, double columns. See page 80.—H.

* For reply to this statement see extract from Review given on p. 105.—H.

Upper Canada correct information on the subject, and to disprove the statement of the writer of the letter, Dr. Ryerson mentioned the following facts:—

The pretensions of the Episcopal clergy began to be disputed by the clergy of the Church of Scotland as soon as it was known that the former had got themselves erected into a corporation. This was, I believe, in 1820.* The subject was brought before the House of Assembly in 1824, and the House in 1824, '25, '26, '27, passed resolutions remonstrating against the exclusive claims of the Episcopal clergy. From 1822 to 1827 several pamphlets were published on both sides of the question, and much was said in the House of Assembly; but during this period not one word was written by any minister or member of the Methodist Church, nor did the Methodists take any part in it, though their ministers were not even allowed to solemnize matrimony—a privilege then enjoyed by Calvinistic ministers—and though individual ministers had been most maliciously and cruelly persecuted, under the sanction of judicial authority. . . . . But in the statements drawn up for the Imperial Government by the Episcopal clergy during the years mentioned, the extirpation of the Methodists was made one principal ground of appeal by the Episcopal clergy for the exclusive countenance and patronage of His Majesty's Government. Some of these documents at length came before the Canadian public; and in 1827 a defence of the Methodists and other religious denominations was put forth by the writer of these remarks in the form of a "Review of a Sermon preached by the Archdeacon of York." Up to this time not one word was said on "the church question" by the Methodists. But it was so warmly agitated by others, that in the early part of 1827 Archdeacon Strachan, an executive and legislative councillor, was sent to London to support the claims of the Episcopal clergy at the Colonial Office. His ecclesiastical chart and other communications were printed by order of the Government, and soon found their way into the provincial newspapers, and gave rise to such a discussion, and excited such a feeling throughout the Province as was never before witnessed. The shameful attack upon the character of the Methodist ministry, whose unparalleled labours and sufferings, usefulness, and unimpeachable loyalty were known and appreciated in the

* In "a Pastoral Letter from the Clergy of the Church of Scotland in the Canadas to their Presbyterian Brethren" issued in 1828, they say:—We did, in the year 1820, petition His Majesty's Government for protection and support to our Church, and claimed, by what we believe to be our constitutional rights, a participation in the Clergy Reserves." Montreal, 1828, p. 2. This Pastoral Letter gave rise to a protracted discussion for and against the Presbyterian side of the question.—H.

Province, and the appeal to the King's Government to aid in exterminating them from the country excited strong feelings of indignation and sympathy in the public mind. The House of Assembly investigated the whole affair, examined fifty-two witnesses, adopted an elaborate report, and sent home an address to the King condemning the statements of the agent of the Episcopal clergy, and remonstrating against the establishment of a dominant church in the Province.* The determination to uproot the Methodists was carried so far in those by-gone days of civil and ecclesiastical despotism, that the Indians were told by executive sanction that unless they would become members of the Church of England, the Government would do nothing for them! In further support of my statement, I quoted four Episcopal addresses and sermons, sufficient to show who were the first and real aggressors in this matter—certainly not the Methodists.

As a sample of Dr. Ryerson's controversial style in 1826, when he wrote the Review of Archdeacon Strachan's sermon (to which he refers above) I quote a paragraph from it. In replying to the Archdeacon's "remarks on the qualifications, motives, and conduct of the Methodist itinerant preachers," which Dr. Ryerson considered "ungenerous and unfounded," he proceeded :—

The Methodist preachers do not value themselves upon the wealth, virtues, or grandeur, of their ancestry ; nor do they consider their former occupation an argument against their present employment or usefulness. They have learned that the Apostles were once fishermen ; that a Milner could once throw the shuttle ; that a Newton once watched his mother's flock. . . . They are likewise charged with "preaching the Gospel out of idleness." Does the Archdeacon claim the attribute of omniscience ? Does he know what is in man ? How does he know that they preach "the Gospel out of idleness?" . . . . What does he call idleness ?—the reading of one or two dry discourses every Sabbath . . . . to one congregation, with an annual income of £200 or £300 ? . . . . No ; this is hard labour ; this is indefatigable industry ! . . . . Who are they then that preach the Gospel out of idleness ?—those indolent, covetous men who travel from two to three hundred miles, and preach from twenty-five to forty times every month ?—who, in addition to this, visit from house to house, and teach young and old "repentance towards God, and faith in our Lord Jesust Christ ?—those who continue this labour year after year . . . . at the enormous salary of £25 or £50 per annum !—these are the men who "preach the

---

* The Report was adopted by a vote of 22 to 8. It stated:—The ministry and instructions [of the Methodist Clergymen] have been conducive—in a degree which cannot be easily estimated—to the reformation of their hearers, and to the diffusion of correct morals—the foundation of all sound loyalty and social order. . . . . No one doubts that the Methodists are as loyal as any other of His Majesty's subjects, etc. Full particulars of this controversy will be found in Dr. Ryerson's "Epochs of Canadian Methodism," pp. 165–218.—H.

Gospel out of idleness !" O bigotry! thou parent of persecution; O envy! thou fountain of slander; O covetousness! thou god of injustice! would to heaven ye were banished from the earth !*

Jan. 22nd, 1831.—In the *Guardian* of this day Dr. Ryerson publishes a letter from the Rev. Richard Watson to the trustees of the Wesleyan University, in Connecticut, declining the appointment of Professor of *Belles Lettres* and Moral Philosophy. He says :—

To *Belles Lettres* I have no pretensions ; Moral Philosophy I have studied, and think it a most important department, when kept upon its true principles, both theological and philosophic. Being, however, fifty years old, and having a feeble constitution, I do not think it would be prudent in me to accept.

During this year (1831) Dr. Ryerson engaged in a friendly controversy with Vicar-General Macdonnell, Editor of the *Catholic*, published in Kingston. This controversy included six letters from Dr. Ryerson, and five from the Vicar-General, published in the *Christian Guardian*. It touched upon the leading questions at issue between Roman Catholics and Protestants. The correspondence was broken off by the Vicar-General.

* In "An Apology for the Church of England in Canada, by a Protestant of the Established Church of England," the writer thus refers to this controversy :— "Our Methodist brethren have disturbed the peace of their maternal Church by the clamour of enthusiasm and the madness of resentment; but they are the way-ward children of passion, and we hope that yet the chastening hand of reason will sober down the wildness of that ferment," etc. Kingston, U.C., 1826, p. 3.—H.

CHAPTER IX.

1831-1832.

METHODIST AFFAIRS IN UPPER CANADA—PROPOSED UNION WITH THE BRITISH CONFERENCE.

OF the events transpiring in Upper Canada during 1831 and 1832, in which Dr. Ryerson was an actor, he has left no record in his "Story." His letters and papers, however, show that during this period he retired from the editorship of the *Christian Guardian,* and that plans were discussed and matured which led to his going to England, in 1833, to negotiate a union between the British and Upper Canadian Conferences. His brother George had gone on a second visit to England in March, 1831. This second visit was for a twofold purpose, viz., to collect money with the Rev. Peter Jones, for the Indian Missions, and also to present petitions to the Imperial Parliament on behalf of the non-episcopalians of the Province. I give extracts from his letters to Dr. Ryerson, relating his experiences of, and reflections on, Wesleyan matters in England at that period. Writing from Bristol, on the 6th of August, 1831, Rev. George Ryerson said :—

> In my address to the Wesleyan Conference here I stated that we stood in precisely the same relation to our brethren of the Methodist Conference in the United States as we do to our brethren of the Wesleyan Conference in England—independent of either—agreeing in faith, in religious discipline, in name and doctrine, and the unity of spirit,—but differing in some ecclesiastical arrangements, rendered necessary from local circumstances. I also expressed my firm conviction that the situation in which we stand is decidedly the best calculated to spread Methodism and vital religion in Canada. This statement did not, I think, give so much satisfaction to the Conference as the others, for what Pope said of Churchmen:
>
> > "Is he a Churchman? then he's fond of power,"
>
> may also be literally applied to Wesleyan ministers, and, I may add, to Englishmen generally. I have reason to know that they would gladly govern us. I was, therefore, very pointed and explicit on this subject. I rejoice that our country lies beyond the Atlantic, and is surrounded by an atmosphere of freedom. A few months' residence in this country would lead you to value this circumstance in a degree that you can scarcely conceive of; and you would, with unknown energy, address this exhortation to the Methodists and to the people of Canada: "Stand fast, therefore, in the liberty wherewith God's providence hath made you free, and in this abound

more and more." I also assured them of our respect and love for them as our fathers and elder brethren, and mentioned my reasons for giving this information to prevent future collision and misunderstanding.

The Conference or Missionary Society have, however, not given up their intention of establishing an Indian Mission in Upper Canada, but, in consequence of my remonstrances, have delayed it. Brother James Richardson's letter to the Missionary Committee, which I submitted, and was told by Rev. Dr. Townley, one of the Secretaries, that they would by no means withdraw their missionary at Kingston, as it was still their intention to establish a mission to the Indians in Upper Canada, and this station would be very necessary to them. I see that they are a little vexed that emigrants from their Societies should augment our membership.

The whole morning service of the Church of England is now read in most of the Wesleyan Chapels, and with as much formality as in the Church. Many of the members, when they become wealthy and rise in the world, join the Church, and their wealth and influence are lost to the Society. Organs are also introduced into many of their Chapels.

In a letter dated London, Feb. 6th, 1832, Rev. Geo. Ryerson writes again to Dr. Ryerson, and says that he and Peter Jones:

By request, met the Rev. Richard Watson, and some others of the Missionary Committee. They wished to consult us respecting the resolutions forwarded to them from your Missionary Committee. They profess that they will not occupy any station where there is a mission, as Grand River, Penetanguishene, etc., except St. Clair. But they declare that as it regards the white population, the agreement with the American Conference ceased when we became a separate connexion. I opposed their views, as I have invariably done, in very strong and plain terms, and explained to them the character and object of the persons who were alluring them to commence this schism. They proposed that we should give up the missions to them. I told them we could no more do so, than they give up theirs. They finally acquiesced, and voted the £300 as Rev. Dr. Townley wrote. At the Conference, at Bristol, I explained that a union of the two Conferences would be inexpedient and unprofitable, any further than a union of brotherly love and friendship.

In another letter to Dr. Ryerson from his brother George, dated London, April 6th, 1832, he says :—

I have been detained so long on expenses, and continually advancing money for the Central Committee at York, that I hope it will be repaid to Peter Jones. I was a long time attending to the business of my mission to bring it to the only practicable arrangement, that is, having it submitted to the Legislature of Upper Canada, with such recommendations and instructions as would give satisfaction to the country by consulting the wishes and interests of all parties. I have never before in my life been shut up to walk in all things by simple faith more than I have for some months past ; yet I was never kept in greater steadfastness and peace of mind, nor had such openings of the Spirit and life of Jesus in my soul. The judgments of God are spreading apace—the cholera is more deadly in London, and it has now broken out in Ireland, and in the centre of Paris, where it is said to be very destructive. You need no other evidence of its being a work of God, than to be informed that it is made the public mock of the infidel population of this city ; a state of feeling and conduct in regard to this pestilence that never, perhaps, was witnessed from any country, and that would make a heathen or Mahommedan ashamed. I have seen gangs of men traversing the streets and singing songs in ridicule of the cholera, and have seen caricatures of it in the windows.

August 29th, 1832.—To-day, in a valedictory editorial, Dr. Ryerson took leave of the readers of the *Christian Guardian*, having been its first editor for nearly three years. In that valedictory Dr. Ryerson said (p. 116):—

I first appeared before the public as a writer, at the age of two and twenty years. My first feeble effort was a vindication of the Methodists, and several other Christian denominations against the uncalled-for attack made upon their principles and character. It also contained a remonstrance against the introduction into this country of an endowed political Church, as alike opposed to the statute law of the Province, political and religious expedience, public rights and liberties. I believe this was the first article of the kind ever published in Upper Canada, and, while from that time to this a powerful combination of talent, learning, indignation, and interest has been arrayed in the vain attempt to support by the weapons of reason, Scripture, and argument, a union between the Church and the world—between earth and heaven; talents, truth, reason, and justice have alike been arrayed in the defence of insulted and infringed rights, and the maintenance of a system of public, religious, and educational instruction, accordant with public rights and interests, the principles of sound policy, the economy of Providence, and the institutions and usages of the New Testament.

Dr. Ryerson also published in this number of the *Guardian* the general outline of the arrangements proposed at Hallowell (Picton) on behalf of the Canada Conference to the English Conference, and designed to form the basis of articles for the proposed union between the two bodies. Rev. Robert Alder was present at the Conference, and was a consenting party to the basis of union.

December 7th, 1832.—The prospects of Union with the British Conference were not encouraging in various parts of the Connexion, and chiefly for the reasons mentioned by Rev. George Ryerson in his letters from England (see pp. 107, 8). Rev. John Ryerson, writing to Dr. Ryerson from Cobourg, also says:—

The subject of the Union appears to be less and less palatable to our friends in these parts, so much so, that I think it will not be safe for you to come to any permanent arrangements with the British Conference, even should they accede to our proposals. I am of the opinion that, except we give ourselves entirely into their hands in some way or another, no Union will take place. I tell the preachers, and they and I tell the people, that, Union or no Union, it is very important that you should go home; that you will endeavour, in every way you can, to convince the British Conference of the manifest injustice and wickedness of sending missionaries to this country.

November 21*st*, 1832.—The proposed union with the British Conference excited a good deal of discussion at this time in various parts of Upper Canada. Dr. Ryerson, therefore, addressed a note on the subject to Rev. Robert Alder, the English Conference representative. I make a few extracts:—

At the Hallowell Conference (1832) the question of the union was principally sustained by my brothers, and was concurred in by the vote of a large majority of the Conference. . . . But in some parts of the country, where Presidential visits have been made, certain local preachers have found out that the Societies ought to have been consulted; that they have been sold ("by the Ryersons,") without consent; that no Canadian will henceforth be admitted into the Conference; that our whole economy will be changed by arbitrary power, and all revivals of religion will be stopped, etc. The first of the objections is the most popular, but they have all failed to produce the intended effect, to an extent desired by the disaffected few. The object contemplated is, to produce an excitement that will prevent me going to England, and induce the Conference to retrace its steps. The merit or demerit of the measure has been mainly ascribed to me; and on its result, should I cross the Atlantic, my standing, in a great measure, depends. If our proposals should meet with a conciliatory reception, and your Committee would recommend measures, rather than require concessions, in the future proceedings of our Conference, everything can be accomplished without difficulty or embarrassment. You know that I am willing, as an individual, to adopt your whole British economy, *ex animo*. You also know that my brothers are of the same mind, and that a majority of the Conference will readily concur. May the Lord direct aright!

Dr. Alder's reply to Dr. Ryerson in February, 1833, was that:

You must look at the great principles and results involved in this most important affair, and not shrink from the duties imposed on you, to avoid a few present unpleasant consequences. It is not for me to prescribe rules of conduct to be observed by you, but I must say, that I am surprised that any circumstance should cause you to waver for a moment in reference to your visit to Europe. If you were to decline coming, would not the many on the other side, who are strictly watching your movements, at once say that the whole arrangements are deceptive, and merely designed to make an impression on me for a certain purpose. You know they would. Of course you will act as you please. I neither advise nor persuade, but say: Be not too soon nor too much alarmed. There are no jealousies, no evil surmisings, no ambitious designs in the matter, but a sincere desire to promote the interests of Methodism and the cause of religion in Upper Canada; and nothing will be desired from, or recommended to, you, but for this purpose.

It is a noble object that we have in view. Rev. Richard Watson takes a statesmanlike view of the whole case, and will, I am persuaded, as will all concerned here, meet you with the utmost ingenuousness and liberality, and, if they be met in a similar manner, all will end well. If you can agree to the following recommendation, I think everything else will easily be settled, viz., to constitute two or three districts, to meet annually, as District Conferences, and to hold a Triennial Conference, to be composed of all the preachers in the Provinces, under a President, to be appointed in the way mentioned in the plan of agreement proposed by your last Conference. Several of your preachers wish it; Bro. Green, the presiding Elder, is in favour of it.

January 10th, 1833.—It being necessary to collect funds to defray Dr. Ryerson's expenses to England, his brother, William, wrote to him from Brockville at this date, giving an account of his success there as a collector. He said:—

After the holidays I commenced operations, and having besieged the doors of several of our gentry, most of whom contributed without much resistance, on most honourable terms, of course, such as paying from $3 to $6, with a great many wishes, and hearty ones too, for your success. More than two-thirds of the sum collected are given by the gentlemen of the village, most of whom expressed and appeared to feel a pleasure in giving, and who have never been known to give anything to the Methodists before on any occasion whatever. Our congregation has greatly increased, so that we now have about five hundred, some say more, in the evening. A majority of the first families in the village attend our chapel. Among many others, Mr. Jonas Jones, and several of the families in the same connection; Mr. Sherwood, the High Sheriff, and several others, most of whom have never been known to attend a Methodist meeting before. You will be surprised to hear that Mrs. James Sherwood has become my warm friend, treating me with the greatest attention and kindness; and also on various occasions speaking most kindly and respectfully of me and all our family, especially yourself.

January 31st, 1833.—Under this date, Dr. Ryerson has recorded in his diary the following tribute to his first wife:—

A year ago this morning, at half-past five o'clock, the wife of my youth fell asleep in Jesus, leaving a son and daughter (John and Lucilla Hannah), the former two years and a half old, and the latter fourteen days. Hannah Aikman (her maiden name) was the daughter of John and Hannah Aikman, and was the youngest of eleven children. Hannah was born in Barton, Gore District, on the 4th of August, 1804. Her natural disposition was most amiable, and her education was better than is usually afforded to farmer's daughters in this country. At the age of sixteen she was awakened, converted, and joined the Methodist Church, of which she remained an exemplary member until her death. I became intimately acquainted with her in 1824, when she was twenty years of age, and after taking the advice of an elder brother, who had travelled the circuit on which they lived, at the strong solicitation of my parents, and the impulse of my own inclinations, I made her proposals of marriage, which were accepted. This was before I had any intention of becoming a preacher in the Methodist Church, either travelling or local.

About this time the Lord laid his afflicting hand upon me;* I was brought to the gate of death, and in that state became convinced by evidence as satisfactory as that of my existence, that in disregarding the dictates of my own conscience, and the important advice of many members of the Church, both

---

* See note on page 86 and page 28.

preachers and lay, in regard to labouring in the itinerant field, I had resisted the Spirit of God; and on that sick, and in the estimation of my family, dying bed, I vowed to the Lord my God, that if He should see fit to raise me up and open the way, I would no more disobey the voice of His Providence and servants. From that hour I began visibly to recover, and, though the exercises of my mind were unknown to any but myself and the Searcher of hearts, before I had sufficiently recovered to walk two miles, I was called upon by the Presiding Elder, and several official members, and solicited to go on the Niagara Circuit, which was then partly destitute through the failure in health of one of the preachers. I could not but view this unexpected call as the voice of God, and, after a few days' deliberation and preparation, I obeyed, on the 24th of March, 1825, the day on which I was twenty-two years of age.

This unanticipated change in the course of my life, while it involved the sacrifice of pecuniary interests and some very flattering offers and promises, presented my contemplated marriage in a somewhat different light; though the possibility of such a change was mentioned as a condition in my proposals and our engagement. And I will here record it to the honour of the dead that she who afterwards became my wife, wrote to me a short time after I commenced travelling, that if a union between us was in any respect opposed to my views of duty, or if I thought it would militate against my usefulness, I was perfectly exonerated by her from all obligations to such a union; that, whatever her own feelings might be, she begged that they would not influence me,—that God would give her grace to subdue them,—that she shuddered at the thought of standing in the way of my duty and usefulness.

Knowing, as I did, that her fondness for me was extravagant, I could not wound the heart which was the seat of such elevated feelings, or help appreciating more highly than ever the principles of mind which could give rise to such noble sentiments, and such martyr-like disinterestedness of soul. In subsequent interviews, we mutually agreed—should Providence permit—and (at her suggestion) should neither of us change our minds, we would get married in three or four years. During this interval, I had at times agitations of mind as to the advantages of such a step, in regard to my ministerial labours, but determined to rely on the Divine promise, "Blessed is the man that sweareth to his own hurt, and changeth not." This promise has been abundantly fulfilled in me. We were married on the 10th of September, 1828. A more affectionate and prudent wife never lived. She was beloved and respected by all that knew her. I never saw her angry, nor do I recollect that an angry or unkind word ever passed between us. Her disposition was sweet, her spirit uniformly kind and cheerful, sociable, and meek. Her professions were never high, nor her joys rapturous. But in everything she was invariably faithful, and ready for every good word and work. In her confidence, peace, and conduct, as far as I could discover, without intermission, the poet's words were clearly illustrated :—

"Her soul was ever bright as noon, and calm as summer evenings be."

Though her piety for years excited my respect, and in many instances my admiration, it was nevertheless greatly quickened and deepened about six months before her death, during the Conference held at York. From that time I believe she enjoyed the perfect love of God. At least, as far as I can judge, the fruits of it were manifest in her whole life.

Several days previous to her death, when her illness assumed a mortal aspect, and she became sensible that her earthly pilgrimage was closing, her usual unruffled confidence rose to the riches of the full assurance of understanding, faith and hope, and she expressed herself with a boldness of language, a rapture of hope, and triumph of faith that I never before witnessed. Passages of Scripture, and verses of hymns, expressive of the dying Christian's victories, triumphs, and hopes, were repeated by her with a joy and energetic fervency that deeply affected all present. Her death-bed conversations and dying counsels were a rich repast and a valuable lesson of instruction to many of her Christian friends. The night before she took her departure, she called me to her and consulted me about disposing of the family and all her own things, with as much coolness and judgment as if she had been in perfect health, and was about leaving home on a few days' visit to her friends. A little before midnight she requested the babe to be brought to her—kissed it—blessed it, and returned it. She then called for the little boy (John), and, embracing and kissing him, bequeathed to him also the legacy of a pious mother's dying prayer and blessing. Afterwards she embraced me, and said, "My dear Egerton, preach the Word; be instant in season and out of season, and God will take care of you, and give you the victory" She then bid an affectionate farewell individually to all. She continued in the perfect possession of her reason, triumphing in the Rock of her salvation, until the messenger arrived and her spirit took its departure with the words, "Come, Lord Jesus," lingering upon her lips. Thus lived and died one of the excellent of the earth,—a woman of good, plain sense, a guileless heart, and a sanctified spirit and life. Such is the testimony respecting her, of one who knew her best.

In his deep sorrow and affliction, at that time, Dr. Ryerson received many sympathizing letters. I give an extract of one from his brother George, dated London, Eng., 29th March, 1832. He says :—

I deeply sympathize with you in your affliction. I know how to feel for you, and you as yet know but a very small part of your trials. Years will not heal the wound. I am, even now, often quite overwhelmed when I allow myself to dwell upon the past. I need not suggest to you the commonplace topics of comfort and resignation, but I have no doubt you will see the hand of God so manifestly in it, that you will say "It was well done." I will further add that the saying of St. Paul was at no time so applicable as at the present (1 Cor. vii. 29, etc.).

The years 1830–1832 were noted in the history of the Methodist Church in Upper Canada for two things : 1st. The establishment of the Upper Canada Academy—the radiating centre of intellectual life in the Connexion. 2nd. The erection of the Adelaide St. Chapel, which for many years was the seat and source of Church life in the Societies. At the Conference of 1830 it was agreed to establish the Upper Canada Academy. In the *Guardian* of the 23rd of April, 1831, Dr. Ryerson gave an account of the new institution and made a strong appeal in its favour. On the 7th June, 1832, the foundation stone of the Academy was laid at Cobourg. On the 16th June, 1833, the new brick church on Newgate (Adelaide) St. was opened for Divine Service. In the *Guardian* of June 19th, Dr. Ryerson says : "For its size—being 75 by 55 feet—it is judged to be inferior to very few Methodist Chapels in America." P. 126.

CHAPTER X.

1833.

UNION BETWEEN THE BRITISH AND CANADIAN CONFERENCES

I UNDERTOOK the mission to England to negotiate a Union between the British and Canadian Conferences with great reluctance. I determined in the course of the year, from various circumstances, to abandon it; but was persuaded by letters from Rev. Robert Alder, the London Missionary Secretary (one of which is given on page 110), and the advice of my brother John, to resume it

The account of my voyage and proceedings in England are given in the following extracts from my journals :—

March 4th, 1833.—This morning at 6 a.m. I left York *via* Cobourg, Kingston, and New York, on my first important mission to England, an undertaking for which I feel myself utterly incompetent ; and in prosecution of which I rely wholly on the guidance of heavenly wisdom, imploring the special blessing of the Most High.

Kingston, March 11th.—I find that considerable excitement, and in some instances, strong dissatisfaction, exists on the question of Union, by misrepresentation of the proceedings and intentions of our Conference respecting it. Full explanations have in every instance restored confidence, and acquiescence. A correction of these misrepresentations, and the reply of the Wesleyan Missionary Committee to the proposals of our Conference have given universal satisfaction, and elicited a general and strong desire for the accomplishment of this all-important measure. My interviews with my brothers (William and John) have been interesting and profitable to me.

Watertown, N.Y., March 12.—Came from Kingston here to-day, twenty-eight miles. This Black River country is very level, and appears to be fertile, but the people generally do not seem to be thriving.

Utica, March 13th.—This is a flourishing town of about 10,000 inhabitants, beautifully situated on the south side of the Mohawk river. I travelled through a settlement and village called Renson, consisting principally of Welsh, where the Welsh language is universally spoken ; there is a *Whitefield* Methodist chapel, but I was told they retained more of the name, than of the genuine spirit of their founder. " Because of swearing the land mourneth."

Hartford, March 16th.—The southern part of Massachusetts and the northern part of this State, are mountainous and rocky and barren. The inhabitants are supported by manufactures, grazing and dairies. They appear to be rather poor but intelligent. In my conversation to-day with a professed infidel I felt sensibly the importance of being skilled in wielding any weapon with which theology, history, science, so abundantly furnishes the believer in the Christian revelation; and never before did I see and feel the lofty superiority of the foundation on which natural and revealed truth is established, over the cob-web and ill-shaped edifice of infidelity.

Hartford, March 17th.—I have attended service three times to-day, and preached twice. Religion seems to be at a low ebb. Yet I have not heard religion spoken of, or any body of religious people referred to, in any other way than that of respect.

New York, March 20th.—I am now about to embark for England, the reason of my long journey from Canada to New York is the slow travel by stage, before any railroads, and the Hudson river not navigable so early.

New York, March 21st.—[Just on the eve of sailing for England, Dr. Ryerson wrote from New York to his brother John, at Hallowell. He said:—

I stayed with the Rev. Dr. Fisk all night and part of two days. I was much gratified and benefited, and have received from him many valuable suggestions respecting my mission to England and agency for the Upper Canada Academy. He was unreserved in his communications, and is in favour of my Mission, as were Brother Waugh, Drs. Bangs, Durbin* and others. They all seem to approve fully of the proceedings of our Conference in the affair.—H.]

New York, March 22nd.—[On the day on which Dr. Ryerson sailed for England, Mr. Francis Hall, of the New York *Commercial Advertiser*, sent him a note in which he said :—

I have just received from a friend in Montreal the following information which I wish you would give to the Rev. Richard Reece, of London:—The Lord has blessed us abundantly in Montreal. Upwards of four hundred conversions have taken place in our chapel since last summer. It is now necessary for us to have a chapel in the St. Lawrence suburbs, and another in the Quebec suburbs immediately. This (said Mr. Hall) for those who know Montreal, is great news indeed. It is equal to an increase of as many thousands in the city of New York; the whole population being only a little more than thirty thousand, a great portion of which are Roman Catholics.—H.]

Dr. Ryerson's journal then proceeds :—

At Sea, April 10th.—On the 22nd ult., I embarked on the sailing ship "York," Capt. Uree, New York. I was sick for fourteen days, ate nothing, thought little, and enjoyed nothing. Feeling better, I was able to read a little.

April 12th.—After twenty days' sail we landed at Portsmouth. Thanks be to the God of heaven, earth, and sea for His protection, blessing, and prosperity! I was greatly struck with the extensive fortifications, and vast dockyards, together with the wonderful machinery in this place; such indications of national wealth, and specimens of human genius and industry.

---

* While in England, Dr. Ryerson received the following note from Rev. Dr. J. P. Durbin, in which he said: After I parted with you at my house, I felt a strong inclination to engage your correspondence for our paper, at least once a week, if possible, for the benefit of our people and country, through the Church. Can you not write us by every packet? Information in regard to English Methodism will be particularly interesting, especially their fianancial arrangements. Do inquire diligently of them, and write us minutely for the good of our Zion.—H.

April 13th.—This morning I arrived in London, and was cordially received by the Secretary of the Wesleyan Missionary Society, and kindly invited to take up my lodgings at the Mission House.

April 14th—Sabbath.—Heard the Rev. G. Marsden preach. In the afternoon this holy man addressed about four hundred Sunday-school children, after which I spoke a few words to them. We then attended a prayer-meeting, where many found peace with God. In the evening I heard the Rev. Theophilus Lessey preach a superior sermon, and I felt blessed.

April 16th.—This evening I preached my first sermon in England, in City Road Chapel, from John iii. 8. This is called Mr. Wesley's Chapel, having been built by him, and left under peculiar regulations. Alongside is Mr. Wesley's dwelling-house, and in the rear of it rest his bones, also those of Rev. Dr. Adam Clarke and Rev. Richard Watson; three of the greatest men the world ever saw. In the front of this chapel, on the opposite side of the street, are the celebrated Bunhill Field's burying ground, among whose memorable dead rests the dust of the venerable Isaac Watts, John Wesley's mother, John Bunyan, Daniel Defoe, etc.

April 21st—Sunday.—To-day I went to hear the celebrated Edward Irving. His preaching, for the most part, I considered commonplace; his manner, eccentric; his pretensions to revelations, authority, and prophetic indications, overweening. I was disappointed in his talents, and surprised at the apparent want of feeling manifested throughout his whole discourse.

April 20th.—This morning I attended the funeral of the great and eminently pious Rev. Rowland Hill, who died in the 89th year of his age. Lord Hill, his nephew, was chief mourner. There was a large attendance of ministers of all denominations, and a great concourse of people. Rev. Wm. Jay, of Bath, preached an admirable sermon from Zech. ii. 2. " Howl fir tree, for the cedar hath fallen." The venerable remains were interred beneath the pulpit.

April 26th.—To-day I heard Rev. Richard Winter Hamilton, of Leeds, an Independent, preach a missionary sermon for the Wesleyan Society. His text was Col. i. 16. It was the most splendid sermon I ever heard.

April 28th.—Heard the Rev. Robert Newton in the morning. In the afternoon I preached a missionary sermon in Westminster Chapel, and in the evening another at Chelsea.

April 29th.—This day was held the Annual Meeting of the Wesleyan Missionary Society, in Exeter Hall, Lord Morpeth in the chair. He is a young man, serious and dignified in his manners. The speeches generally were able and to the point. Collection was £931.

May 1st.—The Annual Meeting of the British and Foreign Bible Society was held in Exeter Hall. Lord Bexley presided. The Bishops of Winchester and Chester, brothers, addressed the meeting. They are eloquent speakers, but the Hon. and Rev. Baptist Noel was the speaker of the day.

May 3rd.—This morning I attended the Annual Breakfast Meeting of the preachers' children, at the City Road Morning Chapel; nearly 200 preachers and their families were present. Rev. Joseph Entwistle spoke, as did Mr. James Wood, of Bristol, myself and one or two others.

May 5th., Exeter.—Left London at 5 a.m. and arrived here at 10 p.m., within a minute of the time specified by the coachman. We passed over the scene of that inimitable tract, " The Shepherd of Salisbury Plain." We were shown the tree under which the shepherd was sheltered.

May 6th.—Rev. Wm. Naylor preached this morning in Exeter, and I preached in the evening.

Taunton, May 7th.—At a Missionary Tea Meeting to-day, deep interest was excited in the cause of the British North American Missions. Taunton is a very ancient town. It existed in the time of the Romans. It was in this town that King Ina held the first Legislative Assembly or Parliament ever held in Britain. It consisted of ecclesiastics and noblemen and enacted certain laws for the better government of the Heptarchy. It was near this town King Alfred concealed himself, and was discovered in the capacity of a cook. Here also stands the Church of St. Mary, a most splendid and ancient gothic building, where that venerable and holy man of God, Joseph Alleine, author of the "Alarm to the Unconverted," preached.

In a letter to a friend in Upper Canada, Dr. Ryerson at this date writes :—

Nottingham, May 29th.—I this morning called upon Mrs. Watson, mother of the late distinguished Richard Watson. She is nearly eighty years of age, and in rather humble circumstances. She is in the possession of a naturally strong and unimpaired intellect, and has apparently not the least vanity on account of the unrivalled talents, high attainments, and great popularity of her son. In conversation she stated the following particulars : That her husband was a saddler ; that he formerly lived and followed his business in Boston-on-the-Humber in Lincolnshire, where Richard was born ; that her husband was the only Methodist in the town, and was the means of introducing Methodism into that town; that his business was taken from him, and he was obliged to leave and remove to another place on account of it; that Richard was very weakly, and so poorly that she carried him when a child on a pillow in her arms ; that when he began to talk and run about he was unusually stupid and sleepy, would drop asleep anywhere ; that he was very tall of his age, and made such advancement in learning, that he read the Latin Testament at five years of age, and had read a considerable part of it before his parents knew that he had been put to the study of Latin; the clergyman, his tutor, thought him older, from his size and mind, or, as he said, he would not have put him to Latin so young ; that Richard had a very great taste for reading; when he was a very small boy, he read the History of England (when not eight years of age), and recollected and related with the utmost correctness all its leading facts ; that he would frequently remain at school after school hours, doing difficult questions in arithmetic for older boys ; that he was bound out, according to his request, to the trade of a house-joiner; that he was most diligent and faithful at his work, and made such rapid advancement in learning the trade, that at the end of two years, his master told his father that he had already learned as much as he could teach him, and that he was willing to give him up if he desired—the best hand in his shop ; that Richard began to go out and exhort when he was fourteen years of age, and that he preached when he was fifteen, and was received on trial by the Conference as a travelling preacher about a month after he was sixteen ; that he was frequently pelted with eggs, and even trodden under foot ; that his own uncle on one occasion encouraged it, saying, "My kinsman does it pretty well, give him a few more eggs, lad" (addressing one of the mob), and that Richard came home frequently with his clothes completely besmeared with eggs and dirt.

I attended the Wesleyan Missionary meeting here and spoke at it. The meeting was highly interesting. It was addressed by Rev. Mr. Edwards, (Baptist) and by the Messrs. Bunting, Atherton, and Bakewell. In this town the noted Kilham made his first Methodist division, and here suddenly ended his life. Here Bramwell got the ground for a chapel in answer to prayer. Near the town runs the River Trent. From Nottingham I went fourteen miles to Mansfield and attended a missionary meeting. I was in the house which was the birth-place of the great Chesterfield, and passed through Mansfield forest, the scene of Robin Hood's predatory exploits.

In his journal Dr. Ryerson says :—

London, June 24th.—I had an interview with Rt. Hon. Edward Ellice, on Canadian affairs; a man of noble spirit, liberal mind, and benevolent heart. He condemned Dr. Strachan's measures, and manifested an earnest desire to promote the welfare of Upper Canada. I gave him an account of the political and religious affairs in Upper Canada with which he expressed himself pleased, and gave me £50 for the Upper Canada Academy.

June 16th.—This day was dedicated, by Rev. Wm. Ryerson, the new brick chapel on Newgate (Adelaide) Street, Toronto. (See subsequent chapter.)

June 24th.—Writing to-day to a valued friend in Upper Canada in regard to his mission in London, Dr. Ryerson told him that he had no doubt of its advantageous results in promoting harmony and peace. He then said :—

I apprehend that Mr. Stanley's appointment to the Secretaryship of the Colonies will not be very beneficial to us. The reason of Lord Goderich and Lord Howick (Earl Grey's son) retiring from that office was that they would not bring any other Bill on slavery into Parliament, but one for its immediate and entire abolition. I understand that Lords Goderich and Howick are sadly annoyed at Mr. Stanley's course.

It will only be for the friends of good government to pray for the re-appointment of Lord Goderich, or insist upon a change in the Colonial policy towards Upper Canada. This part, however, belongs to political men. But I am afraid it may have an unfavourable bearing upon our religious rights and interests.

In Rev. J. Richardson's letter to me, he mentions that the petitions were sent in the care of Mr. Joseph Hume. He is not the person to present a petition to His Majesty on religious liberty in the Colonies, and especially after the part he has taken in opposing the Bill for emancipating the slaves in the West Indies. It has incensed the religious part of the nation against him. He is connected with the West India interest by his wife, and his abandoning all his principles of liberty in such a heart-stirring question, destroys confidence in the disinterestedness of his general conduct, and his sincere regard for the great interests of religion. I leave London this afternoon for Ireland. My return here depends upon whether I can do anything in this petition business.*

It is difficult to get a moment for retirement, excepting very early in the morning, or after twelve at night. It is not the way for me to live. I had, however, a very profitable and good day yesterday. I preached, and superintended a lovefeast in City Road Chapel last evening. It was a very good one, only the people were a little bashful in speaking at first, like some of our York friends who are always so very timid, such as Dr. Morrison, Mr. Howard, and others.

In his journal Dr. Ryerson says :—

June 26th.—According to appointment, I called upon the Earl of Ripon, and was most kindly received. I wished to enquire about the medal promised by His Majesty, William IV., to Peter Jones, and to solicit a donation towards our Academy at Cobourg. His Lordship gave me £5. He expressed his disapprobation of Sir John Colborne's reply to the Methodist Conference in 1831, (see page 98). He stated that he was anxious for the Union between the British and Canadian Conferences, and

---

* In Epochs of Canadian Methodism, Dr. Ryerson says :—When the writer of these Essays was appointed a representative of the Canadian Conference to negotiate a union between the two Conferences in 1833, he carried a Petition to the King, signed by upwards of 20,000 inhabitants, against the Clergy Reserve Monopoly and the Establishment of a Dominant Church in Upper Canada. This petition was presented through Lord Stanley, the Colonial Secretary. Page 221.—H.

was gratified at the prospect of its success.* His Lordship stated that, while in the Colonial Department, he had only received Mr. W. L. Mackenzie as a private individual, and had done no more than justice to him.

June 28th.—I called at the Colonial office, and laid before Mr. Stanley statements and documents relative to the Clergy Reserve Question. Mr. Stanley was very courteous, but equally cautious. I stated that the House of Assembly of Upper Canada had nearly every year since 1825, by very large majorities, decided against the erection of any Church Establishment in that Province, and in favour of the appropriation of the Clergy Reserves to the purposes of General Education; that this might be taken to be the fair and deliberate sense of the people of Upper Canada; that this question was distinct from any question or questions of political reform; that parties and parliaments who differed on other questions of public policy, agreed nearly unanimously in this. He expressed his opinion that the Colonial Legislature had a right to legislate on it, and asked me why our House of Assembly had not done it. I told him it had, but the Legislative Council had rejected the Bill passed by the Assembly on the subject.

July 13th.—In a letter at this date to a friend in Upper Canada, Dr. Ryerson further refers to this and a subsequent interview as follows:—

I have had two interviews with Mr. Secretary Stanley, on the subject of the House of Assembly's Address on the Clergy Reserves, and have drawn up a statement of the grounds on which the House of Assembly and the great body of the people in Upper Canada resist the pretensions and claims of the Episcopal clergy. Mr. Solicitor-General Hagerman has been directed to do the same on behalf of the Episcopal clergy. I confess that I was a little surprised to find that the Colonial Secretary was fully impressed at first that Methodist preachers in Canada were generally Americans (Yankees);—that the cause of the great prosperity of Methodism there was the ample support it received from the United States;—that the missionaries in Upper Canada were actually under the United States Conference, and at its disposal. The Colonial Secretary manifested a little surprise also, when I turned to the Journals of the Upper Canada House of Assembly, and produced proof of

---

* Dr. Ryerson has left no record in his "Story" of the negotiations for this Union. His report, however, on the subject will be found on pages 193, 194, Vol. iv. of the *Guardian* for October 16th, 1833, from which I take the following extracts: On the 5th June, Rev. Messrs. Bunting, Beecham, Alder, and myself, examined the whole question in detail, and prepared an outline of the resolutions to be submitted to the British Conference, and recommended that a grant of £1,000 be appropriated the first year to the promotion of Canadian Missions. On the 2nd August these resolutions were introduced by Rev. John Beecham (Missionary Secretary). They were supported by Rev. Jabez Bunting, Rev. Jas. Wood (now in his 83rd year), and Rev. Robert Newton. A Committee was appointed to consider and report on the whole matter, consisting of the President, Secretary, and seven ex-Presidents, the Irish representatives (Messrs. Waugh, Stewart, and Doolittle), and fifteen other ministers. This Committee considered and reported these resolutions, which were adopted and forms the basis of the Articles of Union. Hereafter, the name of our Church will be changed from "The Methodist Episcopal Church in Canada," to "The Wesleyan Methodist Church in British North America."—H.

the reverse, which he pronounced "perfectly conclusive and satisfactory."

August 8th.—Dr. Ryerson received a touching note at this date from Mrs. Marsden, with explanation of her reluctance to let Rev. Geo. Marsden, her husband, go to Canada as President of the Conference. She says:—

At length my rebellious heart is subdued by reason and by grace. I am made willing to give up my excellent husband to what is supposed to be a great work. I am led to hope that, as a new class of feelings are brought into exercise, perhaps some new graces may be elicited in my own character, as well as that of my dear husband; at any rate it is a sacrifice to God, which I trust will be accepted, and, both in a private and a public view, be over-ruled for the glory of God. I am sure, notwithstanding some repeated attempts to reconcile me to this affair, I must have appeared very unamiable to you; but the fact was simply this, I could not see you or converse with you, without so much emotion as quite unnerved me, therefore I studiously avoided you; but did you know the happiness which dear Mr. Marsden and I have enjoyed in each other's society for so many years, you would not be surprised that I should be unwilling to give up so many months as will be required for this service; but to God and His Church I bow in submission.

This estimable lady did not long survive. She died in six months—just after her husband had returned from America. In a letter from Rev. E. Grinrod, dated March, 1834, he says. Mrs. Marsden died, after a short illness, on 22nd February. She was one of the most amiable and pious of women. Her life was a bright pattern of every Christian virtue. Her end was delightfully triumphant.

The following is an extract from Dr. Ryerson's diary of this year:—

After many earnest prayers, mature deliberation, and the advice of an elder brother, I have decided within the last few months to enter again into the married state. The lady I have selected, and who has consented to become my second wife, is one whom I have every reason to believe possesses all the natural and Christian excellencies of my late wife. She is the eldest daughter of a pious and wealthy merchant, Mr. James Rogers Armstrong. For her my late wife also entertained a very particular esteem and affection; and, from her good sense, sound judgment, humble piety, and affectionate disposition, I doubt not but that she will make me a most interesting and valuable companion, a judicious house-wife, and an affectionate mother to my two children. Truly I love her with a pure heart fervently. I receive her, and hope ever to treat and value her as the special token of my Heavenly Father's kindness after a season of His chastisement. If thou, Lord, see fit to spare us, may our union promote Thy glory and the salvation of sinners!

Dr. Ryerson's marriage with Miss Mary Armstrong, took place at Toronto, on the 8th of November, 1833.

CHAPTER XI.

1833–1834.

"Impressions" of England and their Effects.

ON my return to Canada, after having negotiated the Union of 1833 with the English Conference, accompanied by Rev. George Marsden, as first President of the Canadian Conference, I was re-elected editor of the *Christian Guardian*, and continued as such until 1835, when I refused re-election, and was appointed to Kingston; but in November of the same year, the President of the Conference appointed from England (Rev. William Lord) insisted upon my going to England to arrange pecuniary difficulties, which had arisen between him and the London Wesleyan Missionary Committee.

Except the foregoing paragraph, Dr. Ryerson has left no particulars of the events which transpired in his history from the period of his return to Canada in September, 1833, until some time in 1835. I have, therefore, selected what follows in this chapter, from his letters and papers, to illustrate this busy and eventful portion of his active life.

The principal circumstance which occurred at this time was the publication of his somewhat famous " Impressions " of public men and parties in England. This event marked an important epoch in his life, if not in the history of the country.

The publication of these "Impressions" during this year created quite a sensation. Dr. Ryerson was immediately assailed with a storm of invective by the chief leaders of the ultra section of politicians with whom he had generally acted. By the more moderate section and by the public generally he was hailed as the champion, if not the deliverer, of those who were really alarmed at the rapid strides towards disloyalty and revolution, to which these extreme men were impelling the people. This feature of the unlooked for and bitter controversy, which followed the publication of these "impressions," will be developed further on.

October 2d, 1833.—On this day the Upper Canada Conference ratified the articles of union between it and the British Conference, which were agreed upon at the Manchester Conference on the 7th of August. (See note on page 119.)* At the Conference held this year in York (Toronto), Dr. Ryerson was again elected editor of the *Guardian*. He entered on the duties of that office on the 16th October.

October 30th.—In reply to the many questions put to Dr. Ryerson on his return to Canada, such as: "What do you think of England?" "What is your opinion of her public men, her institutions?" etc., etc., he published in the *Guardian* of this day the first part of "Impressions made by my late visit to England," in regard to public men, religious bodies, and the general state of the nation. He said:—

There are three great political parties in England—Tories, Whigs, and Radicals, and two descriptions of characters constituting each party. Of the first, there is the moderate and the ultra tory. An English ultra tory is what we believe has usually been meant and understood in Canada by the unqualified term tory; that is, a lordling in power, a tyrant in politics, and a bigot in religion. This description of partizans, we believe, is headed by the Duke of Cumberland, and is followed not "afar off" by that powerful party, which presents such a formidable array of numbers, rank, wealth, talent, science, and literature, headed by the hero of Waterloo. This shade of the tory party appears to be headed in the House of Commons by Sir Robert Inglis, member for the Oxford University, and is supported, on most questions, by that most subtle and ingenious politician and fascinating speaker, Sir Robert Peel, with his numerous train of followers and admirers. Among those who support the distinguishing measures of this party are men of the highest Christian virtue and piety; and, our decided impression is, that it embraces the major part of the talent, and wealth, and learning of the British Nation. The acknowledged and leading organs of this party are *Blackwood's Magazine* and the *London Quarterly Review*.

The other branch of this great political party is what is called the moderate tory. In political theory he agrees with his high-toned neighbour; but he acts from religious principle, and this governs his private as well as his public life. To this class belongs a considerable portion of the Evangelical Clergy, and, we think, a majority of the Wesleyan Methodists. It evidently includes the great body of the piety, Christian enterprise, and

* As an example of the manner in which the Union was hailed in some parts of the Province, a gentleman, writing from Merrickville on the 11th December, mentions a gratifying incident in regard to it. He says:—At one Quarterly Conference Love Feast, when the presiding Elder told the assembled multitude that they were for the first time about to partake of bread and water as a token of love under the name of British Wesleyan Methodists, a general burst of approbation proceeded from preachers, leaders, and members, and such a feeling seemed to pervade the whole assembly, as it would be difficult to describe.—H.

sterling virtue of the nation. It is, in time of party excitement, alike hated and denounced by the ultra Tory, the crabbed Whig, and the Radical leveller. Such was our impression of the true character of what, by the periodical press in England, is termed a moderate Tory. From his theories we in some respects dissent; but his integrity, his honesty, his consistency, his genuine liberality, and religious beneficence, claim respect and imitation.

The second great political and now ruling party in England are the Whigs—a term synonymous with whey, applied, it is said, to this political school, from the sour and peevish temper manifested by its first disciples—though it is now rather popular than otherwise in England. The Whig appears to differ in theory from the Tory in this, that he interprets the constitution, obedience to it, and all measures in regard to its administration, upon the principles of expediency; and is, therefore, always pliant in his professions, and is even ready to suit his measures to "the times"; an indefinite term, that also designates the most extensively circulated daily paper in England, or in the world, which is the leading organ of the Whig party, backed by the formidable power and lofty periods of the *Edinburgh Review*. The leaders of this party in the House of Lords are Earl Grey and the Lord Chancellor Brougham; at the head of the list in the House of Commons stands the names of Mr. Stanley, Lord Althorp, Lord John Russell, and Mr. T. B. Macaulay. In this class are also included many of the most learned and popular ministers of Dissenting congregations.

The third political sect is called Radicals, apparently headed by Messrs. Joseph Hume and Thomas Attwood; the former of whom, though acute, indefatigable, persevering, popular on financial questions, and always to the point, and heard with respect and attention in the House of Commons, has no influence as a religious man; has never been known to promote any religious measure or object as such, and has opposed every measure for the better observance of the Sabbath, and even introduced a motion to defeat the bill for the abolition of colonial slavery; and Mr. Attwood, the head of the celebrated Birmingham political Union, is a conceited, boisterous, hollow-headed declaimer.

Radicalism in England appeared to me to be but another word for Republicanism, with the name of King instead of President. The notorious infidel character of the majority of the political leaders and periodical publications of their party, deterred the virtuous part of the nation from associating with them, though some of the brightest ornaments of the English pulpit and nation have leaned to their leading doctrines in theory. It is not a little remarkable that that very description of the public press, which in England advocates the lowest radicalism, is the foremost in opposing and slandering the Methodists in this Province. Hence the fact that some of these editors have been amongst the lowest of the English radicals previous to their egress from the mother country.

Upon the whole, our impressions of the religious and moral character, and influence, of the several political parties into which the British nation is unhappily divided, were materially different in some respects, from personal observation, from what they had been by hear-say and reading.

On the very evening of the day in which the foregoing appeared, Mr. W. L. Mackenzie (in the *Colonial Advocate* of Oct. 30th), denounced the writer of these "Impressions" in no measured terms. His denunciation proved that he clearly perceived what would be the effect on the public mind of Dr. Ryerson's candid and outspoken criticisms on men and things in England—especially his adverse opinion of the English idols of (what subsequently proved to be) the disloyal section of the public men of the day in Upper Canada and their followers.

Mr. Mackenzie's vehement attack upon the writer of these "Impressions" had its effect at the time. In some minds a belief in the truth of that attack lingered long afterwards—but not in the minds of those who could distinguish between honest conviction, based upon actual knowledge, and pre-conceived opinions, based upon hearsay and a superficial acquaintance with men and things.

As the troubled period of 1837 approached, hundreds had reason to be thankful to Dr. Ryerson that the publication of his "Impressions" had, without design on his part, led to the disruption of a party which was being hurried to the brink of a precipice, over which so many well meaning, but misguided, men fell in the winter of 1837, never to rise again.

It was a proud boast of Dr. Ryerson (as he states in the "Epochs of Canadian Methodism," page 385), that in these disastrous times not a single member of the Methodist Church was implicated in the disloyal rebellion of 1837-8. He attributed this gratifying state of things to the fact that he had uttered the notes of warning in sufficient time to enable the readers of the *Guardian* to pause and think; and that, with a just appreciation of their danger, members of the Society had separated themselves from all connection with projects and opinions which logically would have placed them in a position of defiant hostility to the Queen and constitution.

But, to return. The outburst of Mr. Mackenzie's wrath, which immediately followed (on the evening of the same day) the publication of Dr. Ryerson's "Impressions," was as follows :—

The *Christian Guardian*, under the management of Egerton Ryerson, has gone over to the enemy,—press, types, and all,—and hoisted the colours of a cruel, vindictive, Tory priesthood........The contents of the *Guardian* of to-night tells us in language too plain, too intelligible to be misunderstood, that a deadly blow has been struck in England at the liberties of the people of Upper Canada, by as subtle and ungrateful an adversary, in the guise of an old and familiar friend, as ever crossed the Atlantic.

In his "Almanac," issued on the same day, Mr. Mackenzie also used similar language. He said:—

The arch-apostate Egerton, alias *Arnold*, Ryerson, and the *Christian Guardian* goes over to Strachan and the Tories.

Nov. 6th.—In the *Guardian* of this day Dr. Ryerson inserted an extended reply to Mr. Mackenzie, and, in calm and dignified language, gave the reasons which induced him to publish his "Impressions." He said:—

We did so,—1st, As a subject of useful information; 2nd, To correct an erroneous impression that had been industriously created, that we were identified in our feelings and purposes with some one political party; 3rd, To furnish an instructive moral to the Christian reader, not to be a passive or active tool, or the blind, thorough-going follower of any political party as such. We considered this called for at the present time on both religious and patriotic grounds. We designed this expression of our sentiments, and this means of removing groundless prejudice and hostility in the least objectionable and offensive way, and without coming in contact with any political party in Canada, or giving offence to any, except those who had shown an inveterate and unprincipled hostility to Methodism. We therefore associated the Canadian *ultra* tory with the English radical, because we were convinced of their identity in moral essence, and that the only essential difference between them is, that the one is top and the other bottom. We therefore said, "that very description of the public press which in England advocates the lowest radicalism, is the foremost in opposing and slandering the Methodists in this Province."

That our Christian brethren throughout the Province, and every sincere friend to Methodism, do not wish us to be an organized political party, we are fully assured — that it is inconsistent with our profession and duty to become such. Out of scores of expressions to the same effect we might quote quite abundantly from the *Guardian*, but our readers are aware of them.

That the decided part we have felt it our duty to take in obtaining and securing our rights in regard of the Clergy Reserve Question, has had a remote or indirect tendency to promote Mr. Mackenzie's political measures, we readily admit; but that we have ever supported a measure, or given publicity to any documents from Mr. Mackenzie, or any other political man in Canada, on any other grounds than this, we totally deny.

Mr. Mackenzie's attack rests on four grounds: 1. That our language was so explicit as to remove every doubt and hope of our encouraging a "thick and thin" partizanship with him, or any man or set of men in Canada; or, 2. That we did not speak in opprobrious, but rather favourable terms, of His Excellency the Lieutenant-Governor; or, 3. That we expresssd our approbation of the principles and colonial policy of Lord Goderich (now Earl Ripon), and those who agree with him; or 4. That we alluded to Mr. Hume in terms not sufficiently complimentary. If Mr. Mackenzie's wishes are crossed and his wrath inflamed, because we have not entered our protest against His Excellency the Lieutenant-Governor, we could not do so after we had learned the views of His Majesty's Government, in a reply of His Excellency to an address of our Conference about two years ago,* when every unfavourable impression had been removed, and when good-will was expressed towards the Methodists as a people; we have not so learned to forgive injuries—we have not so learned to "honour and obey magistrates,"—we have not so learned our duty as a minister, and as a Christian. We, as a religious body, and as the organ of a religious body, have only to do with Sir John Colborne's administration, as far as it concerns our character and rights as British subjects; His Excellency's measures and administration in merely secular matters lie within the peculiar province of the political journalists and politicians of the day. If our offering a tribute of grateful respect to Lord Goderich, who had declared in his despatches to Canada his earnest desire to remove every bishop and priest from our Legislature, to secure the right of petitioning the King to the meanest subject in the realm, to extend the blessings of full religious liberty and the advantages of education to every class of British subjects in Canada, without distinction or partiality, and in every way to advance the interests of the Province;—if honouring such men and such principles be "hoisting the colours (as Mr. Mackenzie says), of a cruel, vindictive, Tory priesthood," then has Mr. Mackenzie the merit of a new discovery of vindictive cruelty, and with his own definition of liberty, and his own example of liberality, will he adopt his own honourable means to attain it, and breathe out death and destruction against all who do not incorporate themselves into a strait-jacket battalion under his political sword, and vow allegiance and responsibility to everything done by his "press, types, and all?"

* See page 98.

Mr. Mackenzie did not reply to Dr. Ryerson in the spirit of his rejoinder. He was a master of personal invective, and he indulged in it in this instance, rather than discuss the questions raised on their merits. He, therefore, turned on Dr. Ryerson, and, over his shoulders, struck a blow at his venerable Father and his eldest Brother. He said :—

The Father of the Editor of the *Guardian* lifted his sword against the throats of his own countrymen struggling for freedom from established churches, stamp acts, military domination, Scotch governors, and Irish government; and his brother George figured on the frontier in the war of 1812, and got wounded and pensioned for fighting to preserve crown and clergy reserves, and all the other strongholds of corruption, in the hands of the locusts who infest and disturb this Province.

Dr. Ryerson's simple rejoinder to this attack on his Father and Brother was as follows :—

The man who could hold up the brave defenders of our homes and firesides to the scorn and contempt of their countrymen, must be lost to all patriotic and loyal feelings of humanity for those who took their lives in their hands in perilous times.

Nov. 14th.—As to the effect of the "impressions" upon the country generally, the following letter from Hallowell (Picton) written to Dr. Ryerson by his brother John, may be safely taken as an example of the feeling which they at first evoked. It is characterized by strong and vigorous language, indicative of the state of public opinion at the time. It is valuable from the fact that while it is outspoken in its criticism of Dr. Ryerson's views, it touches upon the point to which I have already referred, viz : the separation into two sections of the powerful party which was then noted as the champion of popular rights. Mr. Ryerson says :—

Your article on the Political Parties of England has created much excitement throughout these parts. The only good that can result from it is, the breaking up of the union which has hitherto existed between us and the radicals. Were it not for this, I should much regret its appearance. But we had got so closely linked with those extreme men, in one way or another, that we cannot expect to get rid of them without feeling the shock, and, perhaps, it may as well come now as anytime. It is our duty and interest to support the Government. Although there may be some abuses which have crept in, yet, I believe that we enjoy as many political and religious advantages as any people. Our public affairs are as well managed as in any other country. As it respects the Reformers, so called, take Baldwin, Bidwell, Rolph, and such men from their ranks, and there is scarcely one man of character or honour among them. I am sorry to say it, but it is so. The best way for the present is for us to have nothing to say about politics, but treat the Government with respect. Radcliffe, of the Cobourg *Reformer*, and Dr. Barker, of the Kingston *Whig*, have come out in their true character. Radcliffe is preparing a heavy charge against you. But let them come; fear them not ! I hope they will show themselves *now*. I thought that you, in your reply to W. L. Mackenzie, did not speak in a sufficiently decided manner. You say you have not changed your views; but I hope you have in some respects. Although you never were a Radical, yet have not we all leaned too much towards them, and will we not now smart for it a little? But, the sooner it comes on, the sooner it will be over.

Rev. John Ryerson then gives the first intimation of the existence of that germ of hostility to the recently consummated Union on the part of the British Wesleyan Missionaries in this country—a hostility which became at length so deep and widespread as to destroy the Union itself—a union which was not fully restored until 1847. Mr. Ryerson points out the political animus of the movement, and proceeds :—

You see that the Missionaries are making great efforts to have Kingston and York made exceptions to the general arrangements. Should the English Committee listen to them, confidence will be entirely destroyed. Their object is to make the British Conference believe that we have supported Radical politics to an unlimited extent, and that, therefore, the people will not submit to the Union with such people; they (the Missionaries) are, however, the authors of the whole trouble. Rev. Mr. Hetherington told me that they were getting the back numbers of the *Guardian* to prove that we had been political intimidators ! They say that Mr. Marsden, the President, told the members at Kingston that if they could make it appear that we had done this, they should be exempted from the Union, and be supplied with Missionaries from home.

In a subsequent letter from Rev. John Ryerson, he discusses his brother's "Impressions of Public Men in England," and utters a word of warning to the Methodist people who have allied themselves too closely with the disloyal party. He says :

What will be the result of your remarks in the *Guardian* on Political Parties in England, I cannot say. They will occasion much speculation, some jealousy, and bad feeling. I have sometimes thought you had better not have written them, particularly at this time, yet I have long been of the opinion (both with regard to measures and men) that we leaned too much towards Radicalism, and that it would be absolutely necessary to disengage ourselves from them entirely. You can see plainly that it is not Reform, but Revolution they are after. We should fare sumptuously, should we not, with W. L. Mackenzie, of Toronto, and Radcliffe, of Cobourg, for our rulers! I have also felt very unpleasant in noticing the endeavours of these men (aided by some of our members) to introduce their republican leaven into our Ecclesiastical polity. Is it not a little remarkable that not one of our members, who have entered into their politics, but has become a furious leveller in matters of Church Government, and these very men are the most regardless of our reputation, and the most ready to impugn our motives, and defame our character, when we, in any way, cross their path. There are some things in your remarks I don't like; but, on the whole, I am glad of their appearance, and I hope, whenever you have occasion to speak of the Government, you will do it in terms of respect. I am anxious that we should obtain the confidence of the Government, and entirely disconnect ourselves from that tribe of levellers, with whom we have been too intimate, and who are, at any time, ready to turn around and sell us when we fail to please them.

Nov. 20th.—In another letter to Dr. Ryerson from his brother John, at this date, he says :—

I deeply feel for you in the present state of agitation and trial. My own heart aches and sickens within me at times; I have no doubt, however much of a philosopher you may be, that you at times participate in the same feelings; but, pursuing a conscientious course, I hope you will at times be able to say:

> "Courage, my soul! thou need'st not fear,
> Thy great Provider still is near."

The following sympathetic letter from Dr. Ryerson's friend, Mr. E. C. Griffin, of Waterdown, written at the same time, gives another proof of the unreasoning prejudice of those whose knowledge of the outer world was circumscribed and superficial In England, Dr. Ryerson saw things as they were. He was, therefore, not prepared for the burst of wrath that followed the plain recital of his "impressions" of men and things in England. Mr. Griffin writes :—

The respect I have for you and yours should at all times deter me from bearing evil tidings, yet the same consideration would make it a duty under peculiar circumstances. You have already learned that the public mind has been much agitated in consequence of your remarks in the *Guardian* on Mr. Joseph Hume, M.P., and Mr. Thomas Attwood, M.P. (see page 123). On this Circuit it is truly alarming—some of our most respectable Methodists are threatening to leave the Church. The general impression has obtained (however unjustly) that you have "turned downright Tory," which, in this country, whether moderate or ultra, seems to have but one meaning among the bulk of Reformers, and that is, as being an enemy to all reform and the correction of acknowledged abuses. This general impression among the people has created a feverish discontent among the Methodists. The excitement is so high that your subsequent explanation has seemed to be without its desired effect. I should be glad if you would state distinctly in the *Guardian* what you meant in your correspondence with the Colonial Secretary, when you said you had no desire to interfere with the present emoluments of the Church clergy (or words to that effect); and also of the term "equal protection to the different denominations." You are, doubtless, aware of the use made of these expressions by some of the journals, and, I am sorry to say, with too much effect. These remarks, taken in connection with those against Mr. Hume, is the pivot on which everything is turned against you, against the *Guardian*, and against the Methodists.

A few days later Dr. Ryerson received another letter from Mr. Griffin, in which he truthfully says :—

Perhaps there have not been many instances in which sophistry has been applied more effectually to injure an individual, or a body of Christians, as in the present instance. Whigs, tories, and radicals have all united to crush, I may say at a blow, the Methodists, and none have tried to do so more effectually than Mr. W. L. Mackenzie. He persisted in it so as to make his friends generally believe that the cause of reform was ruined by you. His abuse of you and your friends, and the Methodists, is more than I can stand. He has certainly manifested a great want of discernment, or he has acted from design. I see that the Hamilton *Free Press* has called in the aid of Mr. F. Collins, of the *Canadian Freeman*, to assist in abusing you and your whole family.

From Augusta, Rev. Anson Green wrote about the same time, and in a similar strain, but not so sympathetically. He says :—

I fear your impressions are bad ones. Our people are all in an uproar about them.

Nov, 22nd.—Rev. William Ryerson writing from Kingston at this time, reports the state of feeling there. He says :—

As to the *Guardian*, I am sorry to inform you that it is becoming less popular than formerly. If your English "impressions" are not more acceptable and useful in other parts than they are here, it will add little to your credit, or to the usefulness of your paper to publish any more of them. I know that you have been shamefully abused, and treated in a most base manner, and by no one so much so as by Mr. Radcliffe of the Cobourg *Reformer*. I hope you will expose the statements and figures of the *Reformer* to our friends. It is rather unfortunate that if you did intend, as is said, to conciliate the Tory party in this country, you should have expressed yourself in such a way as to be so much misunderstood.

Nov. 23rd.—Rev. Alvah A. Adams, writing from Prescott, says :—

There are a few disturbances in our Zion. Some are bent on making mischief. You need not be surprised that the Grenville *Gazette* speaks so contemptuously of you and the cause in which you have been, and are still, engaged. There are reasons why you need not marvel at the great torrent of scurrilous invectives with which his useless columns have of late abounded.

Nov. 23rd.—Although not so intended by Dr. Ryerson, yet the publication of his "impressions," had the effect of developing the plans of Mr. W. L. Mackenzie, and those who acted with him, much more rapidly and fully than they could have anticipated. In the second supplement to his *Colonial Advocate*, published November 23rd, Mr. Mackenzie used this unmistakeable language :—

The local authorities have no means to protect themselves against an injured people, if they persist in their unconstitutional career. . . . . . There are not military enough to uphold a bad government for an hour, if the Rubicon has been passed; and well does Sir John Colborne know that although he may hire regiments of priests here, he may expect no more redcoats from Europe in those days of economy. . . . . . He also knows that if we are to take examples from the Mother Country, the arbitrary proceedings of the officers of his government *are such* as would warrant the people to an open and *armed resistance*.

Dec. 6th.—Dr. Ryerson having received a protest from five of his ministerial brethren in the Niagara District,* against his

* Rev. Messrs. David Wright, James Evans, William Griffis, jun., Henry Wilkinson and Edwy Ryerson. The protest was as follows: We, the undersigned ministers of the W. M. Church, desirous to avert the evils which may probably result to our Zion from "impressions" made by certain political remarks in the editorial department of the *Guardian*, take this opportunity of expressing our sentiments for your satisfaction, and to save our characters from aspersion. First. We have considered, and are still of the same opinion, that the clergy of the Episcopal Church ought to be deprived of every emolument derived from Governmental aid, and what are called the Clergy Reserves. Secondly. That our political views are decidedly the same which they were previous to the visit of the editor of the *Guardian* to England, and we believe that the views of our brethren in the ministry are unchanged.

"impressions" he wrote a remonstrance to each of them, but this did not appease them. Rev. David Wright said :—

As an individual I am not at all satisfied either with the course you have taken or the explanation given. Could you witness the confused state of our Church on Stamford Circuit ; the insults we receive, both from many of our members and others of good standing, you would at once see the propriety of the steps we have taken for our defence. Hardly a tea-party or meeting of any kind, but the *Guardian* is the topic of conversation, and the conversion of its editor and all the preachers to Toryism. The Ranters and the Ryanites are very busy, and are doing us much harm. I am more and more convinced of the imprudence of the course you have taken, especially at this trying time in our Church. In Queenston, Drummondville, Chippewa, Erie, St. Davids, the Lane, and Lyons' Creek the preachers are hooted at as they ride by. This is rather trying, I assure you.

Rev. James Evans said :—

You request me not to solicit any to continue the *Guardian* who are dissatisfied, and who wish to discontinue. This is worse than all beside. And do you suppose that, in opposition to the wish of the Conference, and interest of the Church, I shall pay attention to your request? No, my brother, I cannot; I will not. It shall be my endeavour to obtain and continue subscribers by allaying as far as practicable, their fears, rather than by telling them that they may discontinue and you will abide the consequences. I am astonished! I can only account for your strange and, I am sure, un-Ryersonian conduct and advice on one principle—that there is something ahead which you, through your superior political spyglass, have discovered and thus shape your course, while we land-lubbers, short-sighted as we are, have not even heard of it.

Dr. Ryerson, therefore, challenged these five ministers to proceed against him as provided by the Discipline of the Church. In his reply to them, he lays down some important principles in regard to the rights of an editor, and the duty of his ministerial accusers. He said :—

I beg to say that I cannot publish the criminating declaration of which you speak. You will therefore act your pleasure in publishing it elsewhere. The charges against me are either true or false. If they are true, are you proceeding in the disciplinary way against me? Though I am editor for the Conference, yet I have individual rights as well as you; and the increased responsibility of my situation should, under those rights, if possible, be still more sacred. And if our Conference will place a watchman upon the wall of our Zion, and then allow its members to plunge their swords into him whenever they think he has departed from his duty, without even giving him a court-martial trial, then they are a different description of men from what I think they are. If, as you say, I have been guilty of imprudent conduct, or even "misrepresented my brethren," make your complaint to my Presiding Elder, according to discipline, and then may the decision of the Committee be published in the *Guardian*, or anywhere else that they may say. So much for the disciplinary course. Again, if "the clamour," as you call it, against the *Guardian* be well founded, are you helping the *Guardian* by corroborating the statement of that clamour? Can Brother James Evans consistently or conscientiously ask an individual to take, or continue to take the *Guardian*, when he or you publish to the world the belief that its principles are changed? Will this quiet the "clamour?" Will this reconcile the members? Will this unite the preachers? Will this promote the harmony of the Church? Will it not be a fire-brand rather than the "seeds of commotion?" One or two others here got a meeting of the male members of the York Society, and proposed resolutions similar in substance to yours, which were opposed and reprobated by brother Richardson, on the very disciplinary and prudential ground of which I speak, and rejected by the Society. In your declaration you say (not on account of "clamour," or accusations of editors or others, but on account of editorial remarks in the *Guardian*), "you express your sentiments to save your character from aspersion." In this you imply that the editor of the *Guardian* has misrepresented your sentiments, and aspersed your character; and, if so, has he not changed his principles? And, if he has changed his principles, is he not guilty of falsehood, since he has positively declared to the reverse? You therefore virtually charge him with inconsistency, misrepresentation, and deliberate falsehood. Is this the fruit of brotherly love? Again, you say that "our political sentiments are the same as before the visit of the editor of the *Guardian* to England." Is not this equal to asserting that the editor's sentiments are not the same? You therefore say that you love me; that you desire the peace of the Church, and the interests of the *Guardian*, yet you propose a course which will confirm the slanders of my enemies—to implicate me with inconsistency and falsehood—to injure the *Guardian*, and deprive yourselves of the power, as men of honour and truth, to recommend it—to kindle and sanction dissatisfaction among our Church members—to arm preacher against preacher—and to criminate a brother before the public, without a disciplinary trial. You say "our friends are looking out for it." Is this the way, my brother, that you have quieted their minds, by telling them that you also were going to criminate the editor? If this be so, I am not surprised that there is dissatisfaction on your circuit. Brother Evans said that nothing but a denial of having changed my opinions, and an explicit statement of them, would satisfy our friends. I did so, and did so plainly and conscientiously. Yet you do not even allude to this expression of my sentiments, but still insist upon doing what is far more than taking my life—stabbing my principles and integrity. I ask if this is my reward for endangering my life and enduring unparalleled labours, to save the Societies heretofore from being rent to the very centre, and enduring ceaseless storms of slander and persecution for years past in defending the abused character of my brethren? Are they the first to lift up their heel aginst me? Will they join in the hue and cry against me, rather than endure a "hoot," when I am unjustly treated and basely slandered? I hope I have not fallen into such hands.

Dr. Ryerson received at this time a candid and kindly characteristic letter from his youngest brother, Edwy, at Stamford, which indicated that a reaction was taking place in regard to the much discussed "impressions." He says :—

The present agitated state of the Societies, partly from the Union, and, in a greater degree, from your "impressions" (which would have been a blessing to our Societies, had they never been published) make it very unpleasant to ask even for subscriptions to the *Guardian*. We are here in a state of commotion; politics run high, and religion low. "The *Guardian* has turned Tory," is the hue and cry, and many appear to be under greater concern about it, than they ever were about the salvation of their souls. Many again, have got wonderfully wise, and pretend to reveal (as a friend, but in reality as an enemy) the secrets of your policy. Under these unpleasant circumstances, the Ranters have availed themselves of the opportunity of planting themselves at nearly all our posts, and sowing tares in our Societies.

You have received a protest, signed by several preachers, and my name among them. Those were my impressions at the time. Therefore I thought it my duty, in connection with my brethren, to make my protest. I have, however (since seeing the *Guardian*), been led to believe you had not changed from what you were. Many of the preachers are rejoiced that you were put in the editorial chair, and feel strongly disposed to exert their influence that you may not be displaced.

Dec. 2nd.—On this day Dr. Ryerson received a kind word of encouragement from Mr. Alex. Davidson, a literary friend in Port Hope, afterwards of Niagara. He said :—

I have had an opportunity of seeing most of the provincial papers. They exhibit a miserable picture of the state of the press. The conduct of the editors ought, I think, to be exposed. I have been afraid that from such unmerited abuse, you would quit the *Guardian* in disgust, and I am glad to see that, though your mind may be as sensitive as that of any other person, you remain firm.

Another indication of the reaction in regard to the "impressions" is mentioned in a note received from Rev. Ephraim Evans, Trafalgar. He says :—

Mr. Thos. Cartwright, of Streetsville, who had given up the *Guardian*, has ordered it to be sent to him again so that he may not seem to countenance the clamour that has been raised against you. Mr. Evans adds : "I am happy to find that the agitation produced by the unwarrantable conduct of the press generally, is rapidly subsiding ; and, I trust, nay, am certain, that the late avowal of your sentiments, will be perfectly satisfactory to every sensible and ingenuous mind. I am, upon the whole, led to believe that Methodism will weather out this storm also, and lose not a spar."

Dec. 6th.—Among the many letters of sympathy received by Dr. Ryerson at this time, was one from his Father, in which he says :—

I perceive by the papers that you have met with tempestuous weather. I devoutly hope that the Great Pilot will conduct you safely through the rocks and quicksands on either side.

Jan. 6th, 1834.—In a letter from Rev. Anson Green, at Augusta, it was apparent that the tide of popular opinion against Dr. Ryerson had turned. He said :—

I have been very much pleased indeed with the *Guardian* during the last few months. There is a very great improvement in it. In this opinion I am not alone. Your remarks on the Clergy Reserve question were very timely and highly satisfactory. A number of our brethren have wished me to express to you the pleasure they feel in the course which you have pursued as editor. There has been very great prejudice against you in these parts, among preachers and people, but I think they are dying out and will, I trust, shortly entirely disappear. I hope we shall soon see " eye to eye."

March 5th.—In the *Guardian* of this day, Dr. Ryerson intimated that :—

Among many schemes resorted to by the abbettors of Mr. Mackenzie to injure me, was the circulation of all kinds of rumours against my character and standing as a minister. For proof, it was represented that I was denied access to the Wesleyan pulpit in this town. When these statements were made early in the year, the stewards and leaders of the York Society met on the 11th of last January, and passed a resolution to the effect

That being anxious, lest, under exciting circumstances, you might be tempted to withhold your ministrations from the York congregation, they desire their Secretary to inform you that it is their wish, and they believe it a duty you owe to the Church of Christ, to favour it with your views on His unsearchable riches as often as an opportunity may present itself.

As these rumours have now been revived, I published this resolution in the *Guardian* of to-day.

The capital offence charged against Dr. Ryerson in publishing his " impressions " was his exposure of Joseph Hume, M.P., the friend and patron of Mr. Mackenzie. (See pages 118 and 123.) In the *Guardian* of December 11th, Dr. Ryerson fully met that charge. Among other things he pointed out:—

1st. That, having voted for a Church establishment in India, Mr. Hume was the last man who should have been entrusted with petitions from Upper Canada, against a Church establishment in Upper Canada. 2nd. That Methodists emigrating to this country, when they learn that Mr. Hume is regarded as a sort of representative of the principles of the Methodists in Upper Canada, immediately imbibe strong prejudices against them, refusing to unite with them, and even strongly opposing them, saying that such Methodists are Radicals—a term which, in England, conveys precisely the same idea that the term Republican does in this Province. Thus the prejudices which exist between a portion of the Canadian and British Methodists here, are heightened, and the breach widened. 3rd. That even adherents of the Church of England here who were Reformers in England join the ranks of those opposed to us when they know that Mr. Hume is a chosen representative of our views in England; for the personal animosity between the Whigs and Reformers and Radicals in England is more bitter, if possible, than between the Radicals and Tories, and far more rancorous than between the Whigs and Tories. There is just as much difference between an English Reformer and an avowed English Radical as there is between a Canadian Reformer and an avowed Canadian Republican. In the interests of the Methodists, therefore, religiously and politically, the allusion to Mr. Hume was justifiable and necessary. Dr. Ryerson continues:—

I may mention that so strongly impressed was I with these views, that in an interview which I had with Mr. Secretary Stanley, a few days before the Clergy Reserve petitions were presented by Mr. Hume, I remarked that the people of Upper Canada, not being acquainted with public men in England, had sent them to the care of a gentleman of influence in the financial affairs of Great Britain, but that I was apprehensive that he was not the best qualified to advocate a purely legal and religious question. Mr. Secretary Stanley smilingly interrupted me by asking "Is it Hume?" I replied, "It is, but I hope this circumstance will not have the least influence upon your mind, Mr. Secretary Stanley, in giving the subject that important and full consideration which its great importance demands." Mr. Stanley replied: "No, Mr. Ryerson, be assured that the subject will not be in the least prejudiced in my mind by any circumstance of that kind; but I shall give it the most important and grave consideration."

May 24*th.*—Within three months after Dr. Ryerson had stated these facts in regard to Mr. Hume, overwhelming evidence of the correctness of his statement that Mr. Hume was unfit to act as a representative, in the British Parliament, of the people of Upper Canada, was given by Mr. Hume himself in a letter addressed to Mr. W. L. Mackenzie, dated 29th March, 1834. In that letter Mr. Hume stated that Mr. Mackenzie's

Election to, and subsequent ejection from the Legislature, must hasten that crisis which is fast approaching in the affairs of the Canadas, and which will terminate in independence and freedom from the baneful domination of the mother country.

He also advised that

The proceedings between 1772 and 1782 in America ought not to be forgotten; and to the honour of the Americans, for the interests of the civilized world, let their conduct and the result be ever in view.

Dr. Ryerson added: There is no mistaking the revolutionary and treasonable character of this advice given to Canadians through Mr. W. L. Mackenzie. Yet I have been denounced for exposing the designs of such revolutionary advisers!

The following is an extract from Mr. W. L. Mackenzie's remarks in the *Colonial Advocate* on Mr. Hume's letter:—

The indignant feeling of the honest old Reformer (Hume), when he became acquainted with the heartless slanders of the unprincipled ingrate Ryerson, may be easily conceived from the tone of his letter.... Mr. Mackenzie will be prepared to hand the original letter to the Methodist Conference.

June 4th.—In the *Guardian* of this date, Dr. Ryerson replied at length to Mr. Hume's letter, pointing out how utterly and totally false were Mr. Hume's statements in regard to himself. He, in June, 1832, expressed his opinion of Mr. Hume (pages 118 and 123). He then said:—

That was my opinion of Mr. Hume, even before I advocated the Clergy Reserve petition in England,—such it was after I conversed with him personally, and witnessed his proceedings,—such it is now,—and such must be the opinion of every British subject, after reading Mr. Hume's revolutionary letter, in which he rejoices in the approach of a crisis in the affairs of the Canadas, "which will terminate in independence and freedom from the baneful domination of the mother country!" I stated to Mr. Mackenzie more than once, when he called upon me in London, that I could not associate myself with his political measures. But notwithstanding all my caution, I, in fact, got into bad company, for which I have now paid a pretty fair price.... I cannot but regard it as a blessing and happiness to the Methodist connexion at large, that they also, by the admission of all parties, stand so completely distinct from Messrs. Hume and Mackenzie, as to be involved in no responsibility and disgrace, by this premature announcement of their revolutionary purposes.

Oct. 25th.—As to the final result of the agitation in regard to the "Impressions," Rev. John Ryerson, writing from Hallowell (Picton), at this date, says:—

The work of schism has been pretty extensive in some parts of this District. There have as the result of it left, or have been expelled, on the Waterloo Circuit, 150; on the Bay of Quinte, 40; in Belleville, 47; Sidney, 50; Cobourg, 82; making in all 320. There have been received on these circuits since Conference 170, which leaves a balance against us of 150.

REMARKS ON THE RESULT OF THE "IMPRESSIONS."

The result (on the membership of the Societies) of this politico-religious agitation was more or less the same in other parts of the Connexion. The publication of the "impressions" was (to those who had for years been in a state of chronic war with the powers that be) like the falling of the thunderbolt of Jove out of a cloudless sky. It unexpectedly precipitated a crisis in provincial affairs. It brought men face to face with a new issue. An issue too which they had not thought of ; or, if it had presented itself to their minds, was regarded as a remote, if possible, contingency. Their experience of the working of "British institutions" (as the parody on them in Upper Canada was called), had so excited their hostility and embittered their feelings, that when they at first heard Dr. Ryerson speak in terms of eulogy of the working of these institutions in the mother country, they could not, or would not, distinguish between such institutions in England and their professed counterpart in Upper Canada. Nor could they believe that the great champion of their cause, who in the past had exposed the pernicious and oppressive workings of the so-called British institutions in Upper Canada, was sincere in his exposition of the principles and the promulgation of doctrines in regard to men and things in Britain, which were now declared by Mr. W. L. Mackenzie to be heretical as well as entirely opposed to views and opinions which he (Dr. Ryerson) had hitherto held on these important questions. The novelty of the "impressions" themselves, and the bitterness with which they were at once assailed, confused the public mind and embarrassed many of Dr. Ryerson's friends.

In these days of ocean telegraphy and almost daily intercourse by steam with Britain, we can scarcely realize how far separated Canada was from England fifty years ago. Besides this, the channels through which that intercourse was carried on were few, and often of a partizan character. "Downing Street [Colonial Office] influence," and "Downing Street interference with Canadian rights," were popular and favourite topics of declamation and appeal with the leaders of a large section of the community. Not that there did not exist, in many instances, serious grounds for the accusations against the Colonial Office ; but they, in most cases, arose in that office from ignorance rather than from design. However the causes of complaint were often greatly exaggerated, and very often designedly so by interested parties on both sides of the Atlantic.

This, Dr. Ryerson soon discovered on his first visit to England, in 1833, and in his personal intercourse with the Colonial

Secretaries and other public men in London. The manly generosity of his nature recoiled from being a party to the misrepresentation and injustice which was current in Canada, when he had satisfied himself of the true state of the case. He, therefore, on his return to the Province, gave the public the benefit of his observation and experience in England.

In the light of to-day what he wrote appears fair and reasonable. It was the natural expression of pleased surprise that men and things in England were not so bad as had been represented; and that there was no just cause for either alarm or ill feeling. His comparisons of parties in England and in Canada were by extreme political leaders in Canada considered odious. Hence the storm of invective which his observations raised.

He showed incidentally that the real enemies to Canada were not those who ruled at Downing Street, but those who set themselves up—within the walls of Parliament in England and their prompters in Canada—as the exponents of the views and feelings of the Canadian people.

The result of such a proceeding on Dr. Ryerson's part can easily be imagined. Mr. Hume in England, and Mr. W. L. Mackenzie in Canada, took the alarm. They very properly reasoned that if Dr. Ryerson's views prevailed, their occupation as agitators and fomenters of discontent would be gone. Hence the extraordinary vehemence which characterized their denunciations of the writer who had so clearly exposed (as he did more fully at a later period of the controversy), the disloyalty of their aims, and the revolutionary character of their schemes.

This assault on Dr. Ryerson was entirely disproportionate to the cause of offence. Were it not that the moral effect of what he wrote—more than what he actually said—was feared, because addressed to a people who had always listened to his words with deep attention and great respect, it is likely that his words would have passed unchallenged and unheeded.

I have given more than usual prominence to this period of Dr. Ryerson's history—although he has left no record of it in the "Story" which he had written. But I have done so in justice to himself, and from the fact that it marked an important epoch in his life and in the history of the Province. It was an event in which the native nobility of his character asserted itself. The generous impulse which moved him to defend Mr. Bidwell, when maligned and misrepresented, and Sir Charles Metcalfe, whom he looked upon as unjustly treated and as a martyr, prompted him to do full justice to English institutions, and to parties and leaders there, even at the expense of his own preconceived notions on the subject.

By doing so he refused to be of those who would perpetuate an imposition upon the credulity of his countrymen, and especially of those who had trusted him and had looked up to him as a leader of men, and as an exponent of sound principles of government and public policy. And he refused the more when that imposition was practised for the benefit of those in whom he had no confidence, and to the injury of those for whose welfare he had laboured for years.

Dr. Ryerson preferred to risk the odium of interested partisans, rather than fail to tell his countrymen truly and frankly the real state of the case—who and what were the men and parties with whom they had to do in England—either as persons in official life, or as members of Parliament, or writers for the press. He felt it to be his duty to warn those who would heed his warning of the danger which they incurred in following the unchallenged leadership of men whose aim he felt to be revolution, and whose spirit was disloyalty itself, if not a thinly disguised treason.

After the storm of reproach and calumny had passed away, there were thousands in Upper Canada who had reason to cherish with respect and love the name of one who, at a critical time, had so faithfully warned them of impending danger, and saved them from political and social ruin. Such gratitude was Dr. Ryerson's sole reward.

It would be impossible, within the compass of this "Story," to include any details of the speeches, editorials, or other writings of Dr. Ryerson during the many years of contest for civil and religious rights in Upper Canada. The *Guardian*, the newspaper press (chiefly that opposed to Dr. Ryerson), and the records of the House of Assembly contain ample proof of the severity of the protracted struggle which finally issued in the establishment on a secure foundation of the religious and denominational privileges and freedom which we now enjoy. To the Presbyterians, Congregationalists, Baptists, etc., who joined heartily with the Methodist leaders in the prolonged struggle, the gratitude of the country must always be due.— J. G. H.

March 7th.—In the midst of his perplexing duties as editor, and the storm of personal attack which his "impressions" had evoked, Dr. Ryerson received a letter from his Mother. It must have been to him like "good news from a far country." Full of love and gratitude to God, it would be to him like waters of refreshment to a weary soul. His Mother said:—

With emotions of gratitude to God, I now write to you, to let you know that the state of my health is as good as usual. Surely the Lord is good, and doeth good, and His tender mercies are over me as a part of the work of His hands. I find that my affections are daily deadening to the things of earth, and my desires for any earthly good decreasing. I have an increase of my desire for holiness of heart, and conformity to all the will of God. I can say with the poet,

> "Come life, come death, or come what will,
> His footsteps I will follow still."

I long to say, "I live, yet not I, but Christ liveth in me." Besiege the throne of grace, dear Egerton, in my behalf. Pray that the Lord would finish his work, and cut it short in righteousness, and make my heart a fit temple for the Holy Ghost to dwell in. Oh, my son, be continually on your guard. You have need to believe firmly, to pray fervently, to work abundantly. Live a holy life, die daily; watch your heart; guide your senses; redeem your time; love Christ, and long for glory. Give my love to your wife, and to all whom who may enquire for me, and accept a share yourself, from your affection-mother,

MEHETABEL RYERSON.

Charlotteville, March 4th, 1834.

After his return from England, Dr. Ryerson received a letter from Rev. Wm. Lord, dated Manchester, 25th March, 1834, in which he referred to an incident of Dr. Ryerson's visit to his house while in England. He says:—

Your company, I am thankful to say, was very useful to several members of my family. The last time you prayed with us, an influence was received by one or two, the effects of which have remained to this day. I now allude more particularly to ——, who, more than twenty times since, has met me at the door, saying, "Have you a letter from Mr. Ryerson?"

CHAPTER XII.
1834.
EVENTS FOLLOWING THE UNION.—DIVISION AND STRIFE.

DR. RYERSON has left nothing in his "Story" to illustrate this period of his personal history, nor the strife and division which followed the consummation of the union of the British and Canadian Conferences. These untoward events are, however, fully described in the "Epochs of Canadian Methodism," pages 247-311: They arose chiefly out of the differences which disturbed the British and Canadian Methodist Societies in Kingston and other places, and the separation in the Societies generally, caused by the establishment of the Methodist Episcopal Church in 1834.

I have already given, in chapter xi., page 128, an extract of a letter to Dr. Ryerson, from his brother John, indicating the causes of strife between the British and Canadian Societies. I give the following letter, also from the same gentleman, written from Hallowell early in November, 1833, in which he said:—

Brother William and I called on the Rev. Mr. Hetherington at Kingston. He said:—That there could be no union; that we were Radicals; that they would not be united with us; that the District Meetings of Lower Canada, Halifax, etc., intended to make common cause with them; especially they intended to remonstrate against giving up York and Kingston. They also intended to appeal to the British Conference, and if they were not heard by it they would appeal to the British people. If the British Conference will allow its members to throw firebrands, arrows, and death around in this way, and reciprocate their proceedings after this manner with impunity, they are very different men from what I have taken them to be.

Nov. 20th.—In a subsequent letter to Dr. Ryerson, his brother John says:—

I fear much for the Union from the English Missionary party. Should they, from any consideration, undertake to retain Kingston and York, our cause there will be ruined. In case of such an event, I will retire immediately, and bid farewell to the strife and toil in which we have been engaged ever since we have been travelling preachers. Let me know who have thrown up the *Guardian.* You will have seen the Cobourg *Reformer's* attacks. It is of much more importance for you to expose Mr. Radcliffe, the editor, than any one else, and point out that, in his present enmity to Methodist principles, this is not the first time he has endeavoured to break the Methodist ranks, and to sow the seeds of discord among her friends.

I would take good care not to lean a hairsbreadth towards radicalism. One reason of their making this onslaught is to scare you, and induce you to say something which will excite the jealousy of the Government, and the disapprobation of our British brethren, and thereby destroy us with them as they seek to do with other parties.

Nov. 22nd.—What is thus stated by his brother John was corroborated by his brother William, who was stationed at Kingston, and who, in a letter to Dr. Ryerson, said :—

I need not say what my feelings were when I arrived at this place, and found that arrangements had been made by Mr. Marsden, in violation of the understanding with the Conference, and in defiance of the opinions and wishes of every one of our friends in the town and country, whose feelings have not only been wounded and grieved, but have rendered the prospects of a union in this place more than ever entirely hopeless. I have not been considered fit (probably for want of ability) to act as Superintendent of such an important station; I have no authority to receive or expel a member, or even to preside in a meeting of Stewards and Leaders; while my Superintendent is in Montreal or Quebec; whether or not he will so stoop as to visit us at all, we cannot say. Besides being shut out of the British Wesleyan Chapel, every possible means is being used to prevent a single individual of their Society from attending our Chapel; and my field of labour is not only greatly circumscribed, but the prospect of usefulness is nearly destroyed. What my feelings must be, under such circumstances, you can easily judge. I can only say that as soon as I can see a way opened, and can do so consistently, I will not labour as a travelling preacher one day longer.

January 8th, 1834.—His brother John, in another letter to Dr. Ryerson from Hallowell, said :—

Whoever may be the agents in making alterations in our economy, I will not be one. With "improvements," alterations, unions, and disunions, we have been agitated long enough. I am done with such business, henceforth and forever. At our last Conference it was understood, and expressly stated that no alterations would hereafter be attempted; and so we have assured the people. But behold, before they receive that assurance, some alterations are mooted. Do away with the Presiding Elders, lessen the Districts, etc., and a dozen other things which will necessarily follow. The reason urged for these changes is worse than the things themselves—namely: If we don't, the British Missionaries will write to the Superintendents and raise such a storm in England, etc., etc. If this is the way we are to be governed, and if this is the state of the Connexion at home, the Resolutions on Union, on parchment or paper, are a miserable farce. The more I think on this subject, the worse I like it.

In a letter from Kingston to Dr. Ryerson on this subject, Rev. Joseph Stinson says :—

I have done my utmost to promote the union of the two Societies in this town. If things are carried with too high a hand, we shall lose our Kingston Chapel and congregation altogether; and, should the Kingston people shut their Chapel against us, it will be impossible to keep things quiet in Lower Canada. I do not think it necessary to sacrifice the Union to Kingston, nor is it necessary to sacrifice Kingston, because a number of disaffected radicals in the Bay of Quinte like to make the state of things here an excuse for their anti-methodistical proceedings. If there were no Kingston in existence, these men would never cordially love the Union.

April, 1834.—Dr. Ryerson received a letter from the new President of the Canada Conference (Rev. Edmund Grindrod) dated London, England, in which the latter said :—

One object of my visit will be to allay the hostility of our Societies in the Lower Province to their union with us.

Mr. Alder (said Mr. Grindrod) was to have accompanied him, but at Mr. Bunting's suggestion this plan was abandoned in the hope that—

The friends in Lower Canada, when they have had time to reflect, would return to better views and feelings.

Dec. 3rd.—Writing to Dr. Ryerson from Kingston, at this date, Rev. John C. Davidson* says :—

I have been told by the most influential members of the Leaders' Meeting here that pledges to the following effect have been most solemnly given to them by Mr. Alder and Mr. Grindrod, viz :—That the members of the British Society here did not, and were never to make a part of the Societies governed by the Canada Conference; that they were to remain as they always were; that their numbers were to be returned to the home Conference; that our Society was to be merged in theirs; and Kingston become the head of the Missionary establishment in Canada,—always to be the residence of the Superintendent, who was to control and regulate the Kingston Societies; and that the Presiding Elder was to have nothing to do with the town; that a large chapel was to be forthwith built,—to be deeded to the British Conference; and that the minister in charge of Kingston was always to be an Englishman.

Towards the close of this year, the Methodist Episcopal Church in Canada was organized. Full details of this division are given by Dr. Ryerson in the "Epochs of Canadian Methodism," pages 270-288. Happily this separated branch of the great Methodist family is being re-united to the parent stock in 1883. Further reference to the subject is, therefore, unnecessary in this "Story." Nevertheless it should be remembered that in the discussion and controversy which for years followed this event, Dr. Ryerson occupied a foremost place as the champion on the Wesleyan Methodist side.

---

* This gentleman entered the Methodist Church in 1827, joined the Church of England in 1854, and was for many years a minister of a congregation in the Province of Quebec. He died in 1881.

CHAPTER XIII.

1834–1835.

SECOND RETIREMENT FROM THE "GUARDIAN" EDITORSHIP.

AS already intimated in Chapter xi., the publication of Dr. Ryerson's "Impressions" of England, etc., in the *Guardian* of 1833, excited quite a political and social sensation. Public men of all shades of opinion had their feelings at once enlisted for or against the Editor of that paper, and condemned or commended his course accordingly.

Such a result did not cause much immediate concern to Dr. Ryerson. He, as Editor, claimed from the first, and his opponents outside of the Connexion admitted, that in battling for religious equality and denominational rights, he should be left untrammelled. In other words, that as Editor of a leading paper like the *Guardian*, he should be left free to counsel, to advise and warn, and, if necessary, to take strong ground on all questions involving purely civil rights, and the constitutional exercise of the prerogative on the part of the Executive. This was the more necessary, as civil and religious freedom were largely identical in those days of undefined prerogative, irresponsible government, and inchoate institutions.

All parties, therefore, tacitly conceded what the Editor of the *Guardian* claimed—a wide latitude and a reasonable discretion in discussing questions of the day which involved either civil rights or religious freedom. This wise discretion was the more necessary from the fact that the *Guardian* was unquestionably the leading newspaper during these years, and was edited with more than ordinary ability and power.*

* The amount of postage paid by newspapers would be a fair indition of their circulation. For instance, in 1830-1, the postage on the *Christian Guardian* was £228 sterling ($1,140), which exceeded by £6 the aggregate postage paid by the thirteen following newspapers in Upper Canada at that time, viz.:—Mackenzie's *Colonial Advocate*, £57; *The Courier*, £45; *Watchman*, £24; *Brockville Recorder*, £16; *Brockville Gazette*, £6; *Niagara Gleaner and Herald*, £17; *Hamilton Free Press*, £11; *Kingston Herald*, £11; *Kingston Chronicle*, £10; *Perth Examiner*, £10; *Patriot*, £6; *St. Catharines Journal*, £6; *York Observer*, £3. Total £222, as against £228 paid by the *Guardian* alone.—H.

Besides, there were many thoughtful men who took little part in politics, and yet who looked with alarm on the claims and encroachments of the Family Compact,—a powerful and influential party, and dominant alike in church and state. Many of the able public men of the day, who were moderate in their views, were nevertheless the champions of popular rights. These men were Messrs. Bidwell, Baldwin, Dunn, and others. Their influence was strongly felt in the House of Assembly, and was sustained by their great moral worth and high social position. To such men the powerful aid of the *Guardian*, in advocating the principles of equal justice to all parties alike, was indispensable; and from its support they derived much strength, and were greatly aided in maintaining their position in the House and in the country.

It was under these circumstances, and amid the peculiar exigencies of the times, that the *Christian Guardian* became the great organ of public opinion on the liberal side in Upper Canada. It can, therefore, be well understood how at such a time, when the supremacy of party was the question of the hour, the publication of Dr. Ryerson's "impressions"—candid and moderate as they were—fell like a bombshell amongst those in Canada who had set up as political idols such men as Hume and Roebuck in England. To dethrone such idols was of itself bad enough ; but that was not the head and front of Dr. Ryerson's offending. What gave such mortal offence was that Dr. Ryerson saw any good whatever in the moderate English Conservative (though he saw none in the English Tory). And worse still, that he saw many undesirable things in the English Whigs, and nothing good in the English Radicals. To give special point to these criticisms and comparisons Dr. Ryerson stated that :—

Radicalism in England appeared to me to be another word for Republicanism, with the name of King instead of President. . . . and that the very description of the public press, which in England advocates the lowest Radicalism, is the foremost in opposing and slandering the Methodists in this Province. Hence the fact that some of these editors have been amongst the lowest of the English Radicals, previous to their egress from the mother country.

The point of this criticism struck home; and, on the very day on which it appeared, the cap was fitted upon the head of the leading radical of the province. In fact, he placed it there himself, and thenceforth proclaimed war to the knife against the Editor of the *Guardian*. (See page 125.)

With singular ability and zeal did Mr. W. L. Mackenzie carry on this warfare. He at once saw what would be the effect of the new departure. And so promptly and energetically did he denounce the "arch-apostate Egerton, *alias* Arnold, Ryerson" as a deserter, that he secured with little difficulty an impromptu verdict from the public against him. This he the more readily accomplished, by the aid of at least half a dozen editors of newspapers in various parts of the province, while Dr. Ryerson was single-handed. Not only did these editors join with great vigour in the hue and cry against Dr. Ryerson (for they had many scores of their own to settle with their powerful rival), but many of Dr. Ryerson's own brethren were carried away by the sudden outburst of passion against him. Hundreds of the supporters of the *Guardian* turned from him, as a deserter, and many gave up the paper.

It is true that the tide soon turned; and those who had refused at first to heed, or even to listen to, the words of warning uttered by Dr. Ryerson in this crisis, were afterwards glad to profit by them, and thus saved themselves in time from the direful consequences which followed during the sad events of 1837-38.

The effect, however, of that severe and unexpected encounter with irrational prejudice (joined to the hostility of those whose plans were prematurely disclosed and frustrated) was too much for one who, as a Christian minister and a lover of his country, was filled with higher aims than those of a mere politician.

In the course of the discussion which followed, Dr. Ryerson came into contact with some of the more unreasoning of his brethren. (See pages 130-133.) The question was raised as to how far the *Guardian* should be involved in conflicts like the present, which from their very nature introduced an apple of discord into the Connexion, as they partook more of a political than of a religious character. This question was pressed upon members of the Conference by the British Missionaries, whose national prejudices and political sensibilities were, as they alleged, wounded by the adverse strictures of the Editor of the *Guardian* on Church Establishments, the Clergy Reserve question, and kindred topics.

Knowing the impossibility of reconciling views so opposite as those expressed by the British Missionaries and those of the great majority of Canadian Methodists (as represented by the *Guardian*), Dr. Ryerson resolved to retire from the editorship. This, by a vote of his brethren in the Conference of 1834, he was not permitted to do. But, like a wise and prudent counsellor amongst men of differing views, he determined to take the initiative in settling, on a satisfactory basis, the future course of the *Guardian* as to the discussion of political and social questions. At that Conference, therefore, he prepared and submitted a series of resolutions to the following effect :—

1. That the *Christian Guardian*, as the organ of the Conference, shall be properly and truly a religious and literary journal, to explain our doctrines and institutions, and, in the spirit of meekness, defend them when necessary; to vindicate our character, if expedient, when misrepresented; to maintain our religious privileges, etc. 2. To publish general news, etc. 3. That the *Christian Guardian* shall not be the medium of discussing political questions, nor the merits of political parties; as it is injurious to the interests of religion, and derogatory to our character as a religious body, to have our Church amalgamated or identified with any political party.

These resolutions were cordially adopted by the Conference.

October 4th, 1834.—In a letter received by Dr. Ryerson from Rev. G. Marsden, Liverpool, the latter referred to this subject and said :—

Your continuance in office, as editor, is of very high importance; indeed, in some respects it is essential to the consolidation of the Union. Loyalty to our Sovereign, and firm attachment to the British Constitution will be supported by it. You will also be able to defend, and to support sound Wesleyan Methodism; and the foundation being now laid, you will be able to guard it well.

Rev. E. Grindrod, also writing from England, said :—

From the *Christian Guardian*, I perceive that you have had a hard battle to fight, but you have proved victorious; and at a future day, I have no doubt, you will rejoice that the Lord counted you worthy to suffer in the achievement of an object which will probably result in immense benefit to a whole Province for generations to come.

January 28th, 1835.—About this time Dr. Ryerson received a remonstrance on the subject from his brother John, who said :—

The more I think of your leaving the office, the more unfavourably I think of it. There is a tremendous opposition to it in these parts (Hallowell), among both preachers and people. I think it will do the paper a great wrong; you had better remain undisturbed until next Conference."

Feby. 20th.—Rev. William Ryerson, in a kind letter from St. Catharines, said :—

The spirit and feeling displayed in your most interesting letter has made the deepest impression on my mind. I know that you have your own difficulties and troubles, yet they do not appear to prevent the outflow of your sympathy for others. How sincerely do I pray that the God of mercy and truth may graciously support you under all your trials and difficulties, and in His good time bring you out of them, purified as gold. I am exceedingly fearful that we shall have more, and great difficulties, at our next Conference. Every article and word in the *Guardian* is criticised and noted, and made the subject of a large and constant correspondence, especially with the local preachers, in different parts of the Province. We shall be much embarrassed about the editorship of the *Guardian*. Perhaps Providence will point out some suitable person should you retire.

May 27th.—In the *Guardian* of this date, Dr. Ryerson again gave expression to his long-cherished desire to retire from the editorial management of that paper. He did so for reasons already given—

Besides (he said) it was the understanding entered into with the Conference of 1834, when I consented to undertake the duty of editor for one year. It is gratifying to notice that the vituperation of party interest and malevolence are nearly, if not quite, spent. I have, in this and the last two numbers of the *Guardian*, endeavoured to leave nothing for my successor to settle on that score. My editorial career in the past has been during an eventful and agitated period of our Provincial history. I have steadily endeavoured to keep one object in view—the promotion of Christianity and the prosperity of the country. In severing my connection with a large portion of the reading public, I am moved with feelings not easily expressed. My interest in the cause which I have advocated, and in the general welfare of my native Province (which has been intense for years past), will not be less so in any future fields of labour.

When it was found that Dr. Ryerson had finally decided to retire from the editorship of the *Guardian*, various suggestions were made to him as to his future field of labour. The Connexion in Lower Canada were anxious to secure him as a minister there. The question came up at an official meeting in Quebec, and Rev. William Lord, who presided, wrote to Dr. Ryerson on the subject, in May, 1835, as follows :—

Respecting your future appointment to this Province, I may mention that several of the brethren objected to your leaving the Upper Province, lest it should be thought you were sent away in disgrace. I think, however, that I can obtain a station that will be deemed honourable to yourself, and, I think, quite agreeable, affording a fine field of usefulness. I am now sitting in the Quarterly Meeting, and when the question of preachers for the next year came on, I mentioned that I had conversed with you respecting taking a circuit in this Province. They unanimously requested that Brother Wm. Squire and Brother Egerton Ryerson might be appointed to them next year. I shall soon be in York, when I will endeavour to obtain the consent of the friends there, and I think you will be pleased with the place.

As an indication amongst others of the appreciation in which Dr. Ryerson's services were held, Rev. R. Heyland, in a letter to him from Adolphustown, said :—

The people in these parts are very desirous of seeing and hearing the champion who has written so much in defence of Methodism, and rescued the character of our Church from the odium which its unprincipled enemies have been endeavouring to heap upon it for years past. Be so good as to gratify them this once, and come and dedicate our new chapel here.

June 17th.—On this day, for the second time, Dr. Ryerson took leave of the readers of the *Guardian*—having been relieved by the Conference of the duties of Editor, at his own request. He said :—

I was, however, elected Secretary of the Conference, and was stationed at Kingston. In addition, I was appointed, with Rev. William Lord, President of our Conference, a delegate to the American General Conference.

In his valedictory he said :—

In relinquishing my present position my thoughts are spontaneously led back to the period—ten years since—when I first commenced public life. At that time the Methodists were an obscure, a despised, an ill-treated people; nor had their church the security of law for a single chapel, parsonage, or acre of land. . . . Now the political condition and relations of the Methodist connexion are pleasingly changed. Ten years ago there were 41 ministers and 6,875 church members; now there are 93 ministers and 15,106 church members. We may well thank God, therefore, and take courage.

I have no ill-will towards any human being. I freely and heartily forgive the many false and wicked things said of me, publicly and privately. I have written what I thought best for the cause of religion, the cause of Methodism, and the civil interests of the country. I have never received one acre of land, nor one farthing from Government, nor of any public money. I have never written one line at the request of any person connected with the Government. I count it to be the highest honour to which I can aspire to be a Methodist preacher; and in this relation to the Church and to the world I shall count it my highest joy to finish my earthly course.

Dr. Ryerson's wish having been fully gratified, and the Conference of 1835 having relieved him of the editorship, he was stationed at Kingston. This place, of all others, had been the scene of strife and division between the British and Canadian branches of the Church, and was the key to the position held by the British Missionaries in Upper Canada. (See pages 128 and 141). Dr. Ryerson's arrival there and his reception by the people at Kingston are described in a letter which he wrote to his friend, Mr. S. S. Junkin, of the *Guardian* office, dated July 15th:

We have just arrived, and are for the present staying at the house of Mr. Cassidy, the lawyer, where we receive every possible kindness and attention. (See Chapter xxiii.)

I have been very kindly received by the members here. Strong prejudices have existed in the minds of individuals against me. But they are not only broken down, but in the principal cases are turned into warm friendship already. Some who were as bitter as gall, and croaking from day to day that "the glory has departed," are now like new-born babes in Christ; are happy in their own souls, praying for sinners, and doing all they can to build up the cause. I can scarcely account for it. I never felt more deeply humbled than since I came here. I have indeed resolved to give my whole soul, body and spirit, to God and to His Church anew, but I have had scarcely a tolerable time in preaching. Yet the Divine blessing has specially accompanied the Word. On Wednesday night last the fallow ground of the hearts of professors seemed to be completely broken up. On Thursday night I was in the country, but was told the prayer-meeting was the largest that had been held for two years. On Sunday evening we had prayer-meeting after preaching. Several came to the altar, two or three of whom found peace. I closed it at nine o'clock, but some stayed and others came in, and it was kept up until near one o'clock in the morning. On Monday night the altar was surrounded with penitents, and the meeting, I was told (for I was not there), was better than any former one, and was kept up until after midnight. At our preachers and leaders' meeting last night there was a good time. We have preaching and prayer-meeting again to-night. We have formed the leaders' meeting of both chapels into one, to the satisfaction of the brethren on both sides. I now begin to hope for better times. My soul was bowed down like a bulrush for some days after I came here. But I thank God I have a hold upon the salvation of Christ that I had not felt for a long time before; and I do believe the Lord our God will help us and bless us. I have preached at Waterloo twice since I came down. The last time, several penitents came to the altar; two professed to find peace, but it was upon the whole a dry time to me. They are hard cases there. I attended a very blessed quarterly meeting on the Isle of Tanti, on Thursday last. It was the best day to my own soul that I have experienced for years.

I feel like a man liberated from prison; but I have reason to believe that the people are in general amazingly disappointed in my pulpit exercises. They expected great things—things gaudy, stately, and speculative,—and I gave them the simplest and most practical things I can find in the Bible, and that in the plainest way. You would be amused at the sayings of some of the plain Methodist people; they think that it is the "real pure Gospel, but they did not expect it so, from that quarter." I am told that Dr. Barker has said in his *Whig*, that my "pulpit talents are nothing." I am very glad to have this impression go abroad; it will relieve me from distressing embarrassments, and enable me to do much more good in a plain way; for I know the utmost I can attain in the pulpit is to make things plain, and sometimes forcible.

We had a very blessed prayer-meeting last night, after preaching. A considerable number of penitents came to the altar, and some found peace. The work seems to be deepening among the Society. I think we shall have a comfortable and prosperous year.

September 24th. In a subsequent letter to Mr. Junkin, Dr. Ryerson speaks of a sudden and severe bereavement which had overtaken him. He said:—

My poor little son John* has been removed to the other and better

---

* John William, aged six years, one month, and eleven days. (See pages 111 and 113.)—H.

country. He continued to walk about until within ten minutes before his death, on the 22nd inst. After attempting to take a spoonful of milk, he leaned back his head and expired in my arms, without the slightest visible struggle. He has suffered much, but expressed a desire that he might live, so that he could see his little sister. He told me a few days before he died, that he hoped to go to Heaven, because Jesus had died for him, and loved him. I feel as a broken vessel in this bereavement of the subject of so many anxious cares and fond hopes. But this I do know, that I love God, and supremely desire to advance His glory, and that He does all things for the best. I will therefore magnify His name when clouds and darkness envelope His ways, as well as when the smiles of His providence gladden the heart of man. O may He make me and mine more entirely and exclusively His, than ever!

In a letter to Mr. Junkin, dated November 14th, Dr. Ryerson says :—

We all go into one chapel to-morrow, which will complete the Union. Thank the Lord for it! Every one of our members of the "American" Society (so called heretofore) has already taken sittings in the newly enlarged chapel, and all things appear to be harmonious and encouraging. Every pew in the body of the chapel has already been taken by our brethren and intimate friends; and, notwithstanding the new chapel will hold more than both the old ones, we are not likely to have enough sittings to meet the applications that are likely to be made, when it is known out of the Society, though the whole chapel above and below (except one tier around the gallery) is pewed.

I have learned that I shall have to take another trip to England. We had just got comfortably settled here in Kingston; had become acquainted with the people on all sides, and are happy in our souls, and in our work. Nothing but the alternative, as Rev. William Lord deeply feels, of the sinking or success of the Upper Canada Academy, could have induced me this year to have undertaken such a task. But my motto is—"the cause of God, not private considerations."

CHAPTER XIV.

1835—1836.

SECOND MISSION TO ENGLAND.—UPPER CANADA ACADEMY.

SCARCELY had Dr. Ryerson been settled at Kingston in the enjoyment of the freedom and pleasure of his new life as a pastor, than the exigencies of the Upper Canada Academy called him a second time to England. The causes of this sudden call upon his time and energies, on behalf of the Academy, were many and pressing, They were caused chiefly by the miscalculations, if not indiscreet zeal, of Rev. William Lord, who, as President of the Conference and Chairman of the Trustee Board of the Academy, had, by inconsiderate expenditure, plunged the Board into hopeless embarrassment. (See page 166.)

Mr. Lord was sanguine that what he did in Canada, on behalf of the Academy, would, if properly represented, be cordially endorsed by the brethren and friends in England. He, felt that although he himself might not be able to realize these hopes by a personal appeal, yet he was certain that the presence in England of Dr. Ryerson on such a mission would be highly successful. He, therefore, as President of the Canada Conference, called upon him to undertake this task. He furnished Dr. Ryerson with such letters and appeals to influential friends as he hoped would ensure success. Dr. Ryerson, acting on his motto, that "the cause of God, not private considerations," should influence him, obeyed the call, and set out for England on this difficult, and, as it proved, arduous and protracted mission, on the 20th November, 1835.

The nature and extent of the embarrassments of the Academy are stated in the letters written to Dr. Ryerson after he had left for England. His brother John said:—

While you are travelling in England making collections for the Academy, there are, I can assure you, a great many heartfelt prayers and fervent supplications being offered in this country for your success. The whole concern is in an extremely embarrassed state. If Rev. William Lord had not urged us to expenditure, it would have been at least £1,000 better for us, although what he did at the time, he doubtless did for the best. Mr. Lord was the means of inducing the building committee to make an unnecessarily expensive fence, out-houses, furniture, &c., saying at the time that money would be forthcoming, and that John Bull never failed to respond to such calls. We have applied to the Legislature for assistance, but I think with but little prospect of success. Should we not get anything there, and you raise no more than £2,000, we must go down, and the concern be sold. It will require £4,000 or £5,000 to get us out of debt. If you should collect no more than £2,000 before you return home, don't fail to make some arrangements for borrowing two or three thousand more.

Rev. Mr. Lord, writing to Dr. Ryerson, said :—

By the delay in finishing the buildings, and the excitement caused by the falsehood of the ultra-Radicals, confidence was gone, money could not be raised, either by begging or borrowing ; and if something had not been done, the consequence would have been ruinous. I expect that you will have me greatly blamed for not considering before I drew bills on England for the debt, but there was no time. The mischief would have been done before we could have heard. The man would have been arrested immediately,—our character ruined,—societies divided,—and subscriptions would have been withheld. Our difficulties are great, and we must make a desperate effort to extricate ourselves. Everything depends upon your making a good case, which you can do.

In another letter to Dr. Ryerson, from Canada, Mr. Lord said :—

Let me urge you to lose no time in obtaining a Charter and grant from Government. I expect our Radical friends will be using their influence through their friends to prevent your success. Be diligent in procuring subscriptions. You possess great advantages now, by the introductions with which you have been favoured. Mr. Alder tells me that my bills will be dishonoured. If so, in addition to the loss of character, there will be a waste of property in fines, &c. We are all distressed, our drafts are coming due and the Banks have ceased to discount, in consequence of the stagnation of trade, through "stopping the supplies." We have agreed upon a temporary mode of relief, by drawing upon you for about £500. It has given me great surprise and sorrow to ascertain that upwards of £5,000 are wanted to relieve us from our difficulties. What an unfathomable depth this building has reached. You must stay in England until the money is got. Use every effort, harden your face to flint, and give eloquence to your tongue. This is your calling. Excel in it! Be not discouraged with a dozen of refusals in succession. The money must be had, and it must be begged. My dear Brother, work for your life, and I pray God to give you success. Do not borrow, if possible. *Beg, beg, beg* it all. It must be done!

Such were the circumstances under which this important mission was undertaken by Dr. Ryerson. As a set off to these disheartening letters, Dr. Ryerson received the following from some of his brethren in Canada. Rev. Ephraim Evans said :—

I have become a consenting party to your being solicited, at considerable sacrifice of feeling, to undertake a tedious journey at the most untoward season of the year, for the good of the common cause, and I sincerely tender, in common with my Brother James, my best thanks for your kind compliance, and my hearty wishes for your complete success. Indeed I feel most deeply that upon your success depends, under God, the prosperity or downfall of the Upper Canada Academy. Be assured that my most fervent prayers will be daily offered up for your health and safety, for a happy issue to attend your generous endeavours again to promote the interests of the Church of our mutual affection.

I entertain not the slightest hope of being able to procure such a Charter as we would be justifiable in accepting, or any support to the institution from our own Legislature.

Rev. John Ryerson, writing from Hallowell, said :—

Your friends in Kingston (and all the Methodists there seem to be such) spoke much about you and your successful labours there. Brothers Counter, Jenkins, and others, say they are resolved to have you for their preacher next year, on your return from England. I hope and pray that good luck will attend your efforts. Everything depends on the issue of your mission. May the Lord give you favour in the eyes of the people, and good success in your vastly important work.

Rev. Joseph Stinson, writing from Kingston, said :—

We all feel very strange now that you are gone, but be of good cheer; we follow you with our sympathy and prayers. We doubt not but God—that God in whose cause you are making this additional sacrifice, will succeed your labour, and cause all things to work together for your good.

In a letter from London, England, Dr. Ryerson says :—

Mr. Lunn and other friends have arrived from Quebec, and have given me Canadian news, among other items the stations of various ministers: Rev. James Richardson and Rev. J. S. Atwood withdraw from the Conference, and Rev. Mr. Irvine goes to the States. The President and I remain at Kingston. I have been appointed, by a unanimous vote, the representative to the British Conference, and I am to present to Lord Glenelg an Address from the Conference to the King. On the 18th of June, 1836, the Upper Canada Academy was opened, and the Principal (Rev. M. Richey) inaugurated.

Dr. Ryerson added :—

I am to stay in Birmingham, at the house of a worthy and wealthy Quaker, by the name of Joseph Sturge.

At the general meeting of the Missionary Committee, held recently the resolutions of the Committee relative to the withdrawal of the Government grant for the work in Upper Canada were read. Dr. Bunting rose and mentioned its restoration, and kindly and cordially mentioned me as the means of getting it restored. He gave a flattering account of my proceedings in the affair. I thanked him afterwards for his great kindness in the matter.

The labours and result of this, Dr. Ryerson's second mission to England, are given in Chapter xvi., pages 158–166.

CHAPTER XV.

1835—1836.

THE "GRIEVANCE" REPORT; ITS OBJECT AND FAILURE.

AMONGST the Committees of the House of Assembly at this time was a useful one called the "Committee on Grievances." To this Committee was referred all complaints made to the House, and all projects of reform, etc. At the close of the Session of 1835, Mr. W. L. Mackenzie, as Chairman, brought in an elaborate Report which, without being read, was ordered to be printed In that Report, Mr. Mackenzie endeavoured to create a diversion in his favour by showing that while Dr. Ryerson professed to be opposed to Government grants to religious bodies, yet he was willing to receive one for the Wesleyan Conference. The Report stated that :—

> The "British Wesleyan Methodist Conference," formerly the M.E. Church, received £1,000 in 1833, and £611 in 1834, to be applied . . . . "to the erection, or repairing of chapels and school-houses, and defraying the general expenses of the various missions."
> This appropriation to the Methodists, as an Ecclesiastical Establishment, is very singular. In the year 1826 . . . . Dr. Strachan informed the Colonial Minister that the Methodist ministers acquired their education and formed their principles in the United States. . . . . They appealed to the House of Assembly, which inquired into and reported on the matter in 1828.
> Upon another occasion they received a rebuke from Sir John Colborne . . . in answer to the Address of the Conference requesting him to transmit to His Majesty their Address on the Clergy Reserves. Since, however, a share of public money has been extended to and received by them, there seems to have been established a mutual good understanding.

To this Report, Dr. Ryerson replied to the effect—

> That the grant was made to the British Conference in England (over which we had no control) and not to the Canada Conference; that the grant in question was made by Lord Goderich, as part of a general scheme agreed upon in 1832, to aid Missionaries in the West Indies, Western, and Southern Africa, New South Wales, and Canada, "to erect chapels and school-houses in the needy and destitute settlements;" that the Rev. R. Alder had come from England, in 1833, to establish separate and distinct missions from those under the Canada Conference with a view to absorb this grant; that when the Union was formed, in 1833, the missions in charge of the Canada Conference became the missions of the British Conference, and

were managed by their own Superintendent; that the Canadian Missionary Society from that time became a mere auxiliary to the parent Society in England; that the Canada Conference assumed no responsibility in regard to the funds necessary to support these missions; and that, in point of fact, they had cost the British Methodists thousands of dollars over and above any grant received from Lord Goderich as part of the general scheme for the support of missionaries in the extended British Colonies.

Dr. Ryerson, in concluding these explanations, adds :—

We trust that every reader clearly perceives the unparalleled parliamentary imposition that has been practised upon the public by the "Grievance Committee," and their gross insinuations and slanders against the Methodist ministers.

In 1836, the Report of the Grievance Committee came up in the House again. On this subject Rev. John Ryerson wrote in March, 1836, to Dr. Ryerson, in London, as follows :—

The altercations and quarrels which have taken place in the Assembly this session on the part of Peter Perry and W. L. Mackenzie, especially about the "Grievance Report," have raised you much in the estimation of the people. The correctness of your views and statements are now universally acknowledged, and your defamers deserted by all candid men. Political things are looking very favourable at the present time. The extremer of the Radical party are going down headlong. May a gracious Providence speed them on their journey!

To Mr. Perry, Dr. Ryerson replied fully and explicitly. He said:

Mr. Perry has charged me with departing from my former ground in regard to an ecclesiastical establishment in Upper Canada. My editorials and correspondence with Her Majesty's Government will be considered conclusive evidence of the falsity of the charge, and will again defeat the attempts of the enemies of Methodism to destroy me and overthrow the Conference. Another cause of attack by Mr. Perry is, that amongst several other suggestions which I took the liberty to offer to Lord Glenelg, Colonial Secretary, was the appointment of a certain gentleman of known popularity to the Executive Council. Mr. Perry seemed to consider himself as a sort of king in Lennox and Addington, and appears to regard it as an infringement upon his sovereign prerogatives that I should be stationed so near the borders of his empire as Kingston. But many of his constituents can bear record whether the object of my ministry was to dethrone Peter Perry, or to break down the power and influence of a much more formidable and important personage—the power of him that ruleth in the hearts of the children of disobedience.*

March 30th, London.—During his stay in England, Dr. Ryerson had been able to look upon public affairs in Upper Canada with more calmness, and more impartiality, than when he was there in the midst of them as an actor. In that spirit he, at this date, addressed a letter to the *Guardian* on what he regarded as an approaching crisis of the highest importance to the Province. He said:—

---

* Dr. Ryerson's reply to Mr. Perry was afterwards reprinted as an election flysheet, headed "Peter Perry Picked to Pieces by Egerton Ryerson," and circulated broadcast in the counties. It resulted in Mr. Perry being rejected as M.P.P. for Lennox and Addington in the elections of 1836. (See Chapter xxiii.)

It is not a mere ephemeral strife of partizanship; it is a deliberate and bold attempt to change the leading features of the Constitution—a Constitution to which allegiance has been sworn, and to which firm attachment has been over and over again expressed in addresses to the Governor up to 1834. Such being the case, it becomes every man who fears God and loves his country to pause, to think, to decide. I have told the Colonial Secretary, that whilst the Methodist Church asked for nothing but "equal and impartial protection," yet I believed the attachment to the Constitution of the country and to the British Crown, expressed in petitions and addresses from the Methodist Conference and people of Canada, to be sincere, and that they would prove to be so in their future conduct. They had been falsely charged as being Republicans, but they had always repudiated this charge as a calumny. Nor would they be found among those who, like Messrs. Peter Perry and W. L. Mackenzie, had recently avowed their intention to establish republican elective institutions in the Province.

As to the charges of the "Grievance Committee" party, I can truly say that I have never received one farthing of public money from any quarter, and my humble support to my King and country is unsought, unsolicited, and spontaneous.

May 21st—London.—At this date Dr. Ryerson wrote:—

During my exile here in England I have more and more longed for news from Canada, and cooling water to the panting hart could not be more refreshing than late intelligence from my dear native land has been to me. I can now listen with an interest and sympathy that I never did before, to the patriotic effusions of the warm-hearted and eloquent Irishmen, whom I have recently heard, respecting "the first flower of the earth, the first gem of the sea."

The news from Canada presents to my mind strange contrasts. A few years ago efforts were made to prove that the Methodist ministers were the "salaried hirelings" of a foreign republican power. Now efforts are being made to persuade the Canadian public that the same ministers are the salaried hirelings of British power, because they refuse to be identified with men and measures which are revolutionary in their tendencies. Our motto is "fear God and honour the King," and "meddle not with them that are given to change." Many who were influenced to take part in the former crusade have long since given proof of a better spirit; so it will be, I trust, with those who have now been hurried on into the present shameless and malignant opposition, against a cause which has confessedly been of the highest spiritual and eternal advantage to thousands in Upper Canada. I venture to predict that not a few of our partizan adversaries will ere long lament their madness of political idolatry and religious hostility. In the former case, Methodism survived, triumphed, and prospered; in the present case, if we are true to our principles and faithful to our God, He will again "Cause the wrath of man to praise Him, and restrain the remainder of that wrath."

CHAPTER XVI.

1836–1837.

Dr. Ryerson's Diary of his Second Mission to England

THE following is from Dr. Ryerson's diary (which is incomplete) giving the result of his experiences and labours in England, during his second mission there.

London, January 1st, 1836.—I am again in the great metropolis of the Christian world. My wife and I left our native land, and affectionate pastoral charge, on the 20th of November, 1835, and arrived here the 30th of December, after a voyage of tempest and sea-sickness. But to the Ruler of the winds, and the Father of our spirits, we present our grateful acknowledgments for the preservation of our lives. To our Heavenly Father have I, with my dear wife, presented ourselves at the commencement of this new year. O, may we through grace keep our vows, and henceforth abound in every Christian grace and comfort, every good word and work!

We have been most kindly received by the Missionary Secretaries and other brethren; the prospects appear encouraging for the success of our mission: another ground of thankfulness, increased zeal, and faithfulness.

Jan. 2nd.—Called at the Colonial Office to present my note of introduction from Sir John Colborne to Lord Glenelg. We were admitted to an interview with Mr. (afterwards Sir James) Stephen, Assistant Colonial Secretary, who promised to present Sir John Colborne's letter to Lord Glenelg, and inform me when he would receive me. To-day I received a call from my kind and excellent friend, Rev. John Hannah, a thorough scholar, a profound divine, an affectionate, able, and popular preacher. He heartily welcomed us to the country.

Jan. 3rd—Sabbath.—It being the first Sabbath in the year, I attended that most solemn and important service—the renewal of the covenant. It was conducted by Rev. Dr. Bunting, in a manner the most impressive and affecting I ever witnessed. There were but few dry eyes in the chapel. He spoke of the primary design of Methodism as not to oppose anything but sin —not to subvert existing forms of faith, but to infuse the vital spirit of primitive Christianity into them. Dr. Bunting said that the renewal of the covenant was a service peculiar to Methodism, and expatiated on the importance of its being entered upon advisedly, and in humble dependence upon Divine grace. After singing, the whole congregation knelt down, remaining some time in silent prayer. After Dr. Bunting, as their mouthpiece, read the covenant, all then rose and sang "The covenant we this moment make," etc. The Lord's Supper was administered to several hundred persons, and the services concluded with singing and prayer.

Jan. 4th.—I spent the evening at Rev. Mr. Alder's, in company with Dr. Bunting, Rev. John Bowers, and Rev. P. L. Turner. In conversation, the religious and general interests of the Methodist Connexion were introduced. I was no less edified than delighted with the remarks of Dr. Bunting, especially those which related to the former distinction between, and the present confounding of, supernumerary and superannuated preachers, and the desirableness of restoring the ancient distinction. He spoke of the experience requisite to, and evils of general legislation in, Church affairs—introducing matters of legislation into Quarterly Meetings, etc. Dr. Bunting's prayer at parting was deeply spiritual.

Jan. 5th.—Spent the day in writing an article for the *Watchman*, on the present state of the Canadas; and in drawing up some papers on the Upper Canada Academy. Had a pleasant visit from Rev. John Beecham, one of the Missionary Secretaries.

Jan. 6th.—Met at the Mission House with Rev. Richard Reece, President of the Conference. He is, I believe, the oldest preacher who has filled the presidential chair since the days of Wesley.

Jan. 10th, Sunday.—In the morning heard Rev. Mr. Cubitt, and in the evening endeavoured to preach for him.

Jan. 13th.—Received a note from Lord Glenelg fixing the time when he would receive me.

Jan. 14th.—Spent a delightful evening in company with Rev. John Hannah and wife, Dr. Sandwich (Editor of the *Watchman*) and wife, and several others. The conversation principally turned upon the learning of the ancients, and the writings of the early Protestant Reformers and their successors. Dr. Sandwich is a very literary man, Mr. Hannah an excellent general scholar.

Jan. 15th.—Spent the evening with Rev. William Jenkins, an old superannuated minister, in company with several friends. Mr. and Mrs. Jenkins are a venerable couple about 80 years of age.

Jan. 17th—Sabbath.—Heard the Hon. and Rev. Baptist Noel. The Church was plain, the congregation large, and very attentive and solemn. A large number of school children were present; the little girls all dressed alike; they all had prayer and hymn books; they read the responses and sung with the utmost correctness. In the afternoon we went to that splendid monument of art and wealth—St. Paul's. The sermon was more evangelical than I expected. In the evening I preached to a very large congregation in St. George's Chapel, Commercial Road. A gracious influence seemed to rest on the congregation.

Jan. 24th—Sabbath.—Preached in the Hinde-street Chapel. In Surrey Chapel I heard Rev. James Parsons, of York, one of the first preachers of the day. Surrey Chapel is the place of the celebrated Rowland Hill's protracted ministry. Its shape is octagon, and it will seat 3,000 persons. The church service was read well by a person of strong, sonorous voice. At the conclusion of the church service Mr. Parsons ascended the pulpit. His prayer was simple, unaffected, and scriptural. His text was Luke xi. 47-48. His manner was by no means pleasing; he stood nearly motionless, and appeared to be reading his sermon. Yet attention was riveted; the current of thought soon began to rise, and continued to swell, until he came to a pause. Then there was a general burst of coughing; after which the preacher proceeded in an ascending scale of argument, until he had his audience entranced, when he would burst forth upon his captives with the combined authority and tenderness of a conqueror and deliverer, and press them into the refuge city of Gospel salvation.

Jan. 25th.—Attended a Missionary-meeting in Southwark Chapel. Mr. Thomas Farmer, presided. Several spake: one a New Zealander, whose wit and oddities amused all, but profited none.

Jan. 26th.—Had an interview with Lord Glenelg, on the subject of my mission. We can get a charter for the Upper Canada Academy, but assistance is uncertain. His Lordship was very courteous and communicative. He thanked me for the information I gave him concerning the Colonies.

Jan. 31st, Sunday.—Preached twice to-day (in City Road and Wilderness Row). The Lord was with me, and I believe I did not labour in vain.

Feb. 13th.—Had an interview with the Rt. Hon. Edward Ellice; was received with great kindness; he promised to use his utmost influence to promote the object of my mission at the Colonial office.

Feb. 18th.—Called at the residences of several of the nobility; found none at home, but Lord Ashburton, who gave me £5.

Feb. 20th.—Made no progress in the way of collecting; much ceremony is necessary. Have obtained some useful information, and written to Sir Robert Peel on the object of my mission.

Feb. 21st, Sunday.—Heard the Rev. Peter McOwan preach. It was the best sermon I have heard from a Methodist pulpit since my arrival in England. I preached in Great Queen-street Chapel in the evening, on the new birth. I think the Lord was present to apply the word.

Feb. 22nd.—Called upon Lord Kenyon. I was very courteously received; but His Lordship declined subscribing on account of the many objects to which he contributed in connection with America. He expressed his good wishes. I next called upon the Earl of Aberdeen—Colonial Secretary under Sir Robert Peel's government. He expressed himself satisfied with my letters from Upper Canada, but said that he would enquire of Mr. Hay, late under Colonial Secretary, and directed me to call again. I was also received by Dr. Blomfield, Lord Bishop of London. Dr. Blomfield is a handsome and very courteous man. He declined subscribing on account of its not having been recommended by the Bishop of the Diocese; was not unfriendly to my object; said he had a high respect for the Wesleyan body, and considered they had done much good; he had expressed this opinion in print.

Feb. 23rd.—Addressed a letter to Lord Glenelg requesting an early answer to our application, stating our pressing circumstances. Called upon Thomas Baring, Esq., M.P., who gave me £5. I find it very hard and very slow work to get money.

Feb. 24th.—Received an answer from Sir Robert Peel in the negative. His reason is non-connection with Upper Canada! A gentleman of the house of Thomas Wilson & Co. gave utterance to a sentiment which singularly contrasted with the selfishness of Sir Robert Peel. He said: Education was the same thing throughout the world, and that was the light in which this institution should be viewed. His house gave me ten guineas, and have kindly engaged to furnish me with names of other gentlemen.

Feb. 25th.—Obtained £21 for the Academy. The sentiments expressed by two of the gentlemen on whom I called deserve to be recorded. Mr. A. Gillespie, jun., who is connected with Lower Canada, after subscribing £10 and furnishing me with a list of names of merchants engaged in trade with the Canadas, said:—" I am a member of the Church of Scotland, but I have a high respect for John Wesley and Dr. Bunting. I admire the principles of John Wesley, and hope you will abide by them, and that they will be taught in this institution. Above all things keep out Socinianism." I then called on a Mr. Brooking, who said:—" I feel happy in the opportunity of contributing to such an object. I have been in the North American provinces and know that nothing is wanted more than good institutions for the education of youth, and especially under the superintendence of the Methodists. From what I have seen I believe they have done more good in the colonies than any other Church. Though I am a member of the Church of England, I feel it my duty as a Protestant, and a friend to religion, to give my utmost mite to the labours of your ministers in the colonies. I believe in those new countries the Methodists are the bulwark of Protestantism against popery and infidelity, and I am glad you are establishing such an institution."

Feb. 27th.—Received the greatest kindness from Mr. E. H. Chapman, who was in Upper Canada last summer, and had seen the institution at Cobourg. He expressed himself happy in the opportunity to subscribe, and said he had travelled two days with Sir John Colborne. Mr. Chapman considered, of all people, the Methodists the most active and successful in imparting religious instruction to the Colonists.

Feb. 28th—Sabbath.—Preached at Islington; then dined with a Mr. Brunskill, who was well versed in the history of Methodism.

From this date until the close of July there is no record in Dr. Ryerson's diary. From letters written by him to Canada, I therefore continue the narrative :—

Birmingham, April 11th.—During a delightful visit here at the missionary anniversaries I had an opportunity of hearing and conversing with two of the most remarkable men of the present day : William (or, as he is called, Billy) Dawson, the Yorkshire farmer, and the venerable Gideon Ousley, the patriarchal Irish missionary. Mr. Dawson excelled in his own characteristic way any man I ever heard. His great strength lies in a matchless power of graphic description, dramatic imitation, and hallowed unction from the Holy One. He is a man of an age. At the missionary breakfast I sat beside the venerable Ousley, and told him of some of his spiritual children in Canada that I knew. He gave God the praise, and desired me to deliver this message to his old friends and spiritual children in Canada: " I am now in my 75th year, labouring as hard as ever ; am well, and strong. Be faithful unto death. I will meet you in Heaven."

London, June 8th.—To-day my brethren are assembling in Annual Conference at Belleville. It is the first conference in the proceedings of which I have not been permitted to take a part since I entered the ministry. A considerable part of the day I spent in imploring the divine blessing upon the deliberations of my brethren. After reckoning the difference of time, I retired at the hour when I knew they would be engaged in the conference-prayer-meeting in order to unite with them at the throne of the Heavenly grace ; and truly, I found it refreshing indeed to be present in spirit with them in beseeching the continual direction of the Divine Pilot to guide the Wesleyan ship over the tempestuous sea. I long to be with my fellow-labourers in Canada in their toils as well as joys. " If I forget thee," O thou Spiritual Jerusalem of my native land, " let my right hand forget its cunning, and my tongue cleave to the roof of my mouth. Peace be within thy walls, and prosperity within thy palaces !"

June 12th.—Although I find that collecting for the Upper Canada Academy is a wearisome work, yet I must not slacken my exertions so long as our friends in Upper Canada are in such straits for funds. Brother John has written me an urgent letter from Hallowell, in which he says :—I hope the Lord will give you good success in collecting for our Seminary. Everything depends on the success of your exertions. £4,000 is the least that will answer. O, how awfully we have got involved in this painful and protracted business! O, if you can help us out of this mire, the Lord reward you ! I am greatly at a loss what to do. I had concluded to leave, and go to the States; but thought I had better wait your return and take counsel with you. I hope the Lord may direct me !

Dublin, July 2nd.—I have just come over here to the Irish Conference, and was affectionately received by the Irish preachers. While in Dublin I stayed with a very intelligent and kind family. I attended the Irish Conference, which was held in Whitefriar's Street Chapel—a building rented for a preaching-place by the venerable Wesley himself. Here in the midst of the sallies of Irish wit and humour, mingled with evident piety and kindness, I sat down and wrote a letter to the dear friends in Canada.

From this letter I make an extract:—

The preachers are warm-hearted, pious men, some of them very clever; warm in their discussions, abounding in wit; talk much in doing their business; several are sometimes up at a time. They are certainly a body of excellent men. In their financial reports it appears that many of them are really examples of self-denial, suffering, and devotion.

The following are extracts from Dr. Ryerson's diary:—

July 26th.—Attended the Conference at Birmingham. When Dr. Fisk was introduced, the address of the American General Conference was read. Silence and attention were marked until the words "negro slavery" were mentioned, when there was a general cry of "hear, hear," and "no, no, no."

During the Conference a Mr. Robinson was called upon to explain his reason for preaching to a secret society called "Odd Fellows." Dr. Bunting and Dr. Newton had always refused to preach to such societies. Dr. Fisk made some remarks on Masonry in the United States, and the evil of the Methodist preachers being connected with, or countenancing, such societies.

Sept. 2nd.—Presented to Lord Glenelg the Address, to the King, of the Canadian Conference. He read it carefully, and expressed himself pleased with it. He enquired as to the charges against Sir Francis Head, and the appointment of those persons only to office who are truly attached to the British Constitution. I answered his lordship on each of these points mentioned, and assured him of the loyal British feelings of the inhabitants of Upper Canada. I pressed upon him the importance of an early settlement of the Clergy Reserve question. His lordship thanked me for the communications which I had from time to time made to him on Canadian affairs. He requested me to write to him on any matter, relative to the Canadas, I thought proper.

Sept. 4th—Sunday.—Attended the Hon. and Rev. Baptist Noel's Church at 8 a. m., when he administered the Lord's Supper to such as could not attend at any other hour. I communed for the first time in the Established Church. I heard this evangelical minister preach at 11 a.m. Preached myself in Spitalfields in the evening.

Sept. 6th.—Came here (Birmingham) from London on a collecting tour. Have been kindly received by my Quaker friends, the Sturges. In commemoration of the first Wesleyan Conference being held in Birmingham, gold medals were presented to Dr. Bunting and Dr. Newton, and silver medals to representatives of other Conferences—the Irish and American. My name as representative not having been received in time for a presentation at Conference, a medal was subsequently presented to me as Canadian representative, and to Rev. Richard Reece, ex-President, by the ladies of the Society in Birmingham. The addresses on the occasion were made by the President and Secretary—that to Mr. Reece in a few choice words by Dr. Bunting; and to me, in a kindly manner, by Dr. Newton. In reply I acknowledged the unexpected compliment, not as paid to me, but to the country and connexion which I represented.

Sept. 7th.—Have been kindly received by the preachers in Birmingham. Spent a pleasant evening at Mr. Oldham's (son-in-law of Rev. John Ryland), where I met no less than six clergymen of the Established Church; the conversation was wholly of a religious character, perfectly free and social. I was informed that all the clergymen in Birmingham, except one, were truly evangelical. Mr. Ryland told me that Rev. J. A. James had expressed his conviction that there is decidedly more piety amongst the mass of the Established Clergy than among the Dissenting Clergy. It was altogether the most unaffectedly genteel, and truly religious party I have met with in England.

Sept. 9th.—Busy and successful. Very kindly received by the following

Church of England ministers, viz., Rev. Mr. Mosely, Rector, Rev. Dr. Jeune [afterwards Master of Pembroke College], and Rev. William Marsh, who is frequently called the model of the Apostle John, on account of the depth and sweetness of his piety, the purity of his life, and the heavenly expression of his countenance. [His daughter is a noted evangelist and writer, 1883.]

Sept. 10th.—Took tea with Mr. Meredith, a Swedenborgian, upwards of 80, perfectly sincere in his belief, and sweet in his spirit. Also met the celebrated Dr Philip, of South Africa, and the more celebrated John Angel James, of Birmingham. The conversation of the evening was principally turned upon the means by which the great measure of emancipation was carried—the conduct of Mr. Stanley and Mr. Buxton. I was struck with Mr. Sturge's remark, that he "believed such men as Sir A. Agnew, Sir Harry Inglis, and Lord Ashley [now, in 1883, Lord Shaftesbury], were the most honest men in the House of Commons."

Sheffield, Sept. 17th.—Here I met with my old friends, Revs. Messrs. Marsden, Grindrod, and Moss.

Sept. 18th—Sunday.—Preached in Craven street Chapel in the morning, and at Brunswick Chapel in the evening.

Sept. 20th.—Attended the Financial District Meeting. It was stated that 900 persons had seceded in Sheffield in the Kilhamite schism, and yet the finances were better at the end of the quarter than they had been the preceding one. Kind references were made to myself, and the object of my mission.

Dr. Ryerson's Diary ends here. From his letters to Canada I make the following extracts:—

Sheffield, Oct. 5th.—I was in Barnsley on Friday and Saturday; went to Wakefield on Saturday, and preached there on Sunday. Addressed about 40 circulars to gentlemen in Wakefield on Monday morning. Returned to Sheffield and spoke at the Missionary Meeting; begged yesterday; spoke at the adjourned meeting last evening; have been begging to-day. Spent Friday and Saturday in Wakefield; go to Leeds on Saturday evening, and so on. The preachers and friends shew me all possible kindness and attention. The Yorkshire people are very warm-hearted and social. Methodism there presents an aspect different in several respects from that which it presents in London, or in any other part of England I have visited; more warm, energetic, and unaffected—something like Hallowell Methodism in Upper Canada. Oh! I long to get home to my circuit work. Amidst all the kindness and interest that it is possible for piety, intelligence, Yorkshire generosity and wit to impart, I feel like an exiled captive here in England.

Bradford, Oct. 10th.—The time I am here appears very dreary, as I am from morning until midnight in public labours or society of some kind. I have collected £83 last week, and for much of it I have begged very hard—though some think that I do not beg hard enough. It is, however, only one who has been a stranger and had to beg, that can fully appreciate the feelings and embarrassments of a stranger in such circumstances. This work and sacrifice have not been of my own seeking—but against my seeking. I was comfortably settled amongst kind friends in Kingston, but am now cast forth in this distant land, and engaged in the most disagreeable of all employments,—and for what? Oh! it is for the sake of Him to whose cause and glory I have consecrated my life and all. I shall love, honour, and value my pastoral labours more than ever. I hope that they may be more useful. During the past week I have been enabled more fully than for a year past to adopt the language of St. Paul. Gal. ii. 20.

Oct. 11th.—While here I was truly gratified to receive a letter from Miss Clarissa Izard, of Boulogne (France), in which she says:—I trust you will pardon me, sir, for this expression of my gratitude. If it had not been for a sermon preached by you on the 21st of February last, I might have been where hope never cometh; but, blessed be God, now I have a hope—a hope which lifts me above this world, and which, I trust, I shall retain until I obtain the crown of righteousness which fadeth not away.

Among the many pleasing incidents in Dr. Ryerson's otherwise unpleasant duty of collecting funds for the Upper Canada Academy, was the note written from Kensington Palace by command of Her Royal Highness the Duchess of Kent. It was as follows :—

I am commanded by the Duchess of Kent to acknowledge the receipt of your letter of the 22nd inst., and accompanying statement of "The Upper Canada Academy, for the education of Canadian youth, and the most promising youth of converted Indian tribes—to prepare them for schoolmasters." Her Royal Highness is most happy in patronizing, as you request, so useful and benevolent an Institution, and calculated especially to promote the best interests of the native population, the British emigrants, and the aboriginal tribes of that valuable and important British Province. Her Royal Highness desires that her name be placed on the subscription list for £10.

Referring to the great importance of the Upper Canada Academy, and to the services rendered by Dr. Ryerson in connection with its establishment, Rev. William Lord said :—

There have been many circumstances and occurrences connected with this institution which, to my mind, are indicative of Providential interference. The bitterness manifested against it by the enemies of Methodism and of the peace of the country; the difficulties which stood in the way of its completion; the distressing, overwhelming, and unforeseen embarrassments of its funds, which forced the Committee to send you to this country to seek relief, just at a time when the affairs of the Province had arrived at a crisis, and at a time when you could render special service, by communicating with the Home Government—service, allow me to say, greater than any other man could render, or than you could have rendered at any other time or place—the favourable turn which public affairs have recently taken, and, I know, in some degree through your instrumentality; the perplexing and most painful disappointments experienced in obtaining suitable teachers, now happily overcome; the share of public favour which the Academy has obtained on the commencement of its operations; and, lastly, the great services you have rendered the Missionary Society, in the advantage you have secured to our Indian Missionaries by your representations and applications to the Government, are to me reasons for believing God is in this business. You may, I think, take courage, and go on in the name of the Lord. I can sympathize with you; I have also suffered in this cause. I would not endure the anxiety and mental agony I have experienced on account of this institution for any earthly consideration. But if it flourish, I have my reward. And now the reflection that, at much personal risk, I have more than once saved innocent and deserving men from imprisonment, and Methodism from indelible reproach, is cheering and consoling. I will still stand by your side and share in your difficulties. My honour in this matter is united with yours, and the ruin of this institution will be mine.

In a letter from London, dated 21st July, 1836, Dr. Ryerson narrates the difficulties which he had encountered in obtaining a

Charter for the Upper Canada Academy. The correspondence with the Colonial Office embraced twenty-nine letters, and extended over a period of six months. In conducting it, Dr. Ryerson states :—I found those in the Colonial Office, and those who retired from it (during that time) equally favourable to the object of my mission, and equally desirous of promoting the best interests of the Colonies. In his report of the negotiations for the Charter, Dr. Ryerson says :—

The Attorney-General assured me that not only Lord Glenelg, but every member of His Majesty's Government was anxious to accede to my application—that the difficulties were purely legal—that though the doctrines and rules of the Methodist body in Canada were doubtless very sacred, yet they were unknown in law, (in England.) I, therefore, laid before the Crown officers* a copy of the statutes of Upper Canada (which I had borrowed from the Colonial office), and showed the grounds on which we professed to be invested with the clerical character by the statutes of the Province, as well as by the formularies of our connexion, and were recognized as ministers by the Courts of Quarter Sessions; that we might be defined as ministers (for the purposes of the Charter) as in the Marriage Statute of U.C., which would be the same thing as being defined according to the Rules of our Discipline. Placing the question before the Crown officers in this simple light, their scruples were at once removed, and they cordially acceded to my proposition to recognize our ministerial character. As I was required to name in the Charter the first trustees and visitors, and as I had no list of those who had been appointed by the Conference, I was obliged to furnish names myself. I was also required to name in the Charter the time and place of the next Annual Meeting (Conference) of Ministers. I inserted the second Wednesday of June as the time of meeting; Cobourg, or Toronto, as the place of meeting.

With the aid of a professional gentleman (whom I could only get for a small portion of each day) the draft of Charter was prepared after a delay of five weeks. This draft was approved, with the exception of the words: Wesleyan Methodist *Church*, for which the Solicitor-General had substituted the words: Wesleyan Methodist *Connexion*, as the designation of the Body on whose behalf a Charter was to be granted. In a letter to Sir George Grey I stated my reasons why the word *Church* should be retained, as the Wesleyan ministers, under whose superintendence the Academy is to be placed, had been licensed (under the Provincial Statute referred to in the Charter) as Ministers of the Wesleyan Methodist Church in Canada. To these reasons the Crown Officers yielded, and thus the Charter was completed.

I then renewed my application for receiving aid from the Casual and Territorial Revenue of Upper Canada. In reply, I was assured that the Lieutenant-Governor would be directed to bring the claims of the Academy before the notice of the Provincial Legislature.

Dr. Ryerson concludes :—

Thus terminated this protracted correspondence of more than six months, during the whole of which time I was enabled to cleave to and maintain my original purpose; though I had to encounter successive, discouraging, and almost insurmountable difficulties. Not having been able to effect any loan from private individuals, on account of the agitated state of the Canadas— being in suspense as to the result of my application to the Government, I

* Sir J. Campbell, afterwards Chief Justice, and Sir R. M. Rolfe, afterwards a Baron of the Exchequer.

was several months pressed down with anxiety and fear by this suspense, and by reason of the failure of my efforts to obtain relief. In this anxiety and fear my own unassisted resolution and fortitude could not sustain me. I had to rely upon the unfailing support of the Lord, my God.

In my negotiations for the Charter, I was uniformly treated with courtesy and kindness in the Colonial office, and by the several members of His Majesty's Government. Praise God!

In a letter written to Dr. Alder, after Dr. Ryerson had returned from England, the latter said:—

We have not yet received a farthing of the Government grant to our Academy. The Governor's reply still is, there is no money in the treasury; but he has given us his written promise, and offered his word to any of the banks, that it shall be paid out of the first money which had not been previously appropriated. But, strange to say, there is not a bank or banker in Upper Canada that will take the Governor's promise for £100. Mr. Receiver-General Dunn kindly lent, out of his own pocket, to my brother John, about £1,200 for the Academy, upon my brother's receipt, remarking at the same time that he did it upon his credit, and out of respect to the Methodists, but that he could place no dependence upon the word of Sir Francis in the matter. We are thus pressed to beg or borrow in relation to the Academy as much as ever, or even worse, for several of us are individually responsible for £2,200, besides Mr. Farmer's loan of £800. At our recent Academy Board Meeting, the damages of Mr. Lord's protested bills came under consideration. The circumstances of the case are briefly as follows:—Mr. Lord's sincere desire and zeal to promote the interests of the Institution and Connexion generally, were admitted and appreciated by all the brethren; but it appears, 1. That a large portion of the debts were incurred in compliance with the advice of Mr. Lord, and in consequence of his influence as the representative of the British Connexion. He assured the Sub-Committee at Cobourg that money should be forthcoming, and if necessary he would go to England and beg it, that John Bull never stopped when he commenced a thing, etc.; that Mr. Lord did that contrary to the recommendation of the Conference Committee, and against the advice and even remonstrance of the Chairman of the District (John Ryerson), who had been appointed by the Conference to see that the Sub-Committee should not exceed the appropriations of the Conference, as they had done in former years. 2. The premises were mortgaged to Mr. Lord as security for the sum of £2,500, some of which has not been advanced, and the payments of which he did advance were provided for (with the exception of two or three hundred pounds) by the brethren in this Province. 3. After Mr. Lord received information from the Committee in London that his bills would not be honoured, he called a meeting of the Board—stated his difficulties—got individuals to allow him to draw upon them to meet the bills on their return, and sent me to England. 4. Mr. Lord assured our Conference at Belleville, June, 1836, that the brethren here would never be called upon to pay a farthing of the damages for non-payment of his bills. I believe that no man could feel more earnestly desirous to promote the interests of the Canadian Connexion in every respect than he did. It is also the full conviction of our leading brethren that had I attended the American General Conference, instead of being in England, such an arrangement would have been made as to have secured to our Connexion what was due us from the New York Book Concern—which amounts to more than I obtained in England, besides the mortification and mental suffering which I experienced in my most unpleasant engagements, notwithstanding the sympathy and never-to-be-forgotten kindness of many of my fathers and brethren of the parent Connexion.

CHAPTER XVII.

1836.

PUBLICATION OF THE HUME AND ROEBUCK LETTERS.

IN a letter from London, dated 29th April, 1836, Dr. Ryerson said :—

This day week I went to the House of Commons to hear the debates on the motions relative to the Canadas, of which Messrs. Roebuck and Hume had given notice. As Mr. Roebuck was about to bring forward his motion, the House of 202 members thinned to 50 or 60 members. Under these circumstances he postponed it for a week, in the hope that a sufficient number of members would give him an opportunity to make a speech in return for the £1,100 a year paid to him as Agent of "the poor and oppressed Canadians." When Mr. Hume brought forward his motion there were only 43 members present. I thought how much Canada was benefitted by such men who could only command the attention of 50 out of the 658 members of the House of Commons! I know not a man more disliked and despised by all parties in the House than is Mr. Roebuck—a man who has been employed to establish (as he says in one of his letters to Mr. Papineau) a "pure democracy in the Canadas." One of the serious drawbacks to the credit and interests of our country, amongst public and business men of all parties in England, is their supposed connection with such a restless political cynic as Mr. Roebuck, and such an acknowledged and avowed colonial separationist as Mr. Hume.

In regard to these proceedings of Messrs. Hume and Roebuck, Dr. Ryerson writes, in this part of the Story of his Life, as follows :—

It was during the early part of 1836 that I was accosted by almost every gentleman to whom I was introduced in England with words, "You in Canada are going to separate from England, and set up a republic for yourselves!" I denied that there was any such feeling among the people of Canada, who desired certain reforms, and redress of grievances, but were as loyal as any people in England.

After the Canadian elections of 1836, Dr. Charles Duncombe

(afterwards leader of the rebels in the County of Oxford) came to England, the bearer of petitions got up by Mr. W. L. Mackenzie and his partizans, and crammed Mr. Hume to make a formidable assault upon the British Canadian Government. In presenting the Canadian petition Mr. Hume made an elaborate speech, full of exaggerations and mis-statements from beginning to end. I was requested to take a seat under the gallery, and, while Mr. Hume was speaking as the mouth-piece of Dr. C. Duncombe, I furnished Lord Sandon and Mr. W. E. Gladstone with the materials for answers to Mr. Hume's mis-statements. Mr. Gladstone's quick perception, with Lord Sandon's promptings, kept the House in a roar of laughter at Mr. Hume's expense for more than an hour; the wonder being how Mr. Gladstone was so thoroughly informed on Canadian affairs. No member of the House of Commons seemed to be more astonished and confounded than Mr. Hume himself. He made no reply, and, as far as I know, never after spoke on Canadian affairs; and Mr. Roebuck soon ceased to be Agent for the Lower Canada House of Assembly. He has since become an ultra Conservative!

In a letter from London, dated 1st June, Dr. Ryerson says:—
Before Dr. Duncombe arrived in England, and seeing how much injury was being done to the reputation and influence of Canada by these representations, I commenced a series of letters in the London *Times*, designed to expose the machinations and mis-statements of Messrs. Hume and Roebuck in England, in regard to matters in Upper Canada, showing from their own letters to Messrs. Papineau and Mackenzie that they were the first prompters of the project.* To-day I also addressed a letter to Sir George Grey, Under-Secretary for the Colonies, on the political crisis in that Province. After discussing several matters relating to the recent election of a new House of Assembly, I concluded as follows:—As the affairs of the Province will now be taken into consideration by His Majesty's Government, there are three subjects on which I would respectfully request an interview with Lord Glenelg, yourself, and Mr. [Sir James] Stephen. 1. The Clergy Reserve question —a plan to meet the circumstances of the Province, and yet not deprive the clergy of the Church of England of an adequate support. 2. The Legislative Council—how it may be rendered more influential and popular, without rendering it elective, or infringing (but rather strengthening) the prerogatives of the Crown. 3. The Executive—how its just authority, influence

* The British North American Association of Merchants had these letters reprinted from *The Times* newspaper, and a copy sent to each member of Parliament, both of the Lords and Commons. They were signed, "A Canadian."

and popularity may be promoted and established, so as to prevent the occurrence of that embarrassment in which it is now involved, not from improper acts, but from an actual deficiency of the requisite operative means to secure the Royal Prerogative from insult and invasion. I am aware that each of these subjects is surrounded with difficulty, and that no plan proposed will be entirely free from objection, but I should like to state the views which my acquaintance with the Province has impressed on my own mind, and which I have not seen suggested in any official document or public journal, but which have been favourably thought of by two or three respectable gentlemen connected with Canada, to whom I have stated them.

In reply, Lord Glenelg appointed the following Monday for the desired interview. I afterwards embodied the substance of my views in a letter to Sir George Grey.

No further reference is made to this interview by Dr. Ryerson. But in a letter from him, dated 21st July, he says:—

I was applied to, and did, in my individual capacity, communicate to the Colonial Secretary frequently, and in one or two instances at great length, on the posture of Canadian affairs; and the parties and principal questions which have divided and agitated the Canadian public. I repeatedly received the thanks of the Secretary of State for the Colonies, for the pains which I had taken in these matters; but what influence my communications may have had, or may have, on the policy of His Majesty's Government towards the Canadas is not for me to say, as I desired Lord Glenelg not to assume, *prima facie*, as correct, any of my representations, but to examine my authorities—to weigh my arguments—to hear what could be said by others—as I had no friends to recommend to office, and no personal interests to promote, only the religious and general peace and prosperity of the Canadas, and the maintenance of a firm and mutually beneficial connection between these Colonies and the parent State.

I think I have good reason to believe that much more correct and decided views are entertained by His Majesty's ministers and many public men in England, in respect to the interests and government of the Canadas, than were possessed by them six months ago; and that all of those inhabitants of the Colonies, who patriotically maintain their Christian and constitutional allegiance, will ensure the respect, equal and firm protection, and parental regard of their Sovereign and his government, by whatever party it may be administered.

In a letter from London, dated 26th July (page 154), Dr. Ryerson says:—Mr. William Lunn, of Montreal, has just arrived from Quebec. He informs me that—

My letters to the London *Times*, on Hume and Roebuck, have produced the most amazing effect upon the public mind of the Province, of anything that I ever wrote. To the Lord be all the praise for his great goodness, after all our toil and suffering. There is nothing like integrity of principle and faithfulness in duty, in humble dependence upon the Lord, and with an eye to His glory!

CHAPTER XVIII.

1836—1837.

IMPORTANT EVENTS TRANSPIRING IN UPPER CANADA.

DR. Ryerson was absent in England from 20th November, 1835, to 12th June, 1837. On the 15th of January, 1836, Sir John Colborne, by order in Council, endowed fifty-seven Rectories in Upper Canada out of the Clergy Reserve Lands. On the 23rd of that month Sir F. B. Head, the new Governor, arrived in Toronto. On the 14th of January following, he opened the Session of the Legislature. What followed was reported to Dr. Ryerson by his friend, Mr. S. S. Junkin, in a letter, dated, Toronto, 1st May:—

Our Parliament was prorogued on the 20th April, after such a session as was never before known in Upper Canada. You will form some idea of the state of affairs when I tell you that it "stopped the supplies," and the Governor reserved all of the money bills, (twelve)—including that for the contingences of the House,—for the King's pleasure.

The immediate cause of the rupture between the new Governor (Sir F. B. Head) and the House of Assembly—

Arose out of the resignation of the Executive Council. On the 20th February, the Governor (as directed by Lord Glenelg) added three Reformers to his Council, viz.: Messrs. Robert Baldwin, John Rolph, and John Henry Dunn. On the 4th March, these gentlemen and the Conservative members, (Messrs. Peter Robinson, George H. Markland, and Joseph Wells) resigned. They complained that they were held responsible for measures which they never advised, and for a policy to which they were strangers. In reply the Governor stated in substance that he alone was responsible for the acts of his government, and was at liberty to have resource to their advice only when he required it; but that to consult them on all questions would be "utterly impossible." This answer was referred to a Committee of the House of Assembly, which brought in a report censuring the Governor in the strongest terms. On the 14th March, Sir F. B. Head appointed Messrs. R. B. Sullivan, William Allan, Augustus Baldwin, and John Elmsley, as his new Executive Council. On the 17th the House declared its entire want of confidence in the new Council, and stated that in retaining them the Governor violated the instructions of the Colonial Secretary to the Governor, to appoint Councillors who possessed the confidence of the people. Much recrimination followed; at length Sir F. B. Head dissolved the House, and directed that a new election be held.

In regard to this election, Dr. Ryerson, in the "Epochs of Canadian Methodism" (page 226) says:—

Sir F. B. Head adroitly turned the issue, not on the question of the Clergy Reserves, or of other practical questions, but on the question of connection with the mother country, and of Republicanism vs. Monarchy, as had been recommended by Messrs. Hume and Roebuck, and advocated by Messrs. Mackenzie and Papineau. This was successful, inasmuch as those Reformers who would not disavow their connection with Messrs. Mackenzie, Hume and Roebuck, lost their election ; for though not more than half a dozen had any sympathy with the sentiments of Messrs. Hume, Roebuck, Papineau, and Mackenzie, they did not wish to break the unity of the Reform party by repudiating them, and suffered defeat in consequence at the elections. The successful candidates, generally, while they repudiated Republican separation from the mother country, promised fidelity to the oft-expressed and well-known wishes of the people in the settlement of the Clergy Reserve question, which, however, they failed to fulfil.

In a letter to Dr. Ryerson, from Hallowell, his brother William said :—

Our loyal address, a very moderate one, to the Governor, was carried unanimously—all the young Preachers on trial being allowed to vote on that occasion. This is equally gratifying and surprising to all the friends of British supremacy. A gentleman from Montreal, who was present, was so surprised, and I may say, delighted, that he could hardly contain himself. I did not know for a short time, but he would be constrained from the violence of his feeling to jump up and shout. The Conference also adopted a very good address to the King. (See page 162.)

We are on the eve of a new election. The excitement through the country at large exceeds anything I have ever known. There would be very little cause for doubt or fear as to the results, were it not for one of the last acts of Sir John Colborne's administration, in establishing and endowing nearly sixty Rectories. Knowing, as I do, that the public mind is strongly opposed to any measure of that sort, or any step towards legalizing a church establishment, yet I could not believe the feeling was so strong as it actually is. If the elections should turn out disastrously to the best interest of the country, the result can only be attributed to that unjust and most unpolitic act. We are willing to do all that we consistently can, but everywhere the rectory question meets us. While I am compelled to believe that a vast majority are devotedly loyal to our gracious Sovereign, yet the best and most affectionate subjects of the King would almost prefer revolution to the establishment of a dominant Church thus sought to be imposed on us.

In a letter to Dr. Ryerson, from Toronto, his brother John says :—

The late elections agitated the Societies very much in some places, but they are now settling down to "quietness and assurance." I hope that the worst of the storm is over. The Governor is a talented man, but very little magisterial dignity about him. He takes good care to let every one know that *he* esteems every day alike, travelling on Sabbaths the same as other days. Indeed he seems to have no idea of religion at all, but is purely a man of pleasure. His popularity will soon be upon the wane if he does not mend in these respects.

The friends in Kingston are very anxiously looking for your return, and are becoming quite discontented and out of patience. They complained bitterly to me of your long absence, and were anxious to have me stay with them until you return.

CHAPTER XIX.

1837–1839.

RETURN TO CANADA.—THE CHAPEL PROPERTY CASES.

IN this part of the "Story" of his life, Dr. Ryerson has only left the following sentence:—At the Conference held after my return to Canada, in June, I declined re-election as Editor of the *Christian Guardian*, having promised my Kingston brethren, from whom I had been suddenly removed in November, 1835, that I would remain with them at least one year on my return from England.

After Conference, Dr. Ryerson (with Rev. E. Healy) attended as a deputation to the Black River Conference. He said:—

> The Conference was presided over by Bishop Hedding, who, in strong and affecting language, expressed his feelings of respect and love for our Connexion in Canada. In reply, I reiterated the expression of our profound respect and affection for our honoured friend and father in the Gospel; by the imposition of whose hands, I, and several other brethren in Canada, have been set apart to the Holy Ministry. After my return to Kingston, brother Healy and I received from the Black River Conference a complimentary resolution in regard to our visit. In enclosing it to me, Rev. Jesse T. Peck, the Secretary [afterwards Bishop], said:—Allow me humbly, but earnestly, to beg a continuance of that friendship with you, which in its commencement has afforded me so much pleasure.

In August of this year, 1837, the celebrated trial of the Waterloo Chapel case* took place before Mr. Justice Macaulay, at the Kingston Assizes, and a verdict was given against the Wesleyan Methodists. It was subsequently appealed to the Court of King's Bench, at Toronto. Three elaborate judgments were delivered on the case. Rev. John Ryerson was a good deal exercised as to the ill effects, upon the connexional church property, of Judge Macaulay's adverse decision. In a letter to Dr. Ryerson, he said:—

> We are much troubled and perplexed, here in Toronto, about the Waterloo Chapel case. I saw the Attorney-General on the subject to-day. When Judge Macaulay's judgment is published, I hope you will carefully review the whole matter, and lay the thing before the public in such a way as to produce conviction. Everybody is inquiring whether or not you will take up the subject.

---

* Between the Episcopal and Wesleyan Methodists for the possession of the Church property. Waterloo was four miles north of Kingston.

An appeal was made to the King's Bench at Toronto. This Court—

Set aside the verdict of the lower Court, and ordered a new trial. . . At this second trial, as also that respecting the Belleville Church property case, [November, 1837], ... the whole matter was "ventilated," and the result was that the legal decision of the highest judicial tribunal of the land confirmed the Wesleyan Methodist Church as the rightful owner of the Church property, it being the true representative and successor of the original Methodist Episcopal Church in Canada. These litigations extended over more than two years, and the friends of Zion and of peace greatly rejoiced when they were brought to a just and final settlement. (Epochs of Canadian Methodism, pages 278, 279.)

In regard to these three judgments on the case, Dr. Ryerson said :—

During the latter part of this month I have devoted such time as I could spare to a lengthened review for the *Guardian*, of the elaborate judgments of Chief Justice Robinson, and Justices Macaulay and Sherwood, on the Waterloo Chapel case.* The opinion of the Chief Justice displays profound research, acute discrimination, and sound judgment. The opinion of Mr. Justice Macaulay indicates great labour and strict religious scrupulosity. The opinion of Mr. Justice Sherwood betrays great want of acquaintance with the discipline, usages, and general history of Methodism. To the Methodist Connexion the conflict of opinion and confusion of reasoning of these learned judges are most prejudicial and disastrous. I have therefore sought, in the "review," to set forth the true facts of this abstruse case—facts connected with the history of Methodism—facts, with the most material of which I am personally acquainted, and in the progress of which I have been called to act a conspicuous part.

In regard to this "review," Rev. E. Healy wrote to Dr. Ryerson, from Brockville, and said :—

I have read your review of the opinion of the judges, and am happy to see it. What the judges will do with you, I do not know. You are considered, I believe, by some in this part of the country, as part man and part demon. This is one reason, doubtless, why I am also so bad a man, as I have said so much in your favour.

Rev. Hannibal Mulkins,† writing from Whitby on this subject, said :—

The agitation which was anticipated by some of the preachers at the last Conference, and which has existed in some degree has happily subsided, notwithstanding the most vigorous efforts have been made, and all the arts of calumny and misrepresentation, employed to harrass, to worry, and devour.

I was very glad to see your "review" of the opinions of the Judges in the Chapel case. I have read it with much satisfaction. On this circuit, notwithstanding the prejudices of some individuals, it has been perused with general delight, and to our friends in particular it has been highly satisfactory.

* The Review is inserted in the *Guardian*, vol. viii., pages 169-178. The Belleville case was published in pamphlet form.
† This gentleman entered the Wesleyan ministry in 1835, but joined the Church of England in 1840. He was for many years Chaplain to the Penitentiary, at Kingston, and always retained a warm regard for Dr. Ryerson. He died in 1877, aged 65 years.

Dr. Ryerson, in a letter from New York, dated November, 1837, says :—

I have just returned from an extended tour of about 500 miles in the Middle and Southern States, in order to obtain information and evidence relative to the organization of the Methodist Church in America, the character of its Episcopacy, and the powers of the General Conference—points which involve the issue of our chapel property case. From the mass of testimony and information I have been able to collect, by seeing every preacher in this continent who was in the work in 1784, relative to the character of Methodist Episcopacy, and the powers of the General Conference, I feel no doubt as to the result.‡

Rev. Joseph Stinson, in making his report on the same subject, said :—

I spent a whole day with Bishop Hedding, and had much conversation with him about our affairs generally. He told me that the American Methodist Church had never regarded Episcopacy as a Divine ordinance—nor as an essential doctrine of the Church—but as an expedient form of ecclesiastical government, which could be modified by the General Conference, or even dispensed with without violating the great principles of Methodism. The Bishop is of the opinion, however, that if our Courts decide against us, we shall have to return to Episcopacy, and that the first Bishop should be ordained by the Bishops of the American Church.

Dr. Ryerson, in the same November letter, says :—

I have also accompanied Mr. Stinson to render him what assistance I could, in examining Manual Labour Schools, with a view to establishing one for the benefit of our Indian youth—an object of the very greatest importance, both to the religious and civil interests of our aboriginal fellow countrymen. Also to get from the New York Missionary Board a sum of money for the Indian work which was expected from them before our Union with the English Conference.

In a letter to Dr. Alder, written from New York in the same month, Dr. Ryerson said :—

The concern of our preachers and friends on the Chapel case is deep and truly affecting. As I took so responsible a part in the Union, I cannot describe my feelings on this question. At the request of our brethren I have undertaken to do what I could to secure our Church property from the party claiming it. I have travelled nearly 500 miles this week for that purpose. But it is cheering amidst all our difficulties, and the commotions of the political elements, that our preachers, I believe, without exception, are of one heart—that our societies are in peace—that the work of our blessed Lord is reviving in many of the circuits, although the cause in Kingston suffers, and my dear brethren there complain, in consequence of my connexional engagements and absence from them.

‡ The particulars here referred to are given in detail in the "Epochs of Canadian Methodism," pages 279-281.

CHAPTER XX.

1837.

THE COMING CRISIS.—REBELLION OF 1837.

AS Dr. Ryerson had anticipated, the combined effects of the publication of his "impressions," in 1833; his letters exposing the designs of Messrs. Hume, Roebuck, and Mackenzie in 1837; the secession of a section of the Methodist Church, and the disputes consequent thereon (culminating in the Waterloo and Belleville Chapel suits)—in which he took a leading part—provoked the parties concerned to active hostility against him. He had, however, many warm friends, especially among his ministerial brethren. One of these was Rev. John Black, in the Bay of Quinte District,—a quaint, but true and warm-hearted man. In inviting him to take part in the Quarterly Meeting services, at Napanee, Mr. Black indulges in a little playful satire, as follows:—

It appears that there are some amongst us here whom we dare not number amongst your friends, and who prophesied that you would never return from England—that you dare not, etc. Now we wish to afford them living proof of their vanity in prophesying, by your presence amongst them. Besides, on the other hand, the good-hearted brethren amongst us greatly rejoiced on hearing of your successful mission to England, and they wish to see and hear you once more.

Somewhat in Rev. John Black's spirit of kindly raillery, Rev. John C. Davidson, of Hallowell, in inviting Dr. Ryerson to take part in a Camp-meeting (and after mentioning several inducements), said:—

I would mention another inducement for you to come, viz.: the multiplicity of warm friends and virulent enemies you have on this circuit. Your presence and preaching will afford pleasure and profit to your friends, and will very much tend, in my opinion, to disarm the groundless prejudice entertained by many others against you.

In a more serious letter to Dr. Ryerson, dated Cobourg, 16th November, 1837, Rev. Anson Green gives expression to a general feeling of uneasiness and distrust which prevailed everywhere in the country at that time:—

I pity you most sincerely. You have a storm about your ears that you must bear, if you do not bow before it. In these perilous times a man scarcely knows what to advise. I fear that destruction awaits us on either hand. With the Radicals we are Tories ; and with the Tories we are Rebels. It is said by the Rebels here that they have money enough, and men enough, and guns enough, and that the plans are so laid that there can be no mistake. The Government appears to be in possession of these facts. Thus far the proceedings of the Rebels do not show much wisdom, or skill, in laying plans, or in executing them. I am mistaken if they stop short of a civil war.

I very much regret that you should be under the necessity of coming in contact with Governor Head in any one thing. I could not be a rebel ; my conscience and religion forbid it ; and, on the other hand, I could not fight for the Rectories and Church domination. I think them both to be great evils, and I have resolved to choose neither. I believe that in Haldimand and Cramahe townships there are twenty rebels to one sincere loyalist. Brother Wilson, (son of old Father Wilson), says that his life has been threatened for circulating the petition which you sent down, and others are in a similar condition. What will be the effect of all this I cannot say, but I have thought from the beginning that either the Rectories must be abolished, and a suitable disposition made of the Reserves, or a change of Government will ensue. And if the Church party have it all in their own hands to make peace, by allowing other Churches to enjoy equal privileges with themselves, and do not do so, they must bear the responsibility of all the bloodshed and carnage that may ensue. I fear that they are so perfectly infatuated that they will suffer utter destruction, and choose it rather than equal and impartial justice.

On the 5th December, 1837, Dr. Ryerson reached Cobourg on his way to Toronto. When he arrived there, Elders Case and Green, and other friends, thought that as his life had been threatened it would be unsafe for him to proceed to Toronto.* He, therefore, waited there for further news, and, in the meantime, wrote to a friend in Kingston, on the 6th, as follows :—

You will recollect my mentioning that I pressed upon Sir Francis the propriety and importance of making some prudent provision for the defence of the city, in case any party should be urged on in the madness of rebellion so far as to attack it. He is much blamed here on account of his overweening confidence, and foolish and culpable negligence in this respect. There was great excitement in this town and neighbourhood last night. To-day all is anxiety and hurry. The militia is called out to put down the rebellion of the very man whose seditious paper many of them have supported, and whom they have countenanced.

The precepts of the Bible and the example of the early Christians, leave me no occasion for second thoughts as to my duty, namely, to pray for and support the "powers that be," whether I admire them or not, and to implore the defeat of "fiery conspiracy and rebellion." And I doubt not that the sequel will in this, as in other cases, show that the path of

* Dr. Ryerson in his "Epochs of Canadian Methodism," page 314, says :—It had been agreed by W. L. Mackenzie and his fellow rebels, in 1837, to hang Egerton Ryerson on the first tree they met with, could they apprehend him.

duty is that of wisdom, if not of safety. I am aware that my head would be regarded as something of a prize by the rebels; but I feel not in the least degree agitated. I trust implicitly in that God whom I have endeavoured—though imperfectly and unfaithfully—to serve; being assured nothing will harm us, but that all things, whether life or death, will work together for our good if we be followers of that which is good. Let us trust in the Lord, and do good, and He will never leave nor forsake us!

About 700 armed men have left this district to-day for Toronto, in order to put down the rebels. There is an unanimity and determination among the people to quash rebellion and support the law that I hardly expected. The country is safe, but it is a "gone day with the rebel party."

In a graphic letter to Dr. Ryerson, written on the 5th December, by his brother William, at Toronto, the scenes at the *emeute* in that city are thus described:—

Last night, about 12 or 1 o'clock, the bells rang with great violence; we all thought it was an alarm of fire, but being unable to see any light, we thought it was a false alarm, and we remained quiet until this morning, when, on visiting the market-place, I found a large number of persons serving out arms to others as fast as they possibly could. Among many others we saw the Lieutenant-Governor, in his every-day suit, with one double-barrelled gun in his hand, another leaning against his breast, and a brace of pistols in his leather belt. Also, Chief Justice Robinson, Judges Macaulay, Jones, and McLean, the Attorney-General, and Solicitor-General, with their muskets, cartridge boxes and bayonets, all standing in the ranks as private soldiers, under the command of Colonel Fitzgibbon. I assure you it is impossible for me to describe my feelings. I enquired of Judge McLean, who informed me that an express had arrived at the Government House late last night, giving intelligence that the Radicals had assembled in great force at Montgomery's, on Yonge Street, and were in full march for the city; that the Governor had sent out two persons, Mr. A. McDonell and Ald. J. Powell, to obtain information (both of whom had been made prisoners, but escaped).

Dr. Horne's house is now in flames. I feel very calm and composed in my own mind. Brother John thinks it will not be wise for you to come through all the way from Kingston. You would not be safe in visiting this wretched part of the country at the present. You know the feelings that are entertained against you. Your life would doubtless be industriously sought. My dear brother, farewell. May God mercifully bless and keep you from all the difficulties and dangers we are in!

Rev. William Ryerson further writes, on the 8th December:

About 10 o'clock to-day about 2,000 men, headed by the Lieut.-Governor, with Judge Jones, the Attorney-General and Capt. Halkett, as his aides-de-camp, and commanded by Cols. Fitzgibbon and Allan N. Macnab, Speaker of the House, left the city to attack the rebels at Montgomery's. After a little skirmishing in which we had three men wounded but none killed, the main body commenced a very spirited attack on their head-quarters at Montgomery's large house. After a few shots from two six-pounders, and a few volleys of musketry, the most of the party fled and made their escape. The rest of them were taken prisoners. There were also three or four killed and several wounded. After which His Excellency ordered the buildings to be burnt to the ground, and the whole force returned to the city. All the leaders succeeded in making their escape. A royal proclamation has just been issued offering £1,000 for the apprehension of Mackenzie, and £500 for that of Samuel Lount, David Gibson, Silas Fletcher, and Jesse Lloyd; so that now, through the mercy of God, we have peace, and feel safe again, for which we desire to feel sincerely thankful.

Dr. Ryerson, having reached Toronto safely, and knowing how anxious his parents would be to know something definite as to the state of affairs, wrote a letter to his Father on the 18th December, as follows:—

I have been trying to get time to make you and Mother a visit of at least one night; but I find it quite out of my power to secure the enjoyment of so precious a privilege.

It is remarkable that every man, with very few exceptions, who has left our Church and joined in the unprincipled crusade which has been made against us, has either been an active promoter of this plot, or so far connected with it as to be ruined in his character and prospects by the timely discovery and defeat of it! I have been deeply affected at hearing of some unhappy examples, among old acquaintances, of this description. I feel thankful that I have been enabled to do my duty from the beginning in this matter. Four years ago, I perceived and began to warn the public of the revolutionary tendency and spirit of Mackenzie's proceedings. Perhaps you may recollect that in a long article in the *Guardian*, four years ago this winter, headed "Revolutionary Symptoms," I pointed out, to the great displeasure of even some of my friends, what has come to pass.

It is also a matter of thankfulness that every one of our family and marriage connections, near and remote, is on the side of law, reason, and religion in this affair. Such indications of the Divine goodness are a fresh encouragement to me to renew my covenant engagement with my gracious Redeemer, to serve Him and His cause with greater zeal and faithfulness.

I hope, my dear Father, you are employing your last days in preparing for your approaching change, and for standing before the bar of God. My poor prayers are daily offered up in your behalf. Much travelling and other engagements have hitherto prevented me from writing to you as I would; but, hereafter, the first Monday in each month shall be considered as belonging to my dear aged Parents, in praying for or writing to them. My dutiful respects and love to my dear Mother. I would esteem it a great favour and privilege to receive a few lines from you or her.

CHAPTER XXI.

1837–1838.

SIR F. B. HEAD AND THE UPPER CANADA ACADEMY.

LORD Glenelg, as agreed, when Dr. Ryerson was in England, (page 165,) directed Lieutenant-Governor Sir F. B. Head to bring the pecuniary claims of the Upper Canada Academy before the Legislature. This he did in February, 1837. A committee (of which Hon. W. H. Draper was chairman)* brought in an excellent report on the subject. The House of Assembly by a vote of 31 to 10 agreed to advance $16,400 to the Academy. The Legislative Council, on motion of Hon. J. Elmsley, made such onerous conditions as virtually defeated the bill, and no relief was granted. † Dr. Ryerson, then in England, pressed the matter most urgently upon Lord Glenelg, who in April 1837, sent directions to Sir F. B. Head to advance the money without delay. This, on various pretexts, he refused to do; but when the Legislature opened in January, 1838, he sent a message to the House, which Dr. Ryerson, then in Toronto, thus describes, in a letter to a friend at Kingston, dated February 3rd, 1838. He said:—

* At the Conference of this year resolutions of thanks were passed to Mr. Draper, and were sent to him by Dr. Ryerson, the Secretary. Mr. Draper's reply was as follows:—
I feel deeply indebted to the Conference of the Wesleyan Methodist Church for the honour conferred upon me in deeming my humble exertions in the cause of Christian education worthy of their approbation, and I trust I shall never forget their good opinion. I cannot, at the same time, pass by the opportunity of thanking you for the terms in which you have communicated that resolution to me, and of expressing my satisfaction that I have in any degree contributed to the success of your unwearied exertions in behalf of the Upper Canada Academy in England. I sincerely rejoice that you were enabled to obtain that aid for its completion, which was so necessary and so well deserved.

† In a letter to Dr. Ryerson, his brother William thus accounts for the failure to get the grant: To the miserable Missionary grant of £900 to the English Conference we are chiefly indebted for the loss of the Bill for the relief of the Upper Canada Academy, as we are positively informed by our best friends in the House of Assembly. It has also been the means of depriving many of the preachers of a considerable part of their small salary, and in one or two instances, of the whole of it. It has, and still does more to weaken our hands, and to embarrass our labours, and also to strengthen the hands and to increase the number of our enemies, than almost any or all other causes put together.

Instead of giving us the promised money for the Upper Canada Academy, Sir Francis Head has sent a part of the correspondence with Lord Glenelg and with me down to the House of Assembly, with a message in which he implicates me, as also a letter to Lord Glenelg, written a few weeks after my return from England, in which he impeaches me. I have, in consequence, drawn up a petition to the House, filling six large sheets, exposing the whole of his conduct towards us, vindicating myself from the charges contained in his despatches, and proposing to establish every fact which I have stated before a select Committee of the House of Assembly. My petition was presented this morning. According to rule, a petition has to lie on the table for twenty-four hours before it is read. But a motion was made and agreed to, to dispense with the rule, and read my petition. It was then read, and created a great sensation. It was then moved that 200 copies of it be printed, together with all the documents sent down by the Governor, to which the petition referred. After discussion the motion was carried by a vote of 33 to 4. This was, of course, very gratifying to my feelings, as it must be extremely mortifying to the Governor. This is the first petition that has been ordered to be printed by the present—Sir Francis' own—Parliament. The dispensing with the rule, and giving such a petition the preference, was the highest mark of respect which the House could have shown me. I have not felt so much agitated with anything for years, as with this matter. I am now greatly relieved. I feel as if the Lord God of Hosts was on our side. The Governor clearly thought that as he was so greatly lauded and had become so famous a conqueror, we would not dare to come out against him before the public, or meet him face to face before the Assembly.

On the 16th, Dr. Ryerson again writes to Kingston:—

This Academy business is a most painful one to me. The Legislative Council and the House of Assembly have each appointed a select Committee on the subject. But I am afraid we will get nothing until we hear from Lord Glenelg.

My mind has been, and is, in a great degree depressed beyond expression, in regard to our circumstances. My only trust is in Him who has thus far brought us through, and turned the designs of our enemies to our account. For the last two days I have been as low as I was at my lowest in London.

In addition to Dr. Ryerson's petition to both Houses, he made a separate Appeal to members of the Assembly. In it he stated in substance that Sir Francis Head—

Had already issued his warrant for $8,200; that he was informed in December, 1837, not merely verbally, but in writing, by Hon. J. H Dunn, Receiver-General, that he had funds with which to pay the balance ($8,200), yet the Governor refused to issue the requisite warrant for it, on the plea of much business; but said that Mr. Dunn had all the warrant that was necessary. In January he again declined to issue the warrant, and excused himself by saying that Mr. Dunn required no further authority. When, later in the month, Dr. Ryerson had not only removed every variety of objection and excuse, but sent a note from Mr. Dunn saying that he had the necessary funds, Sir F. B. Head stated that he "must see one or two of his councillors." After he had done so, he wrote a note to Dr. Ryerson to say that he had misled him, as to the advance being a grant instead of a loan, etc.

On 21st February, the House of Assembly recommended that the balance be paid over at once. It pointed out that Dr. Ryerson had become personally liable to the banks for $3,400, and Revs. John Ryerson and E. Evans for $2,000 of the balance due; that although grants were constantly being made by the House, yet there was no precedent for a loan; and that as to whether the advance was to be a grant or a loan they would abstain from offering an opinion. This report had the desired effect. The money was paid.

On the 22nd February, Dr. Ryerson was, therefore, enabled to write to his friend in Kingston, to say that

The prayer of my petition has been this day complied with by a unanimous vote of the House of Assembly; and the Hon. Mr. Draper told Brother Evans that His Excellency would issue his warrant for the money as soon as the Address of the Assembly is presented. Not a man in the Assembly would risk his reputation in defence of the conduct of the Governor in this affair. The Report of the Committee was received, and the Address passed two readings last night and one this morning, and without one word from any member of the Assembly in the way of comment or remark. The Committee of the Legislative Council has actually declined entering into the investigation of the subject at all, as had been desired by His Excellency. Thus has Sir Francis Head not only disgraced himself, but helped us.

I thank the Lord for His blessing thus far. We will still trust in Him, and not be afraid. Tories, Radicals, and the Governor, have each had their turn at us. I hope we may now be allowed to live in peace. The result of this affair has in some measure compensated me for the anxiety of mind I have endured.

After this unpleasant controversy with Sir F. B. Head was over, Rev. Anson Green wrote to Dr. Ryerson as follows:—

How do you feel after your brush with Sir Francis? You need not feel very downcast, having attained so triumphant a victory. I doubt not but Sir Francis would willingly pay double the amount claimed by us, if he could have prevented the result which has happened. It is too late, however, to recall it now. I hope he will learn wisdom from the past, and not be so self-willed and headstrong in future. No one seems pleased with him but those whose praise is a reproach.

Rev. W. H. Harvard, in a letter from Kingston, said:—

I am truly pained at the conduct of the Lieutenant-Governor, and sympathize with you in thus being brought into such an unavoidable collision with him. I am more than grieved that he should use us so ungenerously.

I am glad that you are the warrior, for you will combine caution and courage, and will come off more than conqueror. You are at present the centre of our solicitude. I pray that your heart may be comforted and controlled from above. We are the Lord's covenanted, consecrated servants. In His work we are employed. By His Holy Spirit may we ever be actuated and aided!

CHAPTER XXII.

1838.

VICTIMS OF THE REBELLION.—STATE OF THE COUNTRY.

EARLY in 1838 the trials for treason took place. Messrs. Lount and Matthews were found guilty and sentenced to death. Other parties were also tried: among them was Dr. Thomas D. Morrison, a prominent Methodist in Toronto.* In a letter to Dr. Ryerson, at Kingston, his brother John mentions that Dr. Morrison was triumphantly acquitted. He also mentions (as an amusing incident at the trial) the success of the two counsel for Dr. Morrison, in showing that statements entirely contradictory to each other could be fully proved from Sir F. B. Head's own speeches and dispatches. He said:—

Mr. Macdonald, of St. Catharines, stated that Sir Francis had declared in his speech at the opening of the Parliament, that he knew of the rebellion long before it occurred, and that he was the cause of it. Mr. Boswell, of Cobourg, admitted that Sir Francis had said he knew a good deal. But the Governor was very fond of a fine style; he liked rounded periods, or, as Lord Melbourne had expressed it, "epigrammic" flights, so well, that he could hardly make his pen write the words of truth and soberness on such occasions. Mr. Boswell read several extracts from Sir Francis' despatches to Lord Glenelg, which were in direct opposition to the extracts read by Mr. Macdonald. A gentleman whispered to me that anything (no matter what) could be proved from Sir Francis' writings and sayings! In reply to the Attorney-General, Mr. Macdonald said:—That if the suspicion of treasonable motives and doings in others, and not informing or using prompt measures to correct or prevent what might follow, was treason, then Sir Francis was the greatest traitor in the country, for he said he knew all about the proposed outbreak. Mr. Boswell said, that after Sir Francis had seen the "Declaration," and had taken the advice of the Attorney-General, he had sent a despatch to the Colonial Secretary declaring that there was nothing treasonable in the country; that everything was as it should be! To

---

* Dr. Morrison had been a clerk in the Surveyor-General's office,—had, indeed, while there, collected materials for Dr. Strachan's Ecclesiastical Chart,—but, without any charge, or the slightest deficiency in faithfulness and efficiency, was dismissed, for the simple reason that he had become a Methodist! He then devoted himself to the medical profession. He was once elected to the House of Assembly for York, defeating the Attorney-General. He was also once elected Mayor of Toronto. He was the writer's [and the editor's] physician during life; died in great peace, strong in faith, giving glory to God.—"Epochs of Canadian Methodism," pages 188, 189.—H.

demonstrate this, he had sent away all the troops. Thus, you see, the two lawyers made poor Sir Francis prove everything.

The jury returned with a verdict of "not guilty," which caused great cheering, and which could not be suppressed for some time. Several of the jury were warm Tories, but they acquitted the Doctor.

In another letter to Dr. Ryerson, his brother John gives an account of the efforts made to induce Sir George Arthur, the new Governor, to commute the sentence of Lount and Mathews. He says :—

I have signed a petition for the mitigation of Lount and Mathews' punishment, as did Brother William. I have just seen Rev. James Richardson, who has been with Lount and Mathews. Mathews professed to have found peace. Lount is earnestly seeking. A good deal of feeling has been excited respecting the execution of these unfortunate men. A petition signed by 4,000 persons in their behalf was presented to His Excellency. It was agreed that Rev. Mr. Brough (Church of England minister from Newmarket) and I should go and present the Toronto petition, and that we should seek a private interview with him. Instead of having a private interview, we were called into the Council Chamber in the presence of the Executive Council. This was rather embarrassing to me, as I did not wish to say what I had intended to say in the presence of Sir Francis' old Executive Council. After presenting the petition, Mr. Brough introduced the conversation and referred Sir George to me. I told him that I was extensively acquainted with the country,—that I had travelled lately through the Niagara, Gore, Home, Newcastle, Prince Edward, and part of the Midland Districts,—had conversed with a great many persons, many of whom, even persons of high respectability, and were strongly attached to the interests of His Majesty's Government, and the pervading feeling was that the severe penalty of the law should not be executed on those victims of deception and sin. I also read an extract of your last letter to His Excellency [p. 188]—relating to the inexpediency of inflicting severe punishment "in opposition to public sentiment and policy, for political offences," etc. After having listened to me very attentively, His Excellency said, that after the fullest consultation with his Executive, and the most serious and prayerful consideration of this painful matter, he had come to the conclusion that Lount and Mathews must be executed.

I also mentioned to the Governor that you and Rev. J. Stinson had waited on Sir Francis about four weeks previous to the insurrection,—that you informed him of insurrectionary movements about Lloydtown and other places, which you had learned from me,—that you had strongly urged Sir Francis to raise volunteers, and put the city and other places in a state of defence,—that you and I had waited on the Attorney-General next day, and that we had urged these things on him in a similar manner;—but that these statements and advice had been disregarded, if not disbelieved.

In a subsequent letter he thus related the closing scene :—

At eight o'clock to-day, Thursday, 12th April, Lount and Mathews were executed. The general feeling is in total opposition to the execution of those men. Sheriff Jarvis burst into tears when he entered the room to prepare them for execution. They said to him very calmly, "Mr. Jarvis, do your duty; we are prepared to meet death and our Judge." They then, both of them, put their arms around his neck and kissed him. They were then prepared for execution. They walked to the gallows with entire composure and firmness of step. Rev. J. Richardson walked alongside of Lount, and Rev. J.

Beatty alongside of Mathews. They ascended the scaffold and knelt down on the drop. The ropes were adjusted while they were on their knees. Mr. Richardson engaged in prayer; and when he came to that part of the Lord's Prayer, "Forgive us our trespasses, as we forgive those that trespass against us," the drop fell!

In a letter written to Dr. Ryerson the next day, his brother John mentioned a sad incident connected with Lount's trial:

> Lount's daughter, a young woman, was present when her father was condemned. It had such an effect on her, that she went home and died almost immediately afterwards. These are indeed melancholy times! .

The evil effects upon the country of the arbitrary conduct of Sir F. B. Head, are thus described in a letter to Dr. Ryerson from his brother William, dated Toronto, 22nd April:—

> The very painful excitement caused by the execution of Lount and Matthews has in some degree subsided, but dissatisfaction with the state of things is, I fear, increasing from day to day. Emigration to the States is the fear of the hour. It is indeed going on to an extent truly alarming and astonishing. A deputation has been sent from this city to Washington to negotiate with the American Government for a tract of land on which to form a settlement or colony. They have returned, and say that they met with a most gracious reception, encouragement and success beyond their most sanguine expectations. An emigration society has been formed, embracing some of the leading citizens. Its object is to commence a colony in the Iowa Terrritory, on the Mississippi River.* A very large class are becoming uneasy, and many of the best inhabitants of the country, as to industry and enterprise, are preparing to leave. My own spirit is almost broken down. I feel, I assure you, like leaving Canada too, and I am not alone in those feelings; some of our friends whom you would not suspect, often feel quite as much down in the throat as I do. If ever I felt the need of faith, and wisdom, and patience, it is at the present. I have just returned from visiting the prisoners. After all, we know but little of the calamities and miseries with which our once happy land is now afflicted, and yet Sir Francis, the most guilty author of this misery, escapes without punishment; yes, with honour and praise! How mysterious are the ways of Providence —how dark, crooked, and perverse the ways of man.

---

* This disposition to remove from Upper Canada to Iowa was not confined to Toronto and its vicinity. In the following chapter the case of a Mr. John Campbell, M.P.P. for Frontenac county, is mentioned. He was on his way to Iowa when he saw and read Dr. Ryerson's defence of Mr. Bidwell. The reading of that defence changed his plans, and he remained in Canada. (See page 192.)

CHAPTER XXIII.

1795 1861.

Sketch of Mr. William Lyon Mackenzie.

THE story of Dr. Ryerson's life would scarcely be complete without giving some information in regard to the chief opponents whom he encountered in the earlier part of his career—men well known at the time, but whose names and memories are now passing away.

With the exception of Bishop Strachan, no man came so immediately in contact with Dr. Ryerson in the first years of his public life as did Mr. W. L. Mackenzie.

Mr. Mackenzie was born in Scotland, in March, 1795. He died in Toronto, on the 28th August, 1861, in the 67th year of his age. He came to Canada in 1820, and until 1824 was engaged in mercantile pursuits. In May of that year he entered public life, and commenced the publication of the *Colonial Advocate* at Queenston. From that time until near the close of his life, he maintained his connection, more or less, with the press; but he was always on the stormy sea of politics, even when not a journalist. The reasons which induced him to enter public life are thus given in Mr. Charles Lindsey's "Life and Times of Mackenzie," page 40. They are in Mr. Mackenzie's own words, and were written some time after the rebellion of 1837-8 :—

I had long seen the country in the hands of a few shrewd, crafty, covetous men, under whose management one of the most lovely, desirable sections of America remained a comparative desert. The most obvious public improvements were stayed; dissension was created among classes; citizens were banished and imprisoned [Gourley, Beardsley, etc.] in defiance of all law; the people had been forbidden, under severe pains and penalties, from meeting anywhere to petition for justice; large estates were wrested from their owners in utter contempt of even the forms of the courts; the Church of England, the adherents of which were few, monopolized as much of the lands of the Colony as all the religious houses and dignitaries of the Roman Catholic Church had had the control of in Scotland at the era of the Reformation. Other sects were treated with contempt, and scarcely tolerated; a sordid band of land-jobbers grasped the soil as their patrimony, and with a few leading officials, who divided the public revenue among themselves, formed "the family compact," and were the avowed enemies of common schools, of civil and religious liberty, of all legislative or other checks to their own will. Other men had opposed and been converted by them. At nine-and-twenty I might have united with them, but chose rather to join the oppressed; nor have I ever regretted that choice, or wavered from the object of my early pursuit. So far as I, or any other professed reformer, was concerned in inviting citizens of [the United States] to interfere in Canadian affairs, there was culpable error. So far as any of us, at any time, may have supposed that the cause of freedom would be advanced by adding the Canadas to [that] confederation, we were under the merest delusion. Mr. Lindsey adds:—In some respects the condition of the Province was worse than Mr. Mackenzie described it. He dealt only with its political condition.

With a Scotchman's idea of justice and freedom, he felt a longing desire to right the wrongs which he saw everywhere around him. This, therefore, constituted, as he believed, his mission as a public man in Canada, and it furnishes the key to his life and character.

Mr. Mackenzie was a political pessimist. He looked upon every abuse which he attacked, with a somewhat severe, if not a jaundiced, eye. Every evil which he discovered was, in his estimation, truly an evil; and all evils were about of equal magnitude. Besides, in attacking an evil or an abuse, he did not fail to attack the perpetrator or upholder of it also, and that, too, with a strength of invective, or of cutting sarcasm, which brought every foible, and weakness of his, and even those of his father before him, vividly into view. This was the baleful secret of his strength as an assailant; but this, too, caused him to be regarded by his victims with intense dislike, bordering on hatred. This style of attack, on the part of Mr. Mackenzie, did not necessarily arise from anything like vindictiveness, but rather from a keen sense of dislike to what he conceived to be wrong in the thing he was attacking.

In 1849 (12 years after the rebellion), Mr. Mackenzie, in a letter to Earl Grey, used the following remarkable language:—

A course of careful observation during the last eleven years has fully satisfied me that, had the violent movements in which I and many others were engaged on both sides of the Niagara proved successful, that success would have deeply injured the people of Canada, whom I then believed I was serving at great risks. . . I have long been sensible of the errors committed during that period. . . No punishment that power could inflict or nature sustain, would have equalled the regrets I have felt on account of much that I did, said, wrote, and published; but the past cannot be recalled. . . There is not a living man on the continent who more sincerely desires that British Government in Canada may long continue, etc. Page 291, 292.

No man was more unselfish than Mr. Mackenzie. He would rather suffer extreme hardship than accept a doubtful favour. Even in regard to kindly and reasonable offers of help, he was morbidly sensitive (as mentioned on page 298 of his "Life and Times"); and yet, looking at the conduct of many men in like circumstances, he deserved commendation rather than censure for his extreme conscientiousness.

Mr. Mackenzie did the State good service in many things. His investigations into the affairs of the Welland Canal were highly valuable to the country, greatly aided as he was by Mr. (now, Sir) Francis Hincks as chief accountant. His inquiries in regard to the Post Office and Prison management were also useful. Besides, he advocated many important reforms which were afterwards carried out. Mr. Mackenzie was the first Mayor of Toronto.

Towards the close of his life he and Dr. Ryerson were not on unfriendly terms; and when in 1852, as a member of the Legislature he instituted an inquiry into the management of the Educational Depository, he expressed himself satisfied with its usefulness.* At a later period when Mr. John C. Geikie†—then a bookseller in Toronto—commenced his attack upon the Depository in 1858, Mr. Mackenzie thus rebuked him in his *Weekly Message* of April 9th, of that year:—

At one time we thought with the redoubtable Geikie that Dr. Ryerson's book concern was a monopoly, but a more thorough inquiry induced us to change that opinion. We found that great benefits were obtained for the townships, the country schools, and general education through Dr. Ryerson's plan which could in no other way be conferred upon them, etc.

Dr. Ryerson, on his part, felt kindly towards Mr. Mackenzie. He mentioned to the Editor of this book near the close of the year 1860, that on the ensuing New Year's day he (Dr. Ryerson) would call upon and shake hands with his old antagonist, and wish him a "Happy New Year."

---

* Mr. Mackenzie frequently visited the Educational Depository to make inquiries, etc. The Editor of this book had frequent conversations with him on the subject, and explained to him the details of management. He was pleased to know that through the agency of the Depository thousands of volumes of good books were being yearly sent out to the schools.

† Now the Rev. Dr. Cunningham Geikie, of England, and author of the "Life and Words of Christ," and other valuable books. He declined the use of the title of reverend in his controversy with Dr. Ryerson.

CHAPTER XXIV.

1838.

DEFENCE OF THE HON. MARSHALL SPRING BIDWELL.

FROM various papers and letters left by Dr. Ryerson, I have compiled the following statement in regard to his memorable defence of the Hon. M. S. Bidwell, in 1838. I have used Dr. Ryerson's own words throughout, only varying them when the sense, or the construction, or condensation of a sentence, required it. He said :—

On Dr. Duncombe's return to Canada, I believe the conspiracy was commenced by him, Mr. Wm. Lyon Mackenzie, and others, sought to accomplish their objects by rebellion; but in this the great body of Reformers took no part except to supress it. I had warned them that Mr. Mackenzie's proceedings would result in rebellion. I afterwards received the thanks of great numbers of Reformers for having by my warnings and counsels saved them and their families from being involved in the consequences of the rebellion. I was so odious to Mr. Mackenzie and his fellow rebels, that they determined to hang me on the first tree could they get hold of me. Of this, I had proof from one of themselves; yet I afterwards succeeded by my representations and appeals, to get several of them out of prison. My brother John, who was then in Toronto, presented to Governor Arthur and advocated a largely signed petition against the execution of Lount and Matthews. He also read a letter from me (then a stationed minister in Kingston) against their execution, and on the impolicy of capital punishment for political offences.

After the suppression of the rebellion—in the putting down of which the great body of the Reformers joined — the leaders of the dominant party sought, nevertheless, to hold the entire party of the Reformers responsible for that rebellion, and to proscribe and put them down accordingly. The first step in this process of proscription was the ostracism of Mr. M. S. Bidwell, an able and prudent politician, and a gentleman who took a high place in the legal profession. *

---

* According to the books of the Law Society, Mr. Bidwell commenced his legal studies in Kingston, the 14th March, 1816, in the office of Mr. Daniel Washburn,

During my stay in England, from December, 1835, to April, 1837, I had many conversations with Lord Glenelg, Sir George Grey, and Sir James Stephen (Under Secretaries), on the Government of Canada, shewing them that the foundation of our Government was too narrow, like an inverted pyramid, conferring the appointments to all offices, civil, military, judicial, to one party—excluding all others, however respectable and competent, as if they were enemies, and even aliens. I mentioned that not one member of the Reform party, (which had commanded for years a majority in the House of Assembly) had ever been appointed to the Bench, though there were several of them able lawyers, such as Bidwell, Rolph, etc. (Page 169.)

Lord Glenelg, in a despatch, directed Sir F. B. Head to appoint Mr. Bidwell to a judgeship on the first vacancy. Sir F. Head refused to do so, for which he was recalled, and Sir George Arthur was appointed in his place. In the meantime the House of Assembly was dissolved by Sir Francis, and a general election ordered. I had warned the public against Mr. Mackenzie's doings in converting constitutional reform into republican revolution, in consequence of which he attacked me furiously. Peter Perry, in the parliamentary session of 1836, attacked me also, and defended Mr. Mackenzie in a long speech. This speech reached me in England. I sat down and wrote a letter in reply, which reached Canada, and was published there on the eve of the elections, of which I then knew nothing. The constitutional party in Lennox and Addington had my letter printed by thousands, in the form of a large handbill, headed: "Peter Perry Picked to Pieces by Egerton Ryerson ' Although Mr. Bidwell took no part in the controversy, he was on the same electoral ticket with Mr. Perry, and both were defeated. *

and completed them in the office of Mr. Daniel Hagerman, of Ernestown. He was admitted as a barrister-at-law in April, 1821.

Mr. Bidwell was first elected to the House of Assembly in 1824 ; re-elected and chosen Speaker in 1828. On the death of George IV., in 1830, a new general election took place, when the Reform party were reduced to a minority, and Mr. Bidwell was not re-elected Speaker ; but he greatly distinguished himself in the debates of the House. In 1834, a new general election took place ; a large majority of Reformers were returned, and Mr. Bidwell was again elected Speaker. In May, 1836, Sir F. B. Head dissolved the House of Assembly, and Mr. Bidwell and his colleague, the late Peter Perry, were defeated in the united counties of Lennox and Addington, which Mr. Bidwell had represented in Parliament during twelve years. From that time (May, 1836) Mr. Bidwell never attended a political meeting, or took any part in politics.

* As stated by Dr. Ryerson, in the above note, Mr. Bidwell took no part in politics after his political defeat in May, 1836. In a note to Mr. W. L. Mackenzie, dated August 3rd, 1837, Mr. Bidwell said : Having learned from the *Constitution* of yesterday that I was chosen as a delegate to a Provincial Convention, I think it right without delay to inform you . . . that I must be excused from undertaking the duties of that appointment. . . I cannot but regret that my name

The Radical party being defeated at the polls, its leaders: Mr. Wm. L. Mackenzie, Dr. Charles Duncombe, and many others, sought to accomplish by force of arms what they had failed to accomplish by popular elections; the rebellion of 1836-7 was the result. As Mr. Bidwell was known to be the intimate friend of Dr. Rolph, and as Dr. Rolph was thought to be implicated in the rebellion, it was assumed by Sir F. Head that Mr. Bidwell was concerned in it also. But this was perfectly untrue. Besides, Mr. Bidwell entertained the strongest views that not a drop of blood should be shed to obtain the civil freedom of a country—that only moral suasion and public opinion should be employed for such purposes.

Sir F. Head thought that now was the opportunity to revenge himself alike upon Lord Glenelg and the Whig Government, which had ordered him to appoint Mr. Bidwell to a judgeship, and also upon Mr. Bidwell as a former leader of the Reform party who had opposed him. Mr. Bidwell's letters having reached the Governor, he sent for that gentleman. What transpired is thus related by Mr. Bidwell, in a letter written to me some time afterwards:—

Sir Francis assured me that the letters had been sent to him without his orders, and that he never would allow my letters to be opened. I asked him to open them, as I did not wish to have any suspicions about them indulged afterwards; but he refused to do it, and said he had too much respect for me to allow it. Indeed, on the Wednesday previously, I expressly informed the Attorney-General of my own anxiety, (and that I was willing) to undergo the most full and unreserved examination, and to let all my papers be examined.

The terms of my note of the 8th December—the evening of the day of the interview—were dictated, or at least, suggested to me by Sir Francis, and referred particularly to his expressions of personal regard. The object of drawing such a note from me is now apparent—but I was not then aware that he had received orders from Lord Glenelg to make me a Judge.

Before leaving Toronto (as he intimates), and after his arrival at Lewiston, Mr. Bidwell wrote to Sir F. Head (December 11th, 1837), protesting his innocence and against the injustice of the means used to compel him to leave his country.

The conclusion of Mr. Bidwell's note from Toronto is as follows:

I am confident . . that the investigations, which will now of course be made, will fully remove those suspicions from the mind of your Excel-

should have been used without my consent, or previous knowledge, by which I am driven to the disagreeable necessity of thus publicly declining [the] appointment, etc. In the *Guardian* of 27th September, where this letter appears, it is stated that Mr. Mackenzie did not publish it in the *Constitution* until the 20th September—six weeks after he had received it.

In a letter from Mr. Bidwell, dated, the 30th April, 1837, to Dr. O'Callaghan, of Montreal, he said: Retired from public life, probably for ever; I still look with the deepest sympathy on the efforts of those who are actively contending for the great principles of liberty, and good government, etc.—"*Political History of Canada*, 1840—1855, by Sir Francis Hincks, 1877, page 7."

lency, and will prove that I had also no knowledge or expectation that any such attempt [*i. e.* insurrectionary movement] was in contemplation.

To accomplish his revengeful purpose, however, Sir F. Head wrote or inspired an editorial to the Toronto *Patriot* newspaper (then the organ of his Government) stating that as Mr. Bidwell had left the country, under circumstances that proved his consciousness of guilt, it was therefore the duty of the Benchers of the Law Society to erase his name from their rolls.

I was then stationed at Kingston. When I saw the editorial in the *Patriot*, I at once recognized Sir F. Head's hand in it, and was horror-struck at the idea of a man being exiled from his country, and then deprived of his professional character and privileges without a trial! I passed a sleepless night.

The late Mr. Henry Cassidy was then mayor of Kingston; a staunch Churchman and Conservative. His wife was a relative of mine, so a sort of family intimacy existed between us. Mr. Cassidy had been a student in Mr. Bidwell's law-office and was now his law agent. Mr. Bidwell enclosed to Mr. Cassidy the correspondence which had taken place between himself and Sir F. Head and Attorney-General Hagerman, and Mr. Cassidy had shown it to me. The morning after I saw the article in the *Patriot*, proposing the erasure of Mr. Bidwell's name from the books of the Law Society, I went to Mr. Cassidy, saying that I had not closed my eyes all night, in consequence of Sir F. Head's article in the *Patriot*; that I was the only person besides himself who knew the facts of the case, and though I had been assailed by the newspapers of the party with which Mr. Bidwell had been connected, I felt it in my heart to prevent a gross act of injustice and cruelty being inflicted upon a man, in his absence and helplessness, who had introduced and carried through our Legislature the laws by which the different religious denominations held their Church property, and their ministers solemnized matrimony. I asked Mr. Cassidy if he would allow me the use of the letters which Mr. Bidwell had enclosed to him, justifying his own innocence, and showing the injustice done him by the misstatements of Sir F. Head. After some hours of deliberation, Mr. Cassidy consented. I sat down, and over the signature of "A United Empire Loyalist," I detailed the case, introducing as proofs of Mr. Bidwell's innocence the injustice proposed to be inflicted upon him, referring to Mr. Attorney-General Hagerman's own letter, and appealing to the Law Society, and the country at large, against such injustice and against such violation of the rights of a British subject. I got a friend to copy my communication, so as not to excite suspicion.* It was the first article that had appeared in the public press after the rebellion, breathing the spirit of freedom, and advocating British constitutional rights against illegal oppression.†

The effect of this article upon the public mind was very remarkable. As an example, Mr. John Campbell, member of the Legislative Assembly for the County of Frontenac, despairing of the liberties of the country under the "tory" oppression of the day, determined to sell his property for whatever it might bring, and remove to the States. He was on a steamboat on Lake Ontario, on his way to the Territory of Iowa to buy land and settle there, when the newspaper containing my communication fell into his hands; he read it, rose up and said that as long as there was a man in Canada who could write in that way there was hope for the country. He returned home, resumed his business, and lived and died in Canada.

The Attorney-General was annoyed at the publication of his letter to Mr. Bidwell, and attempted a justification of his conduct. At the conclusion of a letter to me, he said that I had concealed my name for fear of the legal consequences of my seditious paper. I at once sat down and wrote the most argu-

---

* Sir Alexander Campbell, now Minister of Justice, in a note to the Editor, thus explains this circumstance:—In the winter of 1837-38, I was a student-at-law, and a resident of Kingston. Dr. Ryerson was then the Methodist minister in charge of the only congregation of that body in town. The rebellion of 1837-8, had led to excited, and very bitter feelings—arrests had been frequent; and it was not prudent for any one to try to palliate the deeds of the rebels, or to seek to lessen the odium which covered their real, or even supposed allies and friends. Dr. Ryerson, however, desired to bring out the facts connected with Mr Bidwell's banishment, and to change the current of public feeling on the subject—but it was not wise to send letters to the press in his own handwriting, or in any other way suffer it to become known that he was the author of the letters in defence of Mr. Bidwell. Under these circumstances he asked me to copy them, and take them to the *Herald* office—then the most liberal paper in Upper Canada. I was proud of the confidence placed in me, and copied the several letters, and went with them to the publisher. The letters were signed in words which I have not since seen, but which remain impressed upon my memory, and which were as follows:—

"I am Sir, by parental instruction and example, by personal feeling and exertion,

A United Empire Loyalist"

The letters constituted an eloquent defence of Mr. Bidwell, who certainly took no part in the counsels of those who were afterwards engaged in the rebellion, when it became evident that they intended to push matters to extremes.

The incident made a great impression on me at the time, and was the beginning of a friendship with which Dr. Ryerson honoured me, and which ended only with his life.

A. Campbell.

Ottawa, 29th December, 1882.

† The defence was afterwards reprinted in a pamphlet on the 10th of May, 1838, with the following title: "The Cause and Circumstances of Mr. Bidwell's Banishment by Sir F. B. Head, correctly stated and proved by A United Empire Loyalist." Kingston, 1838, pp. 16.

mentative paper that I ever penned (and for the recovery of which I afterwards offered five pounds, but without success), reducing the questions to a series of mathematical propositions, and demonstrating in each case from the Attorney-General's own data, that my conclusions were true, and his absurd. I concluded by defying his legal threat of prosecution, and signed my name to the letter.

The effect of my reply to Mr. Attorney-General Hagerman was marvellous in weakening the influence of the first law adviser of the Crown, and in reviving the confidence of the friends of liberal constitutional government.*

Subsequently, (in June, 1838), I received a letter from Mr. Hagerman, in which he stated that in my observations on Mr. Bidwell's case I had made assertions that impeached his character, and desired me to inform him on what evidence I had based my statements. He said:—

> The first assertion is that I was the author of certain remarks published under the editorial head of the *Patriot* newspaper of this city, injurious to the reputation of Mr. Bidwell. . . The second statement is that I desired to procure his expulsion from the Province, because he had been preferred to me for the office of judge.

My reply to Mr. Hagerman was brief and to the point:

> I beg to say, in reply to your letter, that I am not conscious of having made either of the assertions which you have been pleased to attribute to me.

I think it only just to the late Mr. Hagerman to add, that the sharp discussions between him and me did not chill the friendliness, and even pleasantness, of our personal intercourse afterwards; and I believe few men would have more heartily welcomed Mr. Bidwell's return to Canada than Mr. Justice

---

* Some time after Sir George Arthur's arrival as Governor, he sent for me, and stated that his object in doing so was to request me, for the sake of the Government and the country, to withdraw the letter I had written in answer to Attorney-General Hagerman; that it greatly weakened the Government; that my power of argumentation was prodigious, but he believed I was mistaken; that Mr. Bidwell had called to pay his respects to him at Albany, on his way to Canada; and that he (Sir George) believed Mr. Bidwell was guilty, as far as a man of his caution and knowledge could be concerned in the rebellion; and though my argument on his behalf seemed to be irresistible, he believed I was wrong, and that the withdrawal of my letter would be a great help to the Government. I replied that my weekly editorials in the *Christian Guardian* (of which I had consented to be re-elected Editor) showed that I was anxious to suppress the factious and party hatreds of the day, and to place the Government upon a broad foundation of loyalty and justice; that what I had written in the case of Mr. Bidwell had been written by me as an individual and not as the editor of the organ of a religious body, and had been written from the firm conviction of Mr. Bidwell's innocence, and that his case involved the fundamental and essential rights of every British subject; and that, however anxious I was to meet His Excellency's wishes, I could not withdraw my letter. I then bowed myself out from the presence of Sir George, who, from that hour became my enemy, and afterwards warned Lord Sydenham against me as "a dangerous man," as Lord Sydenham laughingly told me the last evening I spent with him in Montreal, at his request, and before his lamented death.

Hagerman himself. Mr. Hagerman was a man of generous impulses. He was a variable speaker, but at times his every gesture was eloquent, his intonations of voice were truly musical, and almost every sentence was a gem of beauty.

The discussion ended there; but no proposal was ever made to, much less entertained by, the Law Society to erase Mr. Bidwell's name from its rolls.

Mr. Bidwell's case did not, however, end here. In 1842, on the recommendation of Hon. Robert Baldwin, any promise given by Mr. Bidwell not to return to Canada—of which no record was found in any of the Government offices—was revoked, in 1843, by the Governor-General (Lord Metcalfe). Mr. Bidwell was also strongly urged to come back, and a promise was given to him by the authority of the Governor-General that all of his former rights and privileges would be restored to him, with a view to his elevation to the Bench. He, however, declined to return. Again, some years afterwards, when Sir W. B. Richards was Attorney-General, he was authorized to offer Mr. Bidwell the position of Commissioner to revise our Statute Law. He declined that offer also.

In conversation, in 1872, with Sir John Macdonald in relation to Mr. Bidwell's early life, Sir John informed me that some years before, he himself had, while in New York, solicited Mr. Bidwell to return to Canada, but without success. Sir John said that he had done so, not merely on his own account (as he had always loved Mr. Bidwell, and did not believe that he had any connection whatever with the rebellion), but because he believed that he represented the wishes of his political friends, as well as those of the people of Canada generally.

Mr. Bidwell was an earnest Christian. He was also a charming companion. A few weeks before his lamented decease, he visited his relatives and friends in Canada, spent a Sabbath in Toronto, occupying a seat in my pew in the Metropolitan Church. While here he presented me with a beautiful likeness of himself on ivory. I have placed it in the Canadian room of our Departmental Museum. I little thought it was my last meeting with him, as I had long anticipated and often intended to visit him in New York, where he promised to narrate to me many incidents of men and things in the Canada of former years, which had not come to my knowledge, or which I had forgotten. A suitable monument would be an appropriate tribute to his memory by our Legislature and country.

The following are extracts of letters written to Dr. Ryerson, by Mr. Bidwell, at the dates mentioned:

May 21st, 1828—Kingston.—I admire and fully approved of your plan (as

I advised Mr. H. C. Thompson) of striking off a large number of copies, in pamphlet form, of your Review of Archdeacon Strachan's Sermon. (See page 68.) I have no doubt it will be really a great service to the country to do so. Indeed, I sincerely think that you could not in any other way be instrumental in promoting so much the cause of Christ, as in the labours which you have undertaken. The concerns of this Colony, as you see in the newspapers, are attracting the attention of the British Parliament; and the decided expression of public opinion here at present will outweigh all that Dr. Strachan and his junto can say and do. My father and I will shortly give the subject of Church Establishment in this Province, contended for by Dr. Strachan, a full and careful examination, and communicate to you the result.

January 19*th*, 1829—*York.*—I rejoice once more to receive a letter from you. . . I sincerely thank you for your congratulations on my elevation to the Speakership. I am sensible how much I need the prayers and counsels of my friends in discharging the duties of my station. I wish Christians would reflect what important consequences may follow from every step taken by those in public life, and especially in the Legislature. . . I send you a copy of Wilbur's Reference Bible, which I beg you will accept as a testimony of my respect and friendship.

March 10*th*, 1829—*York.*—The Marriage Bill has been passed, with amendments made by the Legislative Council. The House is about equally divided on trying questions, so that we often forbear attempting measures which we would wish to pass. This unpleasant state of things produces anxiety, uncertainty, and (worst of all) violent party spirit. I can with great truth declare that I have received but little satisfaction in my public life.

To you and your brother the Province owes a large debt of gratitude. For one, I feel it sensibly, and wish most sincerely that we could have the benefit of your counsel in our House. Two or three such men would be a comfort, a relief, a support, and an assistance, beyond what you have any idea of.

April 6*th*, 1831—*Kingston.*—I am very glad to see your commendations of the Attorney-General.* I think they are just. They are certainly politic and seasonable. Indeed, I had thought of hinting to you the propriety of some such notice of his liberality, etc. I was afraid otherwise the coldness of the courtiers towards him might make him repent of such liberality. But I think that your remarks have come at the right time, and are exactly of the right sort.*

June 14*th*, 1833—*York.*—We have heard with pleasure of your safe arrival in England: and pleasing indeed this has been to your many friends in the Province, whose prayers, good wishes, and friendly recollections, have accompanied you across the Atlantic. . . Mr. John Willson, M.P.P., of Saltfleet, has, within a day or two, obtained from the Receiver-General, on the warrant of the Lieutenant-Governor, £600 of the public money, to aid in building chapels, I suppose, for the Ryanites. (See page 87). The fact was mentioned to me privately this morning, but I deem it so important as to justify and require me to inform you confidentially of it, leaving it to your judgment to use the intelligence in the most discreet manner that may be consistent with the duty you owe to liberty and religion.

It excites surprise, pain, mortification, indignation, and contempt, to see the Executive Government here making unjust and invidious distinctions between His Majesty's subjects in the appropriations of the Clergy Reserves, thereby endeavouring to secure an unconstitutional and corrupt influence, especially after Lord Goderich's declaration in his despatch (which he

---

* These remarks will be found on page 83 of the *Guardian* of 2nd April.

directed to be published), that if any preference was shown to one denomination of Christians more than another, it was contrary to the policy of His Majesty's Government, and against repeated instructions sent to the Government here.

As a Presbyterian I lament the grant to the Presbytery, and will do all I can to get it repealed, for I am convinced it will do injury to liberty and religion, and to the very persons who may wish, or wicked enough, to receive it. I suppose the Province is indebted to Sir John Colborne for these grants. If it is the Government at home, it ought to be known: if it is not, they ought not only to remove Sir John, but also reform this abuse. Have the Government ever given your Society sixpence, or even a foot of land for your chapels?—although it is the oldest and most numerous body of the kind in the Province; is not wealthy, and has rendered the most valuable services, and at a time when no other Church evinced the least interest for the religious instruction or the welfare of the people.

April 12th, 1838—*New York.*—Your letter of the 23rd ult. and its enclosure [the defence], I need not say, have affected me deeply, too much, indeed, for me to describe my feelings. I thank you from the bottom of my heart for this instance of your kindness; not less valued, certainly, because it was unexpected, not to say undeserved. If my misfortunes shall be the means of recovering a friendship which I formerly enjoyed and always prized, I shall feel not a little reconciled.*

I took the precaution some time ago, to send to England a plain, distinct statement of all that had occurred between Sir Francis Head and myself. This was transmitted to a friend to show to Lord Glenelg. My only object was the vindication of my character. I have never had the least expectation of obtaining justice or redress from the Colonial office. There seems in that department utter incapacity. The very persons they select for the Government of Upper Canada are enough to prove this And yet I believe that Lord Glenelg is an able, as well as amiable, devout, good man.

May 15th, 1838—*New York.*—I have received a letter from the gentleman in England, to whom I had written. He had seen Lord Durham, and shown him my letter. He expressed no opinion; but the gentleman thinks that the matter stands favourably before him. He has not yet seen Lord Glenelg.

August 10th, 1839—*New York.*—Mr. Christopher Dunkin† is very anxious

---

* This loss of friendship with Dr. Ryerson may be explained by the following reference to Mr. Bidwell, in a letter from Dr. Ryerson, to his brother John, dated Kingston, 29th May, 1838 :—From an intimate religious friend of Mr. Bidwell, I learn that during the last few years he had acted more after a worldly policy, common to politicians, and had, therefore, partly laid himself open to the censure which he has received. I am also sensible of his prejudices against me of late years, and of the great injury which I have thereby sustained. I had some difficulty to overcome my own feelings in the first instance. But as far as individual feelings and interests are concerned, "it is the glory of man to pass over a transgression," generous as well as just, as we have received help from Bidwell himself when we could not help ourselves, and were trampled upon by a desperate party. If others had seen the letters from Bidwell to Mr. Cassidy, which I have been permitted to read, I am sure the noble generosity of their hearts would be excited in all its sympathies. I do not think, however, that he will ever return to this Province to reside. That appears to be altogether out of the question with him; but that does not alter the nature of the case.

I have replied to Mr. Hagerman with calmness, but with deep feeling. My reply will occupy about eight columns in to-morrow's *Herald*.

† Mr. Dunkin afterwards became a noted politician, and member of the Parliament of United Canada, from 1857, until Confederation. He was the promoter of the "Dunkin Act." He was one of the contributors to the *Monthly Review*,

to have the honour of an introduction to you. I am very happy to be the means of gratifying him. Mr. Dunkin was editor of the Montreal *Courier*, in the latter part of 1837, and beginning of 1838. He was afterwards appointed by Lord Durham on the Commission relating to education, and has latterly resided in the United States.

About the time of Mr. Bidwell's defence, Dr. Ryerson also wrote an explanatory letter to the Colonial Office in regard to his excellent friend, Hon. John H. Dunn, the Receiver-General, whose generous conduct towards the Upper Canada Academy is mentioned on page 166*. In a letter of acknowledgment from Mr. Dunn to Dr. Ryerson, he said:—

> I am very glad to learn from your letter that you have written to Lord Glenelg. It is but just to put His Lordship in possession of facts which may counteract the influence of misrepresentation, and enable His Lordship to exercise his own humane disposition in putting matters right, which have been so wrong and arbitrary towards the individual Mr. Bidwell, whom you have taken the interest in, and trouble, to restore to his position and his country.
> I feel exceedingly obliged for the kind feeling which you entertain towards me. Believe me, that you have only done me justice by mentioning my name to Lord Glenelg. I have laboured hard since I have been in the Province to discharge my duty to my God and my Government. I have entertained different opinions at times of the "Powers here," but they have been the dictates of an honest heart. I cannot guide my opinions to the service of any party. Whatever they may be, I shall lament if they should result in any other than for the best interests and welfare of the Province of Upper Canada.
> You were so good as to read me your letter to Lord Glenelg, on the subject of the late execution of Lount and Matthews. Your version too, of the real meaning of the representation which caused Sir Francis Head to compel us to retire from the Executive Council, is so correct, that I cannot suggest any amendment; besides, I am bound by my oath not to divulge any transaction arising at the Council Board. I shall be very happy to see the letter published. (See page 170.)
> You have seen my name kindly mentioned in the public prints. What has been said has been the spontaneous expressions of other persons, quite unknown to me. I am grateful to those persons who have vindicated me against a party, eager to destroy me, and my family. I leave them to a Judge who knows the secrets of all hearts, and before whom we all shall soon appear. I have had my share of afflictions and troubles in this world,

established by Lord Sydenham in 1841. He was subsequently appointed to the Bench, and died a few years since.

* The Hon. John Henry Dunn was a native of England. He came to Canada in 1820, having been appointed Receiver-General of Upper Canada, and a member of the Executive and Legislative Council. He held the office of Receiver-General until the union of the Provinces in 1841, when the political exigencies of the times compelled him to resign it. He and Hon. Isaac Buchanan contested the city of Toronto, in the Reform interest, in 1841, and were returned. Mr. Dunn received no compensation for the loss of his office, and soon afterwards returned to England, where he died in 1854. He was a most estimable public officer. His son, Col. Dunn, greatly distinguished himself during the Crimean war, and, on his visiting Canada soon afterwards, was received with great enthusiasm, and a handsome sword was presented to him.—H.

and to which I feel little or no attachment whatever. When the heart is sick, the whole body is faint.

Dr. Ryerson (in the *Guardian* of 22nd January, 1840) thus referred to Mr. Dunn as one of the speakers in the Legislative Council on the popular side of the clergy reserve question:—

I was glad to hear Mr. Dunn speak so well and so forcibly,—universally and affectionately esteemed as he is beyond any other public functionary in Upper Canada.

Some months after the exile of Mr. Bidwell, Mr. James S. Howard was dismissed by Sir F. B. Head from the office of Postmaster of Toronto. The alleged ground of dismissal was that he was a Radical, and had not taken up arms in defence of the country. Dr. Ryerson, with his usual generous sympathy for persons who in those days were made the victims of Governor Head's caprice, at once espoused Mr. Howard's cause. In his first letter in the Defence of Sir Charles Metcalfe, he said:—

After the insurrection of 1837-8, unfavourable impressions were made far and wide against the late Postmaster of Toronto, and Mr. Bidwell. But subsequent investigations corrected these impressions. The former has been appointed to office, and Sir F. B. Head's proceedings against the latter have been cancelled by Sir Charles Metcalfe. (Page 16.)

Again, in the "Prefatory Address" to the Metcalfe Defence, he said:—

While God gives me a heart to feel, a head to think, and a pen to write, I will not passively see honourable integrity murdered by grasping faction. . . I would not do so in 1838, when an attempt was made to degrade and proscribe, and drive out of the country all naturalized subjects from the United States, and to stigmatize all Reformers with the brand of rebellion. . . I relieved the name of an injured James S. Howard from the obloquy that hung over it, and rescued the character and rights of an exiled Bidwell from ruthless invasion, and the still further effort to cover him with perpetual infamy by expelling him from the Law Society. (Page 7.)

CHAPTER XXV.

1838.

RETURN TO THE EDITORSHIP OF THE "GUARDIAN."

THE Rebellion of 1837-38 was suppressed by the inherent and spontaneous loyalty of all classes of the Canadian people. Yet, after it was over, the seeds of strife engendered by the effort to prove that one section of the community was more loyal than the other, and that that other section was chiefly responsible for the outbreak, bore bitter fruit in the way of controversy. Dr. Ryerson took little part in such recriminatory warfare. It was too superficial. He felt that it did not touch the underlying points at issue between the dominant, or ruling, party and those who were engaged in a contest for equal civil and religious rights. He, and the other leaders who influenced and moulded public opinion, clearly saw that this recriminatory war was carried on by the dominant party as a mask to cover their ulterior designs—designs which were afterwards developed in the more serious struggle for religious supremacy which that party waged for years afterwards, and which at length issued in the complete triumph of the principles of civil and religious freedom for which Dr. Ryerson and the representatives of other religious bodies had so long and so earnestly contended. (See page 452.)

Besides, Dr. Ryerson was anxious to fulfil the engagement made with the Kingston Society that he would resume his pastoral charge there, after his return from England in June, 1837. He was, however, repeatedly pressed by his friends to write for the *Guardian*, or other newspaper, on the vital questions of the day. In reply to his brother John, who had urged him in the matter, he wrote (March, 1838) saying that he was so happily engaged in his pastoral duties at Kingston that he could not then devote the necessary time to the discussion of public questions. His brother, in remonstrating with him on the subject, said :—

> Your letter affords me great satisfaction, accompanied with sorrow. I am afflicted to think of the state the Province is in. Never did high-churchism take such rapid strides towards undisputed domination in this country as it is now taking. Never were the prospects of the friends of civil and religious liberty so gloomy and desperate as they are now. You say that you have not time to write on these subjects. I will say, if you had, it would not now, I fear, accomplish much. Indeed, it would require the undeviating

course and the whole weight of the *Guardian* to accomplish anything at this time, so completely is all moral power in the country enervated and liberty prostrated.

It is a great blessing that Mackenzie and radicalism are down, but we are in imminent danger of being brought under the domination of a military and high-church oligarchy, which would be equally bad, if not infinitely worse. Under the blessing of Providence there is one remedy, and only one; and that is, for you to take the editorship of the *Guardian* again. Several preachers have spoken to me on this subject lately. One of them said to me (and he could think of nothing else) that that alone would save us and the country from utter ruin, and urged the necessity of the Conference electing you, whether you would consent to serve or not. The truth is, it is absolutely neccessary for the sake of the Church and the country that you reside in Toronto, and have direction of affairs here. I wish all of our proceedings to be calm and moderate, but that we be firm, and that the great principles of religious freedom and equality should be uncompromisingly maintained.

In a subsequent letter to Dr. Ryerson his brother John said:

In fact there is no way of escape out of our troubles but for you to take the *Guardian*. The feeling of dissatisfaction at the present state of things is becoming exceedingly strong among the preachers and people. I participate in their feelings.

Dr. Ryerson yielded to these appeals, and did write for the *Guardian*. In a letter, dated Kingston, April 4th, he said:—

I have recently written at considerable length to Lord Glenelg respecting the Academy and other local matters. What you say in regard to myself, and my appointment next year, I feel to be a delicate and difficult matter for me to speak on. In regard to myself I have many conflicting thoughts. My feelings, and private interests, are in favour of my remaining where I am, if I remain in the Province. I have been very much cast down, and my mind has been much agitated on the subject. For the present I am somewhat relieved by the conclusion to which I have come, in accordance with Dr. Clarke's "Advice to a Young Preacher," not to choose my own appointment, but after making known any circumstances, which I may feel it necessary to explain, to leave myself in the hands of God and my brethren, as I have done during the former years of my ministry. If the Lord, therefore, will give me grace, I am resolved to stand on the old Methodistic ground in the matter of appointment to the *Guardian*.

I thank you for Chief Justice Robinson's address at the trial of the prisoners. It is good. My own views are in favour of lenity to these prisoners Punishments for political offences can never be beneficial, when they are inflicted in opposition to public sentiment and sympathy. In such a case it will defeat the object it is intended to accomplish. It matters not whether that sentiment and sympathy are right or wrong in the abstract; the effect of doing violence to it will be the same. But I would not pander to that feeling, how carefully soever one may be disposed to observe its operations. The fact, however, is, that Sir Francis Head deserves impeachment, just as much as Samuel Lount deserves execution. Morally speaking, I cannot but regard Sir Francis as the more guilty culprit of the two.

I admire, as a whole, Sir George Arthur's reply to the address of the "Constitutional Reformers." There is good in it. They will see the folly of continuing the former party designations, and pretended grounds of complaint. I think, however, that their address will do good, from the large number of names attached to it. I was surprised, and it has created quite a sensation here, that there are so many as 772 in Toronto, who still have the moral courage to designate themselves "Constitutional Reformers." It will teach the other party that they are not so strong, and so absolute in the voice of the country, as they thought themselves to be.

I am satisfied that there never was such a time as from the termination of the trial of the prisoners to the next session of Parliament, for us to stamp upon the public mind at large, our own constitutional, and Scriptural, political, and religious doctrines ; and to give the tone to the future Government and Legislation of the Province, and to enlarge vastly a sphere of usefulness. I shall write some papers for the *Guardian* with this view.

In a letter from Brockville, Rev. William Scott said :—

My humble opinion is, that in order to our safety as a Church—our preservation from high church influence—you must be at Toronto. I assure you that is the opinion of our influential men in this quarter, who understand the state of the province, and the position of Methodism. Permit me to add that the one hour's conversation which I had with you amply repaid me for all the furious battles which I have fought on this circuit in your defence.

Rev. Joseph Stinson, in a letter to Rev. John Ryerson, said:

I am quite of your opinion that your brother Egerton ought to take the *Guardian* next year. There is a crisis approaching in our affairs which will require a vigorous hand to wield the defensive weapon of our Conference. There can be no two opinions as to whom we should give that weapon. We now stand on fair ground to maintain our own against the encroachments of the oligarchy, and we must do it, or sink into a comparatively uninfluential body—this must not be.

As urged by these letters from his brethren, Dr. Ryerson, early in May, 1838, prepared several articles for the *Guardian*. His brother John, who was a member of the Book Committee, thus speaks of the series of articles sent to that paper :—

I cannot express to you how much I am gratified and pleased with your article on "Christian Loyalty." It will, no doubt, do immense good. We have had a regular campaign in our Book Committee, in reading and discussing your articles. The one on "Christian Loyalty" occupied nearly the whole time. Your article on "The Church" is one of the most admirable papers I ever read. Not a word of that is to be altered. Your communication on "Indian Affairs," I cannot speak so highly of. I hope you will pardon me for leaving out some of the severe remarks on Sir Francis. I am afraid they will do harm with the present Government.

At the Conference of 1838, Dr. Ryerson was re-elected Editor of the *Christian Guardian.*. In his first editorial, dated 11th July, 1838, he said :—

Notwithstanding the almost incredible calumny which has in past years been heaped upon me by antipodes-party-presses, I still adhere to the principles and views upon which I set out in 1826. I believe the endowment of the priesthood of any Church in the Province to be an evil to that Church. . . I believe that the appropriation of the proceeds of the clergy reserves to general educational purposes, will be the most satisfactory and advantageous disposal of them that can be made. In nothing is this Province so defective as in the requisite available provisions for, and an efficient system of, general education. Let the distinctive character of that system be the union of public and private effort. . . To Government influence will be spontaneously added the various and combined religious influence of the country in the noble, statesmanlike, and divine work of raising up an elevated, intelligent, and moral population.*

In combatting the idea that his editorial opinions in the *Guardian* were necessarily "the opinions of the Methodists" as a body, and that they were responsible for them, Dr. Ryerson, in the *Guardian* of August 15th, thus defines the rights of an editor:—To be the mere scribe of the opinions of others, and not to write what we think ourselves, is a greater degradation of intellectual and moral character than slavery itself. . . In doctrines and opinions we write what we believe to be the truth, leaving to others the exercise of a judgment equally unbiassed and free.

In the exuberance of loyal zeal, and yet in a kindly spirit which was characteristic of him, Rev. W M. Harvard, President of the Canada Conference, issued a pastoral on the 17th April, 1838, to the ministers of the Church, enjoining them not to recognize as members of the Society those whose loyalty could be impeached. The directions which he gave were:—

Should there be a single individual for whose Christian loyalty the preacher cannot conscientiously answer for to his brethren, in the first place such individual should not be included in the return of membership; and in the second place such individual should be dealt with kindly and compassionately, but firmly, according to the provisions of the Discipline.

No man who is not disposed to be a good subject can be admissible to the Sacraments of the Church. . .

Should any person apply hereafter for admission into our Church, who may be ill-affected to the Crown . . tell him kindly, but firmly, . . that he has applied at the wrong door.

As soon as this extraordinary pastoral had appeared, Dr. Ryerson addressed a letter of some length to the *Guardian*, objecting in very temperate, but yet in very strong language to the doctrine laid down in it by the President of the Conference. Before publication, however, he sent it to Mr. Harvard for his information and perusal. He showed from the writings of John Wesley, Richard Watson, and others, and from examples which he cited (John Nelson, "the apostolic fellow-labourer of John Wesley," etc.) that such a doctrine savoured of despotism, and was harsh and inquisitorial in its effects. He concluded thus:—

None of the various political opinions which men hold, and their respectful and constitutional expression of them, is any just cause of excluding from the

---

* Even at this early date, Dr. Ryerson indicated the comprehensive character of the system of education which he was afterwards destined to found in Upper Canada.

Lord's Table any human being, provided his religious character is unexceptional. The only condition of membership in our Church is "a desire to flee from the wrath to come,"* and none of the opinions mentioned is inconsistent with the fruits by which that desire is evidenced. The Discipline of the Church, or the Scripture itself, does not authorize me to become the judge of another man's political opinions—the Church is not a political association —any man has as good a right, religiously and politically, to his opinions of public matters as I have to mine—and laymen frequently know much more, and are better judges, than ministers in civil and secular affairs.

It can be well understood what would be the effect of the Pastoral, and not less so of Dr. Ryerson's clear and dispassionate disclaimer of the doctrines which it officially laid down.

It required courage and firmness, in the loyal outburst and reaction of those days, to question the propriety or expediency of any reasonable means by which the unimpeachable loyalty of members of the Church could be ascertained. What added to the embarrassment of Dr. Ryerson in discussing such a question was the fact that the Methodists were being constantly taunted with being disloyal. Knowing this, and sensitive as to the disgrace of such a stigma being cast upon the Church, the President felt constrained to take some decisive, and yet, as he thought, kindly and satisfactory means of ridding the Church of members who were the cause, in his estimation, of such a disgrace and reproach to that Church.

Among many other strong letters of commendations of his reply to Mr. Harvard, which Dr. Ryerson received, were two,— one from a representative minister of the Canadian section of the Church, and the other from an equally excellent representative of the British missionaries. Thus:

Rev. Anson Green, writing from Picton, said:—

I was sorry, though not surprised, to hear that you were very much perplexed. I could easily understand your feelings, and quite sympathize with you. Your recent efforts for the peace and prosperity of the Church have very much endeared you to my heart. I am fully prepared to believe the assertion which you made while in England, "that you love Jerusalem above your chief joy." This you have fully proved by your untiring efforts on behalf of the Academy, the Chapels, and on the Church question; but in nothing more, allow me to say, than in the firm, manly, and Christian spirit, in which you have come out, publicly, in defence of the membership of the Church, and of sound principles. I had resolved when Rev. Mr. Harvard wrote to me to carry out the principles of his instructions and Pastoral in this district, to write him a letter respectfully and yet firmly declining to do so. But when I saw the storm gathering in every quarter, I could only exclaim in the despondency of my soul:—When will our brethren cease to destroy us, and when will the Church again have rest from internal commotion and strife! And just at this crisis (a memorable crisis to thousands of our Canadian friends) your excellent rejoinder to Mr. Harvard's Pastoral came out in the *Guardian*. It was a balm to the afflicted heart. It was a precious cordial poured forth. Your letter was sent from house to house, from cottage

---

* These words as to membership are identical with those which Dr. Ryerson uttered fifteen years afterwards in his discussion on the Class-meeting question.

to cottage, and met with unequivical applause from all. The lowering sky began to clear up, and we are encouraged once more to hope for clear sunshine. You have had the courage to speak the truth in opposition to men in high authority. Your letter was in every respect just what it should have been, and thousands do most sincerely thank you for it.

Rev. Joseph Stinson, writing from Simcoe, said:—

As far as I can ascertain, your appointment as Editor of the *Guardian* next year will give general satisfaction. The President's Pastoral and your reply are producing quite a sensation. Most people give Mr. Harvard credit for purity of intention, but regret that the subject of politics has been adverted to by him in such a form. Your remarks on the Pastoral have hushed the fears of many who were greatly disturbed; but some think that your statement of abstract right is carried too far, and may at a future day be appealed to in support of measures which you would utterly condemn.

Some of your old tory friends think that there is design in all you write on these questions, and do not hesitate to designate you by the amiable title of a "jesuit," etc. You can bear all this and much more in carrying out your design, to show them that their tactics are understood, and their proceedings are closely watched, so as to prevent them from obtaining those objects which would be alike unjust to us as a Church, and ungenerous to themselves. It is well that in all of the "burnings which your fingers" have had, you have not yet lost your nails; for I expect that you will need them before long. The high church party have the will, if they can muster the courage, to make a renewed and desperate attack upon you. Fear not; while you advocate the truth, you can defy their rage.

The public mind seems to me to be in a state of painful suspense. The people hate and dread rebellion. They are not satisfied with the present leading political party. They hope to see a new man rise up with sufficient talent and influence to collect around him a respectable party to act as a balance between oppression and destruction. Some talk of a new election; some talk of leaving the country; all seem to think that something must be done; none know what to do. How ought we in this awful crisis (for an awful crisis it is), to pray for the Divine interposition in behalf of our distracted province. . . I saw your venerable father last night. He very much wishes you to write to him.

On the 7th of November, 1838, the first number of the 10th volume of the *Guardian* was issued. In it there is an elaborate article signed by Dr. Ryerson (although he was then Editor), on the state of public affairs in Upper Canada. In his introductory remarks he said:—

From the part I have usually taken in questions which affect the foundations of our Government, and our relations with the Mother Country,—and from the position I at present occupy in respect to public affairs, and in relation to the Province generally, it will be expected that I should take a more than passing notice of the eventful crisis at which we have arrived. In conclusion, he says: Having faithfully laid before the Government and the country the present posture of affairs, and the causes of our present dissatisfaction and dangers, I advert to the remedies: (1. Military defence.) 2. Let the Government be administered as much in accordance with the general wishes of this country, as it is in England. 3. Abolish high-church domination, and provide perfect religious and political equality. 4. Let them be at equal fidelity to obey the authorities when called upon. . . He who does most to bring about this happy state of things in the Province will be the greatest benefactor of his country.

CHAPTER XXVI.

1838—1840.

ENEMIES AND FRIENDS WITHIN AND WITHOUT.

> Any controversialist, whose honest belief in his own doctrines makes him terribly in earnest, may count on a life embittered by the anger of those on whom he has forced the disagreeable task of reconsidering their own assumptions.—CANON FARRAR.

ALL through his public career, Dr. Ryerson had many bitter enemies and many warm and devoted friends. This was not to be wondered at. No man with such strongly marked individuality of will and purpose, and with such an instinctive dislike to injustice and oppression, could fail to come in contact with those whose views and proceedings were opposed to his sense of right. The enmity which he excited in discussing public questions was rarely disarmed (except in the case of men of generous impulses or noble natures) by the fact that he and those who acted with him were battling for great principles—those of truth, and justice, and freedom.

When these principles could not be successfully assailed, the usual plan was to attack the character, and wound the tender sensibilities of their chief defender. This was a mistake; but it was the common error with most of Dr. Ryerson's assailants. And yet those who did so in his presence, and in the arena of debate, rarely repeated the mistake. With all his kindness of heart and warmth of friendship, there was, when aroused, much of the lion in his nature. Few who assailed him in Conference, or made a personal attack upon him in other places of public discussion, could stand before the glitter of his eye when that lion-nature was aroused; and fewer still would care to endure the effect of its fire a second time.

Most of the personal attacks made upon Dr. Ryerson were in writing, and often anonymously. He had, therefore, to defend himself chiefly with his pen. This he rarely failed to do, and with good effect.* On such occasions he used strong and vigor-

---

* Dr. Ryerson, early in his controversial career, adopted Lord Macaulay's motto: No misrepresentation should be suffered to pass unrefuted. We must remember that misstatements constantly reiterated, and seldom answered, will assuredly be believed.

ous language, of which he was an acknowledged master. Very many of these attacks were ephemeral, and not worthy of note. Others were more serious and affected character, and these were more or less bitter and violent. They, of course, called forth a good deal of feeling at the time, but are only referred to now as part of the story of a life, then singularly active and stormy.

The Editor of the Toronto *Patriot* having published extracts from a pamphlet issued in the Newcastle District (County of Northumberland), in 1832, in which attacks were made upon Dr. Ryerson's character, he replied to them in the columns of that paper. In 1828, his circuit was in the Newcastle district, and the person who made these attacks resided in Haldimand, about eight miles east of Cobourg. Among other things, this man said that Dr. Ryerson "read seditious newspapers at his house, on the Sabbath day!" In reply, Dr. Ryerson said :—

As my plan of labour prevented me from reaching this person's locality until Sunday evening, and then preach in the Church there, it would be impossible for me to do as he has alleged. Were I to have done so, I would be unworthy of the society of Christian men. But the author of this libel, which was published by him four years after the alleged circumstance took place, was defeated as a candidate for the House of Assembly, on account of a personal attack which he made upon me at the hustings! *Hinc illæ lucrymæ.* This person also said that I "hoped yet to see the walls of the Church of England levelled to the dust." In my reply to this I said :—I solemnly declare that I never uttered such a sentiment, nor have I cherished any hostility to the Church of England. Some of my friends desired me to take orders in the Church of England [see page 41]; and a gentleman (now an Episcopal clergyman) was authorized by the late Bishop of Quebec to request me to make an appointment to see him on his then contemplated tour through the Niagara District, where I was travelling. After mature, and I trust, prayerful deliberation, I replied by letter declining the proposals made, at the same time appreciating the kindness and partiality of my friends. A short time afterwards, I met the friend who had been the medium of this communication from the late Dr. Stewart. He was deeply affected at my decision. When I assigned my religious obligation to the Methodists as a reason for declining the offer, he replied that all of his own religious feelings had also been derived from them, but he thought the Church required our labours.

Some person having written, professedly from Kingston, a diatribe against Dr. Ryerson, in the London (Eng.) *Standard*, Rev. Robert Alder replied to it, and apprised him of the fact :—

An attack having been made on you in a letter from Kingston, and inserted in the *Standard*, I have been stirred up to write in your defence. I expect also to have a battle to fight with Sir Francis Head, for "I guess" he knows something of your Kingston friend.

From Mr. Alder's reply, I make the following extracts :—

There is no man, either in the Canadas or at home, better acquainted with the former and present state of these fine provinces than Mr. Ryerson, as his letters in the *Times*, signed "A Canadian," testify. Even his Kingston slanderer admits that the facts stated in these letters were, in the main exceedingly correct, indisputably true, and for the publication of which he is entitled to the grateful thanks of every loyal subject throughout British North America. But the malice of an adversary is too often swifter than the gratitude of those who have derived benefit from our services. This is proved in the case of Mr. Ryerson; for while every radical and republican journal in the province has teemed with communications vilifying his character and motives in the strongest terms, a stinted meed of praise has been doled out to him. . . . .

No wonder that persons in this country deeply interested in Canada frequently consulted him; no wonder that the British North American Land Company republished his letters from the *Times* at their own expense. And it is to the honour of the noble lord at the head of the Colonial Department, that he did obtain from so intelligent and influential an individual as Mr. Ryerson, information respecting the state of parties in a country so well-known to him. If his information and advice, and that of another "Methodist Parson" in Canada, had been received and acted upon elsewhere, there is reason to believe that Mackenzie and his traitorous associates would not have been permitted to unfurl the standard of rebellion in the midst of a peaceful and loyal people. (See pages 176 and 183.)

The inspired truth that "A man's foes shall be they of his own household" received many a painful illustration in Dr. Ryerson's history. In 1838, it was reduced to a system. The assailant was often "A Wesleyan," or, "A True Wesleyan," and under the friendly *ægis* of four or five papers, which were usually hostile to Methodism itself, the attack would be made. From numerous examples noted in the *Guardian*, I select a specimen :—

The rebellious *Guardian* is shut against us; its cry is war, havoc, and bloodshed, with Wesley on the lips, but implacable hatred to him in the heart of its editor and his friends. . . One of two things remain for us, either to expel the Ryerson family and their friends from our Society, who are the root of all our misfortunes, or . . for all true Wesleyans to withdraw from them and their wicked adherents, as the Israelites did from Egypt, or a leper.

In Dr. Ryerson's effort to protect individuals who were oppressed, and who had no means of defence, except in the columns of the *Guardian*, he was often virulently assailed, and even his life threatened. On the 22nd December, 1838, he received a letter of this kind from an influential gentleman in Toronto, who threatened legal proceedings unless the name of a writer in the *Guardian* was given to him. He said :—

In reply to your letter of last evening, I have to say that the writer of the communication in the *Guardian*, to which you refer, is one of the "peaceable members of the Methodist Society," whose character had been gratuitously and basely assailed by the Editor of the *Patriot* and his associate. He is a poor man, whose living depends upon his daily industry. Were he a rich man, I might consult with him on the subject of your letter ; but being in those circumstances of life which disable him from sustaining himself against your wealth, and relentless persecution, I at once determine to shield him from your power. I will not, therefore, furnish you with his name.

In the published paragraph of his communication, the writer has asserted that certain things were published some time since in the *Patriot*, respecting the associate of its Editor, and an attempt was made to blast the character and prospects of several unoffending members of the Methodist Society—men, the daily bread for whose families must be taken out of their mouths, if the political or private character of their protectors is, in times like the present, believed to be what this associate has represented it to be. These men do not, like you, get rich upon " wars and rumours of wars ;" their high church zeal would not, like yours, treble their business, and bring them into possession of a tolerable fortune in a few years. It is to blunt the assassinating dagger of a marked, and hitherto privileged slanderer, against the character of such men that I admitted the paragraph in question into the *Guardian*. If you are not the associate of the city Editor in this "crusade against the character of peaceable members of the Methodist Society," then you are exonerated from the remarks in the letters, and the columns of the *Guardian* are open to you for any reparation you can desire. Notwithstanding your attacks upon both my public and private character for years past; notwithstanding your late unprovoked attack upon my private character in a city newspaper ; notwithstanding your late indirect threats upon my life, and the *Guardian* office in the event of an invasion ; notwithstanding all this, and much more, I am still ready to open the columns of the *Guardian* to you, if you think that any kind of injustice has been done you. The letter to which you refer, mentions no name, but adverts to an already published portrait of a certain character who is, upon good grounds, believed to be figuring behind the scenes in this high church warfare against Methodists and others, and who is known to be indiscriminately scattering "firebrands, arrows and death," amongst all of Her Majesty's subjects who will not contribute to the profits of his newspaper craft in crying up his golden idol of a dominant church. It is amusing to see you, sir, who have availed yourself so lavishly, in all time past, of the freedom of the press to assail others, so sensitive at the mere suspicion of a mere report against causeless attacks upon private individuals, having been intended for yourself.

Dr. Ryerson concluded in the following vigorous language :—

Sir,—After having exhausted the resources of a free, I may add a licentious press to destroy me, with a view of extinguishing the principles of civil and religious liberty which I advocate, you and your party now seek to have recourse to the " glorious uncertainty of the law " to accomplish what you cannot effect by free discussion before an intelligent public ; but I am not concerned at your threats. I know the malice of the party of which you are a convenient, active, and useful tool ; I know its resources ; I know its power ; but I also know the ground on which I stand. I know the country for whose welfare I am labouring ; above all, I rely upon the wisdom and efficiency of that Providence, whose administration, I believe, if I can judge of the signs of the times, has better things in store for the inhabitants of Upper Canada (my native land) than the despotism of a dominant oligarchy, upheld and promoted by the persecuting, the anti-British, and anti-patriotic spirit of such partizans as yourself.

Rev. Matthew Richey wrote to Dr. Ryerson from Cobourg, in January, 1839, stating that some of the leading Methodists in Montreal were inducing subscribers to give up the *Guardian*, on the alleged ground of some disloyal sentiments contained in that paper of the 12th December.* Mr. Richey adds:—

> I have written to a leading friend in Montreal, earnestly expostulating with him upon the precipitancy of such a course. I have not failed to apprise him of the bitter hostility of the *Kingston Chronicle*, the *Toronto Patriot*, the *Cobourg Star*, and *The Church*, to Methodism, and to say that, did they read these papers, they would not be surprised at the pungency with which you express yourself on the questions at issue between the arrayed parties of the Province.
> To intimate that the faithful discharge of your duty may expose you to gaol or gibbet . . is not very complimentary to the freedom of the Government under whose protection you are placed. Situated as you are in the burning centre of excitement, and aware of the high hopes, as well as high-handed measures of your opponents, you have great need of patience and forbearance.

The leading Methodists in Montreal to whom Rev. Matthew Richey refers in the foregoing letter, having written to Dr. Ryerson on the subject of their complaint, he replied to them, on the 7th January, as follows:—

> Your letter of the 24th ult. being rather unusual, both in matter and form, seems to demand more than a silent acknowledgment. I shall have much pleasure in complying with your request; but I should despise myself, were I capable of making any reply to the allegation contained in your letter.
> Not a few of you impugned both my motives and principles in former years, I have lived to furnish a practical commentary on your candour and justice, by being the first to excite in the Colonial Office in England a determination to protect British interests in Lower Canada against French ambition and prejudice. I may yet have an opportunity of furnishing a second similar commentary upon your second similar imputation.
> It is true that I am not of the high church school of politics, nor of the Montreal *Herald* school of bloodshed and French extermination; but I, nevertheless, think there still remains another basis of Scripture, justice, and humanity, on which may rest the principles of a loyalty that will sacrifice

---

* The article in the *Guardian* to which reference is made, is the reply of Dr. Ryerson to several Methodists in Toronto who had signed the Address of the British Missionary party to the Governor; and who, in a letter to him, had repudiated the construction put upon the Address by the *Patriot*. Among other things the Editor said: The manly firmness with which the signers of this Address have resisted the cunning wiles of Egerton Ryerson, is a solemn pledge of their love and veneration for the glorious institution of the Empire. . . Thus ever thought we of British Wesleyans; and thus thinking was our impelling motive for persevering for the first three years of our editorial career, in one incessant battering of the pernicious, seditious principles of Egerton Ryerson; the very first number of whose paper betrayed him to us, *flagrante delicto*, a pestilent and dangerous demagogue. . . If his ambition were as legitimate and praiseworthy as his talents are commanding, he would be a far more valuable member of society than he can ever hope to be while hankering to return to the flesh pots of Yankee Episcopal Methodism, etc.

Dr. Ryerson's reply was an elaborate defence of his opposition to the efforts of the *Patriot* party to create a dominant Church, the application of the reserves to high church uses, and the establishment of the fifty-seven rectories.

life itself in the maintenance of British supremacy, in perfect harmony with a vigorous support of the constitutional rights of the subject,—unmoved at one time by the fierce denunciations of revolutionists, and unshaken at another time by the imputations of ultra-sycophantic partizanship.

Twice have the leading members of the Methodist Society in Montreal had the opportunity of insulting (and if their influence could have done it, of injuring) me—and twice have they improved it,—in May, 1834 [see page 148], when I was in Montreal; and in December, 1838—a juncture when a stain might be inflicted upon the character and reputation of any vulnerable minister of the Church that would tarnish his very grave. It is a pleasing as well as singular circumstance, and one that will be engraved upon the tablet of my heart while memory holds her seat, that when in 1834 I was insulted in Montreal, I was invited to preach in Quebec; and now that I am honoured from Montreal a second time in a similar way, I have this day received from Quebec a second token of "respect for my character and love to Methodism" of ten new subscribers to the *Guardian*, with a promise "ere long of from ten to twenty more."*

On the other hand, Dr. Ryerson, in the *Guardian* of October 17th, 1838, exposes the kind of warfare which was carried on against him by the high church party:—

I have been informed, upon the authority of creditable eye witnesses, that the number of the *Patriot* which contained four or five columns of attacks on the Editor of the *Guardian* in his private and public relations, has been carried from house to house for the edification of Methodists; that in one instance the wife of a rector had carried and read the *Patriot* to members of the Methodist Church and friends of the Editor, and then asked if they could be led by such a man as Egerton Ryerson ?

In the *Guardian* of the 31st October, Dr. Ryerson says:—

Another example of this vicious and disgraceful mode of warfare is contained in a pamphlet published at the *Kingston Chronicle* office, with a view of preventing the soldiers from deserting to the United States. . . I copy the following infamous passages, purporting to be written by a deserter [name and regiment not given]:—Well, I deserted. Ryerson never rested till he worked me up to the deed. I was like a child in his hands—he led me as he pleased. . . It was only to get clear off, and then the road to all that I ever wished for was open before me—so said Ryerson, etc. . . Ryerson has two or three more on hand, etc.

Dr. Ryerson adds:—

I had marked other passages of a like character, from the *Patriot*, the *Cobourg Star*, and the *Statesman*. . . Such are the barbarous weapons used to pull down the religious liberties of the people of this Province, and to establish a church domination.

While Dr. Ryerson was at the Conference at Hamilton, in 1839, Rev. D. McMullen, of Hillier, in a letter to him, said:—

I have read the *Guardian* with some attention during the past year. I believe the general principles of political, civil, and ecclesiastical policy advocated in it are such as must be supported and ultimately prevail, or our country will be ruined. Yet, while I admire the talent displayed by you, it

* In a letter to Dr. Ryerson, dated Montreal, 1st February, 1836, Rev. William Lord said:—Rev. Anson Green was here last week and preached. An Upper Canada Presiding Elder preaching with acceptance in Montreal ! Who would have thought of such a thing when brother Egerton Ryerson and even brother Joseph Stinson were denied the pulpit !

is still a question with me whether you, as a Methodist minister, in conducting a religious journal, are justifiable in going the lengths you do in discussions of a political character. I know that your ability and your intimate acquaintance with the state of things in the country, with parties, and all the questions at issue, etc., render you a very competent person (perhaps the most so of any other in the country) to write on these subjects; nor do I think that you ought to bury this talent, but that through some other medium than the *Guardian*, you should employ it for the country's good, and in a way that would occasion less dissatisfaction among our people, and excite and stir up less bad feeling against us and you from without.

At the same Conference, Dr. Ryerson received a strong letter of approval and encouragement from Mr. Hugh Moore, a highly respected and active member of the Church in Dundas. Mr. Moore said:—

I came to Hamilton this morning (13th June) to see you and to strengthen your hands in the course that you have taken, and are taking, in the *Guardian*. I could not get an opportunity of seeing you, so I take this way of assuring you of our hearty approbation and support,—as it is deemed necessary at this time to speak out. Go on; you speak the language of our hearts. I should have seen you at Toronto on my way from Montreal, and have told you of the opinion and feelings of our community here, but time would not permit. It is worthy of note that the people are determined to support you. May God aid and direct you and all that are with you!

Equally hearty was a letter which Dr. Ryerson received from Rev. John McIntyre, in September, 1839,* inviting him to come and preach for him in Perth. In urging him to comply with the request, Mr. McIntyre said:—

If the day is favourable, the people will assemble from all quarters. I know myself of persons who intend to come about 20 miles to hear you. You can have no idea of your popularity in this district, although principally a military settlement. Methodists, Presbyterians, Roman Catholics, and moderate Churchmen, consider you, as some Presbyterians were pleased some time ago to style you, "The Saviour of Upper Canada." Now, to disappoint their just expectation would be almost unpardonable. The people entertain so high an opinion of your abilities, that (as some have lately said) you could speak with five minutes' notice on any subject. I should be extremely sorry that they should ever hold any other opinion; but, at your departure from Perth, the people may say, as the Queen of Sheba did on her visit to Solomon, "It was a true report we heard of his acts, and of his wisdom, and behold the half was not told us."

Rev. G. R. Sanderson, also writing to Dr. Ryerson, said:—

I greatly regret these constant attacks upon you, who have laboured so arduously and struggled so perseveringly for the good of our country, and the settlement of the Clergy Reserves. I am sure, however, that you will have the warmest thanks of all true friends of their country; and that posterity will not withhold that praise which is due you for your indefatigable exertions.

I have already, on page 101, inserted a kindly letter to Dr.

* This gentlemen entered the Methodist ministry in 1835, and joined the Church of England in 1841. He died some years since.

Ryerson from Rev. William Bell, Presbyterian minister, expressive of his sympathy with the course pursued by the *Guardian* on the Clergy Reserve and other questions. The following letters of the same character were from parties outside of Dr. Ryerson's own Church. Thus in 1839, the Congregational Association of Upper Canada passed resolutions approving of Dr. Ryerson's course—the last one of which was as follows:—

We express to the Rev. Egerton Ryerson our thanks for his able and persevering exertions to effect a settlement of the Clergy Reserve question, and our determination to afford him any and every support in his endeavours that it may be in our power to render.

Rev. James Noll in enclosing the resolutions said:—

I feel myself happy, Sir, to be the medium of communicating to you the sentiments and feelings of my brethren at a time when you are insulted and abused as a public disturber, a rebel, and a political demagogue, by those who are willing to sacrifice the peace, and even risk the safety of the Colony . . Allow me to assure you of my admiration of the fair, spirited, and able manner in which you have conducted this important and painful controversy. . . The cause you are advocating is closely identified with the cause of God. Your object is not only the temporal but spiritual welfare of your country, and your friends are the great bulk of its loyal and well-disposed inhabitants.

Rev. John Roaf (Congregational), of Toronto, in a letter to Dr. Ryerson, dated December, 1838, said:—

I am desirous of not omitting one of my duties in relation to the "Church question," and looking to you as the Leader of the non-established parties, am anxious to understand your views upon the rectory question. Should you also think of any other measure by which I and my immediate brethren can support the cause which you are so zealously and efficiently promoting, or can assist in weakening the opposition to which you are subject, I shall be happy in attending to your suggestions.

Mr. William Greig (Baptist), Bookseller, Montreal, in a letter to Dr. Ryerson, dated June, 1839, says:—

As an ardent friend to civil and religious liberty, and an admirer of the course pursued by yourself as Editor of the *Christian Guardian*, I cannot but express my regret at seeing you assailed on all sides, and especially by those for whose good you have been exerting yourself. As a native of Great Britain, I am fondly attached to her civil institutions, and will yield in loyalty to no one. I cannot, therefore, but approve of any lawful and fair measures which will tend to bring all denominations to that level, that every one provide for itself. I therefore say, go on in your present course; keep up the fire, brisk and hot on the enemy, till they are routed. As I see several are withdrawing their subscriptions to the *Guardian*, the friends of civil and religious liberty, of whatever denomination, ought to come in and take their places. Although not a Methodist, please put me down as a subscriber to the *Guardian*.

CHAPTER XXVII.

1778–1867.

The Honourable and Right Reverend Bishop Strachan.

THE Venerable John Strachan, D.D., LL.D., Archdeacon of York, and subsequently (1839–1867) first Bishop of Toronto, was the chief clerical opponent which Dr. Ryerson encountered in the contest for religious freedom and denominational equality during nearly twenty years.

Dr. Strachan was born in Scotland, in April, 1778, and died at Toronto, in November 1867, in the 90th year of his age.

It was a singular coincidence that Dr. Strachan entered the ministry of the Church of England in May, 1803, just two months after Dr. Ryerson was born. Who could then have foreseen the respective careers of these two remarkable men! The one, the virtual founder and administrative head of the Church of England in Upper Canada for upwards of 60 years; and the other, although not the founder, yet the controlling head and leader of the Methodist Church in the Province for nearly the same period.

Dr. Strachan was an uncompromising high churchman. His exclusive views on the "priestly authority, and the catholic and apostolic character of the Church of England," were those of a church optimist, but they were not based upon any profound study of the subject, as his own statement will attest. *

* My mother (he said) belonged to the Relief denomination. . . My father was attached to the Non-Jurants; and although he went occasionally with my mother, he was a frequent hearer of Bishop Skinner, to whose church he was in the habit of carrying me. He died when I was very young, but not before my mind was impressed in favour of Episcopacy. . . I readily confess, that in respect to Church Government, my principles were sufficiently vague and unformed; for to this important subject my attention was never particularly drawn till I came to this country, when my venerated friend, the late Dr. Stewart, of Kingston, urged me to enter the Church, and as I had never yet communicated, that excellent person, whom I loved as a father, admitted me to the altar a little before I went to Quebec to take holy orders, in 1803. Before I had determined to enter the Church of England, I was induced by the advice of another friend (the late Mr. Cartwright) . . to make some inquiries respecting the Presbyterian Church of Montreal, then vacant. (Dr. Strachan's Speech in the Legislative Council, March 6th, 1828, pages 25, 26.)

It is interesting to note the causes which led Dr. Strachan to cling so tenaciously to the idea of "Church and State"—a union which he regarded as sacred, and ordained of God for the maintenance of His cause and Church on the earth. It is no less interesting to understand the reason why Dr. Ryerson as strenuously repudiated and resisted the practical application of the same idea to Canada. The reason in each case may be stated in a few words.

The one from early associations regarded the idea of Scottish parish churches and parochial schools, supported by the State, as eminently Scriptural, if not divinely enjoined from the earliest Jewish times. The other was brought up in a land where such a state of things had never existed, and where the pure gospel had been preached from the earliest times without the aid of a state endowment. He lived in a land, too, where the command to the Christian Church was felt to be fitly expressed by John Wesley, to take the "world as a parish" and preach the Gospel to every creature. The manner in which this command was to be obeyed was indicated by our Lord's example, when He sent forth His disciples with this injunction:—

Provide neither gold, nor silver, nor brass in your purses . . for the workman is worthy of his meat. Matt. x. 9, 10.

Members of the Conference, in Dr. Ryerson's early days, unhesitatingly obeyed the directions of the Conference—many regarding it as the voice of God in the Church—and went forth, without scrip or purse, everywhere, even to the remotest corner of the land, bearing the good tidings, not considering their pecuniary interests,[*] or even their lives dear unto them, so that they might win souls for the Master.[†]

Dr. Strachan's views on the question of State aid to churches

---

[*] The stipends of Methodist ministers in those days were very small. Rev. Dr. John Carroll tells me that the "quarterage" payable to an unmarried Methodist minister in America, at first, was only $60 per annum; then it was increased to $80, at which rate it remained until 1816, when the General Conference fixed it at $100, at which it remained until 1854. The rule for a married minister was double that for a single man, and $16 for each child. Besides quarterage, there was an allowance for travelling and table expenses. Two hundred dollars was the sum for salary, besides travelling and aid expenses, allowed to a minister up to 1854, and even then this sum was rarely ever paid in full.—H.

[†] Rev. H. Wilkinson in a note to Dr. Ryerson, in 1837, thus describes the kind of places to which some ministers had to be sent, and their duties and qualifications when there. He said: I require a man for a mission which lies about 200 miles from Bytown, up the Grand River (Ottawa), and which will be difficult of access in the winter. A suitable person could make his way northwards with some of the rude lumbermen, who now and then go up in companies. The brother would need to be strong in mind and body, and fervent in spirit. He would need to go on foot, and paddle a canoe, or row a boat, as the case might be, and thus reach his appointments in the best way he can.

were clearly, on the other hand, the result of his observations, in Scotland. They are prominently brought out in his memorable speech, delivered in the Legislative Council, on the 6th of March, 1828. He says:—

> Have not the Methodists in this Province . . ever shown themselves the enemies of the Established Church? Are they not at this moment labouring to separate religion from the State, with which it ought to be firmly united? . . Has it not been the primary object of all enemies to regular government . . to pull down religious establishments? . . If they tell me the Ecclesiastical establishments are great evils, I bid them look to England and Scotland, each of which has a religious establishment, and to these establishments are they mainly indebted for their vast superiority to other nations. To what but her Established Church, and the Parochial Schools under her direction, does Scotland owe her high reputation for moral improvement. (Pages 27 and 28.)

Again, in a remarkable letter to his friend (Rev. Dr. Thomas Chalmers, of Edinburgh*), written in 1832, on the Life and Character of Bishop Hobart of New York, Dr. Strachan relates a conversation with that Bishop in which he took him severely to task for extolling the voluntary system of the American Episcopal Church as compared with the endowed State Church of England. I make a few extracts:—

> Let us look at the Episcopal Church of the United States, and see what moral effect it can have on the population, as a source of religious instruction. . . The influence of the two Churches as confined to England and New York (alone) is as one to seventy. . . Such influence on the manners and habits of the people [in that state] is next to nothing, and yet you extol your Church above that of England, and exclaim against establishment! Add to this, the dependence of your clergy upon the people for support—a state of things which is attended with most pernicious consequences. . . but in general, the clergy of all denominations in the United States, are miserably dependent upon their congregations. . . It is the duty of Christian nations to constitute, within their boundaries, ecclesiastical establishments. . . For it is incumbent upon nations as upon individuals, to honour the Lord with their substance. (Pages 41–47.)

Bishop Strachan's early and later writings abound in expressions of similar views. It was not to be wondered at, therefore, that a man of his strong convictions would seek to give practical effect to them in dealing, as opportunity offered, with questions of church establishment and the clergy reserves.

It is true that by his persuasive words and strong personal influence—when the object was the financial benefit of the Church—Bishop Strachan rallied around him many of the

---

* While in the vicinity of St. Andrews I contracted several important friendships, amongst others, with Thomas Duncan, afterwards Professor of Mathematics, and also with Dr. Chalmers, since then so deservedly renowned. We were all three very nearly of the same age, and our friendship only terminated with death, being kept alive by a constant correspondence during more than sixty years. (Bishop Strachan's Charge to his Clergy, June, 1860; page 10.)

leading members of the Church of England in Upper Canada who aided him in his plans for endowing the Church out of the public domain. Yet it is also true that many equally sound churchmen were opposed to these schemes, and saw in them the germ of a fatal canker, which in time would be sure to destroy the Church's missionary zeal, and paralyze all of those noble and generous impulses which characterize a living Church in the promotion of Christian effort in the various departments of Church work. *

As time has passed on the little band of loyal churchmen, who incurred the Bishop's unmerited censure for opposing his exclusive schemes of Church aggrandisement, has increased to thousands in our day. They deeply regret the success of those schemes, and deprecate the existence of clergy reserves and rectory endowments as in themselves fatal to the healthy development of Church work as an active and aggressive force in the Christian life.

It is not necessary to refer here to Bishop Strachan's views in regard to ecclesiastical polity. They are well known. On this matter also many sound churchmen differed widely (and still differ) from his views. Yet Bishop Strachan, while holding such strong and exclusive views, was kindly disposed towards "Sectaries" individually, and lived on terms of personal friendship with many of those whose opinions were opposed to his on church questions. In his Legislative Council speech, already quoted, he says:—

I have been charged with being hostile to the Scotch Church, and with being an apostate from that communion. . . My hostility to the Kirk of Scotland consists in being on the most intimate terms with the late Mr. Bethune and Dr. Spark. . . To both these excellent men I willingly . . pay a tribute of respect. . . Nor have I ever missed an opportunity, when in my power, of being useful to the clergy of the Church of Scotland, or of treating them with respect, kindness, and hospitality. (Page 22.)

Again, in his sermon on "Church Fellowship," preached in 1832, Dr. Strachan says:—

* Speaking of the passage of a Clergy Reserve Bill in 1840, to which the Bishop of Toronto was strongly opposed, Dr. Ryerson says: A considerable majority of the members of the Church of England in both Houses of the Legislature voted for the Bill, and were afterwards charged by the Bishop with "defection and treachery" for doing so. On this point, Lord Sydenham, in a despatch to Lord John Russell, dated, 5th February, 1840, said: It is notorious to every one here, that of twenty-two members (being communicants of the Church of England) who voted upon this bill, only eight recorded their opinion in favour of the views expressed by the Right Reverend Prelate, whilst, in the Legislative Council the majority was still greater ; and amongst those who gave it their warmest support, are to be found many gentlemen of the highest character for independence, and for attachment to the Church, and whose views on general politics differ from those of Her Majesty's Government. (Dr. Ryerson's Criticism on Bishop Strachan's letter to Lord John Russell, dated, February 20th, 1851.)

Widely as we differ from the Roman Catholics in many religious points of the greatest importance, we have always lived with them in the kindest intercourse, and in the cordial exchange of the charities of social life. The worthy prelate, by whom they are at present spiritually governed, has been my friend for nearly thirty years. With the members of the Church of Scotland we associate in the same manner.* . . The merits of our sister Church cannot be unknown to you, my brethren. To me they are familiar, and connected with many of my cherished and early associations. . . Of that popular and increasing class of Christians [the Methodists], who call themselves a branch of our Church, both at home and abroad, I would speak with praise. (Pages 23-25.)

As to his relations with Dr. Ryerson, I here insert two notes from the Bishop to him. The first is dated February 7th, 1838, as follows:—

The Archdeacon of York presents his compliments to the Rev. E. Ryerson, and begs to acknowledge with satisfaction his courtesy in sending him a copy of his excellent sermon on the Recent Conspiracy, which the Archdeacon has read with much pleasure and profit. Such doctrines, if generally diffused among our people, cannot fail of producing the most beneficial effects, both spiritual and temporal.

The second related to the calamity which had befallen the Church of England congregation of St. James', in the destruction of its church building by fire early in January, 1839. Dr. Ryerson at once wrote to the Archdeacon offering him the use of the Newgate (Adelaide Street) Church. On the 6th January, Dr. Strachan replied as follows:—

I thank you most sincerely for the kind sympathy you express in the sad calamity that has befallen us, and for your generous offer of accommodation. Before your note reached me, I had made arrangements with the Mayor, for the Town Hall, which we can occupy at our accustomed hours of worship, without disturbing any other congregation. I and my people are not the less grateful for your kind offer, which we shall keep in brotherly remembrance.

In his Charge to the Clergy in 1853, and again in 1856, he pays a personal tribute to Dr. Ryerson. In the later Charge, speaking of the School system, he says:—

So far as Dr. Ryerson is concerned, I am one of those who appreciate very highly his exertions, his unwearied assiduity, and his administrative capacity.

Dr. Ryerson's last reference to the Bishop is contained in the "Epochs of Canadian Methodism," written in 1880, as follows:

Upwards of fifty years have passed away since my criticisms on Dr. Strachan's "Sermon on the death of the Bishop of Quebec" were written. On the re-perusal of them, after the lapse of so long a time, the impression on my own mind is that Dr. Strachan was honest in his statements and opinions. . . He was more moderate and liberal in his views and feelings in his later years, and became the personal friend of his old antagonist, "The Reviewer," who, he said, had "fought fair." (Page 145.)

* These kindly words the Bishop repeated in substance to the Editor some years since, when talking with him on the subject.—H.

CHAPTER XXVIII.

1791—1836.

THE CLERGY RESERVES AND RECTORIES QUESTIONS.

THE discussion of the Clergy Reserve Question enters so largely into the Story of Dr. Ryerson's Life, that I give in this chapter a short, condensed sketch of its origin and history down to 1837-38. The remainder of the sketch will be developed in an account of the contest preceding the settlement of the question in subsequent chapters.

After the conquest of Canada, in 1760, the right of the Roman Catholic inhabitants to enjoy their religion was guaranteed to them in the Treaty of Paris, Feb. 10th, 1763. In 1774, an Act was passed by the British Parliament (14 Geo. III., ch. 83) by which the right to their accustomed dues and tithes was secured to the clergy of the Church of Rome in the then Province of Quebec (including what was afterwards Upper and Lower Canada). The same Act provided for the encouragement of the Protestant religion, and, for the support of a Protestant clergy, by other tithes and dues.*

In 1791, the Province of Quebec was divided into Upper and Lower Canada, and, in an Act introduced into the British Parliament by Mr. Pitt, provision was made for their government. Sections 35-42 of that Act dealt with the maintenance and support of a Protestant Clergy, and this provision (1) allotted one-seventh of all lands which might be hereafter granted by the King for settlement; and (2) gave authority for the erection of "parsonages or rectories, according to the establishment of the Church of England," to be endowed out of the lands so allotted, etc. (Sec. 38).

The alleged reasons which induced George III. to make provision for the support of religion in the North American Colonies, are set forth, so far as they related to the Protestant

---

* These tithes continued to be collected for the support of a Protestant Clergy until February, 1823, when a declaratory Act, passed by the Legislature of Upper Canada in 1821, was sanctioned by the King to the effect that hereafter "no tithes shall be claimed, demanded, or received by any ecclesiastical parson, rector or vicar, of the Protestant Church within this Province."

religion, by the late Bishop Strachan in a pamphlet which he published in England in 1827.* He mentions the fact that Great Britain, of all European nations, had hitherto made no provision for religious instruction in her colonies. He further states that:—

The effect of this was that emigrants belonging to the Established Church who settled in America, not having access to their own religious ministrations, became frequently dissenters; and when the Colonies (now the United States) rebelled, there was not, among a population of nearly 3,000,000, a single prelate, and but very few Episcopal clergymen.

The folly of this policy was shown in the strongest light during the rebellion; almost all of the Episcopal clergy and their congregations remained faithful to the King, demonstrating by their conduct, that had proper care been taken to promote a religious establishment in connection with that of England, the revolution would not have taken place.†

Aware of the pernicious effects of this narrow and unchristian policy, and sensible that the colonist ought to be attached to the parent state by religious, as well as by political feelings, the great Mr. Pitt determined (in forming a constitution for the Canadas) to provide for the religious instruction of the people, and to lay the foundation of an Ecclesiastical Establishment which should increase with the settlement.

To accomplish this noble purpose, Mr. Pitt advised that one-seventh of the lands should be set apart for the maintenance of a Protestant Clergy. In Upper Canada this appropriation comprises one-seventh of the whole province: but in Lower Canada, one-seventh of those parts only which have been granted since 1791 (pages 2, 3).‡

In a pamphlet published at Kingston, U.C., during the previous year, the substance of Mr. Pitt's remarks on that part of the Bill which authorized the setting apart of these lands, is given as follows:—

Mr. Pitt (House of Commons, 12th May, 1791), said that he gave the Colonial Government and Council power, under the instructions of His Majesty, to distribute out of a sum arising from the tithes for land or possessions, and set apart for the maintenance and support of a Protestant clergy. Another clause (he said) provided, for the permanent support of the Protestant clergy, a seventh portion of the lands to be granted in future. He declared that the meaning of the Act was to enable the Governor to endow and to present the Protestant clergy of the established church to such parsonage or rectory as might be constituted or erected within every township or parish, which now was, or might be formed; and to give to such Protestant clergyman of the established church, a part, or the whole, as the Governor thought proper, of the lands appropriated by the Act. He further

---

* Observations on the Provision made for the Maintenance of a Protestant Clergy in the Provinces of Upper and Lower Canada, under the 31st Geo. III., cap. 31. By John Strachan, D.D., Archdeacon of York, Upper Canada, pp. 44. London, 1827.

† In a letter written by Dr. Ryerson in 1851, he criticised a similar statement then made by Bishop Strachan. He pointed out that Washington and other leaders of the revolution were staunch churchmen.

‡ In no part of Mr. Pitt's remarks on the Bill setting apart land for the Protestant Clergy do I find any intimation of the kind mentioned by Bishop Strachan. Governor Simcoe, however, held these views, which by mistake the Bishop may have attributed to Mr. Pitt. (See next page.)—H.

explained that this was done to encourage the established church; and that possibly hereafter it might be proposed to send a Bishop of the established church to sit in the Legislative Council. (Parl. Reg., vol. 29, pp. 414, 415.)*

Mr. Fox was entirely opposed to these arrangements. He said: By the Protestant clergy, he supposed to be understood not only the clergy of the Church of England, but all descriptions of Protestants. . . That the clergy should have one-seventh of all grants, he must confess, appeared to him an absurd doctrine. If they were all of the Church of England, this would not reconcile him to the measure. The greater part of these Protestant clergy were not of the Church of England; they were chiefly Protestant dissenters. . . We were, by this Bill, making a sort of provision for the Protestant clergy of Canada [of one-seventh of the land] which was unknown to them in every part of Europe; a provision, in his apprehension, which would rather tend to corrupt than to benefit them. (Hansard, vol. 29, 1791, page 108.)

I have carefully gone through the whole of the debate on this subject, but I cannot find one word in it which would indicate that Mr. Pitt, Mr. Fox, or Mr. Burke (the chief speakers), entertained the idea that endowing the clergy had any political significance as a precautionary measure for ensuring the loyalty of the inhabitants. The opinion was expressed that setting apart these lands was the most feasible way (as Mr. Pitt said) of providing "for the permanent support of the Protestant clergy," and of giving "them a competent income." †

In a letter to Dr. Moore, Archbishop of Canterbury, dated December, 1790, Col. J. Graves Simcoe said :—

I am decidedly of opinion that a regular Episcopal establishment . . is absolutely necessary in any extensive colony which England means to preserve, etc. The neglect of this principle of overturning republicanism in former periods, by giving support and assistance to those causes which are perpetually offering themselves to affect so necessary an object, is much to be lamented; but it is my duty to be as solicitous as possible, that they may now have their due influence, etc.

In a "Memoir" written by Governor Simcoe in 1791, he said :

In regard to the Episcopal establishment. . . I firmly believe the present to be a critical moment, in which that system, so interwoven and connected with the monarchical foundation of our government, may be productive of the most permanent and extensive benefits, in preserving the connection between Great Britain and her Colonies.

From various sources I gather the following particulars :—

From 1791 to 1819, the Clergy Reserves were in the hands of the Government, and managed by it alone. For years they yielded scarcely enough to defray the expenses of management. In 1817 the House of Assembly objected to such an appropriation for the clergy, as "beyond all precedent lavish," and complained that the reservations were an obstacle to improve-

* An Apology for the Church of England in the Canadas, etc. By a Protestant of the Established Church of England. Kingston, U.C., 1826, page 11.

† It was in the discussion on this Bill that the long personal friendship which had existed between Fox and Burke was brought to an abrupt termination.—H.

ment and settlement. In 1819, lands were taxed for the construction of roads, and it was contended that the reservations on the public roads should also be taxed.

In 1819, the question was first mooted, as to to the right of Presbyterians to share in the reserves. In March, of that year, thirty-seven Presbyterians of the town of Niagara, petitioned Sir Peregrine Maitland, to grant to the Presbyterian congregation there, the annual sum of £100 in aid, out of the clergy reserves, or out of any other fund at the Governor's disposal. In transmitting this petition to the Colonial Secretary for instructions, Sir P. Maitland mentioned that "the actual product of the clergy reserves is about £700 per annum." In May, 1820, a reply was received from Lord Bathurst, stating that, in the opinion of the Crown officers, the provisions of the Act of 1791, "for the support of the Protestant clergy, are not confined solely to the clergy of the Church of England, but may be extended also to the clergy of the Church of Scotland," but not to dissenting ministers.

In 1819, on the application of Bishop Mountain, of Quebec, the clergy in each province were incorporated for the purpose of leasing and managing the reserves—the proceeds, however, to be paid over to the Government. On the appearance of a notice to this effect in the Quebec *Gazette*, dated, 18th June, 1820, the clergy of the Church of Scotland memorialized the King for a share in these reserves.

In 1823, the House of Assembly, on motion of Hon. William Morris, concurred in a series of resolutions, asserting the right of the Church of Scotland in Canada to a share in the reserves. These resolutions were rejected by the Legislative Council, by a vote of 6 to. 5.

In April, 1824, Dr. Strachan was deputed by the Bishop of Quebec and Sir P. Maitland, to go to England and get authority from Lord Bathurst to sell portions of the reserves. In the meantime, the Canada (Land) Company proposed to purchase all the Crown and Clergy Reserve Lands at a valuation to be agreed on. The clergy corporation having desired a voice in this valuation, the Bishop of Quebec deputed Archdeacon Mountain to press this view on Lord Bathurst. Some misunderstanding having arisen between Lord Bathurst and Archdeacon Strachan, and the Canada Land Company, Dr. Strachan went to England in April, 1826, and was deputed by Lord Bathurst to arrange the differences with Mr. John Galt, Commissioner of the Company This they did by changing the original plan. The clergy lands were exchanged for 1,000,000 acres in the Huron tract. Out of the moneys received from the Canada Company the Home Government appropriated £700 a year to the Church of Scotland clergy,* and the same amount to the clergy of the Church of Rome in Upper Canada.

In June, 1826, the Home Government, on the memorial of the Church of Scotland General Assembly, and an address from the House of Assembly, founded on the resolutions of 1823 (which, as introduced, had been rejected by the Legislative Council), acknowledged the rights of the Church of Scotland clergy to a share of the reserves. In January, 1826, the House of Assembly memorialized the King to distribute the proceeds of the reserves for the benefit of all denominations, or failing that to the purposes of education and the general improvement of the Province. The reply to this memorial was so unsatisfactory that the House of Assembly (December 22nd, 1826), adopted a series of eleven resolutions, deprecating the action of the Home Government in appropriating the clergy reserves to individuals connected with the Church of England "to the exclusion of other denominations"—that church bearing "a very small proportion to the number of other

* In 1830, Presbyterian ministers not of the Church of Scotland, were, on petition to that effect (signed by Rev. W. Smart, Moderator, and Rev. W. Bell, Presbytery Clerk), placed on the same footing as the ministers of the Kirk.—H.

Christians in the province." The Assembly prayed that the proceeds of the reserves be applied to the support of district and common schools, a Provincial seminary, and in aid of erecting places of worship for all denominations of Christians. These resolutions passed by majorities of from 25 to 30 ; the nays being 2 and 3 only. The bill founded on these resolutions was negatived in the Legislative Council (January, 1827). In the year 1826, Dr. Strachan obtained a royal charter for King's College, with an endowment of 225,000 acres of land, and a grant of £1,000 for sixteen years. This charter was wholly in favour of the Church of England, and its obnoxious clauses remained unchanged until 1835.

In March, 1827, Hon. R. W. Horton introduced a Bill into Parliament to provide for the sale of the clergy lands, as asked for by the Bishop of Quebec. This led to a protracted discussion between the friends in the House of the English and Scotch Churches, and requests were made for information on the state of these Churches in Upper Canada. Archdeacon Strachan, then in England, furnished this information in his famous letter and Chart, dated, May 16th, 1827. Objection to giving the clergy corporation power to sell these lands having been made, Mr. Horton withdrew his original bill, and in a new one, which was passed, confined the exercise of this power to the Executive Government.

In March, 1828, the House of Assembly memorialized the King to place the proceeds of the reserves at the disposal of the House for the purposes of education and internal improvement. Mr. Morris' motion to strike out "internal improvement" was lost. In this year a committee of the House of Commons reported against continuing the reservation in mortmain of the clergy lands, as it imposed serious obstacles to the improvement of the colony.

In 1829, two despatches on the clergy reserve question were sent to the Colonial Secretary by Sir John Colborne. In one, dated 11th April, Sir John says : If a more ardent zeal be not shown by the Established Church, and a very different kind of minister than that which is generally to be found in this Province sent out from England, it is obvious that the members of the Established Church will be inconsiderable, and that it will continue to lose ground. The Methodists, apparently, exceed the number of the Churches of England and Scotland. . . If the Wesleyan Methodists in England could be prevailed on to supply this Province with preachers, the Methodists of this country would become, as a political body, of less importance than they are at present.

In this year the House of Assembly passed a bill similar to that of 1828 It was rejected, as in the previous year, by the Legislative Council. In 1830, the same proceedings were repeated with like result.

In December, 1830 (see page 101), a monster petition was agreed to, and afterwards signed by 10,000 persons and sent to England, praying that steps be taken to leave the ministers of all denominations to be supported by the people among whom they labour and the voluntary contributions of benevolent Societies in Canada and Great Britain—to do away with all political distinctions on account of religious faith—to remove all ministers of religion from seats and places of political power in the Provincial Government—to grant to the clergy of all denominations the enjoyment of equal rights and privileges in everything that appertains to them as British subjects and as ministers of the Gospel, particularly the right of solemnizing matrimony—to modify the charter of King's College, so as to exclude all sectarian tests and preferences—and to appropriate the proceeds of the sale of the lands, heretofore set apart for the support of a Protestant Clergy, to the purposes of general education and various internal improvements.

Such was the comprehensive character of the reforms prayed for in this province upwards of fifty years ago. All of these reforms have been long since granted ; but the enumeration of them shows how far off the mass of the people and their ministers were then from the enjoyment of the civil and religious privileges which are now the birthright of every British subject in Canada.

This " programme of reforms " will also show what were the principles for which Dr. Ryerson, and other pioneers of religious freedom in Upper Canada, had to contend half a century ago. Nor was the victory easily won which they achieved. The struggle was a long and arduous one. Each step was contested by the dominant party, and every reform was resisted with a determination worthy of a better cause.

In March 1831, the first attempt was made (on motion of Mr. Hagerman) to deprive the Canadian Legislature of the power to deal with the clergy reserve question. His motion was to revest the reserves in the crown for religious purposes, but it was negatived by a vote of 30 to 7. Although defeated now, the same proposition was frequently made afterwards, and at length with success. In 1839 a provision of that kind was passed, but it failed on technical grounds to receive the royal assent. See chapter xxxi.

In 1831 and 1832, addresses to the King were adopted by the House of Assembly praying, as before, that the reserves be applied to educational purposes. In this year a satisfactory reply from the Home Government, in regard to the clergy reserve question, was communicated to the Legislature, and it was invited to consider the desirability of exercising its power to " vary or repeal " certain provisions for the support of a Protestant Clergy. In 1832 and in 1833, bills to revest the clergy reserve lands in the Crown were read a second time, and, in 1834, one to that effect was finally passed, but was rejected by the Legislative Council. A bill for the sale of the reserves and the application of the proceeds to educational purposes, was passed in 1835, by a vote of 40 to 4, but was again rejected by the Legislative Council. This body in the same year proposed that both Houses should abdicate their functions in regard to the reserves (as they were unable to concur in any measure on the subject), and request the Imperial Parliament to legislate on the subject ! The House of Assembly peremptorily refused, by a vote of two to one, to concur in such a proposition, and read a dignified lecture to the Council on its refusal to pass their measures, or to originate one of its own. The members of the Assembly felt that the influence of the Governor and the members of the Council would be so potent in England, that by it the wishes of the people of Upper Canada, as repeatedly expressed by that House, would be frustrated.* In 1836, the bill of the previous year was passed by the Assembly by a majority of 35 to 5. The Legislative Council amended it so as to leave the matter as before with the British Parliament. This amendment was defeated by the House of Assembly by a vote of 27 to 1, and so the matter ended. In 1837–38 the rebellion took place, leaving the clergy reserve question in abeyance for some time.

On the 15th January, 1836, Sir John Colborne, by order in council, established fifty-seven rectories in Upper Canada, and endowed them out of the clergy reserve lands. This was done at the last moment, and while the successor of Sir John Colborne (Sir F. B. Head) was on his way from New York to Toronto. So great was the haste in which this act was done, that only 44 out of the 57 patents were signed by the retiring Governor; so that only that number of rectories were actually endowed. There is no doubt but that the Constitutional Act of 1791 authorized not only the setting apart of the clergy reserves, but also the erection of "parsonages and rectories according to the establishment of the Church of England," to be endowed out of the lands so allotted. (Sec. 38). But, in Lord Glenelg's opinion, the subject was never submitted for the signification of the King's pleasure thereon. Certain ambiguous words, in Lord Ripon's reply to a private communication from Sir John Colborne, was the authority relied upon for the hasty and unpopular act of the retiring Governor. The legality of the act was frequently questioned, but it was finally affirmed by the Court of Chancery in Upper Canada in 1856. The judgment in the case of the Attorney-General vs. Grasett was that—

Under the statute 31, Geo. III., ch. 31, and the Royal Commission, Sir John Colborne, the Lieutenant-Governor of Upper Canada, had authority to create and endow rectories without further instructions.

* This was abundantly proved afterwards. In the following Parliament an amended bill was carried, by a majority of one vote, in the House of Assembly to place the proceeds of the reserves at the disposal of the British Parliament. Petitions were at once sent to the Queen to induce her to assent to this bill, and the Bishop went to England to present them. Sir George Arthur also lent his aid for the same object. The scheme failed, however, on technical grounds, but was successfully revived the next year. (See *Guardian* 1st January, 1840, and page 249.)—H.

CHAPTER XXIX.

1838.

THE CLERGY RESERVE CONTROVERSY RENEWED.

THE question at issue, when the House of Assembly was elected in 1836 for the parliamentary term ending in 1839, was adroitly narrowed by Sir F. B. Head to the simple one of loyalty to the Crown, or—as Dr. Ryerson, in a letter to Hon. W. H. Draper (September, 1838), expressed it—"Whether or not . . this Province would remain an integral part of the British Empire." Lord Durham pointed out that Sir F. B. Head led the people to believe "that they were called upon to decide the question of separation [from Great Britain] by their votes."

Under such circumstances the clergy reserve question was subordinated to those of graver moment. Besides, even if pledges had been given by members before the election on the subject, they were not felt, as the event proved, to be very sacred. Speaking of this Parliament, Dr. Ryerson, in his letter to Mr. Draper, (already mentioned), said :—

The present Assembly at its first session adopted a resolution in favour of appropriating the reserves for "the religious and moral instruction of the Province." But its proceedings during the second session were so vacillating that it is now difficult to say what the opinions of the members are.

One explanation of this state of feeling was, that the political views of a majority of the members were in harmony with those of the ruling party in the country, and yet were at variance with the views of their constituents on the clergy reserve question. Advantage was taken of the existence of this political sympathy by the leaders of the dominant party, with a view to secure the removal of the clergy reserve question from the hostile arena of the Upper Canada Legislature to the friendly atmosphere of the English House of Commons, and the still more friendly tribunal of the House of Lords—where the bench of bishops would be sure to defend the claims of the Church to this royal patrimony.*

* In his despatch to Lord Glenelg, giving an extract of his speech at the opening of the ensuing session of the Legislature, Sir George Arthur puts this idea in an official form. He says :—That such "a tribunal is free from those local influences and excitement which operate too powerfully here." In his seventh letter to Hon. W. H. Draper on the clergy reserve question, dated January, 26th, 1839, Dr. Ryerson argues the whole question of the re-investment of the reserves at length. He also shows that so far from the "tribunal" here spoken of by Sir

Accordingly, at the third session of this Parliament, Mr. Cartwright, of Kingston, introduced a bill " to revest the Clergy Reserves in Her Majesty "—the first reading of which was carried by a vote of 24 to 5, and passed through Committee of the whole by a vote of 29 to 12. As soon as Dr. Ryerson, then in Kingston, got a copy of this bill he wrote the following letter, on the 13th January, 1838, to the *Guardian :*—

The professed object of this bill is described by its title, but the real object, and the necessary effect of it, from the very nature of its provisions, is to apply the reserves to those exclusive and partial purposes against which the great majority of the inhabitants of this province, both by petition and through their representatives, have protested in every variety of language during the last twelve years—and that without any variation or the shadow of change. The bill even proposes to transfer future legislation on this subject from the Provincial to the Imperial Parliament! The authors of this bill are, it seems, afraid to trust the inhabitants of Upper Canada to legislate on a subject in which they themselves are solely concerned; nay, they will environ themselves and the interests they wish to promote behind the Imperial Parliament! The measure itself, containing the provisions it does, is a shameful deception upon the Canadian public—is a wanton betrayal of Canadian rights— is a disgraceful sacrifice of Canadian, to selfish party interests— is a covert assassination of a vital principle of Canadian constitutional and free government—is a base political and religious fraud which ought to excite the deep concern and rouse the indignant and vigorous exertion of every friend of justice, and freedom, and good government in the country.

My language may be strong; but strong as it is, it halts far behind the emotions of my mind. Such a measure, I boldly affirm, is not what the people of Upper Canada expected from the members of the present Assembly when they elected them as their representatives; it is not such a measure as, I have reason to believe, a majority of the present members of the Assembly gave their constituents to understand they would vote for when they solicited their suffrages. Honourable gentlemen, if I can be heard by them, ought to remember that they have a character to sustain, more important than the attainment

George Arthur being a desirable one to adjudicate on this question, it would be the very reverse.

It should be remembered that in more than one despatch the Colonial Secretary held that the question was one to be settled by the Provincial, rather than by the Imperial Parliament, and declined to interfere with the rights of the Canadian Legislature in the matter. This will be clearly shown in a subsequent chapter. Lord Glenelg's utterances on this question are very emphatic, especially in his despatch dated 5th December, 1835.

of a particular object; they ought to remember that they act in a delegated capacity; and if they cannot clear their consciences and maintain the views and interests of their constituents, they ought, as many an honest English gentleman has done, to resign their seats in the legislature; they ought to remember to whom and under what expectations they owe their present elevation; above all, they ought to remember what the equal and impartial interests of their whole constituency require at their hands.

If, however, every pledge or honourable understanding should be violated; if every reasonable hope should be disappointed; and if the loyal and deserving inhabitants of Upper Canada should be deceived, and disappointed, and wronged by the passage of this bill into a law, petitions ought to be circulated in every part of the province to Her Majesty the Queen to withhold the royal assent from the bill; and I hereby pledge £50 (if I have to sell my library to obtain the amount) for the promotion of that object. Such an act, under the present circumstances of the country, would be worse than a former alien bill, and ought to be deprecated, resisted, and execrated by every enlightened friend of the peace, happiness, and prosperity of the Province.

In reply to a letter from Rev. Joseph Stinson, urging him to come to Toronto and oppose this bill, Dr. Ryerson said:—

For me to leave Kingston, under present circumstances, and go to Toronto would ruin my ministerial influence and usefulness here and blast all our present hopes of prosperity. You know that by my continued and repeated absence, I have already lost fifty per cent. in the confiding hopes of the people, and consequently in very power of doing them good. You know, likewise, that the financial interests of the Society have so lamentably declined that we are already largely in arrears. I cannot, therefore, leave, unless I am positively required to do so by the Book Committee.

A more serious aspect of the matter, however, was presented to Dr. Ryerson in the extraordinary silence of the Conference organ on the subject. In the same letter he said:—

I cannot but feel deeply grieved at not only the tameness but the profound silence of the *Guardian* on this bill. Silence on such a measure, and at such a time, and after the course we have pursued hitherto, is acquiescence in it to all intents and purposes, and may be fairly and legitimately construed so by both friends and enemies. Oh, is it so? Can it be so, that the Editor of the *Guardian* has got so completely into the leading strings of that churchism which is as poisonous in its feelings towards us, and its plans respecting us, as the simoon blast; that he will see measures going forward, which he must know are calculated, nay, intended, to trample us in the dust, and not even say one word, except in praise (as often as possible), of the very men who he sees from day to day plotting our overthrow!

I have also observed, in Dr. Strachan's letters to Hon. Wm. Morris, an attack upon Lord Glenelg, the Colonial Secretary—such a one as would enable us to turn to our account on the clergy reserve question (and against Dr. Strachan's exclusive system) the entire influence of Her Majesty's

Government, which would have great weight both in and out of the House of Assembly. How I have heard Dr. Bunting, Mr. Beecham, and other members of the Committee at home, say that Lord Glenelg is one of the best and ablest men of the present day. At all events, after what we have obtained through his Lordship's instrumentality, I think that silence on our part is disgraceful—apart from considerations of local interests in this battle for right and justice.

Two able and moderate advocates of the settlement of the clergy reserve question were sent to England in 1837 to confer with Lord Glenelg on the subject, viz.: Hon. William Morris on behalf of the Church of Scotland, and Hon. W. H Draper on behalf of the Church of England. In November of that year Dr. Ryerson was requested to draw up a paper embodying the opinions of the leading members of the Conference. This was done, and an elaborate paper on the subject was published in the *Guardian* of January 17th, 1838.* Shortly afterwards Dr. Ryerson addressed a letter to Lord Glenelg on the subject. I only insert the narrative part of it, as follows:—

I was favoured with a conversation on the clergy reserve question with Mr. [Sir James] Stephen, in accordance with your Lordship's suggestion, the day before I left London for Canada (27th April, 1837). After my arrival in this Province it was unanimously agreed to support the plan for the adjustment of that important and long agitated question, which had been mentioned by Mr. Stephen, in the interview referred to.

Sir F B. Head set his face against it from the beginning, and did not wish me to say anything about it publicly. The Attorney-General acknowledged it was equitable, and did not make any serious objection to it.†

Recently a meeting of our principal ministers took place in Toronto, in order to consult upon the measures which it was desirable to adopt in order to promote the settlement of the question at the next session of Parliament.

---

* The paper was signed by Rev. Messrs. Harvard, Case, Stinson, J. Ryerson. W. Ryerson, E. Ryerson, Green, Evans, Jones, Wilkinson, Beatty, and Wright, See also *Guardian* of October 10th, 1838.

† In the *Guardian* of September 12th, 1838, page 180, Dr. Ryerson makes a fuller reference to this matter. Speaking of the Hume and Roebuck letters (page 167), he says: I was indeed—what I never thought of in London—applauded to satiety by the constitutional press of Upper Canada [for these letters], and by many individuals, several of whom, on my landing in Canada last year, gave me no small thanks for the results of the election of 1836. But all that ceased within a week after my return to Canada. . . And why? Because I availed myself of the first opportunity after my return to submit and press upon Sir Francis and the Attorney-General and others, the importance and necessity of an early and equitable settlement of the clergy reserve question, in order to satisfy the expectations of thousands who had voted for constitutional candidates. . . The very moment it was seen that my views and intentions on that subject remained unchanged, I saw a change in the expression of countenances. Sir Francis, indeed, *never* thanked me, for [the letters]; he wished me to say nothing about the clergy reserve question; and within four weeks sent a calumniating letter against me to Lord Glenelg; and the Attorney-General, so far from remembering the estimate he professed (on my return from England) to place upon my services to the Province, sought last winter to get a clause inserted in the Report of the Select Committee on the Upper Canada Academy, impugning my motives and exonerating Sir Francis from the allegations contained in my petition (see page 180), without even investigating its merits, etc.

At the request of the meeting, another gentleman and myself waited upon the Hon. Mr. Draper (who had taken the most official part in previous sessions), and showed him the resolutions agreed to. We stated that if it would embarrass him in promoting the earliest settlement of the question, we would desist from publishing anything on the subject. He expressed himself as highly gratified at our frankness, courtesy, and general views, and said that if his high-church friends had treated him with the same liberality and courtesy he would have been saved from much difficulty and embarrassment, which he had experienced in his previous exertions; but that he thought there could be no objection to our publishing at large our views on the subject. The preparation of the document was assigned to me. When published, it appeared to meet the views of all parties, except the ultra shade of one party, who want the whole of the reserves ; and it is now the most popular plan throughout the Province of settling the question, except that of appropriating the reserves to educational purposes exclusively.

A day or two before the publication of this document, the House of Assembly went into Committee on a Bill to revest the reserves in the Imperial Parliament! Going to Toronto at this time, I did what I could to bring the subject again before the House, and accordingly addressed a letter through the press to Speaker MacNab, of the Assembly, on the importance of an immediate settlement of the question, and also urging the adoption of the plan which had been recently proposed.* These papers appeared to create a considerable sensation among the members of the Assembly; it was agreed on all sides that the question ought to be settled forthwith. But the reluctance of the Crown Officers to take up the subject soon became manifest; and it was not for some weeks after, that the subject could be forced upon them.† Then all (with very few exceptions) professed that the subject ought not to be postponed any longer. But the Crown Officers had no measure prepared, and differed in opinion on the subject—the Attorney-General consenting to the revesting of the reserves in the Crown, the Solicitor-General contending that they should be divided among four denominations (Episcopalians, Presbyterians, Methodists, and Roman Catholics, according to their relative numbers in Great Britain and Ireland!) This proposition had but three or four advocates in the House, including the author of it. Mr. Boulton, seconded by Mr. Cartwright, moved, in substance, that the clergy reserve provision was made for the clergy of the Church of England;—that it does not provide for more than a competent support for them;—that to appropriate it for them would give most satisfaction to the country. This resolution had five votes in favour of it. All these amendments, and several others, having been lost in Committee, the original resolution moved by Mr. Cartwright, to revest the clergy reserves in Her Majesty, for "the support of the Christian religion in this Province," was

* In a letter to a friend, in January, 1838, Dr. Ryerson relates an amusing incident which was characteristic of Sir Allan MacNab's love of a bit of fun. He said :—In conversation one day with Mr. Speaker MacNab, he gravely proposed to me that I should meet Archdeacon Strachan and a clergyman of the Church of Scotland; and for him and other members of the Assembly to hear us put forth our respective claims to the clergy reserves, and for them to say a word now and then if they liked. After having heard the parsons argue the point, some member was to bring such a measure before the Assembly, as we three should propose This rather amusing way of settling the question was evidently by way of a joke, so I made no objection to it. He is to inform me of the time and place for the argument, after having consulted the other parties concerned; but I shall hear no more of it !

† The cause of this apathy will be apparent from the narrative in chapter xxxi., and the note on page 225.

adopted by a majority of three or four. A bill was then brought in and read a first time, and ordered to a second reading next day, but was never afterwards taken up—the exclusive church party being anxious to keep it out of sight. Thus the question is laid over for another year, to the great disappointment and dissatisfaction of thousands who have promptly come forward to the support of the Government of the country.

As an indication of the determination of the party then in power in Upper Canada to carry their scheme for the re-investment of the Reserves in the Crown, before the close of this friendly Parliament, I quote the following extract from a despatch from Sir George Arthur to Lord Glenelg, dated 11th July, 1838 :—

At the first meeting of the Legislature, I propose to cause a bill to be introduced for re-investing the lands reserved for the clergy in the Crown, to be applied for religious purposes, and I have reason to think that it will be carried by a considerable majority.

In June, 1838, Dr. Ryerson became Editor of the *Christian Guardian*. It was, as I have shown, at a most critical period in our provincial history. He was called to that post by the unanimous voice of his brethren. That call, too, was emphasized by the fact that the object of the dominant party in decrying the loyalty of their opponents was now clearly seen; and that, therefore, none but a man of undaunted courage, unimpeachable loyalty, as well as unquestioned ability, could successfully cope with the powerful combination of talent and influence which the ruling party possessed.

Nor should it be forgotten, that in the unfortunate crisis through which the Province had just passed, the prestige of the party which had always claimed the whole of the reserves as the patrimony of the Church of England, had, from political causes, immensely increased. This gave them a double advantage; while, on the other hand, the prestige of the party which for years had firmly and consistently resisted these claims, had, for the same political reasons, as sensibly and as seriously declined.

These facts were well known to every one in Upper Canada at the time. They imposed a double burthen upon those who had the courage (or, it might be said, audacity) to question the righteousness of claims, which—not to speak of the invaluable services and inviolable loyalty of the claimants themselves in the crisis of the rebellion—were by words of the statute, as interpreted by the law officers of the Crown, so clearly given to those claimants.

Such was the position of parties, and the condition of affairs in Upper Canada, when Dr. Ryerson was called to the editorial chair of the leading newspaper in the Province. That he was possessed of the requisite ability and firmness to maintain the rights of a discouraged minority, and resist the then almost unquestioned will of a powerful majority, few doubted. The bold defence of the supposed exiled rebel, Bidwell, proved that neither courage nor talent was wanting. The bitter hatred of the revolutionary party, as expressed in the threat that, should they succeed, their first victim would be Egerton Ryerson, showed that in the new crusade he would have no help (if not covert opposition) from that extreme section of his former friends. Nor, as events proved, could he reckon on any support from the British missionary section of the Methodist community. Indeed, they were hostile to his views, as will be seen in a subsequent chapter.

In entering into this contest, therefore, Dr. Ryerson found that he would have to encounter a threefold enemy—each section of it able, resolute and influential, especially that one practically in possession of the reserves—fighting, as it was, for its very existence, and acting entirely on the defensive.

Soon after Dr. Ryerson entered on his editorial duties he published in the *Guardian* an elaborate series of letters on "The Clergy Reserve Question, as a matter of History, a Question of Law, and a Subject of Legislation," addressed to Hon. W. H. Draper, Solicitor-General. After reviewing the proceedings of the Government and Legislature on the subject down to the end of the session of 1838, he summed up the leading facts which he had established, in the following words :—

> I have stated that the Government has been administered for fourteen years in utter contempt of the wishes of the inhabitants, constitutionally, continuously, and almost unanimously expressed through their representatives and otherwise, on a subject which concerns their highest and best interests, and which, as the history of Great Britain amply shows, has always more deeply interested British subjects than any other. Sir, on the unspeakably important subjects of religion and education our constitutional right of legislation has, by the arbitrary exercise and influence of Executive power, been made a mockery, and our constitutional liberties a deception ; and it is to the influence over the public mind of the high religious feelings and principles of those classes of the population who have been so shamefully calumniated by the Episcopal clergy and their party scribes, that the inhabitants of Upper Canada are not doing in 1838, what Englishmen did do in 1688, when their feelings were outraged and their constitutional liberties infringed, and the privileges of Parliament trampled upon, in order to force upon the nation a system of religious domination which the great majority of the people did not desire.

As the session of the Legislature of 1839 approached, a vigorous effort was made by *The Church* newspaper (the clerical organ), and the *Patriot* (the lay organ) of the church party to influence public opinion in favour of a re-investment of the clergy reserves in the Crown (for the reasons given on page 225.)

It was well known that Dr. Ryerson had strenuously opposed

any reference of the questions to the British Parliament as a pusillanimous, and yet an interested, party abnegation of Canadian rights. He, therefore, prepared and circulated extensively a petition to the House of Assembly on this and kindred subjects. This proceeding called forth a counter petition, urging the Legislature to recognize the principle of an established church, etc. Dr. Ryerson, therefore, lost no time in inserting in the *Guardian* of 24th October, a stirring appeal, in which he urged the Methodist ministers and members throughout the country to sign the petition which he had prepared without delay. He insisted upon the abolition of the rectories surreptitiously established by Sir John Colborne, on the ground that, although authorized by the Act of 1791, yet that their establishment was not in harmony with the terms of the despatch of Lord Ripon, dated November 8th, 1832, which stated that—

His Majesty has studiously abstained from the exercise of his undoubted prerogative of founding and endowing literary or religious corporations, until he should obtain the advice of the representatives of the people in that respect.

He concluded the appeal with these words:—It becomes every man who properly appreciates his civil and religious rights and privileges, and those of posterity after him, to give his name, his influence, and exertions, in the final effort to place those rights and privileges upon the broad foundation of equal justice to all classes of the inhabitants.

In a subsequent appeal, issued in November, he said:—Let every man who has a head to think, a foot to walk, and a hand to write, do all in his power to circulate the petitions for the entire abolition of high church domination, and the perfect religious and political equality of all denominations of Christians. . . The majority of the people of England are willing to have glebes, rectories, tithes, church rates, etc.; but the majority of the people of this Province want nothing of the kind. . . The right of the inhabitants of this Province to judge, and to have their wishes granted on everything connected with the disposition of the clergy reserves, and the proceeds of them, has been formally recognized in gracious despatches from the Throne.

Few in the present day can realize the storm which these petitions and appeals provoked. Every effort was made (as will be seen) to silence the voice and stay the hand of Dr. Ryerson, the chief promoter of the petitions, and the able opponent of the establishment of church ascendancy in Upper Canada. Thus matters reached a crisis in the latter part of the year 1838. So intense was the feeling evoked by the ruling party against Dr. Ryerson's proceeding, that in many places the promoters of the petitions were threatened with personal violence, and even with death, as may be seen by letters published in the *Guardian* at this time. The publication of these letters at the present time would excite feelings of amazement that such a state of things was ever possible in a free country like Canada.

Not only was this policy of intimidation pursued in the rural parts of the country, but the newspapers in Toronto and the larger towns, controlled by his opponents, made a combined assault upon Dr. Ryerson, as the central figure in this movement. On the 19th December, 1838, he inserted an able defence of himself. He said :—

> The question of the Clergy Reserves, or in other words, of a dominant ecclesiastical establishment in this Province, embracing one or more Churches, has been a topic of public discussion for nearly twenty years. For thirty years after the creation of Upper Canada (in 1783) there was no ecclesiastical establishment in the country, except in the letter of an Act of Parliament. During that time there was no weakening of the hands of Government by discussing the question of a dominant church. . . But from the time that the Episcopal clergy commenced the enterprise of ecclesiastical supremacy in the Province, there has been civil and religious discord. The calumnious and persecuting measures they have pursued from time to time to accomplish their purpose, I need not enumerate. For twelve years I have sought to restore peace to the Province, by putting down their pretensions. I have varied in the means I have employed, but never in the end I have had in view, as I have always avowed to them and their partizans, and to the Colonial and Imperial Governments, on every suitable occasion.

It was a favourite weapon of attack to denounce as rebels and republicans all those who opposed the exclusive claims of the then representatives of the Church of England. And this stigma was, in 1838, a personal and social one which every person to whom it was applied resented. But the more such persons resented the charge of disloyalty the more was the charge reiterated, and they were harassed and denounced as "radicals" and "republicans."

In repelling this unfounded charge, Dr. Ryerson did not descend to vindication or explanation. He became in turn the assailant, and began to "carry the war into Africa." With scorn and invective he replied to the charge, and showed that his opponents, with all their boasting and professions of loyalty, had failed to render the necessary aid in time of need. Thus: It has been said that I prevented the militia from turning out when first called upon. . . It is true that I did not exhort any one to volunteer. . . One reason . . was that I desired to have the country furnished with a practical illustration of high-church patriotism and loyalty in the hour of need. The *Church* and the *Patriot* had boasted of their multitudes; but those multitudes shrivelled into a Falstaff's company in an hour which detected the difference between the loyalty of the lip and the heart. . . The elongated countenances in certain quarters for a few days [in December, 1837], will never be forgotten! From the Government House to the poorest cottage the omnipotent power of the *Guardian* was proclaimed as producing this alarming state of things ! Indeed, I received a verbal message from His Excellency on the subject. At this juncture . . the heads of the Presbyterian and Methodist Churches formally addressed [their adherents] exhorting them to rally to the standard of their country, and from that hour we have heard nothing but congratulations and boasts in regard to the readiness . . with which the militia came forward in all parts of the Province at the call of the Government. It has been insinuated that I attacked the local Government. . . The charge is unfounded. When the local Government was attacked for having pursued a different course from that of Lord Durham towards the political prisoners, I reconciled the course of the two administrations. Several numbers of the *Guardian* containing that dissertation were requested for the Government House, and . . were sent to England. . . But when both my position and myself stand virtually . . impugned by proclamation, I am neither the sycophant nor the renegade to crouch down under unmerited imputations, come from whence they may, even though I should suffer imprisonment and ruin for my temerity.

I am at length exhorted to silence, but not my opponents. . . A royal answer was returned to an address of the Episcopal Clergy a few weeks since.* Nor is silence imposed upon me until the entire weight of the Chief Magistracy is thrown into the Episcopal scale. If the injunction had been given to *all* parties . . then we might have felt ourselves in some degree equally protected. . . But at the moment when the Province is turned into a camp—when freedom of opinion may be said to exist, but scarcely to live—when unprecedented power is wielded by the Executive, and the Habeas Corpus Act is suspended, for one party in the Province to have free range of denunciation, intimidation, etc., against Methodists and others . . and then for silence to be enjoined on me and those who agree with me . . does excite, I confess, my

* In their address they designated themselves as the Bishop, Archdeacons, and Clergy of the Established Church *of Upper Canada*; but Sir George Arthur, in his reply, addressed them as the Bishop, Archdeacons, and Clergy of the established Church *of England* in Upper Canada.

anxious concern, as the object of it in regard to myself and a large portion of the country cannot be mistaken.

The despatches of Lord Ripon (Nov. 8th, 1832) and Lord Glenelg (Dec. 15th, 1835) recommended a "comprehensive liberality" in every department, and in all the acts of the Government, they conceded in full the popular demands on the clergy reserve question, and deprecated the establishment of any religious corporations until the advice of the local Legislature had been obtained—these very despatches Sir F. B. Head promised to carry out. . . But has that pledge been redeemed by him? Has it not been grossly violated? . . . In his appointments and dismissals from office, and in the whole tone and spirit of his government, did not Sir F. B. Head become the head of a party instead of the Governor of the Province? . . . The result of his new system of government already is derangement of the currency—insurrection—bloodshed—loss of property—demoralization, by calling large bodies of men from rural to military employments—decrease of population— cessation of immigration—decrease of credit—decrease of revenue—increase of the public debt—decrease of the value of property—increase of popular dissatisfaction—vast military expenditures from the taxes of an overburthened British population—insecurity of person and property, and general distrust. Under these "Church and King" counsels, for two years more, and this province will be a Paradise! . . We have laboured hard to obtain and secure many blessings for our native land, but certainly not such blessings as these!

In connection with this discussion, a Kingston paper stated that Dr. Ryerson was moved by ambitious motives. In reply Dr. Ryerson said:—As to my motives of ambition, etc., my enemies will probably concede to me two or three things. 1. That long before Sir F. B. Head came to Upper Canada I had been honoured by as large a share of popular favour in this province as any individual could reasonably expect or desire. . . 2. That the path to royal favour has been opened as widely to me as it is possible for it to be opened to any clerical individual who has laid it down as a rule, and stated it to Ministers of the Crown and Governors, that he never could knowingly receive a farthing from any quarter, or in any way, which was not pointed out and authorized by the discipline of his Church. But as a love of popular favour has not obliterated from my recollection the rightful prerogatives of the Crown, I cannot see why I should thereby be disqualified from a disinterested maintenance of constitutional rights, especially when many more are immediately concerned in the latter than in the former.

CHAPTER XXX.

1838-1839.

THE RULING PARTY AND THE RESERVES.—"DIVIDE ET IMPERA."

IN dealing with so large and influential a body as the Methodists, made up, as it was years ago, of two distinct elements, somewhat antagonistic to each other, it can easily be understood that the more astute among the high church or "family compact" party clearly saw that their only hope of success in the clergy reserve controversy was by taking advantage of the presence of this antagonistic element in the Methodist body, and to turn it to practical account against Dr. Ryerson, so as to checkmate him in the contest. Queen Elizabeth's motto: *Divide et impera*, was therefore adopted. And every effort was made to intensify the feelings and widen the breach which already existed between the two sections of the Methodists. This was the more easily done by the appeal which was made to the national prejudices of Methodists of British origin, as against the alleged republican tendency of their colonial brethren.* In this effort the ruling party were publicly and privately aided by members of the Missionary Committee in London. To discuss this question now would be practically useless. None but actors in the scenes and conflicts of those times could realize the strong, even bitter, feelings which existed in the chief towns between the two parties at the time. Cherished sentiments of loyalty, strong home feelings, and orthodox Methodist principles, were appealed to, and alternately asserted their influence on opposite sides in the contest.

Added to the difficulty which Dr. Ryerson experienced in conducting the clergy reserve controversy was the fact, that many Methodists of British origin fully sympathized with the claims of the old national and historical Church of England—

---

* Dr. Ryerson, in the *Guardian* of October 31, 1838, says:—Five columns of *The Church*, of the 20th ult., are occupied with an appeal to the old country Methodists, to induce them to oppose the Conference and Connexion in this Province in the clergy reserve question. The Cobourg *Star* follows in the wake of *The Church*, in the same pious crusade. The *Patriot* of the 26th inst. also copies the schismatic appeal of *The Church*.

they held that it was *ipso facto* the "established" church in every British Colony, as often asserted by the Missionary party.

As the clergy reserve question gradually became the absorbing topic of discussion in the country (with Dr. Ryerson as one of the chief leaders in that discussion), it was natural that so important a matter should receive the attention of Conference. This it did at an early date. In 1837 strong resolutions were passed upon the subject, which excited much uneasiness among the English Missionary party. The Rev. W. H. Harvard, President of the Conference, in writing to Dr. Ryerson on the subject after Conference, said :—

Since I came away from the Conference, I have been greatly concerned as to the anti-church impression likely to be made on the mind of our people by our recent resolutions of Conference; and I would fain engage your interest with Rev. E. Evans, our Editor, to accompany them with some saving paragraph on the general principle of an establishment which may keep our people from the danger of imbibing the principle of dissent, the operation of which will always foster a religious radicalism in our body, and the influence of which our fathers at home strongly deprecate. I think with you, that in the altered circumstances of our Colonial relations, we have reason to plead for concessions of equality of rights and privileges which would never be granted in the Mother Country. In that respect I do not dissent from the spirit of the resolutions. But I more and more think and feel that there is a middle path of respectful deference to the principle of an establishment even in the Colonies, which, so modified, would not be injurious, but rather helpful, to our good cause,—and which is a vantage ground on which none of our enemies could touch us. It is true, that from Wesleyan high quarters you have had encouragement to believe an independent stand against Church domination would not be disapproved; yet even there a denial of the principle of an establishment (or that the Government should profess some one form of Christianity, with equal privileges to other Christians) would meet with reprobation; and if not, who does not see, if we take that anti-Wesleyan ground, it may involve the question of Wesleyan consistency on our part, while at the same time it would be in danger of throwing our people into the arms of the Radical-popish-infidel faction, where they will, bear like, be hugged till the breath of piety is pressed out of them. Of course, it would drive away from our congregations many of those pious or well-disposed Church people who occasionally mingle with and derive good from us. It was Mr. Wesley's conviction that the Methodists were in part raised up to spread scriptural holiness in the Church of England, as well as in the world at large. I must repeat my wish, that you had yielded to my suggestion to admit into the resolution the phrases, "that the principle of an establishment should be so administered in this Province as to secure perfect equality of rights and privileges among all other communities."

You may have ulterior views which I am too short-sighted to perceive. But I am fully convinced, that if the *Guardian* does not save us from identification with dissent from the Church of England at this crisis, the real friends of our Zion will bitterly deplore it another day.*

* Even Rev. J. Stinson (who heartily sympathized in many things with the Canadian Methodists), in a letter to Dr. Ryerson, written in February, 1839, said: —I have read your address to Hon. W. H. Draper, on the clergy reserve question,

Here was a broad and distinct declaration of principle, as fully in harmony with the views of the dominant party as they were entirely opposed to those held by the Canadian Conference party. They were perfectly sincere, too, and were uttered by one of the most moderate, and yet most thoroughly representative agents of the British Missionary party in this Province. It can be easily seen how tempting an opportunity it was for the ruling party to foster this feeling amongst the English Missionary section of Methodists, by strong appeals to their well-known loyalty—their respect and love for the old mother-church, which John Wesley so venerated. Even condesension and flattery were employed. *The Church* and other newspapers made appeals with tact and ability* (see page 236); the Lieutenant Governor himself took the trouble to address a letter on the subject direct to the Missionary Committee in London, and Archdeacon Strachan never failed to single out for respectful mention and commendation the representatives of the British Missionary party in Canada, as distinguished from the "disloyal and republican section of the Methodists."†

with considerable attention; and while there is much in it which I admire, I must honestly tell you, *en passant*, that it contains more against the principle of an establishment in this Colony than I like.

* Not satisfied with these strong appeals in the newspapers, resort was had to personal ones, made to leading members of the missionary party. In a kind and yet candid letter which Dr. Ryerson received in November, 1838, Rev. Joseph Stinson says:—I sincerely sympathize with you in your present perplexing and trying circumstances. I heard to-day that some of the dominant church champions are appealing to me to array myself against you. They may save themselves the trouble of making such appeals. Whenever I have differed in opinion with you, I have told you so, and shall do so again,—but shall never, unless you become a revolutionist, either directly or indirectly sanction any factious opposition to you. I think, as Wesleyan Methodists, we ought, openly and fearlessly, to advocate the righteous claims of our own Church; but we ought to do it without detracting from the merits or opposing the interests of that Church which is so closely connected with our Government, as is the Church of England. I know that the exclusive spirit—the arrogant pretentiousness—the priestly insolence—the anti-Christian spirit of certain members of that Church richly deserves chastisement. . . I know that your public services have been undervalued; your faults have been shamefully exaggerated; your motives have been misrepresented; your influence (connected as you are with a large and influential body of Christians) is feared, and your enemies are as bitter as Satan can make them; but, if you are conscious that, in the sight of God, you are aiming at the right object, why not leave your cause in His hands? why so frequently appeal to the people? You may not see it; but there is a recklessness in your mode of writing, sometimes, which is really alarming, and for which many of the members of the Conference of our Society do not like to be responsible. I know well, that the acts of the high church party are far more likely to excite rebellion than your writings. There is a strong, a very strong, feeling against a dominant Church; but a majority of the Province would rather have that, and connection with Great Britain, than republicanism.

† On the other hand, the Editor of *The Church* thus sketched Dr. Ryerson:—As The promoter, if not originator, of prejudices of indigenous growth, against the

Referring to this period, Rev. John Ryerson, in his Historical Recollections of Methodism (as annotated by Dr. Ryerson) informs us that—

After aiding to suppress the rebellion, the *Guardian* resumed the discussion of the clergy reserve question, and insisted that it should be settled. But nothing was farther from the thoughts of Dr. Strachan and Sir George Arthur. They contended that the mooting of the question at such a time was evidence of disloyalty on the part of those who were endeavouring to despoil the Church of its lawful rights. The Editor of the *Guardian* (Dr. Ryerson) was threatened with personal violence, with prosecution, and banishment. Yet the *Guardian* kept on the even tenor of its way; and in proportion to the fury of the monopolists, did the Editor increase his exertions to wrest from them their unjust gains. Then the oppressors of equal rights, seeing that nothing else would do, called into requisition the old craft to divide the Methodists, or, by other influences, to coercively control them.

Sir George Arthur, the amanuensis of Dr. Strachan in these matters, wrote to the Missionary Committee in London of the evil and disturbing doings of the *Guardian*, and called on them for their interference. This flattering appeal received a very complimentary reply. The Committee also wrote to their missionary agents in Canada, directing them to interpose and arrest the unjustifiable course of the *Guardian*. The objection was that the paper "had become party-political;" that "its course was disquieting to the country, and disreputable to Wesleyan Methodism," . . . etc. It is not denied (adds Rev. J. Ryerson), that the *Guardian* at this time was very political for a religious journal. . .

On this Dr. Ryerson remarked—

It is true, as my brother has intimated, that the *Guardian* was "very political," because the Editor was intensely in earnest on the great object for which he had been elected by the Conference. . . The times of his former proposed conciliations and compromises were now past. He felt the awfulness of the crisis and the responsibility of his position. The Reform party had been crushed by the rebellion of 1837, and the Reform press silenced; there was, in fact, no Reform party. The high-church party thought that their day of absolute power and ecclesiastical monopoly had dawned. It had been agreed by Mr. W. L. Mackenzie and his fellow rebels . . that Egerton Ryerson [should be their first victim]. He alone stood above successful calumny by the high-church party, and

Church of England, and as the thoughtless scatterer of the seeds of political error and of antipathy to the national church. Notwithstanding these counteracting influences, the Editor does not despair of seeing the day when Methodists in Canada will join with Churchmen in vindicating the Church's right to the property of the reserves, which will enable them to plant the established church in every corner of these Provinces. And this they will do, not upon the ground merely of filial partiality, but on the most rational security for the permanence and purity of our Protestant faith, etc. Under these circumstances, Dr. Ryerson said:—

I have felt it due to the *Guardian* connexion to enter my protest against the claims of the Episcopal Church, and to combat and explain the opinion of my English brethren as not those prevalent in this Province.

A lengthened communication, embodying those views, appearing on page 109 of the *Guardian* of May 16th, 1838.

backed as he was by his Canadian Methodist brethren, he determined to defend to the last, the citadel of Canadian liberty.
. . He knew that, as in a final struggle for victory between two armies, when that victory was trembling in the scales, the wavering of a single battalion on either side might animate and decide victory in favour of the enemy; so a compromising sentence or ambiguous word from the Editor might rouse the high-church party to increased confidence and action, and proportionally weaken the cause of civil and religious liberty in Upper Canada. The Editor of the *Guardian* had no fear, and he evinced none. . . I contended that all the political questions then pending had a direct or indirect bearing on this great question; . . that I would not be turned aside from the great object in view until it was obtained; that the real object of the Government and of the Missionary Committee was not so much to prevent the introduction of politics into the *Guardian*, as the discussion of the clergy reserve question itself, and of the equal religious rights of the people altogether, so that the high-church party might be left in peaceable possession of their exclusive privileges, and their unjust and immense monopolies, without molestation or dispute.

Rev. J. Ryerson adds: Had Dr. Ryerson "yielded to the dictation of Sir George Arthur's government, and the interference of the London Missionary Committee, one-seventh of the land of the Province might now be in the hands of the Church of England. But the course of the *Guardian* in this matter, however right, brought upon [the Canadian Methodist Church] calamities and sufferings of seven years' continuance."

About a month before the Conference of 1839 met, Sir George Arthur received a reply, by the hands of Dr. Alder, from the Missionary Committee in London (signed by Dr. Bunting and the other Secretaries), which he published in the *Patriot* newspaper. Dr. Ryerson inserted the letter in the *Guardian* of the 22nd May, with these remarks:—

We copy from the *Patriot* a letter, addressed by the Wesleyan Missionary Secretaries in London to Sir George Arthur, disclaiming "all participation in the views expressed in the *Guardian* on the ecclesiastical questions of this Province."

He then goes on to show that the views expressed in the *Guardian* were identical with those embodied in the proceedings of the Wesleyan Conference in Upper Canada from the beginning, and that they were explicitly avowed and understood by both parties at the time of the union of the Conferences in 1833.

The object of the publication of the letter was evidently twofold: 1st. To put a weapon into the hands of the friends of a dominant church in Upper Canada. 2nd. To paralyze the efforts of Dr. Ryerson to secure equal rights for all religious bodies, and thus to weaken his powerful influence as a champion of those rights.

It was a noticeable fact that all of the disclaimers from the British party first appeared in the Church of England organs, and were there triumphantly appealed to as the unbiassed expression of Methodist opinion from headquarters in England. In supplementing Rev. John Ryerson's Historical Narrative of events at this period, Dr. Ryerson stated, in substance, that:—

It was soon found that Sir George Arthur had thrown himself into the hands of the oligarchy on the question of the clergy reserves—he would not consent to have them applied to any other purpose than the support of the clergy, and was anxious to have them revested in the Crown. When Sir George's views and plans were brought before the Legislature, I opposed them. The Missionary Committee interposed (at Sir George's own request) and supported him on that question. However, Her Majesty's Government subsequently set aside the proceedings of Sir George Arthur, upon the very same grounds on which I had opposed them; but that made no difference in the feelings towards me of Dr. Alder and his colleagues.

Early in June, 1839, Dr. Alder addressed a letter to the *Guardian*, explaining and defending his views on church establishments. On the 12th of that month, Dr. Ryerson replied to him at length, and, at the close, put a series of questions to Dr. Alder. From the 2nd and 6th I make the following extracts:—

2. Are you satisfied that you are providentially called of God to attempt to make Methodism an agency in promoting a national establishment of religion in a new country, in the teeth of an overwhelming majority of the inhabitants?

6. Are you warranted from any writings or authority of Mr. Wesley to insist that, "under *no* circumstances," the principle of an establishment shall be abandoned? . . Mr. Wesley and his coadjutors have left it on record, in the minutes of their Conference, as their deliberate judgment, that "there is no instance of, or ground at all for, a national church in the New Testament;" that they "apprehended it to be a merely political institution." How can any true Wesleyan convert that into a matter of faith and religious principle for which Mr. Wesley declared there "was no instance or ground at all in the New Testament?" . . I know that the local Executive is most intent to secure the aid of the Missionary Committee to support the recent re-investment act of spoliation; I believe that your letter . . emboldened and encouraged them in the re-investment scheme, and His Excellency stated some months since that he had written for you to come to this country; they think that they can bargain with you upon more advantageous terms than they can with the Methodist Conference in this Province, but I entreat you to pause before you proceed to insist that that which Mr. Wesley declares . . to be "a merely political institution," forms any part of Wesleyan Methodism.*

---

* With a view to increase the clamour against the Editor of the *Guardian* on this subject, Mr. Alex. Davidson, writing to Dr. Ryerson from Niagara, said:—Dr. Alder's letter to you had been printed and circulated there in the form of a hand-bill. Mr. E. C. Griffin, of Waterdown, writing from Hamilton on the same subject, said: I have learned from brother Edward Jackson what are the feelings of the Society

Dr Ryerson's account of what transpired at the ensuing Conference is in substance as follows :—

Dr. Alder attended the Conference at Hamilton, June, 1839, and introduced resolutions expressive of his views, to which he insisted upon the concurrence of the Conference. The resolutions were discussed for three days. On the last day Dr. Ryerson replied, after which the resolutions were negatived by a vote of 55 to 5.*

At the same Conference Dr. Ryerson was appointed secretary, by a vote of 41 to 14. But it was in regard to the election of Editor that the greatest interest was taken, not so much amongst the Canadian section of the Methodist people as amongst the members of other religious bodies. The *Guardian* stated :—

For the last two months the several provincial journals have renewed their efforts of vehement vituperation against the Editor; . . they have sought and hoped to create a division in the ranks of the Methodist family, and, by thus dividing, to conquer ; they even triumphed by anticipation—so much so, that the Editor of *The Church* oracularly predicted the speedy release of the Editor of the *Guardian* from his editorial duties.

The chagrin which was felt by these parties can be well imagined when the ballot announced that Dr. Ryerson had been re-elected editor, by a vote of 60 to 13! Speaking of this memorable triumph, Dr. Ryerson declared that :—

Never before did I receive, directly or indirectly, so many unequivocal testimonies of respect and confidence, not merely from the Methodist Church at large, but also from members of other churches.

In the meantime (as Dr. Ryerson stated elsewhere) the discussion on the question of a dominant church monopoly and party . . proscription waxed hotter and hotter ; . . rumours prevailed of a change of Governors in Upper Canada; the high church party felt that this was their time, and perhaps their last chance to confirm their absolute power. . . Under these

in Hamilton, respecting the letter of Dr. Alder. He says, that if the leaders' meeting is any index of the views of the entire Society here, they are a "unit" to a man (except the preacher) in their determination to support you in your principles and proceedings.

* The following incident in connection with this vote is mentioned by Dr. Ryerson: Dr. Alder (he said) appeared disappointed and depressed; and, after the close of the Conference I said to him : Dr. Alder, you see how entirely you have mistaken the state of Canadian society, and the views and feelings of the Methodist people. Now, I do not wish that you should return to England a defeated and disgraced man. I purpose to write a short editorial for the *Guardian*, stating that the differences and misunderstandings which had arisen, after having been carefully considered and fully discussed, were adjusted in an amicable spirit, and the unity of the Church maintained inviolate. Dr. Alder appeared delighted and thankful beyond expression. I prepared the editorial. Dr. Alder used and interpreted this editorial on his return to England, to show that the Canadian Conference and its Editor had acceded to all of his demands, and that he had been completely successful in his mission to Canada ! The English Committee adopted resolutions complimentary to Dr. Alder in consequence ; but I did not imagine that Dr. Alder's fictitious representation of the results of his mission would afterwards be made the ground of charges against myself !

circumstances, I stated to the Conference that the moment that the clergy reserve and other questions affecting our constitutional and just rights as British Canadian subjects, and as a religious body, were adjusted, we ought to abstain entirely from any discussions in reference to civil affairs. When Dr. Alder's resolutions were rejected by our Conference, one prepared by myself was agreed to, as follows :—

While this Conference has felt itself bound to express its sentiments on the question of an ecclesiastical establishment in this Province, and our constitutional and religious rights and privileges, and our determination to maintain them, we disclaim any intention to interfere with the merely secular, party-politics of the day.

This resolution, as it afterwards appeared, did not go far enough to meet the wishes and designs of Dr. Alder. He, therefore, brought the matter before the Book Committee, Toronto, in October, 1839. To that Committee he stated at length his decided objection to the course pursued by the *Guardian* since Conference as " a violation of the known design of the resolution adopted by it." Dr. Ryerson, while fully justifying the course which he had pursued, nevertheless tendered to the Committee his resignation as Editor. The Committee, however, instructed Rev. William Case to write to him as follows :—

By request of the Book Committee, I beg leave to communicate the result of their deliberations on the subject of your proffered resignation of the editorship of the *Guardian*. "*Resolved*, That the Committee do not feel themselves at liberty to accept of the resignation of the Editor of the *Guardian*, and that he be affectionately requested to withdraw it, and to continue his services in accordance with the deliberately framed regulations of the Committee until the ensuing Conference, the regulations to which he objects having been adopted, not for the purpose of reflecting in any way upon the Editor; and that we assure him that we have the utmost confidence in his abilty, his integrity, and his anxious desire to promote the best interests of the Connexion."

Dr. Ryerson withdrew his resignation at the time, but resolved to press it at the next Conference. This he did; and peremptorily declined re-election at the Conference of 1840— in fact other and more serious matters were pressed upon him. He thus finally retired from the editorship of the paper which he had established in 1829, and which he had made such a power in Upper Canada. He justly felt that, with the enlarged Methodist constituency which the *Guardian* at this time represented, it would be impossible for him, while great questions remained unsettled, to harmonize the conflicting opinions on politico-religious matters which were then held by opposite and influential sections of the Methodist Church. He clearly foresaw further conflict on these and other inter-connexional subjects, and was, therefore, the more anxious to free himself from the unwise, official trammels, which a hostile, anti-Canadian and unpatriotic party sought to impose upon him.—single-handed as he was. He longed for more congenial work. He also felt that literary freedom was essential to him in his thorough and practical discussion of the all absorbing questions of the day.* This it was well known he could do, in dealing with these questions, not only on their own merits, but with the comprehensive grasp which his enlarged experience, intuitive clearness of perception, and naturally statesmanlike views on grave public questions, eminently qualified him for.

As an illustration of the acknowledged ability, fairness, and conclusiveness of argument with which he dealt with questions which touched the sensibilities and even prejudices of leading members of the British Missionary party in Canada, it is a striking fact that when these gentlemen were not under the direct and potent influence of the Mission House, they were Dr. Ryerson's personal friends, and gave him an active support. This was particularly the case with the late Rev. Dr. Stinson, a man of noble and generous impulses; Rev. W. H. Harvard, always kind and courteous; Rev. Dr. Richey, a man of much refinement and culture, and others. In the important crisis of 1838, both Dr. Stinson and Dr. Richey voted for Dr. Ryerson as Editor. The former wrote a strong letter urging his appointment as Editor. (Page 201.) The latter, on his way to Halifax, after the Conference of 1839, wrote from Montreal to Dr. Ryerson, as follows:—

Sir John Colborne, on whom I called, and by whom I was graciously received, is delighted with the continuance of the Union. So are all our Montreal friends, after my explanations. They will immediately order the *Guardian*. Sir John paid a handsome tribute to your talents, as who with whom I conversed did not? however they might happen to view your course. They all say you commenced admirably,—that the moment the paper passed into your hands, it manifestly improved; and they all approve of your course for the last six months, just about as well as you know I do. Adhere most religiously, my dear brother, to the spirit and letter of the resolutions, by which the Conference has expressed its will that you should be guided. Your friend Joseph Howe† begins, I perceive, to mingle with tories, as they are invidiously designated. I do not wish you to be a tory; and I will not insult you by expressing a desire that you were a high conservative.

I do not flatter you in saying, that on no man in Upper Canada does the peace of our Church and of the Province so much depend, as on yourself. May all your powers be employed for good! Guard against the fascination of political fame. It will do no more for you on a dying bed than it did for Cardinal Wolsey. O! that your fine mind were fully concentrated upon the πολίτευμα of Heaven!

* Dr. Ryerson gave full expression to these views in a letter addressed to the Governor-General in April, 1840. (See chapter xxxiii., page 266.)

† See letter from Mr. Howe to Dr. Ryerson on page 258

CHAPTER XXXI.
1839.

STRATEGY IN THE CLERGY RESERVE CONTROVERSY.

THE year 1839 was somewhat noted for the prolonged and animated discussions which took place in and out of the Legislature on the clergy reserve question. There were some new features in the discussion of the preceding year which had their effect on the clergy reserve legislation of that year. And while they partially ceased to be influential in the discussions of 1839, yet the legislation of that year was practically brought to the same issue as that of 1838, only that it was more decisive. It may be interesting, therefore, to refer to these special features in the discussion of 1838-9.

The first was the final change of tactics on the part of the leaders of the Church of England party in the contest. The second was the persistent and personal efforts which Lieutenant Governor Arthur put forth in behalf of that party, so as to enable them to accomplish their object, and, at the same time, to counteract the efforts of those who were seeking to uphold Canadian and popular rights. The third was (as shown in the last chapter) the plan adopted to foment discord in the Methodist body—which was by far the most formidable opponent of the scheme of monopoly and aggrandisement which the ruling party was seeking to promote.

At this distance of time it is easy to survey the whole field of conflict, and to note the plans and strategies of the combatants. Although efforts had hitherto been made to shift the battle-ground from Upper Canada to England, yet, as the Colonial Secretary had discouraged such efforts as unwise, and as an unnecessary interference with the rights of the Provincial Legislature, the matter was not openly pressed in 1839. Nor was it pressed at all to a conclusion in 1838. For, by a singular coincidence, the very day (29th December, 1837) on which Mr. Cartwright had moved to bring a bill into the House of Assembly to revest the clergy reserve in Her Majesty, Sir George Grey penned a despatch to Sir George Arthur, in which he disclaimed, on behalf of the Imperial Government, any wish or intention to interfere, in the settlement of the clergy reserve question, with the functions of the Provincial Legislature, on the ground that—

Such interference would tend to create a not unreasonable suspicion of the sincerity with which the Legislature have been invited to the exercise of the power [to vary or repeal] reserved to them on this subject by the Constitutional Act of 1791.

It is likely that the publication of this despatch prevented the House of Assembly from proceeding any farther with Mr. Cartwright's bill, than ordering it to a second reading on the 26th February, 1838. In this dilemma the ruling party were evidently at a loss how to act. It required much tact and skill to break the ranks of the chief forces arrayed against the scheme to revest the reserves in the Crown—a scheme distasteful to Canadians generally, and subversive of the legislative independence of Upper Canada. Two methods were therefore adopted: The first was to divide the Methodists (as shown in the last chapter). The second and more astute one was to appeal to the professed loyalty of that class which hitherto had been held up to scorn as disloyal, and denounced as republican in its tendencies, as well as seditious in their conduct. The appeal was varied in form, but it was in substance that as those who made it were not themselves afraid to trust their interests in the hands of the Sovereign, their opponents should be equally trustful in the equal and entire justice which would be meted out to all of her Canadian subjects.* This appeal, from its very speciousness, and the skill with which it was pressed, had its effect in many cases. But, as a general rule, it failed. The object of the decisive change of tactics was too transparent to deceive the more sensible and thoughtful men to whom the appeal was addressed.

The two other methods adopted (already referred to) were only partially successful; but the three combined, no doubt, strengthened the hands of the advocates of the scheme for the re-investment of the reserves in the Crown. They, however, ceased to press the matter upon public attention, being determined to bide their time, and (as events proved), to carry their point in another and more skilful way.

In the meantime, and early in 1839, Dr. Ryerson was deputed by several important circuits to present loyal addresses to Sir George Arthur. This he did on the 2nd February; and in enclosing them to the Governor's secretary, used language which sounds strange in these days of religious equality. He said:—

* In the *Guardian* of September 19th, 1838, the question is put in this form and discussed: "Why do you not appeal to Her Majesty's Privy Council, or to the High Court of Parliament instead of appealing to the public here?" The answer was conclusive.

I feel myself fully authorized, by various communications and my official position, to assure His Excellency that the members of the Wesleyan Methodist Church will not be contented with subordinate civil standing to any other church, any more than the members of the Church of Scotland. They do not, and never have asked for any peculiar advantages; but they feel that upon the principles of justice, by labours, by usefulness, by character, by numbers, and by the principles laid down in royal despatches, they are entitled, in the eye of the law, and in the administration of an impartial government, to equal consideration, and equal advantages with any other church. I am confident that I but state a simple fact, when I express our belief that the Methodist Church, in its doctrines, ministry, and institutions, furnishes as formidable a barrier against the irreligion and infidelity of the times as any other section of Protestantism. Nor is it possible for us—notwithstanding our unfeigned respect for His Excellency—to feel ourselves under any obligations to tender our support to another section of the Protestant Church, whose clergy, in this Province, collectively, officially, and individually (with solitary exceptions), have resisted the attainment of every civil and religious privilege we now enjoy—have twice impeached our character and principles before the Imperial Government—who deny the legitimacy of our ministry, who, in their doctrines respecting Church polity, and several points of faith, do not represent the doctrines of the Church of England, or of the established clergy in England as a body, but that section only of the established clergy that have associated with all arbitrary measures of government against various classes of Protestant non-conformists which have darkened the page of British history, and also the dark ages, notions of rites and ceremonies, and the conductor of whose official organ in this Province has recently represented the Methodist ministry as the guilty cause of those divine chastisements under the influence of which our land droops and mourns. I am sure my brethren, as well as myself, freely forgive the great wrongs thus perpetrated against us; but we feel ourselves equally bound in duty to ourselves, to our country, and to our common Christianity, to employ all lawful means to prevent such exclusive, repulsive, and proscriptive sentiments from acquiring anything more than equal protection in the Province.

I might appeal to circumstances within His Excellency's knowledge, to show that from 1836 to the close of the last session of our Provincial Parliament, I have spared no pains—without the remotest view to personal or even Methodistic advantage—to second, to the utmost of my humble ability, any plan to which the Province might, under all circumstances, be induced to concur, in order to settle the protracted controversy on the clergy reserve question; and that it has not been, until I have had indubitable proofs that that there was no disposition or intention on the side of the Episcopal clergy to yield a single iota any further than they were compelled. It was not until all these circumstances had transpired, that we reluctantly determined to appeal against the exclusive and unjust pretensions of the Episcopal clergy, to the bar of public opinion—a power recognized by our free constitution, and which no party or administration can successfully resist many years.

The reply of the Governor was friendly and conciliatory; but in it he expresses his

Surprise to find that his appeal on a late occasion to the Wesleyan Methodists, to give the Church of England their most cordial support, had been misunderstood and construed into an expression of sectarian preference. By inviting the Methodists to such a course of conduct, His Excellency thought that he was only appealing to a feeling of attachment for the Church of England, which he had always been induced to consider—especially from personal observation—as a badge of "legitimate Wesleyan Methodists" all over the world.

Dr. Ryerson in his remarks on this reply, said :—

The questions at issue about the clergy reserves do not involve the principle of "attachment for the Church of England" from the well known fact that many respectable members of that Church, in every district throughout the Province, concur in the views advocated in the *Guardian* on that question—therefore an appeal to "attachment for the Church of England" as the rule of judgment in this controversy, much less as a "badge of legitimate Wesleyan Methodists," is the very climax of absurdity.

The discussions on the clergy reserve question up to the time when the House reassembled (27th February, 1839), must have convinced the dominant party that it was, and ever would be, hopeless, in the face of the determined opposition which their schemes encountered, to obtain that which they wanted from the local legislature. They could not again openly bring in a bill (as they did last year) to revest the reserves in the Crown, in the face of the declarations of the Colonial Secretary, that—

Imperial Parliamentary Legislation on any subject of exclusively internal concern, in any British colony possessing a representative assembly is, as a general rule, unconstitutional. It is a right of which the exercise is reserved for extreme cases, in which necessity at once creates and justifies the exception. (Lord Glenelg to Sir F. B. Head, 5th December, 1835.)

They therefore adopted what events proved to be a ruse, to accomplish their object. It is true that Sir George Arthur, in his opening speech, urged that—

The settlement of this vitally important question ought not to be longer delayed. . . I confidently hope, that if the claims of contending parties be advanced . . in a spirit of moderation and Christian charity, the adjustment of them by you will not prove insuperably difficult.

The Governor then adroitly added—

But, should all your efforts for the purpose unhappily fail, it will then only remain for you to re-invest the reserves in the hands of the Crown, and to refer the appropriation of them to the Imperial Parliament, as a tribunal free from those local influences and excitements which may operate too powerfully here.

Both Houses, in apparent good faith, sought to carry out the wishes of the Governor as expressed in the first part of his speech. The managers of the scheme indicated in the latter part of the speech initiated a totally different bill in each House, apparently liberal and comprehensive in character, but yet objectionable in detail. Dr. Ryerson felt this so strongly that he petitioned to be heard at the Bar of the House of Assembly against the bill which had been introduced into it. His request was at first granted on the 7th April, by a vote of 24 to 22, but afterwards refused by a vote of 21 to 17. After protracted debates in the House of Assembly and about forty-four divisions, that House sent up its bill to the Legislative Council for concurrence. The Council struck out the whole of the bill after the word "whereas,' and substituted one of its own, and in turn sent it down to the House of Assembly for concurrence. That House, not to be outdone by the other, struck out the whole of the Legislative Council bill, and substituted a bill of its own, totally different from the one first sent up to the Legislative Council, the last clause of which read as follows:—

The moneys to arise, and to be procured and henceforth received for any sale or sales [of clergy reserve lands] shall be paid into the hands of Her Majesty's Receiver-General of this Province, to be appropriated by the Provincial Legislature for religion and education.

The bill thus constructed needed but the alteration of the last five words to adapt it admirably to the object and purpose of the Church party. The Legislative Council, therefore, changed the concluding words in the last clause into the words "Imperial Parliament for religious purposes." In this apparently simple way, but in reality, fundamental manner—and without any attempt at a conference between the Houses, with a view to adjust differences—the Legislative Council, taking advantage of a comparatively thin House of Assembly, made the desired change on the last day of the session. By adroit manœuvring the agents of the Church party carried the bill in the House of Assembly thus altered. In this way they succeeded in destroying the whole object of the bill, as passed by the House of Assembly. Sir George Arthur, in his despatch to the Colonial Secretary, virtually admitted that the passage of the altered bill was due to the fact that it was carried in the House of Assembly by a majority of one vote [22 to 21], in a House of 44 members, and at a late hour on the night preceding the prorogation!

Such were the discreditable circumstances under which the bill re-investing the clergy reserves in the Crown was passed. It, however, required the assent of the Queen before it became law. This it was destined never to receive, owing to a technical objection raised in England in the following October, that such a delegation to the Imperial Parliament could not be made by a subordinate authority. This defeat, however, proved to be a moral victory for the vanquished, as it gave them time for farther deliberation; it incited them to greater caution in their mode of warfare, and induced them to adopt tactics of a more secret and, as it proved, effective character.

CHAPTER XXXII.

1839.

Sir G. Arthur's Partizanship.—State of the Province.

THE bill for revesting the clergy reserves in the Crown barely escaped defeat (as just mentioned) in the House of Assembly, on 11th May, 1839. On the 14th Sir George Arthur sent the bill to Lord Normanby (successor to Lord Glenelg) for Her Majesty's assent, with an elaborate despatch. On the 15th, Dr. Ryerson also addressed to Lord Normanby a long letter on the same subject. In it he called the attention of the Colonial Secretary to the following facts, which he discussed at length in his letter:—

1. That the great majority of the House of Assembly in four successive parliaments had remonstrated against the exclusive pretensions of the Church of England in Upper Canada; and that the claims of the Church of England to be the established Church of the Province had from the beginning been steadily denied by such representatives, and elsewhere.

2. That the ground of dissatisfaction in the Province was not merely between the Churches of England and Scotland, but between the high-church party, and the religious denominations and the inhabitants of the Province generally.

3. That from the beginning the House of Assembly had protested against any appropriation of the clergy reserves being made to the Church of England, not granted equally [for educational purposes] to the other Christian denominations.

4. That notwithstanding the annual remonstrances of the House of Assembly, large grants had been paid since 1827, to the Episcopal Clergy, exclusive of grants by the Imperial Parliament and the Propagation Society.

5. That under these circumstances it was not surprising that there should be a widespread and deeply seated dissatisfaction. It is rather surprising that a vestige of British power exists in the Province.

6. That Sir George Arthur has for the last five months endeavoured—by official proclamations and other published

communications through public offices, and by military influences in various parts of the Province—to prevent any expression of opinion on this subject, even by petition to the Legislature.

7. That the Lieutenant-Governor has been induced to make himself a partizan with the Episcopal Church in the clergy reserve discussion; the entire influence of the Executive has been thrown into that scale; the representation of impartial sovereignty has been made the watchword of party.

8. That under the pretense of resisting brigand invasion, large militia forces have been raised; violent penniless partizans have been put on pay in preference to respectable and loyal men; and these forces have not been placed on the frontier where invasion might have been expected, but have been scattered in parties over many parts of the interior, in order to exterminate discontent by silencing complaint.

These, with a reference to the embarrassed financial condition of the Province, were the chief points to which Dr. Ryerson called the attention of the Colonial Secretary in this elaborate letter.

On the 22nd of the same month (May) Dr. Ryerson addressed another vigorous letter to Lord Normanby, on the clergy reserves and kindred questions. "That letter," he says, he writes "with feelings which he has no language to express."

The main points of the letter were as follows:—

1. For thirty years (up to 1820) nothing was heard of an ecclesiastical establishment in the Province: all classes felt themselves equally free, and were, therefore, equally contented and happy.

2. From the first open and unequivocal pretensions to a state establishment being made, the inhabitants of Upper Canada, in every constitutional way, have resisted and remonstrated against it.

3. Every appropriation and grant to the Episcopal clergy out of the lands and funds of the Province has been made in the very teeth of the country's remonstrance.

4. The utter powerlessness of the representative branch of the Legislature has rendered the officers and dependents and partizans of the Executive more and more despotic, overbearing, and reckless of the feelings of the country.

5. This most blighting of all partizanship has been carried into every department of the Executive Government—the magistracy, militia, and even into the administration of justice. Its poison is working throughout the whole body politic; it destroys the peace of the country; rouses neighbour against neighbour; weakens the best social affections of the human

heart, and awakens its worst passions; and converts a healthy and fertile province into a pandemonium of strife, discontent, and civil commotion.

6. While upwards of $220,000 (besides lands) have been given to the Episcopal clergy since 1827, the grants made by the Imperial Parliament to the clergy of Upper Canada amount to over $400,000, being over $620,000 in all.

7. A very large sum has been expended in the erection of Upper Canada College, on the grounds of King's College, and with an endowment of $8,000 or $10,000 a year. This institution is wholly under the management of Episcopal clergymen, while the Upper Canada Academy, which has been built at Cobourg by the Methodists at a cost of about $40,000, could not without a severe struggle get even the $16,000 which were directed to be paid over to it by Lord Glenelg. The matter had to be contested with Sir F. B. Head on the floor of the House of Assembly before he could be induced to obey the Royal instructions. (Page 179.)

8. In the recent legislation on the clergy reserve question, the high church party resisted every measure by which the Methodist Church might obtain a farthing's aid to the Upper Canada Academy. And, to add insult to injury, the high church people denounce Methodists as republicans, rebels, traitors, and use every possible epithet and insinuation of contumely because they complain, reason, and remonstrate against such barefaced oppression and injustice—notwithstanding that not a single member of that church has been convicted of complicity with the late unhappy troubles in the Province.

9. A perpetuation of the past and present obnoxious and withering system, will not only continue to drive thousands of industrious farmers and tradesmen from the country, but will prompt thousands more, before they will sacrifice their property and expatriate themselves, to advocate constitutionally, openly, and decidedly, the erection of an "independent kingdom," as has been suggested by the Attorney-General, as best both for this province and Great Britain.

10. It rests with Her Majesty's Government to decide whether or not the inhabitants shall be treated as strangers and helots; whether the blighted hopes of this province shall wither and die, or revive, and bloom, and flourish; whether Her Majesty's Canadian subjects shall be allowed the legitimate constitutional control of their own earnings, or whether the property sufficient to pay off the large provincial debt shall be wrested from them; whether honour, loyalty, free and responsible government are to be established in this province, or whether our resources are to be absorbed in support of preten-

sions which have proved the bane of religion in the country; have fomented discord; emboldened, if not prompted, rebellion; turned the tide of capital and emigration to other shores; impaired public credit; arrested trade and commerce, and caused Upper Canada to stand "like a girdled tree," its drooping branches mournfully betraying that its natural nourishment has been deliberately cut off.

In a third and concluding letter to Lord Normanby, Dr. Ryerson uses this language:—

The great body of the inhabitants of this province will not likely again petition on the question of the clergy reserves and a church establishment in this province. They will express their sentiments at the hustings with a vengeance, to the confusion of the men who have deceived, and misrepresented, and wronged them; . . A petition would acknowledge the right of the Imperial Parliament to interfere—which ought not to be admitted. If past expressions of public sentiment will not satisfy Her Majesty's Government, none other can do it; and more efficient means (such as the coming elections), must and ought to be adopted, instead of the fruitless method of asking by petition for what has been guaranteed to the constituencies of the country as a right.

The validity of the recent Act of the Legislature, revesting the reserves in the Crown, never will be acknowledged, or recognized by the electors of this province. Any Ministers of the Crown in England would more than lose their places, who should press through the House of Commons, on the last night of the session, in a thin house, a great public measure which had not only been repealed by four successive parliaments, but had been negatived from six to twelve times during the same session of the existing parliament. Nor would the British nation ever submit to any public measure (much less to loss of the control of one-seventh of their lands, and the infliction upon them of an uncongenial ecclesiastical system) which had been forced upon them.

The declarations of the Representative of Royalty have heretofore been regarded in this province as sacred and inviolable; but the reliance of the Canadian electors upon those declarations from the lips of Sir Francis Head has cost them bloodshed, bankruptcy, and misery. . . The electors will employ the elective franchise to redress their accumulated wrongs to the last farthing.

It is, of course, my good or bad fortune to be assailed from week to week, whether I write or not. . . I am no theorist. I advocate no change in the Constitution of the Province. I have never written a paragraph the principles of which could not be carried out in accordance with the letter and spirit of the established Constitution. I desire nothing more than the free and impartial administration of that Constitution for the benefit of all classes of Her Majesty's subjects. I only oppose or support men, or measures, for the attainment of that object.

Entertaining such strong feelings in regard to the personal conduct of Sir George Arthur in respect to the passage of the clergy reserve bill, Dr. Ryerson felt that he could not accept any social courtesy at his hands. In reply, therefore, to an invitation from Sir George, for Her Majesty's birthday, he felt constrained to decline it. In his letter to the A.D.C., he said :—

After the most mature deliberation up to the last moment in which it is proper to reply, I feel it my duty respectfully to decline the honour of His Excellency's invitation. I most firmly believe that the office of impartial sovereignty has been employed by His Excellency for partial purposes; that an undue and an unconstitutional exercise of the office of royalty has been employed by His Excellency to influence the public mind, and the decisions of our constitutional tribunals on pending and debatable questions between equally loyal and deserving classes of Her Majesty's subjects in this Province; that His Excellency has also employed the influence of the high office of the Queen's representative to procure and afterwards express his cordial satisfaction at the passing of a Bill, in a thin House, on the very last night of the session, the provisions of which had been repeatedly negatived by a considerable majority of the people's representatives, and which deprive the faithful but embarrassed inhabitants of this Province of the control of a revenue and lands sufficient in value to pay off the whole public debt—a proceeding at complete variance with the fair and constitutional administration of a free monarchical government, and the imperial usages since the accession of the present Royal Family to the throne of Great Britain; and, finally, that His Excellency has employed the influence of his high office to the disparagement of the large section of the religious community whose views, rights, and interests, I have been elected to my present offices to advocate and promote.

I beg that my declining the honour proposed by His Excellency may not be construed into any disrespect to His Excellency personally, or to the high office His Excellency holds—for the inviolableness and dignity of which I feel the jealous veneration of a loyal subject—but I beg that it may be attributed solely to a fixed determination not to do anything that may in the slightest degree tend to weaken, but on the contrary, to use every lawful means, on all occasions, to advance those civil and religious interests which I am most fully convinced are essential to the happy preservation of a prosperous British Government in this country, and to the happiness and welfare of the great body of Her Majesty's Canadian subjects.

In order to insure the assent of Her Majesty to the Bill which had been sent to the Colonial Secretary by Sir George Arthur, the authorities of the Church of England in the Province circulated a petition for presentation to the Queen and the British Parliament* containing the following statement and request:—

"Your petitioners, consisting of the United Empire Loyalists and their children, took refuge in this Province after the American Revolution, under the impression that they possessed the same constitution as that of

---

* See note on page 224.

the Mother Country, which includes a decent provision for the administration of the Word and Sacraments according to the forms of the Church of England."

The prayer of the petition was—

That the proceeds of the clergy reserve lands be applied to the maintenance of such clergy, and of a bishop to superintend the same, so that the ministrations of our Holy Religion may be afforded without charge* to the inhabitants of every township in the Province.

Dr. Ryerson, having with difficulty procured a copy of this petition, pointed out in the *Guardian* of July 3rd, 1839: 1st. Its historical misstatements, and denounced the selfish and exclusive character of its demands. He showed in effect that the Province was settled in 1783, whereas the constitutional Act (which was invoked as though it had existed long before that date), was not passed until 1791—eight years after "the United Empire Loyalists and their children took refuge in Upper Canada." 2nd. That for forty years and more, nine-tenths of the United Empire Loyalists and their descendants, with all their "impressions," might have perished in heathen ignorance had not some other than the Episcopal clergy cared for their spiritual interests ; and that after these forty years of slumbering and neglect, and after the incorporation of the great body of the old Loyalists and their descendants into other churches, the Episcopal clergy came in, and now seek, on the strength of these apocryphal "impressions" (which never could have existed), to claim one-seventh of the lands of the Province as their heritage. † In proof of these facts Dr. Ryerson referred to the testimony of fifty-two witnesses, given before a select Committee of the House of Assembly in 1828, and published in full at that time.

* This selfish demand—"that the ministrations of our Holy Religion be afforded without charge to the inhabitants of every township" (in which members of the Church of England were persistently educated in those days)—was most unfortunate in its influence on the Church, and has borne bitter fruit in these later times. Its legitimate effect has been to dry up the sources of Christian benevolence, paralyze the arm of Christian effort, and secularize, if not render impossible, any successful plan of Church extension and missionary work. Witness the almost complete failure (as compared with other Christian bodies) to raise sufficient funds to support even the limited number of Home missions in most of the dioceses, and the nearly hopeless task of infusing a genuine missionary zeal in behalf of the "regions beyond."

† It should be noted, in connection with this petition, that one most important part of its prayer was granted in that year—viz., the appointment of the Archdeacon (who went to England to present the petitions and to receive the appointment) as first Bishop of Toronto. His patent bears date, 27th July, 1839. The other part of the prayer was also granted, but not until 1840, when Lord John Russell, then Colonial Secretary, by an unprecedented and unlooked for stretch of official authority, but no doubt with the assent of his colleagues, introduced a bill into the House of Commons to do what even he and other Colonial Secretaries had deprecated doing—viz., the re-investing of the reserves in the Crown. Dr. Ryerson, then in England, strongly protested against this act of provincial spoliation and legislative invasion, but the bill became law. (See next chapter.)

I have purposely abstained from making any special reference to discussions in the clergy reserve question with which Dr. Ryerson had no connection. An important one, however, took place between Hon. Wm. Morris and Archdeacon Strachan in 1838-39, chiefly in regard to the claims of the Church of Scotland. Mr. Morris, however, did good service in the general discussion.

In November, 1838, Dr. Ryerson received a letter from Thomas Farmer, Esq., of London, England, in regard to the Centenary Celebration, to which he replied as follows:—

Our prospects as a country are rather gloomy. We have lately had the excitement and loss produced by Lord Durham's departure, and the second rebellion in Lower Canada, followed in a few days by a brigand invasion of this province to distract and destroy us. You refer to a Centenary Offering. I cannot say what we shall be able to do. We have not the slightest provision yet for the education of preacher's children ; nor a contingent fund to aid poor circuits, or to relieve the distressed preachers' families ; and an unpaid for Book Room, and not an entirely paid for Academy ;—all of which subjects have engaged our most anxious consideration ;—but in the present entirely unsettled state of our public affairs, we scarcely know what to do in respect to the future. We cannot, therefore, as yet fix upon the objects of our Centenary Offering.

The Methodist Centenary Year occurred in 1839. The Conference set apart the 25th October for its celebration,

By holding religious " services in all of our chapels and congregations, for the purpose of calling to mind the great things which the Lord has done for us as a people ; of solemnly recognizing our obligations and responsibilities to our Heavenly Father; and of imploring, on behalf of ourselves and the whole Wesleyan Methodist family throughout the world, a continuance and increase of religious happiness, unity and prosperity."

Meetings were held all over the Province during the months of August, September and October, for the collection of a centenary offering, to be applied to the Superannuation Fund, Book Room, Parsonages, Missionary, and other objects. Dr. Ryerson, as one of a deputation, attended a large number of meetings. Writing from Brockville, he mentions the fact that he

Stopped at a graveyard, a few miles west of Prescott, to survey the graves of some of the honoured dead. The remains of Mrs. Heck, the devoted matron who urged Philip Embury (the first Methodist preacher in America) to lift up his voice in the city of New York, in 1766, are deposited here.

CHAPTER XXXIII.

1838-1840.

THE NEW ERA—LORD DURHAM AND LORD SYDENHAM.

IN the midst of the gloom which overspread the Province, in consequence of the long continued exercise of irresponsible and arbitrary power on the part of the local executive, Dr. Ryerson, like many other loyal-hearted Canadians, rejoiced at the advent of Lord Durham,—a man possessed of plenary powers to inquire into and report on the grievances existing in Canada. Those who wished to perpetuate the reign of the ruling party, strongly deprecated Dr. Ryerson's advocacy of Lord Durham's schemes of reform. One of the most respectable organs* of that party (Neilson's Quebec *Gazette*) in a complimentary editorial on Dr. Ryerson (in May, 1839), expressed regret that a man "of his undoubted talents and great industry" should have endorsed Lord Durham's system of Responsible Government. In the *Guardian* of the 5th June, Dr. Ryerson replied, pointing out the fair and equitable system of Responsible Government advocated by Lord Durham, as compared with the crude one put forth by Messrs. W. L. Mackenzie and L. J. Papineau. He then illustrates the necessity for the reform proposed by Lord Durham, by referring to the arbitrary and irresponsible acts of Sir Francis Head. He said:—

The published word of the Representative of Royalty had [until Sir F. B. Head's time] been sacred and inviolable in Upper Canada; the majority of the people believed him. In 1836 they elected a House of Assembly in accordance with his wishes. He fulfilled his pledges by dismissing many of the magistrates and militia officers, because they voted against his candidates at the elections, and finished his career by plunging the country into misery, and thereby insuring its ruin.

Now, where (he asked) was the "responsibility" under which . . such a Governor acts? He abuses the confidence reposed in him,—where is his cen..ure? He disobeys the orders given

---

* The organs of that party in Upper Canada spoke of Dr. Ryerson's advocacy of Lord Durham's reforms with far less courtesy, and for obvious reasons.

him from England,—where is his punishment? He ruins men [Bidwell, etc.] whom he was ordered to appoint,—where is their redress, and his accountability? They are exiles, and he is made a Baronet! He disgraces and degrades numbers of persons without colour of reason, or justice, or law—yet they are without redress, and he is even without reproof. He tramples upon the orders from Her Majesty's Government, and attacks her ministers in their places—then returns to England, and boasts of his disobedience. . . And there are those who tell us of the responsibility of our Governors to the Queen and Parliament! . . The history of Sir F. B. Head's administration is enough to make the veriest bigot a convert to "Responsible Government."

For these and other important reasons it can be seen how the great question of the day (in 1839) was that of responsible government for these provinces. Dr. Ryerson and others had written freely on the subject, claiming that the government of the country should be administered, as it was then expressed—" according to the well understood wishes of the people." This could only be done by men representing their wishes, and responsible to the legislature for their exercise of power and for every official act of the Governor.

In October, Dr. Ryerson received a letter on this subject from a well-known advocate of the principle of responsible government in Nova Scotia—Hon. Joseph Howe. He said :—

May I beg your acceptance of a little work on responsible government, the object of which is to advance the good cause in which you have so heartily and with so much ability embarked. It is a great satisfaction to the friends of responsible government here, that the cause has been taken up in Canada by men about whose intentions and loyalty there can be no mistake. So long as we deprive the family compact of their only defence, which the folly of rebels and sympathizers raised for them, and act together without just cause for suspicion that we are anything but what we say, there can be little doubt of ultimate success. Should your electors return a majority favourable to responsibility at the next election, and all the colonies unite in one demand, it will be yielded. Our legislature, and any that can be chosen here, will uphold the principle. So will the majorities in Newfoundland, and Prince Edward Island, and New Brunswick. I cannot speak with certainty, but hope they will soon understand the question thoroughly in that province. It may be necessary for all the provinces to send delegates at the same time to England, to claim to be heard on the subject at the Bar of the Commons and Lords, and to diffuse, through every fair channel, correct views of the question. Think of this, and drop me a line at your leisure.

This Dr. Ryerson did in due time.

The coming of Lord Durham was the first harbinger of better days for Canada. His mission was one of enquiry, and for the suggestion of remedial measures. The mission of Mr. Poulett Thompson (who followed Lord Durham as Governor-

General) was hailed with delight by the people generally. He came to give practical effect to pressing measures of reform— to unite the provinces, and to introduce a new element of strength into the administrative system of the country.

The year 1839 was noted for the enthusiasm with which "Durham Meetings" were held throughout Upper Canada. These meetings were for the purpose of endorsing the famous report of Lord Durham, and for approving of the many valuable reforms which that report suggested. Much opposition and even violence characterized these meetings; but they revived and again inaugurated the right of free speech on public questions. The only record which Dr. Ryerson has left of this period of his history is as follows:—

In 1838 I yielded to persuasion and remonstrances, and was again re-elected Editor, and continued as such until June, 1840, when I relinquished finally all connection with the Editorship of the *Christian Guardian.*

It was during this period, from 1833 to 1840, that the most important events transpired in Upper Canada; the controversy respecting the clergy reserves, and a church establishment, was steadily and earnestly maintained.

The constitution of Lower Canada was suspended for two years, and an Executive Council Government was established in its place. The dominant party in Upper Canada by liberal professions succeeded in the elections, in 1836; but, instead of adopting a just and liberal policy, they sought to exclude all Reformers from a share in the Government as virtual rebels, and set themselves to promote a high-church establishment policy, to the exclusion of the Methodists and members of other religious denominations.

This unwise, unjust, and inverted-pyramid policy laid the foundation for a new agitation. The Methodists were the only party capable of coping with the revived high-church policy to crush out the rights of other denominations and the liberties of the country, and to paralyze their influence. The Presbyterians being divided, the Canadian Conference was not to be deterred, or moved from its principles, avowed and maintained for more than ten years; the result was a contest between the English and Canadian Conferences, which culminated in 1840 in a separation of the two bodies, and a conflict of seven years— wholly political—for London Wesleyan, English superiority, and tory ascendancy on the one side, and Canadian Methodist and Canadian liberty on the other side.

It is not my purpose to enter into detail, except in so far as Dr. Ryerson became an actor in the new scenes and events which followed the appointment of Mr. Charles Poulett Thompson as Governor-General.

Mr. Poulett Thompson arrived in Quebec on the 19th October, 1839, and in Toronto on the 21st November. As Governor-General, he superseded both Sir John Colborne at Quebec and Sir George Arthur at Toronto.

On the 3rd December, the Governor-General opened the Upper Canada Legislature; and on that very day Dr. Ryerson addressed to him an elaborate letter on the chief object of his mission. In referring to the clergy reserve question, he said :—

For sixteen years this question has been a topic of ceaseless discussion; and one on which the sentiments and feelings of a very large majority of the inhabitants have been without variation expressed; notwithstanding that Governor has succeeded Governor, and party has succeeded party. . . From the time when, at the elections of 1824, the sentiments of the country were first called forth to the present moment, its collective voice has demanded, what your Excellency has avowed on another subject, "equal justice to all of Her Majesty's subjects." This question is the parent of social discord in Upper Canada; all the other party questions have originated in this. The elevation of one class above all others in a community where there is little diversity of rank or intelligence, begets a necessity for special means to support that elevation. Hence partizan appointments to office; hence partizan administration of offices; hence party animosities, embittered by the jealousies of conscious weakness on one side, and a deep sense of unmerited exclusion and provocation on the other. . . Hence on the one side a selfish, insolent, baseless ecclesiastical and political oligarchy, and, on the other side, an abused, an injured, and dissatisfied country.

The bill providing for the vesting of the proceeds of the reserves in the Imperial Parliament, to which I have referred in the proceeding chapter, was not sanctioned by Her Majesty. This was "a sore blow and a heavy discouragement" to those who had laboured so assiduously to carry such a bill through the local Legislature. The objection raised to it by Lord John Russell was twofold. The chief reason, however, was thus expressed :—

It appeared to Her Majesty's Government that strong objections existed to this delegation to Parliament by a subordinate authority of the power of legislation. The proceeding should have been by address to the three estates of the Realm, asking them to undertake the decision of the question.

Thus by a stroke of Lord John Russell's pen, the whole of the pet scheme of the ruling party, devised after three months' anxious local legislation, was irrecoverably lost. And yet it was not lost, for by the after careful manipulation of Lord John and his colleagues by Bishop Strachan, Lord Seaton (Sir John Colborne) and Sir George Arthur, that bill afterwards proved to be, for ten years, the basis of a far more sweeping and unjust measure than even the most reckless and partizan member of the Legislature in Upper Canada would have ventured to propose.

When it was known that Her Majesty had declined to sanction Sir George Arthur's bill, steps were taken by the Governor-General to devise such a measure as would meet with the approval of the great mass of the people in Upper Canada. To aid him in accomplishing this desirable end, Mr. Poulett Thompson privately sought the aid of leading public men in the Province. Having obtained their assistance, he, with the advice of his Council, prepared a compromise measure which was designed to be just and equitable to all parties concerned.

On the 6th January, 1840, the Governor-General sent a message to the House of Assembly, in which he thus outlines the measure which, with his sanction, Hon. Solicitor-General Draper submitted to the House:—

The Governor-General proposes that the remainder of the land should be sold, and the annual proceeds of the whole fund, when realized, be distributed [one half to the Episcopal and Presbyterian Churches, and the other half among other religious bodies desiring to share in it] for the support of religious instruction within the Province, and for the promotion there, of the great and sacred objects for which these different bodies are established or associated.

On this bill, Dr. Ryerson remarked:—

From this message, the hopelessness of success in any further attempts to get the annual proceeds of the reserves appropriated to exclusively secular objects, is apparent. . . Up to the present time I have employed my best efforts, by every kind of argument, persuasion and entreaty, to get the proceeds applied simply and solely to educational purposes. . . This is unattainable, and is rendered so by an original provision of our Constitution (of 1791), as stated by the Governor-General.

The bill was fiercely attacked by the then newly-appointed Bishop of Toronto. He denounced it as—

Depriving the National Church of nearly three-fourths of her acknowledged property, and then, in mockery and derision, offering her back a portion of her own, so trifling as to be totally insufficient to maintain her present Establishment; it tramples on the faith of the British Government by destroying the birthright of all the members of the Established Church who are now in the province, or who may hereafter come into it; it promotes error, schism and dissent, and seeks to degrade the clergy of the Church of England to an equality with unauthorized teachers, etc.

The Bishop then uttered, that which events proved to be a memorable and true prophecy, that the Church—

Need be under no great apprehension in regard to any measure likely to pass the Provincial Legislature on the subject of the reserves :—reckless injustice in their disposition will not be permitted; although the Church may appear friendless and in peril, from the defection and treachery of some profes-ing members. . . If any of her children incline to despondency, let them turn their eyes to England, where we have protectors both numerous and powerful, watching our struggles, and holding out the hand of fellowship and assistance. [See next page.]

Dr. Ryerson at once joined issue with the Bishop, and—

Confuted the pretensions of "John Toronto" by the doctrines and statements of "John Strachan," who, when in England in 1827, published a pamphlet in which he stated that "the provincial legislatures have nothing to do, either directly or indirectly, with the Romish Church; but the same legislatures may vary, repeal, or modify the 31st Geo. III., cap. 31, as far as it respects the Church of England.

Dr. Ryerson pertinently asked the Bishop—

How could a "birthright" be "varied, repealed, or modified," as he had admitted that the constitutional act could do, "as far as it respects the Church of England?" Can (he asks) the Legislature "vary or repeal" the deeds by which individuals hold their lands ?—Which of the "dissenting" denominations recognized by law is not as orthodox in doctrine as the Church of England, and far more orthodox than those who endorse the Oxford " Tracts for the Times ?"

The bill was finally passed in the House of Assembly, by a vote of 31 to 7, and in the Legislative Council, by a vote of 13 to 4, notwithstanding a remarkably outspoken and defiant speech from the Bishop. In it he used the following language:

Feeling that the bill provides for the encouragement and propagation of error; inflicts the grossest injustice by robbing and plundering the National Church; that it attempts to destroy all distinction between truth and falsehood; that its anti-Christian tendencies lead directly to infidelity, and will reflect disgrace on the Legislature, I give it my unqualified opposition.

The Bishop again utters his prediction, and stated that what he wanted would be secured in England. He said—

At the same time I have no fear of its ever becoming law. But it may be useful, for its monstrous and unprincipled provisions will teach the Imperial Government the folly of permitting a Colonial Legislature to tamper with those great and holy principles of the Constitution, on the preservation of which the prosperity and happiness of the British Empire must ever depend.

Although it was almost impossible to reason with any one who would deliberately use such extravagant language, yet Dr. Ryerson replied to the Bishop's statements *seriatim*. With a touch of irony, he said :—

After penning such an effusion, the Bishop might well betake himself to the Litany of his Church, and pray the good Lord to deliver him—from all blindness of heart; from pride, vain glory and hypocrisy; from envy, hatred and malice, and all uncharitableness.

The fate of the bill is thus described in a statement on the subject, prepared by Dr. Ryerson. What he details clearly reveals the powerful and sympathetic influences which the Bishop of Toronto was able successfully to bring to bear upon "Henry of Exeter"—the then leader of the Bench of Bishops, —and, through him, upon the other Bishops in the House of Lords. Besides, Sir John Colborne (now Lord Seaton) took strong ground in the House of Lords in favour of the views of his old friend, Bishop Strachan, and aided the English Bishops in giving them practical effect. Thus the reiterated prophecy of the Bishop of Toronto was not uttered without abundant foreknowledge. It proved too true. Knowing this, he no doubt felt free to deal in strong language, both against the Legislature of Upper Canada, and the members of the Church of England in both Houses, who were too patriotic, just and reasonable, as well as far-seeing, to second his efforts to aggrandize the Church at the expense, and against the strongly-expressed and oft-repeated wishes, of the majority of the people of Upper Canada. He said:

On the bill being sent to England (accompanied by a most energetic despatch from the Governor-General, imploring Her Majesty's Government not to disallow, but to sanction it), the Bishop of Exeter moved in the House of Lords, that the question of the right to the clergy reserve property in Canada should be referred to the twelve Judges of England; but the decision of the Judges having proved adverse to the exclusive pretensions of the Bishop of Exeter and his party in England and Canada, the English Bishops then conferred with Lord John Russell, in order to set aside Lord Sydenham's Canadian bill, and introduce one into the Imperial Parliament which would accomplish as far as possible the objects aimed at by referring the question to the Judges. Lord John Russell became a consenting party and agent in this unconstitutional act of injustice and spoliation against the rights and feelings of a large majority of the people of Upper Canada. It was against this act that Messrs. W. and E. Ryerson (then in England), on behalf of the Wesleyan Church in Canada, remonstrated in an elaborate and strongly-worded letter to Lord John Russell—the only communication of the kind made by any religious body in Canada against the bill while it was before the British Parliament, or for several years afterwards.

Knowing the strong influences which had been brought to bear upon Mr. Poulett Thompson against Dr. Ryerson, by Sir George Arthur (page 193), and against the Methodist body generally by interested parties in this discussion, Dr. Ryerson addressed a letter to the Governor-General on the 25th March, 1840, in which he reviewed the course of the *Guardian* and his own attitude on public questions during the preceding ten years. The letter was evidently written with deep feeling, and under a keen sense of the injustice done to the Methodist people by means of the prolonged and persistent misrepresentation of these years. He said:—

I address your Excellency with feelings of the highest respect and strong affection. You are the first Governor of Canada who has exerted his personal influence and the authority of his station, to accomplish that in Upper Canada which has been avowed and promised by every Colonial-Secretary during the last ten years—framing enactments and administering the Government for the equal protection and benefit of all classes of Her Majesty's Canadian subjects. . . In doing so, your Excellency has been told that you have patronized "republicans and rebels." . . The *Guardian*, which you have been pleased to honour with an expression of your approbation, has been charged with opposite crimes from different quarters. . . You have been told that the ministers of the Wesleyan Methodist Church—whose rights you have justly and kindly consulted—have formerly come from the United States; and that the *Guardian*, during the first years of its existence, was nothing but a vehicle of radicalism, disaffection, and sedition. . . As to the former, I may say that the Methodist ministers have not come from . . the United States during the last twenty years. . . As to the latter, I furnish three columns of extracts from the *Guardian*, . . from which the following may be adduced :—

1. That in 1830 I entertained less friendship towards our American neighbours than I do in 1840.
2. That in 1830 I advocated the very principles in the administration of the Provincial Government that your Excellency has declared to be the basis of your administration in 1840.
3. That in 1830 I was as strongly opposed to an exclusive, or sectarian, spirit as I am in 1840.
4. That the very advice which I gave to the electors in 1830, as to their rights and interests, I could now repeat with a view to support your Excellency's administration.
5. That the very principles upon which your Excellency has commenced your administration, . . were actually promised and assured to the people of Upper Canada by a Tory Government in 1830.

In 1830 the Colonial-Secretary and Sir John Colborne proclaimed the "good laws and free institutions," and the non-preference system amongst religious denominations, which your Excellency is determined to carry into practice. . . When the hopes created by these avowals have not only been deferred for these years, but those who have indulged these hopes have been maligned and proscribed for constitutionally seeking a realization of them, you cannot be surprised if many of their hearts have been made sick, and that confidence and hope has yielded to distrust and despair.

The Governor-General, through his private secretary, often requested Dr. Ryerson, while Editor of the *Guardian*, to correct misstatements which were made in regard to His Excellency's proceedings.*

After an interview with His Excellency, at his request, Dr. Ryerson, in a letter dated 4th April, 1840, made a practical sug-

* Thus in a note dated 8th April, 1840, the Private Secretary said :—I know that His Excellency would wish you to comment on Lord John's despatch in the sense in which it is treated in the Montreal *Gazette*. [This was done in the *Guardian* of 15th April.] There is no doubt also that it is absurd in Hon. Henry Sherwood to pretend that he is supporting the Government when he opposes their own Solicitor-General, but not less so in the *Examiner* to support him and oppose Mr. Draper, or to stand up for a kind of responsible government which both His Excellency and Lord John Russell have declared to be inadmissible. I know that His Excellency would wish you to do everything in your power to support both Mr. Draper and Mr. Baldwin. Should any article come out which you consider would interest His Excellency, may I request you to send me a copy.

gestion as to the desirability of establishing the *Monthly Review*, as a means of disseminating the liberal views which he entertained in regard to the future government of this country, and also as an organ of public opinion in harmony with these views. It was at first proposed that Dr. Ryerson should edit the *Review*, but after fuller consideration of the matter he declined, and the editing and management of it was, at his suggestion, placed in the hands of John Waudby, Esq., Editor of the Kingston *Herald*. It was issued in Toronto early in 1841, but ceased on the death of Lord Sydenham, in September of that year. In Dr. Ryerson's letter to the Governor he said :—

> About a fortnight after your Excellency left Toronto, I happened in the course of conversation with Hon. R. B. Sullivan to mention the subject of establishing a monthly periodical, such as I had mentioned to you. Mr. Sullivan was anxious that something of the kind should be undertaken; I stated to him that I understood that your Excellency would highly approve of such a publication, if it could be successfully established. Mr. Sullivan pressed me to prepare a prospectus and submit it for your Excellency's consideration. I drew up a prospectus, and got an estimate of the cost, covering all expenses. Mr. Sullivan fully concurred in the prospectus, except the first paragraph. He was afraid it might be construed into an expression of opinion in favour of "responsible Government," and proposed another paragraph in place of it. The one was as acceptable to me as the other. A feeling of apprehension and embarrassment at the responsibilities of such an undertaking, and the course of exertion which a successful accomplishment of it would require, has deterred me from forwarding, until now, the accompanying prospectus for your Excellency's perusal and signification of your pleasure thereon.*

* The following was the prospectus agreed upon and issued :—

A MONTHLY REVIEW, DEVOTED TO THE CIVIL GOVERNMENT OF CANADA.

The Canadas have been united under an amended constitution; the foundation has been laid for an improved system of government. The success of that constitution will greatly depend upon a correct understanding and a just appreciation of its principles; and the advantages of the new system of government will be essentially influenced by the views and feelings of the inhabitants of the Canadas themselves. At a period so eventful, and under circumstances so peculiar, it is of the utmost importance that the principles of the constitution should be carefully analysed, and dispassionately expounded; that the relations between this and the Mother Country, and the mutual advantages connected with those relations, should be explained and illustrated; the duties of the several branches of the government, and the different classes of the community, stated and enforced; the natural, commercial, and agricultural resources and interests of these Provinces investigated and developed; a comprehensive and efficient system* of public education discussed and established; the subject of emigration practically considered in proportion to its vast importance; the various measures adapted to promote the welfare of all classes of the people originated and advocated; and a taste for intellectual improvement and refinement encouraged and cultivated.

As the Editor's views on all the leading questions of Canadian policy accord with those of His Excellency the Governor-General, who has been pleased to approve of the plan of the *Monthly Review*, it will be enabled to state correctly the facts and principles on which the government proceeds; yet the writers alone will be held responsible for whatever they may advance.

* Dr. Ryerson, who wrote this prospectus, evidently had in view such a system of Education as he afterwards established.

I cannot but see that the public mind in this country is in a chaotic state, without any controlling current of feeling, or fixed principle of action, in civil affairs ; but susceptible, by proper management and instruction, of being cast into any mould of rational opinion and feeling ; yet liable, without judicious direction, to fall into a state of "confusion worse confounded." I know that now is the time—perhaps the only time—to establish our institutions and relations upon the cheapest, the surest, and the only permanent foundation of any system, or form of Government—the sentiments and feelings of the population. But I alone have not the means or the power of contributing to the accomplishment of these objects. To the utmost of my humble abilities and acquirements, I am willing to exert myself ; and that without a shillings' remuneration—although my present salary is less than £200 per annum. I believe the government about to be established in these provinces may be made the most enduring and loftiest memorial of your Excellency's fame, and the greatest earthly blessing to its inhabitants ; and it will be to me a source of satisfaction to contribute towards the formation and cementing of materials for the erection of a monument at once so honourable to its founder, and so beneficial to Her Majesty's Canadian subjects.

The personal influence of your Excellency in Lower Canada will be required to induce two or three of the cleverest men in Lower Canada to contribute to the columns of the *Review* ; especially on questions and subjects which grow out of the state and structure of society in that province. Mr. Sullivan thinks he will be able to contribute one, if not two, articles for each number. I am acquainted with several other gentlemen who are competent to contribute very ably on some subjects. I know from experience that furnishing matter for any periodical, as well as giving it character, must chiefly devolve upon the conductor of it. He must give it soul, if it have any ; he must combine, concentrate, and direct its power. And such a publication, got up under so high and favourable auspices, and properly conducted, and embodying the productions of the leading minds of both provinces, cannot fail to prove an engine of immense and even irresistible moral power in the country ; and must materially contribute to its intellectual as well as political elevation.

As to my own views and feelings, I would greatly prefer retiring altogether from any connection with the press in all discussions of civil affairs in every shape and form, and I can consistently and honourably do so in June. But if this course be not justifiable in the present circumstances of the province; if it be deemed expedient for me still to take a part in public matters, I am sensible I ought to do more than I do now, or can do through the organ of a religious body. The relation, character and objects of the publication I now conduct, impose a restriction upon the topics and illustrations which are requisite to an effective discussion of political questions. Under such circumstances I can neither do justice to myself, nor to the subjects on which I occasionally remark, or might discuss.

I have felt the more disposed to make this communication, because your Excellency's avowed system and policy of Government is but carrying out and reducing to practice those views of civil polity in Canada which have guided my public life, as your Excellency will have observed from the articles and references which have appeared in the *Guardian*. I have been defeated and disappointed heretofore, because the local executive itself has been for the most part rather the head of a party, than the Government of the country, and the opposition, or "Reform" party, has often gone to equal extremes of selfishness and extravagance ; so that I have occupied the unenviable and uncomfortable position of a sort of break-water—resisting and checking the conflicting waves of mutual party violence, convinced that the exclusive and absolute ascendancy of either party would be destructive of the ends of just Government, and public happiness ; a position which, previously to your Excellency's arrival in Canada, I had determined to abandon, as I found myself possessed of no adequate means of accomplishing any permanent good by occupying it.

I think the appearance in this province of Lord John Russell's despatch on "Responsible Government" is timely. The "Reformers" are too fully committed to Government to fly off; and a large portion of the old "Conservative" party are glad of an excuse to change their position. Neither party can triumph, as *both* must concede something. This mutual concession will prepare the way for mutual forbearance, and ultimately for co-operation and union. Having perceived that the Editor of the *Examiner* was seeking, under the pretence of supporting the Government, to get a House of Assembly returned, consisting wholly of the old Reformers, who had identified themselves in 1834-5-6, with the Papineau party of Lower Canada, I thought it desirable to check such a design in the bud, by insisting upon the support of Hon. W. H. Draper, and that he should be returned upon the same grounds as those of Mr. Baldwin. The elucidation and description of this one case will affect the position of parties in the character of the elections throughout the province, and make them turn, not upon Lord Durham's "Report," or any of the old questions of difference, but upon your Excellency's administration. This, I have no doubt, with a little care, will, in most instances be the case. Thus will the members returned from Upper Canada, be isolated from the French anti-unionists of Lower Canada, and be more fully, both in obligation and feeling, identified with the Government. I have not, therefore, been surprised at the *Examiner's* indignation, as it is so ultra, and thorough a partizan, and as it has some discernment, though but little prudence.

In reply, the Private Secretary of the Governor-General said:

I am to express to you His Excellency's approbation of the plans you have suggested, and he desires me to say that he requests that you will visit Montreal, on your way to New York, as he is anxious to see you on the subject contained in your letter.

The Special Council meets this day for the first time.

The Secretary further added:—

His Excellency agrees that the line which you have taken is most judicious. There is no doubt that the gentleman to whom you refer is doing very great mischief both to Hon. Robert Baldwin and the Government, by the extremes to which he is pushing his cry for responsible government, and his opposition to Hon. W. H. Draper.

Dr. Ryerson (who was on his way to the General Conference at Baltimore) in a note, dated Montreal, 4th May, said:—

The Governor-General having kindly invited me to visit him and converse on matters relating to public affairs, I did so, and was most cordially received by him. I also had a long interview with him on Friday afternoon, and am desired to spend the evening with him on Saturday. His Excellency has given every requisite information as to his plans. I am thus enabled to accomplish the object of my visit far beyond what I expected when I left home.

In a letter from New York (dated 9th May) Dr. Ryerson said:—Much to my surprise to-day, while in New York on my way to Baltimore, I received a note from the Governor-General's Secretary, T. W. C. Murdoch, Esq., as follows:—

By direction of the Governor-General I send you the enclosed bill of exchange for £100 stg., the receipt of which I would request you to acknowledge.

You will have seen the English papers which hold out every prospect that both the Union and the Clergy Reserve Bills will be satisfactorily settled. I feel that I may congratulate you, and every friend of Canada, on such a result.

I acknowledged this kind and generous act, but at once returned the Bill of Exchange to His Excellency—at the same time respectfully assuring him, that under no circumstances could I receive anything for what I had done, or might do, to support the policy and administration of Her Majesty's Government, in the peculiar circumstances of the Province.

One of the chief points discussed in Upper Canada, in connection with the proposed union of the provinces, was the effect it would have on the Protestant character of the government and institutions of the county. Mr. John W. Gamble, a public man, and a leading member of the Church of England, in Vaughan, writing to Dr. Ryerson on the subject, said:—

I feel deeply the conviction that the time has now arrived when Protestants must sink all points of minor consideration, and unite in defence of our common faith. The union of the provinces will most assuredly result in giving not only a preponderance, but a large majority to the Roman Catholics in the united legislature; and this taken in conjunction with the plans now in operation for pouring a large Roman Catholic population into these provinces, surely ought not only to excite the fears, but rouse the energies of those who know and love the truth as it is in Jesus. I am altogether ignorant of your opinion upon the union question, but I call upon you as a Protestant to unite with me in endeavouring to avert the threatened calamity.

Mr. Gamble was for many years afterwards an earnest opponent in the Legislature of United Canada of the extension of the Separate School system in the province.

Although greatly enfeebled in health, yet Dr. Ryerson's Mother was enabled to write to him occasionally. In a letter written by her in 1839, after returning from seeing him, she said:—

I suppose you are anxious to know the state of my mind. I yet feel that the Lord is my trust, and I am waiting daily till my change come. I feel that when the "earthly house of this tabernacle be dissolved, I have a house not made with hands, eternal in the heavens." Dear Egerton, I feel very much as I did when I left you—a great deal of weakness. I am anxious to live to see you all once more, perhaps for the last time. Do not neglect to come up, one and all, as soon as convenient, if you only stay one day. When you come fetch some books, such as you think would be profitable for me, and one of your good-sized Bibles; also three of your likenesses. I thought that your Father had brought them up when he came. Do not fail to come up and see us. Don't let me be denied the happiness of seeing you soon.

CHAPTER XXXIV.
1840.
PROPOSAL TO LEAVE CANADA—DR. RYERSON'S VISIT TO ENGLAND.

THE year 1840 is somewhat memorable in the Methodistic history of Upper Canada, for three things: 1st. The final retirement of Dr. Ryerson from the editorship of the *Christian Guardian;* 2nd. Visit of Revs. William and Egerton Ryerson to England, and the painful, yet fruitless, discussions with a Committee of the British Conference on the lapsed Union; 3rd. The annual and special Canada Conferences of that year—at the latter of which the formal separation of the British and Canadian sections of the Conference took place under peculiarly affecting circumstances.

Dr. Ryerson and his brother John attended the American General Conference at Baltimore, May, 1840. In a letter from there he said :—

The Methodist Connexion here are much in advance of us, and, as a whole, even of the British Connexion. I have never seen a more pious, intelligent, and talented body of men than the preachers assembled here at Conference; nor more respectable, intelligent congregations. The manners of the people in these Middle States are very like the manners of intelligent people in Upper Canada—alike removed from the English haughtiness and Yankee coldness—simple, frank, and unaffected. Bishops Roberts, Soule, Hedding and Waugh dined with us to-day. They are venerable and apostolic men. We have had cordial invitations to come to this country, and did we consult our own comfort, brother John and I would do so without hesitation. Bishop Hedding hopes to visit us at our approaching Conference. Rev. R. Newton, of England, will not visit Canada. Mr. —— has told him that it was not worth while to go to Canada; and all that can be said to induce him to come is unavailing. We in Canada are not worth so much trouble, or notice!

In a letter from Baltimore, dated May 25th, 1840, Dr. Ryerson states the reason why he proposed to leave Canada :—

I am still at the General Conference. Rev. Dr. Bangs says that I ought to remain until the close. After much consideration I have decided upon a step which, for many reasons, appears desirable. Instead of coming to this country for a few months, in order to avail myself of some collegiate lectures, to pursue certain branches of science, I have concluded and have made arrangements to take a station in the city of New York for one, if not for two years. My brother John would have done the same if we could have both left Canada this year. If things in the province do not go on better with us he will do so another year. I have seen the new constitution which is about to be adopted by the British Parliament for the future Government of Canada. I do not approve of it. To interfere any more in civil contentions will be wasting the best part of my life to little purpose, for there seems to be no end to such things. To remain in Canada and be silent, will incur the hostility of both parties. The government will regard my neutrality as opposition, and the popular party will view it as indifference to the rights of the people; and, in such circumstances, I shall neither be useful nor happy. While, therefore, I am on good terms with the Government and the country at large, my brother thinks with me that it is by all means best to withdraw from such scenes. I have the offer of one of the three or four largest Methodist Chapels in New York. I shall be appointed to one of the largest and most elegant in the city, where all the great public meetings are held. There are, however, three or four vacant, equally desirable. I much prefer this to my taking a district in Canada. I would not return to the *Guardian* again for any earthly consideration.

Dr. Ryerson went to the Conference at Belleville after his return from Baltimore. Writing from there, he said:—

Previously to proceeding to elect the Secretary, an English brother remarked that he had certain communications from the Committee in London, which he wished to read. I observed that no communications could be read until the Conference was organized, and the Conference could not be organized until the Secretary was elected. The brother persevered, and then stated that the documents referred to me. I then arose, and observed that the proceeding was at variance with law, Methodism, and justice. The Conference was justly roused to indignation by my remarks, which were followed by some observations from my brother John, in the same strain. Not a man spoke in favour of the English brother's proceeding, and he was compelled to withdraw his proposal. Such an anti-Methodistic and barbarous attempt to sacrifice me (as some of the preachers afterwards expressed it), excited a strong feeling in my favour, and, I was told, increased my majority of votes for the Secretaryship. When the Conference balloted for Secretary, the votes stood as follows:—Matthew Richey, 1; Anson Green, 1; Wm. Case, 2; E. Evans, 12; Egerton Ryerson, 43. The circumstance has so deeply affected me, that I feel it to be like tearing soul from body to be separated from brethren who stand by me in the day of trial, and who will not suffer me, as one of them expressed it to me, to be sacrificed at the pleasure of my enemies.* But I see no reason to change my purposes; and

* The more important parts of the painful proceedings at this Conference are given in "Epochs of Canadian Methodism," pages 341-358. The result of this formidable attack on Dr. Ryerson by the English Missionary party before the Canada Conference, is thus stated by Rev. Dr. Carroll: "When the Rev. Matthew Richey's motion of condemnation on the Rev. Egerton Ryerson for his interference in the matter [of the Government grant of £900 to Wesleyan missions] was

my brother John thinks I can do more good to the Connexion by being in New York, than by remaining in Canada.

I desire, with humble dependence upon the wisdom and providence of God, to commit my all to Him. I hunger and thirst after the mind which was in Christ Jesus.

Subsequently Dr. Ryerson wrote, saying :—

My plans in regard to the United States must now be changed. The charges of the London Committee, and the state of the Connexion in regard to the Union, render my absence from the Province, in the judgment of my brethren, unjustifiable and out of the question. Some of the preachers insist that I must go to England, and meet Mr. Alder before the British Conference. Such a mission is not impossible, but, I hope, not probable.

After the election of Secretary, the charges against Dr. Ryerson were read. They were embodied in a resolution to the effect that he had improperly interfered and sought to deprive the British Conference of its annual grant from the Imperial Government for the extension of missions in the province. The resolution was negatived by a vote of 59 to 8, and a series of resolutions sustaining Dr. Ryerson, in the strongest manner, was passed. He and his brother William were appointed as Representatives at the British Conference, with directions "to use all proper means to prevent collision between the two Connexions."

As intimated in Dr. Ryerson's letter from Baltimore, he decided to retire finally from the Editorship of the *Christian Guardian*. This he did at the Belleville Conference, and on the 24th of June, 1840, he laid down his pen as Editor of the *Christian Guardian*, and was succeeded by Rev. Jonathan Scott. In his valedictory of that date, Dr. Ryerson said :—

The present number of the *Guardian* closes the connection of the undersigned with the provincial press. To his friends and to those of the public who have confided in him, and supported him in seasons of difficulty and danger, he offers his most grateful acknowledgments; those who have opposed him honourably, he sincerely respects; those who have assailed him personally, he heartily forgives; and of those whose feelings he may have wounded in the heat of discussion, he most humbly asks pardon. While he is deeply sensible of his imperfections, infirmities, and failings, he derives satisfaction from

put to the Conference, there were only eight in its favour, several of whom, after obtaining further light, wished to change their votes; and fifty-nine against it. Three were excused from voting."—*Case, etc.,* vol. iv., page 298, note.

the consciousness that he has earnestly aimed at promoting the best interests of his adopted church and his native country.

EGERTON RYERSON.

Immediately after the close of the annual Conference of 1840, Dr. Ryerson and his brother William left for England. From his diary, written at that time, he had made the following extracts for this work:—

July 22nd, 1840.—After landing at Liverpool, I called upon an old and kind friend, Mr. Michael Ashton, and I had much conversation with him and Rev. R. Young, on the affairs of our mission. I and my brother William arrived in London on the 23rd. Took up our lodgings with my old hostess, 27 Great Ormond Street. Addressed a note to Lord John Russell, on the object of our mission; an interview was appointed for the next day. Went to the House of Commons in the evening, having an order for admission to the Speaker's gallery, through the kindness of Lord Sandon.

July 24th.—Went to the Colonial office; had a long interview with Lord John Russell, on the Canada Clergy Reserve Bill. Mr. [afterwards Sir James] Stephen was present. We pointed out to His Lordship the injustice of the bill, and the probable consequences if it were passed in its present shape. We spoke at some length, but with great plainness; intimating that we regarded the measure as the forfeiture of good faith on the part of Her Majesty's Government, as the violation of the constitutional rights of the inhabitants of Upper Canada, and as the cause of the unpopularity of the British Government in that country. But his Lordship appeared inflexible, and seemed to regard it essential to conciliate the Bishops, but not essential to do what he considered just in itself, or to fulfil the declarations of Government to the inhabitants of Upper Canada, or to consult their oft-expressed views and wishes. In the afternoon we went to see Mr. Charles Buller, but he was not in town. In going through Hyde Park we saw the Queen and Prince Albert, coming from Windsor. We took a hasty view through Westminster Abbey, and in the evening we called upon the Rev. Mr. Stead, formerly a missionary to India, and received from him many useful suggestions respecting the object of our mission.

July 27th.—Prepared a long letter to Lord John Russell on the Canada Clergy Reserve Bill, now before Parliament. Went to the House of Commons in order to hear the debate on the third reading of said bill. Lord John Russell was not present. But we heard a long debate on the China opium trade, etc. Mr. W. E. Gladstone introduced the discussion. Afterwards Sir Robert Peel spoke on the present position of the Church of Scotland in resisting the decision of the House of Lords. Mr. Fox Maule [Lord Panmure] spoke in reply, and contended that the point for which the General Assembly contended was the right of the people to a voice in the choice of their ministers.

July 28th.—Visited the City Road Chapel Grave-yard, the Bank, various book establishments, and St. Paul's Cathedral.

July 30th.—Left London yesterday; entered the city of York by the southwest gate; got a glimpse of the Minster; the country exceedingly beautiful, and in a high state of cultivation. Heard of the death of poor Lord Durham. The attacks upon him in the House of Lords as Governor-General of Canada, the abandonment of him by the Government, the mortification experienced by him in consequence of the Royal disapprobation at his sudden return from Canada before his resignation had been accepted, are said to have hastened, if not caused his death. His heart seems to have been set upon making Canada a happy and a great country, and I think he intended to rest his fame upon that achievement. He was defeated, disappointed, died! How bright the prospect two years ago—how sudden the change, how sad the termination! Oh, the vanity of earthly power, wealth and glory!

July 29th.—Arrived this morning at Newcastle-upon-Tyne by stage, eighty miles from York. The next morning we went to the Conference, and sent in our cards to Rev. G. Marsden; he came out and kindly received us, and hoped our mission would be for good. We met with a very cool reception from several of the preachers, with whom I was acquainted and on friendly terms during my former visits. Not feeling very well, or very much at home, we enquired our way to our lodgings, and left.

July 31st.—Went to the Conference this morning at 7 a.m. We were furnished with the President's card of admittance, and shown a seat in a corner at the side of the Chapel, and could hear but a part of the debates. In the afternoon we addressed a note to the President, to which we only received a verbal reply.

Aug. 1st.—This morning we were engaged in writing a strong letter to the President concerning our treatment, our position, the objects of our mission, etc., but we were saved the pain of delivering it, as, on our arrival, we were met and introduced as accredited Representatives of the Canada Conference. Rev. J. Stinson and Rev. M. Richey were also introduced at the same time. My brother William then presented the address and resolutions of the Canada Conference. A comfortable seat was now provided for us, in front of the President. Thank God, we now have a right to speak, can take our own part, and maintain the rights and interests we have been appointed to represent!

Aug. 3rd.—The Commitee of the last year on Canadian affairs had met and reported:—That the resolutions of the Committee of which the Canadian Conference had complained we unanimously confirmed, and recommended that the Conference appoint a large Committee to whom the Messrs. Ryerson and the documents of the Canadian Conference be referred.

The cases of Circuits proposed to be divided were next taken up. This caused many amusing remarks. Rev. R. Newton thought they were losing the spirit of their fathers in travelling, who had insuperable objections to solitary stations. Dr. Bunting assigned as a reason for the failure of the health of so many young men, the custom of giving up horses: said it was an innovation; quoted some of the last words of Wesley: "I cannot make preachers—I cannot buy preachers—and I will not kill preachers."

A long conversation ensued on the subject of reading the Liturgy generally, and concluded by a resolution that the Liturgy be read on the principal Sabbath at each Conference. On the subject of reading the Liturgy by the preachers themselves, Dr. Bunting said: It was very well for men to spend their strength in preaching, and let others read the prayers, when Methodism was only a Society supplementary to the Church; but having in the order of Providence grown up into an independent and separate Church, the preachers were something more than mere preachers of the Word—they were ministers of the Church, and ought to read as well as preach.

The address of the Irish Conference was read. Rev. T. Jackson said he could bear testimony to the very respectful manner in which the address of the British Conference had been received by the Irish Conference, and he trusted the brethren would understand the import and bearing of that remark. Rev. Mr. Entwistle referred to the liberality and cheerfulness of the Irish preachers in their difficulties, when Dr. Bunting replied that if they had been in such difficulties their heads would have hung down.

Dr. Ryerson's diary ends here. A full account of the inter-
18

views and discussions with the Wesleyan authorities in England are given in the Epochs of Canadian Methodism, pages 407-426. The result was, that the Committee on the subject reported a series of resolutions adverse to the Canada representatives, which were adopted by the Conference after "more than four-fifths of its members had left for their circuits." The pacific resolutions of the Upper Canada Conference were negatived by a majority, and it was declared "that a continuance of the more intimate connection established by the articles of 1833 [was] quite impracticable."

Thus was ignominiously ended a union between the two Conferences which had (nominally) existed since 1833, and which had promised such happy results, and thus was inaugurated a period of unseemly strife between the two parties from 1840 to 1847, when it happily ceased. What followed in Upper Canada is thus narrated by Dr. Ryerson :—

The English Conference having determined to secede from the Union which it had entered into with the Canadian Conference in 1833, and to commence aggressive operations upon the Canadian Conference, and its societies and congregations, a special meeting of the Canadian Conference became necessary to meet this new state of things, to organize for resenting the invasion upon its field of labour, and to maintain the cause for which they had toiled and suffered so much for more than half a century.

The prospects of the Canada Conference were gloomy in the extreme ; the paucity of ministers, and the poverty of resources in comparison to the English Conference, besides numerous other disadvantages ; but the ministers of the Canadian Conference with less than a dozen individual exceptions, had hearts of Canadian oak, and weapons of New Jerusalem steel, and were determined to maintain the freedom of the Church, and the liberties of their country, whatever might be the prestige or resources of their invaders; and "according to their faith it was done unto them;" out of weakness they waxed strong. They sowed in tears, they reaped in joy. Their weeping seed-sowing was followed by rejoicing, bringing their sheaves with them.

The Special Conference caused by these events was held in the Newgate (Adelaide) Street Church in October, 1840. The venerable Thomas Whitehead, then in his 87th year, opened the proceedings, after which Rev. William Case was elected to preside. Rev. Mr. Whitehead was subsequently elected President. Dr. Ryerson was elected Secretary, but declined, and Rev. J. C. Davidson was appointed in his place. The whole matter of differences between the two Conferences was discussed at great length, and with deep feeling on the part of the speakers. Dr. Ryerson spoke for five hours, and his brother William for nearly three. Finally a series of eleven resolutions were adopted, strongly maintaining the views of the Canadian Representatives to England, and protesting—

Against the Methodistic or legal right or power of the Conference in England to dissolve, of its own accord, articles and obligations which have been entered into with this Conference by mutual consent.

In consequence of the adoption of these resolutions, the following ministers requested permission to withdraw from the Canada Conference with a view to connect themselves with the British Missionary party, viz :—

Rev. Messrs. William Case, Ephraim Evans, Benjamin Slight, James Norris, Thomas Fawcett, William Scott, John G. Manly, Edmund Stoney, James Brock, Thomas Hurlburt, Matthew Lang, John Douse, William Steer, John Sunday, and C. B. Goodrich.

The leave-taking was said to have been very tender and sorrowful. Of the members of the Canada Conference who left it, Dr. Ryerson said :—

Among the ten who seceded from the Canada Conference to the London Wesleyan Committee was the venerable William Case, who took no part in the crusade against his old Canadian brethren, but who wished to live in peace and quietness, with the supply of his wants assured to him in his old, lonely Indian Mission at Alnwick, near Cobourg, isolated alike from the white inhabitants and from other Indian tribes, where he continued until his decease.

The character of this untoward contest with the British Conference party—so far as it related to Dr. Ryerson—can be best understood from the conclusion of his five hours' speech before the Special Conference. He said :—

I am aware that a combined effort has been determined upon and is making to destroy me as a public man, and to injure this Connexion, as far as my overthrow can affect it. I rejoice to know that the strength and efficiency of our Church are not depending upon me; but I am not insensible to the advatages which it is supposed will be gained over the Church if I can be put down. Our adversaries seem to have abandoned the idea of answering my arguments, or of diverting me from my purposes, in regard to my position, and views and feelings towards this Connexion. The only expedient left is that which requires no strength of intellect—no solid arguments—no moral principle—but abundance of confidence, malignity, and zeal. It is the expedient of impeaching my moral integrity, and blackening my character. And this is attempted to be accomplished. One class of adversaries, not by an appeal to reason, or even to official documents, but by the importation and retail from one side of the Atlantic to the other, and one end of the province to the other, and from house to house, of bits and parcels of perverted private conversations—a mode of warfare disgraceful to human nature, much more to any Christian community. History apprizes me that, in such a warfare, some of the best of men have not triumphed until long after they slept in death, when the hand of time and the researches of impartial history did them that justice which the cupidity and jealousies of powerful contemporaries denied them. I know not the present result of existing combinations against myself. On that point I feel little concern, though I am keenly alive to their influence upon my public usefulness. I engaged in the Union, because I believed the principles upon which it was founded were reasonable, and the prejudices against it on all sides were unreasonable. I do not regret the opposition which I have experienced—the reproaches which I have incurred—the labours I have endured; but I do regret—and every day's reflection adds fresh poignancy to my regrets—that in carrying out a measure which I had hoped would prove an unspeakable blessing to my native country, I have lost so many friends of my youth. No young man in Canada had more friends amongst all Christian denominations than I had when the Union took place. Many of them have become my enemies. I can lose property without concern or much thought; but I cannot lose my friends, and meet them in the character of enemies, without emotions not to be described. I feel that I have injured myself, and injured this Connexion, and I fear this province, not by my obstinacy, but by my concessions. This is my sin, and not the sins laid to my charge. I have regarded myself, and all that Providence has put into my hands from year to year, as the property of this Connexion. I can say, in the language of Wesley's hymn—

" No foot of land do I possess,
No cottage in the wilderness;
A poor wayfaring man."

And it is to me a source of unavailing grief, that after the expenditure of so much time, and labour, and suffering, and means, one of the most important measures of my life may prove a misfortune to the Church of my affections and the country of my birth. I have only to say, that as long as there is any prospect of my being useful to either, I will never desert them.

We have surveyed every inch of the ground on which we stand: We have offered to concede everything but what appertains to our character, and to our existence and operations as a Wesleyan Methodist Church. The ground we occupy is Methodistic, is rational, is just. The very declarations of those who leave us attest this. They are compelled to pay homage to our character as a body; they cannot impeach our doctrines, or discipline, or practice; nor can they sustain a single objection against our principles or standing; the very reasons which they assign for their own secession are variable, indefinite, personal, or trivial. But the reasons which may be assigned for our position and unity are tangible, are definite, are Methodistic, are satisfactory, are unanswerable.

The effect of this disruption was disastrous to the peace and unity of the Wesleyan body, especially in the towns and cities.

Some time after the Conference, Dr. Ryerson received the following characteristic letter from the venerable Thomas Whitehead, the President of the Canada Special Conference:—

I have been not a little pleased with the expectation of seeing you this evening, and of hearing you speak of the sorrows and joys of Wesleyan Methodism in Upper Canada. God grant that you and I and all of us, when our labours, sorrows and joys on earth are ended, may meet around the throne of God and the Lamb. Your labours, sorrows and joys for these years past have been unparalleled, and to the present they are increasing. Well, you have been called (with not a few invaluable assistants) to stand up in defence of the Gospel, and have been sometimes placed near the swellings of Jordan; however, you still rejoice in your labours, and the effects thereof, and so do I; and, blessed be God, the Pilot of the Galilean lake is still on shipboard, and he will soon speak peace to the troubled waters, and there will be a great calm. I have no doubt but Brother Green and Brother Bevitt (a comical soul) and yourself have had cold travelling (I hope good lodging) in your western rides; I am persuaded you have met with friends, and a generous people. God bless them!

I greatly rejoice that our brethren in the ministry are faithful, affectionate, and successful in defence of all that appertains to the privileges of the glorious Gospel of the Son of God, long, long preached by the Wesleyan Methodist ministers in the wilds of Upper Canada, and I trust they will, by all Christian means and measures, support Her Majesty's Government in Canada. May the Holy and Blessed God give us peace, and good government in our day. I have been a little vexed with the travelling gab of one of our own former friends, who is pleased to inform the people that you were the sole cause of the late rebellion. I must tell him, the first time I meet with him, that the meaning of his sing-song is not understood, and that if he will explain his hidden meaning, it will be, that he is ready to prove that the Rev. Egerton Ryerson was the sole cause of the rebellion in Heaven, by the fallen angels. In that case no one would mistake his meaning.

In a letter of congratulation, written in May, 1841, to Rev. Dr. Bangs, on his appointment to the Presidency of the Wesleyan University, Middletown, Conn., Dr. Ryerson said :—

I hope and pray that you may be able to continue without abatement to favour and edify the religious public with the rich results of your varied reading and matured thinking. On this ground I desire to express my personal obligations; and not the least for your "Letters to young Ministers of the Gospel," which were the first I recollect of reading. Many of your remarks and suggestions, on the subjects which they treat, have been of great service to me.

Speaking of the rupture of the union between the British and Canadian Conferences, and of alleged personal obstacles which he presented in the way of a reunion, Dr. Ryerson said : —The agents of the London Missionary Committee have not injured the Societies generally; although the scenes of schism which have been and are exhibited in many places are highly disgraceful. I am not aware that Elder Case has taken any active part in these transactions, and he has continued an acting and useful member of the Academy Board, notwithstanding his strange secession from our Conference. I have observed by the discussion, especially in the pamphlet lately published by the Committee in London, that the whole affair is made to appear, as much as possible, a matter of difference between the Committee and me personally, and epithets have been multiplied against me in proportion to the want of facts. I have always resolved not to allow myself to be the ground of difference between two bodies. If I can make this circumstance instrumental in effecting an amicable adjustment of differences, such as would be agreeable and advantageous to my brethren, I have thought it would be best to do so, and retire personally from the Conference, either employing my pen for the religious and general interests of my native land, or seeking a more peaceful field of labour in your part of the world, where I almost wish I had gone last year as proposed—although I know not that I could have done otherwise than I did, in accordance with what is due to personal honour and character.

The Imperial Parliament has disposed of the clergy reserves in a manner the most unfair, unjust, and corrupt, although the old Constitution of Canada provides for the disposal of them by the Provincial Legislature. Wide-spread, secret dissatisfaction exists in the country; a majority of the new Assembly (which has not yet met) are friends of the people, but many are afraid to move, or to say what they think. My own apprehension is that, notwithstanding all exertions to the contrary, under the present system of things the morals and intelligence of the people will be on a level with their liberties. Whether my continued silence in such circumstances is a virtue, or a crime; or whether I should retire from the country, or remain and make one Christian, open, and decisive effort to secure for my fellow-countrymen a free constitution and equal rights among their churches, is a perplexing question to me, as well as to my brothers. It is believed by some intelligent men, who have talked on the subject, that if I would come out as the advocate of the country, there would be no doubt of success, from my knowledge of the subject, from a general, and, as I think, overweening confidence on the part of my friends in my powers of concentration, perseverance and energy, and from the feelings of the country. It is also thought that, if there should be a failure of success, I could then honourably retire to the United States. I am no theorist, but I hate despotism as I do Satan, and I love liberty as I do life; and my thoughts and feelings flow so strongly in favour of the religious and civil freedom of my native country, that with all my engagements and duties, I cannot resist them, at least half of the time. I would be most grateful to you for your opinion on this general matter, irrespective of details, with which, of course, you cannot be acquainted.

To this letter Rev. Dr. Bangs replied as follows:—

I feel much for my Canadian brethren, and I can never be indifferent to their weal or woe. I have never had but one opinion respecting your separation from us, and that is, that it was an erroneous step at the time, originating with the ambition of one man—Henry Ryan. (See page 87.) Regrets, however, are useless now. The die has been cast; but from that unhappy moment you have been tossed about from one point of the compass to another. What a sad condition the people are in, according to your representation! And who shall right them? I suppose you cannot do it, although you cannot be indifferent to their interests, temporal and eternal.

Respecting your leaving the country, I would say, that if your brethren judge it best, you will receive a cordial welcome among us; as I am sure you would from me. In the meantime, you would do well to consult Bishop

Hedding, who presides among us this year. I thank you for the expressions of affection. Whatever of good you may have received from my poor labours, let God have the praise and glory. I never undertook any duties with more appalling feelings than I did the present ones; and yet I have been wonderfully blessed and favoured by providential indications. When I was called to the Presidency of the Wesleyan University, I dared not say no; but I accepted it with a trembling sense of my responsibilities, and thus far I have been greatly blessed and comforted. I shall be glad to see you, and remember that I have a prophet's room, and a bed and a table for you.

From Rev. Dr. D. M. Reese, a noted member of the New York Conference, Dr. Ryerson received the following letter :—

I am at a loss to say what is the opinion of our great men here, touching your Canadian conflict with the British Conference; though all our sympathies are with you. All concur that you have the victory in your pamphlet war. I have not heard a different opinion from any one who has read them. I suppose you may have learned how cavalierly Rev. R. Newton treated Rev. Mr. Gurley, though introduced to him by letters from those to whom Mr. N. was largely indebted here. He refused to introduce him to Dr. Bunting, etc., although this favour was solicited. He neither invited Mr. G. to see him again, nor even called on him. This British reciprocity of American politeness is humiliating, and resembles the treatment you and your brother received at his hands, as well as that of other great men in the Wesleyan Conference towards you.

At the Special Conference of October, Dr. Ryerson was appointed Corresponding Secretary of the Wesleyan Missionary Society of Upper Canada. On the 10th November he issued a statement and appeal on behalf of the Society. In it he indicates definitely the secret causes which led to the disruption of the Union. He said :—

Zealous attempts have been made to lead astray sincere friends of Methodism and religion by the pretense that party politics is the [difficulty]. Never was a pretext more unfounded. . . It will be seen by the proceedings of our Conference— . . and is even admitted in the report of the . . English Conference—that no political party question should, on any account, be suffered amongst us, . . or in our official organ, and that we did not even desire the continued discussion of the clergy reserve question. . . But with even silent neutrality on all questions of civil polity . . , the authorities of the English Conference were not satisfied ; they insisted that we should " admit and maintain, even in this Province, the principle of Church and State Union "—a question which has been the most exciting and baneful topic of party feeling and party organization of any question which has ever been discussed in Upper Canada. They also insisted that we should concede to the Conference in England the right of an " efficient direction over the public proceedings " of the Connexion in this province. . .

These are the real grounds of the difference between the two bodies.

In a letter on this subject, written by Dr. Ryerson, 13th November, he said:—

> Herewith is a copy of a letter which I addressed to the late Rev. Richard Watson in 1831 [see *Guardian* of November 18th, 1840], deprecating the interference of the London Committee with our work in this province, and explaining our views and operations as a body. . . In going one day into the Wesleyan Mission House, when in England in 1833, I found one of the clerks copying that letter into the official books of the Committee. That letter is of some importance on several accounts. It will show that we were just as moderate, and as reasonable, and as constitutional in our views as a body in 1831, as we have been from that time to this, and that the representations to the contrary are the fabulous creations of party feelings. . . [It will also show] that [the London Committee] fully understood our views on the question of a church establishment in Upper Canada, respecting which they have not even pretended that we ever made the slightest compromise; and that we as a body were in a prosperous condition before the Union.

It was not, therefore, without full knowledge of Dr. Ryerson's views on this subject, and of the state of the Methodist body in Upper Canada, that the British Conference in 1833, and again in 1840, sought to interfere with the work in this province and divide the Societies. By Dr. Ryerson's mission to England this evil was averted by a union in 1833, which proved to be but a hollow truce, as the events of 1840 demonstrated.

That the evil genius of Rev. Robert Alder exercised a baneful influence upon both Conferences, is abundantly evident from his own subsequent conduct and other events. And that this was the case is more clearly manifest from the fact that when he ceased to exert any influence in the Connexion, and when Dr. Ryerson and the Canadian Representatives were able to lay the whole case before the British Conference in 1847, that body, led by Dr. Bunting himself, entirely endorsed the consistent action of the Canada Conference in all of this painful and protracted business. He said: "The Canadian brethren are right, and we are wrong." (See a subsequent Chapter on the subject.)

Looking at the facts of the case in the light of to-day, can any one wonder at the pertinacity and zeal with which Dr. Ryerson resisted the unnatural and unwise system of foreign dictation sought to be imposed upon the Canadian Connexion. This he did at a great sacrifice of personal feeling, and of personal friendship, as well as of personal comfort and popularity. He maintained, as he had stipulated in the articles of Union, that "the rights and privileges of the Canadian preachers and Societies should be preserved inviolate." He knew that a Church in a free country like Canada, characterized as it was by Methodistic zeal and vigour, and yet tempered by the moderation of Canadian institutions and manners, possessed within itself a spirit of independence and of growth and progress which would never brook the official control of a Committee thousands of miles away. To be subject to even the generous control of such a Committee, possessed of no practical experience in Canadian matters, would, he knew, doom the Church to a dwarfed, and unnatural, and a miserable existence. Events had already proved to Dr. Ryerson (while the Union during 1839–1840 was in a moribund state) that the Church, controlled by a dominant section of the British Conference, would be a prey to internal feuds and jealousies. In the conflicts that would then ensue spiritual life would die out, missionary zeal would be fitful in its efforts, and every Church interest would partake largely of a sectional and partizan character, destructive alike to the symmetry, growth and harmony of development of a living Church, endowed with rich spiritual life and free and vigorous in its independent action.

To a person of the statesman-like qualities of mind which Dr. Ryerson possessed in so high a degree, these things must have been ever present. They gave evident decision to his thoughts and vigour to his pen. He was no novice in public or ecclesiastical affairs. He had been trained for fifteen years in a school of resistance, almost single-handed, to ecclesiastical domination, and had detected and exposed intrigues,—one of which was of parties in this conflict, which was entirely derogatory to the dignity and independence of Methodism in Canada. (See pages 238–241.)

His knowledge of public affairs and of party leaders gave him abundant insight into the motives and tactics of men bent upon accomplishing pet schemes and favourite projects. And all of this knowledge had so ripened his experience that it rendered him the invaluable and trusted leader in Canadian Methodism, which in those days made his name a household word in the Methodist homes of Upper Canada. This trust and confidence he never betrayed. His unswerving fidelity to his Church and people cost him dearly—the loss of many friends, and the reproaches of many enemies. But he survived it all, and was enabled, under Providence, to mould the institutions of Canadian Methodism and even of his native country. He has left on some of them the impress of his mind and genius, which it is the pride of Canadians to recognize and acknowledge to this day.

CHAPTER XXXV.

1840–1841.

LAST PASTORAL CHARGE.—LORD SYDENHAM'S DEATH.

THE following paragraphs, prepared by Dr. Ryerson, refer to this period of his history:—

In the autumn of 1840, on returning from England, when the English Wesleyan Committee and Conference seceded from the Union with the Canadian Conference, I was appointed to Adelaide Street station in Toronto, which had been filled for two years by the Rev. Dr. Richey—an eloquent and popular preacher. The separation between the two Conferences had taken place the week before I assumed the charge of Adelaide Street station. Dr. Richey had carried off the greater part of both the private and official members of the Church, and I was left with but a skeleton of each. When I ascended the pulpit for the first time, the pews in the body of the church, which had been occupied by those who had seceded, were empty, and there were but scattered hearers, here and there, in the other pews and in the gallery. By faith and prayer I had prepared myself for the crucial test, and conducted the services without apparent depression or embarrassment. I made no pretensions, and had never made any, to pulpit eloquence—the motto of my ministry being to make things plain and strong by previous thought and prayer, and without verbal preparation. I often went from lying on my back in my study, in an agony of distress and prayer, to the pulpit, where a divine anointing seemed to rest upon me, such as I had never before experienced. There were frequent prayer-meetings in my own study, at six o'clock in the morning. The result was, by the Divine blessing, that the church was filled with hearers, and the membership was more than doubled.

At the first Annual Missionary Meeting in the Church after the division, the President of the Executive Council presided; several members of the Government were on the platform, and the collections and subscriptions were more than double those of any previous year. The pretext for this separation of the

English Wesleyan Committee and Conference from the Canadian Conference, was professed loyalty in Church and State; but both the Imperial and Canadian Government of that day approved the position of the Canadian Conference, withdrew and suspended the grant previously made to the London Wesleyan Missionary Committee during the seven years of its

OLD NEWGATE STREET (AFTERWARDS ADELAIDE ST.) WESLEYAN CHURCH, 1832-1872.

hostility to the Canadian Conference, and only consented to its restoration for the joint interests of the two Conferences, and on recommendation of the Representatives of the Canadian Conference, after the reconciliation and reunion of the two Conferences, in 1847.

In October, 1840, Dr. Ryerson addressed a letter of congratulation to Lord Sydenham, on his elevation to the peerage.

He again referred to the publication of the *Monthly Review*, proposed by His Excellency. In regard to the latter he said :—

> The publication of a monthly periodical such as I suggested to your Excellency last spring, appears to me now, as it did then, to be of great importance, in order to mould the thinkings of public men and the views of the country in harmony with the principles of the new Constitution and the policy of Your Excellency's administration, and to secure a rational and permanent appreciation of its objects, and merits ; and it would have afforded me sincere satisfaction to have given a proper tone and charcter to a publication of that kind. But what I have written publicly in reference to the principles and measures of Your Excellency's Government has already been productive of serious consequences both to myself and the Body with which I am connected.
>
> In the discharge of my ecclesiastical duties, I have to devote several hours of four days in each week to visiting the sick, poor, and other members of my pastoral charge, and am preparing a series of discourses on the Patriarchal History, and the Evidences of Christianity, arising from the discoveries of modern science, and the testimony of recent travellers, besides the correspondence and engagements which devolve upon me in the office I hold in the Methodist Church. Under such circumstances the assumption by me of the management of such a periodical is impracticable. I could not do justice to it, nor to my other appropriate duties. I might, in the course of my miscellaneous reading, select passages from established authors, which would be suitable for a miscellany at the end of each number, to illustrate and confirm the principles discussed in the preceding pages of it. I might now and then contribute a general article on the Intellectual and Moral Elements of Canadian Society ; or, on the Evils of Party Spirit; or, on the Necessity of General Unity in order to General Prosperity, etc., etc.; but even in these respects I fear I could not render much efficient aid, from the exhaustion of my physical strength in other labours, and for want of the requisite time for study, in order to write instructively and effectively on general subjects.

In the same letter, Dr. Ryerson thus referred to his determination to take no further part in the discussion of public affairs, owing to the hostility which his support of Lord Sydenham's policy had excited in various quarters* :—

> In retiring from taking any public part in the civil affairs of this country, I beg to express my grateful sense of the frank-

---

* In the *Guardian* of October 7th, 1840, Dr. Ryerson says :—Lord Sydenham well knows the feelings of reluctance and apprehension under which I assumed the responsibility of giving my humble and earnest support to the measures of his government in Upper Canada. . . He well knows that I adopted the course I did with a deep consciousness that it would be attended with personal sacrifice, with no other expectation or wish but justice to the church to which I belonged—equal justice to other churches—and the hope of prosperity to my native country under an improved and efficient system of government. I did not indeed expect that hostility against me from London would be prosecuted to the extent it has been. . . I have incurred the censure of the British Conference for supporting, and not for opposing, the government when it needed my support, and when it was in my power to have embarrassed it. . . As it respects myself personally, I shall not repine at having made the sacrifice, if the new system of government but succeeds, and the land of my birth and affections is made prosperous and happy. Note on page 199.

ness, kindness, and condescension which I have experienced from Your Excellency. You are the first Governor of Canada who has taken the pains to investigate the character and affairs of the Wesleyan Methodist Church for himself, and not judge and act from hearsay ; the first Governor to ascertain my sentiments, feelings, and wishes from my own lips, and not from the representations of others. As a body, considering our labours and numbers, we have certainly been treated unjustly and hardly by the Local Government. Every effort was used here to deprive us of the Royal liberality, and Lord Glenelg's recommendations in regard to the Upper Canada Academy. I think Lord John Russell himself was prepossessed against me by the representations of Rev. Mr. Alder, and probably of Sir George Arthur and others. But by your condescension and courtesy I have been prompted and emboldened to express myself to Your Excellency on all questions of civil government and the affairs of this country, more fully than I have to any man living. My private opinions and public writings have been simultaneously before Your Excellency, together with all the circumstances under which I have expressed the one and published the other. I feel confident, therefore, that however I may be misrepresented by some, or misunderstood by others, I shall have justice in the estimate and opinions of Your Excellency—that I have been anything but theoretical or obstinate—that I have shrunk from no responsibility in the time of need and difficulty—and that my opinions, whether superficial or well-considered, are such as any common-sense, practical man, whose connection, associations, and feeling are involved in the happiness and well-being of the middle classes, might be expected to entertain.

It is not my intention or wish to obtrude my opinions upon your attention, except in so far as may be necessary to acquaint Your Excellency with the interests and wishes of the body whom I have been appointed to represent. In regard to the many other important questions embraced in the great objects of your Government, I shall abstain from any officious interference ; although all that may be in my mind or heart on any subject shall be at the service of Your Excellency when desired.

From what I have witnessed and experienced, I have no doubt that every possible effort will made to prejudice me in Your Excellency's mind, and induce Your Excellency to treat the Methodist body in this province as preceding Governors have done. But I implore Your Excellency to try another course of proceeding, whether as any experiment, or as an act of justice. I am persuaded that Your Excellency has found no portion of the people of this Province more reasonable in their requests, or more easily conciliated to your views and wishes than the Representatives, members and friends of the Wesleyan Methodist Church in Canada ; and, I doubt not, Your Excellency will find them cultivating and exhibiting the same spirit during the entire period (and may it be a long one !) of your administration of the Government of Canada.

On the 8th of the same month, Dr. Ryerson felt himself constrained to address a note to Lord Sydenham in regard to the policy of Lord John Russell's Clergy Reserve Bill, so far as it might affect the question of public education, in which he was deeply interested. He said that he conceived the Bill to be most unjust in its provisions, as he had stated to His Lordship (while it was under consideration of Parliament). He added: Should the partial and exclusive provisions of the measure pervade the views and administration of Government in Canada, in regard to a general system of education, etc., I should utterly despair of ever witnessing social happiness, general educational culture, or unity in this country. But I have no doubt the exclusive powers with which the Bill invests the Governor, will be exerted to counteract the inequality of its other provisions, and that Your Excellency's whole system of public policy will be based upon the principles of "equal justice to all classes of Her Majesty's Canadian subjects." Under these circumstances, I have suggested to the conductor of the *Christian Guardian* (from the editorship of which I retired last June) not to make any remarks on the Bill which may tend to create dissatisfaction ; nor do I intend, for the same reasons, to publish the letter which my brother and I addressed to Lord John Russell on the subject. His Lordship said, indeed, that the Bill was not what he wished, nor could he say it was just ; but he had clearly ascertained that a more liberal one could not be got through the House of Lords, and he thought that that Bill was better than none.

The Hon. Isaac Buchanan, in a letter to the Editor, dated April 1882,—speaking of these times and events—said :—

I was one of Dr. Ryerson's oldest friends and coöperators that have survived him. I was first in Toronto (then York) in 1830. Although not then 20 years of age, I came out to Montreal as a partner in a mercantile firm ; and in the fall of 1831 I came up to York to establish a branch House. From that time I have known Dr. Ryerson, and then formed that high opinion of both his abilities and his character which went on increasing more and more ; so that for the last forty years of his life I have regarded him as Canada's greatest son. Of late years I seldom met him, but when I did, it was an inexpressible pleasure to me, as an interchange of the most unbounded mutual confidences took place between us in our views and objects. He knew my view of religion,—that as with Spiritual Religion (which is nothing to the mind unless it is everything), so with the Religion of Humanity (my name for the removal of all impediments out of the way of the employment, and of the enjoyment of living of our own people)—it will not take a second place, but must be the first question in the politics of every country—otherwise its Government is a mere political machine. He knew my belief that the Church Question being in the way of this people's question, it took the first place among the causes of all the industrial evils in England and Ireland. With me, therefore, it was a *sine qua non* to get quit of our dominant Church nuisance in Canada, viewing it as a thing in the way of the prosperity of the people, and therefore as a thing insidiously undermining their loyalty. I am sure that his views were not far removed from mine in this matter, and yet not a particle of enmity to the Church ever affected me, and, I believe, the same thing was true of Dr. Ryerson. But I felt the insufferable evil of the position it had in this country, not only as usurping the first place in politics, which the Labour Question should occupy, but as rendering the connection with England odious and shortlived. Being one of those sent for by the Governor-General (Mr. Poulett Thompson) on the clergy reserve question, I told His Excellency plainly that although my countrymen, the Scotch, did not hesitate to dissent, as a matter of conscience, they would not be loyal to a government that made them dissenters by Act of Parliament.

Five years previous to this, or in 1835, I had, as an extra of the *Albion* newspaper, published by Mr. Cull, about the time York became Toronto, proposed a plan of settlement for the clergy reserves, fitted to solve the difficulties connected with them, whether Industrial, Educational, or Political. My proposal was that an educational tax should be levied, the payments by each church or sect being shewn in separate columns, and each sect receiving from the clergy reserve fund, in the proportion of its payments for education.

This first attempt of mine to get an endowment for education failed, as there was then no system of Responsible Government. But five years afterwards (in 1840) when my election for Toronto had decided the question of Responsible Government, and before the first Parliament met, I spoke to Lord Sydenham, the Governor-General, on the subject. He felt under considerable obligation to me for standing in the breach when Hon. Robert Baldwin found he could not succeed in carrying Toronto. I told him that I felt sure that if we were allowed to throw the accounts of the Province into regular books, we would show a surplus over expenditure. His Excellency agreed to my proposal, and I stipulated that, if we showed a surplus, half would be given as an endowment for an educational system. Happily we found that Upper Canada had a surplus revenue of about $100,000 a year —half of which the Parliament of 1841 set aside for education as agreed— the law stipulating that every District Council getting a share of it would locally tax for as much more, and this constituted the financial basis of our educational system. Thus I have given you a glimpse of the time when Dr. Ryerson and I were active coöperators.

Dr. Ryerson has left no farther record of his two years' ministry in Newgate (Adelaide) Street circuit, Toronto, than that recorded on page 282. Some incidents of it will be found in the letter of the Rev. Jonathan Scott, editor of the *Guardian*, on page 294. Rev. I. B. Howard, Dr. Ryerson's assistant at the time, has also furnished me with some personal reminiscences of his intercourse with him during the latter year of Dr. Ryerson's pastoral life. He says :—

When I was Dr. Ryerson's assistant in Toronto, upwards of forty years ago (in 1841-2), he was studying Hebrew with a private tutor. As I had previously taken lessons in that language he kindly invited me to unite with him (at his expense) in this study. This I did three times a week at his house. On those days I always dined with him ; and as it was his custom to spend the hour before dinner in devotional reading and prayer, I had the great privilege of spending this hour with him in his study—and I shall never forget the sincere, heart-searching, and devout manner in which he conducted these hallowed exercises, nor the great spiritual instruction and benefit I received from them. His humble confessions, earnest pleadings, and fervent spirit deeply impressed my youthful heart with the fact that he was indeed a man of God.

During that year (one of the few of his regular pastorate) I had also the privilege of frequently hearing him preach, especially during eight weeks of special and very successful revival services, which we held in old Adelaide (then nearly new and known as "Newgate") Street Church. I have frequently heard him preach since that time, mostly on special occasions, and always with pleasure and profit; but never since he left the pastoral work have I heard from him such earnest, powerful and overwhelming appeals to the minds, and hearts, and consciences of men, as when, with the responsibilities and sympathies of a pastor's heart, he delighted, and moved, and melted the large and admiring audiences which attended his ministry. I have always believed, that, had he continued in his pastoral work, he would have been not only an able and popular, but also in an eminent degree a successful soul-saving preacher.

During the year I was with him in Toronto, Dr. Ryerson frequently heard me preach ; and as it was only the second year of my ministry his presence in the congregation was at first a great terror to me ; but the kind words of encouragement, as well as the wise and fatherly counsels which he frequently gave me soon allayed my fears, and led me to regard it rather as a privilege than a cross to have him for a hearer.* Would that every young preacher had such a kind and sympathizing superintendent!

Hon. William Macdougall also bears testimony to the kindness which he experienced from Dr. Ryerson at this period. He says:

About the year 1840, I was living in the township af Vaughan, and like other boys of the same class and age, devoting my winters to school, and my summers to the healthful exercise of the farm. My father was a good farmer, pretty well-to-do, and I, being the eldest son, was second in command. He had purchased two or three uncleared lots in the same township, one of which was designed for me. I was fond of books, and possessed some good ones, besides I had made diligent use of a circulating library in the neighbourhood. We took in a political newspaper, an agricultural monthly, and the *Christian Guardian*. At this point of my career I met Dr. Ryerson. He came into our neighbourhood to attend a missionary meeting, and stopped at my father's house. I was asked to go with him to his next appointment. We were thus alone together for some hours. On the way we chatted about temperance, history, politics, education, etc. The rebellion of 1837, and the political questions that grew out of it still agitated the public mind. He spoke of Mackenzie and Rolph; of Baldwin and Bidwell; of Sir Francis Head and the Family Compact. I discovered that he admired Bidwell, but disliked Mackenzie. He took much pains to explain to me some points in reference to the clergy reserve and rectory questions, and seeing that I was an appreciative listener, he asked me if I would like to be a politician. I said I would, if I thought I could overturn the Family Compact, secure the clergy reserves for education, and drive the Hudson Bay Company out of the

* This the Editor has been assured was also Rev. Dr. Potts' experience of Dr. Ryerson as a hearer, several years afterwards, and during the time that he (Dr. Potts) was pastor of the Metropolitan Church, Toronto.

North-West. He looked at me for a moment with an amused expression. The last plank of my platform seemed to arouse his curiosity. The Hudson Bay Company and its affairs had not then attracted much notice. He asked me why I desired to drive out the Hudson Bay Company. I replied that I had read a lecture by Hon. R. B. Sullivan, on immigration and the movement of population westward, in which he described the Great Valley of the Saskatchewan in colours so glowing, that I wondered why we did not all go there, but on further enquiry I found that a small body of London Fur-traders claimed the whole country as a preserve for musk-rats and foxes, under an old charter from a King who, at the time, did not own a foot of it; that I thought the fur-traders ought to be compelled to give up the good land, *vi et armis*, if need be. He said, "My young friend, your ambition is great; I am afraid you have not considered the difficulties to be overcome." I felt slightly sat upon; but I warmed with my subject, and as I had already made temperance speeches to admiring audiences in the "back concessions," I was not easily disconcerted. He then made the remark which forty years afterwards I recalled to his recollection. "Before you undertake such enterprises you must study law; it is a noble profession, and in this country is the only sure road to success in politics. If I had not felt it my duty to preach the Gospel, I would have studied law myself." I remarked that I had read articles in the *Christian Guardian*, attributed to him, which I had heard people say exhibited a great deal of legal knowledge. He seemed pleased by the compliment, but did not acknowledge the paternity of the articles. After some further conversation as to my studies, etc., he recommended me to begin at once to read Latin, and promised to speak to my father and advise him to let me study law. He kept his promise; my father rather reluctantly consented, telling me that if I left home I would lose the farm. You know the rest.

May I not venture the remark, that if a promising agriculturist was spoiled by that interview, Dr. Ryerson was the spoiler? and, if Canada has derived any benefit from my humble labours as journalist, legislator, executive councillor, etc., he is entitled to a share of the credit, for, as I loved—and still recall with envious regret—the unsophisticated pleasures and contentment of a farmer's life, I would, probably, have pursued the even tenor of my bucolic way but for his advice and kind-hearted mediation.

In the political controversies that agitated the country from 1850 to 1862, we sometimes crossed swords. In 1865, it became my duty, as a member of Government, to carry through Parliament an important measure relating to Grammar Schools. Much to his surprise, I successfully resisted all attempts at mutilation, for which he warmly expressed his acknowledgements. During the serious, and sometimes acrimonious discussions which preceded and followed the Act of Confederation, I enjoyed the benefit of his approving sympathy and wise counsel. Others with better warrant may speak of his great power and achievements as a Christian Minister; but you will permit me to say that I knew him as a generous friend and patron of Canadian youth; as a sagacious and resolute man of affairs; as a staunch defender of the British constitutional system of government; and as a patriotic, true-hearted son of Canada—*Si monumentum requiris—circumspice!*

Dr. Ryerson's pastoral charge of the Toronto City Circuit in 1840-41, and other ministerial duties, engrossed all of his time to the exclusion of other matters. It seemed to have been a positive relief to him to engage in these more congenial pursuits. He rarely used his pen, except on very pressing occasions. He was nevertheless a close observer of passing events, but took no active part in them.

Lord Sydenham frequently availed himself of Dr. Ryerson's counsel and co-operation. Shortly before the death of that able Governor, Dr. Ryerson had gone to Kingston, as requested, on matters of public interest. The unexpected death of Lord Sydenham, on the 19th of September, 1841 (the immediate cause of which was a fall from his horse), called forth a burst of universal sorrow throughout the then newly created Province of Canada. One of the most touching tributes to his memory was penned by Dr. Ryerson, while on his way to Kingston to see him. It was published in the *Guardian* of the 29th September, and republished with other notices in a pamphlet by Mr. (now Sir) Francis Hincks, then editor of the Toronto *Examiner*. From that sketch of Lord Sydenham's career I take the following concluding passages:—

> At the commencement of His Lordship's mission in Upper Canada, when his plans were little known, his difficulties formidable, and his Government weak, I had the pleasing satisfaction of giving him my humble and dutiful support in the promotion of his non-party and provincial objects; and now that he is beyond the reach of human praise or censure—where all earthly ranks and distinctions are lost in the sublimities of eternity—I have the melancholy satisfaction of bearing my humble testimony to his candour, sincerity, faithfulness, kindness and liberality. A few days before the occurrence of the accident which terminated his life, I had the honour of spending an evening and part of a day in free conversation with His Lordship; and on that, as well as on former similar occasions, he observed the most marked reverence for the truths of Christianity—a most earnest desire to base the civil institutions of the country upon Christian principles, with a scrupulous regard to the rights of conscience—a total absence of all animosity against any person or parties opposed to him—and an intense anxiety to silence dissensions and discord, and render Canada contented, happy and prosperous.
> . . The day before his lamented death he expressed his regret that he had not given more of his time to religion. . . The last hours of his life were spent in earnest supplications to the Redeemer, in humble reliance upon whose atonement he yielded up the ghost.

After the publication of this letter in the *Guardian*, Dr. Ryerson received the following acknowledgment from T. W. C. Murdoch, Esq., late private Secretary to Lord Sydenham:—

> I ought to have thanked you before for the numbers of the *Guardian* containing your letter on the death of Lord Sydenham. That letter I have read over and over again with the deepest emotion, and I cannot but feel how much more worthily the task of writing the history of his administration might have been confided to your hands than to mine. That I shall discharge the duty with affectionate zeal and good faith, I hope I need not assure you, but I fear my inability to do justice to so statesmanlike an administration, or to make apparent to others those nice shades of policy which constituted the beauty and insured the success of his government. In the meantine what are we to hope or expect from the new Governor Sir C. Bagot. My principal confidence is that Sir R. Peel is too prudent a man to wish discredit to his administration by allowing the re-introduction of the old, bad system, and that consequently Sir Charles will be instructed to follow out to the best of his ability Lord Sydenham's policy.

CHAPTER XXXVI.
1841.

DR. RYERSON'S ATTITUDE TOWARD THE CHURCH OF ENGLAND.

THE constant references in this volume to Dr. Ryerson's attitude of hostility to the exclusive claims and pretensions put forth on behalf of the Church of England in this province, require some explanation. His opponents sought to neutralize this opposition by endeavouring to make it appear that, because he opposed these claims and ignored these pretensions, he was hostile to the Church of England as a great spiritual power in the land.* He had himself often pointed out the fallacy of this reasoning, and drawn so clear a distinction between men and things in the controversy—the Church and her representatives—that I cannot add any thing to what he has written on the subject. In one letter he said:—

I am often charged with hostility to the Church of England. Did I know nothing of the Church of England except what has been exhibited in this province, . . how could I have any partiality for that Church ? There is a large and growing branch of the Established Church in England that I venerate, admire, and love; but there is a semi-popish branch of it for which I have no such respect, and that is the branch, with a few individual exceptions, which exists in this province. . .

Again, in a letter to Hon. W. H. Draper, on the clergy reserve question, dated October 12th, 1838, he said:—

I would not derogate an iota from the respect claimed by the Church of England on account of the prerogatives to which she is legally entitled [in England]. As the form of religion professed by the Sovereign and rulers of the Empire—as the Established Church of the British realm—as the Church which has nursed some of the greatest statesmen, philosophers, and divines that have enlightened, adorned, and blest the world, she cannot fail to command the respect of all enlightened men, whatever may be thought of the conduct and pretensions of the Canadian branch of that Church—pretensions which have been virtually repudiated in royal charters, and contradicted by the entire civil and ecclesiastical history of the old British colonies.

Dr. Ryerson's attitude to the Church of England was clearly defined in a private and friendly correspondence between him

* I have already on pages 41 and 206 mentioned the overtures which were made to Dr. Ryerson by the late Bishop Stewart of Quebec to induce him to enter the ministry of the Church of England. See also page 97.

and John Kent, Esq., Editor of *The Church* newspaper, in 1841-42. (See page 97.) That paper was established in May, 1837, as the organ of the Church of England in Upper Canada. It was at first edited by Rev. Dr. (afterwards Bishop) Bethune, rector of Cobourg. In 1841, John Kent, Esq., became its editor.* In the religions controversies of those days *The Church*, was ably edited. It was a decided champion of the high church, or Puseyite party, and, as such it came into constant conflict with the Wesleyan Methodists and their organ, the *Christian Guardian*, and especially with its chief editor, Dr. Ryerson. On the 21st December, 1841, Dr. Ryerson wrote a letter for insertion in *The Church*, and accompanied it with a private note to Mr. Kent. From that letter I make the following extracts:—

I, as well as my friends, have been the subjects of repeated strictures in your pages; during the last two years I have replied not a word, nor published a line in reference to the Church of England.

I have stated on former occasions—and perhaps my two years' silence may now give some weight to the statement—that my objections had no reference to the existence, or prosperity, of the Church of England as a Church, but simply and solely to its exclusive establishment and endowment in Upper Canada, especially, and indeed entirely, in reference to the clergy reserves. During the discussions which took place, and which were continued for years, I wrote many strong things; but nothing on the Episcopal form of Government, or the formularies, or doctrines of the Church of England. The doctrines of the Church of England, as contained in the Articles and Homilies, I always professed to believe. On the subject of Church Government, I often expressed my views in the language of Dr. Paley, and in accordance with the sentiments of many distinguished dignitaries and divines of the Church of England, that no particular form of Church Government has been enjoined by the Apostles. I have objected to the Episcopal, or any other one form of Church Government, being put forth as essential to the existence of the Church of Christ, and as the only Scriptural form; but no further. I do not think the form of Church, any more than the form of civil government, is settled in the Scriptures; I believe that both are left, as Bishop Stillingfleet has shown at large, to times, places, and circumstances, to be determined upon the ground of expediency and utility—a ground on which Dr. Paley has supported the different orders of the Church of England with his accustomed clearness, ability and elegance. I know, on the contrary, that much may be said upon the same ground in favour of itinerancy, of Presbyterianism, and of independency.

On the subject of forms of prayer, I have never written; though I have for many years used forms of prayer in private as helps to, not substitutes for, devotion. I believe the foundation of the Church of Christ is not laid in forms, but in doctrines. . .

I believe it would be a moral calamity for either the Church of England, or Church of Scotland, or the Wesleyan Methodist Church, the Congrega-

* "From 1841 to 1843 the editorial management of *The Church* was assumed by Mr. John Kent, who had been a valuable contributor to its pages from the commencement. The excitement, however, amid the clash and din of party strife was too much for him, and the paper came back to its first editor, who held it again . . for nearly four years. . . It gradually lost ground, and died out . . in 1856. Memoir of Bishop Strachan by Bishop Bethune," page 159.

tional, or the Baptist Churches to be annihilated in this province. I believe there are fields of labour which may be occupied by any one of those Churches with more efficiency and success than by any of the others. They need not, and I think, ought not, to be aggressors upon each other. . .

As there were seven Apostolic Churches in Asia, we believe ourselves one of the Apostolic Churches in Canada. . . Those persons, who believe that the instruction, and religious advantages and privileges afforded by our Church will more effectually aid them in working out their salvation than those which they can command in any other part of the general fold of Christ, are affectionately received under our watch-care; but not on account of our approximation to, or our dissent from, the Church of England, or any other Church.

With the settlement of the clergy reserve question ended my controversy with the Church of England, as I have again and again intimated that it would. Churches, as well as individuals, may learn wisdom from experience. I therefore, submit, whether the controversies and their characteristic feelings between the Church of England and the Wesleyan Methodist Church in this province ought not to cease, with the removal of the causes which produced them? . . Whether both Churches are not likely to accomplish more religious and moral good by directing their energies against prevalent vice and ignorance than by mutual warfare?

Dr. Ryerson concludes his letter in the following truthful and striking language:—

I intend no offence when I express my conviction that the Church of England in this province has vastly greater resources for doing good than for warring with other Protestant Churches. I know her weak points, as well as her strong towers. I am not a stranger to the appropriate weapons for assailing the one, and for neutralizing the strength of the other. And you have not to learn that it is easier to deface than to beautify—to pull down a fair fabric than to rear a common structure; and that a man may injure others without benefitting himself. On the other hand I am equally sensible that the Wesleyan Methodist Church has nothing to gain by controversy; but I am quite sure, from past experience, as well as from present aspects, that she has not so much to fear, to risk, or to lose, as the Church of England. If controversy be perpetuated between your Church and our own, I wash my hands from all responsibility of it—even should the duty of self-defence compel me to draw the sword which I had, in inclination and intention, sheathed for ever. History, and our own experience to some extent, abounds with monitory lessons, that personal disputes may convulse churches, that ecclesiastical controversies may convulse provinces, and lead to the subversion of governments. . .

In his private note to Mr. Kent, Dr. Ryerson said:—

I have long been impressed with the conviction that Canada could not prosper under the element of agitation. I supported the Union of the Canadas with a view to their civil tranquility. I believe my expectations will be realized. In our new state of things I desire not to be considered as standing in an attitude of hostility to the Church of England, any more than to any other Church. I have wished and resolved to leave civil and ecclesiastical party politics with the former bad state of things. Travelling, observation and experience, have been a useful school to me, and time will do justice to the merits or demerits of my motives and conduct.

On the 22nd of December, Mr. Kent replied to Dr. Ryerson :—

Do not think that I wish to meet you coldly. I would gladly fling away the weapons of strife. The warfare in which I am engaged, and which I dare not decline, is literally embittering my existence, and pressing upon me very severely. I am not aware that I have in any way personally attacked you, or ever by name, since the commencement of my editorial career. I should hail a day of concord with overflowing joy. I should rejoice to see your powerful, acute, and vigorous mind exerting itself in a manner that we should all consider serviceable to the cause of loyalty and the Protestant religion.

From a glance at your letters, I fondly hope that some gleam of light is breaking in upon us all. My firm conviction is that the doctrine of the apostolical succession will be the bond of union and the cementer of differences, now apparently impossible. You must have studied the question— and how can your vivid and clear mind elude its force? Must there not be some one apostolical mode of conferring the ministerial functions, or must it be open to all, and Quakerism be right? I do not think I have been the assailant. The *Guardian* is outrageously personal and unscrupulous in its misstatements. . . I am far from thinking that I am meek and gentle enough; but I have carefully excluded personalities,—though I readily concede that my course of argument, which pervades all I write or select, has been to cut away the ground from under the feet of every denomination in the province, outside of the Church.

The papists, I firmly believe, are meditating some grand movement all over the world; and it would be glorious indeed if Protestants could find a common centre of union. But what can I, in my humble way, do? I dare not drop the necessity of the apostolical succession,—though I might dwell less upon it, and avoid, as much as possible, as I always have done, to mix it up with offence to other denominations. Yet, as I before intimated, the assertion and maintenance of it, in the simplest and least controversial manner, must ever provoke hostility. It is an endless subject to get upon. . .

I shall be very happy to call on you at an early opportunity, and obtain, or rather revive, the pleasure of your personal acquaintance. It would be the happiest Christmas I ever spent, if it witness the extinction of long theological enmities, and the dawn of an era of Christian concord and love.

On the 29th December, Dr. Ryerson wrote a private note again to Mr. Kent. He said :—I was glad to learn by the last *Church* that you will give my remarks a place in your columns, and that you cordially and elegantly respond to the general spirit and design of them. . . .

I have had a correspondence with the Editor of the *Guardian* in reference to the mode of conducting it, in regard to the Church of England, and in some other respects. I am happy to be able to say that he has at length yielded to my reasonings and recommendations, and will, I have no doubt, conduct the *Guardian* in accordance with the general views expressed in my communications to you.* To-day's *Guardian*, as you see,

* From Dr. Ryerson's letter to Rev. J. Scott, Editor of the *Guardian*, I make the following extracts :—I take the liberty to mention two or three things that I

presents a visible and agreeable improvement in the points referred to.

I blame you not for your strict and high principles as a churchman, but I do not think that you do now make sufficient allowance for difference of forms and ceremonies in the common faith of Protestantism. I think you should allow as much as Archbishop (Lord Keeper) Williams has done, and as much as is involved in the passage quoted by him from Irenæus. Why have seen in the *Guardian* which have caused me some pain and concern. I refer to your mode and style of controversy with "*The Church.*" During, and since my late tour to the West, I have heard several preachers and some others allude to it, and nearly all in terms of regret. I set down the questions as they occur to my own mind.

1. We have no controversy with the Church of England as a Church Establishment. We have disclaimed opposing, or doing anything to disparage the Church Establishment in England. . . 2. Then on the subject of church polity. Your articles, especially the series entitled "Dissent, etc., No Wonder".—were put forth as a defence. . . But which of our institutions did they defend? The burden of them went to prove that the Church of England is unscriptural in its polity, union with the state, etc. Suppose all this were true, would it prove that our own Church is apostolic and Scriptural? To prove that our neighbours are black, does not prove that we are white. We do not profess to build up ourselves upon the ruin of any body else, or to be "foragers" upon others, although we readily accept members of other churches when they offer themselves. To prove that Presbyterian ordination is valid (as did the valuable series of articles copied by you from the *Wesleyan Magazine*, and Powell, on Apostolic Succession) defends our ordination. To prove that the Church of England is wrong and rotten from beginning to end cannot be a defence of ourselves. It may, indeed, please some of our friends; but it also tends to prove that we are settled enemies to the Church of England in all its forms and features, as well as in its union with the state.

Far be it from me to look upon the things I have mentioned as characteristics of the *Guardian;* I look upon them as blemishes, and as drawbacks from its usefulness—objects which I know are scarcely less dear to your heart than life itself. If we narrow our own foundations by such sweeping denunciations against the Church of England, and strictures on persons without our communion, . . we multiply our opponents, and reduce the circulation of our journal within the circle of our own members.

I am sensible of my own errors, deficiency and unworthiness; but I have felt that I should not do my duty to you as a brother beloved, and one from whom I have received too many proofs of regard, and so much aid in my labours, without thus telling you what was in my heart.

Rev. Mr. Scott at first felt aggrieved and disappointed on receiving this letter and a personal correspondence between him and Dr. Ryerson ensued, which, however, ended satisfactorily. In a letter to Dr. Ryerson, written in 1864—23 years afterwards,—Mr. Scott thus recalls the reminiscence of his career as Editor of the *Guardian.* He says:—My esteemed friend: You and I have not always thought alike (and what is manliness worth that is not independent enough to disagree?) but as age advances I have an increasing pleasure in recalling to mind the years, when you were Superintendent of old Adelaide street Church, and I was your supplementary helper,—in joint intercession with the humbled at night—in the damp basement, and during the day pursuing the penitents in dirty taverns, and the dens of dirtier March [now Lombard] street, the sainted Mrs. S. E. Taylor praying for us; and Christ won many souls. Since then what progress Scriptural Christianity—Methodism—has made in Canada! I trust that when you repose in the tomb, and I am beneath some quiet sod of loved Canada, we shall meet those again for whose salvation we laboured. In the words of an ancient wish: May your last days be your best days! Mr. Scott entered the ministry in 1834; and died at Brampton, May 5th, 1880, aged 77.

should we be "unchurched" any more than the continental churches?

Mr. Kent, in reply to Dr. Ryerson (31st December), said:—

I trust you will think that in the remarks which I have made on your letter in *The Church*, I have met your overtures in a pacific and cordial spirit. I am sure that my remarks will be much more acceptable to churchmen, so far as such remarks are friendly to you, than they will be to others not belonging to our pale. I have not consulted a soul about what I have written, nor have I shown your pleasing reply to my first note to any one save good and safe Mr. Henry Rowsell; though I should like to show it to Rev. H. J. Grasett, and Bishop Strachan. You need never be afraid of what you say to me in confidence. . . It is certainly much more consistent in you (provided only you get rid of Mr. Wesley's authority, and then, by the way, you destroy your genealogy and succession) to call yourselves a Church, than to be of the Church and not in it. . . You are said to possess some fine old Divinity works. You cannot have read them without some approximation to our Church.

You are not in the position of the continental Churches. No constraint is upon you. You can get Episcopacy, if you desire it. Neither does the Church of England stand relatively towards you, as the Gallican Church towards the Huguenots. You admit the purity of our doctrine, and do not consider our discipline unscriptural. If you were to read Bishop Stillingfleet on Separation, I think you would open up new trains of thought. I just became so staunch an Episcopalian, from viewing the matter extrinsically of Scripture and history, and was led to conclude, from the nature of things, that there can be but one valid ministry.

You are certainly a *Prospero*. You have waved your magic wand over the *Guardian*. I saw it in an instant, and saw that you had done it. I purposely, in my editorial, abstained from all allusions to our confidential intercourse, or I would have thanked you for this exercise of your healing influence.

It is by no means an unpleasing marvel that you and I, on the last day of 1841, should be conversing so pleasantly and amicably. I trust that peace and amity will flourish still more!

Do me the favour to accept a slight New Year's gift at my hands.

Dr. Ryerson wrote a reply to the strictures of *The Church* newspaper, and on the 26th addressed a private note on the subject to Mr. Kent, in which he said:—

. . The great difference between us seems to be that I value what I hold to be the cardinal doctrines, and morals and interests of Christianity, above either Churchism or Methodism. So that those interests are advanced, either through the Church of England, or Church of Scotland, or any other Protestant Church, I therein do rejoice and will rejoice. You make the Church of England first of all—essential to all—all in all; and that all who are not in the Church of England are enemies to the Church of Christ, "strangers to the covenants of promise, and aliens from the commonwealth of Israel." . . It is true you have exempted me by way of compliment; but no intelligent man would wish to hold his religious intercourse and standing on the tenor of a compliment; and that too at the expense of his ecclesiastical connexion and general principles. If I cannot but be viewed as an enemy of the Church of England as a Methodist, it is a poor compliment to tell me that I am friendly to it as a man. I do not understand the hair-splitting casuistry which separates the man from the Christian. . .

I believe in your perfect sincerity and personal disinterestedness and kindness, but I must say that you do not appear from the last *Church* to suppose it possible for a man to think in a different channel from yourself without endangering his title to the skies, or to common sense, and without absolutely forfeiting his claim to orthodox Christianity. I refer not all to your maintenance of apostolic succession, but to your unqualified reprobation of the motives, feelings, and character of all who are not of your own fold. How different are the sentiments and spirit of Bishop Onderdonk's essay in support of the "Divine Right of Episcopacy" from those of your articles in the last *Church*? Now, though we may be without the attributes of what you believe to be a scripturally constituted Church, we are not without the attributes and feelings of men. . . The apparatus of the Church of England is surprisingly powerful when spiritually, rightly, and comprehensively applied; but to build your structure like an inverted pyramid, and to rouse every one not of you into warfare against you, does not appear to me to be sound in theory, or wise in practice.

Mr. Kent, in a private reply, dated 3rd February, said:—

I have read your letter over so as to prepare my remarks. In doing this I anticipate no trouble. On the contrary, I hope to strengthen my position and give greater weight to my axioms respecting the duties of Churchmen in withholding aid from all religious societies unconnected with the Church. I find, however, that your tone of remark is excessively warm and indignant; and, deeming from the tenor of your conversation on Thursday last, that you have doubts on your mind respecting church government, and feeling convinced that if ever you are led to subscribe to the indispensable obligations of episcopacy, . . you will admit the validity of my reasons for acting and writing as I do—under all these circumstances I feel bound to ask you to meditate whether you will not withdraw your letter. I give you my sacred honour that I do not dread its effects. But I feel this, that should you ever experience and avow a change of opinion in reference to the matters that are now engaging your attention, it will be brought up against you by your enemies, and may altogether prove a constant embarrassment. Should you withdraw it, 1 will only mention the matter to Mr. Grasett, who has already seen it. Should you determine on its insertion, it shall appear next Saturday.

Dr. Ryerson did not withdraw his letter, and it appeared in *The Church* of February 5th. The personal correspondence, however, ended here.

In accounting for his decided opposition to a church establishment in Upper Canada, Dr. Ryerson said:—

Before I was twenty years of age I had read Paley's Political Philosophy, including his chapters on the British Constitution and a Church Establishment; Locke on Government, and especially Blackstone's Commentaries, particularly those parts on the Rights of the Crown and the Rights of the Subject. From Paley I learned that a Church Establishment is no part of Christianity, but a means of supporting it, and a means which should be used only when the majority of the people are of the religion thus supported. From Blackstone I learned that the Church of England is the Established Church of England and Ireland, but not of any colony, except under one or more of three conditions, none of which existed in Upper Canada. Upon the grounds, therefore, furnished by Blackstone and Paley, I opposed the erection of a Church Establishment in Upper Canada, without touching the question of a Church Establishment in England.

Dr. Ryerson in a letter to a friend, thus refers to his early experiences in regard to the Church of England:—

Although I had no opportunity of attending the service of the Church of England until I was nearly twenty years of age, I made the Homilies and Prayer Book, with the Bible, very constant companions of travel and subjects of study. I drew my best pulpit illustrations from them, at the very time that I was controverting the pretensions of the leaders of that Church to exclusive establishment and supremacy in Upper Canada; and, in so doing, I had the sympathies and support of a large portion of the members of the Church of England, in addition to the unanimous support of the members of other religious denominations. I felt that I was preaching the Protestant Reformation doctrines of the Church of England; and throughout life I have loved the Church of England with all its faults, only second to that of my own church. I declined the offer of ordination in the Church of England [page 206] several months after I commenced preaching on a Methodist circuit, simply and solely upon the ground that I was indebted to the Methodists for all the religious instruction and influences I had experienced. I believed that I would be more useful among them, though my life would be, as then appeared, one of privation and labour. During the first four years of my ministry, my salary amounted to less then one hundred dollars per annum, and during the next twelve years (after my marriage) my salary did not exceed six hundred dollars a year, including house rent and fuel.

In a letter written on the 28th October, 1843, to the Editor of the *Guardian* by Dr. Ryerson, he says:—

It is still, as it has long been, the position with the Editor of *The Church* and writers of his school to represent the efforts of other Churches to maintain their own equal rights and privileges as hostility to the Church of England. . . Who proposed peace, and who has perpetuated war—agressive war? [page 292.] . . Who is it that proclaims bodies prior to his own in Western Canada as "Dissenters," and seeks by every species of unfair statement and insinuation to injure and degrade them—both politically and religiously—and substantially maintaining that Civil Government itself is an appropriate Providential instrument to put down "dissent." For one, I have as yet been silent under this provocation, insult, and proscription.

Circumscribed must his views be who does not perceive that "Puseyism," both in a religious and civil point of view, will soon become a far more important question for the consideration and decision of the inhabitants of Western Canada than that of the seat of Government, or than even that of the University. And the day is hastening apace, when it will be a prime matter of inquiry with them to determine . . whether they will quietly consent to have their civil rights and liberties placed in any form in the hands of men who regard the great majority of their Christian fellow-subjects as unbaptized heathens and aliens in a Christian country. Such is the issue to which *The Church* is bringing matters in Western Canada.*

In a journey from Kingston to Toronto by stage, which Dr. Ryerson made in February, 1842, Bishop Strachan was a fellow passenger. Dr. Ryerson thus speaks of the agreeable intercourse which he had with the Bishop on that occasion :—

For the first time in my life I found myself in company with the Lord Bishop of Toronto. He was accompanied by Mr. T. M. Jones, his son-in-law, and Mr. Jarvis (Indian Department), very pleasant companions, nor could I desire to meet with a more affable, agreeable man than the Bishop himself. It would be unpardonable to introduce remarks . . of one's neighbours . . into travelling notes in any form, but there has been something so peculiar in the relations of "John Toronto" and "Egerton Ryerson," that I must beg, in this instance, to depart from a general rule. Conversation took place on several topics, on scarcely any of which did I see reason to differ from the Bishop. He spoke of the importance to us of getting our College at Cobourg endowed—that an annual grant was an insufficient dependence—that as the clergy reserve question had been settled by law, we had as much right to a portion of the clergy lands as the Church of England—that as we did not desire Government support for our ministers, we ought to get our proportion appropriated to the College, as religious education was clearly within the provisions of the Clergy Reserve Act. Valuable suggestions, for which I thanked his lordship. I took occasion to advert to what had excited the strongest feelings in

* In this connection see the significant conclusion of the note on page 291.

my own mind, and in the minds of our people generally—namely imputations on our loyalty to the Government and laws of the country. The Bishop, with his characteristic energy, said that what he had written on the subject he could at any time prove —that he never represented or supposed that the Methodist body of people were disaffected; nor had he represented or supposed that those preachers who had been born and brought up in the country were disloyal; but he was satisfied that such was the case with the majority of those who used to come from the United States. I felt that the whole matter was one of history, and not of practical importance in reference to present interests; and I was much gratified in my own mind to find that the real question, as one of history, was the proportion of preachers who formerly came from the United States, and the character and tendency of their feelings and influence; for no preachers have come from the United States to this country these many years, and we have none but British subjects in the Canada Conference.

After parting with the Bishop at Cobourg, in analyzing the exercises of my own mind, I found myself deeply impressed with the following facts and considerations:—

1. That the settlement of the clergy reserve question had annihilated the principal causes of difference between those individuals and bodies in this province who had been most hostile to each other.

2. That how much asperity of feeling, and how much bitter controversy might be prevented, if those most concerned would converse privately with each other before they entered into the arena of public disputation.

3. That how much more numerous and powerful are the reasons for agreement than for hostility in the general affairs of the country, even among those who differ most widely on points of religious doctrine and polity.*

* This incident might also form a fitting sequel to chapter xxvii, page 213.

CHAPTER XXXVII.

1841-1842.

VICTORIA COLLEGE.—HON. W. H. DRAPER.—SIR CHAS. BAGOT.

AMONGST the last public acts performed by Lord Sydenham was the giving of the Royal assent to a Bill for the erection of the Upper Canada Academy into a College with University powers. This he did on the 27th August, 1841. Dr. Ryerson thus refers to the event, in a letter written from Kingston on that day :—

> The establishment of such an institution by the members of the Wesleyan Methodist Church in Canada attests their estimate of education and science; and the passing of such an act unanimously by both Houses of the Legislature, and the Royal assent to it by His Excellency in Her Majesty's name, is an ample refutation of recent statements and proceedings of the Wesleyan Committee in London . . while the Act itself will advance the paramount interests of literary education amongst Her Majesty's Canadian subjects. . . For the accomplishment of this purpose, a grant must be added to the charter—a measure . . honourable to the enlightened liberality of the Government and Legislature. When they are securely laying a broad foundation for popular government, and devising comprehensive schemes for the development of the latent resources of the country, and the improvement of its internal communication, and proposing a liberal system of common school education, free from the domination of every church, and aiding colleges which may have been established by any church, we may rationally and confidently anticipate the arrival of a long-looked for era of civil government and civil liberty, social harmony, and public prosperity.

In October, 1841, Dr. Ryerson was appointed Principal of the newly-chartered College, and on the 21st of that month, he opened its first session by a practical address to the students.

At the close of that address he said :—

> His late Most Gracious Majesty William IV., of precious memory, first invested this institution, in 1836, with a corporate charter as an Academy—the first institution of the kind established by Royal Charter, unconnected with the Church of England, throughout the British Colonies. It is a cause of renewed satisfaction and congratulation, that, after five years' operation as an Academy, it has been incorporated as a College, and financially assisted by the unanimous vote of both branches of the Provincial Legislature,—

sanctioned by more than an official cordiality, in Her Majesty's name, by the late lamented Lord Sydenham, one of whose last messages to the Legislative Assembly was, a recommendation, to grant £500 as an aid to the Victoria

UNIVERSITY OF VICTORIA COLLEGE, COBOURG.

College. . . We have buoyant hopes for our country when our rulers and legislators direct their earliest and most liberal attention to its literary institutions and educational interests. A foundation for a common school system in this province has been laid by the Legislature, which I believe will at no distant day, exceed in efficiency any yet established on the American Continent ;* and I have reason to believe that the attention of Government is earnestly directed to make permanent provision for the support of colleges also, that they may be rendered efficient in their operation, and accessible to as large a number of the enterprising youth of our country as possible.

Dr. Ryerson, although appointed Principal of the newly chartered Victoria College in October, 1841, did not relinquish his pastoral duties as Superintendent of the Toronto City Circuit until the Conference of June, 1842. His appointment as General Secretary of the Wesleyan Missionary Society, in 1840, necessitated his constant attendance during the winter season at missionary-meetings. Correspondence, consultation, and committee meetings filled up such time as he could spare from his duties as Superintendent of the Circuit. His was indeed a busy life; and by his untiring energy and industry he was enabled to give more than the usual time to the various departments of the Church's work. His aid and counsel was constantly being sought in these things, and was as freely given as though he had the most abundant leisure at his command. In February, 1842, he went to Kingston to attend its missionary anniversary. While there he says :—

> In an interview which I had with Sir Charles Bagot, the new Governor-General, it affords me a satisfaction I cannot express, to be able to say that, in advancing the interests of Victoria College, and in securing the rights and interests of our Church, Sir Charles Bagot will not be second to Lord Sydenham—that while, as a man and a Christian, His Excellency is a strict and conscientious churchman, as a Governor he will know no creed or party in his decisions and administration. . . I believe that it is a principle of His Excellency's Government, in public appointments, etc., qualifications and character being equal, to give the preference to native and resident inhabitants of the province—those who have suffered in the privations, have grown with the growth, and strengthened with the strength of the country. Sir Charles has the wisdom and experience of sixty-three years, and the buoyant activity of our public men of forty. If I mistake not, the characteristics of his government will be impartiality and energy — not in making further changes, but,—in consolidating and maturing the new institutions which have been established amongst us—in obliterating past differences, in developing the latent resources of the country, and in raising up a " united, happy, and prosperous people."

In March, 1842, the question was raised as to the right of ministers of the Wesleyan Methodist Church in Canada, who had been members of the old organization of the Methodist

---

* This memorable prophecy as to the future of our educational system was evidently made by Dr. Ryerson under the conviction that the verbal promise made to him by Lord Sydenham in 1841, —that he should have the superintendence of that system—would have been carried out by his successor, Sir Charles Bagot. There was no written promise, however, on the subject, and he and his friends were greatly surprised at the singular appointment made in May, 1842. It was not until 1844 that Dr. Ryerson received the promised appointment—the reward (as was then most unjustly alleged against him) of services rendered to Sir Charles Metcalfe in the crisis of that year. (See, however, chapter xliii. on Dr. Ryerson's appointment as Superintendent of Education.)

Episcopal Church in Upper Canada, to solemnize matrimony, or for the Conference legally to hold church property. Dr. Ryerson prepared a case on the subject, and submitted it to Hon. R. S. Jameson, the Attorney-General, for his opinion. The opinion of the Attorney-General was conclusive in favour of these rights, and thus this troublesome question, so often raised by adversaries, was finally set at rest.

The transition period between the death of Lord Sydenham and the arrival of his successor, Sir Charles Bagot, was marked by much uncertainty in political matters. In September, 1842, Dr. Ryerson wrote to his friend, Mr. John P. Roblin, the Liberal M.P.P. for Prince Edward county, on the apparently threatening aspect of affairs Mr. Roblin, in his reply, dated Kingston, September 16th, said:*

The political sea has indeed appeared rough; the clouds were dark and ominous of a dreadful storm. But I am happy to say that they have passed away, and the prospect before us is now favourable. There were in the House quite a large majority against ministers; this they plainly saw, and, therefore, shaped their course to avert the blow. Hon. W. H. Draper stated distinctly that it was, and had been, his opinion, that the Lower Canadians should have a fair proportion of members in the Executive Council, and for that purpose he had no less than three times tendered his resignation; that he was ready to go out, and would do so at any moment. Hon. R. Baldwin certainly occupies a proud position at present, and may continue to do so, if he is not too punctilious. The arrangement, which it is understood has been come to, is that Messrs. Ogden, Draper, and Sherwood go out, and that Mr. L. H. Lafontaine comes in as Attorney East; Mr. Baldwin, Attorney-General West; Mr. T. C. Aylwin, Solicitor-General East; Mr. James E. Small, or some other Liberal, as the third man. This will make a strong Government, for it can command a large majority in the House. It is true that the gentleman you mentioned, and a few others will be dead against it, but they are a small minority, and will form a wholesome check.

No man would regret more than I would to see the country thrown into confusion at this time. I entertain a high opinion of the Governor-General (Sir Charles Bagot.) He certainly has shown a disposition to do everything he consistently could to give satisfaction to the prominent party, and being (as he is) of the Tory school, and appointed by a Tory ministry, he certainly is deserving of much credit for going as far as he did to meet the views of the Reformers.

The following was the only record left by Dr. Ryerson of his principalship of Victoria College:—At the end of two years' labours in the station of Adelaide Street Church (the predecessor of the present Metropolitan Church), I was again wrested from my loved work by an official pressure brought to bear upon me to accept the Presidency of Victoria College, which was raised from Upper Canada Academy to a College, and opened and inaugurated, in 1842, as a University College.

On the 3rd of August, 1842, the Wesleyan University at

* This correspondence illustrates one phase of the political history of the times.

Middletown, Connecticut, conferred on the Principal of Victoria College the degree of D.D. His old and valued friend Francis Hall, Esq., proprietor of the New York *Commercial Advertiser*, was the first to convey to him the pleasing intelligence. He said:

> Perhaps this will be the first communication from Middletown which announces to Victoria College that its head is.Rev. Egerton Ryerson, D.D. May you long live to enjoy the distinguished title! I hope to take you by the hand in a few days, and congratulate you personally.

On the 21st of June, 1842, Dr. Ryerson was, with appropriate ceremonies, formally installed as Principal of Victoria College. The Editor of this volume well remembers what a joyful day it was for the College; and how heartily and kindly the new Principal spoke words of encouragement to each of the students then present. On that occasion he delivered a carefully prepared inaugural address, which was afterwards published in pamphlet form and widely circulated. On the 10th September, he sent a copy of the address to Hon. W. H. Draper. In his note Dr. Ryerson called Mr. Draper's attention to what he conceived to be the defective nature of the provisions for the education of law-students, before their entrance on the study of the law (pages 24 and 25 of the address). To this Mr. Draper replied on the 16th. He also added an explanation in regard to his present position in the Government. He said:—

> I have perused your address with much satisfaction. The Law Society of Upper Canada, by appointing a well-qualified examiner last term, will, I think, forward your views as to the education which should precede the study of that profession.
>
> By the recent changes which have taken place, I have no longer the right to visit Victoria College officially; but I hope that I may be favoured with an opportunity of doing so in my private capacity.
>
> You will not, I trust, consider it intrusive in me to briefly state the cause of my retirement from the Cabinet. I have long considered the Government in a false position, while the French Canadians saw in the Council no person acquainted with their wants and wishes—able and willing to look after their interests, and in whom they had confidence. Apprehending from what took place in the beginning of last session that they might refuse to take office with me, I signified several months ago my readiness to retire if that were the case. In July I renewed that offer. And now, when a negotiation was opened on, it appeared that they would not come in without Mr. Baldwin. I again offered my resignation, because, taking the view I do of his conduct when we were last in Council together, I feel I should not be in that body if he were there also. From that moment I ceased to advise or have anything to do with the matter. Had every other part of it been satisfactory to me, or had it been altered so as to make it satisfactory, nevertheless his being brought in inevitably put me out. Should you hear my conduct canvassed and misunderstood, this explanation will, I trust, set it right.

To Mr. Draper's letter Dr. Ryerson replied, and on the 7th October again wrote, asking him to deliver an address to the students at the opening of the session. In his letter Dr. Ryerson said:—

20

I deeply regret any occurrence which would deprive Canada of the advantage of your official counsels. I have observed your public conduct throughout, and it has been such in my estimation, as I have felt it a pleasurable duty to appreciate and defend, even in the most doubtful and trying circumstances. You now enjoy the proud distinction of advising and assisting, on public grounds, to form a government, from which, on personal grounds, you have felt it your duty to retire. You cannot suppose that I entertain a less exalted opinion of your disinterestedness and high sense of honour, when the strong opinions I have again and again expressed of it, have been more than realized by your present patriotic and noble course of proceeding.

In regard to the address which I have solicited you to deliver at the opening of the next session of our College, I desire to state that you will of course make it long or short, as you like, although I should like it long. It is my intention to get, if possible, some gentleman of high public standing and literary talent to deliver an address at the commencement of each collegiate year. I think that such addresses will have a salutary influence upon the taste and feeling and ambition of the students; and the notices and publication of them in the newspapers will tend to elevate the standard of the public taste, and will, I think, be useful to public men themselves. I shall be gratified, and I am sure good will ensue, from your appearing before the public in a somewhat new character.

To this letter Mr. Draper replied, on the 10th October:—

I find that, consistently with my professional engagements at the different assizes (which are now of paramount importance to me), I cannot prepare an address so as to do justice to your request. If it involved only the attendance on the day, I would cheerfully make some sacrifice to accomplish it; but there is more, for I would wish, if I undertook the task, to perform it well, and try to approximate the favourable expectation of those who were willing to entrust it to me; and for this end I cannot devote time enough out of the short interval between this and the latest day named by you. Accept my assurance that I feel great reluctance in declining your proposal. The compliment it conveyed was highly gratifying to me under existing circumstances, and I should have felt sincere pleasure in exerting my humble abilities in favour of an institution to which, when I had fuller opportunities, I had endeavoured to be of use (page 179). Accept my acknowledgements for the kindness and courtesy of your other remarks in reference to myself.

Sir Charles Bagot did not long hold the office of Governor-General. Like Lord Sydenham, he was unexpectedly stricken by the hand of death, at Kingston, on the 19th May, 1843. A sketch of his life and character was prepared by Dr. Ryerson and published in the Kingston *Chronicle*. In that sketch he said:—

Sir Charles Bagot has created throughout the length and breadth of United Canada the settled and delightful conviction that its Government is henceforth to be British, as well as Colonial—and, as such, the best on the continent of America; that Canadians are to be governed upon the principle of domestic, and not transatlantic, policy; that they are not to be minified as men and citizens, because they are colonists; that they are (to use the golden words of Sir Robert Peel) "to be treated as an integral portion of the British Empire."

This sketch was very favourably received by the leading public men of Canada, and, after it appeared in the *Chronicle*, was reprinted by Stewart Derbyshire, Esq., Queen's Printer, who, in a letter to Dr. Ryerson on the subject, said :—

Your letter in the *Chronicle* has attracted high admiration in the quarters most competent for criticism, and it is felt you have done a real service to the country. Supposing your wish is to diffuse the sentiments of your letter, I have taken the liberty of giving it to our printers of the *Canada Gazette* to set up in handsome type, 8 octavo pages, and shall strike off 1,000, and send about, giving away a good many, and putting the rest at bookstores at a very small price. The common run of people do not value what they do not pay for. Have I acted in this in accordance with your wishes —or do you interdict the publication ? Many extra copies of the *Chronicle* were struck off, and about forty copies sent to-day to England by the steamer " Great Western." Sir Robert Peel, Lord Stanley, and Sir Charles Buller had one each.

Dr. Ryerson assented to the republication of his letter.

In the light of after events, the following extract from a letter received by Dr. Ryerson from Hon. R. B. Sullivan, dated Kingston, 21st July, 1843, is somewhat interesting. Mr. Sullivan had placed one of his sons under Dr. Ryerson's care at Victoria College. After referring to matters relating to the education of youth, Mr. Sullivan proceeded :—" I hope that our friendship will be a sufficient inducement to you to teach my boy that upon his own good conduct under Providence his future happiness depends, and to give him that steadfastness of mind which lads naturally want. In asking these things of you, I place myself under no common obligation. There is no man in Canada of whom I would ask the same. My doing so of you arises from a respect and regard for you personally, which has grown as we have been longer acquainted, and which no prejudices on the part of those with whom I have mixed, and no obloquy heaped upon you by others, have ever shaken."

It is pleasant to get a kind word from those who approve of one's course. It is pleasanter to get it from those who have been indifferent, or even hostile. Thus, in a letter from Rev. Matthew Holtby to Dr. Ryerson, written in March, 1842, he said :

Soon after I arrived here from England, I became acquainted with you and your writings, and ever since, I have watched your course, often with painful and prayerful anxiety. It is long since I doubted the propriety of your public conduct, or the justice of your cause ; but as I observed the storm gathering around you, and the winds blowing into a hurricane, from all the cardinal points at once, I have had my fears, that you might faint in the apparently unequal conflict. Thank God, he has delivered you—he has enabled you to stand at the helm, and to steer the Old Ship into smoother water. But we may rest assured that our foes are not dead. I only wish you may manifest as much nautical skill in a calm, as you have in the long storm, and I doubt not but all will be well.

CHAPTER XXXVIII.
1843.
EPISODE IN THE CASE OF HON. MARSHALL S. BIDWELL.

AS mentioned in Chapter xxiv., page 188, an effort was made in 1843 to induce Hon. M. S. Bidwell to return to Canada. Copies of the correspondence on the subject were enclosed to Dr. Ryerson, by the Hon. Robert Baldwin, in a letter dated Kingston, 5th June, 1843, as follows:—

I enclose you copies of letters which I am sure will afford you much pleasure. At present this communication of them must be confidential, as you will see by their date that they have not yet reached their object himself. But after the warm interest you have taken in the cause of my friend, at a time when any interference on my part would have been worse than useless, I feel it due to you to make you early acquainted with what has taken place. I have seen, with much pleasure, that you have carried out the intention you hinted to me when I last had the pleasure of seeing you at Kingston. Your admirable letter must have had a good effect. I see that some little popguns were let off at you on the occasion, but they are too puny to excite anything but a smile at their imbecility.

I regret much my inability to have been present at your last annual examination, but hope to be more fortunate another year.

The Hon. Robert Baldwin's letter to Mr. Bidwell, enclosed to Dr. Ryerson, dated Kingston, 2nd June, 1843, was as follows:—

I have great pleasure in being able to transmit to you a copy of a note addressed by me to His Excellency the Governor-General, with a copy of that of Mr. Secretary Harrison, conveying His Excellency's reply, which, I am happy, so distinctly removes every obstacle to your return to what has been in all essentials your native country; and that without the descent on your part, by even a single step, from the high ground which you have always maintained in relation to your unjust expatriation.

I will at present only stop to assure you of the sentiments of unabated affection and respect with which you have ever continued to be regarded in this country, during the whole period of your exile, and to express my conviction of the satisfaction with which your return will be hailed by all your former friends, and by many even of your former political opponents—in which satisfaction, I trust, I need scarcely add that no one will more sincerely participate than myself.

The following is a copy of Mr. Baldwin's note to Sir Charles Metcalfe, the Governor-General, dated 25th May:—

Mr. Robert Baldwin, having been informed by Mr. Secretary Harrison that with reference to the case of Mr. Bidwell, which Mr. Baldwin had the honour of bringing under the notice of the Governor-General shortly after his assumption of the Government, His Excellency only requires a request to be made to him as a foundation for his directing that the pledge taken from that gentleman, in his departure from Upper Canada, should be cancelled, and giving His Excellency's sanction for the introduction into Parliament of a Bill to restore to Mr. Bidwell the political rights of which his residence abroad, under pressure of that pledge, has deprived him, Mr. Baldwin respectfully begs leave to make that request.

The letter in reply, of Mr. Secretary Harrison to Hon. Robert Baldwin, dated 29th May, was as follows:—

I am commanded by the Governor-General to inform you, in reply to your note of the 25th inst., that His Excellency considers it right that whatever pledge may have been given by Mr. Bidwell on his departure from Upper Canada, to preclude his return, should be cancelled. The letter of that gentleman to the then Lieutenant-Governor, Sir Francis Bond Head, supposed to contain such a pledge, is not to be found in the archives of the Secretary's office. I am, therefore, directed to say that the pledge is considered as cancelled, and that the letter, if ever found, may be returned.

I am also further desired to acquaint you that in the event of Mr. Bidwell's proposing to return, His Excellency will give his sanction to the introduction into Parliament of a Bill to restore to that gentleman the political rights of which his residence abroad, under pressure of his pledge, has deprived him.

On the 14th August, 1843, Hon. Robert Baldwin wrote the following letter to Dr. Ryerson:—

I send you a copy of a letter from our friend, Mr. Bidwell, in answer to my letters to him. The original I have sent up to my father, but had a copy made for you, knowing the interest you have ever taken in his case.

Hon. M. S. Bidwell's letter to Hon. Robert Baldwin, dated New York, 31st July, 1843, was as follows:—

I hardly know how to commence my answer to your letter after so long a delay which has been unintentional and unexpected, and in a great measure unavoidable. I might, indeed, and ought to have written to you when I first received it, but I then hoped it would be in my power to make you a short visit in compliance with your invitation. On this point I was kept in suspense by the state of Mrs. Bidwell's health, and was besides very laboriously occupied with indispensable professional engagements. With this frank explanation I throw myself upon your indulgence to pardon my delay.

Never, my dear friend, for one moment have I doubted your kind and friendly feelings, or your anxiety that I should be treated with justice and liberality by the Government, and I have never ceased to be gratified that I was honoured with the friendship of one whose wishes and talents have, for many years, commanded my respect. Amidst the dejection of spirits and perplexity of mind that I have suffered, this consideration has afforded me great consolation.

Your communication has now taken me by surprise. You will add to your former obligations if you will make suitable acknowledgements for me to His Excellency for the answer which, by his directions, Mr. Secretary Harrison returned to your letter.

All that I have learned of Sir Charles Metcalfe's character and measures has filled me with the highest respect, and with a confidence that Canada will be governed by him with wisdom, justice, and liberality. Loving that country, this confidence has been a source of great joy to me.

Let me add that, in my judgment, Sir Robert Peel in all his measures, since his last appointment has shown a wise moderation and conciliatory spirit, and an anxious desire for the true welfare of the vast Empire beneath the sway of Her Majesty's sceptre.

I would gladly make you a visit at once if I could, but I should feel great pleasure to see you here. I shall do with great pleasure what I can to make the visit agreeable to you. I have heard with concern of the feeble health of your venerable father. I cannot tell you with what deep interest and great respect I think of him. He has been the consistent friend of constitutional liberty through evil report as well as good report. Amidst perfidy and violence, folly and bigotry and intolerance, he has presented a rare and happy example, which I admire, of an enlightened and cultivated mind supporting the great principles of the British Constitution with discriminating zeal, constancy of purpose, and moderation of temper. I beg that you will do me the favour when you write to him to present my most affectionate and respectful regards.

I perceive that Mr. Secretary Harrison alludes to the possibility of my returning to Canada. I cannot fail to feel, as long as I live, a deep interest in that country, and the most ardent wishes for its prosperity. But I have formed no plans for a change of residence. A constant attention to my business, which is necessary for the support of my family, has left me no time to form plans.

With a gratified sense of your kindness and with great regard and affection, your friend, MARSHALL S. BIDWELL.

To this letter from Mr. Bidwell, Hon. Robert Baldwin replied on the 12th August, as follows :—

I have, believe me, great pleasure in acknowledging the receipt of your letter, as well on account of its relieving me, to a certain extent at least, from apprehensions that Mrs. Bidwell's health was the cause of your silence.

I cannot, however, conceal my disappointment at the last paragraph of your letter, in which, though you do not altogether shut out the hope of our having you again amongst us . . The obligations in regard to Mrs. Bidwell's health which you wrote (as precluding such consideration for the present) are, however, too sacred for even friendship to venture upon more than a repetition of those assurances, which my former letter contained, of the feelings of affection entertained towards you in this country, and the satisfaction which your return would afford. I, however, find it impossible to do otherwise than indulge in the pleasing anticipation of again seeing you amongst us, not as a mere visitor, but as once more a Canadian, in fact as well as in feeling. We have not, and certainly for the generation to which we belong, shall not, have any subjects of equal importance, in a pecuniary point of view, to those which seek the aid, and reward the exertion, of your professional talents where you are. It seems, therefore, to partake somewhat of selfishness to wish to withdraw you from an arena worthy of your great talents, to appropriate those talents to a sphere so much more limited. Be that as it may, I will indulge the hope, so long as you do not forbid it. In the meantime, could you not take a leave of absence for a few weeks during the coming Autumn Assizes, and amuse yourself with holding some briefs on some of them here? We have now five Circuits—the Eastern, Midland, Home, Niagara, and Western. Mr. Justice Jones takes the Eastern, Mr. Justice McLean the Midland, the Chief Justice the Niagara, and Mr. Justice Hagerman the Western. Nothing would give me more pleasure than to see you thus renew your relations with our bar ; even if you should not do so with a view to a final return to it. Let me know soon, in a post or two, if possible, as well as the circuit you mean to go on. . . . Now as I have gone on with this scheme, I find myself grow warm on it, so do not throw cold water upon it by a negative.

If I could do so with any propriety, I would avail myself of your kind invitation to visit you at New York for the purpose, not only of seeing you, but of urging this my suit in person. But I assure you it is out of my power to do so. Parliament is called for 2nd September, and I shall not have a moment's leisure from this time till the Session is over. You must recollect that, as a Parliament man, I am comparatively but a young hand, and I have to try and make up for want of experience by hard work; though I find it by no means a sufficient substitute.

I complied in substance with your request to make your acknowledgements to His Excellency for the answer, which by his direction, Mr. Secretary Harrison returned to my letter; but lest I should do so less appropriately then I ought, I took the liberty of letting you speak for yourself, by showing His Excellency your letter.

Your opinions of the Governor-General and of Sir Robert Peel entirely agree with my own. But I regret to say that some of our friends, and of our firm friends too, seem to me to forget what has been accomplished because everything is not done at once, or, because some things are done not exactly as they would have them. This impatience is much to be regretted. If I were one whom it was necessary to keep up to the mark, as it may be called, it might be excusable, but they do not even profess to think that to be the case as respects the points in question. Their display of dissatisfaction, therefore, has only the effect of lessening the weight of the party in Upper Canada in the eyes of both the Head of the government here and the Imperial authorities at home. But I did not mean to make this a letter of complaint; but the fact is, I am just now smarting under an ebullition of violence on the part of our friends in Toronto, on the subject of Mr. Stanton's appointment to the Collectorship there, which almost involuntarily led me into these remarks. You will, I hope, excuse me.

My dear father, I am happy to say, appears by his last letters to be rather better. I fear much, however, that the improvement cannot be considered of a permanent character. As the Governor-General kept your letter till yesterday, I was only able to send it up to him to-day. It will, I am sure, afford him much gratification.

I hope you will excuse the length of this epistle, and rebuke me by the shortness of your reply, which need contain no more than six words, to wit: "I will ride the circuit." I believe "ride" is the professional term; at least used to be so, though it may belong to the era of Mr. Justice Twisden, if not a still more remote one, rather than at present. . . You see how inclined I am to run on, so that lest I should transgress beyond endurance, I will conclude at once, with the assurance of my warm and continued regard.
Ever your affectionate friend, R. B.

CHAPTER XXXIX.

1844.

EVENTS PRECEDING THE DEFENCE OF LORD METCALFE.

THE defence of Lord Metcalfe, the Governor-General of Canada, who succeeded Sir Charles Bagot in 1843, was unquestionably the most memorable act of Dr. Ryerson's long and eventful life.

His previous training for twenty years in the school of controversy in relation to civil and religious rights; his personal intercourse with leading statesmen in England on Canadian affairs; his contests for denominational equality with successive Governors in Upper Canada, and his counsels and suggestions, (offered at their request), to such notable representatives of Royalty in Canada as Lord Durham, Lord Sydenham, Sir Charles Bagot, and Sir Charles Metcalfe, put it beyond the power of even the most captious to question the pre-eminent qualifications of Dr. Ryerson to discuss, in a practical and intelligent manner, the then unsettled question of responsible government as against the prerogative—a question which had arisen between Sir Charles Metcalfe and his late Councillors. In the chapter which Dr. Ryerson had prepared for this part of the Story of his Life, he thus refers to his intercourse with, and relations to, the distinguished Governors whom I have mentioned. He said :—

In 1839 a Royal Commission was issued to Lord Durham to investigate the affairs of Canada, and report thereon to Her Majesty. While engaged in his important duty he sent for and conferred with me repeatedly, and treated me with such consideration, as that on leaving him he would accompany me to the door and open it for me, shaking hands with me most cordially. After his return to England he sent me a copy of his famous Report (addressed by himself) before it was laid on the table of the House of Lords. On receiving in advance this report of Lord Durham I published in the *Guardian*, with appropriate headings, extracts from that part of it which related to the establishment of responsible government and its administration in Canada, and then lent the extracts and the type on which they were printed to Mr. (afterwards Sir) Francis

Hincks for insertion in the *Examiner* newspaper, of which he was at that time proprietor and Editor. I afterwards aided Lord Sydenham in every way in my power to allay the party passions and animosities of the past, and to establish responsible government upon liberal principles, irrespective of past party distinctions, comprehending Hon. W. H. Draper and Hon. Robert Baldwin in the same administration—a union or coalition which did not long survive the life of Lord Sydenham—Mr. Baldwin declaring his want of confidence in Mr. Draper, and retiring from the government. Soon afterwards, Mr. Baldwin and his friends succeeded to power under Sir Charles Bagot.

This was the state of things until 1843, when Sir Charles Bagot died, and Sir Charles Metcalfe was appointed to succeed him. I had the melancholy pleasure of offering a tribute (in the form of an obituary notice) to the character and administration of both Lord Sydenham and Sir Charles Bagot—papers much noticed and widely circulated at the time as the best specimens of any writing which had ever appeared; but I had a genial theme and good subjects in both cases. Sir Charles Metcalfe was popular with all parties at first; but after a few months a difference arose between him and his Councillors as to the appointment of the Clerk of the Peace of the County of Lanark, and then on the principle of appointments to office; or in other words, the exercise of the patronage of the Crown.

To understand the character of this famous and much misrepresented controversy, and how I became involved in it, some preliminary and explanatory remarks are necessary :—

It is to be observed in the first place, that one chief subject of complaint by "Reformers" for many years—nay from the beginning—was the partial exercise of the patronage of the Crown, appointing magistrates, officers of militia, judges, etc., from men of one party only, in whose behalf every kind of executive favour was bestowed for years. This was the purport of their complaints in the various petitions and addresses of "Reformers" to the Earl of Durham, Lord Sydenham, Sir Charles Bagot, etc., who necessarily promised that the Governments should henceforth be conducted upon the principles of justice, "according to the well understood wishes of the people," of whom "Reformers" claimed to contribute a large majority, and even of the liberal Conservative members of the Church of England. But singular to say, on the occurrence of the first vacancy, the Reform government urged upon Sir Charles Metcalfe the appointment of one of their own party, irrespective of the superior claims, as the Governor conceived (on the ground of service, experience and fitness), of a deserving widow and her orphan son. The circumstances were as follows :—

Amongst the early gentlemen immigrants in the County of Lanark was a Mr. Powell, a man of wealth and education; but in attempting to clear and cultivate a farm in a new country, he soon expended his means and became reduced in circumstances. He was appointed Clerk of the Peace, and discharged its duties for many years, when he sickened and died. During the two years' sickness which preceded his death, the duties of office were discharged satisfactorily by his son, who was then about twenty or twenty-one years of age. On the death of her husband, the Widow Powell proceeded to Kingston to plead in person before Sir Charles Metcalfe for the appointment of her son to the office vacated by the death of her husband, and as the only means of supporting herself and family. One can easily conceive the effect of such an appeal upon Sir Charles Metcalfe's benevolent feelings. He declined the advice of his Councillors for a party appointment, and determined to appoint the widow's son to the office rendered vacant by the death of her husband, and one which he had successfully discharged for nearly two years. The Council, instead of resigning on the fact of the appointment, sought to obtain from Sir Charles Metcalfe a promise that he would henceforth act upon their advice. He said he would always receive and consider their advice, but would give no promise on the part of the Crown as to how far he would pledge the prerogative in advance and act upon that advice. On this the Councillors resigned, charging Sir Charles Metcalfe with violating the principles of responsible government. This he positively denied. The circumstances of the case were so mystified by the statements made, that general prejudice was excited against Sir Charles Metcalfe, and the Councillors seemed for the time to have the country at their backs.*

I was at that time President of Victoria College; and the late Hon. Wm. Hamilton Merritt, returning from Kingston at the sudden close of the Session of Parliament held there, stopped the stage in front of the College, called to see me, and asked me what I thought of the occurrences between the Governor-General and his Councillors. I told him that, from what I had heard, my sympathies were with the Councillors. He answered that I was mistaken; that the Councillors were clearly in the wrong; that they had made a great mistake, and were endangering principles of government for which he had so long contended. He then stated the particulars of what had transpired, and referred me, in confirmation of his statement, to the documents and correspondence which would all be printed in a few days. I replied, that if what he (Mr. Merritt) stated was correct, Sir Charles Metcalfe was an injured man, and that the new system of responsible government was likely to be applied in a way contrary to what had always been professed by its

---

* As an indication of outside opinion on this question, I insert the following note, written by Rev. Anson Green, on the 31st December, 1843, to Dr. Ryerson. Mr. Green said: I cannot see why the Executive Council should resign at the present time, for they stated in the House that both Mr. Stanton, Collector at Toronto, and the Speaker of the Legislative Council were appointed by their advice. I think they should have waited until His Excellency refused to ask or take their advice, and not force him to make pledges. In my opinion both parties have acted indiscreetly. I have reason to believe that a majority of the Reformers from Upper Canada, in Parliament, would be happy to support Hon. S. B. Harrison, if he could form a ministry from the majority on the question at issue.

advocates. Mr. Merritt requested me to examine for myself the documents and correspondence to which he had referred, but enjoining secresy as to his conversation with me—and which I never mentioned to any human being during his life.

After Mr. Merritt returned to St. Catharines he wrote to Dr. Ryerson early in January, 1844 on the subject, as follows:—

There can be little doubt that both the Governor and his late administration have erred. A conciliatory spirit would have avoided this crisis; they had an opportunity of placing this Province in a most enviable situation—they have neglected, or did not possess the ability to avail themselves of it; and I am sorry to say, that I am neither satisfied with their measures, nor can I place confidence in their judgment. At the same time I feel so thoroughly convinced of the necessity of having under the control of our Legislature the entire management of our internal concerns—without which any attempt at a thorough reformation would be useless—that I have my apprehensions, that any movement which would have a tendency to check its onward progress, would be injurious—the principle does not appear to be fully understood, or fully conceded. The time has not arrived—nevertheless I feel satisfied the Governor-General would admit it, and act fully up to it with any Cabinet which possessed his confidence, and thus bring it into action much earlier than persisting in the opposite course. On the other hand, you are subject to the imputation of abandoning men who resigned for the maintenance of that principle, and few can doubt the honesty of purpose of Lafontaine and Baldwin.

Being thus placed on the horns of a dilemma, the wisest plan is, perhaps, to let matters take their course—at all events I have made up my mind to do so. I should be most happy to hear from you on the subject, knowing you have given those subjects much attention; and believing that your mind is devoted to promoting the best interests of your fellow countrymen, your opinions are received with attention, and always carry great weight with me.

To this letter from Mr. Merritt, Dr. Ryerson replied on the 20th January, 1844, as follows:—

After you called upon me, I turned my attention to the state of our public affairs, and reflected on them from various points of view. I concluded to state my views to His Excellency, if he requested me to do so, and also to Hon. S. B. Harrison, if I should see him.

Dr. Ryerson having gone to Kingston at the request of Sir Charles Metcalfe, saw Mr. Harrison, who urged him to state his views fully to the Governor-General. In the same letter to Mr. Merritt, Dr. Ryerson said:—The next day, in compliance with His Excellency's expressed wish, I laid before him the result of my reflections on the present state of our affairs, in an interview of three hours and a half. In them His Excellency expressed his full concurrence, and thanked me cordially for the trouble I had taken to wait upon him and state at large what he considered of so much importance. In addition to the question at issue between Sir Charles Metcalfe and his late Councillors, Dr. Ryerson discussed with him the subject of the reconstruction of his Cabinet. The result he thus states in his letter to Mr. Merritt :—I cannot of course enter into every one of the subjects to which I referred in my conversation with the Governor-General. Mr. Harrison has doubtless written to you on the whole matter. The result was that Mr. Harrison will take office if you will.*

As to your superior qualifications for the position offered you, there can be but one opinion in the country. I am satisfied that, without the slightest sacrifice of principle or consistency —upon the broadest principles of responsible government, and in harmony with the best interests of the country—you can accept of office. I think that when the views I have expressed to His Excellency are fairly and fully stated to the country, you would, in office, have a large majority of at least the Upper Canada members of the present House of Assembly to support you : and, in case of a general election, I doubt not but you would have an ample majority in the new Parliament. Should you consent to take office, I think you need not fear the result. I think there is a fair opportunity for you to render a great service to the country, and to establish still more widely and permanently an already honourable reputation of no common order.

I shall be glad, at your earliest convenience, to learn the result of your deliberations. I should also be happy to see you, if you should soon proceed to Kingston. Whatever the Governor-General may have heretofore thought of either the theory or practice of responsible government, he is certainly right on the subject now. And when His Excellency avows what Sir F. Head denied, and offers everything that has been demanded, surely, as far as principles of government are concerned, the country wants, and ought to have, no more. I think it will be a fearful calamity to the country, if we drive Sir Charles Metcalfe away from us. I doubt whether England can produce his like for Canada.

To this letter Mr. Merritt replied, on the 25th January :—

I regret to say that my own private affairs, arising from circumstances which have occurred since I saw you, prevent my assuming any situation under the Government which must necessarily occupy my undivided attention. I have heard from and replied to Mr. Harrison to the same effect.

* In regard to this proposal, Mr. Harrison wrote to Dr. Ryerson on the 17th of January, to say that he had an interview with the Governor-General, and that : His Excellency expressed himself favourably disposed upon all the points touched upon, and was willing to consider the means of carrying out the objects contemplated. It appears, therefore, to me, that the matter may be arranged if our friend Merritt can be persuaded to join. I have written to him in that view. Should that be the case, I am prepared, and a communication should be made to Hon. W. H. Draper, which I will make immediately upon hearing from you and Mr. Merritt. As Mr. Draper will be here by the latter end of this week, it would be better, on hearing from Mr. Merritt, that you should be here yourself.

No person can more regret the unfortunate position in which we are placed than I do, and I agree with you that the loss of Sir Charles Metcalfe will be a public calamity. I have no doubt he will honestly carry out the principles of responsible government, and with a competent council, who understand what the country requires, and with competent individuals to carry those measures into effect, he would render more essential service to Canada than any former Governor whatever.

I am under some apprehension that you mistake the feelings of the majority of Upper Canada members. A mere majority would ensure defeat; they must act in a body to give a majority in the present House; and from recent indications, there appears to be a change in the minds of those who were under very different impressions some time since. Although I was under a different impression some time since, I cannot see any chances of a new ministry being sustained, unless by a dissolution. 1. A majority seems indispensable to secure which the Reformers of Upper Canada must unite—and every Conservative must support them also;—the first cannot be relied on, therefore it is unnecessary to discuss the second. Most of the present members will feel themselves committed by their recent vote; they will all be pressing for a new election; and shape their course to the prevailing opinions. No ministry can have time to bring their measures before the public to produce any general impression; and no ministry can have confidence in the ultimate success of the wisest measures. In short, they will have no chance to exercise their ability, with a view of commanding success. Whereas, were a new election to take place (on the declaration by the Governor-General, that from the difficulty he experienced in making up a ministry which would command a majority of the present House, in conformity to the principles he avowed), the Governor-General could appeal to the people to return a representation from which he could select a Council possessing their confidence. Such an appeal would not be inconsistent with his former declarations, which must have been predicated on his obtaining a Council which would command a majority. Under such circumstances members would feel very naturally a much greater anxiety in sustaining any ministry with a chance of four years to test their measures, than as many days, as in the present instance. As far as I am individually concerned, even in that case, I could not accept of office unless I succeeded in arranging my own personal concerns, which I hope to effect during the season.

I hear that in this district a strong feeling prevails in favour of the late ministry, who resigned, as they believe, to support the principle of responsible government; and they cannot understand that the Governor-General adheres to the same. This impression is natural; and it takes a long time to remove error. No man doubts the motives of Mr. Baldwin; none other of the administration is named, or possesses the least weight. I have not moved about or corresponded with a single member of the House, and I shall remain as passive as possible.

I fully agree with you, that with the present Governor-General a fair opportunity offers to carry out useful projects; nay more, I am sure that one half of the present revenue now wasted, could be saved (not less than £100,000) for useful objects; but I cannot at present assist in carrying it into effect, which you cannot regret more than I do.

In a note received from Mr. Civil Secretary Higginson, dated 10th April, he gave Dr. Ryerson the reasons for the unexpected delay in the formation of a new Cabinet. Hon. S. B. Harrison had also written to him on the same subject, so far as he and the other proposed Upper Canada members were concerned. Mr. Higginson said :—

The formation of a permanent Council has been most vexatiously, but unavoidably, delayed, owing to the extraordinary timidity—I can call it by no more appropriate name—of our friends in Lower Canada—the most eligible of whom have hitherto shrunk from the responsibility they would incur by the acceptance of office. Hon. D. B. Viger, who is still in Montreal, and who ought from long experience, to have a good knowledge of his countrymen, expresses himself confident of the result, and is of opinion that the delay, of which we complain, produces good and strengthens His Exellency's position. It is very evident that it has a different effect in the West; and it is to be hoped that as soon as the Montreal election is over (of which, barring violence, Mr. Molson is certain) immediate steps will be taken to fill up the offices now vacant.

In reply to Mr. Higginson's note, Dr. Ryerson said :—

I do not think that much evil arises at the present time, even in Canada West, from delay. Could the vacancies be filled up two or three months ago, the government would have secured the support of thousands who have since swelled the ranks of the ex-Councillors. But the loss by delay was, I think, incurred to its full extent during the months of January, February, and March. The proceedings of the late meeting of the Leaguers in Toronto have doubtless added something to their strength. But some portions of these very proceedings will meet them in a way they little expect—not, to be sure, before a jury of twelve men, as did the nine months' proceeding of O'Connell and his associates, but before the jury of the whole country, and upon principles sanctioned by the Constitution and history of England, which, I believe more confidently than when I wrote last, will result in a triumphant acquittal and justification of the Vice-Regal defendant.

On the 23rd May, Mr. Civil Secretary Higginson wrote to Dr. Ryerson, as follows :—

You will be sorry to hear that Hon. Mr. Harrison has failed to make certain private arrangements which he so much hoped for, and that he has declined to take office. He is, therefore, unable to join the Cabinet.

CHAPTER XL.

1844.

PRELIMINARY CORRESPONDENCE ON THE METCALFE CRISIS.

WITH a view to a thorough understanding of the question at issue between Sir Charles Metcalfe and his Councillors, the following statement by Dr. Ryerson is necessary :—

After the conversation with Hon. W. H. Merritt, in January, 1844, and after subsequent communications with him on the subject, I most carefully and minutely examined the documents and correspondence and other statements of parties, and was satisfied of the correctness of Mr. Merritt's statements and conclusion. The question then arose in my own mind, whether, after I had so much to do in the establishment of responsible government and was morally so largely responsible for it, I should silently witness its misapplication, and see a man stricken down for maintaining, as the representative of his Sovereign, what Reformers had maintained in all previous years—that the patronage of the Crown, like the administration of justice, should be administered impartially according to merit, without respect to religious sect, or political party.

Dr. Ryerson also states (26th February) that :—After a prolonged and interesting interview with the Governor-General, I addressed a letter to him on the subject of that interview. In it I said : In looking over what I have from time to time, during the last eight years, written on the best government for Canada, I find that I have invariably insisted upon precisely the same views which I expressed to your Excellency, and with a frequency and fulness that I had no recollection of when I was honoured with the late interviews by you. These views were then warmly responded to by that portion of the public for whom I wrote. I am, therefore, the more fully (if possible) convinced of their correctness and importance to the best interests of Canada, and that they will be sustained when properly brought before the public—at least in Western Canada.

In reply to a note from Mr. Civil Secretary Higginson, dated 2nd March, Dr. Ryerson, on the 7th, addressed a reply of some length to His Excellency. In it he said :—

The aspect of things in Western Canada has clearly changed for the worse during the last two months—since my first interview with Your Excellency in January. The party of the opposition have become organized—organized under circumstances more formidable than I have ever witnessed in Canada. Their ranks and influence have been increased by numbers who, two months since, were neutral, and who could have been forthwith brought to the side of constitutional government. Private letters to me (on which I can rely) speak in a very different tone as to the state of public sentiment and feeling. Unless a change to a very considerable extent be affected in the public mind, I think a dissolution would rather strengthen than weaken the ex-Council party. I am confident I do not overrate their strength—and it is a dangerous, though common error, to underrate the strength of an adversary. They are likewise organizing their party, and exciting the public mind to such a degree as to prevent any sentiments or measures from the present administration from being regarded or entertained at all. Such being the case, I have felt that delay has been loss. Whether that loss can be repaired presents to my own mind a problem difficult of solution.

Speaking of his former relations with the Lieutenant-Governors of Upper Canada, Dr. Ryerson said:—

I love liberty, personal and public, as much as any man. I have written much in its defence; but as much as I love liberty, and as ultra liberal as some may have supposed me to be, I have always regarded an infringement of the prerogative of the Crown as a blow at the liberty of the subject, and have, in every instance, resisted and repelled it as such. I did so in support of Sir F. Head in 1836. I did so in support of Sir George Arthur, in the difficult and painful task of administering the criminal law after the insurrection of 1837. I did so in support of the Royal instructions and recommendations of which Lord Sydenham was the bearer and agent; but in each instance, after having been lauded without measure, I was abandoned, or pursued, without protection or mercy. Sir Francis Head took offence at certain communications which Rev. Dr. Alder and Rev. Peter Jones justly made to the Imperial Government respecting his treatment of the Indians, and swore that, "as he had put down the radicals, he would now put down the Methodists;" and the Bishop of Toronto avowed and rejoiced that, radicalism having been extinguished, "the Church" would and should be maintained inviolate in all its (assumed) rights and immunities. Sir George Arthur having got through his many difficulties (in the course of which he gave me many thanks) determined, when the Session of the Legislature came, not to split with the Bishop of Toronto; not to grant, under any circumstances, the Methodists more than a mouse's share of public aid, and none at all except as salaries for their clergy, actually employed. He embodied these views in resolutions, and employed Hon. R. B. Sullivan to advocate them in the Legislative Council.

It was with extreme reluctance that I could at all assent to the measure of Union of the Canadas. The agents of the London Wesleyan Committee vehemently opposed it, and wished me to write against it. I wished to remain neutral. Lord Sydenham most earnestly solicited my aid—promised a just measure on the clergy reserve question, and assured me against any hostility of the agents of the London Committee, of all the protection and assistance that the Government could give. He died,—and I have been left, without the slightest assistance or protection on the part of the Government, to meet alone the hostile proceedings and influence of the London Wesleyan Committee. In order to sustain myself in these reverses, and especially in the last, but most painful one, I have been compelled to put forth physical and intellectual efforts that I am absolutely incapable of repeating.

I have adverted—even at the expense of being tedious and egotistic—to these unpleasant details, that Your Excellency may fully understand and appreciate my present position, and my caution in embarking in another conflict without a reasonable hope that I will not be made a victim of abandonment and of oppression, after I have employed the utmost of my humble efforts in support of the principles of the constitution and prerogatives of the Crown.

In the present crisis, the Government must of course be first placed upon a strong foundation, and then must the youthful mind of Canada be instructed and moulded in the way I have had the honour of stating to Your Excellency, if this country is long to remain an appendage to the British Crown. The former, without the latter, will only be a partial and temporary remedy.

Anything like a tolerable defence of Your Excellency's position—anything approaching to an effective exposure of the proceedings of the late Council in their demands, the grounds of their resignation, their explanation, their tribunal of appeal, their variations of position, the principles and consequences involved in each step of their course, and the spirit and doctrines they now exhibit, appears to me to be a desideratum. They could be convicted out of their own mouths on every count of the charges they have brought against the Governor-General, and from the same source might evidence be adduced that they advocate sentiments and sanction proceedings which are unknown to the British Constitution, and which appertain only to an independent state. Yet, in place of exposition, and arguments and illustrations that would tell upon the public mind, we have nothing but puerile effusions, thread-bare assertions, and party criminations—nothing that would convince adversaries and make friends of enemies. Your Excellency's replies, and a few passages in the Montreal *Gazette*, and in a pamphlet which lately appeared in the Kingston *Chronicle*, are all that I have seen which are calculated to produce practical effect upon the public mind. Hon. D. B. Viger's pamphlet is too limited in its range of topics, and too speculative and refined to be effective upon any other than well-educated statesmen.

The desideratum required I would attempt to supply, and then devise measures, put forth publications, and employ efforts to direct the public mind into new channels of thinking, and furnish the youthful mind with instruction and materials for reading that would render this country British in domestic feeling, as I think it now is intentionally in loyalty. To do anything effectual toward the accomplishment of such a task, my position should be made as strong as possible. At best my qualifications for a work so difficult and varied are extremely limited, but more especially under present circumstances.

After weighing the matter carefully, and pondering (in comparing small things with great) upon the part which Bishop Burnet took in settling the disordered elements of British intellect after the revolution of 1688, I have resolved to do as he did—place my humble services at the disposal of my Sovereign—and in whatever situation Your Excellency is of opinion I can render most service to the government and the country under existing circumstances. I will hazard the enterprise, and stand or fall with the Governor-General in the present crisis, notwithstanding the increased cloudiness of our political atmosphere. I would rather aid as a private individual, and as an independent volunteer in the service of the Crown and country—as I have been on former occasions—than be placed in any official situation.

To this letter Dr. Ryerson received the following reply from Mr. Secretary Higginson, dated 12th March :—I am directed to convey to you the expression of the Governor-General's cordial thanks for the public spirited offer of your able and valuable services in the present crisis of public affairs; an offer which His Excellency accepts with a high degree of satisfaction, feeling confident that you will bring most efficient aid to the Government.

On March 18th Dr. Ryerson replied to this note from Mr. Higginson. He said :—I think there will be but little difficulty in disentangling the question from the perplexing confusion in which it has been involved, and placing it upon the true issue as to a government of party, or of justice. If, in elucidating and applying it, I can incorporate some of Lord Brougham's fulminations on the evil of party with my own conceptions, I may be able to add the occasional discharge of a cannon, or the bursting of a bombshell, to the running fire of ordinary musketry. Though

I am no stranger to contests, I cannot divest myself of palpitations at the approach of an engagement. When once the fire has commenced, I feel but little concern except to keep cool and good-natured, and to have an ample supply of ammunition for all exigencies—satisfied of the righteousness of the cause and the government of an over-ruling Providence.

In February the Rev. John Ryerson wrote to Dr. Ryerson on the Metcalfe crisis, and said:—

While I believe that the late Executive Council, in the main, and in principle, was right, and Sir Charles wrong, yet I am very far from endorsing all that the Council did as right. I think that they should not have resigned when they did. I think they were guilty of a breach of trust in throwing up office in the midst of a session of Parliament, and when many important measures were pending. I think, as the "antagonism" which caused the resignation of the late Council existed before the Parliament was convened, that they should then have resigned, or remained in office until the prorogation. . . .

You are not to suppose from these remarks that I have turned politician, or that I am intermeddling with things which do not belong to me. I have been endeavouring to attend to my appropriate work; and though continually pressed with questions, soliciting my opinions respecting passing events, I have said as little on all these matters as possible, and I am identified with no party. Indeed, the state of my health is such as to admonish me to think about other things than worldly politics, and I blush to think that I have written so much respecting them. Powerfully convincing reasoning, with truth on your side, might produce a great effect among our people; but at the present more than nine-tenths of them, in these western parts, are the supporters of the late Executive Council.

In reply to a letter from his brother John, asking his opinion on the pending dispute between Sir Charles Metcalfe and his late Councillors, Dr. Ryerson wrote on April 3rd, and said:—

Of the general measures of the late Council I cordially approve. I cannot say so of their dispute with the Governor-General. Of the policy which he or they had pursued, I have nothing to say. In that they might have been right, and he wrong. But, according to British practice, they ought to have resigned on what he had done, and not on what he would not promise to do. If the Crown intended to do just as they desired the Governor-General to do, still the promise ought not to be given, nor ought it to have been asked. The moment a man promises to do a thing he ceases to be as free as he was before he made the promise. It is essential principle that in the British Constitution that the Crown should be free—should be undefined in its prerogative. The exercise in that prerogative may be checked in various ways; but to bind it by promises is to infringe its constitutional liberty. If the Queen were to bind herself by promise, or declaration, that she would not appoint any person contrary to Sir Robert Peel's advice, how could she refuse to make O'Connell a peer, or appoint him Lord

Chancellor of England if Sir Robert were to insist upon it? How could she ever get clear of Sir Robert by differing with him on a question of policy, if she were to bind herself beforehand to act according to his advice? Would it not be virtually giving the regal power into his hands?

Dr. Ryerson then proceeded to illustrate the views which he held on this subject :—

I can find examples in English History since 1688, of British Sovereigns having done just as Sir Charles Metcalfe is alleged to have done; I can also find examples of ministers resigning on account of what such Sovereigns had done; but I can find no example of any minister resigning on account of what the Sovereign would not promise to do on the subject of consultation and possible appointments.

I have seen it alleged, that the Governor-General was not bound to act upon the advice of his Council, only to ask it before he made any appointment. But the Governor-General did take the advice of the Council, in regard to the appointments of the Clerks of the Peace, both in the Bathurst and Dalhousie districts. Yet he is blamed as much for not acting upon it as if he had acted without taking it. But in Mr. Hincks' writings, and in all the papers advocating the same sentiments, I observe that it is contended that the Governor-General should act upon, as well as take, the advice of his Council. If so, what is he but their amanuensis—the recorder of their decrees?—the office which Sir Charles Bagot sustained on account of his illness; but whose example, in such circumstances, can not be laid down as a general rule.

Responsible government was a mere theory with the late Council, or until they came into office under Sir Charles Bagot. They had thought and reasoned about it, but they had never acted upon it, until then; what they learned under the government of a sick and dying man was not adapted to make them perfect practitioners. So they were about as wise and as raw in the business practically, as was Sir Charles Metcalfe, who had doubtless thought, and read, and reasoned upon the subject also. The unskilfulness of inexperience, with good intentions, seems to me to have been evinced in the whole proceeding.

Of course it was considered, on the impulse of the moment, good policy to take a stand upon the principle of responsible government, and not upon the propriety, or policy, of certain appointments. By taking the latter ground, all might be lost; by taking the former ground, all would be gained, and a great deal of glory too, in the course of a few days, or a few weeks at most. But it has turned out otherwise. The question of prerogative has been brought up—a constitutional and imperial question. As such the British Government have decided upon it. . . It is now no longer a question between the late Councillors and Sir Charles Metcalfe, but between them and Her Majesty's Government. I see, therefore, nothing in prospect but a renewal of the scenes of 1837, and 1838, only on a larger scale. Whether the point contended for is worth that price, or will be even obtained at that price, is problematical. I see no alternative, unless some enlightening, healing agency interpose. I pray for the safety of our Zion and people, especially, while I implore Divine interposition in behalf of our beloved country.

I am no party man—I have never judged—I cannot judge questions according to party, but according to constitutional principles and history. On the first blush I was favourably impressed with the position and resignation of the late council; but when I came to examine their position, as I had done Hon. Mr. Draper's speech on the University question by the light of history (it being a new question), I came to the conclusions that I have stated above. I think the most general impression in the country, and perhaps amongst the members of our Church, is that which first struck my own mind; but I think it is contrary to the principles and practice of the British Constitution.

During one of his visits to Kingston, early in 1844, Dr. Ryerson called at the office of his old friend, Hon. J. H. Dunn (one of the late Councillors), who had desired to see him. Mr. Dunn was not in when he called. He therefore, on his return to Cobourg addressed him as follows:—My brother John told me that you had asked him what I thought of the late differences between the Governor-General and his Council. After all that I have read and learned, I think very much of them as I did of the differences between the late Lord Sydenham and Hon. Robert Baldwin. You then asked me (at the Lambton House) whether I approved of your remaining in office, or of Mr. Baldwin's resigning. You will recollect my reply, that I thought Mr. Baldwin ought to have waited until an actual difference arose between him and other members of the Council on some measure, or measures; and that he ought not to have resigned on account of an alleged want of confidence, or theoretical difference of opinion. So I think in the present case. After stating your views to Sir Charles Metcalfe, you ought to have waited until some act, or acts, had taken place in contravention of these views, and which act, or acts, you were not disposed to justify; or if you thought it your duty to resign, then it appears to me you should have resigned on some acts which had been performed, and which you would not justify, and on the policy involved in which you were prepared to appeal to the country. But to resign upon a conversation, and not upon specific administrative acts, appears to me to be without precedent. It has brought up the question of prerogative, the constitutional decision of which, rests of course, with the supreme tribunals of the Empire. I think Mr. Baldwin's conscientious theoretical rigidness has led to an error, praiseworthy in its motives, but not the less an error—an error which in private life would have attracted no attention, but in public life makes a great noise, and may lead to serious consequences. I could wish with all my heart that you were in your late office, which you have so long and so faithfully filled.

In a note to Dr. Ryerson, on various matters, dated April 10th, Mr. Civil Secretary Higginson said:—

The Reform League in Toronto are making unusual exertions, and as you may have seen by their late resolutions, no longer conceal their real object, but in defiance of all their machinations, and they are not over scrupulous as to their means, truth and honesty of purpose, backed by loyal hearts and liberal measures, must and will prevail.

To this note Dr. Ryerson thus replied on the 12th April:—
I think the public feeling in Canada West is now stationary; or since the rumour of my appointment as Superintendent of Education (and how it got afloat I cannot imagine) is rather turning in favour of the Governor-General. The reason seems to be this: The opponents of His Excellency represent him as weak—as supported by nobody but a weak ultra-party. It has been alleged by both my friends and enemies, that whether the best or worst man in Canada, I have not hesitated to face in succession the united press and councils of each of the two ultra-parties in Canada, and succeeded in each instance to reduce them from a large majority to a small minority—deriving no advantage from the victories, except as some suppose, the pleasure of humbling my enemies. It is the impression of great numbers of persons, and to an extent and degree which has often amused me, that whatever cause I espouse, be it good or bad, will succeed; and that I never undertake a thing, however apparently impracticable, without a certainty of success. Though such a feeling increases the difficulty of every step of a man's career, it furnishes him with capital to begin with. My life having been bound up with the two great principles of constitutional monarchy on the one hand, and equal civil and religious principles in Canada on the other, all who really desire such a government, without regard to the domination of a party, . . seem to think the Governor-General will succeed if I have resolved to espouse his government. . .

From this state of mind in the case of many Reformers, and from what I have learned from other sources, I am satisfied that, notwithstanding the efforts to inflame party spirit—to produce party blindness, and create party organizations—there is still a spirit of candour and enquiry (all I ask) amongst a large portion of the Liberal party which will furnish an ample fulcrum for a lever that will overthrow the enemy. I think that June will probably be the best time for the application of such a lever. The opposition can do nothing more at present. June is rather a leisure month for reading—the hay and wheat harvest will come on in July, August and September,—during which time agitators can do but little, and then I suppose will come the session of the Legislature. I hope to produce a vindication of His Excellency that will do no discredit to him, and shake, if not confound, his enemies, and exhibit such a platform of government as will appeal to every candid, common sense, sound British subject, best adapted to promote the best interests and greatest happiness of Canada. . .

To vindicate injured worth, either in high or humble life, has, on different occasions, afforded me peculiar pleasure, and I contemplate, even as a pleasing task (though painful from the occasion) the purpose and opportunity of doing so in respect to so noble a subject and so good a cause as that with which His Excellency is identified. When the Government once assumes the attitude of strength, many who are now neutral, or perhaps professedly leaning to the apparently stronger party, will come over avowedly to the Crown. The timidity of the secret friends of the government in Lower Canada is an infirmity (I think of a majority of mankind) which requires as much pity as it deserves censure. All Greeks are not Spartans. Ten men seem to be made for work, where one is constituted for war. I have found it so in the hour of peril; when I have been left almost alone, though I found abundance of helping and co-operating friends as soon as the tide of victory began to turn in my favour. I think it will be so with the government in less than twelve months—at least in Upper Canada. The League organization in Toronto is the most formidable affair that has ever been formed in western Canada. I am told that its funds are large also,—several thousand pounds—but I think its power can be broken.

In a note to Dr. Ryerson from Mr. Higginson, dated 23rd of May, he said:—You will of course have seen the manifesto just hatched and brought forth by the League, jesuitically and cleverly enough put we must admit; it will no doubt be widely circulated, and it is very desirable that an antidote to the poison should be as extensively communicated to the people; and who in the province is so capable as yourself for such a task? If you would take up the arguments *seriatim*—you could prove their fallacy without much difficulty. The fabric being founded upon misapprehension and falsehood, must go with a run. I confess I long to see these ambitious party-men unmasked.

CHAPTER XLI.
1844.

SIR CHARLES METCALFE DEFENDED AGAINST HIS COUNCILLORS

ON the 27th May, 1844, Dr. Ryerson issued the first part of his memorable Defence of Sir Charles Metcalfe, not only against the attacks of his late Councillors, but also against those of the all-powerful League which had been formed against him on the 24th March, under the auspices of the Toronto Reform Association. The Manifesto of that famous League was dated on the 16th May. Its issue at once decided Dr. Ryerson to enter the lists in defence of Sir Charles, and the prefatory note to his rejoinder was written on the 27th May. From the introductory portion of it I make the following extract:—

> Rev. Egerton Ryerson . . proposes . . to prove [from the] testimony of his late Advisers . . that His Excellency is entitled to the verdict of the country on every count of the indictment got up against him.
>
> Sir Charles Metcalfe may say to the people of Canada, as Themistocles said to the Athenians who were incensed against him, "Strike, but hear me!"
>
> . . If Leonidas,* with three hundred Spartans, could throw themselves into the Thermopylæ of death for the salvation of their country, it would ill become one humble Canadian to hesitate at any sacrifice, or shrink from any responsibility, or even danger, in order to prevent his own countrymen from rushing into a vortex, which, he is most certainly persuaded, will involve many of them in calamities more serious than those which followed the events of 1837.

The following account of this memorable controversy was written by Dr. Ryerson himself. It has been slightly abridged and a few explanatory notes added:—

After much consideration, but without consulting any human being, I determined to enter the arena of public discussion to set forth and vindicate the true principles of responsible government, and to defend Sir Charles Metcalfe, as I had before defended Mr. Bidwell, from the unjust attacks made upon him; and I published an introductory paper avowing my purpose. My friends generally and the country at large were against me. My elder brother, John, a life-long Conservative, on first meeting

* By a singular popular error, which this sentence may have suggested, it was stated and generally believed that the Defence of Lord Metcalfe by Dr. Ryerson was written and published under the *nom de plume* of "Leonidas."

me after the publication of that introductory paper, said, "Egerton, you have ruined yourself, for nine-tenths of the people are opposed to the Governor-General." I answered, "I know it; but I believe that nine-tenths of the people are mistaken, and that if they will read what I am about to write they will think as I do."

The contest was severe; the ablest and most meritorious public men in the province were arrayed on the opposite side; but I felt that truth and justice did not rest on numbers—that there was a public, as well as an individual, conscience, and to that conscience I appealed, supporting my appeal by reference to the past professions of Reformers, the best illustrations from Greek, Roman, and English history, and the authority of the best writers on constitutional government, and moral and political philosophy, and the highest interests, civil and social, of all classes of society in Upper Canada. For months I was certainly the "best abused man" in Canada; but I am not aware that I lost my temper, or evinced personal animosity (which I never felt), but wrote with all the clearness, energy, and fire that I could command.

The general elections took place in October, 1844, and in all Upper Canada (according to the *Globe's* own statement) only eight candidates were elected in opposition to Sir Charles Metcalfe! Such a result of a general election was never before, or since, witnessed in Upper Canada.

It has been alleged again and again, that Sir Charles Metcalfe was opposed to responsible government and that I supported him in it. The only pretext for this was, that in the contest with Sir Charles Metcalfe his opponents introduced party appointments as an essential element of responsible government, which they themselves had disavowed in previous years when advocating that system of government. The doctrine of making appointments according to party (however common now, with its degenerating influences) was then an innovation upon all previously professed doctrines of reformers, as I proved to a demonstration in my letters in defence of Sir Charles Metcalfe.

Sir Francis Hincks, in an historical lecture delivered at Montreal, in 1877, has revived this charge against Sir Charles Metcalfe, and has attempted to create the impression that there was a sort of conspiracy between the late Earl of Derby and Lord Metcalfe to extinguish responsible government in Canada. For such an insinuation there is not a shadow of reason, though the author may have thought so, from his strong personal feelings and former party views, as one of the actors in the struggle.

I was in England during the latter part of 1844 and 1845, when the Earl of Derby was Colonial Secretary, and had more than one conversation with him on Canadian affairs; and I know that the Earl of Derby had no more intention or desire to abolish reponsible government in Canada than had Sir Francis Hincks himself. The Earl of Derby had, indeed, fears lest the party in power, under the new system, should act upon the narrow and prescriptive principles and spirit of the old tory party, and wished to see that with the new system an enlarged policy would extinguish the hatreds, as well as the proscriptions, of the past, and unite all classes in the good government and for the advancement of the country. This was the view of Lord Metcalfe; and this was the view advocated in my letters in his defence, which may be appealed to in proof that the essence of that contest was not responsible government, but as to whether or not the distribution of the patronage of the Crown should be dispensed upon the principles of party, or on those of justice and morality.

I may add an illustrative and curious incident on this subject:—On the passing of the Imperial Act for confederating the British North American Colonies into the Dominion of Canada, and its proclamation, I wrote and published an address to the people of Upper Canada in 1868, suggesting to them to forget the differences of the past, and the principles and spirit in which they should introduce the new system of government, and build up for themselves a united and prosperous nation. A few days after the publication of this address, I met in the street, an honourable gentleman, who had been one of the party opposed to Sir Charles Metcalfe, a member of a Liberal government, a life-long Reformer. He complimented me on my recent address to the people of Upper Canada; but added, "The great mistake of your life was the letters you wrote in defence of Lord Metcalfe." I answered, "Do you think so?" "Yes," said he, "that was the great mistake of your life." "And," said I, "you approve of my recent public address?" "Yes," he answered, "I think it is the best thing you ever wrote." "Well," said I, "do you know that that address with the exception of the introductory and concluding paragraphs, is a reproduction, word for word, of my third letter in defence of Lord Metcalfe, counselling my fellow-countrymen as to the principles and spirit in which they should act in carrying into effect the then new system of responsible government!" He exclaimed, "It cannot be! I have these letters." I said, "It can be; and it is so; and if you will compare my third letter in defence of Lord Metcalfe with my recent address, you will find that I have not omitted an illustration from Greek, or Roman, or English history, or an authority from standard writers, on political or moral science, or a petition or address from Reformers from the rebellion of

1837 to the establishment of responsible government under Lord Sydenham and Sir Charles Bagot in 1840-42 ; that I have not added to, or omitted, a word, but have repeated *verbatim et literatim* in 1868, in regard to confederate government, what I advised the people of Canada in 1844 in regard to responsible government. And now, I continued, " who has changed ? you or I ?" " Oh," he said, "circumstances alter cases." " Truly," I said, " circumstances alter cases ; but circumstances don't change principles ; I wrote on the principles and spirit of government irrespective of party." On such principles I have endeavoured to act throughout my more than half a century of public life— principles, the maintenance of which has sometimes brought me into collision with the leaders of one party, and sometimes in opposition to those of another party ; but principles which I have found higher and stronger than party.

A day or two after the issue of Dr. Ryerson's first paper in defence of Sir Charles Metcalfe, Hon. Isaac Buchanan sent to him copies of letters which he had written to Hon. Joseph Howe, Halifax, and to Civil Secretary Higginson, Kingston, on the Metcalfe controversy. In this letter he said :—

It is with infinite pleasure that I see you have publicly come out to tell the truth as to politics and public men. The fact is, politics in a new country are either the essential principles of society or parish business. In both cases every man is interested, and to a less extent than in an old state of things, where in a hereditary educated class, there are natural guardians of the public virtue. Is it objectionable that clergymen interefere in the arrangement of detail for the happiness of the country? But it is, as I have always maintained, their most imperative duty to hold and express an opinion on constitutional politics. The priests in Lower Canada, from not doing so, permitted the rebellion of 1837. I, myself, care nothing, and never did care anything, for party politics in Canada ; and, in my mind, the distinction has always been more marked between these and constitutional politics than I have been able to explain.

Dr. Ryerson did not attend the opening of Conference at Kingston, in June, 1844. Mr. Higginson wrote to him on the 12th to express his disappointment at not seeing him there, and added :—

Of your letters—your admirable letters—I only hear one opinion, that they are most powerful, unassailable ; and this the opposition press appears to find them, for I can perceive no attempt to answer the convincing arguments adduced by you. They merely abuse you and impugn your motives : lying and misrepresentation are their favourite weapons.

You will have heard of the discovery of the Orange Plot, the conspiracy between Sir C. Metcalfe and Ogle R. Gowan to upset the Government !

We had a very satisfactory communication from Lord Stanley, by the last packet, entirely approving of the " dignified and temperate " conduct of the Governor, and assuring him of the strenuous support of Her Majesty's Government, in resisting the "unreasonable and exorbitant pretensions of the late Cabinet." Shall we see you again before we move to Montreal? Sir Charles goes to the Falls, and then returns to Kingston, which he leaves on the 20th for Montreal.

From Mr. Higginson Dr. Ryerson received the following interesting letter, dated Montreal, 20th July:—

As you will no doubt think it right, after you complete the series of your admirable and unanswerable letters, to expose the fallacy and falsehood with which Hon. R. B. Sullivan, as "Legion," endeavours to bolster up his arguments in reply to them, I think the enclosed *précis* of a conversation that took place between the leader of the French party in the late Council and myself, early in May last, will convince you that His Excellency did not write his despatch of the 23rd of that month, quoted in the debate by Lord Stanley, upon insufficient grounds, or in ignorance of the real sentiments and inclinations of his then advisers. Letter No. 5 of "Legion," in referring to this despatch, charges His Excellency with what he calls paraphrasing, or, in other words, misrepresentation, as no men in their senses could have made such demands as the late Council are stated to have urged. The words made use of by His Excellency are not theirs, it is true; but did not the opinions expressed by Mr. Lafontaine, their leader, bear out the assertion? I regret that Lord Stanley did not quote what followed. I have given the meaning, rather than the words, of the dictatorial Councillor; but I have not in the slightest degree exaggerated the substance of his discourse. I ought to add that the conversation originated in a rumour of His Excellency's intending to appoint a Provincial Aide-de-camp, of whom Mr. Lafontaine did not approve; and that, although addressed to me, I could only suppose that it was intended for the ears of His Excellency. You will, of course, not believe the newspaper statements of Sir Charles having sent for Mr. Lafontaine. Ever since our arrival here the French party have been urging that the only way of getting out of our difficulties is by allowing Messrs. Lafontaine and Baldwin to resume their places—as the French people believe that they cannot enjoy responsible government without them. To this His Excellency cannot consent. What the result may be is not quite clear; our future plans have been delayed by this negotiation, which, though still pending, must terminate in a day or two. I hope that under any circumstances we shall be able to meet the present Parliament, if not with a majority, at least with a strong minority.

The following is the *Précis* to which I refer :—

Mr. Lafontaine said: Your attempts to carry on the government on principles of conciliation must fail. Responsible government has been conceded, and when we lose our majority we are prepared to retire; to strengthen us we must have the entire confidence of the Governor-General exhibited most unequivocally—and also his patronage—to be bestowed exclusively on our political adherents. We feel that His Excellency has kept aloof from us. The opposition pronounce that his sentiments are with them. There must be some acts of his, some public declaration in favour of responsible government, and of confidence in the Cabinet, to convince them of their error. This has been studiously avoided. Charges have been brought against members of the Council, in addresses, and no notice given to them, viz.: Mr. B. was even mentioned by name, or at least by office, and will declare on the first day of the session that it is only as a member of responsible government that he for one would consent to act. If he supposed for a moment that Sir Charles could introduce a different system, he would resign. In fact, the Governor ought to stand in the same position towards his Cabinet as Her Majesty does. They cannot be prepared to defend his acts in Parliament if done without their advice—instance the case of the Collector of Customs' intended dismissal. No new-comers ought to be appointed to office. Declares his disinterestedness, as his party—*i. e.* the French Canadians—must carry the day. The Conservatives would be just as ready to join them as those that have—has no desire for office for office's sake. If the Governor does not take some steps to denounce and show his disapprobation of Orangeism, his not doing so will be construed into the reverse, and the system will extend, and bloodshed will follow. The other party will organize—and they would be great fools if they did not—no Orangemen to be included in Commissions of the Peace—no justice at present for Catholics in Upper Canada. A law for the suppression of illegal societies does exist, but very difficult to discover members of them and to execute the law. Conciliation is only an attempt to revert to the old system of government—viz: the will of the Governor. It must fail. Lord Stanley decidedly adverse to the Lower Canadians; does not forget their expunging one of his despatches from their journals—it was so impudent. Trusts the Home Government will accept the proposed civil list; they will never have so large a one offered again. In conclusion, Sir Charles Metcalfe's great reputation places him in an eminently favourable position for carrying out Sir Charles Bagot's policy, by which alone the Province can be satisfactorily governed. A declaration by Government to this effect would put a stop to political agitation which the opposition keep alive as long as they have the slightest hopes of office—all they care for. Let them know that the game was up, and all would go right, and many come round. The differences of religion in Upper Canada will always prevent amalgamation; you must make them all of the same, like ourselves in Lower Canada. French language clause in Union Bill must be expunged.

On the 26th July Dr. Ryerson replied to Mr. Higginson—

I shall make use of the enclosure *Précis* in substance when I come to reply to "Legion"—which will, of course, not be until he shall have got through his series.

The "Defence" of Sir Charles Metcalfe consisted of nine papers, in which the whole question at issue was fully discussed. In concluding the ninth, Dr. Ryerson said:—

I have written these papers . . as a man who has no temporal interest whatever, except in common with that of his native country—the field of his life's labours—the seat of his best affections—the home of his earthly hopes; —up to the present time I have never received one farthing of its revenue. I know something of the kinds and extent of the sacrifices which are involved in my thus coming before the public. If others have resigned office, I have declined it, and under circumstances very far less propitious than those under which the late Councillors stepped out. . . I have no interest in the appointment of one set of men to office, or in the exclusion of any other man, or set of men, from office. I know but one chief end of civil government—the public good; and I have one rule of judging the acts and sentiments of all public men—their tendency to promote the public good. . . I am as independent of Messrs. Viger, Draper and Daly, as I am of Messrs. Baldwin, Sullivan and Hincks. . . I might appeal to more than one instance in which the authority and patronage of the Governor did not prevent me from defending the constitutional rights of my fellow-subjects and native country. . . The independent and impartial judgment which I myself endeavour to exercise, I desire to see exercised by every man in Canada. I believe it comports best with constitutional safety, with civil liberty, with personal dignity, with public duty, with national greatness. With the politics of party—involving the confederacy, the enslavement, the selfishness, the exclusion, the trickery, the antipathies, the crimination of party, no good man ought to be identified. . . With the politics of government—involving its objects, its principles, its balanced powers, its operations—even against the encroachments of any party—every British subject has much to do. Civil government, as St. Paul says, "is an ordinance of God." Every Christian . . is to see it not abused, or trampled under foot, or perverted to party or sectional purposes; but he is to seek its application to the beneficent ends for which it was designed by our common Creator and Governor. Such have been the ends for which the people of Canada have long sought its application; such have been the ends sought by the Governor-General.

Dr. Ryerson, in his letter to Mr. Higginson (26th July) said:

I have now concluded my defence of His Excellency against the attacks of his late councillors. I have done the best I could. As to its influence upon the public mind, I am, of course, not responsible. I cannot compel persons to read, think, or reason, however I may do so for them. In some places, I am told, a most essential change has taken place in the public mind, in consequence of the perusal of my letters. In other places, passion has prevented the perusal of them, and numbers of persons have just become calm enough to desire to peruse them, and are anxiously waiting for the pamphlet edition.

I have not yet heard of any one who has read them all, who has not become convinced of the correctness of my reasoning. But it is the opinion of persons who have far better means of judging than I have, that the effect of them the next two months will be much greater than during the last two months. The violent feelings which the whole party of the Leaguers sought to excite against myself have, to a great extent, subsided, and a spirit of inquiry and reflection is returning to the public mind. I believe nothing has been done to circulate my articles among the mass of the people—beyond the ordinary newspaper agency. I believe that were my ninth number itself printed and widely circulated in Upper Canada in tract form, it would prepare the way for the success of a just administration, consisting of any persons whom His Excellency might select—at least so far as the great majority of the people of Western Canada is concerned. I think the decision of the Imperial Government on the whole question should be laid before the Legislature in a despatch. The matter would be thus brought to a single issue, and I doubt not but the prerogative would be placed upon the true foundation.

To proceed again to legislation, without a distinct settlement of this question, appears to me derogatory to the dignity of the Crown itself (both in England and Canada) and unsafe in every respect; and unjust to both His Excellency and to all who have supported him. I think also that the Hon. Mr. Draper ought (if necessary) to be supported as strongly as ever George III. supported Mr. Pitt. Mr. Draper has thrown himself into the breach, and defended and supported the Government in no less than three emergencies, when others have abandoned, and even sought to overthrow it. I think that Mr. Draper ought not to be made a sacrifice, without an appeal to the people. Much prejudice and passion have, of course, been excited by the Leaguers since last January, and they have formed a regular and extensive organization; but a reaction has already commenced; the backbone of their power is broken. They can form branches, associations, and threaten us as they did a few months ago; but not a few amongst themselves are wavering. If the Government will act with liberality and energy, and the Home Government transmit an official decision on the question at issue, to be first submitted to the Legislature and then to the people, I believe His Excellency's exertions will be crowned with a glorious victory, to his own credit, the honour of the British Crown, the strengthening of our connection with the Mother Country, and the great future benefit of Canada.

As to myself: when I commenced this discussion I did not know what might be my own fate in respect to it. I wished, at least, to do my duty to my family; to quiet their apprehension, and not embarrass and distrust my own mind, while undertaking a task of so great magnitude.

In regard to the past: I have completed my task to the best of my humble ability. The satisfaction of having done my duty is all the acknowledgment or commendation I desire, or can receive. With my present experience, I might perform the task in a manner more worthy of the subject, and more to my own satisfaction. I hope, however, an occasion for such a discussion may not occur again in Canada. The hostile personal feelings excited against me in some quarters will, I hope, be lived down in time. The disclosures which have been made of the alleged sins of my public, and even private life, have not, I trust, brought to light one dishonourable act, one republican or unconstitutional sentiment, even under the severest provocations, and grossest abuse.

Dr. Ryerson had written to the Governor-General early in August on several matters. He received a reply from Mr. Secretary Higginson on the 15th of that month. In it he says:—

The Governor-General looks forward to the pleasure of seeing you soon, when he will have an opportunity of personally expressing his warmest thanks for your admirable and unanswerable letters in defence of the Queen's Government. His Excellency feels very much indebted to you for the zeal and ability that enabled you to perform, in so truly an efficient manner, the arduous task which your patriotism and public spirit induced you to undertake. Upon other important subjects adverted to in your letter, His Excellency will be very happy to have personal communication with you when you come down. Our object now is to complete the Council, as far as may be practicable, without the body of the French party, who doggedly refused to take part in any Administration of which Messrs. Lafontaine and Baldwin are not members. Mr. William Smith, of the Montreal Bar, accepts the Attorney-Generalship, for the duties of which he is said to be well qualified. He is a Liberal in politics, and has always been looked on as a friend of the French party. The Hon. Mr. Morris is willing to take the Receiver-Generalship, and I hope that Mr. W. H. Merritt will now find himself at liberty to join the Council. The Crown Lands Department will still remain unfilled ; and perhaps it is well that that door should be still kept open.

Mr. Billa [now Hon. Senator] Flint, of Belleville, in a letter dated 14th August, in correcting an error in one of Dr. Ryerson's Metcalfe letters on a matter of fact, adds :—

I hope soon to read your pamphlet, but in not reading your letters heretofore, I have been enabled to answer the attacks of your enemies, not on the grounds of a consent, but upon other, and I trust better ground, that of not condemning a man unheard, as is the case in this part of the community, and as I have stated that you must be near right from the fact that your enemies dare not publish your productions.

With a view to aid Dr. Ryerson in his personal defence, Hon. Isaac Buchanan wrote to him on the 22nd August, and said:—

As I think you may feel called on to answer the personal attacks made upon you, or, at all events, to defend the ministerial character from those who deprive it of all manliness and independence, I send you Hetherington's "History of the Church of Scotland." On one page, and in the note referred to, you will find the methods and conduct of Knox explained. It will be the best, as well as the most truthful policy on your part, to show your agreement with this great character. The effect will be great, not only on the Methodist Scotch, but all other Scotch in the Colony, for we are all for national, instead of party, freedom ; we prefer our country to our party.

It may be my fondness for my country; but I think no other country, or people, have ever shown that indomitable love of equal justice and rational, because national freedom, as opposed to party supremacy, as we have done in Scotland.

I feel sure that you may make some happy illustrations from Hetherington's History to enlighten the public on the present state of affairs, when we are about to be enthralled by party tyranny, and do much to revive the spirit :

"Ne'er will I quail with down-cast eye
Beneath the frown of tyranny;
In freedom I have lived, in freedom I will die."

The history of our Church is not only the history of Scotland, but the history of the world's freedom from the tyranny of men, or parties.

Dr. Ryerson had written to His Excellency in regard to the issue of his letters in a pamphlet with a full index. To this letter Mr. Higginson replied on the 19th August:—

I am desired by His Excellency to repeat his thanks for your continued exertions in support of Her Majesty's Government.

Your index to the pamphlet will be exceedingly useful. I should like very much to have the pamphlet translated into French, for the benefit of the Lower Canadians, and perhaps I shall be able to accomplish it. I should be obliged by your ordering a few hundred copies to be sent to me for distribution in the Eastern Townships.

CHAPTER XLII.

1844—1845.

AFTER THE CONTEST.—REACTION AND RECONSTRUCTION.

DR. RYERSON naturally took a deep interest in political affairs at this time, and Sir Charles Metcalfe kept him fully informed of events transpiring at the seat of Government. In a letter, dated 19th August, 1844, Mr. Civil Secretary Higginson said to him :—

You will be glad to hear that Hon. D. B. Papineau accepts a seat in the Council. The Inspector-General and Solicitor-General of Lower Canada are the only offices unprovided for. As to Mr. W. H. Merritt, the state of his private affairs may operate in his case, as in that of Mr. Harrison. If it should prove so, the Hon. James Morris may be induced to join the Council, and a very worthy representative of the Upper Canada Constitutional Reformers he would be. Whether the present Parliament is to be met again, or to be dissolved, remains for discussion. Sir Charles inclines to meet them, and I think we can do with a majority, albeit a small one, to support the Government.

Mr. Higginson wrote to Dr. Ryerson, Sept. 8th, and said:

Dissolution or no dissolution, still undetermined Thorburn declines office. We must have an Inspector-General, and from the Upper Canada Liberals. Where are we to find one fit for the duties?

Dr. Ryerson addressed a letter, on the 10th September, to Hon. W. H. Draper, in reply to Mr. Higginson's note—

I need scarcely say that I congratulate you most heartily on your formal appointment as Attorney-General, and on the important additions which have been made to your strength in the Council. Would not Mr. Scobie make a good Inspector-General? He is said to be a good financier. His private character, sound principles, and moderate feelings, are all that you could desire. After much reflection, and conversation with some judicious persons who have travelled more than I have throughout the country, and have better opportunities of forming an opinion than I have, I am inclined to think that you will gain much more than you can lose, by meeting the present Parliament, and declaring your views, and taking your stand upon the true principles of responsible government. I make these remarks, because I spoke rather in favour of a dissolution when I saw you last.

To this letter Hon. W. H. Draper replied, on the 17th :—

I acknowledge the force of your arguments against a dissolution, but at the same time it appears to me you have not weighed the arguments on the other side. These may be concisely stated. 1st. That the ensuing session will be one certainly preceding a general election, and therefore, one in which popular doctrines have their fullest force. 2nd. That members having committed themselves by the vote of last session would fear to retrace their steps and brave the charge of inconsistency at such a time. 3rd. That the ex-ministers would have an opportunity, which they would not neglect, of presenting a new question for the country. You have sickened them of the first question; they would like a second, better selected, if they could get it. For example, if they moved a committee to inquire how the Government has been administered during the last ten months, would they not be very likely to carry it? Information can do no harm; enquiry is a right of the House, etc., etc. Who would venture to oppose when the committee was granted? No business would be done till it had reported. Whatever the report—and if they got a majority on the committee, we may judge its character—their point would be gained, and they would have a new issue to try before the country; a new topic of inflammatory harangue, and studious misrepresentation. Whether this would be their move I cannot say, but they would do something tending to a similar end. The experience of 1836 will teach them not to make a dead set against doing business, or granting supplies, etc. They will make that a consequence, and if possible force the Government to a dissolution, thus casting the onus of doing no public business on the Government. Again, although not meeting the present House may be considered as an admission of inferiority there, I think this less injurious than that the new Administration should be beaten there; and I cannot in any way anticipate a different result. After going over the list in every way I see no just ground for hoping for victory there. Again, of those in whom we might place some hope of a vote in a crisis, there are some who will not be in their places. Col. Prince certainly will not, and I doubt much if Hon. W. H. Merritt, or Mr. Thorburn can. Does no other Upper Canadian Reformer suggest himself? I confess that I am at a great loss. Neither Harrison nor Merritt can take office, as they say, because of their private affairs. Hon. James Morris has given up politics. I have not failed to note your observation respecting Mr. Scobie, and have brought the matter before the Council.

To this letter Dr. Ryerson replied on the 19th September:—

You will observe that my remarks had reference almost exclusively to the best means of augmenting the elective suffrage in favour of the Government. The facilities for circulating knowledge amongst the mass of the people are so very imperfect, that it takes a long time, and great exertions, even out of the ordinary channel, to inform the great body of the people on any subject.

In the present instance, the Tory party, although they approve of my letters, do not take pains to circulate them gratuitously. It is amongst the persons opposed to the Governor-General, that the reading of them is the most important. That class of persons cannot be supposed to be very solicitous to procure publications against their own sentiments and feelings, although they—at least very many of them—would readily read them if they were put into their hands. I have scarcely heard of an individual who has read all my letters who does not adopt the sentiments of them—how strong soever his feelings might be against the Governor-General. It was with a view, therefore, of gaining over to the Government a larger portion of the electors, that I proposed delay, and the intermediate means of fully informing the public mind.

From the considerations which you assign, I do not see that you can do otherwise than dissolve the House. I can easily conceive how some persons can absent themselves from a short session, and thus weaken the Government more than others could strengthen it by their presence and support; and that popular movements may be devised to shift the question and embarrass you.

You will probably not gain as many elections now as you would six months or three months hence; but what you may not gain in numbers you may gain in the moderation of new members, or in a new House; especially if you can reduce the majorities of opposition members who may be returned, and hold before them in a new House the possibility of a second dissolution.

Dr. Ryerson then sums up his suggestions as follows:—

The great question then is, How can you come before the country forthwith to the best advantage? I would take the liberty of offering the following suggestions, which have probably occurred to yourself, with others that I shall not mention: 1. Ought not the views of the Government, on the great questions, be put forth in some more authoritative, or formal and imposing way, than has yet been adopted? I know not whether it would be in order for the Governor-General to issue a proclamation in some such form as Lord Durham adopted, when he made his extraordinary appeal to the inhabitants of British North America. In such a document, whatever ought to be the form of its promulgation, the question and doctrine of responsible government should be stated with an explicitness that will leave the ex-Council party no room to cavil, or justify further resistance on that subject. You have this advantage, that you can state your case as you please, and as fully as you please, to the country. 2. Ought there not to be more effective means used than have yet been employed to circulate the refutations of the ex-Council's publications amongst their own supporters? Every one you gain from that side counts two, in more ways than one. And from what I have understood, I am persuaded the chief desideratum is to furnish them with the refutations of the attacks of the late Councillors. A proper improvement of means for nearly two months might accomplish a great deal, and would soon reduce them to a minority, in a large majority of the counties in Upper Canada.

On the 18th September, Mr. Higginson wrote to Dr. Ryerson:

The question of meeting the present Parliament, or of going to the people, has at last been decided in favour of the latter measure. There was so much to be said, *pro* and *con*, that it was a most difficult point to decide. If the Government could have reckoned with any degree of certainty upon a majority in the House, which they unfortunately could not, there would have been the strongest reasons, as your brother so forcibly put them, for not dissolving. Your suggestion to Hon. Mr. Draper as to Mr. Scobie filling the Inspector-Generalship, engages the attention of His Excellency and the Council. Can the gentleman referred to command a seat? I fear not.

They complain of a great want of information in the Colborne District. I mean Dr. Gilchrist's portion of it, where they see nothing but the Peterborough *Chronicle*. Mr. Hickson may be depended on as far as he can be of use in circulating some of your wholesome truths. As there will now be no opportunity of speaking to the people from the Throne previous to the elections, some other mode must be taken to ensure our not coming before the country upon a wrong issue, and such language used as the masses can readily comprehend. It is to the electors we must look for victory, and that Sir Charles Metcalfe will triumph I entertain no doubt.

In acknowledging an official letter to His Excellency, Mr. Higgins on(October 10th) informed Dr. Ryerson that he should receive an official reply through Mr. Daly. He then added:—

I doubt not that you will outlive all the abuse that foul-mouthed radicalism can heap upon you.

It is, as you know, impossible to calculate with any degree of certainty upon the results of the elections until the polls are tested; but, I think I may assert with safety that our prospects in Lower Canada are by no means so discouraging as our enemies, and, I believe, some of our friends, would make it appear. Of the latter, there is a class that stand still with their arms folded, fancying that there must be a majority against the Government, and that it will be taken by the Home authorities as an evidence of the impossibility of working responsible government.

In sending letters of introduction to friends in England, Hon. George Moffatt, of Montreal, wrote to Dr. Ryerson in October to say :—

As to the result of the Metcalfe contest, returns have been received from more than half of the constituencies in the two sections of the Province, and it is gratifying to find that the Governor-General is assured of having a good working majority in the Assembly. I have no fears about him, and my only anxiety now is that things may not be again grossly mismanaged at the Colonial Office. Unfortunately, however, Sir Charles Metcalfe's health is very precarious, and should he resign, it will be of the utmost importance that a statesman of ability and character should be sent out to succeed him.

I drew your attention to the ungrateful conduct of the returned exiles, generally; and if proof were wanting of the entire failure of the conciliation system in this section of the Province, it would only be necessary to refer to the active part taken by these men in the late contest.

Hon. Peter McGill, of Montreal, in his letter of introduction to Sir Randolph Routh, thus referred to Dr. Ryerson :—

The Rev. Egerton Ryerson, with whose name you, and every one connected with Canada, must be familiar, has recently been doing the State some service, by his eloquent writings in defence and vindication of Sir Charles Metcalfe's Government, and in support of law, order, and British Connection.

Having applied to His Excellency for letters of introduction to parties in England, Mr. Secretary Higginson writes :—

I have the pleasure to enclose an introduction from His Excellency to Lord Stanley, and letters to old friends of his and mine, Mr. Trevelyan, of the Treasury, and Mr. Mangles, M.P.

How nobly and strongly Upper Canada has come out! She will send us at least thirty good men and true, who will not be overawed by a French faction. From this section of the Province we shall have, on the lowest calculation, thirteen or fourteen, which gives us a majority of five or six to commence with, and that will doubtless increase.

From no one did Dr. Ryerson receive during the Metcalfe contest more faithful and loving counsel then from his old friend, Rev. George Ferguson. Mr. Ferguson had been a brave soldier before he entered the ministry, in 1816, and he was, up to the time of his death, in 1857, a valiant soldier of the cross. In a letter to Dr. Ryerson, in September, 1844, he said :—

> My esteemed friend, beloved brother, (and may I add) dear son: These epithets you know come from a warm heart; a heart of friendship, affection, and love, without dissimulation. If you have a friend in this little wicked and deceitful world it is George Ferguson. I have watched you in all your movements from first to last with great anxiety and deep concern. Your welfare and prosperity I have, do, and will rejoice in; and when you are touched in character, or otherwise, I feel it acutely. When I understood what you intended to undertake, and hearing the clamour among the people, I felt awful, not that I feared that any production or argument coming from your pen would be controverted successfully. I believe that your last production is unanswerable on logical, constitutional, and fair, honest principles, but I was afraid that it would not accomplish the end for which it was designed; for the people, generally, had run mad, formerly by the word "reform," and now they are insane by the word "responsible." I fear that the Governor will lose the elections in Canada West. Your pamphlet may, it is true, be a text book to the next Parliament, and keep them right from fear. I was not afraid that you had committed yourself with the Conference and the Church after all the fuss preachers and people made in this respect, (and I am of opinion many would have been glad of it) but I had my serious fears that it would injure your enjoyments in religion, and be a source of temptation that would cause you to leave the ministry. But I hope and pray that one who has stood against all the bribes, baits, and offers made to buy him, when but a boy, will be upheld. Oh! no, no; having Christ in the soul, walking with God, having secret communion and fellowship with the Deity continually, with your talents and qualifications what a treasure to the Church! and the good you would be made the happy instrument of doing! This is true honour, real dignity, true popularity, and eternal wealth. I would rather go to the grave with you dying well, than ever hear that my beloved Egerton was lost to the Church. But, my dear son, you have need to watch, to stand fast, to be strong, and acquit thyself as a man; to have an eye single to the glory of the Lord, to keep the munition, to watch the way. You never will be out of danger till you get to heaven. Be much in secret prayer and communion with your Maker. These simple truths come from a father in his 29th year of his ministry—one that is, in every sense of the word, superannuated, and one that will shortly be known no more.

Hon. R. B. Sullivan (under the *nom de plume* of "Legion") in a series of thirteen letters, with appendix, extending to 232 pages of a pamphlet, replied to Dr. Ryerson's Defence of Lord Metcalfe. These letters were afterwards reviewed by Dr. Ryerson in a series of ten letters, extending to 63 pages of a pamphlet. This review was in the form of a rejoinder, but in it no new principles of government were discussed. Dr. Ryerson's "Defence" proper, was originally published, as was his review of "Legion's" letters, in the *British Colonist*, then edited by the late Hugh Scobie, Esq. The Defence was afterwards published in pamphlet form, and extended to 186 pages.

CHAPTER XLIII.

1841–1844.

Dr. Ryerson Appointed Superintendent of Education.

THE alleged "reward" which Dr. Ryerson was positively asserted to have received from Lord Metcalfe for his memorable Defence of that nobleman, was long a favourite topic on which Dr. Ryerson's enemies loved to dilate. Beyond the fact that the appointment was finally made by the administration of Sir Charles Metcalfe, upon the recommendation of Hon. W. H. Draper, there was nothing on which to base the charge of such a *quid pro quo* having been received by Dr. Ryerson for his notable Defence of the Governor-General.

In point of fact, the appointment was first spoken of to Dr. Ryerson by Lord Sydenham himself, in the autumn of 1841. The particulars of that circumstance are mentioned in detail in a letter written by Dr. Ryerson to T. W. C. Murdoch, Esq., Private Secretary to Sir Charles Bagot, on the 14th January, 1842. Dr. Ryerson said :—

In the last interview with which I was honoured by [Lord Sydenham], he intimated that he thought I might be more usefully employed for this country than in my present limited sphere; and whether there was not some position in which I could more advantageouly serve the country at large. I remarked that I could not resign my present official position in the Church, with the advocacy of whose interests I had been entrusted, until their final and satisfactory adjustment by the Government, as I might thereby be represented as having abandoned or sacrificed their interests; but that after such adjustment I should feel myself very differently situated, and free to do anything which might be beneficial to the country, and which involved no compromise of my professional character; that I know of no such position likely to be at the disposal of the Government except the Superintendency of Common Schools (provided for in the Bill then before the Legislature), which office would afford the incumbent a most favorable opportunity, by his communications, preparation and recommendation of books for libraries, etc., to abolish differences and jealousies on minor points; to promote agreement on great principles and interests; to introduce the best kind of reading for the youth of the country; and the not onerous duties of which office would also afford him leisure to prepare publications calculated to teach the people at large to appreciate, upon high moral and social considerations, the institutions established amongst them; and to furnish, from time to time, such expositions of great principles and measures of the administration as would secure the proper appreciation and support of them on the part of the people at large. Lord Sydenham expressed himself as highly gratified at this expression of my views and feelings; but the passing of the Bill was then doubtful, although His Lordship expressed his determination to get it passed if possible, and give effect to what he had proposed to me, and which was then contemplated by him.

Apart from this statement of the intentions of Lord Sydenham, it is also clear that the determination of Sir Charles Metcalfe to appoint Dr. Ryerson to a position in which he could carry out a comprehensive scheme of Public School Education, in Upper Canada, was come to some time before the question of the difference between Sir Charles Metcalfe and his late Councillors had engaged Dr. Ryerson's attention, and even at a time when his impressions on the subject were against the Governor-General. This conclusion was arrived at by Sir Charles Metcalfe, after full and frequent conversations with Dr. Ryerson on the subject of the University Bill. With a view to avail himself of Dr. Ryerson's knowledge and judgment on that subject, he directed his Private Secretary to address the following note to him on the 18th of December, 1843:—

> One of the many important subjects that at present engages the attention of the Governor-General your Church is particularly interested in, and His Excellency is, therefore, desirous of having the benefit of your opinion upon it. I mean the consideration of the arrangements that are now necessary in consequence of the failure of the University Bill introduced last session. I beg to add that His Excellency will be happy to have some conversation with you on the question to which I allude, the first time you may visit this part of the province.

Not having been able to go at once to Kingston, Dr. Ryerson wrote to the Governor-General in regard to the University Bill. His Secretary replied early in January, saying:—

> When it suits your convenience to come this way, His Excellency will have an opportunity of fully discussing the subject touched upon in your letter.

Dr. Ryerson soon afterwards went to Kingston and saw Sir Charles Metcalfe on the subject. In a letter written to Hon. W. H. Merritt shortly after this interview, Dr. Ryerson said:—

His Excellency's object in desiring me to wait upon him had reference to the University question, on which he intends, with the aid of Mr. Draper, etc., to have a measure brought into the Legislature, which I think will be satisfactory to all parties concerned. I took a day to consider the questions he had proposed. In the meantime I saw Mr. S. B. Harrison and stated to him the opinions I had formed. Of their correctness and importance, and practicability he seemed to be fully satisfied, and urged me to state them to His Excellency.

In a letter from Dr. Ryerson, published in the *Guardian*, and dated 28th October, 1843, the character of Mr. Baldwin's University Bill is thus described:—

It is a measure worthy of the most enlightened government; and is, I have reason to know, entirely the production of Hon. Attorney-General Baldwin. . . In the discussion [on the University question] the authorities of Victoria College have taken no part. We have remained perfectly silent and neutral, not because we had no opinion as to the policy which has been recently pursued in converting a Provincial ministry into a Church of England one * . . because we, as a body, had more to lose than to gain by any proposed plan to remedy the abuse and evil complained of. As a body, we gain nothing by the University Bill, should it become a law; it only provides for the continuance of the small annual aid which the Parliament has already granted; whilst, of course, it takes away the University powers and privileges of Victoria College—making it a College of the University of Toronto. Our omission, therefore, from the Bill would be preferable, as far as we, as a party, are concerned, were it consistent with the general and important objects of the measure. But such an omission would destroy the very character and object of the Bill. As a Provincial measure, it cannot fail to confer unspeakable benefits upon the country. Viewing the measure in this light, the Board of Victoria College have consented to resign certain of their rights and privileges for the accomplishment of general objects so comprehensive and important.

In a written statement on this subject prepared by Dr. Ryerson for this volume he says:—

Towards the close of 1843, Sir Charles Metcalfe determined to prepare and give effect to a liberal measure on the University question—on which subject Hon. Robert Baldwin had proposed elaborate and comprehensive resolutions. Sir Charles Metcalfe sent for me to consult with me on the University question, as I was then connected with one of the colleges. I explained to His Excellency my views, and added that the educational condition of the country at large was deplorable, and should be considered in a system of public instruction, commencing with the Common School and terminating with the

---

* The second resolution adopted by the Victoria College Board, on the 24th October, 1843, says:—the noble and comprehensive objects of the amended Charter have been entirely defeated; and the abrogated, sectarian Charter has been virtually restored, by the partial and exclusive manner in which appointments to that institution have been made, and its affairs managed; apart from the misappropriations of large portions of its funds.

University; being connected and harmonious throughout, and equally embracing all classes without respect to religious sect or political party. Sir Charles was much impressed and pleased with my views, and expressed a wish that I could be induced to give them public effect.

Dr. Ryerson then goes on to say :—I remarked to Sir Charles that Lord Sydenham, a few days before his sudden death, had proposed the same thing to me, and that had he survived a few weeks, I would likely have been appointed, with a view of organizing a system of Elementary Education; but that as Lord Sydenham died suddenly, and as I scorned to be an applicant to Government for any office, I mentioned the fact to no member of the Government. In May, 1842, another gentleman was appointed Assistant to the Provincial Secretary as Superintendent of Education. He was treated as a clerk in the office of the Provincial Secretary, having no clerk himself, and having to submit his drafts of letters, etc., to the Provincial Secretary for approval. [For particulars of this appointment, see p. 347.]

After this interview Dr. Ryerson, on the 26th February, wrote to the Governor-General on the University Question. Mr. Secretary Higginson replied, and at the conclusion of his letter repeated the offer which Sir Charles Metcalfe had made at the close of the year:—The Governor-General is so sensible of the great value of the aid you would bring to the Government in the intellectual improvement of the country, that he anxiously hopes, as suggested. that some arrangement may be devised satisfactory to you to obtain your co-operation; and His Excellency will keep his mind bent on that object, and will be happy to hear any further suggestion from you with a view to its accomplishment.

Early in this month (February, 1844), Dr. Ryerson's appointment as Superintendent of Education has been talked of. His brother John wrote to him on the 6th of March, recalling the fact of that appointment having been the subject of conversation with Sir Charles Bagot and some members of the Cabinet in 1842. Rev. John Ryerson then went on to say:—

You know that when your appointment to the office of Superintendent of Education was talked of in Toronto, in 1842, I was in favour of your accepting the appointment. The appointment that was made I thought a most unwise one, and the late Executive greatly lowered themselves in making it. Whenever I have thought of the thing since, I have felt disgusted with the late Government, that they should have been guilty of such a shameful dereliction of duty and honour as not, at least, to have offered the appointment to you.

In reply to this letter, Dr. Ryerson said :—

As liberal as the Council of Sir Charles Bagot were in many

things, they rejected the application of every Methodist candidate for office. Making appointments upon the principles of party, they must be given only to one of the party; a system of appoiniment which holds out a poor prospect to the Methodist who makes religion first, and party not more than second—especially when he may have as a rival candidate one who makes party everything, and religion nothing.

To this letter Rev. John Ryerson replied :—

I am very well pleased with the idea of your being appointed to the office of Superintendent of Education—an office for which, I think, you are better qualified than any other person in the Province, and an office in which you can be of more service to the Church, and the country generally, than in any other way. . . You say the appointment is not political. . . Yet, is it true, in point of fact, that the appointment is not political? . . Would any person be continued in the office who would not support the Government for the time being? . . Did not Lord Sydenham create this office for the very purpose of connecting the incumbent with the Government, and did he not have you in his mind's eye when he influenced this part of the enactment? . . There is no doubt, however, that in case of the Baldwin Ministry again coming into power, the stool will be knocked from under you. And we should not forget that the success of the Governor-General, in carrying out his contemplated measures, respecting the University, Colleges, etc., depends upon the Parliament; and I have very little expectation of his being able to secure the support of the present Parliament, in connection with every other Ministry but the late ones; and what will be the result of another election, who can tell?

In corroboration of the foregoing statements, Hon. Isaac Buchanan, in a letter to the Editor of this volume dated 24th March, 1883, says :—

Being on the other side of the Atlantic from the fall of 1841 to that of 1843, I was not in circumstances to know to what extent the name of Dr. Ryerson was discussed prior to the appointment of Mr. Murray [in May, 1842]; but I cannot believe that the minds of many who knew him to be the fittest man, could have been otherwise than on Dr. Ryerson. On the contrary, I believe that nothing prevented him being gladly offered the originating of an educational system for Upper Canada—a Province which he knew so well and loved so much —but the most unworthy church prejudices of parties who had influence with the Government of the day, for it was known to be a herculean task which no one could do the same justice to as Dr. Ryerson, and which few men (however great as scholars themseves) could have carried through at all.

Thus from the foregoing statements of Dr. Ryerson, Rev. John Ryerson, and Hon. Isaac Buchanan, the following facts clearly appear:—

1. That Dr. Ryerson was offered the appointment of Superintendent of Education by Lord Sydenham in 1841, and "had he survived a few weeks [Dr. Ryerson] would likely have been

appointed, with a view of organizing a system of Elementary Education " for Upper Canada.

2. That Dr. Ryerson's appointment as Superintendent was "the subject of conversation with Sir Charles Bagot and some members of his Cabinet in 1842."

3. That the failure to appoint Dr. Ryerson was due to the fact that the Cabinet of Sir Charles Bagot—the Governor himself being unable to act—"rejected," as Dr. Ryerson himself stated, "the application of every Methodist candidate for office;" or, as Hon. Isaac Buchanan states : " Nothing prevented [Dr. Ryerson] being gladly offered the originating of an educational system for Upper Canada, but the most unworthy church prejudices of parties who had influence with the Government of the day."

4. That the appointment of Dr. Ryerson by Sir Charles Metcalfe was due to the discussion on the comprehensive scheme of education which took place between Dr. Ryerson and Sir Charles Metcalfe, on the University question, late in 1843.

It may be proper to state that the appointment of Rev. Robert Murray in May, 1842, was a surprise to the public, as the Editor of this volume well remembers, and was, as Rev. John Ryerson states, " a most unwise one." Mr. Murray was a minister of the Church of Scotland at Oakville. He was chiefly known at the time as an anti-temperance writer[*]; but had never been known to have taken any special interest in education. He was intimate with Hon. S. B. Harrison, who owned mills at Bronte, a few miles west of Oakville, where Mr. Harrison resided for some years. To Mr. Harrison, the then leader of the Government, Mr. Murray was indebted, as was then understood, for the appointment.

[*] In September, 1839, Rev. Robert Murray, of Oakville, published a series of lectures on "Absolute Abstinence." From a review of these lectures, by Dr. Ryerson in the *Guardian* of the 18th of that month, I make the following extracts :—

We confess we have seldom read anything so illiberal and sweeping. . . The principle of total abstinence is wholly repudiated, and temperance societies are forbidden an existence. . . But such a work . . shall not by us be allowed to go forth without the accompaniment of our decided reprobation This is not the day for encouragement to be given to the drunkard, nor this the time when a Minister of the Gospel is . . to fill the cup of death and present it to his fellows without an attempt being made to dash it to the ground.

The following extract from the second lecture, relating to the fulfilment of a certain prophecy in the book of Jeremiah, is given by Dr. Ryerson :—

"Many of you, I am persuaded, have witnessed this prophecy fulfilled to the very letter. Have you never seen young men making themselves cheerful with malt liquors, while the young maids were producing the same effect with the blood of the grape? Nor is there the slightest doubt on my mind, that the prophet hailed this event as a special manifestation of the great goodness of God."

It was in reference to the author of such opinions, and the advocate of such views, that Rev. John Ryerson used the language quoted on the preceding page.

Rev. John Ryerson having written to his brother Egerton, asking if the rumour of his appointment as Superintendent of Education was true, Dr. Ryerson replied, on the 3rd April:—

As to the appointment to which you allude, it is but a rumour. No appointment has yet been made. Should it take place, it will not require my removal from Cobourg. Whatever has been proposed to me on that subject, has been proposed with a view of giving body, form, practical character and efficiency, to a system of general education, upon these non-sectarian principles of equal justice which have characterized my life. Nothing political is involved in the appointment—although it was at first proposed to give me a seat in the Council! The education of the people has nothing to do with the dispute with Lord Metcalfe, of which you speak. I do not think it would become me to refuse to occupy the most splendid field of usefulness that could engage the energies of man, because of the dispute which has arisen.

On the 12th April, Dr. Ryerson replied to a letter from Mr. Secretary Higginson, in which he said:—

Dr. Bethune, the Editor of *The Church*, has indeed protested against my proposed appointment;* but I understand that a majority of the members of his own congregation at Cobourg approve of the appointment. Mr. Boswell, M.P.P., and Mr. Sheriff Ruttan (the most influential churchmen in the District), have expressed themselves in favour of it in the strongest and warmest terms; as have Mr. Keefer, of Thorold (who is a magistrate of wealth, leisure and benevolence,—was foreman of the Grand Jury at the late assizes in the Niagara District, and has, at the request of the District Council, consented to superintend the schools in that district); also Dr. Beadle, who is an old resident, and I believe, an American Presbyterian.

Up to this time (April), Dr. Ryerson had decided to take no part in the controversy between Sir Charles Metcalfe and his Councillors, but to devote his energies to the great work of founding a system of education for his native country. Much to the surprise of his friends, and (as he says in his prefatory paper) "without consulting a human being," he felt that it was his duty—after the issue of the manifesto of the Toronto League—to relinquish the work assigned to him, and once more to take up his pen in defence of one whom he believed to be in

---

* On the 19th October, 1844, Dr. Ryerson was appointed Superintendent of Education for Upper Canada. Of his appointment, Rev. Dr. Bethune, Editor of *The Church*, on the 25th October, said:—It was an impolitic and a heartless step, as regards the Church of England in this colony, to raise to the office of Superintendent an individual who has thriven upon his political obliquities, and who owes his fame, or rather his notoriety, to his unquenchable dislike to the National Church. In a moment of danger we can forget the injury; but it must not be thought that we shall sit quietly beneath the wrong.

Rev. Dr. Bethune subsequently changed his opinion of Dr. Ryerson, and, when Bishop of Toronto, referred to him in some of his public utterances in very kind and complimentary terms.

the right, and yet who was left single-handed to meet the storm of popular clamour which had been excited against him by combined and powerful enemies. Dr. Ryerson, therefore, determined to decline the appointment offered to him, and to abide the issue of the impending contest in which he proposed to take a prominent part. In the opening remarks of this memorable "Defence," he said :—

I was about entering upon the peaceful work—a work extensive and varied beyond the powers of the most untiring and vigorous intellect—a work down to this time almost entirely neglected—of devising and constructing (by the concurrence of the people, through their District Councils) a fabric of Provincial common school education—of endeavouring to stud the land with appropriate school-houses—of supplying them with appropriate books and teachers—of raising a wretched employment to an honourable profession—of giving uniformity, simplicity, and efficiency to a general system of elementary educational instruction—of bringing appropriate books for the improvement of his profession within the reach of every schoolmaster, and increased facilities for the attainment of his stipulated remuneration—of establishing a library in every district, and extending branches of it into every township—of striving to develop by writing and discourses, in towns, villages and neighbourhoods, the latent intellect, the most precious wealth of the country—and of leaving no effort unemployed within the limited range of my humble abilities, to make Western Canada what she is capable of being made, the brightest gem in the crown of Her Britannic Majesty. Such was the work about to be assigned to me; and such was the work I was resolving, in humble dependence upon the divine aid, to undertake; and no heart bounds more than mine with desire, and hope, and joy, at the prospect of seeing, at no distant day, every child of my native land in the schoolgoing way; and every intellect provided with the appropriate elements of sustenance and enjoyment; and of witnessing one comprehensive and unique system of education, from the a, b, c, of the child, up to the matriculation of the youth into the Provincial University, which, like the vaulted arch of heaven, would exhibit an identity of character throughout, and present an aspect of equal benignity to every sect, and every party upon the broad basis of our common Christianity.

But I arrest myself from such a work—leave it perhaps for other hands, and the glory of its accomplishment to deck another's brow; and, if need be, to resign every other official situation; and, unsolicited, unadvised by any human being—inwardly impelled by a conviction of what is due to my Sovereign, to my country, to a fellow-man—I take up the pen of vindication, of reasoning, of warning and appeal, against criminations and proceedings of impending evil, which, if they be not checked and arrested, will accomplish more than the infamous ostracism of an Aristides, render every other effort to improve and elevate Canada abortive, and strew in wide-spread desolation over the land the ruins of the throne and its government.

From the date of Mr. Higginson's letter (12th April) until the 7th of September nothing was done in regard to the appointment of a Superintendent of Education. On the latter day, however, Mr. Higginson wrote to Dr. Ryerson as follows :—

We find a great difficulty in making a provisional arrangement for the Educational duties. The University authorities require the immediate services of a mathematical professor, and His Excellency proposes Mr. Murray for the office, which will, it is hoped, be a satisfactory arrangement to all parties; but Mr. Murray cannot hold both positions, even for a time. Under these circumstances it appears to be worthy of consideration, whether your appointment ought not to take place at once, which would not, of course, interfere with your projected visit to Europe in November, when it might be easier to make some proper temporary provision for the performance of your duties during your absence. His Excellency is aware that you were in favour of deferring your nomination until after your return from Europe; and if you should adhere to this opinion, you may, perhaps, be able to suggest some means of meeting the apparent difficulty.

On the 18th September, Mr. Higginson addressed another note to Dr. Ryerson, in reply to one from him, in which he said:

You will have learned from my last note that Sir Charles approved of all your suggestions, except the non-announcement of your appointment. As you see reason to alter your opinion on this point, the difficulty is removed, and you shall be gazetted in the last week of the month, as you propose. I wish, with you, that the College question could be settled in England, if we could only prevail on the contending parties to agree to a case of facts. This might be accomplished, and I am not without hope that some scheme may be devised to which no party will have just ground of objection. I shall write to you upon this subject as soon as anything is determined on.

At this point I resume the narrative which Dr. Ryerson had prepared for this volume in regard to his appointment:—
In September, 1844, a vacancy occurred in the Professorship of Mathematics in the University of Toronto, by the resignation and return to England of Mr. Potter; and as the gentleman who had been appointed to the Education branch of the Secretary's Office, was reputed to be an excellent mathematician, and had high testimonials of his qualification, he applied for the professorship; evidently feeling the anomalousness of his position, and his inability and powerlessness to establish a system of Public School Education.*

The Governor-General appointed him to the Mathematical Professorship, and formally offered the Education Office to me. I laid the official letter containing the offer before the executive authority (a large committee) of my Church, and was advised to accept it. But as I had determined to abide by the decision of the country as to the principles of its future government, on which I was then appealing to it, I determined not to accept of office until I should know the result of that appeal.

After the endorsement of my views by all the constituencies of Upper Canada, with eight exceptions, I felt no hesitation in

* In regard to this appointment, the Hon. Isaac Buchanan, in a letter to the Editor of this volume, dated March, 1883, said:—I was one of the first to see the necessity of our getting Dr. Ryerson to take hold of our Educational system, and I shared the somewhat delicate duty of getting our esteemed friend, Rev. Robert Murray (whom we had got appointed Assistant-Superintendent of Education), to accept a professorship at the Toronto University, when Rev. Dr. Ryerson succeeded to the vacant post in 1844

accepting an office which had been some months before offered to me. The draft of my official instructions, stating the scope and design of my appointment and of the task assigned to me, was written by myself, at the request of Mr. Secretary Daly, afterwards Governor in Australia.

During my connection with the Education Department—from 1844 to 1876—I made five educational tours of inspection and enquiry to educating countries in Europe and the United States. I made an official tour through each county in Upper Canada, once in every five years, to hold a County Convention of municipal councillors, clergy, school-trustees, teachers and local superintendents, and thus developed the School system as the result of repeated inquiries in foreign countries, and the freest consultation with my fellow-citizens of all classes, in the several County Conventions, as well as on many other occasions.

During the nearly thirty-two years of my administration of the Education Department, I met with strong opposition at first from individuals—some on personal, others on religious and political grounds; but that opposition was, for most part, partial and evanescent. During these years I had the support of each successive administration of Government, whether of one party or the other, and, at length, the co-operation of all religious persuasions; so that in 1876 I was allowed to retire, with the good-will of all political parties and religious denominations, and without diminution of my public means of subsistence.

I leave to Dr. J. George Hodgins, my devoted friend of over forty years, and my able colleague for over thirty of these years, the duty of filling up the details of our united labours in founding a system of education for my native Province which is spoken of in terms of strong commendation, not only within, but by people outside of the Dominion.

Note.—It is the purpose of the Editor of this book (in accordance with Dr. Ryerson's oft expressed wish) to prepare another volume, giving, from private letters, memoranda, and various documents, a personal history of the founding and vicissitudes of our educational system from 1844 to 1876 inclusive.

CHAPTER XLIV.
1844–1846.

Dr. Ryerson's First Educational Tour in Europe.

DR. RYERSON left Canada for Europe in November, 1844, on his first educational tour through Europe. He visited and examined into the educational systems of Belgium, France, Italy, Bavaria, Austria, the German States, and Switzerland. He kept a full diary of his travels. Much of it is out of date, but I shall give those portions of it which relate to his personal history, and his impressions of men and things. The epitome of these travels which he had prepared is as follows:—

England.—Scenery of Essex and Kent from the Thames; landing in Holland; its scenery, palaces, school system, schools, universities, museums, principal cities and towns, churches, canals and roads.

Belgium.—From Utrecht to Antwerp—cathedral, churches, schools, museums; Rubens' paintings; Brussels—schools; Hôtel de Ville, etc.; field of Waterloo; Belgian school system; Howard's Model Prison; convent; university buildings.

France.—Journey to Paris; curiosities and peculiarities of Paris; acquaintance with the Protestant clergy; my residence and employments there for three months, to qualify myself to speak as well as write official letters, etc., in the French language.

From Paris to Rome.—Modes of travel; places viewed on the way; Orleans, Loire, Lyons, Rhone, Avignon, Nismes, Montpellier, Arles; antiquities; Marseilles, Genoa, Leghorn, Civita Vecchia, to Rome.

Rome.—Three weeks among its antiquities, palaces, churches, colleges and schools.

June 13th, 1845.—Naples; the peasants on the way from Rome to Naples; Vesuvius, Herculaneum, Pompeii, museums, hospitals, college, schools.

June 20th.—In a steamer from Naples to Leghorn, thence in a hired coach to Pisa and Florence,—beautiful country, and highly cultivated. Employed four weeks in studying the institutions and peculiarities of Florence; no beggars or Jesuits allowed in Florence; the grand Duke a father to his people.

July 19th.—Proceeded to Bologna, re-enter the Papal dominions, and crossed the Appenines; views; a Normal School at Bologna, containing 1,000 pupils, and a Foundling Hospital with 3,000 children.

July 23rd.—Left Bologna in a vetturina, in company with two agreeable gentlemen, a German and an American; Ferrara; reached the Po, where we entered Austrian dominions; when we entered the first custom-house in Italy, the head officers of which did not ask for money, and declined it when offered to them. Crossed the Adige; interesting places; thence to Venice, where I spend four days in that wondrous city.

Bavaria.—In a stage by the Trent, through the Tyrolese Alps to Munich, capital of Bavaria, where I employed nineteen days in visiting its schools and museums, conversing with the professors.

From Munich by stage to Ratisbon; down the Danube to Luiz and Vienna—the most perfect city in its buildings, streets, and gardens I had visited. Gave a day to go down the Danube to the capital of Hungary.

Bohemia.—From Vienna, through Bohemia, by the first train on the then new railroad to Prague; women working on the railroad.

Saxony and Germany.—From Prague to Dresden—visits to schools; thence to Leipsic—visits to public buildings, schools, and university; thence to Halle—Franke's foundations, and other schools; to Wittemburg—Luther and Melancthon.

Prussia.—Berlin, Sept. 8th.—Examination of its various institutions, schools, and its university; Hanover, Cologne, Mayence, Wiesbaden, Frankfort, Strasbourg, Bâle, Zürich; school of M. Fellenburg; Lausanne—Geneva—to Paris.

Episode in my European travels, 1844, etc.—Acquaintance and travel with a Russian nobleman, who becomes a Catholic priest—the Pope's Nuncio at the Court to have the Canadian school regulations for Separate School translated and published in the Bavarian newspapers; also requested me to be the bearer of a medal to Cardinal Antonelli. Rome; presentation to, and interview with, the Pope.

London—February 22nd, 1845.—Started this morning in company with a young Russian nobleman (Dunjowski), for the Continent. We commenced our voyage on the Thames, wending our way amidst shoals of craft of all descriptions. The most prominent object in the river was the new "Great Britain" iron steamer; she seemed to preside Queen of the waters; excelling every other ship, as much in the beauty and elegance of her form, as in the vastness of her dimensions. On our left lay Essex, rising gradually at a distance from the river; the undulating surface presents a high state of cultivation, variegated by stately mansions, farm-houses, and villages. On the right lay Kent, remarkable for its historical recollections. The chalk-hills near Purfleet, the men working in them, also the lime and sand, attracted my attention as a novelty I had never before witnessed. We had a tolerable view of Gravesend, the great thoroughfare of south-eastern England. We passed the ancient village of Tilbury Fort, and Sheerness. We arrived at Holland on Sunday morning (about twenty hours from London), but could not ascend the river to Rotterdam on account of the ice. We therefore steamed to Screvinning, a village on the sea-shore, about three miles from the Hague. There were about fifty fishing-boats lying on the shore, high and dry, with their prows to the sea, as the tide was out. I was struck with their shortness, breadth, strength, and clam-like shape of their bottoms, with a portion in the centre perfectly flat. The speed of these curiously-constructed crafts is considerable; they sail close to the wind; having boards at the side as a substitute for a keel. Our mode of landing was novel. The boats were run aground, when several stout Dutch sailors jumped into the water nearly waist deep, and each took a passenger on his shoulders, soon placing him on *terra firma*. I have travelled in a great variety of ways, but I was never before placed on a man's shoulders, astride of his neck; but in this way I took my leave of the German Ocean. There is not a rock to be seen on the shore; which consists of fine sand thrown up from the sea, and forms a bank about twenty feet high; the highest land on the coast of Holland, forming a ridge from one to three miles wide along the northern coast. Screvinning is principally inhabited by fishermen. The road to the Hague is perfectly straight, level, and smooth, lying between two rows of oak trees, one row of which divides between it and a collateral canal—the accompaniment of every road throughout Holland. At 5 p.m. we went to the French Protestant Church, the place in which the famous Saurin delivered his eloquent discourses. The congregation was thin; my emotions and recollections of Saurin contrasted with the present preacher and congregation. The pulpit was at the side; the form of the church was amphi-theatrical. I noticed old Bibles, and Psalms; the text was Luke xxiii 27-28. A moderate preacher, calm, solemn and graceful; baptisms after the service. Went from the French to the English Church; only fifteen persons were present, including ourselves. I spoke to the clergyman (Mr. Beresford), introducing ourselves, and the object of our mission.

February, 24th.—Went to the British Embassy with Rev. Mr. Beresford; from thence to the Royal Library; and then proceeded to the Chinese and Japanese collection of curiosities; then on to the Gallery of Paintings; some very exquisite. From thence to the residence of the Russian (Greek) clergyman, Chaplain to the Queen of Holland, who kindly shewed us the Queen's private apartments—refined taste, and great magnificence. Then on to a Protestant school, of about 800 poor children, which is supported by subscription. The King is a subscriber to the amount of 1,000 guilders. The teachers consist of a head master and four assistants. No monitors; admirable construction of the seats; excellent order of the children; rod never used—shame, the chief instrument of correction; fine specimens of painting; Scriptures read, and prayers four times a day; salary of the head master 1,000 guilders, and assistants from 300 to 400; books furnished to the children, and all the stationery; an excellent building, well-ventilated, comfortably warm, and perfectly clean; the children remain from six to twelve years of age. Saw the British Chargé d'Affaires, who procured me a general letter of introduction to teachers, etc., throughout Holland, from the Minister of the Interior. Visited the largest and principal free school at the Hague; it contains about eleven hundred children, girls and boys, taught by a head-master, aided by a second, and five other under-masters, and five assistants, lads from fifteen to eighteen years of age. No master ever sits, or has a seat to sit on. Were conducted by the Russian clergymen to the palace again ; the state apartments were splendid indeed; collection of paintings extensive and most select; hot-houses and gardens delightful. Spent the evening with this gentleman, and was deeply interested in his conversation on his own labours, and the customs and character of the Hollanders.

February 25th.—Left the Hague for Leyden. The country perfectly level, looking like a low meadow won from the empire of water by the industry of man, intersected by dykes and canals, interspersed with villas and good private dwellings; here and there a wood of twenty or fifty years growth. On our way we visited Dr. de Rendt, who keeps the most select private school in Holland for the first class of nobility and gentry.

February 26th—Leyden.—Attended the University, and conversed at large with the Inspector of Schools for the district, Mr. Blusse, who gave the history, and explained the whole system of elementary education in Holland. Visited six schools, admirable upon the whole. Three thousand poor children are taught in them, at an expense to the State. Visited the Museum, University, and Library; then proceeded to Haarlem, examined the schoolrooms of the celebrated Mr. Prinsen and afterwards heard his own views of the essentials of a good system of popular education: his remarks were profound and practical. He remarked, "a good system of education consists in the men. Theory and practice make the teacher. The government of the head, how acquired and how exercised. Few books; much exposition." His business for forty-four years has been to make school-masters. Religious instruction, history of his own career and of his own school. Afterwards examined Casler's monument and the church; heard the organ, and proceeded to Amsterdam.

Feb. 27th—Amsterdam.—Had some talk with the Government Inspector of Schools. Visited a school, taught by a Roman Catholic, in which there were 950 children in one room, all quiet, and all attentive. There were four masters and twelve assistants. They have prayers four times a day.

Feby. 28th.—Went to Saundau. Reflections on Peter the Great. Visited the palace, its paintings and museum. Took supper with the Rev. Mr. Jameson, Episcopal clergyman.

March 1st—Belgium.—Proceeded to Utrecht, thence to Antwerp.

March 2nd—Sunday.—Went to the cathedral; paintings by Rubens; earnestness and oratory of the preacher. Went to St. Pauls; the streets very quiet.

March 3rd.—Visited the Jesuit's church, and three schools; phonic and Lancasterian method of teaching. Visited the museum, the city, the view from the tower of the cathedral, statues of Rubens, of the Virgin and Saviour. Proceeded to Brussels; visited three schools; courteously received; arrangements good. Visited the Hotel de Ville; Gobelin tapestry; history of Clovis; abdication of Charles V. Paintings. Reflections.

March 4th.—Spent three hours in examining the field of Waterloo. Went to Nivelles and visited the Normal School for south Belgium; all the arrangements perfect. Returned to Brussels.

March 3rd.—Left Brussels for Ghent; met a commissioner at the railway station, and visited the Government Model School ; the views of the intelligent master were very excellent. Called on a Doctor to whom I had a letter of introduction. He explained the school system of Belgium with great clearness. Visited the prison, the celebrated establishment that excited the admiration of Howard, and after the model of which several prisons in England and America have been built. There were about twelve hundred prisoners—arrangements wonderful, discipline apparently perfect—kept by twenty-eight men. Visited a poorhouse, a benevolent establishment to assist poor old people; about three hundred inmates; grateful feelings, sympathy. Visited the celebrated convent, containing about eight hundred nuns, who come and remain voluntarily ; none, it is said, have ever left. Visited the university buildings—the best I have seen on the continent ; lecture-rooms very fine. Left for Lille, in France; courteously treated at the French custom house.

March 8th—Paris.—On our way from Lille we crossed a branch of the Rhine and the Meuse on the ice; country level and well cultivated; passed Cambray and other towns. Walked to the park, Tuileries, to the Triumphal Arch of Napoleon—a world of magnificence.

March 9th.—Studying French; walked through and around the Palais Royale in the boulevards—noble, splendid.

March 10th—Suuday.—Attended the Wesleyan chapel—about one hundred present—then the English Church; thence to the Madeleine Church—most magnificent; congregation vast; music and chanting excellent beyond description; discourse read; paintings and sculpture fine; church built by Napoleon.

March 11th.—Went to Dr. Grampier, the director of the French Protestant Evangelical Mission, a pious man, an able author, at the head of an excellent institution having missions in Africa as well as in different parts of France.

March 12th.—Removed to new lodgings ; tolerably comfortable.

March 13th.—Went to the university; heard lecture on history ; Attended an evening party at Dr. Grampier's; was introduced to several gentlemen of rank and wealth. Singing and reading of the Scriptures ; much pleased with the party ; as many ladies as gentlemen; assembled at eight, broke up at eleven o'clock.

March 14th.—Heard a most splendid lecture on astronomy from the celebrated Arago; audience very large; the professor had no notes; the subject was light—comets, causes of the changes in the color of the stars, etc., etc.; lecture two hours, much cheered.

March 15th.—Went to the French Chamber of Deputies; saw Guizot. Difference between the French Chamber of Deputies and the British House of Commons struck me—1st. The more ample accommodations for members; 2nd. The little attention which appeared to be paid to the President of the Chamber; 3rd. In the members going to the tribune to speak, and reading their speeches; 4th. In the position of the different officers of the House; 5th. The fine appearance of the servants, and the very convenient accommodations for them; 6th. The superior accommodations for strangers. Heard two lectures at the university, one on mineralogy; lecture good; specimens numerous—the other on electricity; splendid lecturer; fine illustrations.

March 16th—Sunday.—Went to the Oratoire, the principal Protestant place of worship; about seventy catechumens admitted; the dress of the females white. Sermon by Mr. Monod; text—*"Mon fils, donne-moi ton coeur;"* very practical and impressive; the singing peculiarly touching. He is a complete talking machine; read from Lamartine, as did M. Delille beautifully and effectively.

March 17th.—Close application to the study of French all day. Anecdotes at breakfast respecting the pride of Victor Hugo. Walked along the Seine, then across the river into Notre Dame—the Westminister Abbey of Paris—worthy of the appellation.

March 18th.—Pursued my studies till 7 p.m., when I attended a party given by Count Gasparin, M.H.D., who, with his father, is styled the Wilberforce of France—the one being a member of the House of Peers, the other of the House of Deputies. They are regarded as the representatives of Protestantism in the French Legislature. Had a good deal of conversation with Dr. Grampier, on the strength, state, and prospects of Protestantism in France; also the mode of instructing young persons for public recognition in the Church, and admission to the Holy Communion. These catechumens are instructed two or three times a week, for six months, in the evidences, doctrines, and morals of Christianity. They are then examined, and if they shew themselves qualified, they are publicly admitted. The ceremony of admission takes place twice a year, a little before Easter, and at Pentecost. None are admitted under fifteen years of age. Dr. Grampier considered that Protestantism was decidedly gaining upon Popery; and that his own university had been as successful amongst the Catholics, as amongst Protestants, in genuine heart conversions; that whole congregations in some parts of France had embraced Protestantism. His remarks respecting Guizot were interesting and curious. The mother of this great man is now eighty-four years of age, a woman of great vigour of mind; a saint, and nursing-mother in Israel; she offers daily prayers for her son. Guizot is an orthodox Protestant, employed Dr. Grampier to instruct and prepare his children for the Holy Communion, but never goes to church himself, but has told Dr. Grampier that he prays every day. He has been much afflicted in the loss of two wives whom he greatly loved; and also of a son, about twenty-one, a young man of most amiable disposition, great acquirements, talents and virtues. Conversed also with Count Gasparin, who appears to be a truly converted man; spoke of the inefficiency of a formal religion, and the necessity of the religion of the heart. Mentioned the readiness of Roman Catholics to hear Protestant missionaries. He believes that God is about to do a great work in France. The Count is an author; his father has been Minister of the Interior.

March 19th.—Heard lecture on chemistry by Prof. Dumas, one of the ablest chemists of the present day, and a most eloquent lecturer.

March 20th—Good Friday.—Went to hear a Protestant clergyman, one of the most pious and able ministers in Paris; his manner unaffected, eloquent, and impressive. No organ; singing good, all sang. It being a holy day, crowds were everywhere; streets for miles were filled with three, and sometimes four lines of carriages, of all descriptions; the broad sidewalks were literally crowded with pedestrians, forming solid masses from twenty to fifty feet wide, and extending two miles. Order was preserved by soldiers and cavalry, stationed at short distances. I never saw such a moving mass of people, embracing, no doubt, every nation in Europe and America. The attractions of the harlequins, jugglers, hucksters, etc., of all descriptions, surpass imagination. I walked to Napoleon's Arch of Triumph; observed the inscriptions and remarkable figures on that elegant and extraordinary structure; ascended to the top, and there enjoyed one of the most magnificent views I ever beheld, embracing all Paris and its environs for many miles, the day being cloudless; the serpentine Seine, the richly cultivated country, its parks, its gardens, its arcades of trees, its villas, churches, colleges, hospitals, palaces, squares, and monuments, together with the elegant Tuileries, the noble Louvre, the magnificent Champs Elysées, the playing fountains, the spacious streets, and the moving masses of people, presented a scene which for variety, splendour, and I may add, solemnity, could not be excelled by any prospect that might have been commanded on the pinnacle of Jerusalem's Temple. In fifty years the mass of this vast multitude will be numbered amongst a bygone generation; and these stately works of art shall perish. What a worm am I amongst such a multitude! yet I am destined to immortality; have but a few years to live in a probationary state, but an eternity to exist!

March 21st.—Went to the Louvre to see the paintings; about two thousand in number; some large and splendid, many beautiful, and some affecting; none of the paintings from sacred history equal those I have seen in England, Holland, and Belgium, especially in Antwerp.

March 22nd—Easter.—Went to the Oratoire, where a discourse was delivered, and the Lord's Supper celebrated. The preacher, Mons. Venueil, was so impressive and affecting that the greater part of the congregation were in tears several times. Being Easter Sunday, his subject was the resurrection of Christ. He reminded me of Saurin. The spectacle presented of the communicants standing around a long table, and the minister in the midst, at one side, distributing the emblems with suitable addresses, reminded me of pictures I have seen of Christ at the Last Supper. The catechumens who had been received on the previous Sabbath, first partook. I, for the first time, communed with French Protestants, and I felt it good to be there. I attended the Wesleyan chapel; service in French; congregation about seventy-five; preacher (a little Frenchman), quite animated; he quoted many passages of Scripture, chapter and verse, proving the universality of the Atonement. The communion followed.

March 24th, 1845.—This day I am forty-two years of age! My life is more than half gone, at the best. The recollections of the past year are painful and humiliating beyond expression. It has been the least spiritual year of my Christian life. For some weeks past I have been revived in my purposes, devotions and enjoyments. By God's grace, my future life and labours shall be His. I have never before felt so keenly the weakness and depravity of the human heart; nor have I ever felt so deeply the necessity and the sufficiency of the atoning blood of Christ. He is all. All is wretchedness and death without Him.

March 26th.—Worked very hard at my French studies; much discouraged, but must not abandon my efforts to speak a new language. Visited the Pantheon—wondrous structure—a sovereign's pride, and a nation's monument. Visited the tombs of the dead; ascended to the dome—magnificent view; fine paintings in fresco. My impressions will never be effaced. This evening was in company with Count Gasparin and his noble father, and Mr. Monod, one of the principal Protestant ministers in Paris. Mr. Monod spoke strongly of Puseyism; mentioned that he was at a school this week where there were twelve Protestant young ladies sent from England to be educated in a Papal school, and every one of them had become Roman Catholics. He told me there was no intercourse between the Protestants in France and Holland; he considers vital religion is advancing in Holland.

March 27th.—Went to the Observatoire; heard lecture from Mons. Arago; room crowded. Visited the beautiful gardens of the Luxembourg.

March 30th.—Heard Mons. Armand Delille (my host) preach, in Dr. Grampier's Church; impressive service, and a comfortable place of worship outside the gates of the city.

March 31st.—Commenced receiving lessons in French from Mons. O. De Lille; believe I shall soon be able to speak. The name of God be praised for His help and blessing!

April 2nd.—Went to the College (Sorbonne); heard a lecture on Botany.

April 3rd.—Was strongly talked with for not speaking French; Oh, that God would help me; I desire to employ it to His honour. Heard Mons. Arago on Astronomy.

April 5th.—Commenced conversing in French, in good earnest. Heard a lecture by Mons. Depretz on Modern History, in which the eloquent lecturer drew a parallel between France and Rome, and the reign of Augustus and the career of Buonaparte, of course in favour of the latter.

April 6th—Sabbath.—Attended church both morning and evening. Received this morning a present of several books in French from the pious author of them; read the description and reflections upon "Jésus Bénissant les Enfants"; was deeply affected with the remembrance of the manner in which my most pious and excellent mother brought me, in various ways, to the Saviour, when I was a little boy. I owe my all to her, as a divinely-owned instrument, in my early conversion and dedication of myself to God and His Church. She is now on the verge of heaven—may grace strengthen me to meet her there.

April 7th.—Heard four lectures this day on law, chemistry, theology, and philosophy. The lecture on theology was on the authenticity of the Scriptures—comparing the prophecies of Isaiah with the narrative of the evangelists. Lecture on philosophy was devoted to an admirable analysis of Locke.

April 8th.—Attended four lectures at the university at 9 o'clock. "Droit de la nature et des nations," (in the college of France) by Mons. de Postels; "Poésie latine," by M. Patin, the subject was Horace; "Anatomie, physiologie comp. et zoologie," by De Blainville; much of geological theory; "Physique-Acoustique," by M. Despretz; musical instruments.

April 9th.—Have attended five lectures: "Histoire de Littérature Grecque," by Egger; "Histoire Ecclésiastique," by l'Abbe Jager; "Botanique anat. et Physiologie Végétales," by Payer; "Théologie Morale," by l'Abbe Receveur.

April 10th.—Attended three full lectures, and part of a fourth. 1st. Eloquence latine—Cicero, by M. Hanet; 2nd. Histoire Moderne, by M. Michelet, celebrated, (Collége de France) crowded audience and much applause; 3rd. Littérature Grecque; 4th. Histoire Moderne, par M. Sornement. I understood more than I ever did before. The name of the Lord be praised!

April 11th.—Attended five lectures. 1st. Civil Law of France; 2nd. Astronomical Geography; 3rd. Sacred Literature; 4th. Botany and Vegetable Physiology; 5th. French Eloquence. Read French and English with a young collegian. The name of the Lord be praised for the goodness of this day, and for the success of my labours!

April 12th.—Was enabled to make a long recitation this morning, and have attended five lectures at the university. Received a parcel from London, furnishing me with Canadian papers; how refreshing is news from home in a foreign country. Thus has my heavenly Father blest me with all good things.

April 13th—Sabbath.—Attended service at the Chapelle Tailbout; M. Bridel preached on prayer; thence to the Wesleyan Chapel, which was crowded. Read the religious intelligence from Canada. I rejoice to hear of the doings of my brethren; the success of the work in their hands; hope still to labour with them.

April 14th.—Attended four lectures at the university, besides my studies. I pray my heavenly Father to assist and prosper my exertions. I can do nothing without confidence in Him. To the glory of His name shall the fruit of my unworthy labours be consecrated.

April 15th.—Attended the meeting of the "Société des Introits généraux du Protestantisme français." Proceedings commenced with prayer. The meeting was addressed by a number of pasteurs; most of the speakers had notes. Also attended the annual meeting of the "Société des Traités religieux" in the Chapelle Tailbout; report well read; speeches short and energetic.

April 16th.—Attended the Conference of the Protestant Pastors, in the Consistory of the Oratoire. About sixty present; the proceedings opened with prayer. The President then asked the members present to propose the subject of their friendly conversation; several were proposed. Two hours brotherly conversation took place on the duties, powers, and interests of the synod. Most of those who spoke had notes; delivered their sentiments sitting; were asked in order. Attended the twenty-fifth anniversary of the "Société Biblique Protestante;" commenced with prayer and singing. The Count de Gasparin spoke extemporaneously, and with great elegance and ease. A number spoke with energy and force; the last speaker selected passages to show that the Gospel is not incomprehensible to the vulgar, as Romanists assert; also attended the annual meeting of the "Société Evangélique de France;" Chairman read a very short address; several spoke; M. de Gasparin concluded by prayer.

April 17th.—Attended the Conference of Pastors; the proceedings the same as yesterday. At the annual meeting of the "Société des Missions Evangélique;" the chair was occupied by a venerable old man, who seemed, from the allusions made, to be an old friend and supporter of the Society. The aged President read with a feeble voice a short address. There were nine speakers; the last the venerable Monod, who delivered a charge and parting address to the young men who were going to Africa. He embraced in his address the marrow of the Gospel, its power, its promises, its preciousness. The young men were deeply affected, as were all present. He directed them to the power and promises of Christ; assured them of the continued sympathy of the Protestant pastors and churches of France. Another pastor volunteered a few words of address to the young men, on the distribution of religious tracts, and everywhere proclaiming themselves as the missionaries of Christ from France. There was a most affectionate greeting of pastors and old friends. In the Consistory Chapel of the Oratoire de l'Église, there are four busts of ministers whose memory is cherished by their survivors. The names and epitaphs are as follows:—(1) F. Methezet—"Il se repose de ses travaux et ses œuvres le suivent." (2) J. A. Barbant—"Je sais en qui j'ai cru." (3) J. Monod—"Christ est ma vie, et la mort est gain." (4) P. H. Marron—" O mort où est ton aiguillon ! O sépulcre où est ta victoire !"

April 18th.—Attended the annual meeting of the "Société Biblique Françoise et Etrangère." Count de Gasparin in the chair; speeches spirited;

details of report interesting and encouraging. Went to Dr. Grampier's; a social meeting of pastors, to converse and pray on the subject of Missions; subject of conversations; the Missionary work and spirit. From thence went to an annual party, where there was much of fashion and elegance; magnificent tea; peculiar manners; conversed with Mr. Touse, an English clergyman, and with M. G. de Gasparin.

April 19th.—Attended the annual meeting of the "Société pour l'encouragement et l'instruction primairie le protestants de France." The Protestants are not satisfied with the system of mixed schools; they wish to have exclusively Protestant schools. The report was full, explicit, and decided. Several speeches from the principal Protestant ministers, dwelling upon religious instruction in primary schools. Attended the morning conference; nothing new in the proceedings; but there was a marriage; but neither groomsmen nor bridesmaids. Address of the pastor. The bride led by her father, the brother-in-law leading the bridegroom; salutations of friends; the presentation of the wedding-ring by the father of the bride; presentation of a Bible to the newly-married couple; touching offering to the poor.

April 20th—Sabbath.—Went to the "Institution des Diaconesses de l'Église Evangélique de France." The situation is delightful. Several addresses and statements of affairs. Employed the evening in religious study. Witnessed much lightness among certain ministers of the Protestant Reformed Church. The prevalent views here respecting the sanctity of the Sabbath are very different from those which prevail either in England or Canada.

April 25th.—Visited several schools of the Protestant dissenters in Paris —called "Ecoles Gratuités." The first was the Female Normal School, containing nineteen pupils. I was impressed with the admirable arrangement of the school and its appliances, as well as the taste and neatness of the botanical garden. The dormitory was plain, neat, and airy; in it on the wall were pasted the following passages of Scripture, viz., Psalms xv. 5., Amos iv. 12. There were two schools for boys and girls attached to the institution, but these several departments constitute one school—all Roman Catholic children taught by Protestants, on strictly Protestant principles. The priests make no opposition. People independent of the priests.

April 26th.—Pursued my studies with encouraging success. Visited M. Toase who gave me useful information.

April 27th—Sabbath.—Heard M. Toase; went afterwards to the Madeleine; building magnificent; passed through the garden of the Tuileries; a paradise of a place; shades; walks; grass-plots; lakes; fountains; fish; statues; amusements; but, alas! what profanation of the Sabbath!

April 30th.—Went to Versailles; grand and little Trainon, magnificent.

May 1st.—The King's birthday and fête; illuminations; fireworks; appearance of the King Louis Philippe on the balcony of the palace. The Tuileries; the Champs Elysées; booths; fêtes; riding; examples of physical strength; girls riding; jumping; great multitudes; good order preserved; Church of St. Roch; music; saw Lord Cowley; his kindness in lending me his ticket for the House of Peers; getting recommendations from the Government; documents on education, etc.

May 3rd.—Visited Notre Dame; Hôtel-Dieu; Chambre des Pairs; Chapelle; gallery of paintings; nuns; few peers present; old men; session short; not imposing; fine paintings in the Chapel; admirable selection in the gallery; answer from Lord Cowley.

May 8th.—Have devoted several days to study, nothing worthy of remark.

May 9th.—Left Paris for Lyons; on the top of the diligence on the railroad to Orleans, level, fertile country; passed through Orleans; saw Cathedral; Jeanne d'Arc; Loire; historical recollections.

May 12th.—Examined the curiosities of the town; rough-looking people; homage to the Virgin; "Hôtel du Midi;" view from the Observatoire; Roman antiquities.

May 13th.—Left Lyons in a steamer for Avignon; confluence of the Rhone and Soane; varied, beautiful, and sometimes bold; romantic scenery on the Rhone. Vienne; vineyards; wines; St. Villars; Pontius Pilate; river very narrow and crooked; Roch de Tain; Hannibal; vista of the valley of the Isère; Alps; Valence; St. Pay; Peroy; wine of St. Peroy; Castle of Crupol; Drôme; Montilvart; Viviers; rocks; canal; Ardiche; "Paul St. Esprit," great curiosity; Roquemon; women carrying stones; noble and extensive work on the banks of the river, and in the erection of new bridges.

May 14th.—Avignon; wall; view from the tower of the Cathedral; visit it; paintings very beautiful; palace; inquisition; left Avignon for Beaucaire; river uninteresting; thence to Nismes by railway; poor country; asses and mules used; women shoeing them; people athletic, but very passionate and quarrelsome.

May 15th.—Examined the antiquities of Nismes; truly wonderful and interesting.

May 16th.—Arrived at Montpellier; narrow streets; Citadel Fountaine; promenade; Jardin des Plantes; Mrs. Temple's tomb; read a passage from Young's Night Thoughts there; Bannia Palm; Ecole de Médicine; Cathedral; Museum of Painting.

May 17th.—Returned to Nismes; revisited the Amphitheatre and the Maison Carée; beautiful in proportion and execution. Returned to Beacaise; visited the Castle; very high, and remarkably strong; crossed the river to examine a castle, now a prison; historical recollections of both castles. Visited the Church dedicated to St. Martha; curious front. Visited St. Martha's Tomb; felt awful in the grim darkness, rendered barely visible by the flickering lamp; inscription at the head of the Tomb: "Solicita Noritubatur; singular well; old women in the Church; the Image of St. Martha, with its knees and feet worn by kissing. Procceded to Cette; the Amphitheatre is by no means as well preserved as that of Nismes, but larger; the walls immeasurably thick. Saw the remains of a Roman theatre; its curious workmanship attests its former magnificence.

May 18th—Sabbath.—Back at Marseilles, but no Sabbath here; theatres all open, and crowds pressing into them; saw some curious handbills about the Pope granting indulgences; holy water in the churches; children using it.

May 20th.—Coast from Marseilles, bold, varied, picturesque; barren rocks; vineyards and olive trees; entrance into the bay and harbor of Genoa very beautiful.

May 21st.—In Genoa the streets are very narrow; the buildings very high; the city clean; all preferable to Paris; left for Leghorn.

May 22nd.—At Leghorn, visited Smollet's tomb. At Pisa, saw the leaning tower; baptistry, etc.

May 23rd.—Entered Rome at sunset. We could see St. Peter's more than fifteen miles off.

May 25th.—Commenced visiting the churches of the city. 1. Temple of Antonius; column to his honour, and his victories inscribed. 2. Church of St. Ignazia; tomb of Gregory XV. 3. Pantheon of Agrippa—built 22 B.C., of Oriental granite brought from Egypt. The obelisk is from the Temple of Isis. 4. In the second chapel to the left, Raphael was buried in 1520. He gave orders to his scholar Lorenzetto to make the statue of the Virgin, behind which he is buried. It is ornamented by gold and silver offerings of trinkets, rings, and bracelets. 5th. Piazza della Minerva—formerly Temple of Minerva, another of Isis, another of Serapis, now a church obelisk. Statue of Michael Angelo. 6. Roman College. 7. Palace of Prince Doria. In the picture gallery I was especially struck by a beautiful painting of the Holy Family; also Titian, by himself, his last work. Visited the Church of St. Joseph—under which was the Mamertine Prison, where St. Paul was confined. Arch of Titus. The Church of St. Peter's in Vincola has twenty pillars from the Diocletian Bath, two of them Oriental granite. Michael Angelo's last work is a marble figure of Moses, with the two tables of the law under his right arm,—magnificent. There are also twelve magnificent marble figures of the twelve apostles.

May 26th.—Church of St. Maria, in Villicella; festival in honour of St. Fillippo. High mass was celebrated in presence of the Pope and cardinals. I stood near the altar, and had a good view of them all. The Pope passed twice within a few feet of me; was carried in a splendid chair by twelve men, who passed up the aisle into the vestry. He is eighty years of age, good looking and walked with a firm step; he blessed the people as he passed. The cardinals kissed the Pope's hand, the priests his toe or foot. Next went to the Church of the Jesuits, where there is a splendid representation of Religion, giving the foot to Protestant heresy in the person of Luther and Calvin.

June 1st—Sunday.—Went to the Roman College to the worship of the congregation of Jesuits. In another hall a discourse was being delivered to the pupils, some four hundred being present. At St. Paul's, was shown the house in which St. Paul resided during two years a prisoner in Rome. Witnessed an extraordinary but most impressive service in the celebrated Amphitheatre, where, it is said, 200,000 Christians were put to death in two centuries.

June 6th.—During the last five days have been studying Italian, and revisiting some of the more remarkable remains of Roman antiquities, colleges, and schools; also a prison for women, well managed and arranged; much attention is paid to their religious instruction.

June 10th—Sabbath.—Visited the Churches of St. John, and Maria Maggiore; visited one of the most important and interesting schools of the Christian Brothers; 400 pupils taught by four masters; 4,000 pupils are taught by the same fraternity. Visited also the College of Propaganda; was shewn by the Rector over the whole establishment; it is wonderful, the influence of which is felt in all lands; he shewed me the oldest and most curious MSS. I ever saw.

June 14th.—Arrived at Naples, after a stage journey of thirty hours. Peasants very lazy; passed the murdered body of a man. As we advanced we observed a great change in the manners and habits of the people.

June 15th—Sabbath.—Vesuvius was splendid last night, to a degree, I understand that has not been seen since 1839. Visited the Poor House; the establishment accommodates upwards of 2,000.

June 16th—Visited Pompeii, and Herculaneum, and Vesuvius. Met with the Jesuit Prefect of Educational Institutions; and a Priest from the United States. From the Jesuit I obtained a full account of the educational institutions in Naples; from the American Priest much useful information on various subjects. Ascended Mount Vesuvius; when we reached the summit my face was burnt; lava falling all round us—God of dreadful majesty, who art a "consuming fire!" Beheld here the setting sun—God of glory who art "the light of the world!" Descending we reached our hotel about midnight; thank God for His protection and mercy.

June 18th—Went to the museum to examine the antiquities of Herculænum and Pompeii. Left for Leghorn.

June 20th—Pisa.—Took a coach with two other gentlemen; a beautiful ride of eight hours along the valley of the Arno, from Pisa to Florence. The best cultivated country, and the best looking peasantry I have ever seen; the river walled, and the bridges fine.

June 24th.—The celebration of the Feast of John the Baptist, commenced by a chariot race, after the fashion of the chariots in the games of the Greeks and Romans.

June 26th.—The Grand Duke of Tuscany will not allow Jesuits in his dominion; but in Naples the Jesuits are all powerful—confessors to the king and royal family—and that even an artist cannot get employment who has not a Jesuit for a confessor.

July 19th.—This day I leave Florence after four weeks of study, and acquaintance with its schools, arts and science.

July 20th—Bologna.—Crossed the Appenines, and had a view of the Adriatic. Visited the Scoules Normali, containing upwards of 1,000 pupils.

July 23rd.—Left Bologna in a vetturina for Ferrara, in company with a German and two Americans. Ferrara is fallen, forsaken, solitary.

July 25th.—Crossed the Po in a curious ferry-boat, and entered the Lombardo-Venetian dominions of Austria. Here I met with the first instance in Italy of money not being asked by Custom House officers; every part of the proceeding indicated dignity unknown to the Papal States. Crossed the Adige by a ferry; passed through Monselice, near which is the town and castle of Este. North of Este is Argna, or Argnota, where Petrarch retreated, dwelt, and died ! Next passed through Battaglia and Padua ; on the left is Abano, the birth-place of Livy. Gothic laggia, vast hall, said to be the largest unsupported roof in the world, built by Frate Giovanni; bust and tomb of Livy.

July 30th.—Came on to Venice, where we spent four days; a wondrous city.

August 4th.—Have been in Munich nineteen days; visited its museum, churches, elementary schools, &c., &c.; conversed with many professors.

August 25th.—Left Munich; passed through Landsport; arrived at Ratisbon; visited Valhalla; descended the Danube to Liuz.

Sept. 3rd.—The city of Vienna is the most perfect I have seen, in its buildings, streets, gardens, etc.; it would furnish me with materials for a volume were I a writer of travels.

Sept. 4th.—Came through Bohemia by the first railroad train from Vienna to Prague, where I remained two days. The houses in the villages through which we passed, were all of one story, thatched with straw; the peasants wear skins, and women work on the railroads.

Sept. 5th.—Left Prague in a small steamer for Dresden; visited Dr. Blockman's school; every appurtenance; very complete schools, both public and private. From thence on to Leipsic; visited all the principal buildings; visited the Burgher school, designed for the education of the middle ranks, and those of the upper ranks, if desired.

Sept. 15th and *16th.*—From Leipsic went on to Halle (in Prussia); visited the schools on Franke's Foundations; several farms belong to the establishment; there are six schools, rather small; there are free scholars, orphans, and money scholars. Went to the University.

Sept. 17th—Wittemburg.—This morning visited the church in which Luther first preached the doctrines of the Reformation, and where both Luther and Melancthon are buried; I ascended the pulpit, and there prayed that the spirit of the Reformation might more abundantly rest upon me; I experienced strong sensations on entering the church; it is a plain building with a few monuments; the statue (bronze) of Luther is in the market-place, with the words :—

"Ist's Gottes Werk, so wird's bestehen;
Ist's Menschen, so wird's untergehen."

We then visited the house in which Melancthon lived, now being repaired; Luther's chamber in the convent; his study, with his chair, table, and stove; his library, his bed-room; at his table I knelt and prayed, and renewed my covenant with my God. I afterwards visited the place where Luther burnt the Pope's Bull.

Sept. 18th—Berlin.—Employed the day in visiting the great schools of this magnificent city: Frederick William Gymnasium, Dorothean Higher City School, Royal Red School, embracing both the classical and scientific departments; went over the establishment.

Sept. 19th.—Visited the University and Picture Gallery; went through all the apartments of the City Trade School; the collection of apparatus and specimens to carry out the course of instruction is perhaps the most complete in Prussia, in schools of this class.

Sept. 20th.—Potsdam—a magnificent place; went into the Court, and visited several of the rooms of the Royal Military School—a noble establishment; visited the Normal School; witnessed the teaching of two of the pupil-teachers,—both used the blackboard, and both appeared thorough masters of what they were teaching, using no books,—other pupil-teachers were looking on; never saw a finer class of young men.

Sept. 23rd.—Berlin. Dined with the British Ambassador, and had an interview with the Prussian Minister of Public Instruction; witnessed the semi-annual parade of the Prussian army—more than 10,000 men; saw also the King of Prussia and the Empress of Russia.

Sept. 24th.—Hanover. Passed through several townships; visited the Palace; saw the gold and silver plate, much of which belonged to former British Sovereigns; visited Herrenhausen, favourite residence of George I. and II. of England.

Sept. 28th.—Cologne. Visited Cathedral and Churches; saw the tomb of Charlemagne, and the house in which Rubens was born.

Oct. 1st.—Bonn. Saw the University buildings; saw the great Catholic Normal School, at Bright.

Oct. 2nd.—Mayence. Ascended the Rhine from Bonn,—embracing all the magnificent scenery of this celebrated river.

Oct. 3rd.—Visited Wiesbaden, capital of Hesse-Cassel; went to Frankfort; visited Burgher School there, 700 children. Birth-place and monument of Gœthe.

Oct. 5th.—Strasburg. Left Frankfort; passed through Darmstadt; heard two sermons in French, and one in German; visited the magnificent Cathedral, and Normal School.

Oct. 7th.—Zurich. Came to Bâle yesterday; arrived here this morning; visited the great Cantonal Industrial School—noble building.

Oct. 8th.—Cargon. Obtained much information from the director of the Gymnase, Real and Higher Burgher School here.

Oct. 9th.—Berne. Travelled through a mountainous and picturesque country to Papiermühle; walked three miles to the celebrated school of M. de Fallenberg; had the whole system explained—gymnasium, real, intermediate, poor, and limited to the number of thirty; dined at the Agricultural School,—situated on a gentle hill, in the midst of the valley of Switzerland, surrounded by mountains,—I have been abundantly repaid in spending a whole day in surveying such an establishment.

Oct. 11th.—Lausanne. Fine view of the Alps; visited the garden where Gibbon finished his History on the rise and fall of the Roman Empire.

Oct. 12th.—Geneva. Arrived here in heavy rain; attended three services; visited the tomb of Sir H. Davy; had a fine view of Mt. Blanc; left for Paris.

CHAPTER XLV.
1844–1857.

EPISODE IN DR. RYERSON'S EUROPEAN TRAVELS.—POPE PIUS IX.

ONE of the many episodes in my European travels which I have been requested by many to narrate led to my presentation to Pope Pius IX., and is as follows:—

On my arrival in England on my first educational tour, near the end of 1844, I was invited to a Christmas dinner party at the house of an English clergyman, where I was introduced to a young Russian nobleman, by the name of Dunjowski, who had attended lectures in several German universities, and came to England to learn the English language, in which he soon became a proficient. During his residence in England he became acquainted with a number of distinguished men, noblemen and others; among whom were the late Rev. Dr. Chalmers. This young Russian nobleman, having learned that I was on a tour of investigation of the educational institutions of Europe, proposed before the close of the evening to join me in investigating the educational institutions of western and central Europe, with a view to his writing an account of them on his return to St. Petersburg. I accepted his proposal; and in the course of a few weeks we commenced our tour through Holland and Belgium to Paris, of which some account will be found in the extracts from my Journal in the preceding Chapter.

At Paris my Russian friend conceived the idea of attending another course of lectures on some branch of Roman law at Tubigen. We parted, but he changed his mind, and instead of attending an additional course of lectures in a German university, he proceeded to Rome. A few weeks after my arrival there, I felt a tap on my shoulder at the dinner table, and, on looking up, I recognized my young Russian friend, who was already speaking Italian, with as much fluency as he had spoken English, French, and German, when we parted at Paris six weeks before.

We renewed our travels together, after having completed our tour of Rome, with its antiquities and institutions; we proceeded to Naples by stage, where we spent several days in examining its College of Nobles and other educational institutions, including its antiquities of Herculaneum and Pompeii, Vesuvius, etc. In the College of Nobles we met an American Priest, who was President of the Roman Catholic College at Georgetown, near Washington, and invited him to take a seat in our carriage the next day on an excursion to Herculaneum and Pompeii. In the course of the day a religious discussion took place between the American Priest and the Russian, who was very fond of controversy. I took no part in it, but I thought the Priest had rather the best of it. The result was, my Russian friend was persuaded to go into a house of retirement near Rome, and devote some weeks to solitary prayer, fasting, and meditation. I never afterwards saw him or heard from him for eleven years, though I remonstrated with him, and wrote him from Florence, entreating him to reconsider what he was doing; but he said that what I spoke and wrote rather confirmed him in his course, than diverted him from it.

When making my third educational tour on the Continent of Europe, I was, with my daughter, at Munich, in Bavaria, about the beginning of 1857, and while at dinner at our hotel, I felt two hands placed upon my shoulders; on looking up, I recognized, notwithstanding his present dress, my old friend, Dunjowski, who embraced and kissed me as a brother. After dinner we retired to the parlour, and talked over the past. I asked him what he had been doing these eleven years, how he had become transformed from a Russian nobleman, scholar, and lawyer, into a Roman Catholic priest, in full canonicals. He told me that after we separated at Naples, eleven years before, he went into a house of retirement at Rome, and by prayer, fasting, and meditation, devoted himself to God and His Church, without reserve of rank, fortune, or country; that he had ultimately decided to be a Catholic; that he had studied theology four years in France; that he had been appointed a Missionary to the North, and had been some years a Missionary to the Lapps, and had preached before the Kings of Denmark and Sweden; that he was then Missionary Apostolic to all the Catholic Missions in Europe and America, north of latitude 60; and that he might yet visit Canada. This extraordinary man had mastered the languages of the various countries in which he hed travelled and laboured, and gave my daughter specimens of his writing in twenty-seven different languages. I never knew a man of more disinterestedness, more devotion, and singleness of purpose, than Mr. Dunjowski. He was up and out at prayers to his church before five o'clock, in the terribly cold mornings the last of December and the beginning of January, in one of the coldest capitals of Europe.

On the other hand he asked me what I had been doing during the last eleven years. I replied that I had devised and brought into operation a system of public instruction, which had been approved by the Government and Legislature, and by the people at large, whom I had consulted, in the several counties of Upper Canada. He wished to know what I had done in respect to his co-religionists. I shewed him the provisions of our School Act, and the Regulations founded upon it in respect to Roman Catholics in Upper Canada. My Russian friend thought that nothing could be more just and fair than these clauses of the law and regulations, and requested permission to shew them to the Pope's Nuncio (an Italian Archbishop), at the Court of Bavaria. The Pope's Nuncio was so pleased with them, that he requested the loan of them until he got them translated into German, and published in the Bavarian newspapers, to shew how fairly the Roman Catholics were treated under the Protestant Government of Upper Canada The Pope's Nuncio afterwards desired me to call upon him; and during the interview, after some complimentary remarks, requested me to be the bearer of a medal from the King of Bavaria to Cardinal Antonelli, at Rome. I readily accepted the honour and the office, and found the Pope's arms and seal a ready passport when I got in a tight place among the avaricious Italian Custom House officers.

Dr. Ryerson thus describes his interview with Pope Pius IX.:

On my arrival at Rome I duly delivered my letters of introduction, and the King of Bavaria's medal to Cardinal Antonelli who received me with the utmost courtesy, offered me every facility to get pictures copied by my own selection at Rome, and proposed, if acceptable to me, to present me to His Holiness the Pope. I readily accepted the attentions and honours offered me; but told the Cardinal that I had a young daughter, and young lady companion of hers, whom I should wish to accompany me; His Excellency said, " By all means."

On the day appointed we went to the Vatican. Several foreign dignitaries were waiting in an ante-room for an audience with the Pope, but the Methodist preacher received precedence of them all. "Are you a clergyman?" asked the Chancellor, who conducted me to the Pope's presence; "I am a Wesleyan minister," I replied. "Ah! John Wesley. I've heard of him," said the Chancellor, as he shrugged his shoulders in surprise that a heretic should be so honoured above orthodox sons of the Church. We were then in due form introduced to the Pope, who received us most courteously, and stood up and shook hands with me and with whom I conversed (in French) for nearly a quarter of an hour; during the conversation His Holiness thanked me for the fairness and kindness with which he understood I had treated his Catholic children in Canada. Before the close of the interview, His Holiness turned to the young ladies (each of whom had a little sheet of note paper in their hands) and said, "My children, what is that you have in your hands?" The girls curtsied respectfully, and told His Holiness that they brought these sheets of paper in hopes His Holiness would have the condescension and kindness to give them his autograph. He smiled, and wrote in Latin the benediction: "Grace, mercy, and peace from God our Father, and Jesus Christ our Lord," and then kindly gave them also the pen with which it was written.

Thus ended our interview with Pope Pius IX., of whose unaffected sincerity, candor, kindness, and good sense, we formed the most favourable opinion, notwithstanding the system of which he is the head.

Dr. Ryerson also mentions another interview which he had:—

In addition to my letters of introduction to Cardinal Antonelli, my Russian friend, Dunjowski, gave me a letter of introduction to Father Thyner, the keeper of the Archives at Rome, and an intimate personal friend of the Pope; in which letter he referred to the school systems of Upper Canada, in reference to Roman Catholics. Father Thyner wished to see the Canadian school law and regulations, and shewed and explained them to the Pope, who afterwards spoke of their fairness and kindness, in my interview with His Holiness.

Father Thyner was once Librarian to the King of Prussia, and being a Roman Catholic, he went to Rome, where his varied learning and high character soon obtained him a high position at the Vatican. He, as well as the Pope, in his early life was an enemy of the Jesuits, and was regarded by them as such throughout his whole life.

I had a severe illness of some weeks at Rome, during which Father Thyner visited me almost daily, but never said one word to me on the grounds of difference between Roman Catholics and Protestants.

During my last visit to England in 1876-7, I spent part of a day at the residence of the Rev. Wm. Arthur, A.M., who showed me the works in his library from which he had derived the principal materials of his masterly work on *The Pope and The People*. Among other works he shewed me some volumes written by Father Thyner, containing an account of the proceedings of the Council of Trent. "Why," I said, "I know Father Thyner personally," and related my acquaintance with him. Mr. Arthur said in reply, "This work is the chief source of my knowledge of the proceedings of the Councils of Trent;" and added, "Father Thyner having determined to publish an account (which had never before been published) of this Council, was forbidden to do so, and banished, or driven from Rome, when he went to Hungary, and published his great work on the Councils."

I have observed in the papers, that Father Thyner died in Hungary a year or two since. He was a man of profound learning, of fervent devotion, of great moderation in his views, of uncompromising integrity. I visited him in his convent, near Rome, and drank the juice of the grape grown in his own garden, and pressed by his own hand.

CHAPTER XLVI.

1844—1876.

Ontario School System.—Retirement of Dr. Ryerson.

ALTHOUGH I hope to be able to prepare a record of the private and personal history of the founding of our System of Public Education, and of the vicissitudes through which it passed, as requested by Dr. Ryerson (page 350), yet in this chapter I give a brief outline of the principles of that System.

After his educational investigations in Europe, in 1844-1846, Dr. Ryerson prepared an elaborate Report on a "System of Public Instruction for Upper Canada," which was published in 1846. In that report he says:—

By Education, I mean not the mere acquisition of certain arts, or of certain branches of knowledge, but that instruction and discipline which qualify and dispose the subjects of it for their appropriate duties and appointments in life, as Christians, as persons in business, and also as members of the civil community in which they live.

A basis of an educational structure adapted to this end should be as broad as the population of the country; and its loftiest elevation should equal the highest demands of the learned professions; adapting its gradation of schools to the wants of the several classes of the community, and to their respective employments or professions, the one rising above the other—the one conducting to the other; yet each complete in itself for the degree of education it imparts; a character of uniformity, as to fundamental principles, pervading the whole: the whole based upon the principles of Christianity, and uniting the combined influence and support of the government and the people.

The branches of knowledge which it is essential that all should understand, should be provided for all, and taught to all; should be brought within the reach of the most needy, and forced upon the attention of the most careless. The knowledge required for the scientific pursuit of mechanics, agriculture, and commerce, must needs be provided to an extent corresponding with the demand, and the exigencies of the country; while, to a more limited extent, are needed facilities for acquiring the higher education of the learned professions.

With a view to give a summary sketch of Dr. Ryerson's exposition of the system of Public Instruction which he desired to establish, I give the following additional extracts from his first Report. After-combating the objection which then existed in some quarters to the establishment of a thorough system of primary and industrial education, commensurate with the population and wants of the country, he remarked:—

The first feature then of our Provincial System of Public Instruction, should be universality. The elementary education of the whole people must, therefore, be an essential element in the legislative and administrative policy of an enlightened and beneficent government. Nor is it less important to the efficiency of such a system that it should be practical than that it should be universal. The mere acquisition, or even the general diffusion of knowledge, without the requisite qualities to apply that knowledge in the best manner, does not merit the name of education. Much knowledge may be imparted and acquired without any addition whatever to the capacity for the business of life. . . History presents us with even University Systems of Education (so called) entirely destitute of all practical character; and there are elementary systems which tend as much to prejudice and pervert, not to say corrupt, the popular mind as to improve and elevate it.

The state of society, then, no less than the wants of our country, requires that every youth of the land should be trained to industry and its practice, whether that training be extensive or limited.

Now education, thus practical, includes religion and morality; secondly, the development to a certain extent of all our faculties; thirdly, an acquaintance with several branches of elementary knowledge.

By religion and morality, I do not mean sectarianism in any form, but the general truth and morals taught in the Holy Scriptures. Sectarianism is not morality. To be zealous for a sect and to be conscientious in morals are widely different. To inculcate the peculiarities of a sect and to teach the fundamental principles of religion and morality are equally different.

I can aver, from personal experience and practice, as well as from a very extended inquiry on this subject, that a much more comprehensive course of biblical and religious instruction can be given than there is likely to be opportunity for in elementary schools, without any restraint on the one side, or any tincture of sectarianism on the other—a course embracing the entire history of the Bible, its institutions, cardinal doctrines and morals, together with the evidences of its authenticity.

With the proper cultivation of the moral feelings, and the formation of local habits, is intimately connected the corresponding development of all the other faculties, both intellectual and physical. The great object of an efficient system of instruction should be, not the communication of so much knowledge, but the development of the faculties. Much knowledge may be acquired without any increase of mental power; nay, with even an absolute diminution of it. (See Chapter li.)

In founding the System of Public Instruction, Dr. Ryerson wisely laid down certain great principles which he believed to be essential to the success of his labours. These general principles may be thus summarized: 1. That the machinery of education should be in the hands of the people themselves, and should be managed through their own agency; they should, therefore, be consulted in regard to all school legislation. 2. That the aid of the Government should only be given where it can be used most effectually to stimulate and assist local effort in this great work. 3. That the property of the country is responsible for, and should contribute towards the education of the entire youth of the country, and that as a complement to this, "compulsory education" should necessarily be enforced. 4. That a thorough and systematic inspection of the schools is essential to their vitality and efficiency. These, with other important principles, Dr. Ryerson kept steadily in view during the whole thirty-two years of his administration of the school system of Ontario. Their judicious application has contributed largely, under the Divine blessing, which he ever sought, to the wonderful success of his labours.

Notwithstanding the zeal and ability with which Dr. Ryerson had collected and arranged his facts, analyzed the various systems of education in Europe (largely in Germany) and America, and fortified himself with the opinions of the most eminent educationists in those countries, yet his projected system for this province was fiercely assailed, and was vehemently denounced as embodying in it the very essence of "Prussian despotism." Still, with indomitable courage he persevered in his plans, and at length succeeded in 1846 in inducing the legislature to pass a School Act which he had drafted. In 1849 the Provincial administration personally favourable to Dr. Ryerson's views went out of office, and one unfavourable to him came in. The Hon. Malcolm Cameron, a hostile member of the cabinet—although he afterwards became a personal friend of Dr. Ryerson—having concocted a singularly crude and cumbrous school bill, aimed to oust Dr. Ryerson from office, it was (as was afterwards explained) taken on trust, and, without examination or discussion, passed into a law. Dr. Ryerson at once called the attention of the Government (at the head of which was the late lamented Lord Elgin) to the impracticable and un-Christian character of the bill, as under its operation the Bible would be excluded from the schools. Rather than administer such an Act, Dr. Ryerson tendered the resignation of his office to the Government. The late Honourable Robert Baldwin, C.B., Attorney-General (the Nestor of Canadian politicians, and a truly Christian man), was so convinced of the justness of Dr. Ryerson's views and remonstrance, that he took the unusual course of advising His Excellency to suspend the operation of the new Act until Dr. Ryerson could prepare a draft of a bill on the basis of the repealed law, embodying in it, additional to the old bill, the result of his own experience of the working of the system up to that time. The result was that a law passed in 1850, adapted to the municipal system of the Province, so popular in its character and comprehensive in its provisions and details, that it is still (in a consolidated form) the principal statute under which the Public Schools of Ontario are maintained.

The leading features of that measure may be briefly summed up under the four following heads :—

1. The machinery of the system was mainly adapted to the circumstances of Upper Canada, from the school laws of the Middle (United) States.

2. The method of supporting the schools by a uniform rate upon property was adopted from the New England States.

3. The Normal and Model schools (established in 1847), were projected after those in operation in Germany.

4. The school text-books were originally adapted from the series then in use in Ireland, and acceptable to both Protestants and Roman Catholics.

In 1850, Dr. Ryerson, while in England, made preliminary arrangements for establishing the Library, and Map and Apparatus Depository in connection with his department; and in 1855 he established Meteorological Stations in connection with the County Grammar Schools. In this he was aided by Colonel (now General) Lefroy, R.E., for many years Director of the Provincial Magnetical Observatory, at Toronto. Sets of suitable instruments (which were duly tested at the Kew Observatory) were obtained, and in 1855, the law on the subject having been amended, twelve stations were selected and put into efficient working order. In 1857 Dr. Ryerson made his third educational tour in Europe, where he procured at Antwerp, Brussels, Florence, Rome, Paris, and London an admirable collection of copies of paintings by the old masters; statues, busts, etc., besides various articles for an Educational Museum in connection with the Department. In 1858-60, Dr. Ryerson took a leading part in the discussion in the newspapers, and before a committee of the legisture, in favour of grants to the various outlying universities in Ontario, chiefly in terms of Hon. Robert Baldwin's University Bill of 1843. He maintained that "they did the State good service," and that their claims should be substantially recognized as colleges of a central university. He deprecated the multiplication of universities in the province, which he held would be the result of a rejection of his scheme. In consideration of his able services in this contest, the University of Victoria College conferred upon him the degree of LL.D. in 1861.

In 1867 he made his fourth educational tour in England and the United States. On his return, in 1868, he submitted to the Government a highly valuable "special report on the systems and state of popular education in the several countries of Europe and the United States of America, with practical suggestions for the improvement of Public Instruction in Upper Canada." He also made a separate and extensive "Report on Institutions for the Deaf and Dumb and Blind in Various Countries."

In a letter to a friend, Dr. Ryerson thus explained the principles upon which he conducted the educational affairs of the Province for upwards of thirty-one years. He said:—

During these years I organized the school system and administered the Education Department upon the broad and impartial principles which I had advocated. During the long period of my administration of the Department, I knew neither religious sect nor political party—I knew no other party than that of the country at large—I never exercised any patronage for personal or party purposes—I never made or recommended one of the numerous appointments of teachers in the Normal or Model Schools, or Clerks in the Education office, except upon the ground of testimonials as to personal character and qualifications, and on a probationary trial of six months.

In this way only competent and trained persons were appointed to the Normal and Model Schools, and to the Education Office, when a vacancy occurred by resignation or death. Each employé below the one who had resigned or died was advanced a step if deserving; and the most meritorious lad was selected from the Model school, or on other testimonials, and placed at the bottom of the list, and trained and advanced according to his merits in the work of the Education Department. Each one, thus felt, that he owed his position not to party, or personal patronage or favour, but to his own merits, and respected himself and performed his duties accordingly.

I believe this is the true method of managing all the Public Departments, and every branch of the public service. I believe it would contribute immensely to both the efficiency and economy of the public service. Needless and inefficient appointments would not then be made; and it would greatly elevate the standard of action and attainments, and emulate the ambition of the young men and youth of the country, when they know that their selection and advancement in their country's service depended upon their individual merits, irrespective of sect or party, and not as the reward of zeal as political party hacks in elections and otherwise, on their own part, or on that of their fathers or relatives.

The power of government in a country is immense, for good or ill. It is designed by the Supreme Being to be "a minister of God for good," to a whole people (without partiality, as well as without hypocrisy), like the rays of the sun; and the administration of infinite wisdom and justice, and truth and purity. But when government becomes the mere agency of party, and its highest gifts the prizes of party zeal and intrigue, it loses its moral prestige and power; and from the corrupt fountain would flow polluted streams into every Department of the public service, which would corrupt the whole mass of society, were it not for the counteracting and refining influences which are exerted upon society by the ministrations and labours of the different religious denominations.

I know it has been contended that party patronage, or, in other words, feeding partizans at the public expense. is an essential element in the existence of a government. This is the doctrine of corruption. The Education Department—the highest public department in Upper Canada—existed for more than thirty years without such an element, and with increased efficiency and increased strength in the public estimation, during the whole of that period. Justice and virtue, and patriotism and intelligence, are stronger elements of power and usefulness than those of buying and rewarding partizans; and if the rivalship and competition of public men should consist in who should best devise and promote measures for the advancement of the country, and who should exercise the executive power most impartially and intelligently, for developing and promoting the interests of all classes, then the moral standard of government and of public men would be greatly exalted, and the highest civilization of the whole country be advanced. But I will not pursue this topic any further. The truths I state are self-evident.

For many years after Confederation Dr. Ryerson felt that the new political condition of the Province—which localized as well as circumscribed its civil administration of affairs—required a change in the management of the Education Department. He, therefore, in 1869 and 1872, urged upon the Government the desirability of relieving him from the anomalous position in which he found himself placed under the new system.

The reasons which he urged for his retirement are given in a pamphlet devoted to a "Defence" of the System of Education, which he published in 1872, and are as follows :—

When political men have made attacks upon the school law, or the school system and myself, I have answered them. Then the cry has been raised by my assailants, and their abettors, that I was "interfering with politics." They would assail me without stint, in hopes of crushing me, and then gag me against all defence or reply.

So deeply did I feel the disadvantage and growing evil of this state of things to the Department and school system itself, that in 1868 I proposed to retire from the department. . . My resignation was not accepted ; . . when, two months later, I proposed that, at the commencement of each session of the legislature, a committee of seven or nine (including the Provincial Secretary for the time being) should be elected by ballot, or by mutual agreement of the leading men of both parties, on the Education Department; which committee should examine into the operations of the Department for the year then ending, consider the school estimates, and any bill or recommendations which might be submitted for the advancement of the school system, and report to the House accordingly. By many thoughtful men, this system has been considered more safe, more likely to secure a competent and working head of the department, and less liable to make the school system a tool of party politics, than for the head of it to have a seat in Parliament, and thus leave the educational interests of the country dependent upon the votes of a majority of electors in one riding. This recommendation, submitted on the 30th January, 1869, was not adopted ; and I was left isolated—responsible in the estimation of legislators and everybody else for the Department—the target of every attack, whether in the newspapers or in the Legislative Assembly, yet without any access to it, or to its members, except through the press, and no other support than the character of my work and the general confidence of the public.

In 1876, however, Dr. Ryerson was permitted to retire on full salary from the responsible post which for nearly thirty-two years he had so worthily and honourably filled.

CHAPTER XLVII.
1845—1846.
ILLNESS AND FINAL RETIREMENT OF LORD METCALFE.

IN a letter to Dr. Ryerson from Mr. Higginson, dated 27th May, 1845, he thus refers to Lord Metcalfe's increasing illness:—

I wish that I could answer your inquiries about Lord Metcalfe's health in a satisfactory manner. The torturing malady with which he is afflicted is no better; and although there is no decided change for the worse, yet there is in my mind too much reason to apprehend that the disease, though slow in its progress, keeps constantly advancing and threatens farther ravages. The pain is incessant and unabated. The resignation with which he suffers, and his unyielding determination to remain at his post as long as his presence can serve Canada, inspires a feeling of veneration which I will not attempt to describe. He seems to be quite prepared to realize, if necessary, that noble sentiment—

"Dulce et decorum est pro Patria mori."

Mr. Higginson again wrote to Dr. Ryerson, from Montreal, on the 28th of October, as follows:—

As bad news travels fast, you will probably have heard before this reaches you of the aggravation of the painful malady from which Lord Metcalfe has so long suffered. No other man, in his present lamentable condition, would think of administering the Government. He seems quite ready to die in harness, if necessary, but is determined not to leave here as long as he can, at any sacrifice of personal considerations, continue to discharge the duties. I hope and believe that Her Majesty's Government will not hesitate to relieve him as soon as a successor can be found—it would be inhuman to delay any longer. How much of Canada's weal or woe depends upon the selection? It is far easier to mar than to mend the triumph my inestimable friend has achieved—to weaken than to strengthen its effects.

Mr. Higginson wrote to Dr. Ryerson on the 18th December:

I, two days ago, had the pleasure to receive your kind and feeling letter of the 11th. It will afford me great satisfaction to communicate to my suffering friend the grateful sentiments to which you give expression.

Lord Metcalfe's retirement was, as you justly observe, strictly a providential dispensation. He remained at his post until it pleased the Almighty to render him physically incapable of discharging all its duties; and he was quite prepared to die at it, in the service of his country. The terms in which the Queen's permission to return home was acceded are, beyond measure, gratifying and complimentary. I shall have much pleasure in reading the despatch to you the first time we meet. Of the fearful malady, I can only say that its onward progress seems to be beyond human control, and that I entertain no hope of its being arrested. But the surgical skill of Europe may, and I earnestly pray to God will, alleviate the intensity of the blessed man's sufferings.

After Lord Metcalfe had returned to England, the Hon. D. Daly, Secretary of the Province, wrote to Dr. Ryerson, who had returned to Canada, on the 20th December, as follows:—

Your disappointment was naturally great at missing the only opportunity that, in all human probability, can be afforded you in this world of seeing our lamented and excellent Governor. In his late and most severe suffering, the greatness of that most inestimable man's character was, if possible, more resplendent than under the trials to which you saw him subjected. May he enjoy a peaceful termination to his useful existence! We can know nothing certain of his successor until the news of which he is the bearer has reached England, his relinquishment of the Government having been left entirely to his own free will. He had the comfort of knowing how fully his services were appreciated by his Sovereign; and his removal was effected in the most gratifying way by Her Majesty's command.

On the 9th May Dr. Ryerson wrote a farewell letter to Lord Metcalfe, from which I make the following extract:—

Having passed Your Lordship on the ocean, and being disappointed of the privilege of ever seeing you again in this world, I wrote by the first packet after my arrival to Mr. C. Trevelyan, requesting him to have the goodness to convey to Your Lordship the expression of those sentiments of gratitude and affectionate respect which I can never fail to cherish while memory remains. . .

In Your Lordship's retirement and suffering, . . I think it wrong to intrude further than to state my deep sympathy in your sufferings, and that my supplications are offered up daily to the God of all consolation, that He would grant you patience, resignation, and a " sure and certain hope of a glorious resurrection to everlasting life;" and to assure Your Lordship that my life shall be sacredly devoted to the work in behalf of the youthful and future generations of Canada, for which Your Lordship's kindness has done so much, to enable me to qualify myself. With, these the strongest feelings of my heart, I have, etc.

The final letter received from Mr. Higginson was dated Montreal, June 10th, 1846 :—

I beg you to accept my cordial thanks for your very kind communication of the 30th ult. I am not insensible to the high honour that has been conferred upon me by our Sovereign —far beyond my humble merits; but I have great satisfaction in feeling that I won it fighting shoulder to shoulder with you and the other advocates of those great British Constitutional principles of Government, for which we contended, and which were so fiercely assailed by the British Democratic party, who, I earnestly trust may never again be able to make head in Canada. That I, in the slightest degree contributed to the victory will be to me a source of pride. To the eminent Pilot who directed us no one knows better than yourself how much is due. Would that he had been spared to perfect the good work. My latest account of his health encourages the hope that I may yet be permitted to see him again.

We closed the session yesterday, which was got through with success, and I hope with some advantage to the public interests.

I regret very much that I have not had the pleasure of seeing you since your return from Europe. Farewell!   J. M. H.

The appointment which Mr. Higginson received from the Queen was that of Governor of Antigua. In his reply to an address from the Wesleyan missionaries of that island, on his arrival, he thus referred to his experience of that body in Canada:—

I have had frequent opportunities of witnessing in various quarters of the globe the untiring exertions of your brethren in the sacred cause of religion and humanity, and whether in the sultry heat of Asia, . . or struggling against the rigours of a Canadian winter, I have always found the Wesleyan missionaries animated by the same benevolent and philantrophic spirit, and undaunted by obstacles, however appalling, manifesting the same discreet zeal to spread far and wide the healing influence of the holy Gospel of Christ.

CHAPTER XLVIII.

1843–1844.

CLERGY RESERVE QUESTION RE-OPENED.—DISAPPOINTMENTS.

EXTRAORDINARY efforts were put forth (as shown in Chapter xxxiii., page 263) by the leaders of the Church of England party in Upper Canada to prevent the Royal assent being given to Lord Sydenham's Clergy Reserve compromise Bill of 1841. Equally strenuous efforts were successfully made to ensure the fulfilment of Bishop Strachan's prediction that the rejected Bill of Lord Sydenham would form the basis of an Imperial Act, which would secure to the national Churches of England and Scotland, for all time, the lion's share of the proceeds of George the Third's ill-fated gift to Canada of the clergy reserves. Lord John Russell, the pretentious and vacillating Secretary of State for the Colonies at the time, proved himself to be, in this matter, a pliant instrument in the hands of Henry of Exeter. This prelate endorsed, *con amore*, all the extreme views of the Bishop of Toronto; and with the aid of Lord Seaton (Sir John Colborne) and the Bench and Bishops in the House of Lords, compelled the Government to perpetuate an act of legislative usurpation and injustice, which even the tyros in constitutional law, as applied to the Colonies, were wont at the time to instance in the press as examples of history repeating itself—quoting, as an illustration, the ill-advised Imperial legislation in the case of the Stamp Act, etc.

By a singular fatality, which often attends arbitrary and unjust proceedings, the success of the scheme, which had been so carefully prepared, and carried through the British Parliament in the interests of the Church of England, was destined to become a source of weakness to that Church, and a foreboding of financial disaster. On the 29th December, 1843, the Attorney and the Solicitor-General of Canada (as stated by the Bishop of Toronto in his pastoral letter of the 10th of December, 1844) reported that having attentively examined the provisions of the acts for this subject, it was their opinion that the proper construction of the law threw upon the revenues of Canada the burthen of making up any deficiency in the clergy reserve fund, in paying the usual and accustomed allowances and stipends to the Ministers, . . and, while that deficiency lasted, the Imperial Treasury could not be called upon to make any payments to the two Churches. (See page 4 of Pastoral.)

The Bishop then charges the Provincial Government with being the cause of this financial difficulty, and accounts for the deficiency in the fund by the mismanagement of that Government. He adds further on :—

> But, alas! the mismanagement has increased, pending these difficulties; and while my clergy are left in a state of destitution, large sums continue to be wasted in remunerating services which are really worse than useless, and this to such an extent as to render hopeless the expectation that the clergy reserve fund will ever answer the wise and holy purpose for which it was established.

In this dilemma the Bishop states what he had done to extricate the Church out of its difficulty. In doing so, he uses language which partakes more of the character of a wail than of a simple statement of facts. He also draws a most gloomy picture of the prospective religious state of Upper Canada, should the dearly prized, and as dearly bought, Imperial Clergy Reserve Act prove, after all, to be an apple of Sodom.

It is curious to notice how the Bishop, in his despairing outburst, studiously ignores the active and successful labours of the several voluntary churches—whose claims to a share in the reserves he had so strongly and selfishly opposed—churches which were even then actively engaged in "spreading scriptural holiness throughout the land," without the aid of a penny from the State. In his Pastoral, the Bishop says :—

> I applied to the venerable [Propagation Society] in England to advance, in the meantime, the salaries (only £100 per annum each) to my five suffering clergy,—assuring the Society that I had the fullest conviction it would be repaid as soon as it was decided which Government was liable. . . The Society paid the stipends for the year ending 30th June, 1843, but have declined since that time to continue the advance. . . In consequence, my five clergymen have been left without their stipends since June, 1843 [to December, 1844], . . and this large and increasing Diocese [then the whole of Upper Canada], already so destitute of the means of public worship (if the statute be allowed to operate as it has done for the last four years), will, in a spiritual sense, become, through half its extent, a wilderness. Not only are five clergymen in a state of want, but two parishes are left vacant, and the process is unhappily going on. . . I have brought this disheartening and deplorable state of things under the notice of the Provincial Government. . . I have pressed [the matter] upon His Excellency the Governor-General. . . But all that was in my power to do has been without avail (page 6).

I also quote the foregoing passages from this noted Pastoral, as they throw a vivid side-light upon the course of the Bishop in so vehemently pursuing the shadow of a state endowment for the Church of England in Upper Canada. The subsequent utterances of the Pastoral show how persistently the otherwise clear-headed and practical chief ruler of that Church shut his eyes to the remarkable success and vitality of the non-endowed Churches in the Province, and how much he deplored the necessity of adopting their successful voluntary system in his own church.* He says :—

I represented to His Excellency, in May last, that, "on a review of this unfortunate subject . . the distress of my five clergymen, and the desolation with which it menaces the Church, it involves consequences so calamitous and imminent as to justify the representative of the sovereign in assuming more than ordinary responsibility in arresting their progress. . .
On the 31st October, I again brought this painful subject at great length before the Provincial Government, and stated that, having failed to receive relief, I could only see one way left of mitigating the evil, and that is by an appeal to my people on the present critical situation of the Church, and in behalf of my destitute clergymen. It is indeed a step which I take with extreme reluctance, and which, were it possible, I would most willingly avoid. . . (page 6.)

In a remarkable document, which the Bishop published in 1849, on "*The Secular State of the Church in the Diocese of Toronto*," he furnishes a painful and striking commentary on the effect of his own teaching: that it was the duty of the State to support the Church, and thus relieve the people of the chief obligation of supporting the Gospel amongst them. Speaking of "contributions to the Church within the Province," he says :

Till lately we have done little or nothing towards the support of public worship. We have depended so long upon the Government and the [Propagation] Society, that many of us forget that it is our bounden duty. Instead of coming forward manfully to devote a portion of our temporal substance to the service of God, we turn away with indifference, or we sit down to count the cost, and measure the salvation of our souls by pounds, shillings, and pence. . . While we are bountifully assisted, and seldom required to do more than half; yet we are seen to fail on every side (page 19).†

On pages 34—40 of this pamphlet, Bishop Strachan is very severe on the clergy to whom Bishop Fuller refers, whom he accuses of putting forth efforts " to disturb the peace of the diocese—efforts which were rapidly being organized into some-

---

* In process of time, the necessities of his Church compelled the Bishop to adopt a new financial scheme, which he laid before his clergy in 1841, one main feature of which was to incorporate the voluntary principle with a system of moderate grants—such as has been the rule adopted for some years by the Mission Board of the Diocese of Toronto.

† In sending a copy of this pamphlet some years ago to the Editor of this volume, Archdeacon Fuller (now Bishop of Niagara), said :—This able and interesting document. . . . was drawn out from the late Bishop by the growing dissatisfaction amongst the clergy and laity, in consequence of Bishop Strachan managing the whole of the clergy reserve fund, without consulting anybody, and managing to get several thousand pounds of arrears paid to himself, as Bishop, and his protegé, the present Bishop [Bethune], made Archdeacon of York, with a salary of £365 a year as Archdeacon, while he could not find means to pay the missionaries more than £100 a year.

thing of a regular system of agitation, so common . . among the traders in politics" (page 34).

An agitation having been commenced by the Bishop and clergy in Western Canada, in 1843, for "better terms" and an amendment to the Imperial Clergy Reserve Act of 1840, the question was re-opened. The effect of this re-opening of the question was deprecated by Dr. Ryerson and others. Early in January, 1844, Mr. Surveyor-General Parke sent to Dr. Ryerson the copy of a letter written by Rev. Prof. Campbell, of Queen's College, Kingston, in which Mr. Campbell sets up the claim of the Kirk of Scotland, having a branch in Canada, as such, to a portion of the Canadian clergy reserves. Mr. Parke says:—

The writer of the letter arrives at two other conclusions, which, I think, are based on error, and calculated to interfere materially with the rights of the other bodies of Protestant Christians : namely, that the Kirk in Canada participate in the clergy reserves, solely by the right it has as a branch of the Kirk in Scotland ; and that other bodies of Christians participate in them merely as an act of favour. To the first of these conclusions I entirely object, on the ground that the Act confers the reserves, purely and solely, on Canada, and for the benefit of interests and persons, absolutely within Canada. To the second conclusion or statement of the Professor, that is, that other bodies participate as a matter of favour, I object on every ground on which it is possible for equity to place the subject. What! shall the unexampled toils, and incessant labours of the early and later Methodists, and other pioneers of the christianizing of Canada, have doled out to them, as a matter of simple grace, and a body in Scotland, who never knew nor participated in the labour of sowing the seeds of the Gospel through the length and breadth of the land, claim as a matter of absolute right, for one of its branches, a participation in lands, purely Canadian in fact and law ? This I can never assent to ; it was the question on which, as a Methodist, I first became a Canadian politician, and it is the question on which I yet feel the keenest. I desire to call your attention to the matter, and solicit a correction from you of errors which, I think, are insidiously calculated to mislead the public mind, and make uphill work in combating other questions which may arise in unfortunate Canada, bye-and-bye. Some of the Kirk folks would monopolize for themselves, as far as they dare, and the Church of England too ; but the general community, who have borne the burden and heat of the day—fought and won the battle—should not in any way have their interests and feelings trifled with by the unreasonable claims of a few, who at comparatively a late day entered the field.

As the agitation increased, Dr. Ryerson, who was in England in 1845, addressed a letter to Lord Stanley, Colonial Secretary, in January, on the injustice to the non-episcopal churches of the Act of 1840. He said :—

There is a subject which, in connection with transpiring circumstances in Canada, deeply involves the future condition of the government of Canada, and which can be considered by your Lordship alone : I refer to the withholding, to the present time, from the Wesleyan Methodist body in Upper Canada all benefit of the Act passed for the settlement of the clergy reserve question—a question which certain parties in Canada propose to re-open, with a view of depriving the Church of England of what is considered a disproportionate share of the proceeds of the clergy reserves. The advantage afforded by such a subject of agitation would be eagerly seized upon by the leaders of the opposition in Parliament. The Wesleyan Methodist body in Upper Canada (now numbering 131 regular ministers, and 24,000 communicants), has for many years possessed and does still possess the casting vote between the contending political parties in that country; and should they join in the agitation contemplated, nothing but military power will prevent the wresting out of the hands of the Church of England their—the chief—pecuniary advantages which it derives from public sources. Hitherto the leading members of the Wesleyan Methodist body have declined any public agitation on the subject—though solicited by influential parties—contenting themselves with private communication to the Government until they should find them hopelessly unsuccessful. Should not their case be considered? I have reason to believe that they will at their next annual meeting, to be held in June, commence an appeal to the public and to the Local Legislature on the injustice done them; as they have ascertained that all the leading lawyers in Upper Canada of both parties, as well as three successive Governors considered them wronged in the manner in which they alone, of the four great leading denominations of the country, have been excluded from the benefits of an act, to the basis of which Lord Sydenham never could have obtained the consent of the Canadian Legislature without their most decided support.

I should deeply lament the re-agitation of the clergy reserve question in Canada. Such a step, on the part of the great Wesleyan body there, would doubtless be attended by the strengthening of the opposition in the Legislature, and to probable withdrawal of the support of several members from the present Government. In an interview with the official Committee of the Wesleyan body, shortly before I left Canada, I promised them to bring the subject before your Lordship during my stay in England. They, therefore, deferred appealing to the Local Legislature to interpose in their behalf, until they should learn the result of such an appeal to your Lordship. . .

I cannot suppose that it has been the wish of your Lordship, any more than the intention of the Crown officers, to perpetuate the exclusion of the Wesleyan Methodist Church in Canada from their confessedly-just claim of which they have already been deprived for a period of four years. The amount of the claim is less than one-half of what has been secured to the Roman Catholic Church in Upper Canada—less than one-third of the amount paid the Church of Scotland, and less than one-tenth of what has been guaranteed to the Church of England. The Wesleyan body, whose members in Upper Canada have increased eight thousand during the last four years, will be satisfied on the payment of the sum admitted in their behalf. And I submit that the sanctioning of it by your Lordship will, in my humble opinion, be far better, even as a matter of policy—apart from higher considerations—than affording just ground for an agitation, the consequences of which cannot be easily foreseen.

No relief was, however, afforded by a change in the administration of the Act of 1840. The Act itself remained unrepealed until 1853.

CHAPTER XLIX.

1846–1848.

RE-UNION OF THE BRITISH AND CANADIAN CONFERENCES.

DURING and before the period of the Metcalfe Controversy events were transpiring in Methodist circles in which Dr. Ryerson took an active part, and in which he was deeply interested.*

Important correspondence on the relations to each other of the British and Canadian Conferences took place in 1842. But as the issue of the contest between these Conferences was so prolonged, and involved so many important questions—religious and public—I think it desirable to give a brief preliminary outline of the origin of the difficulties between the two bodies. This is the more necessary, as Dr. Ryerson's own personal history and conduct became, from a variety of circumstances, most prominently mixed up with these controversies. His letters to the Government on the subject, and to the Missionary Secretaries, now first published, are also valuable Methodist historical documents—although they partake largely of a per-

---

* In a letter to him from the Rev. A. Green, dated November, 1842, the desirability of a union with the Episcopal Methodists was pressed upon his attention. Mr. Green said:—The Episcopal Methodists are gaining ground in many circuits. It would be of much service to us, could we take them on board the old ship again. I learn from Brother Richardson that they are anxious for this, and that Mr. Reynolds would give up his claims, and many of their preachers would retire, could they effect it. But in some parts of the Province the re-union would be opposed; and some members have said, that they would even join the English missionaries if we were to be united with them (the Episcopals). You are a wise man, tell us what we should do. If we do not take steps soon, it will be entirely too late. I understand that they talk of having a Bishop elected soon,—and should Mr. Richardson or Mr. Smith be appointed, it would add greatly to the influence of the party; and yet I cannot now see what steps we could safely take, until we settle the English Union question, for they would take advantage, I fear, of such a reconciliation, to prejudice the old country members against us.

I wish also to obtain your views upon the propriety of petitioning the Governor-General, at once, for a share of the public money granted for the purchase of Sabbath-school books. The sum of £150 goes into the hands of Dr. Strachan annually, for that purpose; and where is it? We are never benefited a farthing by it! Could we obtain one-half, or even one-third of the sum for our schools, it would be of great service to them.*

* I have no copy of the reply sent to this letter. The letter itself, however, shows what subjects were being discussed in Methodist circles in 1842.

sonal character—as he was the foremost figure in all of these connexional contests. They are highly characteristic of the courage and self-sacrifice of the writer.

Methodism, after its introduction into Upper Canada in 1790, was organized into a Church by preachers from the United States. In 1811, when Upper Canada was on the eve of being the theatre of war with the United States, several American preachers who had been appointed to Canada declined to come, while those here (Messrs. Roads and Densmore) applied to the Canadian Government in 1812 for leave to return to their own country.* Nevertheless, after the war, and on the representation of persons prompted by high churchmen, the London Wesleyan Missionary Society sent out missionaries to four of the larger towns in Upper Canada. This schismatical policy was pursued by the British Conference until 1820, when the American General Conference sent Rev. John (afterwards) Bishop Emory, as a deputation to that Conference to remonstrate. The result was that the following resolutions were passed by the British Conference in that year (1820):—

1. That as the American Methodists and ourselves are but one body, it would be inconsistent with our unity, and dangerous to that affection which ought to characterize us in every place, to have different societies and congregations in the same towns and villages, or to allow of any intrusion on either side into each other's labours.

2. That this principle shall be the rule by which the disputes now existing in the Canadas, between our missionaries, shall be terminated.

In transmitting these and several other resolutions on the subject to the British Missionaries in Canada, the Secretaries (Rev. Joseph Taylor and Rev. Richard Watson) said:—

We know that political reasons exist in many minds for supplying even Upper Canada, as far as possible, with British Missionaries; and, however natural this feeling may be to Englishmen, and even praiseworthy when not carried too far, it will be obvious to you that this is a ground on which, as a Missionary Society, and especially as a Society under the direction of a Committee which recognizes as one with itself the American Methodists, we cannot act.

The British Conference loyally observed this compact from 1820 until 1833. At that time (Dr. Ryerson says) the advocates of a dominant church establishment, though in a small minority in the House of Assembly, were all powerful in the Executive and Legislative Councils, and employed very naturally all the resources at their command to perpetuate their supremacy. For this purpose they appealed to the Wesleyan Missionary Committee in England, and solicited them upon the ground of their loyalty to the Church of England and to the Throne to send out Missionaries to Upper Canada, offering $4,000 per annum out of the Crown revenues to assist in so loyal a work. The Eng-

* Epochs of Canadian Methodism, pages 292–294.

lish Wesleyan Missionary Committee sent out a representative agent, who contended that the engagement into which the English Conference had entered with the American General Conference in 1820, through Dr. Emory, to leave Upper Canada to the Canadian preachers, was no longer binding since the Conference in Canada has become separate from that in the United States, and the English Committee was therefore free to send missionaries into any part of Upper Canada. The Canadian Conference was thus confronted by a double danger —the danger of division in their congregations, and the danger of increased power against their claims to equal rights and privileges; and a two-fold duty devolved upon them—to prevent division if possible, and, at the same time, to secure the attainment of their own constitutional rights.

In the meantime other disturbing influences occurred. In 1824, an agitation was commenced, with a view to take the appointment of the Presiding Eldership out of the hands of the Bishops, and make the office elective by the annual Conferences. The Presiding Elders of Upper Canada (Rev. Henry Ryan and Rev. William Case) opposed this change, and, in consequence, failed in their election by the Genesee Annual Conference as delegates to the General Conference. Mr. Ryan was chagrined at this result, and on his return to Upper Canada commenced to agitate for an entire separation from the American Church. A memorial to that effect was sent to the General Conference. The request was not granted, but the Canadian work was set off to itself as the "Annual Conference of the Methodist Episcopal Church in Canada." This was not what Mr. Ryan wanted, and it displeased him. The theme of his complaint was "the domination of republican Methodism and the tyranny of Yankee Bishops." He therefore, set himself again to agitate for entire independence. Finally, after having been the means of stirring up personal strife all through the Connexion, the Conference of 1827 directed that he should be reproved and admonished by Bishop Hedding in presence of the Conference. This was done. Next day Mr. Ryan withdrew from the Conference. (See chapter vii.)

The high-church party encouraged Mr. Ryan in his disaffection; and when he withdrew, and set up a separate church organization, Dr. Strachan actually sent Mr. Ryan $200 to assist him in his schismatical efforts! (Epochs, page 305.) Hon. John Willson, Speaker of the House of Assembly, and formerly a Methodist, joined the high-church party, and did all he could to aid and encourage Mr. Ryan. Thus, in addition to the £50 sent to Mr. Ryan by Ven. Archdeacon Strachan, to aid him in his schismatical crusade against the Conference, a Government grant of £666 ($2,664) was made to the new organization at the instance of Mr. Willson in 1833, and £338 ($1,352) in 1834. (Epochs, page 359.)

The cry of disloyalty having been again raised, the Government and clerical party (for they were one under the control of the Archdeacon of York), lost no time, therefore, in maturing a plan to induce the British Conference again to undertake the occupancy of Upper Canada as missionary ground, and forthwith to send missionaries into the province for that purpose. A correspondence was opened between the head of the Canadian Executive Government, Sir John Colborne, and the Wesleyan Missionary Committee, on the subject of the new missionary enterprise into Upper Canada. (Epochs, page 305.) The result was, that in May, 1832, without notice, an intimation was received that the Rev. Robert Alder, and twelve missionaries were to be sent out to Canada. With a view to avert the calamity of again having hostile Methodist camps in every city and town in Upper Canada, Rev. John Ryerson suggested to Dr. Ryerson that the Canada Conference should endeavour to form a union with the British Conference, and thus secure harmonious action instead of discord and disunion. This was done, and provisional arrangements were made with Dr. Alder at the Hallowell Conference of 1832, subject to the ratification of the British Conference. This ratification was made, and took effect in 1833, and the union continued for four or five years only.

About the year 1840, a considerable controversy arose in regard to the payment of an annual grant of £900 by the Government, in aid of the general work of the Church. It may be well, therefore, to state the circumstances under which this grant was made, and then point out the personal causes which intensified the feeling of estrangement between the English and Canadian Conferences.

In a letter on this subject to the Provincial Secretary, dated 28th December, 1842, Dr. Ryerson said :—

Rev. Robert Alder was in Upper Canada in the spring and summer of 1832, negotiating on the subject of the grant and the union, which Sir John Colborne was anxious to promote. The Canadian Conference, aided by Dr. Alder's counsels, agreed to propose certain articles of union with the English Conference. Those articles contemplated a financial, as well as ecclesiastical union ; and Dr. Alder expressed his conviction that the English Conference would grant £1,000 per annum out of its Contingent Fund, to aid our Conference, besides the aid granted out of the Mission Fund, in aid of Missions in Upper Canada. A copy of these proposed articles of union was forthwith laid before Sir John Colborne by Dr. Alder, and published in the *Guardian*, of the 29th August, 1832, five days after which Sir John Colborne wrote to Lord Ripon, recommending a grant to the Wesleyan Committee of £900 per annum [on terms of the comprehensive scheme mentioned on page 155].

But the Government delayed making any payment until October, 1833, after the ratification of the union by both bodies. In the meantime, however, the English Conference declined granting any aid out of their Contingent Fund, and had a clause inserted in the Articles of Union against any claims upon the funds of the English Conference on the part of the Canadian Preachers. Of this clause in the Articles of Union the Government seems never to have been made aware until Lord Sydenham came to Upper Canada in 1839.

In a long and valuable historical letter to Mr. Murdoch, Chief Secretary to Sir Charles Bagot, dated May, 1842, Dr. Ryerson further said :—

The first payment of the grant was made in October, 1833, a few days after the final ratification of the Articles of Union by the Canadian Conference; so that every payment of the grant was made and applied according to the "usage" prescribed by the Articles of Union. . .

Dr. Ryerson then discussed various matters relating to their "usage," and the articles of Union, and proceeded : Some weeks after Lord Sydenham's arrival in Toronto, His Lordship sent for me—as I was afterwards informed, at the recommendation of Sir Allan MacNab, Receiver-General Dunn, and others—but the interview, and one or two subsequent ones, related entirely to the objects of his Lordship's mission, in accomplishing which, he desired all the aid I could give him. The last week of the year 1839, and the first week of 1840, Lord Sydenham spent in seeing various parties and concerting a measure on the clergy reserve question. He sent for the Rev. Messrs. Stinson and Richey (agents of the London Wesleyan Committee) as well as for me. As all the present difficulties grew out of these interviews of the London Wesleyan Committee's agents and myself, with Lord Sydenham, I think it important to state the substance of them, and the evidence on which I make my statement.

First as regards myself. The proposed measure being intended to secure a continued payment of grants already made out of the Casual and Territorial Revenue, and the Clergy Reserve Fund, to the parties receiving them, I submitted to Lord Sydenham that, as the three principal denominations (Church of England, Church of Scotland, and Roman Catholics) received large aid out of one or both of these funds, it was clear that unless some assistance was granted to the Wesleyan Methodist Church before the passing of the Clergy Reserve Bill, and tranferred with other charges by the provisions of the Bill, we would be effectually excluded from obtaining any aid for a series of years. I submitted to Lord Sydenham an application, which I had been directed to make, in behalf of the Upper Canada Academy—now Victoria College. His Lordship acceded to the justice of my views, but replied that aid was given to us also in the form of an annual grant. I replied, and sought to impress upon his Lordship, that the grant referred to by him had not been made to the Canadian Conference, and did not operate to its advantage, but to the sole advantage of the Wesleyan Missionary Society in England; and, at his request, I prepared a statement of the case in writing. It will be seen by the date of my letter that these communications took place January 2nd, 1840. It is perfectly clear, therefore, that up to that time there could have transpired between Lord Sydenham and myself, nothing relative to the transfer of the grant.

On the same day, Rev. Messrs. Stinson and Richey (agents of the Wesleyan Committee) had an interview with Lord Sydenham. They told him that the union between the English and Canadian Conferences was not likely to continue; and prayed (in their memorial, written the day after) "that the sum intended for the Wesleyan Methodist Church in Canada, should be given to the Wesleyan Methodists, who are now, and who may be hereafter, connected with the British Wesleyan Conference." I believe Lord Sydenham's laconic reply was, that he had to do with religious bodies in Canada, not in England.

It will be seen that the communication of Messrs. Stinson and Richey, as well as mine, served to impress Lord Sydenham that there was not an identity of interests between the English and Canadian Conferences, as he had supposed, and, as His Lordship said, Her Majesty's Government also supposed.

A day or two after Messrs. Stinson and Richey's interview with Lord Sydenham, I waited upon him, when I was given to understand that a memorial had been presented to him in behalf of the British Conference, on the ground of an anticipated dissolution of the Union. My feelings of surprise and indignation, and my remonstrances against such a monstrous proposition, may be easily conceived. It is known that Lord Sydenham, from the very first, viewed such a proposition with disapprobation; it was on this occasion also that His Lordship apprised me of the conclusions he had come to on the subject of any proposition for a grant to the Canadian Conference, previously to passing the Clergy Reserve Bill; that he was satisfied that the Canadian Conference had a just claim to assistance; that it did not derive any practical benefit from the grant to the London Committee, but that it ought to do so, as such were the original intentions of the Government in making it. Lord Sydenham stated his recollection of the intention of the Government in 1832 to be—and perhaps the recollections of Lord Stanley may be to the same effect—that it was supposed by the Government, from communications from Upper Canada, that the Wesleyans here were not quite as (conservatively) loyal as was desirable; that it being understood they were willing to unite with the English Conference, the Government thought it advisable to enable the English Conference to assist them, as it would exert a salutary influence upon their feelings and usefulness. Thus was the grant made; but from the peculiar nature of the articles of Union, the leading objects of the grant had never been accomplished, as the Canadian Conference had to support all its own members and institutions—except a few missions—as much since, as before the Union. He had, therefore, determined to write to Lord John Russell, and recommend a different distribution of the grant; believing that to accomplish the original and benevolent objects in Canada, it ought to be placed under the entire control of the Canadian Conference. In these views I did, of course, gratefully concur, although I never fully understood until then the intentions of the Imperial Government in making the grant. I also thought the course proposed would defeat the intimated project of breaking up the Union, and furnish real aid to the Church of which I was appointed advocate and representative. Leaving the matter in the hands of Lord Sydenham, I had no intention of saying anything more upon the subject, until, nearly a fortnight afterwards, when His Lordship requested me—as I was so familiar with the subject—to furnish him with a written statement of the financial relations of the English and Canadian Conferences, in regard to the grant, etc., as it would aid him in preparing his despatch to Lord John Russell. I did so. The letter, written at the request of Lord Sydenham, was intended as a memorandum for his Lordship. But he thought it best to transmit a copy of it with his own despatch to Lord John Russell, by whom it was enclosed to the Wesleyan Committee; and hence the present controversy. That letter is dated 17th January, 1840.

I cannot but feel that I labour under great disadvantages in the present discussion, from the numerous representations and statements which the Wesleyan Committee have made to the noble Secretary of State to my disadvantage. My standing, as a public man, is my all, and therefore, however small relatively, is as important to me as a kingdom to a monarch.

As the Wesleyan Committee have made me so prominent a subject in this affair, I have offered to submit to His Excellency, Sir Charles Bagot, or to the Executive Council—or to His Excellency and the Executive Council—or to the Lord Bishop of Toronto; or to the Moderator of the Synod of the Church of Scotland in Canada—or to the Lord Bishop of Toronto and the Moderator of the Scotch Synod—and to bind myself in any penalty to abide by the decision of such tribunal. When the Wesleyan Committee are accusers, judge, and jury in their own case, it is not likely they will be very impartial; but if there is a shadow of truth or justice in their accusations and statements, I have given them full opportunity to secure the confirmation of them, by the highest tribunals, in the country of my life and labours.

The Wesleyan Committee declined to refer the matter in dispute to an independent tribunal, and Dr. Alder wrote to members of the Canadian Conference impugning Dr. Ryerson in the strongest terms, insisting upon his withdrawal of certain things which he had written, and making various threats. Dr. Ryerson decided then to address a final letter to Rev. Messrs. Bunting, Beecham and Hoole, Missionary Secretaries. This he did on the 19th October, 1842. This letter, and the preceding letter, are doubly valuable from the fact that they embody a number of interesting details of the interviews and correspondence between Lord Sydenham and Dr. Ryerson, and also between Sir Charles Bagot and Dr. Ryerson, which have not hitherto been published. There is a tone of manly dignity and independence in this letter which commends itself, and which were characteristic of Dr. Ryerson in his best moods as a controversialist. From the letter, which extends to thirty-four foolscap pages I make the following extracts. He said :—

I wish the most extended success to the general labours of the Wesleyan Missionary Society, however much they have sought to retard those of the Canadian Conference; nor have I ever objected to their labours among the "destitute white settlements" and heathen tribes of Canada; I only object to their works of schism, and division. . . Did you ever think of sending missionaries, or of employing your money and men, in our regular circuits, before the breaking up of the Union?— Kingston, or Belleville, or Toronto, or Hamilton, or Brantford, or London, etc. ? places where there is no more need of missionary men or missionary money than there is in City Road, or Great Queen street circuits in London—places in which it is notorious that the soul, body, and strength of your societies consists, not in converts from the world, but in secessions from the Canadian Conference. When, therefore, four-fifths of your missionaries (so called) in Western Canada are employed on regular circuits of the Canadian Conference, is it surprising that I should complain, remonstrate, and condemn?

The burden of Dr. Alder's letter is that I have been the first, gratuitous, and wanton aggressor upon the character and motives of those "to whom the British Conference has entrusted the transaction of its most important business;" and, as such, the author and fomenter of the difficulties between the British and Canadian Conferences. And it has been more than once intimated on your part that if I, the Jonah, were thrown overboard, the commotion of the Methodistic element of Western Canada would soon cease, and mutual confidence and joy would be restored to the whole ship's company. . . Need I add, that in the columns of your *Watchman* newspaper, and in the pages of pamphlets, and in your *Wesleyan* in Canada, not only my public conduct, but my character, my motives, my principles, have been impugned without delicacy or restraint? Need I add, that the Canada Conference and myself have been the defendants, and you the assailants, throughout? That in Dr. Alder's letter to Lord John Russell the proceedings of the Canada Conference are represented as revolutionary?

I am also impeached in almost every form of phraseology—the Christian integrity and loyalty of my brethren and myself have been impugned by your agents throughout this country—our fields of labour have been invaded, and our flocks divided, while our principles and feelings have been resented as dangerous to the safety and interests of the State. Yet Dr. Alder complains of the occasional exposure of these things in the *Guardian*, and is rampant at the application of the word divisionists, to those of your missionaries who are dividing our regular societies, and establishing rival congregations on our regular circuits! . . But, in reply, there may be opposed to the unanimous resolutions of your Conference, adopted in Liverpool, in 1820, and the whole tenor and spirit of the New Testament, especially the writings of St. Paul, who denounces partialities for Peter, or Paul, or Apollos, as pretext for schisms in the Church of God.

Then as to my desire to protract litigation. Does my having done all in my power to have the affair referred to a third party —to any impartial tribunal you might prefer—evince the truth of such a charge? Or does your refusing to agree to any such reference look most like desiring to protract hostilities? Great Britain and other civilized nations have more than once submitted their differences to the decision of a third party; ancient churches did the same; I have advocated the same; you refuse; your refusal does not certainly argue a consciousness that you are right, or a desire for peace, whatever else it may argue.

Furthermore, as to my own feelings and conduct, I will let the following memorandum, which I presented at the late session of the Canada Conference, speak in reply to your various allegations:—

I hereby resign my seat in the Conference of the Wesleyan Methodist Church in Canada.

I do not resign my membership in the Conference, but I resign all privilege and right to take part in its deliberations, or even to be present at its sittings. I hold myself as much as ever responsible and subject to the Conference, and am as ready as ever to do all in my power to defend the Conference and Institutions of the Church when necessary; but I voluntarily relinquish participating in any way whatever in its Executive or Legislative Councils. The following are the considerations which have induced me to take this step:—

1. My presence and participation in the proceedings of the Conference have been represented as forming an insuperable obstacle to any adjustment of differences between the Wesleyan Conference in England, and this Conference.

2. I prefer the unity of Methodism, and an honourable adjustment of differences between two branches of the great Methodist family, to the exercise of any influence I may possess, or may be supposed to possess in the Councils of this Conference; or to the profit and pleasure I may derive from attending the annual deliberations of my reverend and beloved brethren.

3. I can now take this step without incurring any imputation upon my character, and without injuring the interests of the Conference, or of the Church at large.

I respectfully request that this memorandum may be inserted in the journals of the Conference, as an official record and recognition of this my voluntary act.

(Signed)   EGERTON RYERSON.

HALLOWELL, June 14, 1842.

You will see from the above memorandum, that I proposed to relinquish all except my connection with a church which I had joined in obedience to conscience, and my connection with a field of labour to which I believed myself called by the voice and providence of God. My request was laid upon the table of the Conference for a day, and then pressed by me with as much propriety as I could employ on such a subject, but, with one exception (Andrew Prindel), was unanimously rejected, it being insisted that I should not be allowed to change my relations to the Conference, in any respect, on account of your differences with me. To relinquish my connection with the Church, and my labours as a Methodist minister, involve considerations which ought not to yield to the impulse of passion, or bow to the suggestions, of expediency. By God's grace, therefore, I hope to be able to "stand in my place to the end of the day," say or do what you may. . .

Dr. Alder and his Canadian friends have advised you from the beginning that my standing and influence in Canada was merely political; that I was aware of this, and was, therefore, determined to employ myself in political affairs in order to gratify my ambition. My assertions to the contrary were, of course, rejected and scorned by you. Well, nearly three years have elapsed since, by common consent, I have had nothing whatever to do with the civil affairs of Canada, as all the public men in it know. My own conduct, therefore, has thus far refuted one part of the statements of your informers. As to the other part, has my standing as a public man declined? or, have all parties, during that period, awarded me a testimony of regard more gratifying than that which I had ever before received from any party?

You were also told that my principles were revolutionary, and were so viewed by the wealth and intelligence of this country, which would support you and repudiate me and those connected with me. What do you now see, but the Government at home and in Canada adopting the very system of administration, both in religious, educational, and civil affairs, which I maintained many years ago to be most suitable to the social condition of this Province; and the wealth and intelligence of our population (save a little knot of Puseyite ultras) rejoicing in its establishment; and the country in happy tranquility, and blooming with prosperity, under its operations? What do you see but Her Majesty possessing a strength far more formidable than that of swords or bayonets, in the hearts of her Canadian subjects? What do you see, but three branches of the Legislature unanimously incorporating as a College, with the privileges of a University, an institution under the direction of the Canada Conference (which you had repudiated), and in compliance with an application which I had the honour to have advocated, and according to the provisions of a Bill, *verbatim et literatim*, which I drew up? What do you see, but that same Legislature, with equal unanimity, granting £500 to the same institution, and lately, by the recommendation of His Excellency, Sir Charles Bagot, renewing that grant as an annual aid to the institution, now presided over by the individual against whom all your attacks have been directed? Can I but feel a grateful, as well as a dutiful attachment to a Government so perfectly consonant with my own feelings? Can I but feel an honest pride, retrospecting the past, and looking abroad upon the present, to see in the constitution and spirit of Her Majesty's Canadian Government my own views and wishes carried out to the very letter? Can I but rejoice, to see several members of the Government on our College Board and Senate—and to be aided by their counsel, abilities, and influence?

I advert to these facts with heart-felt thankfulness, as a practical vindication of my life and character against your imputations, and as an indication strong, if not providential, that I have, in the main at least, endeavoured to do my duty to my God, my Sovereign, and my country. . . Unconnected as I am with any party, and on friendly terms with leading men of all parties, countenanced by the Government, aided by the Legislature, and sustained by the public, I can, by the divine blesssing, employ my humble abilities, even under the weight of Dr. Alder's frowns, to rearing up a large body of well instructed youth, and a considerable number of ministers, who, I hope, will be a blessing to this their country, and to the church, and who will, doubtless, do justice to me when both Dr. Alder and myself shall be receiving our reward according to our respective works, "whether they be good or bad." . .

My differences with you are wholly of a public and official character; personally I esteem and honour you as much as I ever did, and wish you God speed in your general works of faith and divine labours of love. . .

The only persons in England with whom I have the slightest personal difference are Dr. Alder and Mr. Lord, for their uncalled for and unjust personal attacks upon me. I cherish no ill-feeling towards them. But I ask not your indulgence; I fear you not; I know and admire you as distinguished servants of the Most High, but as greatly mistaken as to what truly appertains to one hundred and twenty-one itinerant ministers, and a large and growing branch of the Wesleyan body in Western Canada—a body now beginning, like yourselves, to raise up a regularly educated as well as a zealous ministry. . .

This epistle shall be my witness to the Government, to the church, and to posterity, that the dreadful disgrace and varied evils of perpetuating the present unseemly violation of Methodistic and Christian unity in Upper Canada, and the creation and continuance of unnatural and unchristian schisms and divisions in a Christian church, lie not at my door; and that for the sake of peace, I have offered to do all that could be demanded of me by reason of Christianity. . .

As the Government is interested in this controversy, I shall deem it my duty to enclose a copy of the present letter to His Excellency the Governor-General, with a request that His Excellency will have the goodness to forward it to Her Majesty's Secretary of State for the Colonial Department, that Her Majesty's Government, both at home and in this country, may fully understand the present posture of this affair, at least as far as you and myself are concerned, and with whom lies the responsibility of this continued controversy.

For the reasons given above to the Secretaries of the Wesleyan Conference in England, Dr. Ryerson transmitted a copy of his letter to them to Sir Charles Bagot, on the 10th December, 1842, accompanied with an explanatory letter, from which I extract the following narrative connected with this matter:—
Two weeks before the late Lord Sydenham's arrival in Toronto (in November, 1839), at a meeting of the agents of the London Committee, and the Executive Committee of the Canadian Conference, every matter of misunderstanding and jealousy, as

far as I know, was satisfactorily settled. It was explicitly agreed on all sides, and recorded, that I should press the settlement of the clergy reserve question. On other things it was my wish and aim to remain neutral. This I did, until some weeks after Lord Sydenham's arrival. Parties were very equally divided on the question of the union of the Canadas, and the terms on which it should be effected. I was then Editor of the *Guardian;* I was desired by the agents of the London Wesleyan Committee and their friends (and some of my own friends), to oppose the union of the Canadas; Lord Sydenham sent for me, and earnestly solicited me to advocate it, and assured me that it should involve no change in the principles of our Constitution, but even secure greater privileges to the people of Canada, and that it was the only hope of Canada. He promised, in case he could get the Union measure through the Canadian Legislature, to apply himself to the settlement of the clergy reserve question, in accordance with such principles as I had expressed, and which he understood to be general in Upper Canada. After much consideration, I consented to give a decided support to the Government in that great measure. The agents of the London Committee were greatly offended, and were sure, as were many others, that Lord Sydenham would not be supported by the Imperial Parliament, and threatened a breaking up of the union between the English and Canadian Conferences; and in about three weeks afterwards, they intimated to Lord Sydenham that the union between the two bodies would not be continued, and sought to get the Methodist portion of the proceeds of the clergy reserves secured to those who should be connected with the British Wesleyan Conference. Lord Sydenham, learning the circumstances in which I was placed, opposed by the agents of the London Committee and all the opponents of the union of the Canadas, and by the "radical reform" portion of the press, for assenting to the application of the clergy reserves to religious purposes at all, and by many of the members of my own Church, because I assented to a Bill which recognized the Churches of England and Scotland by name, and not the Methodist Church, —assured me of all protection and support that his Government could give. I asked for nothing but a due consideration and protection of the interests of the Church which I represented. Of this I received repeated assurances; and when, a few months afterwards, Lord Sydenham received from Lord John Russell, a copy of Dr. Alder's first letter to his Lordship, Lord Sydenham not only renewed the private expression of his views and purposes, but introduced them voluntarily in an answer to a congratulatory address of the Canadian Conference. In reference to these very matters, out of which the present question has arisen, Lord Sydenham thus expressed himself, and pledged the faith of his Government. He said :—

Whilst I administer the affairs of the Canadas, it is my duty to look to the feelings of the people of that country; and you will find me ever ready and willing, whenever any question connected with the Executive Government may arise, to support the reasonable views, and maintain the just rights of your society, as expressed through your recognized authorities within these Provinces.

When it was ascertained that the English Conference would not abide by the articles of union, and that several months' delay had taken place without carrying out the views which Lord Sydenham had expressed—that an Act on the clergy reserve question had been passed by the Imperial Parliament, different in several important respects from that which Lord Sydenham had got through the Canadian Legislature, it was our intention to have the claims and interests of our Church in respect both to the grant and clergy reserves, brought under the consideration of the Canadian Legislature. But previously to taking this step, I was directed to proceed to Kingston (June, 1841), to ascertain what measures the Government were disposed to adopt; when I learned from Lord Sydenham that he had been empowered to settle the question of the grant, and that in that and all other respects he would consult the interests of our Church to the utmost of his power. It was not his wish to communicate his decision officially until near the close of the session of the Legislature, which, unhappily, proved to be the end of his life. What has since transpired is within the personal knowledge of Your Excellency.

After all this correspondence, the question of reunion with the British Conference was often and earnestly discussed privately between leading members of the Canadian and British Conferences, as well as in the American Methodist journals.*

In October, 1843, Rev. Joseph Stinson, then in Sheffield, England, wrote to Dr. Ryerson on the subject, and said:—

There is a strong desire on the part of many of our most influential ministers that the work in Canada should be consolidated and made one. It is certainly most desirable that there should be one vigorous, united, and pros-

* Dr. Thomas Bond, Editor of the New York *Christian Advocate*, having suggested in December, 1842, the basis of settlement of the differences between the English and Canadian Conferences, Rev. W. M. Harvard wrote from Quebec to Dr. Bond, dissenting from his proposition. Dr. Bond, in a letter to Dr. Ryerson, commenting on Mr. Harvard's objections, thus refers to the Canadian Connexion:

The Canada Conference was sound in the faith, and well affected to primitive Wesleyan discipline, and when it came of age, the Methodist Episcopal Connexion allowed them, and aided them, to go to housekeeping by themselves. We knew of no objection on either subject, when we, with the kindest of feelings, have now hinted at the possibility of an amicable arrangement between our British and Canadian brethren.

perous Methodist Church; in which the pure doctrines of Methodism, and of the Gospel, shall be preserved, and a refuge for those who really want to be saved shall be presented—to all those, I mean, who prefer our religious system to any other. Now, my dear sir, allow me to say, that I think that the only two men in the world who can effect this most desirable object, are yourself and Dr. Alder. If any plan could be adopted by which you and he could be reconciled to each other, the work would be done; and it will not be done effectually, I fear, until this is the case. I still entertain the hope of spending many happy and useful years in Canada; and I thank you sincerely for your kind offer with reference to Cobourg. I cannot forget the happy, and, I may say, holy hours we have spent together before God in prayer; and I hope and trust we shall yet be found side by side in the Church militant and in the Church triumphant.

Rev. Joseph Stinson wrote again in December, and was very urgent in regard to the reunion of the Conferences. He says:

Let us still labour and pray for the great object of union. Every day, and every aspect which the Church and the world presents, deepens the conviction of my mind of its necessity, and I hope we shall live to see a united and prosperous Church in Canada, against which the gates of hell cannot prevail. We are now very busy with our Educational movements. We intend to raise £200,000 in seven years, and we shall, by the Divine blessing, succeed. Our people were never more united, and truly Methodistical in their feelings and purposes. God has a great work for us to do in the world, and if we are but faithful, we shall be a greater blessing to our Empire than we have ever been.

In November, 1844, after his arrival in London, Dr. Ryerson addressed a letter to his two friends, Rev. Joseph Stinson and Rev. G. Marsden, on the Union question. From Mr. Stinson he received a reply, from which the following is an extract:—

I heartily congratulate you on your promotion. I pray that you may be happy and useful in the interesting and responsible station assigned you by the providence of God and the Government of your country. I hope your visit to this country may be one of those Providential events which will lead to the accomplishment of an object which lies as near to my heart now as it ever did—the unity of our Methodist interests in Canada. The aspects of the times at home and abroad surely are plainly indicating that our very existence as a Church depends, in no small degree, upon our unity. In the meantime, if I can, by any little influence I have, be able to effect a reconciliation between you and our friends at the Mission House, nothing on earth will afford me so much pleasure.

Rev. G. Marsden, in his reply to Dr. Ryerson, said:—

Often have I reflected with deep interest on the whole of that very important affair—the union of the two bodies; and though it was afterward dissolved, I firmly believe that the union at that time was of God. It gave a favourable opportunity for our Conference reviewing and improving the code of Discipline, and I hope that it is now rendered permanent. In that respect I believe you in Canada are on good ground; and I could almost wish that it may be unalterable. There may be attempts made, under the pretence of improvements, to alter in future our Book of Discipline, but I trust that those preachers who were at the Conference when the Discipline was settled and solemnly agreed upon, will not hastily adopt any material alterations.

The union was also providential as it occurred before the rebellion commenced. So far it appeared to be in the order of Providence; and though in a few years the union was dissolved, yet you have gone on well in Canada, and the Lord has prospered you.

The position which you now occupy is one of great importance, as it respects the future good of Canada. If the youth of that country be trained up in sound Christian principles, the country, as it respects the inhabitants, may become one of the finest in the world. The old countries are formed, yours is in some measure yet to be formed; and as is the education, such in all probability will be the inhabitants in future.

Dr. Ryerson after his arrival in England, also addressed a letter to Dr. Bunting, dated December 11th, 1844, as follows:—

I desire your acceptance of the accompanying publication [relating to the Metcalfe controversy]. The Prefatory Notice and Address will explain to you the circumstances under which it was written.

I take the liberty of presenting you with this publication, not merely from feelings of profound respect for yourself personally, but also for the following reason:—That you may have the best possible proof of the sentiments which I have ever inculcated upon the public mind in Canada, and which are current among the ministers and members of the Wesleyan Methodist Church in that country. In appendix No's. 3 and 4, pages 171-178, I have made extracts from what I wrote between the years 1838 and 1841, the period, in August, 1840, during which both my sentiments and conduct were impugned in your presence. You will probably recollect that I then stated that my principles were strictly British, and such alone as could perpetuate British authority in Canada. The fact that the present Governor-General of Canada, and Her Majesty's present Government—apart from a candid inquiry into the nature of them—have staked their character and authority in Canada upon those principles, is ample proof of their constitutional orthodoxy and essential importance; and the manner in which Sir Charles Metcalfe has been, and is, supported in Upper Canada, is sufficient evidence of their influence over the public mind there, without your expending some three thousand pounds a year of missionary money within the bounds of the regular self-supporting and missionary-contributing circuits of the Canada Conference in order to teach us loyalty. (See pages 282, 283.) Since I was last in England, I have not written a word on civil affairs, except a short obituary notice of the late Sir Charles Bagot (which was not inserted in the *Christian Guardian*, any more than what I have recently written) until the publication which I herewith transmit. By referring to pages 134, 153, 164, you will find that I have not, even as an individual, written for party, or in the spirit of party, but with a view of giving and securing the application of a Christian interpretation of the fundamental principles of the British Constitution, and of all good government.

I am thankful that I have been permitted to live and give to the British Government in England, and to the public in Canada, a more tangible and abiding proof of my principles and feelings than the representations which were made of them in your presence in 1840.

It may not be improper for me to add, that the appointment with which the Government has honoured me, in placing under my direction, the public educational instruction of the youth of Upper Canada, was not accepted by me, until after my ministerial brethren, officially, as well as unofficially, expressed their approbation of my doing so.

After the Conference of 1845, Dr. Ryerson (then in Europe) received a letter from Rev. John Ryerson, in which he said :—

The Conference received a note from the sub-Secretary of the British Conference, enclosing certain resolutions which had been passed two years ago, appointing a committee to settle matters with the Canada Conference respecting the differences between the two Connexions. Our Conference appointed a similar committee, and the Secretary was directed to communicate to the British Conference, and request it to make some proposals for settlement, as they had rejected all the proposals which we had made. In fact, parties here have taken advantage of the overtures which we have made to injure the Canada Conference, while there is no move on the part of the British Conference to indicate that they even desire a settlement. For my own part, I would have gone so far as to have made the proposal which you suggested; but I could not influence a majority of the Conference to do so. The belief here is gaining ground that the British Conference has no intention to settle the differences ; that they are only tampering with us, and, at the same time, they are striving to get the £700. I believe that no settlement can be effected until that grant matter is adjusted, and that no grant will be paid until that settlement is made. I cannot forget the reprehensible conduct of the Missionary party, in sending a missionary to Bytown, at the very time that they were pretending to negotiate a settlement with us! Still I am anxious to do almost anything to effect an adjustment of our misunderstandings; but I fear that the British Conference, influenced by the Missionary party here, will accede to no feasible plan of settlement—at all events, not while these men are kept here, and are allowed to have the influence in England which they seem to possess.

You are aware, of course, that a party in Toronto have for these six months being publishing a paper, the object of which is by agitation among our people, to drive the Conference to censure you and your political writings. The Radical party in the Conference tried to get that body to pass some such resolutions as Rev. C. R. Allison introduced at Brockville, but they totally failed. The Conference in reply to two memorials—the one from Brantford, and the other from Cobourg—defended the resolutions passed at Brockville on political matters, and the pastoral address of the same year, and remarked that it saw no reason to say more than it had said. This was sadly mortifying to the parties opposed to you. However, every effort of that party in this and other questions totally failed. They were left in most miserable minorities in everything they undertook of a party and revolutionary character. The party has assailed all of our funds, especially our Missionary Society and Victoria College. Indeed, there was nothing connected with our institutions which they have not tried to injure, taking good care to connect your name with everything, so as to let the Church know that you would be a sacrifice entirely satisfactory to them.

Political matters in the country are in a state of great quiet. I think the present Government has got on strong ground—being assailed by the two extreme sharks—the *Pilot* and the *Patriot*. . . The impartiality and high-minded justice of the Governor-General are becoming more and more apparent. Indeed, I do not think the Radicals will be able to recover their power in any degree while Lord Metcalfe remains, certainly not if he continues, in defiance of party strife, to administer the Government as it has been administered since the present Council has been organized.

The University Question is a most perplexing one, and the Ministry will find the utmost difficulty to so devise a plan of settlement so as to satisfy a majority of the people and carry the House with them.

After this correspondence on the Union question had taken place little was done and less resulted from it. When Dr. Ryerson returned to Canada, he wrote to Rev. Peter Jones, then in England, to see Rev. Dr. James Dixon, and urge him to come to Canada. In February, 1846, Rev. Mr. Jones replied:—

On receiving your letter I lost no time in calling upon Dr. Dixon, who appeared pleased with the invitation from our Executive Committee. He said that if he could see that his visit to Canada would bring about a reconciliation between the two Conferences, he would be most happy to go. I am very glad that the Committee have invited him to come and inspect the state of affairs. I believe that the invitation will do much good, whether Dr. Dixon goes or not, as it will be seen that our Conference is anxious for a settlement, and courts investigation.

I do assure you that we are getting very homesick; and I am heartily tired of the work of begging. I shall be glad when we are again quietly settled in our own wigwams.

In reply to this invitation, Rev. Dr. Dixon wrote a letter to Rev. Dr. Ryerson, in March, in which he foreshadowed the important Methodistic legislation which resulted in the establishment of the General Conference which met at Toronto in 1874, with Dr. Ryerson as its first President. Dr. Dixon said:—

My own idea is that a measure much more comprehensive than that of a mere settlement of these disputes is needed. The time must come when the North American provinces will be united ecclesiastically, by having a General Conference of their own, in connexion with the Provincial or District Conferences, after the manner of the United States. Things must come to this at no remote period; and this being the case, it seems reasonable to consider such a scheme in connection with the measure now under review. To do the thing well will require, of course, very much and mature deliberation. In case such a measure should be thought of, some form of fellowship, some bond of union—must be recognized betwixt the British Conference and such a body as I contemplate. Here is a ticklish point—it is at this point that all splits and quarrels begin. But clearly the line of justice, religion, and a Christian experience may be discovered, if honestly sought. I am deeply convinced myself that the organization of such a body as I refer to must, in the nature of things develop the energies of Methodism in the Provinces infinitely more vigorously than can be secured by the action of a distant government.

I venture to throw this out as my general feeling and impression. Of course, it has been thought of by others as well as myself; and I found the other day from Rev. Peter Jones that the subject is engaging the attention of different parties on your side of the water. Could you not open a discussion on this question in your periodicals? But it should be free from party bias, from angry passions, from national views and partialities; indeed, the discussion of such a subject requires the highest reason, philosophy and statesmanship. If a calm head and pure patriot could be found amongst you to argue such a point, it would be clearing the ground. Of the soundness of the principle that the Methodist body ought to be one in all the adjacent colonies; and I am convinced that it would be wise and expedient to establish as soon as men's minds are prepared for it, such an establishment as a general colonial Conference. And in the present state of things, I conceive it would be useful to receive a certain amount of British influence in such a Conference. You cannot do very well without us; and on this side there would be great alarm at the idea of an entire separation. But all these are questions of detail.

Let me say now, that I have a strong desire to visit your Provinces—I should like above all things to obey your call; but I see it possible not only to do no good, but to do harm, by exasperating parties on my taking up an independent position. Let me say, I think the object we desire is being promoted by your communication; and I hope that either myself, or some other one better fitted, will, ere long, appear amongst you as a messenger of peace. I long to see it.

It would afford Mrs. Dixon and I the highest gratification to see you in this country again—to have the very great delight to see you by our fireside, and experience over again some of the happy moments we dearly enjoyed in your friendly society. Thank God there is a Christianity infinitely above ecclesiastical divisions, and sub-divisions; and there is a depth of feeling and affection in the human heart which cannot be destroyed by the miserable squabbles of nations and churches.

At the Conference held at Kingston, after the receipt of this letter from Rev. Dr. Dixon, it was considered expedient to send a deputation from Canada to the English Conference. Rev. John Ryerson and Rev. Anson Green were selected for this important mission and soon left for England. In a letter to Dr. Ryerson from his brother John, dated Bristol, August 1st, he says that :—

The difficulties in the way of any proper adjustments of our differences seem to be almost insurmountable. Prejudices so strong and so extensive, have been excited against us that we, as the representatives of the Canada Conference, are looked upon with shyness, if not fear and contempt. Our situation is anything but pleasant; it is even distressing and painful. . . Rev. Joseph Stinson is most cordial and affectionate, and is doing his utmost to further the object of our mission and promote peace in Canada; this is also the case of Rev. William Lord.

Subsequently Rev. John Ryerson wrote to say that :—

Dr. Alder presented the address of our Conference, and also the certificate of our appointment to the British Conference. It was moved by Dr. Bunting, and seconded by Dr. Alder, that the address be received, and that we be affectionately and cordially requested to take a seat in the Conference. The resolution was opposed, and it called up a warm debate. The opposers contended that their connection with the Canada Conference and its matters had only been a source of trouble and injury to themselves, and that, as the Union was now dissolved, they should keep aloof from all intercourse with us. The resolution was warmly supported by Doctors Bunting, Alder, Beaumont, Dixon, Mr. Lord, and Mr. Stinson. It at length passed triumphantly, and all things are coming out right, and will end well.

Rev. John Ryerson again wrote to Dr. Ryerson from Bristol:

Although we took our seats in the Conference last week, yet we were not formally introduced until yesterday. It is clear that Dr. Alder and others were resolved that we should not take our seats on the platform, but Mr. Lord and Mr. Atherton (the President) and others were resolved that we should. The President accordingly stated that the brethren from Canada, Representatives of the Canada Conference, would be introduced to the Conference, and would take their seats on the platform, which we did. What Dr. Alder may hereafter do, I know not; up to this time his conduct has been cold and repulsive; he, however, continually declares that he is in favour of an adjustment of matters in Canada.

In looking at matters here, I cannot express the painful anxiety of my mind; sometimes I can neither eat nor sleep, and it quite destroys all the satisfaction which I might otherwise enjoy from a visit to England. Had I known that things would be as I find them, I should never have come to England. I left Canada distressed in mind about our mission; the distress has only continued to increase every day since. Were I to follow the strong impulse of my mind, I should leave at once and return to America.

All this was changed, however; and on the 15th September Rev. John Ryerson thus writes to Dr. Ryerson as to the final issue of negotiations with the British Conference:—

After four days' conference in committee on Canada affairs, the whole business was brought to a happy and most amicable conclusion. When I wrote my last letter I was under most painful apprehensions respecting the results of our mission. Little change took place in the bearing of the leading men towards us, until we met in committee on the 9th inst. Then a most full, frank, and undisguised explanation of all missionary and domestic matters was entered into. After this full unburthening of ourselves, the one to the other, a totally different feeling seemed to come over Drs. Bunting, Alder, and the whole committee—which consisted of about thirty leading members of the British Conference. In consequence of the strong feeling which exists chiefly in Lower Canada, the British North American plan mentioned by Dr. Dixon in his letter to you, was thought not practicable at present. The plan of settlement to which we have agreed, is a union with the British Conference, on a basis similar to that by which the British and Irish Conferences are united. The British Conference appoints our President and the Superintendent of Missions, as in the former union; all of our missions become missions of the Wesleyan Missionary Society; our Missionary Society is auxiliary to their Society. The £700 grant is to be placed under the Missionary Committee, to be appropriated for missionary purposes in Canada. On the other hand, all the regular British Missionary circuits in Canada, are to be placed under the Canada Conference, the same as any other circuits; and there are to be no missionary districts; but the missionaries are to be members of the different districts in the bounds of which their missions are situated. The missionaries are to be stationed by our Stationing Committee, the same as other ministers. The British Conference is to appropriate £600 sterling annually to our contingent fund; and the Missionary Committee is to place £400 at the disposal of our Conference for contingent purposes.

More kindness, more nobleness of sentiment and feeling, I never witnessed than was manifested towards us after we had succeeded in removing suspicion, and allaying fears, etc. In the course of the conversations, your name came up frequently, but always in terms of great respect; only they all seemed to think that you got astray in the matter of the disruption of the union. I assured them, however, that no man in Canada was more desirous of a settlement of differences than you were, and in order to the attainment of it, you were desirous that all the past should be forgotten, and that henceforth in these matters all should become new. I assured Dr. Alder that no man in Canada would receive him more cordially than you would. This assurance seemed to be very gratifying to him and all the other ministers present.

On the 24th November, 1846, after the return of the Conference delegation from England, Dr. Ryerson addressed the following letter to Drs. Bunting and Alder:—At the suggestion of my brother, Rev. John Ryerson, and in accordance with my own feelings, I take the liberty of addressing you a few lines on adjustment of differences between the English and Canadian Conferences, and the concentration of the work of Methodism in Upper Canada. In the arrangement which has been mutually agreed upon. between your Committees and the Canadian Representatives, I entirely concur. Into the consideration of a measure so purely Christian and Wesleyan, I have never allowed, and could not for a moment allow, any sense of personal injury to enter. I have had the pleasure of expressing to the Conferential Committee of the Canadian Connexion my appreciation of the honourable and generous arrangement to which you have agreed, and to propose a resolution expressive of the concurrence of that Committee in that arrangement, to which it assented cordially and unanimously. I have also had the pleasure of moving that Rev. M. Richey be invited to occupy the relation to Victoria College which I have for some years sustained, and to which the College Council has also unanimously agreed. Nor shall I hesitate to use every exertion in my power to complete and render beneficial an arrangement so honourable to the British Conference, and so eminently calculated to promote the best interests of Methodism in Western Canada.

Your treatment of my dear and most beloved brother, John, I regard and acknowledge as a favour done to myself. I did not do myself the honour of calling upon you personally when I was in England, nor should I feel myself at liberty to do so even now, were I again to visit London. It is not that you have objected to many things that I have said and done, and have expressed your objections in the strongest language. In this you have acted as I have done, and for which I ought not either to respect or love you the less. But, in your resolutions of April, 1840, you were pleased to charge me " with an utter want of integrity ;" and in a subsequent series of resolutions, you were pleased to represent me as unworthy of the intercourse of private life. These two particulars of your proceedings attracted the painful notice of the late Sir Charles Bagot before I ever saw him, and, I have reason to believe, made no slight impression on the mind of his successor, the late venerated Lord Metcalfe; and they have sunk deeply into my own heart. But I have not so much as alluded to them in my official intercourse with my Canadian brethren, nor will I do so; and as a member of the Canadian Conference, I shall (if spared) receive and treat Dr. Alder with as much respect and cordiality as I ever did, and shall do my best to render his contemplated visit to Canada agreeable to himself, and successful in its objects. I have, more than once, through the press, disclaimed any imputation upon his integrity, motives, or character; but with his recorded declaration of my "utter want of integrity," and my unfitness for social intercourse in private life, I feel that my own conduct towards him should be confined to official acts and official occasions; in which I shall treat him with as much cordiality as I would any other member of the English Conference. Had it not been for the two particulars in your former proceedings to which I have referred, I should have as readily sought the opportunity of paying you my personal respects, during my recent visit to England, as I did in 1836.

I have thought this explanation, at the present moment, due both to you and to myself. I assure you at the same time of my personal regard, and of my desire and purpose to promote, in every possible way, the great objects which you have proposed, viz., the amicable reunion between the English and Canadian Connexions. [The *amende* was subsequently made.]

In order to place the English and Canadian reunion question fully and fairly before the English Wesleyan public, Dr. Ryerson was requested to prepare an article on the subject for the London *Watchman*. This he did. Rev. M. Richey writes from Montreal, on the 28th June, 1847, and thus acknowledges the service which Dr. Ryerson had rendered in this matter:—

Your promptitude in preparing an article for the *Watchman*, and the ability, as well as noble spirit of Wesleyan catholicity by which it is characterized, have afforded to Dr. Alder the highest satisfaction. The article perfectly corresponds to the ideal he had conceived of a production adapted to place the whole matter before the transatlantic public so as best to accomplish the important object. The article will doubtless appear in the earliest impression of the *Watchman*, to the joy of thousands of hearts. He has also to acknowledge the receipt of the address of the Canada to the British Conference. Permit me to assure you that Dr. Alder and myself most affectionately reciprocate your expressions of kindness and regard, and we have every confidence that no elements will be ever hereafter permitted to disturb either our ecclesiastical relations or our personal friendship.

On his return from Canada, Dr. Alder wrote to Dr. Ryerson,

under date of the 17th September, expressing his grateful feelings at the result of his visit. He said :—

I assure you of the recollection which I cherish of the candid and manly part which you took, both in public and in private, in connexion with the various important matters of business which were brought before us during the sittings of the last Conference in Toronto, as well as previous to the meeting of that assembly. I have not failed in my communications since my return, to do you that justice to which you are so well entitled; and I trust, as I doubt not you do, that the good understanding which has thus been restored, will be as permanent as it is gratifying. Much will depend upon you, as well as upon myself, in securing the harmonious working of the union which has been accomplished; and I shall always be happy to receive from you free and full communications, which will be regarded by me as confidential.

Dr. Alder in a subsequent letter, to Dr. Ryerson, said :—

In the *Watchman* I have prefaced an account of our Missionary Anniversary by a few observations, in which I have taken occasion to bear testimony to the spirit and conduct of your brother William, as well as of your own, with a view, not merely to perform an act of justice to you, but to prepare the way for the appointment of one, or you both, coming, either now, or at some future period, in a representative character, to our Conference,—an arrangement which, I am persuaded, will be productive of much good in various ways.

In carrying out practically so great a measure as that of the union, difficulties of no ordinary kind will be felt. I have pressed upon, and fully explained our financial matter to, Earl Grey, who has, I believe, written to Lord Elgin on the subject. I think I have made Earl Grey understand the peculiarity of our case. You must press the matter on your side.

In the union matter you must have the greatest practical freedom of operation. I have explained my views to Dr. Dixon, your new President, who sailed last Saturday in the best of spirits.

In a fraternal letter, written in July, 1847, to the Rev. Dr. Olin, President of the Wesleyan University, Middletown, Conn., Dr. Ryerson gave some particulars as to the union with the British Conference. He said :—

You have, doubtless, ere this, heard that a complete adjustment of past differences between the Wesleyan Conferences in England and Canada, has been effected, and that provision has been made for a perfect *oneness* of their interests and labours in Upper Canada. This important object has been accomplished with a cordiality, and unanimity, and devotion, that I have never seen surpassed, and without the loss—so far as has yet been ascertained —of a single minister or member of either body, and to the universal satisfaction and even joy of both parties. We look upon it with gratitude and wonder, as the Lord's doing, and as marvellous beyond expression in our eyes.

In a reply to this letter written to Dr. Ryerson, in September, 1847, Dr. Olin discusses the question of the Union, and also the relations of the Church, North and South, on the Slavery question :—

I do most cordially rejoice at the happy termination of your negotiations with the Wesleyan body in England. I must confess, however, that I have been somewhat disappointed at the results of your attempts to get on as an independent Conference. In theorizing upon the subject, I have concluded that union would be far more likely to embarrass than to facilitate your movements. I have since learned that there were disturbing influences not discernible by observers at a distance, growing out of the occupancy of the field by conflicting agencies; the heterogenous character of your population and the power of home associations, etc. I rejoice that you have overcome these various obstacles, and are likely to have harmony for the future. All parties will probably be warned and instructed by the temporary interruption in your connexional relations. All must be now deeply impressed with the importance of forbearance and concessions after an experience so memorable of the necessity of union.

I deeply regret that you should have received anything but kindness from our side of the line. I think I can assure you that, as a Church, our sympathies are, and have been, strongly with you; but the natural and spontaneous feelings of the Body are not well expressed; and they are in imminent danger of being perverted on certain questions, which, unfortunately, become party questions amongst us. The Methodist Episcopal Church is passing through a crisis. It has fallen upon her to decide momentous questions under peculiar temptations to error. The ministers are pure and high, above all liability to be influenced by corrupt motives; but we are calamitously enough thrown into a position where we must judge between ourselves and our brethren, with powerful interests and more potent prejudices to mislead us. Beyond all reasonable doubt, we are coming to an issue for which, it is my opinion, the Church of Christ, the world and history, will not cease to reproach us. And yet we are coming to that issue with a good conscience, honestly, so far as party spirit and blind prejudice, and the most unfortunate leading, has left us the power of being honest. I wish my convictions of the right were not quite so unchangeably settled. It would afford me unspeakable relief to be able to suspect that the predestined course of the Church could be other than a flagrant violation of justice. I would gladly surrender my opinion, if I could avail myself of even the benefit of a doubt in favour of retraction. How we shall hereafter be looked upon by the world, is a consideration of less interest than another which perpetually thrusts itself upon my fears—what will God pronounce upon our policy? My only hope is in the indulgence wont to be extended to errors, and even to high offences which are the result of haste, excitement, or prejudice. All of these mitigations may be claimed in anticipation in behalf of the measures which will certainly prevail at our next General Conference. Of the vast majority, which will deny to the South what I esteem their unquestionable rights, I am sure I shall never suspect a man of doing an intentional wrong. I hope your public sentiment and your press will enable to temper their disapprobation with this needful infusion of charity.

After his return to England Rev. Dr. Dixon, in a letter to Dr. Ryerson, thus referred to the impression which his visit to Canada made upon him. He said:—

My impressions are strong respecting the importance of Methodism in Canada. It is at present a glorious religious element in the country, and will become much more powerful. The colony is destined to become, either in its present, or some new connection, a great empire. It is consequently of great importance to adapt your religious system to existing things, preserving points of doctrine.

I must say, that I never think of my intercourse with you; my journeys with your brother; my connection with the Conference; and the kindness of the brethren, but with feelings of intense interest. In imagination, I try to live everything over and over again. Many faces and persons are imprinted on my mind; and almost every scene through which I passed lives in vivid reality. I am often journeying down your glorious lakes and rivers, gazing on your woods and forests, and stretching myself in the expanse, as if there were room to live and breathe. Then, the affection and kindness of everybody! The people and the scenery agree. All is magnificent in America. I hope you may be able, by the divine blessing, to preserve the purity of religion amongst you. I have strong feelings on one point—viz.: the necessity of giving to all our movements an evangelic and aggressive character. We Methodists are so fond of organizations of every sort, and hence of legislating and placing everything under rule and order, that we leave no room for extension and for development. I am convinced that a religious system which does not act on the evangelic principle; and, moreover, have good people free to work and exercise the divine affection, must break down.

I consider myself much more in the character of an observer now, than an actor in anything. I have finished my mission, as regards public work. It ended in Canada; and the above are my last, and, I believe will remain, my unalterable convictions. Our danger is over-legislation; cramping the energies of living piety by decrees and rules; laying too much weight on the springs of individual movement; destroying the man in society, the committee, etc.

I am glad to hear that you preach constantly. This is all that I care about —to endeavour to do some little good in the way of saving souls. Noble work this! So let me intreat you never to let your other avocations interfere with this glorious calling. It is painful to see some men merge the ministerial character in some pitiful clerkship—some book-keeping affair. And worst of all, these parties take it into their head, generally amongst us, to consider themselves and their office as much higher than that of the messengers of Christ!

Two deaths of notable representative men in Canadian Methodism occurred during 1846:—Rev. Thomas Whitehead and Rev. James Evans. Rev. Thomas Whitehead was the venerated representative of the early pioneers of Methodism in Upper Canada, and Rev. James Evans was a remarkable type of the self-sacrificing and devoted missionaries of that Church in the great North-west. A brief sketch of each of these ministers will illustrate points in the history of Methodism in Upper Canada, without which the account of Dr. Ryerson's career and labours would be incomplete,—especially as he had to do with both of these ministers during his lifetime. Rev. Mr. Whitehead was one of these so-called "Yankee Methodists," whom Dr. Ryerson so often and so strenuously defended against the charge of disloyalty; and Rev. James Evans was one of the five brethren with whom he remonstrated so earnestly and yet so kindly in 1833. (See page 131.)

Rev. Thomas Whitehead was in many respects a strongly-marked representative man. He was elected President at the memorable Special Conference held, in the dark days of the Church, in 1840. (Page 274.) A characteristic letter from him to Dr. Ryerson will be found on page 276. Mr. Whitehead was born in Duchess County, New York, in December 1762, when it was still a British Province. He was, therefore, not a "Yankee Methodist," but a United Empire Loyalist. He commenced his ministry in 1783, and went on a mission to Nova Scotia and New Brunswick, where he remained from 1786 until 1804. In September, 1806, he was sent by Bishop Asbury to Upper Canada, where he resided for forty years. He preached his last sermon on Christmas Day, 1845. He was in the ministry 62 years, and died at Burford in January, 1846, aged 83 years.

Rev. James Evans was one of the most noted missionaries of the North-west; and was specially so from the fact that, by his wonderful inventions of the syllabic character in the Cree language, he has conferred untold blessings upon the Indian tribes and missions of all the Churches in that vast North-West territory, in which he only was permitted to labour for six years.

Mr. Evans was born in England in 1800. He was converted in Upper Canada, and in 1830 entered the Christian ministry, and was a member of the Canada Conference from that year. In 1840 he volunteered his services as a missionary to the North-west. At his station of Norway House, he devoted himself to his great work. Rev. E. R. Young, in the *Canadian Methodist Magazine* for November, 1882, thus speaks of Mr. Evans' eminent service to the mission cause by his famous invention. He says:—

> The invention of what are known as the syllabic characters was undoubtedly Mr. Evans' greatest work, and to his unaided genius belongs the honour of devising and then perfecting this alphabet which has been such a blessing to thousands of Cree Indians. The principle on which the characters are formed is the phonetic. There are no silent letters. Each character represents a syllable, hence no spelling is required. As soon as the alphabet is mastered, the student can commence at the first chapter in Genesis and read on, slowly of course, at first, but in a few days with surprising facility.
>
> When the invention became more extensively known, and other Churches desired to avail themselves of its benefits, the British and Foreign Bible Society nobly came to the help of our own, and the kindred Churches having missions in the North West, and with their usual princely style of doing things, for years have been printing, and gratuitously furnishing to the different Cree Indian missions, all the copies of the Sacred Word they require.

Rev. Mr. Young relates an interesting anecdote connected with this alphabet, which occurred when he was a missionary in the North-West. During Lord Dufferin's visit there he conversed with Mr. Young in regard to the Indians in these distant regions, and expressed his solicitude for the welfare and happiness of these wandering races, and made general enquires in reference to missionary work among them. Mr. Young adds:—

> In mentioning the helps I had in my work, I showed him my Cree

Indian Testament, in Evans' Syllabic Characters, and explained the invention to him. At once his curiosity was excited, and jumping up he hurried off for pen and paper, and had me write out the whole alphabet for him, and then with that glee and vivacity for which His Lordship was so noted, he constituted me his teacher, and commenced at once to master them. Their simplicity, and yet wonderful adaptation for their designed work became clearly recognized by him, for in a short time he read a portion of the Lord's Prayer. Lord Dufferin became quite excited, and, getting up from his chair, and holding the Testament in his hand, exclaimed, "Why, Mr. Young, what a blessing to humanity the man was who invented that alphabet! Then continuing, he added, "I profess to be a kind of literary man myself, and try to keep up my reading of what is going on, but I never heard of this before. The fact is," he added, "the nation has given many a man a title, and a pension, and then a resting-place, and a monument in Westminster Abbey, who never did half so much for their fellow-creatures." Then turning to me again, he asked, "Who did you say was the author, or inventor of the characters?" "The Rev. James Evans," I replied. "Well, why is it, I never heard of him before, I wonder?" he answered. My reply was, "Well, my lord, perhaps the reason why you never heard before of him was, because he was a humble, modest Methodist preacher." With a laugh he replied, "That may have been it," and then the conversation changed. (Pages 437, 438.)

The following are examples of the

CREE SYLLABIC CHARACTERS.

▽ △ ▷ ◁ ā, e, oo, ah.
∨ ∧ > < pā, pe, poo, pah.
∪ ⊃ ⊂ ⊃ tā, te, tooh, tah.
⌒ ⌊ ⌄ ⌊ chā, che, choo, chah.
𐊾 σ ꝺ ꝗ nā, ne, noo, nah.
ꝗ ρ ჿ σ kā, ke, koo, kah.
⌐ ⌈ ⌐ ⌊ mā, mee, moo, mah.
ꝡ Ꝣ ꝑ ⱨ sā, see, soo, sah.
⋖ ⋗ ⋖ ⋗ yā, yee, yoo, yah.

The following is the mode of forming words:—

L σ ⊂ Mah-ne-tooh—Great Spirit.
▷ ⌈ ⌈ Oo-mee-mee—Dove.
ꝗ < σ Nah-pah-ne—Flour-making.

CHAPTER L.

1846—1854.

MISCELLANEOUS EVENTS AND INCIDENTS OF 1846-1854.

AFTER his return from England, Dr. Ryerson was engaged in the preparation of his Report on a "System of Public Instruction for Upper Canada," from which I have given extracts on page 368. In that report he gave the broad outlines of his proposed scheme of education, and fully explained the principles of the system which he proposed to found. He also prepared a draft of a Bill designed to give effect to some of the most pressing of his recommendations.

In a letter to a friend, dated 18th April, 1846, he said:—My report on a system of public elementary instruction occupies nearly 400 pages of foolscap. It will explain to all parties what I think, desire, and intend. But I would not hesitate to resign my situation to-morrow, and take my place and portion as a Methodist preacher, if I thought I could be as useful in that position to the country at large. My travels have added to my limited stock of knowledge, but they have not altered my principles, or changed my feelings.

To another friend he wrote about the same time:—As the science of civil government is the most uncertain of the uncertain sciences, if I should fail in my exertions—if counteracting influences should intervene which I cannot now foresee, and give success to the opposition against me, or paralyze my influence—I would not remain in office a day, or would I retain it any longer than I could render it a means of strength to our system of government as well as of good to the country. I would rather break stones on the street than be a dead weight to any government, or in any community.

It may be of interest at the present time to learn what was Dr. Ryerson's opinion of Mr. Gladstone in 1845. Writing in the *Guardian* of March 18th, 1846, in reply to strictures on that statesman, Dr. Ryerson said:—During my late tour in Europe, I was one evening present at the proceedings of the British House of Commons, and heard Mr. Gladstone, the Secretary of State for the Colonies, avow a change in his opinions in regard to ecclesiastical and educational matters. Sir Robert Peel's Government had determined to establish several colleges in Ireland, not connected with the Established Church. Mr. Gladstone, in his book on "Church and State," had maintained that the National Church was the only medium through which the Legislature ought to instruct the nation in every department of knowledge. . . . There was, therefore, a complete antagonism between Sir Robert Peel's policy and Mr. Gladstone's book. On the night I was present, Mr. Gladstone . . frankly stated that he had written a book advocating an opposite policy to that which Her Majesty's Government had deemed it their duty to pursue, in establishing secondary colleges in Ireland; that further reflection and experience had convinced him that his views were not correct; that he fully concurred in the policy of the Government in respect to those colleges, and should, as an individual member of Parliament, give it his support; but that should he do so as a Minister of the Crown, after having publicly avowed very different sentiments, he would not be in a position to place his motives of action above suspicion. To exonerate himself, therefore, from the imputation, or suspicion, of being actuated by a love of office or power, to support, as a Minister of State, what he condemned as an author, he resigned his office; and to do. justice to his present convictions of what he conceived the interests of Ireland demanded, he avowed his change of opinion, and his determination to support the Irish policy of Sir Robert Peel, with whom he declared he cordially concurred in every measure which had been discussed in the Cabinet.

Sir Robert Peel followed in a beautiful and touching speech—appealing to the sacrifice which the Cabinet had made in the loss of so able a member as Mr. Gladstone, as a proof of the sincerity of the Government, and the strength of its convictions in its Irish educational policy.

The conduct of those two distinguished statesmen (Dr. Ryerson adds) towards each other on that occasion, presented one of the finest examples of strong personal friendship between two public men that I ever witnessed.

No man excelled Dr. Ryerson in his respect and love for his parents. This was apparent from many incidents, and from the tone of his mother's and father's letters to him, as given in this volume. He generally wrote to them at the beginning of each year. His letter dated Toronto, 1st January, 1847, is, however, the only one which I have. It is as follows:—

MY DEAR AND MOST VENERATED PARENTS,—

As heretofore, the first work of my pen is employed in presenting to you my filial respects, and offering you my dutiful and affectionate congratulations at the commencement of another year,—lifting up, as I most earnestly do, my heart to Almighty God, that, having brought you at so advanced an age to the beginning of this year, He will make it the happiest, as well as the holiest of your lives! I cannot but regard the lengthening out of your earthly pilgrimage so much beyond the ordinary period of human life—so much beyond what I expect to reach—as a special means and call of God to become fully ripe for heaven. You stand a long time on the margin of eternity—may that margin prove the verge of eternal glory! As the body grows feeble, may the soul grow strong! As the bodily sight becomes dim, may the heavenly vision become brighter, and the heavenly aspirations and assurances stronger! How great the privilege, and how soul-cheering the thought, especially at the approach of death, to know that "your life is hid with Christ in God." It is in safe keeping, and the disclosure of it bye-and-bye will be glorious beyond conception; for "when Christ, who is our life, shall appear, shall we then appear like Him in glory." The sufferings of the present life, however severe and protracted, are not worthy to be compared with the glory which that life shall reveal. O, my dear parents, may that glory be yours in all the fulness of its splendour, and in all the perfection of its beatitudes!

I thankfully acknowledge the receipt of the two pairs of socks—the last of the many like tokens of my Mother's affection, and the work of her own hands. I scarcely ever put them on without a gush of feeling which is not easily suppressed. They every day remind me of the hand which sustained my infancy and guided my childhood, and the heart which has crowned my life with its tenderest solicitudes, and most fervent and, I believe, effectual prayers. Praised be God above all earthly things, for such a Mother! May I not prove an unfaithful son!

We are all well. I was at brother George's to-day. I hope to see you in the course of the winter. Each of the family unite with me in expressions of dutiful respect and affection to you. Please remember me to all those who reside with you, and to all relatives, and old acquaintances and neighbours.

With daily prayers at the family altar for your health, comfort and happiness, and anxiously desirous of hearing from you, I am, my most honoured Parents, your affectionate son,

Toronto, 2nd January, 1847.   EGERTON RYERSON.

Between Dr. Ryerson and Rev. Peter Jones a life-long friendship existed. In a note to Dr. Ryerson, dated Credit, Nov. 1st, 1847, Mr. Jones says : I had the pleasure of receiving a set of your School Reports, for which I thank you from the bottom of my heart, and I trust I shall receive much valuable informa-

tion which may prove beneficial in our Indian School schemes.*
My brother, I thank you for all the kindness you have ever
shown to me and my dear family, and I hope and pray that the
friendship which was formed between us many years ago will
last for ever. Pray for us. Rev. Peter Jones had been an inmate of Dr. Ryerson's house during his last illness in 1856.
As the crisis approached he desired to return to his own home
in Brantford. After he reached there, Ven. Archdeacon Nelles
visited him, and in a note to Dr. Ryerson, dated 25th June,
said:—Mr. Jones has been gradually sinking ever since his return
from Toronto. He enjoys great peace of mind, and I believe
truly trusts on that Saviour whom he has so often pointed out
to others as the only refuge and hope of poor sinners. May
my last end be like his.

After the change of administration, consequent on the result
of the recent elections, it was confidently stated that Dr. Ryerson would be removed from office. Having written to his
brother John on the subject, his brother replied, on the 9th of
February, 1847, as follows : It is quite certain that combined and
powerful efforts are being made against you by certain parties,
no doubt with a determination to destroy you as a public
man, if they can. The feeling of the "radical" party is most
inveterate. They are determined, by hook or by crook, to turn
you out of the office of Chief Superintendent of Education. All
the stir among the District Councils, and about the school law,
etc., are but the schemes and measures set on foot by the party
in power for the purpose of compassing the great object in view
of ousting the " Superintendent of Education."

In a letter which I received from Dr. Ryerson, while at the
Belleville Conference, dated June 13th, 1848, he said:—Every
distinction has been shown me in the appointments and arrangements of the Conference; and I believe the great body of the
preachers will sustain me in all future contingencies.

The Conference thus far has been the most delightful I ever

---

* Being a member of the Conference Committee appointed to confer with the Government on the establishment of Manual Labour Schools for the Indians, Rev. Peter Jones, in writing to Dr. Ryerson from the Credit, on the subject, in September, 1844, said :—You will be glad to see that our Indian brethren have subscribed liberally, which shews their ardent desire to have Manual Labour Schools established amongst them. We forwarded a copy to the Governor-General, and His Excellency was pleased to approve of the liberality of the Indian tribes. From the manner in which His Excellency has always spoken of Indian Manual Labour Schools, I am sure that he will take great pleasure in aiding their establishment. As you have access to the ears of our Great Father at Montreal, may I beg the favour of your explaining to him the object of my visit to England, and the necessity of His Excellency's sanctioning the payment of my expenses. As I intend to visit England for the purpose of augmenting the funds of the Manual Labour Schools, I think at least my expenses should be paid out of the Indian subscriptions of $400.

attended. I took the evening service of yesterday, and preached with considerable freedom to an immense congregation; text, John xvii. 17—first part of verse.

There has been an advancement in every department of the interests of our Church during the year. This is very encouraging, and a ground of special thankfulness.

Judge then of Dr. Ryerson's surprise and of mine on seeing the following paragraph in the *Globe* newspaper, about the same time:

> It is said that Egerton Ryerson is trying to get the Methodist Conference to deprive him of his clerical standing, because of his holding a permanent Government situation.

In the course of his reply, Dr. Ryerson said:—When the situation in connection with elementary education was offered to me, in February, 1844, before replying to the offer, I laid the letter containing it before the large Executive Committee of the Wesleyan Conference, and was authorized by that disinterested body to accept of the appointment. When, in the latter part of the May following, I placed the appointment again at the disposal of the Government, as absolutely as if no offer had ever been made or accepted, and determined in June not to accept it under any circumstances, should the offer again be made, a written address was got up to me, numerously signed by the Wesleyan ministers of the Conference which assembled that month, requesting me not to refuse it, should the offer be again made; and it is to the influence of that judgment, in which I confided more than in my own feelings, that the *Globe* and some other papers are indebted for the opportunity and privilege of abusing me in my present position these last four years. Sir, the Wesleyan Conference is as incapable of entertaining such a proposition as you have attributed to me, as I am indisposed to make it; and, though I am not insensible to the honour and importance of my educational office, I hold it as in all respects consistent with my relations and obligations to the Church, through whose instrumentality I have received infinitely greater blessings than it is in the power of any civil government to bestow.

At the proper time I shall be prepared to show that I was personally as disinterested (whether right or wrong) in what I wrote in 1844, as in what I wrote in 1838 and 1839 in connection with the names of Marshall S. Bidwell and J. S. Howard, Esquires. I have ever maintained since 1827 what appeared to me right and important principles, regardless of man in high or low places, and favour or oppose what party it might. I have never borrowed my doctrines from the conclaves or councils of party, nor bowed my neck to its yoke; nor have I made my office subservient to its interests in any shape or form, but to the interest of the country at large, so far as in my power, irrespective of sect or party. I should contemn myself if I could perform one act or say one word to court party favour, or avert party vengeance, if such exists. I shall do as I have done, endeavour faithfully to perform the duties and fulfil the trusts imposed upon me, and leave the future, as well as the past, to the judgement of my native country, for the equal rights of all classes of whose inhabitants I contended in "perilous times," and for years before the political existence of the chief public men of any party in Canada, with the exception of the Hon. William Morris.

The question, incidentally raised by the *Globe* newspaper, after the Conference of 1848, as to Dr. Ryerson's retaining a ministerial *status*, while holding and administering a civil office was brought up at the next Conference, held at Hamilton, in June, 1849. In a letter to me from the Conference, dated 11th of the month, he said:—I brought my position before the Conference in consequence of a remark from one of the preachers, saying, while Mr. Playter's case was under consideration, "that there was a general opposition among the members of the Conference, occupying the position that Mr. Playter did, or a civil situation." Several of the senior members of the Conference spoke in a very complimentary way respecting me; and a strong satisfaction was expressed from all parts of the Conference with my position—the manner in which I had filled it, and consulted the interests of the Church—expressing their earnest desire that I would continue in it.

In a letter to Dr. Ryerson from his brother, Rev. E. M. Ryerson, from Brantford, on July 2nd, 1848, it would appear, from the foregoing, that some hostile movement was being generally formed against him. His brother said:—I found upon my return from Conference to Brantford that the general topic of conversation was your dismissal from your present office. When I told them it was not the case, some rejoiced, while silent grief and disappointment were visible on the countenances of others.

Dr. Ryerson having been called to Montreal on educational matters, in April, 1849, wrote a letter to me from that city, dated 27th of the month, in which he gave a graphic account of the state of the city during the crisis at that time:—You may well imagine my surprise and regret, on reaching Lachine yesterday, to learn that the Parliament House had been burnt, together with a noble library of 25,000 volumes, containing records of valuable books which can never be replaced. On arriving in Montreal, I found nothing but confusion and excitement, which, instead of subsiding, are increasing, and it is apprehended that to-morrow will be a more serious day than any that has preceded it. Yesterday, the court of the Government House was filled with soldiers, while the street in front of it was crowded with a multitude, who saluted every appearance of any members of the Executive Council, or any of their Parliamentary supporters with hisses and groans. This continued from one o'clock until eight or nine o'clock in the evening. Mr. Lafontaine came out in care of Colonel Antrobus and soldiers, to get into a cab, and he was pelted with eggs and stones. Not one of the Ministers can walk the streets. Last night Mr. Lafontaine's house was sacked, and his library destroyed; and Mr. Hincks' house was also sacked, but he had removed nearly all of his furniture, as well as his family. The scene of to-day was similar to that of yesterday. This afternoon a meeting of several thousands of persons was held in the Champs de Mars. I heard some of the speeches. They were moderate in tone, but the feelings of disgust and contempt for Lord Elgin exceed all conception. There have been two vast assemblages this evening—the one French, the other British—in different parts of the city. Companies of soldiers have been stationed in the streets between them, preventing persons going from one party to the other. I have heard their shoutings since I commenced this letter.

The next day Dr. Ryerson wrote to me again to say:—Nothing has occurred in the city since last night, worth noticing. Soldiers meet you at every turn almost. Two companies of soldiers were stationed to-day in the building in which the Legislative Assembly met. There was a long debate on the causes of the recent disturbances, and strong protestations from all sides of the House against "annexation."

An opportunity to appoint Hon. M. S. Bidwell to the Bench in Upper Canada having occurred, Dr. Ryerson, on the 3rd September, 1849, addressed the following letter to Hon. Robert Baldwin, urging the appointment:—There is one subject I take the liberty of mentioning, although it is contrary to my practice to interfere in any matter of the kind; but the peculiarity of it may excuse me on the present occasion. I allude to the appointment of Mr. Bidwell as one of the new judges in Upper Canada. The recent history of Europe affords many illustrations of circumstances being seized upon by despots to compel the departure of valuable and dreaded men from their own country. You know that it was under such circumstances that Mr. Bidwell was compelled to leave Canada. You know that it was the order of the Imperial Government to elevate Mr. Bidwell to the Bench, that prompted Sir Francis Head to adopt the course towards him that he did. You know, likewise, how long, and faithfully, and ably, Mr. Bidwell laboured to promote the principles of civil and religious liberty which are now established in Upper Canada; and that at a time when great responsibility and obloquy attached to such advocacy. Mr. Bidwell was the author, as well as the able advocate of the laws by which the religious denominations in Upper Canada hold Church property, and by which their ministers solemnize matrimony. I believe he has never altogether abandoned the hope of returning to Canada; but I believe he has felt that he was entitled to the offer of that position, which the Home Government contemplated conferring upon him in 1837. I felt it too delicate a question to propose to Mr. Bidwell when I saw him the other day; but my friend Mr. Francis Hall, of the New York *Commercial Advertiser* (who sees and converses with him every week), expressed his full conviction that Mr. Bidwell would accept a Judgeship in Upper Canada—that Mr. Bidwell had constantly taken the Canadian Law Reports, and procured the Canadian and English Statutes, and kept up his reading of them as carefully as if he had lived in Canada. I believe the appointment of Mr. Bidwell would be an honour to the Canadian Bench, and an act of moral and political gratitude most honourable to any party, and of great value to Upper Canada. You are aware of the reasons for which I feel a deep interest in this subject, and which will, I trust, excuse in your mind the liberty I take—believing, as I do, that it will be as grateful to your feelings as it will be noble in your character, to remember a man to whom our common country is so much indebted.

To this letter Mr. Baldwin replied, on the 20th September

With respect to the principal object of your letter, you need not, I assure you, have made any excuse for introducing it, even independently of the part taken by you formerly with reference to the case of my friend Mr. Bidwell, and which alone would give you a just claim to address me. I can never feel any suggestion, no matter from what quarter, having his good for its object, to be an intrusion on me, and be assured that nothing could have afforded me greater pleasure than to have had it in my power to have advised his appointment to the Bench. Nor have I ever ceased to do all that I could with propriety to get him to put himself in the position which might lead to such a result. You are aware of the steps I took in 1843 to have his pledge to Sir Francis Head cancelled. I sent you, I think, the correspondence respecting it. (See page 308.) On that being done, I wrote him a letter of which I preserved a copy, from which I send you one. By this you will see how earnestly I pressed him to return then. Had he come in, as I suggested, it was my intention to have offered him the Crown business on whichever of the Circuits he might have chosen. I have subsequently, as often as I felt I dared to do so, urged his return. But it has been felt impossible, until he had placed himself in the position of a practitioner, as formerly, at our own, and not at a foreign, Bar, to advise his appointment to the Bench of the Province. For myself, although friendship might have led me to have overlooked, or overstepped, this difficulty, my judgment, when appealed to, forced me to admit, with my colleagues, that the objection was insuperable.

I am not acquainted with the income he realizes from his profession in New York, but I doubt not it is much beyond what could be obtained in Toronto. Still, if he really does wish to return to Canada, the time is most propitious as far as professional prospects are concerned. Mr. Sullivan, Mr. Blake, and Mr. Esten being taken from the Bar leaves a space to be filled that, I should say, offers the best possible opening.

Had Mr. Bidwell been in his proper professional position here when the Government was called upon to appoint to the places now filled, or on the eve of being filled, by those gentlemen, there is not one of those high judicial positions to which it would not have been at once a pride and a pleasure both to myself and my colleagues to have advised his appointment. Vice-Chancellor Jameson's health, too, will probably ere long lead to his retirement. When that time arrives, will our friend's continued absence be still a barrier to the gratification of our wishes?

If the affairs of the Province shall be then conducted by the same Councils as now sway them, I may say, with almost the same confidence of that future as I do of the past, that it will be the only obstacle to such gratification. I should add, too, that last winter one of my colleagues who, as well as myself, has always taken a particular interest in Mr. Bidwell's return to the Province, wrote to him, informing him of the Judiciary measures intended to be introduced by the Administration, and giving him to understand as distinctly as could properly be done, that, if he had returned to this country when those measures were to go into operation, it would afford us and our colleagues the greatest pleasure to have it in our power to advise his being placed in a situation alike agreeable to his tastes, deserving of his talents, and satisfactory to the public at large. And though, when he wrote first, he expressed some doubt of the Bills becoming law during the last session, yet shortly after, when it was felt expedient to carry them through, he again wrote to inform Mr. Bidwell that this would be done if the sanction of Parliament was obtained to the measures. Whether, in my letters to Mr. Bidwell, on the subject of his return, I have appeared to him not to speak with sufficient warmth, I know not. It has, at all events, not been from indifference to the object. I certainly have felt that, in the uncertainty that must for the future attach to political power, there was a great responsibility in urging one in good business elsewhere to leave that and throw his fortunes again in with us here. I am naturally cautious, and my caution may have led me to speak less warmly than I felt, particularly when I found my first appeals unsuccessful. But he ought, and I hope, does, appreciate my motives. It is true his ear may be poisoned by having had unjust suspicions poured into it. I know I have never afforded any just grounds for such suspicions, and I feel confident that his generous nature would have been far above conceiving any such, had they not been suggested by others. I am, however, perhaps doing wrong. It may be that none such have ever been thought of by anyone. I trust it is so. If otherwise, it is but just to myself to say that they are the foulest, basest and most malignant that mortal ever breathed.

Rev. Dr. Bangs attended the Conference at Brockville in 1850, as a delegate from the American General Conference. On his return to New York he wrote a letter to Dr. Ryerson on the 3rd July:—

I think my trip to Canada was one of the most pleasant tours I ever made, and shall reflect upon it with peculiar delight. I have commenced, as you will perceive by the *Christian Advocate*, to give the public an account of my visit to your Conference.

The pleasure we enjoyed in our visit to Canada, and especially your hospitality at Toronto, makes us feel truly thankful to God for such hallowed friendships, and reminds us more forcibly than ever of that eternal union which the spirits shall enjoy in a future world.

Dr. Ryerson made a second educational trip to Europe in October, 1850. Writing to me from London on the 8th November, he said:—The day before yesterday, I left Lord Elgin's note of introduction, with my card, at the Colonial Office; the same evening I received a note, appointing yesterday for an interview. Mr. (afterwards Sir B.) Hawes, the Under-Secretary was present. It was most agreeable and gratifying. Lord Grey seemed much delighted with what had been done, educationally, in Upper Canada; and of which he was until then, entirely ignorant. Mr. Hawes asked if I had published any report of my tour in Europe, or the results of it; and as I happened to have a copy of each of the documents I brought with me, I presented Lord Grey with copies of them. He seemed surprised that he had not seen them before, and said he must write to Lord Elgin to send him a copy of each of them for the office. The conversation extended to the United States—our system of Government as contrasted with theirs, etc. Lord Grey and Mr. Hawes appeared entertained and pleased. His Lordship offered to aid me in any way, in his power, that I might devise; and asked me to dine with him.

Last evening, I received from Lord Grey letters of introduction to the Marquis of Lansdowne (President of the Privy Council Committee of Education) to the Rt. Hon. T. B. Macaulay, and Mr. Lingard, successor of Sir J. P. Kay Shuttleworth, and an unsealed letter of introduction from Mr. Hawes, to Sir Henry Ellis, Librarian of the British Museum, in which he said: This will be presented to you by Dr. Ryerson, of Canada, who has rendered great services to the cause of education, not only by his writings, but by his great exertions.

Both Lord Grey and Mr. Hawes seemed to know something about me; and the above copy of note shows the spirit in which they are desirous of aiding me. I shall now commence my work here in good earnest.

Lord Grey introduced the subject of the Toronto University, and of the Bishop of Toronto's Mission to this country, and when he found that I had a copy of the amended University Bill, and the proceedings of the Wesleyan Conference on the subject, he requested them for perusal. In my next interview with His Lordship I shall introduce the subject of the clergy reserves.

I have been very cordially received at the Wesleyan Mission House. I was affected to see Dr. Buntifig's great bodily weakness, and surprised to see his intellect clear, quick, and powerful as ever. When he walks, he can only step about six inches at a time. I expect to hear him on Sunday morning, in the same Chapel (Spitalfields Chapel—a once French church, in which the eloquent Saurin has preached, and made a collection for the refugee Huguenots to the amount of £3,000) in which I preached last Sunday, and aided in administering the Lord's Supper.

On the 10th January, 1851, Dr. Ryerson addressed the following note to Sir Benjamin Hawes, from Paris: I saw Cardinal Wiseman on the strength of your kind note of introduction. He appeared to be pleased with the compliment which my call involved—invited me to hospitalities which I think it would not be prudent for me to accept, and promised to have a list of popular (but not denominational) reading books prepared, and the books selected for my inspection on my return to London.

I most fervently hope that you will be prepared to bring before Parliament, early in the approaching session, a Bill to settle the Canadian clergy reserve question—the only remaining obstacle to the social harmony of Canada, and to its affectionate and permanent union with the Mother Country.

In 1852, the new buildings of the Education Department and Normal School, as shown in the accompanying engravings were completed. For Dr. Ryerson's Office see page 422.

Being in England in 1853, Dr. Ryerson wrote to me there :—

I was glad to learn that Lord Elgin was to go in the same steamship with you from Boston. I have no doubt it will have proved interesting to him as well as to you, and perhaps useful to you. I miss you very much from the office, but I do not like to employ any more aid without sanction of the Government, though I could get no one to take your place. I would wish you to write me what Lord Elgin may have thought or said as to our doings and plans of proceeding. If the Library plan succeeds, it will achieve noble results.* I feel that our success and happiness in the Department are inseparably united.

In 1854 Dr. Ryerson was appointed a member of Commission to enquire into matters connected with King's College, Fredericton, N.B. His fellow-commissioners were Hon. J. H. Gray, Dr. Dawson, Hon. J. S. Saunders, and Hon. James Brown. Mr. Grey the Chairman, in transmitting the Report of the Commission to the Provincial Secretary of New Brunswick, said :—

I beg to express, with the full conscience of my fellow-commissioners, our acknowledgment of the very valuable assistance offered us by Dr. Ryerson. His great experience, and unquestioned proficiency in all subjects connected with Education, justly entitles his opinions to great weight.

* Lord Elgin always referred to Dr. Ryerson's library scheme in his educational addresses, as the "Crown and Glory of the Institutions of the Province."

The Ontario Education Department, and Normal and Model Schools, Erected 1851.

Education Department, showing Dr. Ryerson's Office for 25 Years, in the S. W. Angle of the Main Building in Front.

CHAPTER LI.

1849.

THE BIBLE IN THE ONTARIO PUBLIC SCHOOLS.

EARLY in 1849 an important crisis occurred in the history of our Public School system, the evil effects of which were only prevented by the prompt and emphatic protest on the part of Dr. Ryerson, and the equally prompt measures taken by Hon. Robert Baldwin in the matter. The event to which I refer was the hurried passage of a revolutionary School Bill at the end of a Session of Parliament by parties hostile to Dr. Ryerson— a Bill the effect of which would have been the exclusion of the Bible and religious teaching and influence from our Public Schools. In regard to that calamitous event, Dr. Ryerson stated that within three hours of learning that such a Bill was law he informed Mr. Baldwin that the office of Chief Superintendent of Education was at his disposal.

I was absent from Toronto at this time. Dr. Ryerson therefore wrote me a letter on the subject, dated December, 1849, in which he said:—I am happy to say the scandalous School Bill of last session is upset. The members of the Government (including the Governor-General) have examined my letter to Mr. Baldwin, of July last, and have come entirely into my views. Mr. Malcolm Cameron is also out of office, and is striving to create opposition against his former colleagues. Some of the extreme radical papers (*Examiner, Mirror, Canada Christian Advocate, Provincialist,* &c.,) all state that I had tendered my resignation, and had been persuaded by one or two members of the Government to withdraw it, and they speak piteously of the Government having succumbed to me. The *Canada Christian Advocate* says I have watched my opportunity to get "Mr. Baldwin and the Government under my thumb." I have been permitted to publish the correspondence of July last, and it has placed me in this new and proud position. I thank God for His goodness in thus opening before me a wider field of usefulness than ever, and for sealing at so early a period, with His approbation, adherence to great principles of Christian truth and social advancement, irrespective of men or parties. I shall commence the New Year with new courage and hope, and I am anxious to see you that we may together devise and prosecute the best means to promote our great work.

The circumstances under which this abortive School Bill, as it proved, of 1849, was passed, is thus described by Dr. Ryerson in a letter written ten years afterwards (in 1859):—

From 1846 to 1849 a host of scribblers and would-be school legislators appeared, led on by the *Globe* newspaper. It was represented that I had plotted a Prussian school despotism for free Canada, and that I was forcing upon the country a system in which the last spark of Canadian liberty would be extinguished, and Canadian youth would be educated as slaves. Hon. Malcolm Cameron, with less knowledge and less experience than he has now, was astounded at these "awful disclosures," and was dazzled by the theories proposed to rid the country of the enslaving elements of my Prussian school system. Mr. Cameron was at length appointed to office; and he thought I ought to be walked out of the office. Messrs. Baldwin and Hincks (as I have understood), thought I should be judged officially for my official acts, and that, thus judged, I had done nothing worthy of evil treatment. The party hostile to me then thought that, as I could not be turned out of office by direct dismissal, I might be shuffled out by legislation; and a School Bill was prepared for that purpose. That Bill contained many good, but more bad provisions, and worse omissions, but of which only a man who had studied the question, or rather science, of school legislation could fully judge. Mr. Cameron was selected to submit it to his colleagues, and get it through Parliament. He executed his task with his characteristic adroitness and energy. Mr. Hincks never read the Bill, and had left for England before it passed. Mr. Baldwin, amid the smoking ruins of a Parliament House and national library, looked over it, and thought from the representations given him of its popular objects, and a glance at the synopsis of its provisions, that it might be an improvement on the then existing law, while the passing of it would gratify many of his friends. On examining the Bill, I wrote down my objections to it, and laid them before the Government, and proceeded to Montreal to press them in person. I left Montreal in April, 1849, with the expectation that the Bill would be dropped, or essentially mended. Neither was done; the Bill was passed in the ordinary manner of passing bills during the last few hours of the Session; and within three hours of learning that the Bill was law, I informed Mr. Baldwin that my office was at his disposal, for I never would administer that law.

As to the effect of Mr. Cameron's Bill on Dr. Ryerson's future, he said:—The new Bill on its coming into operation, leaves me but one course to pursue. The character and tendency of the Bill clearly is to compel me to relinquish office, or virtually abandon principles and provisions [in regard to the Bible in the Schools] which I have advocated as of great and vital importance, and become a party to my own personal humiliation and degradation—thus justly exposing myself to the suspicion and imputation of mean and mercenary conduct. I can readily retire from office, and do much more if necessary, for the maintenance of what I believe to be vital to the moral and educational interests of my native country; but I can never knowingly be a party to my own humiliation and debasement. I regret that an unprecedented mode of legislation has been resorted to to gratify the feelings of personal envy and hostility. I regard it as a virtual vindication of myself against oft-repeated allegations, that it was felt I could not be reached by the usual straightforward administration of Government. Lately, in the English House of Lords, the Marquis of Lansdowne stated, that Mr. Lafontaine had returned to Canada, and boldly challenged inquiry into any of the allegations against him in reference to past years. I have repeatedly done the same. No such inquiry has been granted or instituted. Yet I am not only pursued by the base calumnies of certain persons and papers, professing to support and enjoy the confidence of the Government, but legislation is resorted to, and new provisions introduced at the last hour of the Session, to deal out upon me the long meditated blows of unscrupulous envy and animosity. But I deeply regret that the blows, which will fall comparatively light upon me, will fall with much greater weight, and more serious consequences, upon the youth of the land, and its future moral and educational interests. . . Acting, as I hope I do, upon Christian and public grounds, I should not feel myself justified in withdrawing from a work in consequence of personal discourtesy and ill-treatment, or a reduction of means of support and usefulness. But when I see the fruits of four years' anxious labours, in a single blast scattered to the winds, and have no satisfactory ground of hope that such will not be the fate of another four years' labour; when I see the foundations of great principles, which, after extensive enquiry and long deliberation, I have endeavoured to lay, torn up and thrown aside as worthless rubbish; when I see myself deprived of the protection and advantage of the application of the principle of responsible government as applied to every other head of a Department, and made the subordinate agent of a Board which I have originated, and the members of which I have had the honour to recommend for appointment; when I see myself officially severed from a Normal School Institution which I have devised, and every feature and detail of which are universally commended, even to the individual capacities of the masters whom I have sought out and recommended; when I see myself placed in a position, to an entirely novel system of education at large, in which I can either burrow in inactivity or labour with little hope of success; when I find myself placed in such circumstances, I cannot hesitate as to the course of duty, as well as the obligations of honour and self-respect. . . I think it is my right, and only frank and respectful, on the earliest occasion to state, in respect to my own humble labours, whether I can serve on terms and principles and conditions so different from those under which I have, up to the present time, acted; though I cannot, without deep regret and emotion, contemplate the loss of so much time and labour, and find myself impelled to abandon a work on which I had set my heart, and to qualify myself for which I have devoted four of the most matured years of my life.

Having now fulfilled my promise—to communicate to you, in writing, my views on this important and extensive subject—I leave the whole question in your hands.

The result of this letter was, the suspension and abandonment of the Act of 1849, and the preparation and passing of the Act of 1850.

Now Mr. Cameron might naturally feel deeply at the repeal of his own Act without a trial; but after he had time for further examination and reflection, and a more thorough knowledge of the nature and working of the system I was endeavouring to establish, I believe no man in Canada more sincerely rejoiced than Mr. Cameron at the repeal of the Act of 1849, and no man has more cordially supported the present system, or more frankly and earnestly commended the course I have pursued.*

The letter to Mr. Baldwin was written on the 14th July, 1849. Speaking of it, Dr. Ryerson said:—

In the former part of that letter I stated the circumstances under which the Act of 1849 had passed, and the fact that my remonstrance against it had not been even read. I then stated what I considered insuperable objections to it. I will quote part of my eighth and tenth objections:—the former relating

* Mr. Cameron's avowals on the subject are frank and manly. On the occasion of his nomination for the County of Lambton, in October, 1857, he thus referred to the School System, and to its founder:—
On the whole, the system had worked well, the common schools of Canada were admirable, and had attracted the commendation of the first statesmen in the United States, and even in Great Britain they proposed to imitate Canada. He was opposed to Dr. Ryerson's appointment politically, but he would say, as he had said abroad, that Canada and her children's children owed to him a debt of gratitude, as he had raised a noble structure, and opened up the way for the elevation of the people.

to the exclusion of ministers as school visitors—the latter relating to the exclusion from the schools of the Bible and books containing religious instruction. They are as follows:—

> Another feature of the new Bill is that which precludes Ministers of Religion, Magistrates, and Councillors, from acting as school visitors, a provision of the present Act to which I have heard no objection from any quarter, and from which signal benefits to the schools have already resulted. Not only is this provision retained in the School Act for Lower Canada, but Clergymen—and Clergymen alone—are there authorized to select all the school books relating to "religion and morals" for the children of their respective persuasions. But in Upper Canada, where the great majority of the people and Clergy are Protestant, the provision of the present Act authorizing Clergymen to act as School Visitors (and that without any power to interfere in school regulations or books) is repealed. Under the new Bill, the Ministers of religion cannot, therefore, visit the schools as a matter of right, or in their character as Ministers, but as private individuals, and by the permission of the teacher at his pleasure. The repeal of the provision under which Clergymen of the several religious persuasions have acted as visitors, is, of course, a virtual condemnation of their acting in that capacity. When thus denuded by law of his official character in respect to the schools, of course no Clergyman would so far sanction his own legislative degradation as to go into a school by suffrance in an unministerial character. . . The character and tendency of such a change in connection with the Protestant religion of Upper Canada, in contrast with a directly opposite provision in connection with the Roman Catholic Religion of Lower Canada, must be obvious to every reflecting person.
>
> To the school-visiting feature of the present system I attach great importance as a means of ultimately concentrating in behalf of the schools the influence and sympathies of all religious persuasions, and the leading men of the country. The success of it, thus far, has exceeded my most sanguine expectations; the visits of Clergy alone during the last year being an average of more than five visits for each Clergyman in Upper Canada. From such a beginning what may not be anticipated in future years, when information shall become more general, and an interest in the schools more generally excited. And who can estimate the benefits, religiously, socially, educationally, and even politically, of Ministers of various religious persuasions meeting together at quarterly school examinations, and other occasions, on common and patriotic ground, and becoming interested and united in the great work of advancing the education of the young.
>
> The last feature of the new Bill on which I will remark, is that which proscribes from the Schools all books containing "controverted theological dogmas or doctrines." [Under a legal provision containing these words, the Bible has been ruled out of schools in the State of New York.] I doubt whether this provision of the Act harmonizes with the Christian feelings of members of the Government; but it is needless to enquire what were the intentions which dictated this extraordinary provision, since construction of an Act of Parliament depends upon the language of the Act itself, and not upon the intentions of its framers. The effect of such a provision is to exclude every kind of book containing religious truth, even every version of the Holy Scriptures themselves; for the Protestant version of them contains "theological doctrine" controverted by the Roman Catholic; and the Douay version of them contains "theological dogmas" controverted by the Protestant. The "theological doctrine" of miracles in Paley's Evidences of Christianity is "controverted" by the disciples of Hume. Several of the "theological doctrines" in Paley's Moral Philosophy are also "controverted;"

and indeed there is not a single doctrine of Christianity which is not controverted by some party or other. The whole series of Irish National Readers must be proscribed as containing "controverted theological doctrines;" since, as the Commissioners state, these books are pervaded by the principles and spirit of Christianity, though free from any tincture of sectarianism.

I think there is too little Christianity in our schools, instead of too much; and that the united efforts of all Christian men should be to introduce more, instead of excluding what little there is.

I have not assumed it to be the duty, or even constitutional right of the Government, to compel any thing in respect either to religious books or religious instruction, but to recommend the local Trustees to do so, and to provide powers and facilities to enable them to do so within the wise restriction imposed by law. I have respected the rights and scruples of the Roman Catholic as well as those of the Protestant.

By some I have been accused of having too friendly a feeling towards the Roman Catholics; but while I would do nothing to infringe the rights and feelings of Roman Catholics, I cannot be a party to depriving Protestants of the Text-book of their faith—the choicest patrimony bequeathed by their forefathers, and the noblest birthright of their children. It affords me pleasure to record the fact—and the circumstance shows the care and fairness with which I have acted on this subject—that before adopting the Section in the printed Forms and Regulations on the "Constitution and Government of the Schools in respect to Religious Instruction," I submitted it, among others, to the late lamented Roman Catholic Bishop Power, who, after examining it, said, [he could not approve of it upon principle, but] he would not object to it, as Roman Catholics were fully protected in their rights and views, and as he did not wish to interfere with Protestants in the fullest exercise of their rights and views.

It will be seen that New England or Irish National School advocates of a system of mixed schools did not maintain that the Scriptures and all religious instruction should be excluded from the schools, but that the peculiarities of sectarianism were no essential part of religious instruction in the schools, and that the essential elements and truths and morals of Christianity could be provided for and taught without a single bitter element of sectarianism. The advocates of public schools meet the advocates of sectarian schools, not by denying the connection between Christianity and education, but by denying the connection between sectarianism—by comprehending Christianity in the system, and only rejecting sectarianism from it. The same, I think, is our safety and our duty. . . .

Dr. Ryerson concludes this part of his letter with these emphatic words: Be assured that no system of popular education will flourish in a country which does violence to the religious sentiments and feelings of the Churches of that country. Be assured, that every such system will droop and wither which does not take root in the Christian and patriotic sympathies of the people—which does not command the respect and confidence of the several religious persuasions, both ministers and laity—for these in fact make up the aggregate of the Christianity of the country. The cold calculations of unchristianized selfishness will never sustain a school system. And if you will not embrace Christianity in your school system, you will soon find that Christian persuasions will soon commence establishing schools of their own; and I think they ought to do so, and I should feel that I was performing an imperative duty in urging them to do so. But if you wish to secure the co-operation of the ministers and members of all religious persuasions, leave out of your system the points wherein they differ, and boldly and avowedly provide facilities for the inculcation of what they hold in common and what they value most, and that is what the best interests of a country require.

Speaking in a subsequent letter of another feature of this question of the Bible in schools, Dr. Ryerson says: The principal opposition which, in 1846 and for several years afterwards, I encountered was that I did not make the use of the Bible compulsory in the schools, but simply recognized the right of Protestants to use it in the school (not as an ordinary reading book, as it was not given to teach us how to read, but to teach us the way to Heaven), as a book of religious instruction, without the right or the power of compelling any others to use it. The recognition of the right has been maintained inviolate to the present time; facilities for the exercise of it have been provided, and recommendations for that purpose have been given, but no compulsory authority assumed, or right of compulsion acknowledged; and the religious exercises in each school have been left to the decision of the authorities of such school, and the religious instruction of each child has always been under the absolute authority of the parents or guardian of each child. . . Now many a parent may not exercise the right of using the Bible as a text-book of religious instruction for his child in school, but would even such parent (much less every Protestant parent) be willing to be deprived of that right?

To the objection that the Bible is "often read in a formal and perfunctory manner without any real benefit being derived from it by the pupils," Dr. Ryerson replied: Is not the Bible often read in the family, and even in the Church, "in a formal and perfunctory manner," without any benefit to either reader or hearers: but should we, therefore, take away even "the abstract right of reading the Bible" in the family and in the Church?

To the objection urged against the reading of the Bible in the schools because "a majority of the teachers are utterly unfit to give religious instruction," Dr. Ryerson replied: The reading of the Bible and giving religious instruction from it are two very different things. The question is not the competency of teachers to give religious instruction, but the right of a Protestant to the reading of the Bible by his child in the school as a text-book of religious instruction. That right I hold to be sacred and divine.

To a rejoinder that "the cry for the Bible in the schools is a sham," Dr. Ryerson thus replies: Apart from religious instruction, apart from even the reading of the Bible in the schools, the right of having it there—its very presence there—is not "a sham," but a sign, a symbol of potent significance. The sign of the Cross . . is not a "sham," but a symbol precious to the hearts of hundreds of thousands of our brethren; the coat of arms which stands at the head of all royal patents, nor the sparkling crown which encircles the brow of royalty, is not "a sham," but a symbol which speaks more than words to every British heart; the standard that waves at the head of the regiment, nor the flag that floats at the ship's masthead is not "a sham," but a symbol that nerves the soldier and the sailor to duty and to victory. So the Bible is not "a sham," but a symbol of right and liberty dear to the heart of every Protestant freeman, to every lover of civil and religious liberty—a standard of truth and morals, the foundation of Protestant faith, and the rule of Protestant morals; and "the cry" for the Bible in the schools is not a "sham," but a felt necessity of the religious instructor, whether he be the teacher or a visiting superintendent or clergyman,—is the birthright of the Protestant child, and the inalienable right of the Protestant parent. . .

No man attaches more importance than I do to secular education and knowledge, and few men have laboured more to provide for the teaching and diffusion of every branch of it; yet, so far am I from ignoring the Bible, even in an intellectual point of view, that I hesitate not to say, in the language of the eloquent Melville, that—

Whilst every stripling is boasting that a great enlargement of mind is coming on the nation, through the pouring into all its dwellings a tide of general information, it is right to uphold the forgotten position, that in caring for man as an immortal being, God cared for him as an intellectual, and that if the Bible were but read by our artizans and our peasantry, we should be surrounded by a far more enlightened and intelligent population, than will appear to this land, when the school-master, with his countless magazines, shall have gone through it, in its length and its breadth.

With a view to supply an omission, and to provide a Manual on Christian Morals for the schools, Dr. Ryerson, in 1871, prepared a little work, entitled *First Lessons in Christian Morals*. This work was recommended by the Council of Public Instruction for use in schools. It was objected to by the *Globe* newspaper on several grounds. To each of these objections Dr. Ryerson replied. The first and second objections referred to alleged errors and defects in style. In a letter on the subject, written in April, 1872, Dr. Ryerson said:—

Your third objection is against any book of religious instruction being recommended for use in the public shools. To this objection I reply, firstly, that the want of such a book has been not only felt, but expressed, from different quarters. Secondly, the Irish National Board have not only books on this subject, in their authorized list of school text books, but the Council of Public Instruction has long authorized three of them; each of which contains more reading than any one book of mine. Thirdly, in the Toronto University College, not only is Paley's "Evidences of Christianity" an authorized text book, but also Dr. Wayland's "Moral Science," of the most essential parts of which my books are an epitome.

A fourth objection is that I have given a summary of the "Evidences of Christianity," in respect especially to the inspiration of the Scriptures, miracles, and mysteries. In reply, I observe, first, that if young men, before they finish their collegiate education, should be fortified on this ground, it is equally necessary that those youths who finish their education in the public schools should not be left unarmed on this point. Secondly, pupils in the public schools of the fourth and fifth years are quite as capable of understanding the few pages in which I have condensed and simplified the answers to the common infidel objections, as are young men at college to master the large text books prescribed on the subject. Thirdly, the Irish National Board has provided a book on the subject to which I have devoted two lessons. On the list of text books authorized by the Irish National Board is one entitled, "Lessons on the Truth of Christianity, being an appendix to the Fourth Book of Lessons, for the use of Schools." This book enters far more largely into the subject of miracles than I have done, besides the additional two lessons of answers to infidel objections.

A fifth objection is that I have pointed out the defects of the teachings of Natural Religion, and shown the superiority of the teachings of Revelation over those of Natural Religion. In this I have followed the example of Rev. Dr. Wayland, President of Brown University, R. I.

A sixth objection is, that I have not confined myself to those "laws which regulate our natural obligations;" that I have taught the "positive institutions" of Christianity, such as repentance, faith, reading the Scriptures, personal devotion, family worship, attendance at public worship." In this I have also followed Dr. Wayland. In the conclusion of this letter Dr. Ryerson offers this "apology" for writing his little book on "Christian Morals:" Besides desiring a small amount of religious teaching, one hour (Monday morning) in the week, for the senior pupils of the Public Schools, which the trustees and parents might approve, I did desire a united test'mony on the part of Protestantism, as there is a united testimony on the part of Roman Catholicism, as to religious teaching in the schools. One County Inspector writes, that the Roman Catholic priest, in a separate school which the Inspector visited, said, "Your schools are atheistic. You don't acknowledge God." The same charge has been often repeated by the same authority against the public schools. While I have provided and contended for full provision by which the Roman Catholics could teach their own children in their own books of religious instruction, I did desire that there might be a somewhat corresponding unity of testimony and teaching in religious principles and duties of common agreement among Protestants, being first most strongly impressed with its feasibility by the remarks of the late excellent Rev. A. Gale, who, when principal of Knox's Academy, on closing a public examination of the pupils, said that he was persuaded, from his own experience, that all needful religious teaching could be given to pupils at schools without infringing upon any denominational peculiarity. I had long meditated, and at length sought to realize this grand idea in our public schools. One discordant note has interrupted the harmony. The responsibility of the failure, if it is to be a failure, is not with me. I hope the Protestant Christians of Canada will yet realize it, and that my country will yet enjoy the untold advantages of it, though I may die without the sight.

CHAPTER LII.

1850—1853.

THE CLERGY RESERVE QUESTION TRANSFERRED TO CANADA.

THE re-opening of the clergy reserve question by Bishop Strachan, with a view to obtain relief in the temporary distress mentioned in Chapter xlviii., proved to be a fatal step, so far as his hopes for securing "better terms" were concerned In the next year after he had issued his pastoral appeal for help, the clergy reserve fund yielded an increase, "and an expectation of a gradual increase annually was officially expressed." ("Secular State of the Church," page 11.)

The Bishop's complaint against the Provincial Government (Chapter xlviii., page 379) was that its management of the clergy reserve lands was wasteful and extravagant. An effort was therefore made, in 1846, to vest these lands in the religious bodies then entitled to a share in the income derived from their sale. Mr. Gladstone communicated with the Governor-General on the subject, with this view, in February, 1846. The proposal, was, however, viewed with alarm, as well as was the fact that such efforts being made in England showed that, as in 1840, so in 1846, the rights of the Canadian people to this patrimony could be at any time alienated or extinguished by the Imperial Government, without the official knowledge or consent of the Canadian Parliament.

These two facts, when they became known and appreciated by the people of Upper Canada, led to the taking of decisive steps to prevent them from becoming realities. The representatives in the Canadian House of Assembly of the Bishop of Toronto sought to get an address to the Crown passed, with a view to vesting a portion of the lands in the Church Society of Toronto. Hon. Robert Baldwin warned the friends of the Bishop of the impolicy and imprudence of such a proposition, and pointed out that if the clergy reserve question was thus re-opened, the former fierce agitation on the subject would be resumed, which might "end in the total discomfiture of the Church." His warning was unheeded, and although the motion for vesting the lands as proposed was rejected, by a vote of 37 to 14, yet the Bishop in his charge, delivered the next year (in June, 1847), said :—

> After all, our great desire continues to be to acquire the management of what is left to the Church of the reserves; and why this reasonable desire is not complied with remains a matter of deep regret (page 19).

The question thus brought before the Legislature, led to its being brought before the people, until it became a subject of discussion in political meetings and election contests. Finally, in 1850, the Government of the day secured the passage in the House of Assembly of an address to the Crown, praying for the repeal of the Imperial Clergy Reserve Act of 1840. In that address it is stated that—

> During a long period of years, and in nine successive sessions of the Provincial Parliament, the representatives of the people of Upper Canada, with an unanimity seldom exhibited in a deliberative body, declared their opposition to religious endowments... The address further pointed out that the wishes of the people were thwarted by the Legislative Council, a body containing a majority avowedly favourable to the ascendancy of the Church of England. That the Imperial Government, from time to time, invited the Provincial Parliament to legislate on the subject of these reserves, disclaiming on the part of the Crown any desire for the superiority of one or more particular Churches; that Your Majesty's Government, in declining to advise the Royal assent being given to a Bill, passed by a majority of one, for investing the power of disposing of the reserves in the Imperial Parliament, admitted that from its inaccurate information as to the wants and general opinions of society (in which the Imperial Parliament was unavoidably deficient), the question would be more satisfactorily settled by the Provincial Legislature; that subsequently to the withholding of the Royal assent from the last-mentioned Bill, the Imperial Parliament passed an Act disposing of the proceeds of the clergy reserves in a manner entirely contrary to the formerly repeatedly expressed wishes of the Upper Canadian people, as declared through their representatives, and acknowledged as such in a message sent to the Provincial Parliament by command of Your Majesty's Royal predecessor.
>
> That we are humbly of opinion that the legal or constitutional impediments which stood in the way of provincial legislation on this subject should have been removed by an Act of the Imperial Parliament; but that the appropriation of revenues derived from the investment of the proceeds of the public lands of Canada, by the Imperial Parliament, will never cease to be a source of discontent to Your Majesty's loyal subjects in this Province; and that when all the circumstances connected with this question are taken into consideration, no religious denomination can be held to have such vested interest in the revenue derived from the proceeds of the said clergy reserves, as should prevent further legislation with reference to the disposal of them; but we are nevertheless of opinion that the claims of existing incumbents should be treated in the most liberal manner; and that the most liberal and equitable mode of settling this long-agitated question, would be for the Imperial Parliament to pass an Act providing that the stipends and allowances heretofore assigned and given to the clergy of the Church of England and Scotland, or to any other religious bodies or denominations of Christians in Canada, and to which the faith of the Crown is pledged, shall be secured during the natural lives or incumbencies of the parties now receiving the same... subject to which provision the Provincial Parliament should be authorized to appropriate as, in its wisdom, it may think proper, **all revenues**

derived from the present investments, or from those to be made hereafter, whether from the proceeds of future sales, or from instalments on those already made.

As the agitation proceeded, Bishop Strachan and Dr. Ryerson again became involved in it. The Bishop took the lead, and addressed a letter to Lord John Russell on the subject. Dr. Ryerson at once joined issue with the Bishop, and prepared the following able rejoinder in reply to the Bishop's letter. He said :—

The statements of the Lord Bishop of Toronto, in his letter to Lord John Russell, dated Canada, February 20th, 1851, and in his Charge delivered to the clergy of the Diocese of Toronto, in May, 1851, relate to the same subjects, and appear to be designed for perusal in England, rather than in Canada. These statements, as a whole, are the most extraordinary that I ever read from the pen of an ecclesiastic, much less from the pen of a Bishop of the Church of England, and an old resident and prominent actor in the affairs of the country of which he speaks. These statements are not only incorrect, but they are, for the most part, the reverse of the real facts to which they refer; and where they are most groundless, they are the most positive. To discuss them *seriatim* would occupy a volume. I will, as briefly as possibly, notice the most important of them under the following heads :—

1. The circumstances and objects of the original Clergy Land Reservation.

2. The position of the Church of England in Canada, and the professed wishes of the Lord Bishop.

3. The conduct of the Imperial and Canadian Governments towards the Church of England.

4. The effect of the union of the two Canadas on the proceedings and votes of the Legislative Assembly in regard to the Church of England.

5. Public grants to the Church of Rome, and the endowment of that Church in Lower Canada.

6. The Toronto University and Public Schools.

I am to notice in the first place the statements of the Lord Bishop respecting the circumstances and objects of the Clergy Land Reservation. He speaks of it as having been suggested by the circumstances of the American revolution, and as having been intended as the special reward of those who adhered to the Crown of England during that seven years' contest.

The Bishop says :—

At the close of the war, in 1783, which gave independence to the United States, till then colonies of the British Crown, great numbers of the inhabitants, anxious to preserve their allegiance, and, in as far as they were able, the unity of the empire, sought refuge in the western part of Canada, beyond the settlements made before the conquest under the King of France. These loyalists, who had for seven years perilled their lives and fortunes in defence of the throne, the law, and the religion of England, had irresistible claims when driven from their homes into a strange land (yet a vast forest), to the immediate protection of government, and to enjoy the same benefits which they had abandoned from their laudable attachment to the parent State.

The Bishop subsequently states [See Chapter xxviii., page 219] that the object of the Constitutional Act of 1791 was

> More especially to confer upon the loyalists such a constitution as should be as near a transcript as practicable of that of England, that they might have no reason to regret, in as far as religion, law, and liberty were concerned, the great sacrifices which they had made.

Allusions of this kind pervade a considerable part of the Bishop's letter, and furnish the first example, within my knowledge, of any writer attempting to invest the dispute between the American colonies and the mother country with a religious character; when every person the least acquainted with the history of those colonies, and of that contest, knows that the question of religion was never alluded to on the part of the colonists—that General Washington and other principal leaders in the revolution were professed Episcopalians—that the Church of England did not exist as an established church in any of those colonies, unless adopted as such by the local legislature, as in the case of Virginia—and that in the northern and eastern parts of those colonies, whence the first emigration to Upper Canada took place after the peace of 1783, the Church of England never did exist as an established church. Therefore, for the "religion of England" in that sense, those "loyalists" never could have "perilled their lives and fortunes;" nor could they have been influenced by any predilections for an establishment which they had never seen. The Bishop says truly that:

> The noble stand which the Province made against the United States in the war of 1812, in which the attachment of its inhabitants to the British empire was a second time signally displayed, brought the country into deserved notice.

But nothing can be more fallacious than the claims he would found upon this fact, any more than those of the American revolution of 1776, to the clergy reserve land. For the Lord Bishop himself, when Archdeacon of York, in a printed discourse on the death of the first Bishop of Quebec, represents the benefits of the establishment as "little felt or known" in Upper Canada, and states that down to the close of the American War of 1812—namely, in 1815—there were but five clergymen of the Church of England in that vast province. And a few years afterwards, December 22nd, 1826, the Upper Canada House of Assembly, consisting of the representatives of the Loyalists and their sons, who had twice "signally displayed their attachment to the British empire," adopted, by the extraordinary majority of 30 to 3, the following remarkable and significant resolution :—

Resolved, that the Protestant Episcopal Church in the Province bears a very small proportion to the number of other Christians, notwithstanding the pecuniary aid long and exclusively received from the benevolent society in England by the members of that Church, and their pretensions to a monopoly of the clergy reserves.

The original Loyalist settlers of Upper Canada, and their immediate descendants, must be held to have understood their own feelings and sentiments better than the Lord Bishop : and the almost unanimous expression of such sentiments, through their representatives twenty-five years since, together with other circumstances to which I have referred, show how greatly mistaken is his Lordship, and how perfectly baseless are his assumptions and frequent allusions and appeals in reference to the hopes, wishes and sentiments of the original settlers of Upper Canada as a ground of claim to the clergy reserves in behalf of the Church of England.

I have next to say a few words on the Bishop's statement as to the position of the Church of England in Canada, and the professions which he makes in respect to her position. He says, "Our position has, for some time, been that of a prostrate branch of the National Church;" and that position he, in another place, calls " a condition of inferiority to other religious denominations;" and he says, "she has been placed below Protestant dissenters, and privileges, wrested from her, have been conferred upon them." As to the position in which the Bishop would wish the Church of England in Canada to be placed, he says, "We merely claim equality, and freedom from oppression."

These expressions are deeply to be regretted, when it is perfectly notorious that the pre-eminence and peculiar civil advantages claimed by the Bishop for the Church of England, have been the ground of all the disputes which have agitated the Legislature and people of Upper Canada for more than twenty-five years; when every person of the least intelligence in Canada knows that the Church of England, besides other large educational and pecuniary patronage of government, enjoyed until 1840 an exclusive monopoly of the clergy lands which the Legislative Assembly of Upper Canada long contended, and which the judges of England have decided, extended by law to Protestants generally—that the Church of England enjoys at this moment the greater part of the annual proceeds of the sales of those lands, besides rectory endowments of portions of them—that every political and religious party in

Canada awards every thing to the Church of England that they ask for themselves—" equality and freedom from oppression." During the present session of the Legislature, Bills have passed the Assembly giving the Church of England in Lower Canada all the facilities of holding property and managing her affairs which have been desired by the Bishop of the Diocese, as had been granted a few years since in Upper Canada; and when it was objected that privileges were given by such Bills to the Church of England not possessed by any other religious persuasion, it was replied that others might obtain them by asking for them, and the Bills in question were passed with only two dissentient votes.

I repeat the expression of my regret that the Bishop should draw entirely upon his imagination for such statements, and that his feelings should prompt him to represent objections to his own particular views and pretensions as oppression and persecution of the Church of England.

The next class of the Bishop's statements which I shall notice, relate to the conduct of the Imperial and Canadian Governments towards the Church of England. Throughout his voluminous documents the Bishop represents the conduct of government, both Imperial and Colonial, as hostile to the Church of England; and employs, in some instances, terms personally offensive. The great question at issue is thus stated by the Bishop himself in his recent charge to his clergy:—

> In 1819, the law officers of the Crown gave it as their opinion that the words Protestant clergy embraced also the ministers of the Church of Scotland, not as entitling them to endowment in land, but as enabling them to participate in the proceeds of the reserves, whether sold or leased. In 1828, a select committee of the House of Commons extended the construction of the words Protestant clergy to the teachers of all Protestant denominations; and this interpretation, though considered very extraordinary at the time, was confirmed by the twelve Judges in 1840.

In his letter to Lord John Russell, the Bishop alludes to two of these decisions in terms peculiarly objectionable, while he omits all reference to the latter. He says:—

> The Established Church of Scotland claimed a share of those lands, or the proceeds, as a National Church within the Empire; and in 1819, the Crown lawyers made the discovery that it might be gratified, under the 37th clause of the 31st of George III., chap. 31. Next, the select committee of the House of Commons, in 1828, on the Civil Government of Canada, influenced by the spurious liberality of the times, extended this opinion of the Crown lawyers to any Protestant clergy.

The Bishop thus impugns the impartiality and integrity of the opinions expressed by the law officers of the Crown in England, and by the select committee of the House of Commons, sarcastically calling the one a "discovery," and ascribing the other to "spurious liberality;" while he declares that the Act 3 and 4 Victoria, chapter 78 (which only carried partially into effect the decision of the twelve judges, and was, as he states, agreed to by the Archbishop of Canterbury and the other Bishops in London), "deprived the Church of England in Canada of seven-twelfths of her property."

In other documents the Bishop has designated this Act "an act of spoliation," and "robbery" of the Church of England.

When the Bishop employs language of this kind in respect to Acts of Parliament and the official opinions in regard to their provisions, he cannot reasonably complain if other parties should respect them as little as himself, much less regard them as a "final settlement" of a question to which they have not been parties, and against which they have always protested. Under any circumstances, it is singular language to be employed by a person towards a government by whose fostering patronage he has become enriched. The fact is, that the successive Governors of Upper Canada have been members of the Church of England; that the principal cause of their unpopularity, and the most serious difficulties which both the Imperial and local governments have had to encounter in the colony, have arisen from their efforts to secure as much for the Church of England, in the face of the popular indignation and opposition, so much inflamed and strengthened by the irritating publications and extreme proceedings of the Bishop himself. It is understood that the report of the committee of the House of Commons on the civil government of Canada, in 1828, was written by Lord Stanley. However that may be, the sentiments of that report on the clergy reserve question were strongly expressed by his Lordship in his speech on the subject, 2nd May, 1828; and he and the other distinguished men who investigated the subject at that time, know whether they were "influenced by a spurious liberality" in the conclusion at which they arrived, or whether they were guided by a sense of justice, and yielded to the weight of testimony. At all events, the grave decision of the twelve judges of England to the same effect ought to have suggested to the Bishop other terms than those of "spurious liberality," "spoliation," and "robbery," and to have protected not only the "powers that be," but the great majority of the Canadian people, from the shafts of his harsh imputations.

Here I think it proper to correct the Bishop's repeated references to the origin and circumstances of the differences of opinion in Upper Canada, as to the import of the words "Protestant clergy," and the "right of dissenting denominations" to participate in the benefit of the clergy reserves. He represents those differences as having originated with the clergy of the Kirk of Scotland, and that the idea that any other than the clergy of the Church of England had a right to participate in the benefit of the reserves was never entertained in Upper Canada until the friends of the Kirk of Scotland commenced the agitation of the question.

So far from this representation being correct, it appears that the first submission of the question to the law officers of the Crown in England took place at the request of Sir P. Maitland, in reference, not to the clergy of the Kirk of Scotland, but to "all denominations" of Protestants—a question on which Sir P. Maitland, then Lieutenant-Governor of Upper Canada, states in a despatch to Earl Bathurst, dated 17th May, 1819, that there was not only a "difference of opinion" on the subject, but "a lively feeling throughout the Province." It appears that certain "Presbyterian inhabitants of the town of Niagara and its vicinity" (not at that time in connexion with the Church of Scotland), petitioned Sir P. Maitland for "an annual allowance of £100 to assist in the support of a preacher," to be paid "out of funds arising from the clergy reserves, or any other fund at His Excellency's disposal." In transmitting a copy of this petition to Earl Bathurst, Sir P. Maitland ("York, Upper Canada, 17th May, 1819,") remarks as follows:—

The actual product of the clergy reserves is about £700 per annum. This petition involves a question on which I perceive there is a difference of opinion, viz., whether the Act intends to extend the benefit of the reserves, for the maintenance of a Protestant clergy, to all denominations, or only to those of the Church of England. The law officers incline to the latter opinion. I beg leave to observe to your Lordship, with much respect, that your reply to this petition will decide a question of much interest, and on which there is a lively feeling throughout the Province. [See page 221.]

Earl Bathurst's reply to this despatch is dated "Downing Street, 6th May, 1820, and commences as follows:—

Having requested the opinion of His Majesty's law officers as to the right of dissenting Protestant ministers, resident in Canada, to partake of the lands directed by the Act of the 31st George III., c. 31, to be reserved as a provision for the support of a Protestant clergy, I have now to state that they are of opinion that though the provisions made by the 31st George III., c. 31, ss. 36 and 42, for the support and maintenance of a Protestant clergy, are not confined solely to the Church of England, but may be extended also to the clergy of the Church of Scotland, yet that they do not extend to dissenting ministers, since the terms Protestant clergy can apply only to the Protestant clergy recognized and established by law.

It is thus clear that the question of the right of different Protestant denominations to participate in the benefit of the clergy reserves did not originate in any claims or agitation commenced by the clergy of the Church of Scotland; that as early as the beginning of 1819, (only four years after the close of the last American War, during which, as the Bishop truly says, "the attachment of the inhabitants to the British empire was a second time signally displayed,") there was "a lively feeling throughout the Province" on the subject. The first Loyalist settlers, and their immediate descendants, were opposed to the Bishop's narrow construction of the Act 31st George III., chapter 31 ; their representatives in the Legislative Assembly maintained invariably the liberal construction of the Act ; the select committee of the House of Commons in 1828, on the Civil Government of Canada, after taking evidence as to the intentions of the original framers of the law, expressed the same opinion, and that opinion was ultimately confirmed by the decision of the twelve judges in 1840. The Bishop is, therefore, as much at fault in his facts on this point, as he is in the language he employs in reference to Imperial legal opinions, and an Imperial Act of Parliament.

It now becomes my duty to examine another large class of statements, which I have read with great surprise and pain ; and which are, if possible, less excusable than those which I have already noticed. I refer to the Bishop's statements in regard to the influence of the union of the two Canadas on the votes and proceedings of the Legislative Assemby of the united Province, on the question of the clergy reserves.

The Bishop, in his letter to Lord John Russell (referring to the Address of the Legislative Assembly, at the session of 1850, to the Queen), states as follows :—

Before the union of Upper and Lower Canada, such an unjust proceeding could not have taken place, for, while separate, the Church of England prevailed in Upper Canada, and had frequently a commanding weight in the Legislature, and at all times an influence sufficient to protect her from injustice. But since their union under one Legislature, each sending an equal number of members, matters are sadly altered.

It is found, as was anticipated, that the members returned by dissenters uniformly join the French Roman Catholics, and thus throw the members of the Church of England into a hopeless minority on all questions in which the National Church is interested.

The Church of England has not only been prostrated by the union under that of Rome, and the whole of her property made dependent on Roman Catholic votes, but she has been placed below Protestant dissenters, and privileges wrested from her which have been conferred upon them.

In his recent charge to the clergy of his Diocese, the Bishop remarks again :—

So long as this diocese remained a distinct colony, no measure detrimental to the Church ever took effect. Even under the management and prevailing influence of that able and unscrupulous politican, the late Lord Sydenham, a Bill disposing of the clergy reserves, was carried by one vote only—a result which sufficiently proved that it was not the general wish of the people of the colony to legislate upon the subject.

I shall first notice that part of the Bishop's statement which relates to Upper Canada, before the union with Lower Canada. The Bishop asserts it not to have been "the general wish of the people of the colony to legislate upon the subject" of the clergy reserves; that the Church of England prevailed, and had sufficient influence to maintain what he regards as her just rights. The Bishop has resided in Upper Canada nearly half a century, and such a statement from him, in direct contradiction to the whole political history of the Province during more than half that period, is difficult of solution, though perfectly easy of refutation. I have already transcribed one of a series of resolutions, adopted by the Legislative Assembly as early as December, 1826, by a majority of 30 to 3, objecting entirely to the exclusive pretensions made in behalf of the Church of England. But I find that nearly a year before this, namely, the 27th of the January preceding, the House of Assembly of Upper Canada adopted an Address to the King on the subject, in which it is stated, respectfully, but strongly,—

That the lands set apart in this Province for the maintenance and support of a Protestant clergy ought not to be enjoyed by any one denomination of Protestants to the exclusion of their Christian brethren of other denominations, equally conscientious in their respective modes of worshipping God, and equally entitled, as dutiful and loyal subjects, to the protection of Your Majesty's benign and liberal Government; we, therefore, humbly hope it will, in Your Majesty's wisdom, be deemed expedient and just, that not only the present reserves, but that any funds arising from the sales thereof, should be devoted to the advancement of the Christian religion generally, and the happiness of all Your Majesty's subjects of whatever denomination; or if such application or distribution should be deemed inexpedient, that the profits arising from such appropriation should be applied to the purposes of education and the general improvement of this Province.

The following year (January, 1827), the House of Assembly passed a Bill (the minority being only three), providing for the sale and application of the whole of the proceeds of the reserves for purposes of education, and erection of places of public worship for all denominations of Christians. And, on examining the journals, I find that from that time down to the union of the Canadas in 1841, not a year passed over without the passing of resolutions, or address, or bill, by the House of Assembly of Upper Canada, for the general application of the proceeds of the reserves, in some form or other, but always, without exception, against what the Bishop claims as the rights of the Church of England in respect to those lands.

It is difficult to conceive a more complete refutation than these facts furnish of the Bishop's statement, that the Church of England prevailed in Upper Canada, and had a commanding weight in the Legislature; nor could a stronger proof be required of "the general wish of the people of the colony to legislate upon the subject," than such a course of procedure on the part of their representatives for so many years during successive Parliaments, and amidst all the variations of party and party politics on all other questions.

It is also incorrect to say that the Bill of Lord Sydenham in 1840 "was carried by a majority of one vote only." A Bill did pass the Assembly of Upper Canada the year before, by "a majority of one vote only;" but that was a Bill to re-invest the reserves in the Imperial Parliament for "general religious purposes,"—a Bill passed a few hours before the close of the session, during which no less than forty-eight divisions, with the record of yeas and nays, took place in the Assembly on the question of the clergy reserves; and after the Assembly had passed, by considerable majorities, both resolutions and a Bill to give the Church of England one-fourth of the proceeds of the clergy reserves, and the other three-fourths to other religious denominations and to educational purposes—a Bill which, with some verbal amendments, also passed the Legislative Council, and against which the Bishop, joined by one other member, recorded an elaborate protest. But just at the heel of the session, and after several members of the Assembly voting in the majority had gone to their homes, a measure (which had been previously negatived again and again) was passed by a "majority of one vote only" (22 to 21), to re-invest the reserves —a measure which the law officers in England pronounced "unconstitutional," as the manner of getting it through the Canadian Legislature was unprecedented. [See page 249.]

But the measure of Lord Sydenham was carried in the Assembly by a majority of 4, and in the Legislative Council (of which the Bishop was a member and voted against the bill) by a majority of 8. A considerable majority of the members of the Church of England of both Houses of the Legislature voted for the bill, and were afterwards charged by the Bishop with "defection," and "treachery" for doing so. [See page 262.] On this point Lord Sydenham, in a despatch to Lord John Russell, dated Toronto, 5th February, 1840, stated as follows:—

It is notorious to every one here, that of twenty-two members being communicants of the Church of England who voted upon this Bill, only eight recorded their opinion in favour of the views expressed by the right reverend Prelate; whilst in the Legislative Council the majority was still greater; and amongst those who gave it their warmest support are to be found many gentlemen of the highest character for independence and for attachment to the Church, and whose views in general politics differ from those of Her Majesty's Government.

After this epitome of references to the proceedings of the people of Upper Canada, through their representatives, from 1825 to 1840, on what the Bishop terms the "rights" and "patrimony" of the Church of England, it is needless to make more than one or two remarks on his statements as to the influence of the union of the Canadas on the proceedings and votes of the Legislative Assembly upon the subject. My first remark is, that the question of the clergy reserves has not been introduced into the present Legislative Assembly by any member, or at the solicitation of any member, from Lower Canada. I remark, secondly, that though there is not a Roman Catholic among the forty-two members elected for Upper Canada; yet when a resolution was introduced into the Assembly, both at the last and during the present session, expressing a desire to maintain the present settlement of the clergy reserves, as provided in the Act, 3 & 4 Vic., chap. 78, only sixteen in the first instance, and thirteen in the second, voted for it—only about one-third of the members for Upper Canada. Should, therefore, the union of the Canadas be dissolved to-morrow, the Bishop would be in as hopeless a minority as he was before the union. The following remarks of a recent speech of Mr. Lafontaine (the leader of the Roman Catholic French members of the Assembly) will show how entirely groundless are the Bishop's imputations upon that portion of the Assembly.

> He thought the clergy reserves should be fairly divided among the Protestant denominations, and that they should be altogether taken out of the hands of the Government, as the only way to take them out of the reach of agitation. He thought the rectories were vested rights, and should not be disturbed, unless by due process of law, if, as was pretended, they were improperly obtained. If there were any claims in the Act of 1791 which seemed to connect the Church of England to the State, though he did not think they did, they might be repealed, and the Bishop of Toronto seemed to be of opinion that that might be done. Let the appointment of the incumbents to the rectories, too, be taken from the Government, if it were thought proper, and given to the Church for other uses. He merely suggested that without wishing to impose it. He would conclude with one reflection: Let his Protestant fellow-countrymen remember they would never find opposition to their just rights from Roman Catholics and French Canadians. The latter had repeatedly passed Acts in Lower Canada to give equal rights to those who were called dissenters, and Jews, which were rejected by members of the Church of England in the Council, and it was worthy of remark that, at a moment when in England a pretended aggression had given occasion for persecution, the Church of England here had to rely upon Catholics to protect it against the aggression of other Protestant sects.

I shall now make a few observations on the Bishop's statements respecting government grants to the Church of Rome, and the endowments of that Church in Lower Canada. The Bishop, framing his statements with a view to the Protestant feeling of England, inveighs in general terms against the Government on account of its alleged patronage of the Church of Rome; makes exaggerated statements on one side, and omits all references to facts on the other side which would enable the Protestants of England, to whom he appeals, to understand the part which he has himself taken in favour of grants to the Church of Rome, the manner in which those grants are paid at the present time, and the alliance which he has long endeavoured, and would still wish to form with that Church in respect to endowments. The Bishop says :—

> In Upper Canada, the Roman Catholic clergy do not, at present, exceed seventy in number, and the provision for their support is very slender. It depends chiefly on their customary dues, and the contributions of their respective flocks ; unless, indeed, they receive assistance from the French portion of the Province, where the resources of the Romish Church are abundant.

Now, while the Bishop presents an overdrawn and startling picture of the emoluments of the Church of Rome in Lower Canada, he omits all statements of public grants and payments to the clergy of that church in Upper Canada. The Bishop must know, that in addition to their " customary dues, and the voluntary contributions of their flocks," the clergy of the Church of Rome receive £1,666 per annum, and that that sum is paid out of the clergy reserve fund under the provisions of the very Act, 3 & 4 Vic., chap. 78, for the perpetuation of which he contends. The first instructions to support the Roman Catholic clergy in Upper Canada out of public funds, were given by Earl Bathurst, in a despatch to Sir P. Maitland, dated 6th October, 1826, and which commenced in the following words :—

> You will receive instructions from the Treasury for the payment, from funds to be derived from the Canada Company, of the sum of £750 per annum, for the salaries of the Presbyterian ministers, and a similar sum for the support of the Roman Catholic priests.

But what is remarkable is, that this very policy of granting aid to the Roman Catholic priests in Upper Canada, for which Government has been so much blamed by the Bishop's friends in England, was urged by, if it did not originate with, the Bishop himself. For, in a speech delivered by the Bishop in the Legislative Council of Upper Canada, 6th March, 1828, and afterwards published by himself, I find his own statement of his proceedings in this matter, as follows :—

> It has always been my wish to see a reasonable support given to the clergy of the Church of Scotland, because they belong to a Church which is established in one section of the empire ; and to the Roman Catholic Church because it may be considered as a concurrent church with the establishment in the sister Province ; and to this end I have, at all times, advised the leading men of both those churches to make respectful representations to His Majesty's Government for assistance, leaving it to Ministers to discover the source from which such aid might be taken.— His Excellency, the Lieutenant-Governor of this Province (Sir P. Maitland), having represented in the strongest manner to His Majesty's Government the propriety of making some provision for the clergy in communion with the kirk, and also of the Roman Catholic clergy resident in Upper Canada, a reference was made to me on that subject,

while in London, in June, 1826. On this occasion I enforced, as well as I could, the recommendations made by His Excellency, in respect to both churches.

Thus four months before Earl Bathurst sent out instructions to give salaries to Roman Catholic priests in Upper Canada, the Bishop states that he urged it upon the favourable consideration of His Lordship. The Bishop then significantly adds:—

> I did flatter myself that they would have been satisfied, as indeed they ought to have been, and that henceforth the clergy of the two denominations, the Roman Catholic and Presbyterian, while discharging their own religious duties, would cordially co-operate with those of the establishment in promoting the general peace and welfare of society. It is gratifying to me to state that, as far as I know, the Roman Catholic clergy, during this contest, have observed a strict neutrality.

However ingenious it may be, I cannot regard it as ingenuous that the Bishop should promote the endowment of the Roman Catholic clergy in this country in order to secure their political alliance and support against other Protestant denominations, and then appeal to Protestants in England against the Government and Legislature in Canada, because of the countenance given to the Church of Rome. It is hardly fair for the Bishop to act one part in Canada and another in England; and it is fallacious and wrong to represent the votes of Roman Catholics as exerting any influence whatever on the state of the question in Upper Canada—as of the twenty-five Roman Catholics who voted on the question last year, twelve voted on one side and thirteen on the other; and they are known to hold the opinion declared by their leader, Mr. Lafontaine, that the proceeds of the clergy reserves belong to the Protestants of the country in contradistinction to Roman Catholics.

The Bishop's statements in regard to the endowments of the Roman Catholic Church in Lower Canada are most extravagant. They cannot affect, in the least, the merits of the question which has so long agitated Upper Canada; and they appear to be introduced merely for effect in England, where the social state and position of parties in Canada are little known or understood. It is needless to examine the Bishop's statements on this subject in detail; but I will make two or three remarks, to show the fallacy of both his assertions and his reasoning. He gives no data whatever for his perfectly gratuitous and improbable assumption of four hundred parish priests in Lower Canada at a salary of £250 each, exclusive of those employed in colleges, monasteries, and religious houses, making, he says,

> The revenue of the Roman Catholic Church in Lower Canada, £100,000 per annum, a sum which represents a money capital of at least £2,000,000!

This imaginary estimate of the Bishop is simply absurd, and supposes in Lower Canada ten-fold the wealth that really exists.

The Bishop also gives a return of the seignorial lands of several religious orders of the Roman Catholic Church in Lower Canada, then invests those lands with a fictitious value, and sets them down as representing "a capital of £700,000!" whereas the rights to these lands are simply seignorial, and the annual revenue arising from them does not amount to threepence per acre. The Jesuits' estates, 891,845 acres—by far the largest item in the Bishop's paper—are in the hands of the Government, and not of the Roman Catholic Church at all.

The fallacy of the Bishop's reasoning on this point will appear from the facts, that the British Crown has never made a grant or endowment to the Roman Catholic Church in Lower Canada, or to any religious order of that Church; that whatever lands or endowments that Church or its religious communities may possess, were obtained either from the Crown of France, and therefore secured by treaty, or by the legacies of individuals, or by purchase. The island of Montreal was obtained by purchase; the rights are merely seignorial, or feudal, and yield to the seigneurs £8,000 per annum.

There is, therefore, no analogy whatever between endowments thus obtained and held, and lands appropriated by the Crown for certain general objects, which have been vested in the hands of no religious community, and over which Parliament has expressly reserved the power of discretionary legislation.

I shall now offer a few remarks on the Bishop's statements respecting the Toronto University and system of public schools in Upper Canada. As these are questions which have been set at rest by local legislation, by and with the sanction of the Imperial Government, I need only refer to the Bishop's statements so far as to remove the erroneous impressions and unjust prejudices which they are calculated to produce.

In reference to the Bishop's statements, that "graduates in holy orders are declared ineligible as members of the Senate," I remark that such graduates are and have been members of the Senate from the commencement. And when the Bishop pronounces the University "essentially unchristian," he must have known that not only a Parliamentary law, but a University statute, exists for the religious instruction and worship of all the students of the University; whereas, when the Bishop had the management of it, no provision whatever existed for the religious instruction and worship of any of the students except members of the Church of England. The statement, therefore, of the Bishop, that—

There is at present no Seminary in Upper Canada in which the children of conscientious churchmen can receive a Christian and liberal education, is contradicted by the fact that the children of many churchmen, as "conscientious" as the Bishop himself, are receiving such an education at a "Seminary in Upper Canada."

The lands out of which the University has been endowed were early set apart by the Crown, not on the application or recommendation of any authority or dignitary of the Church of England, but on the application of the Legislative Assembly of Upper Canada; and the cause of all the agitation on the subject is, that the Bishop, unknown to the Canadian people, and by representations which they, through their representatives, declared to be incorrect and unfounded, obtained a University Charter in England, and the application of those lands as an endowment, which the Legislative Assembly never would recognize. And now that that Assembly has at length got these lands restored to the objects for which they were originally appropriated, but from which they had for a time been alienated, the Bishop seeks, by the most unfounded imputations and representations, to do all in his power to damage a Seminary which he ought to be the first to countenance and support.

In his recent charge to his clergy, the Bishop has sought to damage the public elementary schools; and here his statements are equally at fault with those noticed in regard to the University. The Bishop says, "Christianity is not so much as acknowledged by our School law." This statement is contradicted by the 14th section of the School Act, and the general regulations which are made under its authority, headed, "Constitution and government of schools in respect to religious instruction," and which commence with the following words:—

As Christianity is the basis of our whole system of elementary education, that principle should pervade it throughout.

The Bishop says again:—

To take away the power of parents to judge and direct the education of their children, which is their natural privilege from God, as our schools virtually do, will never be allowed in Great Britain.

The Bishop makes this statement in the face of the express provision of the 14th section of the School Act, which declares that "pupils shall be allowed to receive such religious instruction as their parents or guardians shall desire."

The Bishop furthermore states that "the Bible appears not among our school books," and says also that the "system is not based on a recognition of the Scriptures." It would be strange if the Bishop were ignorant that in a lengthened correspondence, printed by order of the Legislative Assembly, the Chief Superintendent of Schools objected to any law or system which would exclude the Bible from the schools,—that the Government sanctioned his views,—that his annual reports show that the Bible is used in the great majority of the schools in Upper Canada. By the returns of last year, the Bible was used in 2,067 of the 3,059 schools reported—being an increase of 231 schools over those of the preceding year in which the Bible was used.

The Bishop likewise says:—

A belief of Christianity is not included among the qualifications of schoolmasters; and I am credibly informed that there have been instances of candidates for schools disavowing all religious belief.

There is no law to prevent the vilest persons from being "candidates" for any office, even that of holy orders; but "candidates for schools," and "school-masters," with legal certificates of qualification, are two very different things. According to the school law, no person can be a legally qualified teacher, or receive any portion of the school fund, without appearing before a County Board of Examiners (who consist, in all cases, more or less of clergymen), produce to them "satisfactory evidence of good moral character," and be examined and approved by them. Even the name of the church to which the "school-master" belongs is specified, and the annual reports of the Chief Superintendent of Schools include this item of information. A teacher may also, at any time, be dismissed for intemperance or any immoral conduct. It is notorious that the standard of qualification for teachers, both moral and intellectual, and the provisions and regulations for religious instruction in the schools, are much higher, and more complete and efficient, than under a former school law which the Bishop himself introduced into the Legislature, when he was Chairman of the Provincial Board of Education.

Again, the Bishop states that

All that is wanting is, to give power to the different boards or authorities to grant separate schools to all localities desiring them.

This is precisely what the school law provides; for the 24th section of the Act expressly authorizes and empowers the Board of School Trustees in each city or town, "to determine the number, sites, kind and description of schools which shall be established in such city or town." The Boards of School Trustees may therefore establish as many "separate schools" in all the cities and towns in Upper Canada, as they shall think proper. But they are not willing to establish such separate schools as the Bishop desires; and when an amendment to the school law was proposed at the last session, to compel the local "boards or authorities" to do so, it was almost unanimously rejected. The Bishop says, indeed, referring to this circumstance, that "when the Church of England requested separate schools for the religious instruction of her own children, her prayer was rejected by the votes of Romanists." The fact is, that that proposition received the votes of but five members of the Legislative Assembly, in which there are upwards of fifty Protestants.

It is lamentable to see the Bishop making such statements to damage and pull down the educational institutions of the country, merely because they are not under his denominational control, and subservient to his denominational purposes,—a system of schools which he has, from the commencement, endeavoured to establish in Upper Canada, and for which he has agitated the country these many years. That I do the Bishop no injustice in this statement, I may remark, that in his letter to the Under-Secretary of State for the Colonies, in 1827, applying for the so-much-agitated Charter of the Provincial University, he states his object to be, that the clergy of the Church of England in Upper Canada may "acquire by degrees the direction of education which the clergy of England have always possessed." Now that the Legislative Assembly, since the establishment of free constitutional government, have defeated the peculiar objects of the Bishop, he labours by groundless imputations and statements to bring the whole system of public instruction into contempt. It is to be hoped that such efforts will be as unsuccessful in England as they have been in Canada, where his appeals for agitation have not been responded to by one out of ten of the congregations of the Church of England, and are not sustained by the greater part of the members of the Church of England in both branches of the Legislature. Not a petition has been presented by members of the Church of England against the present system of public schools, except one, adopted by a meeting presided over by the Bishop, and signed by himself; and the Legislative Council within the last few days, by a majority of more than two to one, concurred with the Legislative Assembly and Administration in regard to the clergy reserves and University. The Bishop's extreme policy and proceedings have been and are a great calamity to the Church of England in Canada—a calamity which can only be mitigated and removed by the discountenance of such proceedings, and by the adoption of a more Christian and judicious policy on the part of members of the Church, both in England and in Canada.

In reviewing the history of this question from 1840 until its final settlement by the Canadian Parliament, in 1854, Dr. Ryerson said :—

Messrs. William and Egerton Ryerson had been appointed representatives of the Canadian to the British Conference in 1840. On their arrival in England, they found Lord John Russell's Bill for the disposal of the Canadian Clergy Reserves to the Churches of England and Scotland before Parliament; and, as representing the largest religious denomination in Upper Canada, they requested an interview with Lord John Russell on the subject of His Lordship's Bill before Parliament. In the interview granted, they pointed out to His Lordship the injustice, impolicy, and danger of the Bill, should it become law, and respectfully and earnestly prayed His Lordship to withdraw the Bill; but he was inflexible, when the Messrs. Ryerson prayed to His Lordship to assent to their being heard at the Bar of the House of Commons against the Bill; at which His Lordship became very angry—thinking it presumptuous that two Canadians, however numerous and respectable their constituency, should propose to be heard at the Bar of the British House of Commons against a measure of Her Majesty's Government. But the Messrs. Ryerson knew their country and their position, and afterwards wrote a respectful but earnest letter to His Lordship against his measure, and faithfully warned him of the consequences of it if persevered in; they went so far as to intimate that the measure would prove an opening wedge of separation between Great Britain and the people of Upper Canada; and lest they should be considered as endeavouring to fulfil their own predictions, they did not publish their letter to Lord John Russell, or write a line on the subject for more than ten years—knowing that a wound so deep would, without any action or word on their part, fester and spread so wide in the people of Upper Canada as ultimately to compel the repeal of the Act or sever their connection with Great Britain. The result was as they, Messrs. Ryerson, had apprehended; for in 1853 the Act was repealed by the British Parliament.*

Early in 1852, the Government of which Earl Grey was Secretary of State for the Colonies, was superseded by that of the Earl of Derby, with Sir John Pakington as Secretary of State for the Colonies, who, in a despatch to Lord Elgin, dated April 22nd, 1852, says:—

By a despatch from my predecessor, Earl Grey, of the 11th July last, you were informed that Her Majesty's then servants found themselves compelled to postpone to another Session the introduction of a Bill into Parliament giving the Canadian Legislature authority to alter the existing arrangements with regard to the clergy reserves.

With reference to that intimation, I have to inform you that it is not the intention of Her Majesty's present advisers to propose such a measure to Parliament this Session. "The result would probably be the diversion to other purposes" of the clergy reserves than "the support of divine worship and religious instruction in the colony."

Sir John Pakington was soon undeceived as to the continued Canadian sentiment on the subject, for Sir Francis Hincks, then Inspector-General and Premier of Canada, who happened to be in London on official business on behalf of the Canadian

* Earl Grey had intended to propose its repeal in 1850-51, and had requested the writer of these papers (who was then on an educational tour in Europe) to remain in England in order to furnish His Lordship with data and details to enable him to answer objections which might be made to his Bill in the House of Lords, and wrote to Lord Elgin, then Governor-General of Canada, requesting the protracting of Mr. Ryerson's leave of absence for two or three months. But the Bill had to be deferred until another Session, and Mr. Ryerson returned immediately to Canada. (See page 455.)

Government, enclosed to Sir John Pakington an extract from a report, dated 7th April, 1852, approved by His Excellency, in which the Executive Council said:—

> The assurances of Her Majesty's late Government that such action would be taken, had prepared the people of Canada to expect that no further delay would take place in meeting their just wishes upon a question of such paramount importance to them; the Council, therefore, recommend that their colleague, the Inspector-General, be requested by the Provincial Secretary to seek an interview with Her Majesty's Ministers, and represent to them the importance of carrying out the pledges of their predecessors on the subject of the clergy reserves, and thus empower the Colonial Legislature to deal with the question in accordance with the well-understood wishes of the people of Canada.

The Derby ministry resigned office in December, 1852, and the Duke of Newcastle succeeded Sir John Pakington as Secretary of State for the Colonies. On the 15th January, 1853, the Duke adressed a despatch to the Earl of Elgin announcing the decision of the new ministry to propose the repeal of the Imperial Act of 1840, which was sucessfully accomplished.

After the passing of the Imperial Act transferring the final settlement of the clergy reserve question to Canada, a coalition Government was formed by the aid of Sir Allan McNab, called the Hincks-Morin Ministry. After protracted negotiation (with the beneficiaries under the Imperial Act) and discussion in the Legislature, a Bill was passed providing for the interests of these claimants, but "secularizing" the remaining proceeds of the reserves to municipal purposes. This was the last of the Acts assented to by Lord Elgin previous to his departure from Canada. Sir Edmund Head, his successor, speaking on this subject, said:—

> An Act assented to by my predecessor has finally settled the long pending dispute with regard to the clergy reserves, and it has done so in such a manner as to vindicate liberal principles, whilst it treats the rights of individuals with just and considerate regard.

Thus was a struggle of more than twenty-five years ended, equality before the law of all religious denominations established, and constitutional rights of the people of Upper Canada secured, to their great joy. But the Bishop of Toronto, whose policy and measures had caused so much agitation in Upper Canada, regarded this settlement of the clergy reserve question as an irreparable calamity to the Church of England in Canada. On the 16th of March, 1853, the Bishop addressed a letter to the Duke of Newcastle, of which the following are extracts:—

> Power and violence are to determine the question; vested rights and the claims of justice are impediments to be swept away. Hence the spoliation sought to be perpetrated by the Legislature of Canada has no parallel in

colonial history. Even in the middle of the American Revolution, the old colonists, during the heart-burnings and ravages of civil war, respected the ecclesiastical endowments made by the Crown against which they were contending. . . .

The grants made by the Crown were all held by the same tenure—whether to individuals or corporations—not reservations for certain purposes, with power expressly given to Colonial Assemblies to "vary or repeal" them. The Bishop proceeded :—

I feel bitterly, my Lord Duke, on this subject. Till I heard of your Grace's despatch, I had fondly trusted in Mr. Gladstone and his friends, of whom you are one, notwithstanding the present doubtful Administration; and I still argued in my heart, though not without misgivings, that the Church was safe. I have cherished her with my best energies for more than half a century in this distant corner of God's dominions; and after many trials and difficulties I was beholding her with joy, enlarging her tent, lengthening her cords, and strengthening her stakes, but now this joy is turned into grief and sadness, for darkness and tribulation are approaching to arrest her onward progress. Permit me, in conclusion, my Lord Duke, to entreat your forgiveness if, in the anguish of my spirit, I have been too bold, for it is far from my wish or intention to give personal offence. And of this rest assured, that I would most willingly avert, with the sacrifice of my life, the calamities which the passing of your Bill will bring upon the Church in Canada.

There is a touching pathos in the close of this letter; but the Bishop himself lived to see his apprehended calamities turned into blessings; for the most prosperous and brightest days of the Church of England in Upper Canada have been from 1853 to the present time.

CHAPTER LIII.

1851.

PERSONAL EPISODE IN THE CLERGY RESERVE CONTROVERSY.

DR. RYERSON made another educational tour in Europe in 1850–51. While in London, early in 1851, Earl Grey sought Dr. Ryerson's counsel on the clergy reserve question, which had been lately re-opened in Canada. The proceedings and result of the interviews which he had with Earl Grey, are detailed in several letters which he wrote to me from London during a period of four months. I give such extracts from these letters as will explain the nature of Dr. Ryerson's conferences with Earl Grey on the subject. His first letter was written on the 7th February, in which he said:—

You will rejoice to learn that Her Majesty's Government have adopted the prayer of the Canadian Legislature on the question of the clergy reserves, and have determined to bring forward a measure on the subject. Whether Lord Grey will desire me to remain longer on account of the question I have not had time to learn. Mr. [afterwards Sir Benjamin] Hawes says that he will procure me admission to the speaker's gallery to hear Lord John Russell bring forward his measure on the Papal Question.

In a letter written by Dr. Ryerson the following week, dated 14th February, he enclosed to me a confidential letter on the clergy reserve question, in which he explained the likelihood of his being detained in England by Lord Grey in connection with it. He said:—

I send this to you, so that you may know all the circumstances which are likely to protract my stay for some months in this country; and for the same reason, and that you may co-operate with me, I entrust you with the perusal of my confidential letter—another proof of my unreserved confidence in your prudence and fidelity. I think it would not be well for you to mention anything as to my probable delay in England, and especially as to the reasons of it, until it becomes known to the public.

My position is, indeed, a gratifying one, after so long labour and so much abuse in connection with the great clergy reserve question, that I should be desired to aid in its final settlement according to the voice of the people of Canada, and should now be called upon to aid Lord John Russell himself to undo his own measure of 1840, against which I then protested. I am sure you will be prepared to perform any additional labour to enable me to fulfil such a mission. I trust that I will be enabled to confer a benefit upon Canada. It is a gratifying position in which such a concurrence of circumstances will place me, and my personal character and history in regard to a question which has engaged so large a portion of my past life—the ground of all the opposition I formerly met with from the London Wesleyan Committee and Conference. Verily there is a God that ruleth over all things, that makes the wrath of man to praise Him, that rules in ways we know not of. We should indeed fear Him, bow down in the dust before Him, but at the same time most calmly and implicitly trust Him. Please write me as to the effects produced by Lord Grey's despatch, the manner in which it is received, etc.

In a letter, dated 13th March, Dr. Ryerson said :—

I have received a letter from a member of the Government in Canada, expressing a wish that I would remain in England until after the great Exhibition, as the Canadian Parliament would not meet until May. This, in anticipation of what Lord Grey has desired, has quite settled my mind on the subject of remaining until May or June.

I shall remain in Paris until I am wanted in London on the clergy reserve question—I suppose until the middle of next month. Listening some hours each day in Paris to some of the most learned men in Europe, giving the results of all their researches and reflections on various branches of literature and science, will be of great advantage to me in my future lectures, writings and labours, and this I shall continue until the voice of war on the clergy reserves shall echo across the Atlantic. I suppose my presence in England at this time will be a great annoyance to the exclusive Church party, and it will perhaps make them more cautious than they might otherwise be in their statements.

As the ministry in England continue firm, I hope no effort will be wanting in Canada to sustain Lord Grey, should an opposition be raised against his proposed bill, the bringing in of which may be delayed some time by the late long ministerial crisis in England.

In a letter, dated 11th April, Dr. Ryerson said :—

In regard to the clergy reserves, I have been inclined to think the Bishop of Toronto and his friends would not attempt to renew the agitation of the clergy reserve question in Canada, but would prepare the strongest statement of their case for the Parliament here, in the mouths of some of their ablest friends in both the Commons and Lords, and thus take the Government here by surprise, and try and defeat the Bill in the Lords, after having reduced the majority in favour of it in the Commons as much as possible.

On the 18th April, 1851, Dr. Ryerson wrote again :—

The Scotch Presbytery of Kingston, U. C., have sent a petition to the House of Commons against Lord Grey's Bill, or against complying with the prayer of the address of the Canadian Assembly, and sent to me with the request that I would prepare an answer to it. I think of preparing my answer in the form of a communication or two to the *Times* newspaper, and thus bring the whole subject before the Members of Parliament and the public. Should I succeed in this, Lord Grey may not think my longer stay to be necessary. I am anxious to get away as soon as possible; the season is advancing, and I have so much to do before the close of it in the autumn.

Business and embarrasments have so accumulated in the House of Commons that it is pretty nearly decided to bring the clergy reserve Bill into the Lords by Lord Grey himself, and he expects to do so about the middle of May. Should it be brought into the Lords, of course there would not be so long delay there before deciding the question one way or the other. But the chances are so strong against its success if brought into the Lords first, that Lord Grey is unwilling to adopt that course until it is seen that that is the only alternative. If it should be lost in the Lords now, he, of course, thinks it would soon be carried by a pressure from Canada, such as the rejection of the Bill by the Lords would probably call forth.

On the 25th April, Dr. Ryerson wrote :—

The late crisis has made no change in the intentions of the Government in regard to the clergy reserve question. I send you a copy of the *Times* of the 23rd instant, the day before yesterday, in which you will see the first of my papers on " The Clergy Reserves of Canada." The second and third will occupy a column and a half or two columns, each. I finished and handed in the remaining papers this morning. Lord Grey spoke to me twice on the subject of writing something for the press, and Mr. Hawes, the last time I saw him, seemed to think the Bill would be lost in the House of Lords, but the Government would send out a despatch to Canada saying that the question was not abandoned, but would be brought forward again the next Session. I have thought this was a very poor consolation for the loss of the Bill, and that it was best to see what could be done. I have written strongly, and with an express view to the House of Lords—confining myself wholly to the question of the right of the people of Canada to judge and decide in the matter. What may be the effect of these papers, I cannot, of course, tell ; but if Lord Grey should be of opinion that the publication of them will supersede the necessity of my longer stay for that purpose, I will leave as soon as possible—by the third week in May.

I wrote fully to Dr. Ryerson on this subject, pointing out the relation of parties in Canada on this subject, and deprecating his taking any further active part in the discussion which had become so heated in this country. On the 2nd May, Dr. Ryerson replied :—

What you have communicated on the clergy reserve question has changed my mode of proceeding in some respects ; and the second and third articles I prepared for the *Times* will not appear as first intended ; but I will explain by and by. I was at the great Exhibition yesterday. It was the grandest of all grand affairs I ever witnessed. I had a place near the centre, within a few feet of the " Iron Duke," until he left to join the procession.

On the 9th May, Dr. Ryerson wrote his final letter :—

On reflection, and from what I found to be the relations of parties in Canada, and the turn the clergy reserve question was likely to take, I came to the same conclusion you have expressed in your last letter—not to come into collision with any party on the question, beyond what is expressed in the short article in the *Times* newspaper—namely, that Canada should judge for itself on the question. I have determined to furnish Lord Grey with a memorandum of facts and principles on the question. I have seen Lord Grey and stated my wish not to remain longer, and not to be further mixed up with the question—that I was now on good terms with all parties—had thus great facilities for usefulness—that party agitation in Canada was becoming violent—two extreme parties, uniting against the Ministerial measure. I told him that I would furnish him with a memorandum, with all the chief points of the question on which he was likely to be opposed. He seemed to be disappointed, but said if I thought my Department would suffer by my longer absence, he would not insist upon my staying. I told him that all parties would approve of my staying for the Great Exhibition, and that I thought a memorandum, such as I would prepare on the question of the clergy reserves, would be as serviceable as my presence, etc.

MEMORANDUM ON THE CLERGY RESERVE QUESTION.

The following is the memorandum which Dr. Ryerson prepared for Lord Grey on the clergy reserve question, and to which he refers in his letter to me of the 9th May, 1851:—

Fully concurring in the remark of the Bishop of London, in a late reply to the deputation of the inhabitants of St. George's, Hanover Square, that "there is no kind of intestine division so injurious in its character and tendency as that which is grounded on religious questions;" and firmly believing, as I do, that the long continuance of Canada as a portion of the British Empire depends upon the proceedings of the British Parliament on the question of the clergy reserves, I desire, as a native and resident of Upper Canada, as a Protestant and lover of British institutions, to submit the following brief observations on that question, in order to correct erroneous impressions in England, and to induce such a course of parliamentary proceedings as will conduce to the honour of Great Britain, and to the peace and welfare of Canada:—

1. My first remark is, that this is a question agitated for more than twenty-five years, almost exclusively among Protestants in Canada, and the agitation of which, at the present time, has not, in any way whatever, been promoted by Roman Catholic influence. An attempt has been made in some quarters to create a contrary impression in England; but that I am correct in my statement will, I think, appear from the following facts:—First, though the question of the clergy reserves nominally relates to Lower as well as Upper Canada (since the union of the two Canadas under one Legislature), it is historically and practically an Upper Canadian question. The agitation of it originated in Upper Canada; it never was agitated in Lower Canada before the union of the two provinces; it is discussed chiefly by the Upper Canada press, and pressed most earnestly by the Upper Canada members of the Legislature. So strongly is it viewed as an Upper Canadian question, that a considerable portion of the press of Upper Canada has objected to Lower Canadian members of the Legislature interfering in its discussion or influencing its decision by their votes. Secondly, all the Upper Canadian members, both of the Executive Council and of the Legislative Assembly, are Protestants. Of the forty-two members of the Legislative Assembly elected in Upper Canada, not one of them is a Roman Catholic; of the five Upper Canadian members of the Executive Council, all are Protestants, and all were in favour of the late Address of the Assembly to the Queen, praying for the repeal of the Imperial Act, 4 & 5 Vic., chap. 78, and for restoring to the people of

Canada the constitutional right of judging for themselves as to the disposal of the clergy reserve lands in that country. It ought, therefore, to be remembered in England, that this question relates chiefly to Upper Canada, which is, for the most part, a Protestant country, and which has not a single Roman Catholic in the Legislative Assembly.

2. I remark, in the next place, that it is not a question of Church and State union, or whether the State shall contribute to the support of religion in one or more forms. It is whether the Canadian people shall judge for themselves as to the mode of supporting their religious worship, as well as to the religious creed they shall adopt. This right was clearly secured to them by their constitutional Act of 1791, 31st George III., chap. 31, but was taken from them by the Imperial Act of 1840, 3 & 4 Vic., chap. 78. In what manner the people of Canada, through their representatives, may exercise the constitutional right, the restoration of which they claim, for the support of religion, I am not prepared to say. But whether they shall exercise wisely or not that, or any other right constitutionally vested in them, is a matter appertaining to themselves, and not to parties in England. I am not to be the less anxious for the restoration to my country of its constitutional rights because it may not exercise them wisely, or exercise them in a manner opposed to my personal views and wishes. The constitutional rights of legislation in Great Britain may not have always been exercised most judiciously, but who would adduce that as an argument for the annihilation of those rights, or against the existence of constitutional freedom in England? Is Canada to be made an exception to this rule?

3. I remark, thirdly, that neither is this a question which affects the vested rights of any parties except those of the people of Canada generally. When one-seventh of the wild lands of Canada was reserved for the support of a Protestant clergy, by the Act of 1791, 31st George III., chap. 31, the Canadian Legislature, created by the same Act, was invested with authority, under certain forms, to "vary or repeal" the several clauses relating to that clergy land reservation. That vested right the people of Upper Canada possessed from 1791 to 1840. All other vested rights are subordinate to those of a whole people, and are not to be exalted above them. The Canadian Legislative Assembly has proposed to secure all parties who have acquired rights or interests in the revenue arising from the sales of the clergy reserve lands during the lives of the incumbents or recipients; but, beyond that guarantee, it claims the right of "varying or repealing," as it shall judge expedient, the landed reservation in question, and the application of the revenues arising from it.

4. The real question for consideration in England being thus separated from other questions with which it has sometimes been erroneously and injuriously confounded, I proceed to remark that the Imperial Act 3 and 4 Vic., chap. 78, is at variance with what the Imperial Governments without exception and without reservation, for twenty-five years, have admitted and avowed to be the constitutional rights of the people of Canada. It has at all times been admitted in the first place, that the Act 31st Geo. III., ch. 31, which created a legislature in Canada, and authorized the clergy land reservation, invested the Canadian Legislature with authority to legislate as to its disposal, and the application of revenues arising from it; and secondly, that whatever legislation might take place on the subject should be in harmony with the wishes of the Canadian people. The Imperial Act 3 and 4 Vic., ch. 78, deprives the Canadian people of that right of legislation which they had possessed for forty years, and does violence to their wishes and opinions in the disposal which it makes of the revenues of the lands in question. Now the rights of the people of Canada on this subject were explicitly stated by the late Sir George Murray in 1828, by the Earl of Ripon in 1832, by His late Most Gracious Majesty in a message to the Legislature of Upper Canada in 1833, and by Lord Glenelg in 1835 and 1836. I give a summary of the whole in the words of Lord Glenelg, in a despatch to the Lieutenant Governor of Upper Canada, dated December 5, 1835, in reply to an attempt on the part of the latter to induce Imperial legislation on the subject. Lord Glenelg says, in behalf of the Imperial Government, that

> Parliamentary legislation on any subject of exclusively internal concern, in a British colony possessing a representative assembly, is as a general rule unconstitutional. It is a right of which the exercise is reserved for extreme cases, in which necessity at once creates and justifies the exception.

After showing that no necessity existed for setting aside the constitutional rights of the Canadian people, Lord Glenelg expresses himself in the following language of enlightened political philosophy :—

> It is not difficult to perceive the reasons which induced Parliament, in 1791, to connect with a reservation of land for ecclesiastical purposes, the special delegation to the Council and Assembly of the right to vary that provision by any Bill which, being reserved for the signification of His Majesty's pleasure, should be communicated to both Houses of Parliament for six weeks before that decision was pronounced. Remembering, it should seem, how fertile a source of controversy ecclesiastical endowments had supplied throughout a large part of the Christian world, and how impossible it was to foretell with precision what might be the prevailing opinions and feelings of the Canadians on this subject at a future period, Parliament at once secured the means of making a systematic provision for a Protestant clergy, and took full precaution against the eventual inaptitude of that

system to the more advanced stages of a society then in its infant state, and of which no human foresight could divine the more mature and settled judgment.

In the controversy, therefore, respecting ecclesiastical endowments, which at present divides the Canadian Legislature, I find no unexpected element of agitation, the discovery of which demands a departure from the fixed principles of the constitution, but merely the fulfilment of the anticipations of the Parliament of 1791, in the exhibition of that conflict of opinion for which the statute of that year may be said to have made a deliberate preparation. In referring the subject to the future Canadian Legislature, the authors of the Constitutional Act must be supposed to have contemplated the crisis at which we have now arrived—the era of warm and protracted debate, which, in a free government, may be said to be a necessary precursor to the settlement of any great principle of national policy. We must not have recourse to an extreme remedy, merely to avoid the embarrassment which is the present, though temporary, result of our own legislation.

I think, therefore, that to withdraw from the Canadian to the Imperial Legislature the question respecting the clergy reserves, would be an infringement of that cardinal principle of colonial government which forbids parliamentary interference, except in submission to an evident and well-established necessity.

In January, 1840, the two branches of the Legislature of Upper Canada passed a Bill (the Legislative Assembly by a majority of 28 to 20, and the Legislative Council by a majority of 13 to 4) relative to the clergy reserve—provided for the interests of their existing incumbents, and dividing the proceeds of the sales of said lands among various religious persuasions according to a census taken once in five years, and leaving each religious persuasion free to expend the sum or sums to which it should be entitled according to its pleasure, whether for the support of its clergy, the erection of places of worship, or for purposes of education. Though the great majority of the people of Upper Canada desired the application of the proceeds of these lands for educational purposes only; yet a majority of both branches of the Legislature agreed to a compromise which could be defended as just to all parties, whatever preferences might be entertained on the subject in the abstract. But instead of the Royal assent being advised to be given to that Canadian Bill on a local Canadian question, a new Bill was introduced into the Imperial Parliament, giving about three-fourths of the proceeds of the clergy reserves (including past and future sales) to the clergy of the churches of England and Scotland, giving nothing to any other church, but leaving the remaining one-fourth (or half of future sales) at the discretionary disposal of the Executive for religious purposes. This part of the Imperial Act has proved inoperative to this day; and should any religious persuasion receive any portion of this comparative pittance of the clergy land funds, it would do so not as a matter of right (as do the Churches of

England and Scotland in receiving their lion's share), but at and during the pleasure of any party in power—a position in which no religious community should be placed to the Executive, and in which the Executive ought not to be placed to any religious community. Such an Act can be justified upon no principle of justice or sound policy, and is at variance with the almost unanimous and often recorded wishes of the people of Upper Canada. The *Christian Examiner*—a monthly organ of the Church of Scotland in Upper Canada—expressed not only the general sentiments of the members of that Church, but also of people at large, in the following words, contained in an elaborate editorial which appeared in that publication a few months before the passing of the Imperial Act of 1841:

Year after year, at least during the last decade, the general sentiment in this colony has been uttered in no unequivocal form, that no church invested with exclusive privileges derived from the State, is adapted to the condition of society among us. It cannot be doubted that this is the conviction of nine-tenths of the Colonists. Except among a few ambitious magnates of the Church of England, we never hear a contrary sentiment breathed. Equal rights upon equal conditions is the general cry. And although several Assemblymen of the present House have chosen to misinterpret the public voice, and to advocate a different principle, we doubt not that on their next appearance before their constituents, they will be taught that this is not the age, nor this the country, in which the grand principle of equal rights can be departed from with impunity.

Now, although the Imperial Act of 1840 may have induced "a few magnates" of the Church of Scotland to unite with other "magnates," whom they once considered "ambitious," in denying the "grand principle of equal rights" to their more numerous Methodist brethren, and other religious persuasions, yet the "convictions of nine-tenths" of the Canadian people remain unchanged; nor will they, because of the changed circumstances of a few clergymen of the Church of Scotland, suffer "the grand principle of equal rights to be departed from with impunity."

5. I observe, likewise, that the continuance of the Imperial Act of 1840 is desired by a mere fraction of the Canadian population, while its repeal is demanded by that country at large. The assertions of any interested parties on a matter of this kind are of little weight against the proceedings and statements of the representatives of the people. The Address of the Legislative Assembly to Her Majesty must be regarded as the authoritative and true expression of the opinions and wishes of the Canadian people. It is true, there was diversity of opinion as to the manner in which the incumbents on the clergy reserve fund should be dealt with, and also as to certain other declarations contained in the Address of the Assembly ; but no member

of the Canadian Legislature ventured to justify the provisions of the Imperial Act, and very few ventured to vote in favour of its continuance, even upon the ground of expediency, in behalf of the "magnates" of two favourable Churches. When the resolutions of the Address to Her Majesty were moved in the Legislative Assembly of Canada on this subject, an amendment was moved by the supporters of the present exclusive privileges of the Churches of England and Scotland in Canada an amendment which contained the following words :—

That in the opinion of this House it is inexpedient to disturb or unsettle, by resolution or enactment, the appropriations or endowments now existing in Upper and Lower Canada for religious purposes; that the well-being of society and the growing wants of the various Christian bodies in Canada demand that the several provisions of the Imperial Act 3 and 4 Vic., cap. 78, should be carried out to their fullest extent.

In favour of the amendment, that is, in favour of the continuance and operations of the Imperial Act of 1840, voted sixteen; against it voted fifty-two. Who would think of perpetuating a law in England at variance with the sentiments of three-fourths of the members of the House of Commons, and even of a large proportion of the constituency of Great Britain? Could the present constitution of government in England be maintained, could revolution be long prevented, if laws were retained on the statute book condemned by three-fourths of the Commons, and more than three-fourth of all classes of people in the land, and those statutes involving religious questions? And is that to be perpetuated in Canada which would not be retained in England for a month?

6. Into the origin and progress of the controversy connected with the clergy reserves, it is needless for me to enter. They are sufficiently stated in the Address of the Legislative Assembly of Canada to the Queen, a copy of which is herewith annexed, together with the majorities by which each of the thirty-one clauses of the Address was separately voted. It will be seen that the first twenty-three clauses of the Address were carried by a majority of 52 to 18; the 24th clause by 51 to 20; the 26th clause by 48 to 19; the 27th and 28th clauses by 47 to 20; the 29th clause by 36 to 34; the 30th clause by 40 to 28; the 31st clause, containing the prayer of the Address, by 45 to 23. The only clause of the Address, therefore, in favour of which the majority of the Assembly was not large and decided, was the 29th; and in a vote to that clause, I have shown that the smallness of the majority was occasioned by objections to different parts of the clause upon quite opposite grounds, of three classes of members—the sixteen supporters of the present pre-eminence of the Churches of England and Scotland, a section

of the Roman Catholic members, and what in England would be called the extreme dissenters. In the vote referred to, I have explained the ground of the opposition to this clause by each of these three classes of members. It will be seen that the 29th clause is rather speculative than practical, and does not affect the character and completeness of the Address, every other clause of which was carried by a large majority. It is, however, curious to remark, that while the supporters of the present exclusive privileges of the Churches of England and Scotland are indebted to the assistance of Roman Catholic members for the only vote in which the minority was large; yet in England some of these same parties represent the Address as having been carried chiefly by Roman Catholic votes, with a view of destroying all Protestant institutions in Canada.

7. No enlightened and candid person can look at the religious history and social state of Canada and desire the perpetuation of the Imperial Act 3 and 4 Vic., ch. 78. It is now quite sixty years since Upper Canada was formed into a province with a representative government. Its population was then 7,000 souls; it is now about 700,000. During the first and most eventful half of that sixty years, the ministrations of the Churches of England and Scotland can scarcely be said to have had an existence there. The present Bishop of Toronto, in a discourse published on the occasion of the death of the first Canadian Bishop of the Church of England, states that down to the close of the war between Great Britain and the United States in 1815, there were but four resident clergymen or missionaries of the Church of England in all Upper Canada—a statement which is confirmed by the annual reports of the Society for the Propagation of the Gospel in Foreign Parts; and the same reports will show how few were the clergy of the Church of England in that province down to a recent period. We learn from the same authority, that till 1818 there was but one clergyman of the Church of Scotland in Upper Canada, and that in 1827 there were but two. It is, therefore, clear that during the first half of its sixty years' existence as a province, Upper Canada must have been indebted almost entirely to other than clergy of the Churches of England and Scotland for religious instruction; yet during that thirty years, it is admitted that the people of Upper Canada were a religious, an intelligent, and loyal people. To whom the people of that province were mainly indebted for their religious instruction, and for the formation and development of their religious character, appears in a report of a Select Committee of the Upper Canada House of Assembly, appointed in 1828, on the religious

condition of the country, and before which fifty witnesses, chiefly members of the Church of England, were examined. I quote the following words from the report of that Committee, (which was adopted by the Assembly by a majority of 22 to 8), a report which was partly prepared in reference to a letter addressed by the present Bishop of Toronto to His Majesty's Secretary of State for the Colonies in 1827:—

The insinuations (says the report) in the letter against the Methodist clergymen, the committee have noticed with peculiar regret. To the disinterested and indefatigable exertions of these pious men this province owes much. At an early period of its history, when it was thinly settled, and destitute of all other means of religious instruction, these ministers of the Gospel, animated by Christian zeal and benevolence, at the sacrifice of health, and interest, and comfort, carried among the people the blessings, and consolations, and sanctions of our holy religion. Their influence and instruction have been conducive in a degree which cannot be easily estimated, to the reformation of the vicious and to the diffusion of correct morals, the foundation of all sound loyalty and social order.

This religious body has now 180 regular ministers in Upper Canada, about 1,100 churches and preaching places, and embraces in its congregations one-seventh of the population.* Yet this oldest religious community in Upper Canada, together with the Free Presbyterian Church of Canada, the United Presbyterian Church, the Baptists and Congregationalists, are treated as nobody by the Imperial Act, while the more modern Churches of England and Scotland are exclusively endowed, and that by setting aside legislative rights which the Constitution of 1791 had conferred upon the people of Upper Canada! In Great Britain the Established Churches are associated with the early and brightest periods of British history, and are blended with all the influences which distinguish and exalt British character; but the feelings and predilections arising from such reminiscences and associations are not the proper rule of judgment as to the feelings, predilections and institutions of Canadian society. As Englishmen best know their own feelings and wants, and claim and exercise the sole right of judging and legislating for themselves; so do the people of Canada best know their own wishes and interests, and ought to judge and legislate for themselves in all local matters which do not infringe any imperial prerogative. No Englishman can refuse this who wishes to do to others as he would have others do to him.

8. But it should also be observed, that down to the passing of the Imperial Act of 1840, the influence of the Church of Scotland itself was adverse to any such act of partiality and injustice, and in favour of applying the proceeds of the clergy reserves even to educational as well as religious purposes. The

* Since the foregoing was written, it has been ascertained that the Wesleyan Methodists number 142,000, or more than one-fifth of the entire population (1850).

discussion of this question was first introduced into the Legislative Assembly of Upper Canada in 1823, by the Hon. William Morris—a gentleman of great respectability, and who has always been regarded and acknowledged as the guardian of the interests, and representative of the sentiments, of the Church of Scotland. December 22nd, 1826, Mr. Morris moved a series of resolutions on this subject, of which the following are the 9th and 10th:

9. *Resolved,*—That it is the opinion of a great proportion of the people of this Province that the clergy lands, in place of being enjoyed by the clergy of an inconsiderable part of the population, ought to be disposed of, and the proceeds of their sale applied to increase the provincial allowance for the support of district and common schools, and the endowment of a provincial seminary for learning, and in aid of erecting places of public worship for all denominations of Christians. [Carried by a majority of 31 to 2.]

10. *Resolved,* That it is expedient to pass a Bill, authorizing the sale of the clergy lands within this Province, for the purposes set forth in the foregoing resolution; and to address His Majesty, humbly soliciting that he will be graciously pleased to give the royal assent to said Bill. [Carried by a majority of 30 to 3.]

On the 28th of the same month, Mr. Morris reported a draft of Bill for the sale of the clergy reserves, pursuant to the foregoing resolutions. The Bill passed the Assembly by a majority of 20 to 3; was sent to the Legislative Council, and was rejected. Similar attempts to legislate having in like manner and from the same cause proved abortive, another address to the King on this subject was adopted by the Assembly in March, 1831, and supported, if not introduced, by Mr. Morris. That address, which was adopted by a majority of 30 to 7, contains the following words:—

That a large majority of the inhabitants of this Province are sincerely attached to your Majesty's person and government, but are averse to any exclusive or dominant Church. That this House feels confident that, to promote the prosperity of this portion of your Majesty's dominions, and to satisfy the earnest desire of the people of this Province, your Majesty will be graciously pleased to give the most favourable consideration to the wishes of your faithful subjects. That, to terminate the jealousy and dissension which have hitherto existed on the subject of the said clergy reserves—to remove a barrier to the settlement of the country, and to provide a fund available for the promotion of education, and in aid of erecting places of worship for various denominations of Christians: it is extremely desirable that the said land reserved should be sold, and the proceeds arising from the sale of the same placed at the disposal of the Provincial Legislature, to be applied exclusively for those purposes.

This address was replied to the January following, 1832, by a formal message from the King, from which I extract the following sentences:—

The representations which have at different times been made to His Majesty and his Royal predecessors of the prejudice sustained by his faithful subjects in Upper Canada, from the appropriation of the clergy reserves,

have engaged His Majesty's most attentive consideration. . . It has, therefore, been with peculiar satisfaction that, in his inquiries into this subject, His Majesty has found that the changes sought for by so large a portion of the inhabitants of Upper Canada, may be carried into effect without sacrificing the just claims of the established Churches of England and Scotland.
. . . His Majesty, therefore, invites the House of Assembly of Upper Canada to consider how the powers given the Provincial Legislature by the Constitutional Act to vary or repeal this part of its provisions, can be called into exercise most advantageously, for the spiritual and temporal interests of His Majesty's faithful subjects in the Province.

It will be seen that the Address to the Crown and reply, above quoted, contemplated the application of no part of the proceeds of the clergy lands for the support of the clergy of any religious persuasion, but the application of the whole to the promotion of education, and in aid of erecting places of worship. I do not make these references to advocate this view of the question, but to show that the Crown has long since assented to the alienation of the whole of the proceeds of the reserves from the support of the clergy of any Church, should the Canadian Legislature think proper to do so, and that the Church of Scotland in Upper Canada agreed with the other religious persuasions, and the great majority of the Canadian people, in the advocacy of such an alienation of said reserves. The same parties cannot now object on constitutional and moral grounds to what they heretofore advocated on those same grounds.

9. It has, however, been alleged that the people of Canada have acquiesced in the provisions of the Imperial Act, and are satisfied with it. At the time of passing the Imperial Act, in 1840, and down to within the last two years, the discussion of questions relating to the organization and system of government itself occupied the attention of the public mind in Canada; but no sooner was the public mind set at rest on those paramount and fundamental questions, than the Canadian people demanded the restoration of their rights on the question of the clergy reserves. What they have felt for two years, and often and strongly spoken, through the local press and at the hustings, they now speak in the ears of the Sovereign of the Imperial Parliament. That there must be deep and general dissatisfaction in Canada on this subject, will appear from the following circumstances: (1) The Imperial Act infringes the rights, and contravenes the wishes of the Canadian people; (2) It inflicts an injustice and wrong upon the great majority of the religious persuasions in that country, where the "convictions of nine-tenths" or rather ninety-nine one-hundreths, of the inhabitants are in favour of "equal rights upon equal conditions," among all classes and persuasions; (3) The Legislative Assembly, by

a majority of 51 to 20, declare that the Imperial Act, "so far from settling this long agitated question, has left it to be the subject of renewed and increased public discontent;" (4) The comparative silence of the Wesleyan body—the oldest, the most numerous, and the most unjustly treated, of all the excluded denominations—is expressive and ominous. Its representatives, having proceeded to England in 1840, remonstrated against this Bill, then before Parliament; they sought the assent of Her Majesty's Secretary of State for the Colonies to be heard at the Bar of the House of Commons against it, and having been refused, they presented to him, July 27th, 1840, a most earnest remonstrance against the Bill. On the Bill becoming law, they silently submitted, and on grounds which were explained, a few months since, by the official organ of the Wesleyan Methodist Church in Canada, in the following words:—

On Lord John Russell's Bill becoming a law, the question was changed from a denominational to a Provincial one—from an ecclesiastical to a constitutional one. It was no longer a question between one denomination and another, but a question between Upper Canada and the Imperial Parliament. As Canadians, and acting in behalf of a large section of the Canadian community, the representatives of the Wesleyan Methodist Church expressed their convictions, their feelings, and their apprehensions to Her Majesty's Government while the question was pending before Parliament; but when the execrable Bill became an Imperial Law, it was as much out of place for them as clergymen, or of any religious persuasion to strive to fulfil their own predictions, or set on foot a Colonial civil contest, as it would have been pusillanimous in them not to have remonstrated before the consummation of such an act of wrong against the people of Upper Canada. The question is now being taken up in the right place, and, we trust, in the right spirit.

10. Under such circumstances it is impossible that the question can long remain in its present state, and it is for the Imperial Parliament to say what shall be done. It is admitted upon all hands that the members of the Churches of England and Scotland in Canada are more wealthy in proportion to their numbers, and, therefore, less needful of extraneous aid than the members of any other religious persuasion ; and in proportion to their numbers and wealth will be their comparative influence and advantages in the proceedings of their own Legislature. It is a grave question, whether the Imperial Parliament will place itself in an attitude of hostility to the Legislative Assembly and people of Canada for the sake of conferring questionable pecuniary distinctions upon the clergy of the two most wealthy denominations in that country ? Should any members of Parliament be disposed to pursue this course, and hazard this experiment, I beg them to pause and consider the following questions :—

(1) Can the real interests of the Churches of England and

Scotland themselves be advanced by occupying a position of antagonism to the acknowledged equal rights of the great majority of the people of Canada? And is it desirable that these Churches should be the instruments and emblems of wrong to a country, rather than natural and powerful agencies of its unity, advancement, and happiness? Interested parties in Canada may not be able to see this, but British and Christian statesmen ought not to overlook it.

(2) Ought the members of the Churches of England and Scotland, who take a part in public affairs in Canada, and who may be candidates for popular power, to be placed in circumstances in which they must either war against the position and authorities of their own Church, or war against all other religious persuasions, or retire from public life altogether?

(3) What will be the natural, or apparently inevitable, result of thus singling out two classes of Canadian people, and distinguishing them from all others by pecuniary endowments, and sustaining them in that position, not by the free Legislature of their own country—not by the original principles of their constitution of government to which Canada may have pledged itself—but by a recent Imperial Act, to the preparing or provisions of which the Canadians were no parties, and against which they protest? Is it likely that the will or predilections of a transatlantic House of Lords, so largely composed of and influenced by one class of ecclesiastical dignitaries, can long determine the mutual relations of religious persuasions in a country constituted as Canada is, and bordering on the northern free Anglo-States of America? What the Canadians ask they ask on grounds originally guaranteed to them by their constitution; and if they are compelled to make a choice between British connection and British constitutional rights, it is natural that they should prefer the latter to the former? It is also to be noted that the Imperial Act in question has to be administered through the local Canadian administration. Such is the machinery of the Act. The revenue that it appropriates is Canadian, and it is worked through Canadian agency—through Canadian heads of departments, responsible to the representatives of the people of Canada. Should the Canadian people, then, find that their respectful and earnest appeal to the Imperial Parliament, through the Sovereign, is in vain, they will naturally look to their own resources and elect representatives at the ensuing general elections who will pledge themselves to oppose the administration of the Imperial Act—representatives who will support no Inspector or Receiver-General that will be responsible for the payment of even any warrant for moneys under such Act. The consequence must soon be, not only

injury to existing incumbents whom the Canadian Assembly now propose to secure, but collision between the Government and the Legislative Assembly, and ultimately between the latter and the Imperial authorities; and finally, either the establishment of military government in Canada (an impossibility), or the severance of that great country from Great Britain. On the other hand, if the reasonable demand and constitutional rights of the people of Canada be regarded in this question, I believe Canada will remain freely and cordially connected with the Mother Country for many years, if not generations, to come. I will conclude these observations in the expressive words of Lord Stanley, to the spirit of which I hope every British statesman will respond. On the 2nd of May, 1828, in a speech on this subject, Lord Stanley expressed himself in the following terms:—

That if any exclusive privileges be given to the Church of England, not only will the measure be repugnant to every principle of sound legislation, but contrary to the spirit and intention of the Act of 1791, under which the reserves were made for the Protestant clergy. 1 will not enter further into it at present, except to express my hope that the House will guard Canada against the evils which religious dissensions have already produced in this country and in Ireland, where we have examples to teach us what to shun. We have seen the evil consequences of this system at home. God forbid we should not profit by experience; and more especially in legislating for a people bordering on a country where religious intolerance and religious exclusions are unknown—a country to which Parliament looked in passing the Act of 1791, as all the great men who argued the question then expressly declared. It is important that His Majesty's Canadian subjects should not have occasion to look across the narrow boundary that separates them from the United States, to see anything there to envy.

CHAPTER LIV.

1854—1855.

Resignation on the Class-Meeting Question.—Discussion.

THE last important connexional discussion in which Dr. Ryerson was engaged was on the Class-Meeting Question. For years he had objected, chiefly privately, amongst his brethren, clerical and lay, to making attendance at class-meeting a condition of membership in the Wesleyan Methodist Church of Canada. For various reasons, few members of the Conference desired to have the subject publicly discussed in Conference. They felt that a serious practical difficulty surrounded the question itself—difficulties which could not be surmounted by public discussion. Many of them also knew that in calmly discussing, without personal feeling, the abstract principle involved in the rule, it would be found that their judgment and loyal feeling to the Church would go one way, while their uniform practice in the administration of the rule would often be at variance with both, owing to peculiar circumstances. On the other hand, Dr. Ryerson thought, that not only should preaching and practice in this matter agree, but that theory and practice should also agree. And hence he felt that as his preaching and practice agreed in opposition to the rule, he was not loyal to the Church in ministering at her altars, while he was heartily and conscientiously opposed to the fundamental rule of membership prescribed by that Church. Hence, on the 2nd of January, 1854, he addressed the following letter to the Rev. Dr. Wood, President of the Wesleyan Methodist Conference (I omit extraneous matter):—

I hereby resign into your hands, my membership in the Conference, and my office as a minister of the Wesleyan Methodist Church—herewith enclosing my parchments of ordination, thus taking my place among the laity of the Church.

I have resolved to take this step after long and serious deliberation, but without consulting any human being. I take this step, not because I do not believe that the Wesleyan ministry is as fully authorized as the ministry of any other branch of the universal Church, to exercise all the functions of

Christian priesthood; not because I do not as unfeignedly as ever subscribe to all the doctrines of the Wesleyan Church; not because I do not profoundly honour the integrity and devotedness of the Wesleyan ministry; not because I do not think that Christian discipline is as strictly, if not more strictly, maintained in the Wesleyan Church than in any other Christian Church in the world.

But I resign (not my connection with, but) my ministerial office in the Wesleyan Church, because I believe a condition of membership is exacted in it which has no warrant in Scripture, nor in the practice of the primitive Church, nor in the writings of Mr. Wesley; and in consequence of which condition, great numbers of exemplary heads of families and young people are excluded from all recognition and rights of membership in the Church. I refer to attendance upon class-meeting—without attendance at which no person is acknowledged as a member of the Wesleyan Methodist Church, however sincerely and cordially he may believe her doctrines, prefer her ministry, and support her institutions, and however exemplary he may be in his life.

I believe the class-meetings, as well as love-feasts, have been and are a means of immense good in the Wesleyan Church, and that both should be employed and recommended as prudential and useful, means of religious edification to all who may be willing to avail themselves of them. But attendance at love-feast is known to be voluntary and not to be a condition of membership in the Church; so I think that attendance at class-meeting should also be voluntary, and ought not to be exalted into an indispensable condition of membership in the Church; I am persuaded that every person who believes the doctrines, and observes the precepts and ordinances enjoined by our Lord and His Apostles, is eligible to membership in the Church of Christ, and cannot, on Scriptural or Wesleyan grounds, be excluded from its rights and privileges upon the mere ground of his or her being unable to reconcile it to their views to take a part in the conversations of class-meetings.

The views thus stated, I have entertained many years. After having revolved the subject in my mind for some time, I expressed my views on it in 1840 and 1841. . . But since my more direct connection with the youth of the country at large, and having met with numbers of exemplary persons who prefer the Methodist Church to any other, but are excluded from it by the required condition of attending class-meeting, besides thousands of young people of Wesleyan parents and congregations, I have become more deeply than ever impressed with the importance of the question, to which I referred in remarks made at the last and preceding Conferences. I had intended until within a short time to defer any decision on the step I now take until the next annual Conference, and until after bringing the question in the form of distinct propositions before the Conference; but, after the best consideration in my power, I have thought it advisable to resign my office in the Church at the present time—fearing the revival and results of unpleasantnesses from my bringing the question formally before the Conference, . . and from a deep conviction that I should no longer delay taking the most effectual means in my power to draw the attention of the ministry and members of the Wesleyan Church to this anomaly in her Disciplinary regulations, and secure, if possible, to tens of thousands of persons the rights and privileges of membership in that branch of the Church of Christ which they prefer—rights and privileges to which I am persuaded they are justly entitled upon both Scriptural and Wesleyan grounds.

I do not think it is honest or right for a man to hold the office of a minister in a Church, all whose essential regulations, as well as doctrines, he cannot justify and recommend. I say essential regulations; for there may be many regulations and practices in a Church of which a minister may not approve, and the existence of which he may deplore, but which would not prevent him from maintaining, as usual, his relations and course of labour. An enlightened Christian mind can and will, without any compromise of principle, allow a wide latitude in modes of proceeding, and in matters of opinion, taste, and prudence. But a regulation which determines who shall and who shall not be recognized as members of the Church of Christ, involves a vital question, the importance of which cannot be overrated, and which must be determined by Divine Revelation, and not by mere conventional rules.

Now, while as an individual I may value and wish to attend, as far as possible, all prudential as well as instituted means of grace in our Church, I cannot as a teacher, by word or office, declare that all persons who will not attend class-meetings, in addition to observing all the ordinances of Christ, should be rejected and excluded from the Christian Church. I cannot say so—I cannot think so—I cannot believe it Scriptural or right, in respect to great numbers of estimable persons, and of the sons and daughters of our people, who believe Wesleyan doctrines, who respect and love the Wesleyan ministry, support Wesleyan institutions, are exemplary in their lives, and who wish to be members of the Wesleyan Church, but who, from education, or mental constitution, or other circumstances, cannot face much less enjoy, the developments and peculiarities of the class-meeting. I have met and sympathized with many who have sought to reconcile their views and feelings to the personal speakings and communications of class-meetings, but who could not succeed; and not being allowed otherwise to enjoy the privileges of membership in the Wesleyan Church, were driven to seek admission into some other Christian communion.

Our Lord and His Apostles have prescribed no form of religious communion but the Lord's Supper. The New Testament meetings of Christian fellowship, in which the early Christians edified one another, are appropriately adduced as the exemplars of Wesleyan love-feasts—that voluntary and useful means of religious edification. But it is remarkable that a person may neither attend love-feast nor the Lord's Supper, and yet retain his membership in the Wesleyan Church, while he is excluded from it if he does not attend class-meeting, though he may attend both the Lord's Supper and love-feast, as well as the preaching of the word and meetings for prayer. Nay, I find in the latter part of the section of our Discipline on "Class Meetings," that the minister in charge of a circuit is required to exclude all "those members of the Church who wilfully and repeatedly neglect to meet their class," but to state at the time of their exclusion, "that they are laid aside for a breach of our rules of Discipline, and not for immoral conduct." I know of no Scriptural authority to exclude any person from the Church of Christ on earth, except for that which would exclude him from the kingdom of glory, namely, "immoral conduct." But here is an express requirement for the exclusion of persons from the Wesleyan Church for that which it is admitted is not "immoral conduct," namely, neglect of class-meeting. This is certainly going beyond Scriptural authority and example.

I have said that I do not regard as Wesleyan, or having the sanction of Mr. Wesley, the making attendance at class-meeting an essential condition of membership in the Church of Christ. Mr. Wesley declared that the sole object of his labours was, not to form a new sect, but to revive religion in the Church and in the nation; that each class was a voluntary society in the Church, but was no more a separate Church organization than a Bible Society, or Temperance Society, or Young Men's Christian Association, is a separate Church organization. Nor did Mr. Wesley regard the admission of persons into, or exclusion from, any one of his societies as affecting, in the slightest degree, such person's Church membership. Nay, Mr. Wesley insisted that all who joined his societies, in addition to attending class-meeting, and the ministrations of his preachers, should regularly attend the services and sacraments of the Church of England. In his sermon "On Attending Church Service," Mr.

Wesley says, "it was one of our original rules, that every member of our society should attend the church and sacrament, unless he he had been bred among Christians of another denomination." In his Tract, entitled "Principles of a Methodist Further Explained," (written in reply to the Rev. Mr. Church,) Mr. Wesley says:—

> The United Society was originally so called, because it consisted of several smaller societies united together. When any member of these, or of the United Society, are proved to live in known sin, we then mark and avoid them; we separate ourselves from every one that walks disorderly. Sometimes if the case be judged infectious (though rarely) this is decided openly; but this you style "excommunication," and say, "does not every one see a separate ecclesiastical communion?"

Mr. Wesley replies:—

> No. This society does not separate from the rest of the Church of England. They continue steadfast with them both in the apostolical doctrine, and in breaking of bread, and in prayers.

And in further reply to the charge, that in excluding disorderly persons from his society, he was usurping a power committed to the higher order of the clergy, Mr. Wesley says:—

> No; not in the power of excluding members from a private society, unless on the supposition of some such rule as ours is, viz.: "That if a man separate from the church, he is no longer a member of our society."

These passages (from scores of similar ones in Mr. Wesley's works), are sufficient to shew what Mr. Wesley understood and intended by admission into, or exclusion from, any one of his societies—that it did not in the least affect the relations of any person to the Church of which he was a member. Now, the rule which Mr. Wesley imposed as a condition of membership in a private society in a Church, we impose as a condition of membership in the Church itself.

It is also worthy of remark, that attendance at class-meeting is not required of members in the general rules of the society—those very rules which our ministers are required to give to persons proposing to join the Wesleyan Church.

In those rules no mention is made of class-meeting, nor is it there required that each member shall meet the leader, much less meet him in a class-meeting, in the presence of many others; but that the leader shall see each person in his class, and meet the minister and stewards once a week. Yet, by constant and universal practice, we have transferred the obligation from the leader to the member, and made it the duty of the latter (on pain of excommunication), to meet the former in class-meeting; an obligation which is nowhere enjoined in the general rules. In those rules it is said:

There is only one condition previously required of those who desire admission into these societies—a desire to flee from the wrath to come, and to be saved from their sins.

The rules then truly state, that wherever this desire is really fixed in the soul, it will be known by its fruits. These fruits are briefly but fully set forth under three heads. (1) By doing no harm. (2) By doing good. (3) "By attending all the ordinances of God: such as, the public worship of God; the ministry of the word, either read or expounded; the Supper of the Lord; family and private prayer; searching the Scriptures, and fasting or abstinence. These are the general rules of our societies, all of which we are taught of God to observe, even in His written word, which is the only rule, and the sufficient rule, both of faith and practice." Now, neither class-meeting nor love-feast is mentioned among the "ordinances of God" enumerated in the general rules of the society; nor is it mentioned in Mr. Wesley's Large Minutes of Conference among the instituted means of grace. So far as the general rules themselves are concerned, there is nothing which makes attendance at class-meeting a condition of membership, even in Mr. Wesley's societies as he originally instituted them; nor did the idea of holding class-meetings at all occur to Mr. Wesley until after the general rules were drawn up and published.* But what was not re-

* Mr. Wesley's own account of the origin of the office of class-leader and class-meetings, illustrates the accuracy of what I have stated. The office was first created at Bristol, 15th February, 1742, for financial purposes alone. A few weeks afterwards, it was instituted for religious purposes also; and for the twofold object of religion and finance, it was embodied in the General Rules, which were drawn up and signed by Mr. Wesley, 1st May, 1743; but in which there is no mention made of class-meeting, or of the duty of any member to meet in class. In his "Plain Account of the People called Methodists," Mr. Wesley thus states the origin of the office of class-leader and the institution of class-meetings.

At length (says he,) while we were thinking of quite another thing, we struck upon a method for which we have had cause to bless God ever since. I was talking with several of the Society in Bristol (Feb. 15, 1742,) concerning the means of paying the debts there, when one stood up, and said, 'Let every member of the Society give a penny a week till all are paid.' Another said, 'But many of them are poor, and cannot afford to do it.' 'Then,' said the other, 'put eleven of the poorest with me, and if they can give anything, well: I will see them weekly; and if they can give nothing, I will give for them as well as for myself. And each of you will call upon eleven of your neighbours weekly, receive what they give, and make up what is wanting.' It was done. In a little while some of these informed me, they found such and such an one did not live as he ought. It struck me immediately, This is the very thing we have wanted so long. I called together the Leaders of the classes (so we used to term them and their companies,) and desired that each would make particular inquiry into the behaviour of those whom he saw weekly. They did so. Many disorderly walkers were detected. Some turned from the evil of their ways. Some were put away from us. Many saw it with fear, and rejoiced in God with reverence. As soon as possible, the same method was used in London, and in all other places. The following is Mr. Wesley's account of the first appointment of class-leaders in London, extracted from his Journal, Thursday, March 25, 1742: I appointed several earnest and sensible men to meet me, to whom I showed the great difficulty I had long found of knowing the people who

quired by the general rules soon became a condition of membership in another way—this was by the system of giving tickets. Mr. Wesley says in his Plain Account of People called Methodists:

> As the society increased, I found it required still greater care to separate the precious from the vile. In order to this, I determined, at least once in three months, to talk with every member myself, and to inquire at their own mouth, as well as of their leaders and neighbours, whether they grew in grace and in the knowledge of our Lord Jesus Christ. To each of those whose seriousness and good conversation I had no reason to doubt, I gave a testimony under my own hand, by writing their name on a ticket prepared for that purpose. Those who bore these tickets, wherever they came, were acknowledged by their brethren, and were received with all cheerfulness. These tickets also supplied us with a quiet and inoffensive method of removing any disorderly member. He has no ticket at the quarterly visitation (for so often the tickets are changed); and hereby it is immediately known that he is no longer of the community.

It was at length required by a minute of the Conference, (as our own discipline enjoins,) that a preacher should not give a

> desired to be under my care. After much discourse, they all agreed there could be no better way to come to a sure, thorough knowledge of each person, than to divide them into classes, like those at Bristol, under the inspection of those in whom I could confide. This was the origin of our classes at London, for which I can never sufficiently praise God; the unspeakable usefulness of the institution having ever since been more and more manifest. In his "Plain Account of the People called Methodists," Mr. Wesley says, "At first they (the Leaders) visited each person at his own house; but this was soon found not so expedient, and that on many accounts." Mr. Wesley assigns several reasons for this change, and proceeds to answer several objections to class-meetings. The following passage shows the exact ground on which Mr. Wesley based the institution of class-meetings:
>
> Some objected, 'There were no such meetings when I came into the society first; and why should there be now? I do not understand these things, and this changing one thing after another continually.' It was easily answered: It is a pity but they had been from the first. But we knew not then either the need or the benefit of them. Why we use them, you will easily understand, if you will read over the Rules of the Society. That with regard to these little prudential helps, we are continually changing one thing after another, is not a weakness or fault as you imagine, but is a peculiar privilege which we enjoy. By this means we declare them all to be merely prudential, not essential, not of divine institution.
>
> Now, while it is proper for each person, as far as may be consistent with his circumstances and views of duty, to use every prudential means of doing and getting good, yet the observance of nothing but what is Divinely instituted should be imposed as a condition of membership in the Church of God. To make attendance at class-meeting that condition, is to require what the Lord hath not commanded, and to change essentially the character and objects of a means of good which Mr. Wesley (with whom it originated) declared to be "merely prudential, not essential, not of divine institution."
>
> That Mr. Wesley conceived the basis of a church should be much more comprehensive than the rules he drew up and recommended in regard to the "little prudential helps" which were suggested to him from time to time, is obvious from the eighth of his twelve reasons against organising a new church—reasons published many years after the preparation and adoption of all his society rules. His words are as follows: "Because to form the plan of a new church would require infinite time and care, with much more wisdom and greater depth and extensiveness of thought than any of us are masters of."

ticket of membership to any person who did not meet in class. In our own Discipline, in the section on class-meetings, will also be found the following question and answer:—

Question.—What shall be done with those members of our church who wilfully and repeatedly neglect their class?

Answer.—1. Let the chairman, or one of the preachers, visit them whenever it is practicable, and explain to them the consequence if they continue to neglect, viz., exclusion.

2. If they do not attend, let him who has charge of the circuit exclude them (in the church), showing that they are laid aside for a breach of our rules of discipline, and not for immoral conduct.

By this added ministerial authority and duty, a condition of membership in the society is imposed which is not contained in the General Rules, and which subjects a member to exclusion, for that which is acknowledged to be "not immoral conduct."

This appears a strange regulation in even a private religious society within a Church; but no objection could be reasonably made to any such regulation in such a society, if its members desired it, and as it would not affect their Church membership. But the case is essentially different, when such society in a Church becomes a Church, and exercises the authority of admitting into, and excluding from the Church itself, and not merely a society in the Church.

In England, and especially in the United States and Canada, the Wesleyan Societies have become a Church. I have repeatedly shewn in past years, that they have become organized into a Church upon both Wesleyan and scriptural grounds. I believe the Wesleyan Church in Canada is second to no other in the scriptural authority of its ministry and organization. Believing this, I believe that exclusion from the Wesleyan Church (either by expulsion or refusal of admission) is exclusion from a branch of the Church of God—is an act the most solemn and eventful in the history and relations of any human being—an act which should never take place except upon the clear and express authority of the word of God.

Far be it from me to say one word other than in favour of every kind of religious exercise and communion which tends to promote the spiritual-mindedness, brotherly love, and fervent zeal of professing Christians. That class-meetings (notwithstanding occasional improprieties and abuses attending them), have been a valuable means in promoting the spirituality and usefulness of the Wesleyan Church, no one acquainted with her history can for a moment doubt; and I believe that myriads on earth and in heaven have, and will ever have, reason for devout thankfulness and praise for the benefits derived from class-meetings, as well as from love-feasts and meetings for prayer. But attendance upon the two latter is voluntary on the part of the members of the Wesleyan Church; and what authority is there for suspending their very membership in the Church of God on their attendance upon the former? The celebration of the Lord's Supper, and not class-meeting, was the binding characteristic institution upon the members of the primitive Church. So I am persuaded it should be now; and that Christian faith and practice alone (and not the addition of attendance upon class-meeting,) should be the test of worthiness for its communion and privileges. While, therefore, as an individual I seek to secure and enjoy all the benefits of the faithful ministrations and scriptural ordinances of the Wesleyan Church, I cannot occupy a position which in itself, and by its duties requires me to enforce or justify the imposition of a condition of membership in the Church of Christ, which I believe is not required by the Holy Scriptures, and the exclusion of thousands of persons from Church membership and privileges, to which I believe they have as valid a right as I have, and that upon the sole ground of their non-attendance at a meeting, the neglect of which our own Discipline admits, does not involve "immoral conduct," and which Mr. Wesley himself, in his Plain Account of the People called Methodists, has declared "to be merely prudential, not essential, not of divine institution."

It is passing strange, that while the Wesleyan Church is the avowed "friend of all and enemy of none"—is the most Catholic of any Protestant body towards other religious communions—she should close the door of admission into her own fold even to attendance upon class-meeting. I regard it as the misfortune rather than the dishonour of the Wesleyan Church, that she repels thousands that seek her communion rather than relax this term of admission. If her success has been so great under disadvantages unparalleled, I cannot but believe, that, with the same divine blessing, and upon a basis of membership less narrow and more scriptural, the Wesleyan Church, would, beyond all precedent, increase her usefulness, and enlarge her borders.

I will not permit myself to dwell upon associations and recollections which cannot be expressed in words, any more than they can be obliterated from the memory, or effaced from the heart. Though I retire from councils in the deliberations of which I have been permitted to take a part during more than twenty-five years, and relinquish all claims upon funds to which I have contributed for a like period, I should still deem it my duty and privilege to pray for the success of the former, and continue my humble contributions to the latter; while I protest in the most emphatic way in my power against shutting the doors of the church upon thousands to whom I believe they should be opened, and against making that essential and divine, which, as Mr. Wesley says, "is merely prudential, not essential, not of divine institution." I hope the day is not remote when the Wesleyan Church will be as scriptural in her every term of membership as she is in her doctrines of grace and labours of love.

To this letter of resignation, Rev. Dr. Wood, President of the Conference, replied on the 4th of January:—

To accept the enclosed documents would be assuming a responsibility at variance with my judgment and affections. If the proposal you make of withdrawing from the Methodist ministry be ever received, it must be with the concurrence of the collective Conference ; or, should the question require immediate attention, that of its executive committee. I shall be glad to see the enactment of any regulation which will promote the usefulness of our Church to the benefit of a large and intelligent class of adherents now receiving no recognition beyond their contributions to our institutions ; and also the adoption of practical measures by which the youth baptized by Wesleyan ministers may be more personally cared for, and affiliated to our ordinances. Your distinguished ability and matured experience eminently qualify you as a safe legislator and counsellor on such grave questions, which by some cannot be separated from ancient usages greatly blessed to the growing spirituality of true believers, without injury to the vital character of the Church. After so long and useful a career, your separation from our Conference and work would be a connexional calamity. You stand among the few in Canada to whom the present independent and legal position of the Wesleyan Church stands deeply indebted, Future generations of ministers and people will partake, imperceptibly to themselves, of the advantages a few of the more gifted and noble-minded brethren struggled and contended for against so many obstacles. You are as capable of remedying anything wrong, or supplying anything wanting within the Church, as you were many years ago, to overcome impediments to her usefulness without.

Nothing further was done in the matter until at the Belleville Conference of 1854 Dr. Ryerson moved the following resolution :—

1. That no human authority has a right to impose any condition of membership in the visible Church of Christ, which is not enjoined by, or may be concluded from the Holy Scriptures.

2. That the General Rules of the United Societies of the Wesleyan Methodist Church being formed upon the Holy Scriptures, and requiring nothing of any member which is not necessary for admission into the kingdom of grace and glory, ought to be maintained inviolate as the religious and moral standard of profession, conduct and character, in regard to all who are admitted or continued members of our church.

3. That the power, therefore, of expelling persons from the visible Church of Christ, for other than a cause sufficient to exclude a person from the kingdom of grace and glory, which the fourth question, and answers to it, contained in the second section of the second chapter of our Discipline, confer and enjoin upon our ministers, is unauthorized by the Holy Scriptures, is inconsistent with the Scriptural rights of the members of Christ's Church, and ought not to be assumed or exercised by any minister of our Church.

4. That the anomalous question and answers referred to in the foregoing resolution, be, and are hereby expunged from our Discipline and are required to be omitted in printing the next edition of it. (See page 477.)

These resolutions having been negatived by a considerable majority on the 12th June, Dr. Ryerson wrote to the President:

The decision of the Conference this afternoon on the scriptural rights of the members of our Church, and the power of our ministers in respect to them, makes it at length my painful duty to request you to lay before the Conference the letter which I addressed to you the 2nd of last January, and that you will consider that letter as now addressed to the Conference through you.

I hereby again enclose you my parchments of ordination. I propose to do all in my power to promote those important measures in regard to the college and means for the regular training of received candidates for the ministry which have been recommended by the Conference. I cannot attempt to add anything more to what is contained in my letter of the 2nd January, expressive of what I feel on the present occasion, except to say that, although I gave no intimation during the discussion of the result of the decision on this subject upon my own official relations to the Conference, I retire from it with feelings of undiminished respect and affection for my Reverend Brethren, and my earnest prayer for their welfare and usefulness.

In reply to this letter Dr. Wood said:—

The purpose you aim to accomplish can be effectually secured by a different resolution to that introduced yesterday; if you will stay and hear what the brethren may say about the appointment of a large committee to take up this subject before I lay your resignation before them, I shall feel much gratified. I again say, I look upon your proposed withdrawal with deep sorrow, and must say, I cannot bring myself to believe that on such grounds you can be justified in taking so serious a step.

Dr. Ryerson did attend the Conference as suggested, after which he wrote to Dr. Wood:—

I listened with delight and hope to the observations and recommendations which you made. I anticipated happy results from the appointment of the very large committee which you nominated, and which might be considered as representing the sentiments and feelings of the Conference. But from the lengthened meeting of that committee, in the evening, it was clear that no disposition existed to modify the power of ministers to expel persons from the Church for non-attendance at a meeting which, in the 12th section, chap. 1st, page 47, of our own Discipline, taken from the writings of Mr. Wesley, is declared to be "prudential," even among Methodists—that thus the highest and most awful penalty that the Church can inflict—a penalty analagous to capital punishment in the administration of civil law—is to be executed upon members of the Church for the omission of what our own Discipline does not exalt to the rank of a "prudential" means of grace among Christians, —only among Methodists.

It was also clear that views of baptism prevailed (I cannot say how widely) at variance with the 17th Article of Faith in our Discipline,* and altogether opposite to those set forth by Mr. Wesley in his sermons and in his Treatise on Baptism.

But that for which I was not prepared (which I supposed to have been settled, and which I therefore assumed), was the obviously prevalent opinion against the Church membership of children baptized by our ministry. It will be recollected that I had not proposed any other condition or mode of admitting persons into our Church from without, than that which already exists amongst us; but I urged in behalf of both parents and children, the practical recognition of the rights and claims of children who were admitted and acknowledged as members of the Church by baptism, as implied in our Form of Baptism, and according to our Catechism, and according to what the Conference unanimously declared at Hamilton, in 1853, our Church holds to be among the privileges of baptized persons,—namely, that "they are made members of the visible Church of Christ." Persons cannot, of course, be members of the "visible" Church of Christ without becoming members of some visible branch or section of it; and it is not pretended that children baptized by our ministry are members of any other visible portion of the Church of Christ than the Wesleyan. To deny, therefore, that the baptized children of our people are members of our Church, and that they should be acknowledged as such, and as such be impressed with their obligations and privileges, and as such be prepared for, and brought into, the spiritual communion and fellowship of the Church, on coming to the years of accountability, is, it appears to me, to make the Sacrament of Baptism a nullity, and to disfranchise thousands of children of divinely chartered rights and privileges. Mr. Wesley, in his Treatise on Baptism, in stating the third benefit of baptism, remarks:—

By baptism we are admitted into the Church, and consequently made members of Christ, its Head. The Jews were admitted into the Church by circumcision, so are the Christians by baptism.

Mr. Wesley, speaking of the proper subjects of baptism, says:

If infants are capable of making a covenant, and were and still are under the evangelical covenant, then they have a right to baptism, which is the

---

* The following is the Article of Faith referred to :—

XVII. *Of Baptism.* Baptism is not only a sign of profession, and mark of difference, whereby Christians are distinguished from others that are not baptized, but it is also a sign of regeneration or the new birth. The baptism of young children is to be retained in the church.

entering seal thereof. But infants are capable of making a covenant, and were and still are under the evangelical covenant.

The custom of nations and common reason of mankind prove that infants may enter into a covenant, and may be obliged by compacts made by others in their name, and receive advantage by them. But we have stronger proof than this, even God's own word: "Ye stand this day all of you before the Lord,—your captains, with all the men of Israel; your little ones, your wives, and the stranger,—that thou shouldst enter into covenant with the Lord thy God."—Deut. xxix. 10-12. Now, God would never have made a covenant with little children, if they had not been capable of it. It is not said children only, but little children, the Hebrew word properly signifying infants. And these may be still, as they were of old, obliged to perform, in aftertime, what they are not capable of performing at the time of their entering into that obligation.

The infants of believers, the true children of faithful Abraham, always were under the Gospel covenant. They were included in it, they had a right to it, and to the seal of it; as an infant heir has a right to his estate, though he cannot yet have actual possession.—Vol. x., English Edition, pp. 193, 194. Vol. vi., American Edition, pp. 16, 17.

Again, Mr. Wesley's third argument on this subject is so clear, so touching, and so conclusive, that I will quote it without abridgement, as follows:—

If infants ought to come to Christ, if they are capable of admission into the Church of God, and consequently of solemn sacramental dedication to Him, then they are proper subjects of baptism. But infants are capable of coming to Christ, of admission into the Church, and solemn dedication to God.

That infants ought to come to Christ, appears from his own words: "They brought little children to Christ, and the disciples rebuked them. And Jesus said, Suffer little children to come unto me, and forbid them not; for of such is the kingdom of heaven."—Matt. xix. 13, 14. St. Luke expresses it still more strongly: "They brought unto him even infants, that he might touch them."—xviii. 15. These children were so little, that they were brought to him; yet he says, "Suffer them to come unto me:" so little, that he "took them up in His arms;" yet he rebukes those who would have hindered their coming to Him. And his command respected the future as well as the present. Therefore His disciples or ministers are still to suffer infants to come, that is, to be brought, unto Christ. But they cannot now come to Him, unless by being brought into the Church; which cannot be but by baptism. Yea, and "of such," says our Lord, "is the kingdom of heaven;" not of such only as were like these infants. For if they themselves were not fit to be subjects of that kingdom, how could others be so, because they were like them? Infants, therefore, are capable of being admitted into the Church, and have a right thereto. Even under the Old Testament they were admitted into it by circumcision. And can we suppose they are in a worse condition under the Gospel, than they were under the law? and that our Lord would take away any privilege which they then enjoyed? Would He not rather make additions to them? This, then, is a third ground. Infants ought to come to Christ, and no man ought to forbid them. They are capable of admission into the Church of God. Therefore they are proper subjects of baptism.—Vol. x., English Edition, pp. 195, 196. Vol. vi., American Edition, pp. 17, 18.

Upon these Wesleyan and Scriptural grounds, I believe that the promise and privileges of membership in the Church belong to the baptized children of our people as well as to their parents;

that the parents have a right to claim this relationship and its privileges for their children until such children are excluded from the Church by the lawful acts of its executive authorities. Otherwise, the youth baptized by our ministry are in the most pitiful and degrading religious position of the youth of any Church that recognizes the doctrine of infant baptism; and it appears to me that we ought rather not to baptize infants at all, or recommend their parents to take them to other churches for baptism, than thus to treat the feelings of such parents, and to regard their children as having no more membership and privileges in our Church than the rest of the youth of the land, or even the world at large.

It is happily true, that many of the children of our people, as well as those of other people, are converted and brought into the Church under the faithful ministrations of the Word; but how many ten thousand more of them would never wander from the Church, would more easily and more certainly be led to experience all the power of inward religion and the blessings of Christian fellowship, were they acknowledged in their true position and rights, and taught the significancy, and obligation, and privilege of all that the outward ordinances and their visible relations involve were intended to confer. It ought to make a Christian heart bleed to think that our largest increase of members, according to returns over which we are disposed to congratulate ourselves, falls vastly short of the natural increase of population in our own community, apart from the increase of the population of the country at large, and, therefore, that perhaps five or more persons are sent out into the world, as worldlings, from the families of our Church, while one is retained or brought into it from the world by all our ministrations and agencies. The prophets did not deny to a Jew his membership in the Jewish Church, in order to make him a Jew inwardly. Mr. Wesley did not un-church the tens of thousands of baptized members of the Church of England to whom he successfully preached salvation by faith: he made their state, and duties, and privileges, as baptized members of the Church of Christ, the grounds of his appeals; and this vantage ground was one great means of his wonderful success.

But I will not enlarge. I will only add, that as in former years, I, with others, maintained what we believed to be the rights of Canada and of our Canadian Church against pretensions which have long since been withdrawn, and the erroneous information and impressions connected with which have long since been removed; so, I now feel it my duty to do what I can to secure and maintain the Scriptural and Wesleyan rights of members of our Church against the exercise of ministerial authority which has no warrant in Scripture nor in the writings of Mr. Wesley; and I feel myself specially called upon by my position in respect to the youth of the country, as well as by my strong convictions, to claim and insist upon the Scriptural and Wesleyan rights of church membership in behalf of the many thousands of children baptized by our ministry—believing upon both Scriptural and Wesleyan grounds, it is due to such children and to their parents.

I have no object in view, beyond what is avowed in this correspondence. If I have had any personal ambition, it has been more than satisfied both in the Church and in the country at large. I have nothing more to seek or desire, than to employ the short and uncertain time that remains to me in striving to become more and more meet for the intercourse of the saints in light, to mature and promote for my native country the great educational system in which I am engaged, and to secure to all members of our Church, and to all parents and children baptized into it, what I am persuaded are their sacred rights and privileges. I am satisfied that Scriptural and Wesleyan truth will, as heretofore, prevail, and that the Conference and the Church will yet rejoice in it, however it may, for the moment, be clouded by error and misrepresentation, or impeded by personal feelings, groundless fears, or mistaken prejudice.

On the 13th June Dr. Ryerson made a request to the Conference that the documents connected with his resignation be published in the *Guardian*. He said:—

I wish the church to know the reasons which have influenced me on this occasion—especially as I believe them to be both Wesleyan and Scriptural. As I have for thirty years contributed to all the funds of the preachers and Church, without receiving or expecting to receive a farthing from them, and from the period and kinds of labours I have performed in the Church, and from my wish to live in connexion with it, I think my letters of resignation might at least not be withheld from the members of our Church. If any expense attend the publication of the correspondence between us, I will defray every farthing of it.

I do not think any other member of the Conference is called upon to do as I have done—my circumstances being peculiar. But I do not wish to be wronged and blackened by misrepresentations; I only desire that my brethren and old friends through the land may be permitted and enabled to read my own reasons and views on this the last occasion of my official intercourse with them.*

* I have understood, nevertheless, that a resolution was adopted expressing the sense of the Conference as to my past labours in the Church; but the publication of it has been suppressed in the official organ, as also in the printed minutes, of the Conference.

The correspondence in the subsequent pages shows with what feelings and sentiments I retired from the councils of the Conference; and I could not have supposed that any members of that body were capable of excluding from the public records of its proceedings what the Conference had deemed a bare act of justice to an

This request was denied, so that Dr. Ryerson published the documents in a pamphlet himself. In doing so he said:—

A more vitally important and deeply affecting subject can scarcely be laid before the Wesleyan community; but in order to present it to the pious judgment of that body at large, I have had no other alternative than to assume the position I now sustain—otherwise being compelled to observe, as in past years, a strict silence beyond the walls of the Conference room. But from what I have witnessed and heard in that room, I appeal to the calm consideration of the intelligent and devout members of the Wesleyan Church, either in their closets with their Bible before them, or at their firesides with their children around them. Whether I have or have not overrated the importance of the question, I leave everyone to decide after reading the following correspondence. It will be seen that the question is not one of a personal nature—is not one which ought to excite any unkind feeling between persons who may take different views of it. The question is as to whether, on the Wesleyan Conference assuming the position and functions of a distinct and independent Church, a condition of membership has not been imposed which is a departure from the principles of Mr. Wesley and the doctrine and practice of the Apostolic and Primitive Church—a condition which ignores the church relation, rights and privileges of the baptized children of the Wesleyan body, and excludes thousands from its membership upon unscriptural and un-Wesleyan grounds. It will be seen by an extract on page 20, that Mr. Wesley's disciplinary object in giving quarterly tickets was, "to separate the precious from the vile," "to remove any disorderly member;" but in vain have I sought for an instance of Mr. Wesley ever excluding, even from his private societies in a Church, an upright and orderly member for mere non-attendance at class-meeting. That, however, he might have consistently done in a society in a Church, if he had thought it expedient to do so, as it would not have affected the membership of any parties in the Church

individual who had laboured nearly thirty years in connection with it, and often performed most difficult services and labours in its behalf. Such a proceeding will reflect more dishonour upon its authors than upon me, in the judgment of every honourable and Christian mind in Upper Canada, of whatever persuasion or party. I am happy to believe that this poor imitation of the system of the "Index Expurgatorius" cannot blot from the memories of an older generation in the Church recollections of labours and struggles of which the expurgators know nothing but the fruits—among which are the civil and religious privileges they enjoy.

I have also been credibly informed that, while the real grounds of my resignation and the judgment of the Conference upon my conduct and labours during many years' connection with it, are withheld from the Wesleyan public, insinuations are circulated, that my resignation has been dictated by ulterior political objects—an idea which I have never for one moment entertained, and which is foreign, as far as I know, to the thoughts of every public man in Canada.

to which they belonged. The three paragraphs of our Discipline, containing three sentences against which I protest, had no place in the Minutes of Conference finally revised and printed by Mr. Wesley in the year of his death; nor do they exist in the Minutes of the British Conference to this day. From what is therefore modern and unauthorized by Scripture, by the practice of the Primitive Church, or by Mr. Wesley, I go back to first principles, and say, as did Mr. Wesley to Dr. Coke and Mr. Asbury, when he sent them to organize the Societies in America into a Church, let us "simply follow the Scriptures and the Primitive Church."

It is often said that "nobody objects to attending class-meeting except those who have no religion." Persons who thus judge of others show more of the Pharisaical, than of the Christian, spirit, and evince but little of the "wisdom that cometh from above" in thus "measuring others by themselves." The following correspondence shows that I am second to none in my appreciation of the value and usefulness of class meetings; but I have had too much experience not to know that the best talkers in a class-meeting are not always the best livers in the world; and I attach less importance to what a person may say of himself in a class-meeting, than to uprightness in his dealings, integrity in his word, meekness in his temper, charity in his spirit, liberality in his contributions, blamelessness in his life. Doings, rather than sayings, are the rule of Divine judgment. . .

It may not be improper for me to observe, that there are ministers who loudly advocate attendance at class-meeting as a Church-law, and yet do not observe that law themselves perhaps once a year, much less habitually, as they insist in respect to private members; and the most strenuous of such advocates pay no heed to the equally positive prohibitions and requirements of the discipline in several other respects, especially in regard to band-meetings, which were designed, as the Discipline expressly states, "to obey that command of God, 'confess your faults one to another, and pray for one another, that ye may be healed.'" I am far from intimating, or believing, that there are many advocates of class-meeting tests of this description. But history shows, from our Lord to the present time, that the most vehement advocates for the "mint, annise and cummin" of particular tests and forms, are not proportionably zealous for the "weightier matters of the law." It is easier for men to impose and enforce law upon others than to observe it themselves. But when a man's words and actions contradict each other, the argument of his actions is the more forcible, as well as the more honest and sincere.

It has likewise been alleged, that if attendance at class-meeting be not made a church-law, and the capital punishment of expulsion be not attached to its violation, class-meetings will fall into disuse. I answer, this is beside the question. The question is, whether there is such a law in the Bible? Has our Lord or His Apostles given authority to any conclave or conference to make such a law? Our Lord and the Apostles knew better than their followers what was essential to membership in the Christian Church, as well as what was essential to its existence and prosperity. I may also observe, that if the existence of class-meetings cannot be maintained except by the terror of the scorpion-whip, or rather executioner's sword, of expulsion from the church, it says little for them as a privilege, or place of delightful and joyous resort. My own conviction is, that if class-meetings, like love-feasts, were maintained and recommended as a privilege and useful means of religious edification, and not as a law, the observance of which is necessary to membership in the visible Church of Christ, but made voluntary, like joining the Missionary Society, class-meetings would be more efficient and useful than they are now, and attendance at them would be more cordial and profitable, if not as, or even more, general. But what might be or not be in any supposed case, is foreign to a question as to what is enjoined in the law and testimony of the Holy Scriptures as essential to discipleship with Christ.

It is well known that meeting in class, by a large portion of the members of the Wesleyan Church, is very irregular—that their absence from class-meeting is the general rule of their practice, and their attendance the exception. Yet such persons are not excluded, as it would involve the expulsion of the greater part of the members of the body, including several of its ministers. It is, therefore, so much the more objectionable, and so much the more wrong, to have a rule which ignores at one sweep the membership of all the baptized children of the body, which sends and keeps away the conscientious and straightforward, who would not think of joining a religious community without intending habitually to observe all its rules, and yet, after all, habitually disregarded by a large portion of both preachers and people, and is made, as far as my observation goes, an instrument of gratifying individual hostility, rather than a means of promoting the religious and moral ends of Christian discipline.

It is, however, the bearing of this question upon the relationship and destinies of the youth of the Wesleyan body that has most deeply impressed and affected my own mind, as may be inferred from the correspondence on the subject. It requires less scriptural zeal, and an inferior order of qualifications, and it is much more exciting and easy, to minister or attend at special meetings, and in the ordinary public services of the Church, than to pursue "in season and out of season" the less conspicuous and more detailed labour of teaching and training up children and youth in the knowledge and experience of the doctrines of Christ, and thus secure them to the Church, and to the Saviour, and secure to them the "godliness which has the promise of the life that now is, and of that which is to come."*

And what is the result of the general adoption (with a few fine exceptions), of the former in preference to the latter—instead of the union of both? It is the humiliating and most painful fact that the great majority of Methodist youth are lost to the Church, if not lost to Christ and to heaven—that in a large proportion of instances, Methodism is not perpetuated to

* Of the utter insufficiency of public ministrations alone, even for grown up Christians, much more for children, Mr. Wesley thus speaks in his large and authorized Minutes of Conference :—"For what avails public preaching alone, though we could preach like angels? We must, yea, every travelling preacher must, instruct them from house to house. Till this is done, and that in good earnest, the Methodists will be little better than other people. Our religion is not deep, universal, uniform; but superficial, partial, uneven. It will be so, till we spend half as much time in this visiting, as we now do in talking uselessly." "For, after all our preaching, many of our people are almost as ignorant as if they had never heard the gospel. I speak as plain as I can, yet I frequently meet with those who have been my hearers many years, who know not whether Christ be God or man. And how few are there who know the nature of repentance, faith and holiness. Most of them have a sort of confidence that God will save them, while the world has their hearts. I have found by experience, that one of these has learned more from one hour's close discourse than from ten years' public preaching." "Let every preacher having a catalogue of those in each society, go to each house. Deal gently with them, that the report of it may move others to desire your coming. Give the children the instructions for children, and encourage them to get them by heart. Indeed, you will find it no easy matter to teach the ignorant the principles of religion. So true is the remark of Archbishop Usher— 'Great scholars may think this work beneath them. But they should consider, the laying the foundation skilfully, as it is of the greatest importance, so it is the masterpiece of the wisest builder. And let the wisest of us all try, whenever we please, we shall find that to lay this ground-work rightly, to make the ignorant understand the grounds of religion, will put us to all our skill.'" "Unless we take care of the rising generation, the present revival will be *res unius aetatis* (a thing of one generation); it will last only the age of a man."

There are several ministers who earnestly labour in the spirit of these extracts from Mr. Wesley's Minutes of Conference—printed the year of his death. But their labours are the promptings of individual zeal and intelligence, and not dictated or backed by the authoritative example of the ministry and Church at large, or the recognition of the Church relations of the interesting subjects of their instructions. The effect of the general disuse or neglect of systematic individual instruction of children, not speaking of such instruction of adult members, and reliance upon public ministrations and meetings alone, must be instability of religious profession, want of clear and acute views of the grounds, doctrines, nature, institutions and duties of religion, indifference to all religion, or wandering from denomination to denomination according to circumstances or caprice; but in all cases the loss to the Wesleyan Church of the greater part of the harvest which she should and might gather into the garner of Christ.

the second generation of the same family—that in the great majority of instances it is only so perpetuated very partially, and in very few instances to all the children of Methodist parents; while there is each year the conversion of only a few hundreds, or thousands, mostly from without. The return of prodigals, and the accession of strangers and aliens to the body, are indeed causes of thankfulness and rejoicing; but prevention is better than cure—piety from childhood is better than reformation in manhood. The judgment of the Apostle upon him "who neglects to provide for his own house," even in temporal matters, is well known; and must there not be a radical defect and wrong in any religious organization which loses the great majority of its own youth, and depends largely on infusions from without for the recruit of its numbers? Such an organization may do much good, and widely extend in many places for the time being, especially in a new and unsettled state of society; but the vital element of permanent strength and lasting prosperity is wanting, where, by its repulsion or neglect, the great majority of its baptized youth are alienated from, and lost to its communion. It is not in the promise of God, or in the genius of Scriptural Christianity, that "children trained up in the way they should go," will, in many instances, much less generally, depart from it in after years. . .

Impressed with the magnitude of the wrongs and evils above referred to, dreading personal collision in the Conference, anticipating but little success from it, and feeling uncertain as to how few were likely to be the days of my earthly career, and believing that a special duty was imposed upon me in this respect by Providential circumstances, I addressed to the President, the 2nd of January, . as the most likely means, without collision with any person or body, to draw practical attention to the subject, on the part of both the ministry and the laity of the Church. . . I have the satisfaction of knowing that, if the first efforts of my pen, after joining the Conference in 1825, were to advocate the right of the members of the Church to hold a bit of ground in which to bury their dead, and the right of its ministers to perform the marriage service for the members of their congregations, my last efforts in connection with the Conference have been directed to obtain the rights of Christian citizenship to the baptized children and exemplary adherents of the Church. While I maintain that each child in the land has a right to such an education as will fit him for his duties as a citizen of the state, and that the obligations of the state correspond to the rights of the child, so I maintain, upon still stronger and higher grounds, that each child baptized by the Church is thereby enfranchised with the rights and privileges of citizenship in it, until he forfeits them by personal misconduct and exclusion, and that the obligations of the Church correspond to the rights of the child. I also maintain that each member of Christ's visible Church, has a scriptural right to his membership in it as long as he keeps the "commandments and ordinances of God," whether he attends or does not attend a meeting which Mr. Wesley (who instituted it), declared to be "merely prudential, not essential, not of divine institution," and for not attending which he never excluded, or presumed to authorize excluding, a person from Church membership. It is a principle of St. Paul, in the 14th chapter of Romans, of all true Protestantism, as well as of the writings of Mr. Wesley, "in necessary things unity, in non-essentials liberty, in all things charity."

In a letter, written from Quebec to a dear friend in Toronto, Dr. Ryerson thus refers to his religious experience at that time of personal trial on the class-meeting question. He said :—In compliance with the entreaties of the Hon. James Ferrier and the Rev. Wm. Pollard, I preached here last Sunday evening, and perhaps seldom with so much effect—certainly, never in Lower Canada. The congregation was very large; many members of the Legislature were present; and some were much affected. I had felt condemned for not preaching in New Brunswick when solicited; and I have felt that I have done right in obeying the powers that be in this respect in Quebec. I am solicited to remain and preach here again next Sunday, as many public persons have expressed disappointment at not having heard me last Sunday evening. A leading member of the church from Montreal was so comforted and edified, that after having spent the evening in my room until after ten o'clock, he went to write out all of the discourse he could remember. The friends here seem delighted to think I will still preach, and say that I would sin against God and man if I refused. My discourse on Sunday was the result of my reflections and prayer here without books or notes; and I feel much better since I consented to do what all seemed to think I ought to do. They are quite satisfied with the course I have adopted, and think it will result in great good, if I will not refuse to preach. The words of St. Paul (1st Cor. ch. 9, verse 16), in a chapter to which I opened the other day, have affected me much; and I know not that I can otherwise do so much good during the very few years at most that now remain to me, as to preach when desired by those who have authority in the matter, in any church or place. I feel deeply humbled under a sense of my own unfaithfulness, and am amazed at the great goodness, long-suffering and compassion of God towards me.

CHAPTER LV.
1855.

DR. RYERSON RESUMES HIS POSITION IN THE CONFERENCE.

ALTHOUGH the great majority of the Conference of 1854, after much conflict of feeling—in which regret and sympathy were mingled—rejected the resolutions proposed by Dr. Ryerson on the class-meeting question, yet sorrow at the loss from their councils of so distinguished a man as Dr. Ryerson prevailed amongst them. This feeling deepened as the year advanced, and much personal effort was made to induce him to consent to some honourable means by which his return to the ministerial ranks could be secured. At length, as the Conference year neared its close, he yielded to the wishes of his friends, and, on the 26th May, 1855, addressed the following letter to Rev. Dr. Wood, President of the Conference :—

From the conversations which have taken place between you, my brother, and some others of our ministers and myself, in reference to my present and future relations to the Conference and to the Church, I think it but respectful and an act of duty to state my views in writing, that there may be no misapprehension on the subject, and that you may adopt such a course as you shall think advisable.

When I wrote my letters of resignation of office in the Church, the one dated 2nd January, 1854, and the other the 12th day of June following, I had but faint expectations of being in the land of the living at this time. In what I wrote and did, I acted under the apprehension of having no longer time for delay in attesting, in the most decisive and practical way in my power, what I believe to be the divine rights of members of the visible Church of Christ whether they are baptized children or professing Christians. Since then I have reason to be thankful that the alarming symptoms in respect to my health have in a great measure subsided, and that I have the prospect of being able to continue my labours with undiminished strength and vigor, at least for some time to come.

In my first letter to you I stated and explained at length my belief that making attendance at class-meeting an essential condition of membership in the Church of God, is not only requiring what is not enjoined in the word of God, but excluding, on other than scriptural grounds, exemplary persons from the Church of Christ, and unchurching the baptized children of our people who, as well as their parents, are scripturally entitled to membership in the Church. Having given the subject much further consideration during the last twelve months, and having examined all the works on it within my reach, I am, if possible, more fully confirmed in the views I expressed last year, as both Wesleyan and scriptural, than when I penned them. And it is not unworthy of remark, that the only two newspapers in Canada which have combatted my views have been *The Church* and *The Catholic Citizen*; and both of these papers have done so upon the ground that my views were not compatible with the due authority of the Church to decree dogmas, rites and ceremonies. I acknowledge myself a heretic according to their creed of ecclesiastical authority; and I confess that the position I have been unexpectedly compelled to assume during the last two or three years as to the right of every man to the Bible, and the rights of individuals and municipalities against compulsion in regard to taxation for the support of sectarian schools, has more deeply impressed upon my mind than ever that the Bible is the only safeguard of civil liberty, and that "the Bible only ought to be the religion of Protestants;" and especially in a matter so important as that which determines who are members and what are the conditions of membership in the Church of Christ.

I must, therefore, in all frankness and honesty, still declare my conviction that there is no scriptural authority for the power which is given to a minister, by the answers to the 4th question in the 2nd section of the 2nd chapter of our Discipline, to exclude a person from the Church of God for what is expressly stated not to be "immoral conduct," namely, not attending a meeting which is not ranked among the ordinances of the Church in the General Rules of our Societies, which the 12th section of the 1st chapter of our Discipline does not enumerate among the "prudential means of grace," even among Methodists, and which Mr. Wesley stated to be "not spiritual, not of divine institution." I would never exercise such authority myself; I never have exercised it; but I will not assume to judge those who think and act otherwise.

I beg, however, that it may not be forgotten, that while I thus speak and quote the authorities of the Church in respect to class-meeting as a test or condition of Church membership; yet as a prudential means of grace and a mode and means of Christian fellowship, I regard class-meetings (as stated in my former letters above referred to), as well as love-feasts and prayer-meetings, as of the greatest value and importance. But when I think of class-meeting being converted into a condition of membership in the Church of Christ, and thus made the occasion of excluding from its pale the whole early generation of our people and many other sincere Christians, I cannot view it as I would wish, and as I could otherwise do, with the same feelings that I view love-feasts and prayer-meetings.

In regard to the other aspect of the question, as it applies to the baptized children of our people, and in which the nature and office of Baptism are involved, I feel it to be of such vital importance that I must beg to make some observations which I hope may not be considered out of place, or prove altogether useless.

The circumstances which have caused me to feel so strongly on this point were stated in my letter to you on the 2nd January, 1854, and afterwards more fully justified in my letter of the 12th of June following; and it is with no small degree of surprise that I have found my views misapprehended and pronounced unsound. It has been alleged that they involve baptismal regeneration. Nothing can be further from the fact. What I maintain is simply what is stated in the 17th Article of Faith professed by our Church, and by the catechism used in the Methodist Church on both sides of the Atlantic, and what is set forth at large in the writings of Mr. Wesley and Mr. Watson. Baptism, like the Lord's Supper, is an outward sign; but, of course, neither can be that of which it is the sign.

Baptism (as the 17th Article of our Faith expresses it), is not only a sign of profession, and mark of difference whereby Christians are distinguished from others that are unbaptized, but it is also a sign of regeneration, or the new birth.

What I maintain is, that baptism is the outward and visible sign, while regeneration, or the new birth, is the inward spiritual grace; that by baptism we are born into the visible Church of Christ on earth, while by the Holy Ghost we are born into the spiritual or invisible Church of Christ in heaven, the same as in the Lord's Supper; there is the visible act of the Church and of the body of communicants, and the invisible act of the Saviour by the Holy Ghost and of the soul of the communicant. The two are distinct; the one may not accompany the other; but they may, and often do, accompany each other. The parent should bring his child in faith to the Lord's baptism, the same as the communicant should come in faith to the Lord's Supper. The communion of the Lord's Supper is the act of a professed member of Christ's visible Church; the receiving of the Lord's baptism, is receiving the seal of membership in Christ's visible

Church, that "mark of difference whereby Christians are distinguished from others that are not baptized." Hence in the Wesleyan catechism, the question is asked,—

What are the privileges of baptized persons? The answer is,—They are made members of the visible church of Christ; their gracious relation to Him as the Second Adam, and as the Mediator of the New Covenant, is solemnly ratified by divine appointment; and they are thereby recognized as having a claim to all the spiritual blessings of which they are the proper subjects.

I maintain, therefore, that the language of our Articles of Faith and Catechism, as well as of our Baptismal Service and the writings of Mr. Wesley, explicitly declares baptism an act of the Church by which it receives the children baptized into its bosom—that all baptized children are truly members of Christ's visible Church, although they be not communicants in it until they personally profess the Faith of their Baptism, and evince their desire to flee from the wrath to come by the negative and positive proofs so briefly and fully enumerated in the General Rules of our societies.

The Church membership of baptized children is known to be the doctrine of all parties in the Church of England, as well as of Mr. Wesley. It is equally the doctrine of all sections of the Presbyterian Church, in which the baptized children are regarded as members of the Church, but not communicants until they make a personal profession of conversion, and receive a token or ticket of admission to the Lord's Supper. On this point it is sufficient to cite the following passages from the fifteenth chapter of the fourth book of Calvin's Institutes.

Baptism is a sign of initiation, by which we are admitted into the society of the Church, in order that being incorporated into Christ, we may be numbered among the children of God. . . For as circumcision was a pledge to the Jews, by which they were assured of their adoption as the people and family of God, and on their parts professed their entire subjection to Him, and, therefore, was their first entrance into the Church; so now we are initiated into the Church of God by baptism, are numbered among His people, and profess to devote ourselves to his service. . . How delightful is it to pious minds, not only to have verbal assurances, but even ocular proof, of their standing so high in the favour of their heavenly Father, that their posterity also are the objects of his care! This is evidently the reason why Satan makes such great exertions in opposition to infant baptism: that the removal of this testimony of the grace of God may cause the promise which it exhibits before our eyes gradually to disappear, and at length to be forgotten. The consequence of this would be an impious ingratitude to the mercy of God, and negligence of the instruction of our children in the principles of piety. For it is no small stimulus to our education of them in the serious fear of God, and the observance of His law, to reflect, that they are considered and acknowledged by Him as His children as soon as they are born. Wherefore, unless we are obstinately determined to reject the goodness of God, let us present to Him our children, to whom He assigns a place in His family, that is, among the members of His church.

Richard Watson, the great expounder of Wesleyan Christian

doctrine, treats this subject elaborately in the third chapter of the fourth part of his Theological Institutes. I will only quote the following sentences :—

Infant children are declared by Christ to be members of His Church. That they were members of God's Church, in the family of Abraham, and among the Jews, cannot be denied. . . The membership of the Jews comprehended both children and adults; and the grafting-in of the Gentiles, so as to partake of the same "root and fatness," will, therefore, include a right to put their children also into the covenant, so that they, as well as adults, may become members of Christ's Church, have God to be their God, and be acknowledged by Him, in the special sense of the terms of the covenant, to be His people. . . . " Whosoever (says Christ) shall receive this child in my name, receiveth me ;" but such an identity of Christ with His disciples stands wholly upon their relation to Him as members of His "mystic body, the Church." It is in this respect only that they are "one with Him ;" and there can be no identity of Christ with "little children" but by virtue of the same relation, that is, as they are members of His mystical body, the Church ; of which membership baptism is now, as circumcision was then, the initiatory rite. . . The benefits of this Sacrament require to be briefly exhibited. Baptism introduces the adult believer into the covenant of grace and the Church of Christ ; and is the seal, the pledge, to him, on the part of God, of the fulfilment of all its provisions, in time and in eternity ; whilst on his part, he takes upon himself the obligation of steadfast faith and obedience. To the infant child, baptism is a visible reception into the same covenant and church, a pledge of acceptance through Christ—the bestowment of a title to all the grace of the covenant as circumstances may require, and as the mind of the child may be capable of receiving it ; and as it may be sought in future life by prayer, when the period of reason and moral choice shall arrive. It conveys also the present blessing of Christ, of which we are assured by His taking children in His arms, and blessing them ; which blessing cannot be merely nominal, but must be substantial and efficacious. It secures, too, the gift of the Holy Spirit in those secret spiritual influences, by which the actual regeneration of those children who die in infancy is effected ; and which are a seed of life in those who are spared to prepare them for instruction in the word of God, as they are taught by parental care, to incline their will and affections to good, and to begin and maintain in them the war against inward and outward evil, so that they may be divinely assisted, as reason strengthens, to make their calling and election sure. In a word, it is, both as to infants and adults, the sign and pledge of that inward grace, which, though modified in its operations by the difference of their circumstances, has respect to, and flows from, a covenant relation to each of the Three Persons in whose one name they are baptized,—acceptance by the Father—union with Christ as the head of His mystical body, the Church—and communion with the Holy Ghost. To these advantages must be added the respect which God bears to the believing act of the parents, and to their solemn prayers on the occasion, in both of which the child is interested ; as well as in that solemn engagement of the parents which the rite necessarily implies, to bring up their child in the nurture and admonition of the Lord.

To these impressive words of Richard Watson, I add the following equally impressive extract from the pastoral address of the Wesleyan Conference in England to the Societies under its charge in 1837 :—

By baptism you place your children within the pale of the visible Church, and give them a right to all its privileges, the pastoral care of its ministers, and as far as their age and capacity will allow, the enjoyment of its ordinances and means of grace. These children are not offshoots of the Church, enjoying only a distant relation to it, but they are of it, as a fact; they are grafted into the body of Christ's disciples; they are partakers of an initiatory and provisional state of acceptance with God, and can forfeit their right to the fellowship of the saints only by a course of sin. Besides, when this sacred ordinance is regarded by parents in the spirit of prayer and faith, it cannot be unaccompanied by the divine blessing. Grace is connected with every institution of the Christian Church; and when children are constituted a part of the flock of Christ by being placed within the fold, they have a peculiar claim on the care of that good Shepherd who "gathereth the lambs with his arms and carries them in his bosom;" and they will receive instruction, spiritual influences, tender care, and the exercise of mercy, agreeing with the relation in which they stand to God. On these grounds we affectionately exhort you to place your beloved offspring within the "courts of the house of our God," and amongst the number of His family, by strictly attending to this divinely appointed ordinance of our Saviour.*

Dr. Ryerson's views were, therefore, the same in 1834 as they were in 1854—that by Baptism children stand in the relation of members of the Church, and should be enrolled in its registers, and entitled to its privileges, until they, by their own voluntary irregularity or neglect, forfeit them. The coincidence mentioned, and the consistency of the views expressed by Dr. Ryerson twenty years before, are very remarkable.

Now what are these solemn and affecting words of John Calvin, of Richard Watson, and of the British Conference, but a mockery and a snare, if the baptized children are not to be acknowledged and treated as members of the visible church of Christ? Ought not then children baptised by the Wesleyan ministry to be recognized and cared for as members of the Wesleyan Church? It is absurd, and leaves them in a state of religious orphanage, to say that they are members of the visible Church of Christ, but not members of any particular branch of it. As well might it be said, that the children born in Canada, are members of the Canadian family, but not members of any particular family in Canada. To be the former without being the latter, would indeed allow them a country, but would leave

---

* As early as 1834, Dr. Ryerson was deeply impressed with the correctness of these views. Having, in the *Guardian* of the 9th of April, 1834, called the attention of his ministerial brethren to the pressing duty of giving effect to the section of the Discipline on the "Instruction of Children," he proceeded to point out in the *Guardian* of the 23rd of that month, the privileges which baptism confers upon Methodist children, fortifying his views by the following quotation from Rev. R. Watson's Institutes:—Baptism introduces the adult believer into the covenant of Grace, and the Church of Christ. . . To the infant child it is a visible reception into the same covenant and Church. . . In a word, it is both to infants and adults a sign and pledge of that inward grace, which has respect to and flows from a covenant relation to each of the three persons, in whose one name they are baptized—acceptance with Christ as the Head of His mystical body, the Church, and of communion of the Holy Ghost.

them without a home, without a parent, without a protector, without an inheritance—homeless, houseless, destitute orphans. Is this the relation in which the baptized children of our people are to be viewed to the Church of their parents? In doing so, are not the most powerful considerations, motives and influences brought to bear upon both parents and children? In not doing so, is not the greatest wrong inflicted upon both, the ordinance of baptism virtually ignored, and its blessings lost? But in denying that any one is or can be a member of the Church except one who meets in class, are not the baptized children of our people refused a place within its pale? deprived of their baptismal birthright, before they are old enough to forfeit it by transgression? shut out from the family of God's people, and as practically unchurched as if they had never received a Christian name, in the name of the Father, of the Son, and of the Holy Ghost? I cannot reflect upon the subject or contemplate its consequences, without the deepest pain and solicitude. I will pursue it no further, but will leave it with you and those on whom the responsibility of deciding upon it devolves.

It will be remembered that I have never said anything as to the mode of receiving adult persons from without into the Church; nor as to the class of members who alone should be eligible to hold office in the Church; nor have I entertained the idea that any other than the scriptural summary of Christian morality contained in the General Rules of our Societies should be applied to all members of the Church, whether in full communion or not. Nor have I other than supposed that all persons recognized as a part of the Church, would, as far as circumstances can permit, be registered as classes, and called upon regularly by a leader or steward for their contributions in support of the ministry and other institutions of the Church, the same as persons meeting weekly in a class. What I have said applies wholly and exclusively to the Church relation and rights of the baptized children of our people, and to the rights of persons otherwise admitted into the Church, who, I believe, ought not to be excluded from it except for what would exclude them from the kingdom of grace and glory.

Anything appertaining to myself personally is unworthy of mention in such a connexion. I banish from my mind and heart the recollection and feeling of anything I consider to have been uncalled for and unjust towards myself on the part of others. Though I have resigned the ecclesiastical or outward authority to exercise the functions of the Christian ministry, I have never regarded myself as a secular man; I have felt, and do feel, and especially with improved health, the inward, and, I trust, divine conviction of duty to preach, as occasion may offer and strength permit, the unsearchable riches of Christ to dying men. And if after the past publication and foregoing statement of my convictions on the point of Church Discipline and its administration, as affecting baptized children and other scripturally blameless members of the Church, and my purpose to maintain them on such occasions, and in such manner as are sanctioned by the Discipline, the Conference thinks it proper and desirable that I should resume my former relations to it and to the Church, I am willing to cancel my resignation, and to labour, as heretofore, to preach the doctrines and promote the agencies of the Church which I have sought by every earthly means in my power, though with conscious unfaithfulness before God, to advance during the last thirty years, and which are, I believe, according to the Scriptures, and calculated to promote the present and everlasting well-being of man.

The reading of this letter at the London Conference of 1855 led to a great deal of discussion and various explanations, which unfortunately afterwards resulted in much misunderstanding and recrimination. The Conference, however, with a unanimity and heartiness which reflected great credit for its calm judgment and Christian love of unity, passed the following resolution by a nearly two-thirds majority :—

> That while this Conference declares its unaltered determination to maintain inviolate the position held respecting the views contained in Dr. Ryerson's communications of last year, and upon which his resignation was tendered and accepted; yet upon the application which the latter part of Dr. Ryerson's present communication contains, this Conference restores him to his former standing and relations to the Conference and the Church.

After the resolution was passed, Dr. Ryerson went to the Conference at London, and in a letter which he wrote to me, dated January 9th, he said :—

My entrance into the Conference was cordially greeted. I was very affectionately welcomed and introduced by the President, Rev. Dr. Wood, after which I briefly addressed the Conference, and I have since taken the same part in the proceedings as heretofore.

After a long discussion yesterday, a very important change was made in the Discipline. By this change a minister may be stationed in the same circuit during five years, if requested by the quarterly meeting. A prominent member made a long and violent speech against it. I replied at length, and stated the general grounds on which I thought the change recommended by the Stationing Committee should be adopted. After the adoption of the resolution, I congratulated the Conference on this indication of progress in a direction to what was regarded as heretical when I first introduced the proposition five years ago. Some preacher said I was a little too soon. I said perhaps I had the misfortune of having been born a few years too soon. Another said that he supposed I expected that other changes would also follow. I replied, time would show. I was informed that all (even Messrs. Jeffers and Spencer) expressed a desire for my return to the Conference. The lengthened discussion was based upon certain parts of my letter to Mr. Wood, which it was held were not courteous, but a bearding of the Conference. On the other hand, it was contended that my sentiments even on the class-meeting condition of membership were the practice of those very preachers who objected to them. Examples were given, much to the surprise of certain parties, who professed to be the greatest sticklers on the subject. It was professed by all, without exception, that but for certain phrases in my letter (to the sentiments of which, it was maintained, the Conference would be committed by the resolution proposed) the vote in regard to me would have been unanimous.

Amongst other congratulatory letters received by Dr. Ryerson, none were more gratifying to him than the following characteristic letter from Rev. John Black, in township of Rawdon, written on the 16th of June :—

My good Mr. Lever, of Sidney, in a letter from the Conference, informs me that "Dr. Ryerson is once more among his brethren, and, as usual, taking an active part in the affairs of Conference." Athough three of my children were confined to bed by sickness, yet on hearing such news I was almost ready for a shout.

Permit me to say that your departure from us at Belleville, twelve months ago, lay heavy on my heart; and now to hear the above intelligence is good to my soul. For many years I have been much attached to Mr. Egerton Ryerson. We were "taken on trial" at the same time, and together were ordained to the great work of the ministry. And although you, Mr. R., have been near the head, and I, Mr. B., near the foot, yet we are in the same ranks, fighting the battles of the Lord, and exercising our talents in behalf of truth and righteousness. I know that your time is precious, yet I believe you will spare a minute or two in reading a few lines from your affectionate, and now almost worn-out, friend and well-wisher. Long may you live for the purpose of using your talents for the benefit of Church and State! This fervent wish stands at a distance from mere compliment and from flattery, and is the free emotion of a Methodist heart.

CHAPTER LVI.
1855–1856.

PERSONAL EPISODE IN THE CLASS-MEETING DISCUSSION.

I HAVE already referred to the character of the discussion which resulted in Dr. Ryerson's restoration to the Conference. In the heat of that discussion some things may have been said by Dr. Ryerson's friends which were not warranted by the terms of his letter of the 26th of May; or what was said may have been construed (designedly or otherwise) into an admission or assurance on Dr. Ryerson's part that he would cease to agitate the question, or that he would hold his opinions in abeyance.

The discussion on the Class-meeting question was the chief event in the proceedings of the Wesleyan Conference of 1855. Yet not the slightest reference to the subject, or to Dr. Ryerson's return to the Conference was made in the report of the proceedings which were published in the *Guardian* of the 13th and 20th of June in that year. It was not until some time after the adjournment of the Conference, and the departure of Dr. Ryerson for Europe, that the subject was mentioned in that paper, and what did appear was apparently an afterthought.*

After Dr. Ryerson had gone, an editorial appeared in the *Guardian* of the 27th of June from which the following is an extract:—

---

* Dr. Ryerson left Toronto for Quebec immediately after Conference, to confer with the Government there on matters connected with his Department. While there he wrote to me a private letter as follows:—

At Mr. Attorney-General Macdonald's suggestion I have been appointed Honorary Commissioner at the Paris exhibition. Mr. Macdonald also endorsed my recommendation for your appointment as Deputy Superintendent with an increased salary. His Excellency appointed you yesterday according to my recommendation, and you will be gazetted on Saturday. . . Sir Edmund Head has given me very flattering letters of introduction to Lord Clarendon and Lord John Russell. . . I leave here for Boston on my way to England. . . I have no doubt but that you will do all things in the best manner, and for the best. I fervently pray Almighty God greatly to prosper you, as well as guide and bless you in your official duties.

We did not notice in our summary account of the proceedings of the Conference the return of Dr. Ryerson to his former position with that body, but as erroneous statements have appeared in the paper respecting it we think proper to give the facts of the case.

A short time previous to the sitting of the Conference Dr. Ryerson addressed a letter to the President, in which he stated that his views remained unaltered respecting the points of difference between himself and the Conference; he expressed a desire to resume his ministerial duties in the Church. The communication was accompanied with a verbal assurance that his own peculiar views on the questions at issue would be held in abeyance in deference to the determination of the Conference to maintain inviolate those parts of the Wesleyan Discipline to which his communication referred. This was the position in which the application of Dr. Ryerson was presented to the Conference, and, after a somewhat animated discussion on the subject, the resolution [for his re-admission] was adopted by nearly a two-thirds majority.

Immediately on the publication of this article, I sent it to Dr. Ryerson at Boston, where he was about to take the steamer for England. He at once replied to the Editor, and sent the letter to me for insertion in the *Guardian*. In his private note to me, dated 3rd July, he said:—

I think the *Guardian's* statement is the most shameful attack that was ever made upon me—one that I did not expect even from him—one that I would not have believed had I not seen it. What may be the end of this affair, I cannot yet see. But I am satisfied in my own conscience as to the course I have pursued, and as to my present duty. As to rescinding the clause of the Discipline relating to the exclusion of persons for not attending classmeetings, no determination was expressed to enforce it. On the contrary, it was declared to be a dead letter in many places. What I maintained was, that the practice and the rule should be in harmony. You will see what I have said to the Editor of the *Guardian* in a private note.

Remember me affectionately to all; and may Almighty God prosper you in your educational work during my absence.

The following is a copy of the private letter to Rev. J. Spencer, which accompanied Dr. Ryerson's reply to the editorial:

I was not a little surprised and pained at your unfair and unjust statement respecting me, and especially after what passed on my leaving the Conference, and your careful silence on the subject until I had left home, and would not therefore be likely to have it in my power to furnish an antidote until your injurious statement had accomplished its object as far as possible. But I am thankful that, through the prompt kindness of Mr. Hodgins, and by that means alone, I have been furnished with a copy of the *Guardian* in time to write a hasty reply before embarking for the other side of the Atlantic. I have requested Mr. Hodgins to take a copy of my communication to you, as I have not time to transcribe it. You can as easily command my letter to the President of the Conference as you did the resolution of the Conference. I ask for no indulgence or favour; I ask for nothing but truth and justice.

I will thank you to inform Mr. Hodgins as early as possible as to whether you intend to perpetuate the wrong you have done me, by refusing to insert my letter to the President of the Conference, and the note I have this evening addressed to you in reference to your statement. I wish Mr. Hodgins to inform me of the result by the next mail to England, and also to act otherwise by me as I would by him in like circumstances.*

Having got Dr. Ryerson's reply to the *Guardian's* attack of 27th June, inserted in the Toronto city papers, I wrote to him to that effect. His reply is dated, London (Eng.,) 3rd August:—
I thank you sincerely for the pains you have taken in regard to my letter to the *Guardian*. I am thankful that, by your zeal and good management, the Methodist body, as well as the public at large, will have an opportunity of learning my own views from my own pen; but considering the intended course

---

* The antagonism between Mr. Spencer (now Editor of the *Guardian*) and Dr. Ryerson was of long standing. Thirteen years before the date of this attack upon Dr. Ryerson, Mr. Spencer was proposed, in 1842, as a candidate for a Mastership in Victoria College. Dr. Ryerson advised him to attend the Wesleyan University at Middletown, Conn., so as to fit himself for the post. He did so. But the Board of Victoria College refused to appoint him. He was very indignant, and so expressed himself to Dr. Ryerson. He afterwards wrote to him a letter (in 1842) as follows :—You were no doubt surprised at the remarks I made to you, and perhaps you thought they were unnecessarily harsh and severe, and made under the momentary impulse of exited feelings. If so, you are mistaken. I spoke deliberately, though strongly. You know the circumstances under which, at your request, I went to the College, and that the situation, though congenial to my feelings, was not sought for by me. Of the decision of the members of the Board, to give the Principal permission to employ me part of the year, I express my decided disapprobation. Now, Sir, I consider such a resolution a downright insult. Had I come before that Board as a stranger, or under the character of a mercenary hireling, and one concerning whose qualifications you were entirely ignorant, then there would have been some appearance of propriety in making such a proposition, as a safeguard, and against imposition. But I am a member of that Conference under whose direction the affairs of that institution are placed; its interests are closely connected with those of the Church of which I am now, and expect to remain, a member. I believed I could render greater service to the Church in labouring to promote the prosperity of that institution. I trust I have yet too much of public spirit, and too ardent a desire for the prosperity of our College, to wish to remain there if my labours were not conducive to its efficiency. But what is the spirit of that resolution? "Why, we wish to get rid of you, and the easiest way to do it is, to employ you for a specified time, and then we can dismiss you with propriety. But the absurdity of that resolution is its most prominent feature. I intend, at the first opportunity, to express my mind more fully to you personally upon this subject." In one of his letters in this controversy, Dr. Ryerson thus refers to this Victoria College episode. He says: In regard to Mr. Spencer, I am aware of his feelings toward me during these many years; ever since he failed to procure an appointment to the Chair of Chemistry and Natural Philosophy in Victoria College, for which he had devoted a year of special preparation. I believe he has attributed his disappointment to me, and that I had not acted toward him in a brotherly way, in not securing his appointment, as he supposed I could have done from my connection with the College. The fact was, I recommended his appointment, at least for a trial, but my recommendation was not concurred in by any other member of the Board, as Dr. Green and others know.

of the *Guardian*, and what he alleges to be the feelings of many others, I have great doubts whether I can be of any use to the Wesleyan body, or of much use to the interests of religion in connection with the Conference, and that I shall rather embarrass, and be a burden to my friends in the Conference, than be a help to them. My only wish and aim as a minister is, to preach the evangelical doctrines I have always proclaimed, and which are preached with power by many clergymen of the Church of England and Presbyterian Churches, and often more forcibly, than by many Methodist ministers.

I confess, from what you state, I see no prospect of effecting the changes in the relation and privileges of baptized children, and the test of membership in the Methodist Church, which I believe to be required by the Scriptures, and by consistency. I apprehend that anything proposed by me on these subjects will be made the occasion of violent attacks and agitation, and that personal hostility to me will be made a sort of test of orthodoxy among a large party in the Conference and in the Church—thus exposing my friends to much unpleasantness and disadvantage on my account, and reducing, if not extinguishing, all opportunities on my part to preach, as I should be (as in times past) wholly dependent upon the invitations of others.

From this incident a private and confidential correspondence on the subject was maintained for months between Dr. Ryerson in Europe and myself, in Canada.

It was clear to my mind at the time that the Editor took an unfair advantage of Dr. Ryerson's absence from the country to injure (as he supposed) his brother in the ministry. In this he was mistaken; and, in his chagrin, he attacked me personally in the *Guardian* for my zeal on behalf of Dr. Ryerson. Events proved that my interposition was opportune and just; and that, had I not done so, the Methodist people would have been improperly and cruelly misled, and irreparable injustice would have been done to the character and motives of a noble and generous man, who, in this instance, ought not to have been held responsible for the utterances of warm hearts, but of possibly indiscreet tongues.

I speak advisedly when I say that I understood perfectly well the two men with whom I had to deal. Rev. James Spencer was well known to me, when I was a student at Victoria College forty years ago. He was a good man, no doubt; but no student at that College ever thought of comparing him with the Principal of the College. How he ever got to be Editor of the *Guardian* was always a mystery to me. I never had the slightest difference with him—quite the reverse; but no comparison could be instituted between James Spencer and Egerton Ryerson.

In this matter I had no personal feeling. Both men were Methodists, while I am an Episcopalian, and both have gone to their final account. Moreover, the question was not one of doctrine, or of denominational preference. It was one of simple justice and fair play between man and man. Hence, I took the earliest opportunity of apprising Dr. Ryerson of the unjust and anomalous position in which he had been placed by the Editor of the *Guardian*.

The following private letters were successively received by me from Dr. Ryerson while he was in Europe:—

Paris, 23rd August.—I enclose my answer to Rev. James Spencer. I wish you would have it inserted in the *Globe* and *Colonist*. As you are acquainted with all the circumstances in Canada, being on the spot, if you think it best to abridge, omit, or modify the words of any part of my communication, I would wish you to do so. Whatever course I may think it my duty to pursue in future, I wish in this communication to preserve that tone of remark which can give no offence to any minister or member of the Wesleyan Church. I will not be the offending party, and the responsibility of a wider breach between the Conference and myself will not be with me. What course duty may require me to pursue, I still leave to the direction of Infinite Wisdom, and to future consideration. . .

The Queen is in Paris this week, during which all business in my way seems to be suspended. She is received with great enthusiasm. We have seen her and the Emperor two or three times.

Paris, 30th August.—Rev. Dr. Wood's denial of my having given him any pledge, or any thing that would be so construed, is full and decided, and if my brother John says anything at all, it will be, I have no doubt, less than I have stated in my letter. But still the main question of my position in the Conference is unaffected by these disclaimers. It appears from Mr. Spencer's statement (in which he seems to be sustained by others) that the terms of my letter were not acted upon or complied with by the Conference, but that the Conference acted upon a verbal assurance that I never made, or authorized. The simplest and most natural way for me to act, is, to withdraw my letter on these grounds, and to decline availing myself of, or recognizing an act of, the Conference based upon what I never proposed or authorized. Thus the responsibility of this irregular and absurd proceeding will rest with others, and I will stand, in the maintenance of all that I have stated and done, with the advantage of having acted a most conciliatory part. But what I shall do must not be decided upon hastily, as I act for life, and finally. If it ultimately appears to me, as it does at present, that there is no consistent or justifiable ground on which I can remain a member of the Conference, it will then be for me to consider whether I can occupy the position of a layman, or enter the ministry of some other section of the Christian Church. I would like to have your own impressions and views on this point, in reference to my future standing and usefulness in Canada.

Paris, 20th September.—In my reply to Mr. Spencer I did not allude to the cases of Montreal and Quebec. Perhaps the disclaimer which has been adopted by quarterly meetings in those places may require from me a remark or two. What I said was founded upon what was told me on reliable authority that no preacher had enforced, or dare enforce, the rule. I understand the same at Quebec. I have been assured, and I have no doubt the enquiry will establish the fact, that there are men, trustees of the Churches, in either or both Montreal or Quebec, who do not meet in class, and whose names are not, and I think whose names never have been, on any class book. But I think the natural and necessary effect of the whole is, to terminate my connection with the Methodist Church. I still remain undecided; but I see no other course on the ground of consistency, propriety, or duty, as well as of religious enjoyment. But this is only to yourself. The remaining question will be whether I should remain a private member of a Church, or enter another Church. On this point I am quite undecided. May I be divinely directed!

In a further letter directed to me from Paris in September, 1855, Dr. Ryerson discussed the whole question at issue. After pointing out the unfair conduct of the Editor of the *Guardian* in attacking and misrepresenting a member of the Conference, and then saying that his columns were closed against any further discussion of the subject, Dr. Ryerson said:—The Editor of the *Guardian* and others represent me as hostile to class-meetings. This may do injury, in the estimation of some persons, to a means of religious edification which I regard as one of the most efficient human agencies for promoting spiritual-mindedness among religious people. The responsibility of such a proceeding is with themselves. The Editor of the *Guardian* represents this as a matter of dispute between the Conference and myself. This is wholly incorrect. The resolution of the Conference is avowedly based upon my letter, and upon that alone. That record cannot be falsified. The variation between the wording of the resolution of the Conference and the latter part of my letter referred to in it, is not of the slightest consequence. The acts of the Conference, as well as of the Legislature, are to be judged of, not by what may have been said by individual members in the course of discussion, but by its attested records and official papers.

Now with the same truth and propriety that my assailants charge me with having written against class-meetings, might I charge them with being opposed to prayer-meetings and love-feasts, and even the Lord's Supper, because they do not make the observance of all or of any one of these institutions (though the latter is expressly instituted by our Lord himself), a condition of membership in the Church of God. Because I have avowed my long-settled conviction that class-meetings ought not to be exalted above all the other ordinances and institutions of religion—giving as an authority the words of John Wesley himself—am I to be charged with having written against class-meeting? So far from having written against these meetings, I have expressed myself in the strongest terms in their favour; and I repeat that, after the public preaching of the Word, and the Lord's Supper, I believe class-meetings have been the most efficient means of promoting personal and vital piety among the members of the Wesleyan Societies.

Yet I am not insensible to the fact that Mr. Wesley found the prototype of this kind of religious exercises, not in any institution or practice of the Primitive Church for fifteen hundred years, but in a society of Monks called *La Trappe*, whose ardent piety Mr. Wesley greatly admired, the lives of some of whose members (such as the Marquis de Renty, etc.,) he wrote, and whose manual of piety (Imitation of Jesus Christ) he translated and abridged, for the use of his own Societies, and several of whose questions in conducting what may be called their weekly band or class-meetings, Mr. Wesley adopted, translated and modified, for conducting his own meetings of a similar character. These weekly exercises in the Societé de la Trappe were eminently instrumental in reforming, and kindling the flame of devotional piety among its members; and Mr. Wesley found them equally useful among the members of his own Societies, and so they have continued till the present time. But will any Wesleyan minister in England or Canada—will any man of intelligence and honesty—venture to assert that Mr. Wesley ever intended that attendance at such weekly exercises should be an essential condition and fundamental test of membership in the visible Church of God? Will any one assert, or can he believe, that Mr. Wesley ever could have anticipated, or supposed, that such an application would, or could, be made of an institution which he expressly stated to be "merely prudential, not essential, not of divine origin?" But I am again met with the charge, on another ground, of having departed from Mr. Wesley. It is said, in substance: "Mr. Wesley has committed class-meeting to us as a trust; it is not for us to inquire into the origin of the institution; it is our duty to maintain inviolably the trust committed to us—which trust Dr. Ryerson has violated." In reply, I remark that the statement of the question itself is fallacious, and the charge groundless. In the first place, the question assumes, what is contrary to fact, that Mr. Wesley instituted and committed the trust of class-meetings as a condition of membership in the visible Church of God, whereas he instituted and transmitted it as a means of grace among the members of a private society in a church. In the next place, the trust of class-meetings was only one part of a system which Mr. Wesley committed as a trust to his followers. The one part of that trust was as sacred as another, and the connection of one part with another is essential to the fulfilment of the obligation. Now one part of Mr. Wesley's trust, and that on which he insists ten times more voluminously and vehemently than he ever spoke of class-meetings, was that his followers should attend the services of the Church of England, should receive the ordinances of Baptism and the Lord's Supper in it, should abide in the Church of England, and that whenever they separated from the Church of England they separated from him. These are so many trusts that Mr. Wesley committed to his followers in England, and on which he insisted as tests of membership in his Society; and in connection with these trusts, he committed the trust of class-meetings—" as the observance and practice of members of a private society in the Church of England." Have Dr. Bunting and others, who charge me with being anti-Wesleyan, fulfilled these trusts committed to them by Mr. Wesley? Have they not wholly separated from the Church of England—ordaining their own ministers, administering the ordinances, claiming and exercising all the attributes of a Church, as much as the authorities of the Church of England herself. And while Mr. Wesley disclaimed exercising the office of excommunicating Church members, and denied that admission into or exclusion from his Societies was admission into or exclusion from the visible Church of Christ, my accusers exercise this authority in the highest degree—confessedly and avowedly admitting into and excluding persons from the visible Church, and making the attendance at class-meeting a test of Church-membership—which Mr. Wesley never believed, much less authorized. I leave it, therefore, to the judgment of every man of common sense to say whether there is the shadow of a reason for the pretensions and charges of my assailants. I am not surprised that Dr. Bunting and others should feel sensitive on the class-meeting test of church-membership, as it so enormously increases clerical power—the ruling idea of Dr. Bunting's legislation throughout his whole life. It virtually places the membership of each member in the hands of the minister. The quarterly class ticket, signed by the minister, is the only proof and title of membership for each member. If the minister withholds this (and he may be prompted to do so on many grounds, personal and others, irrespective of any suspicion, much less charge, against the moral or religious character of the member) the member is deprived of his membership, and this I believe has occurred in more than twenty thousand instances, in England, during the last six years, during which period the connection has experienced the lamentable and unprecedented loss of nearly a hundred thousand members, the fruits of the labours of an age.

London, 5th October.—I know that my brother John was not pleased with my letter to Mr. Wood, read in the Conference. He told me so on the way to the Conference; he wished me to write a short letter, couched in general terms, and that the affair might be passed over in the Conference as quietly as possible—believing that to be the best way to accomplish the object I had in view. In this I could not agree with him, and stated that unless received in the terms of my letter, I did not wish to be received at all; nor did I wish the letter read if any opposition were apprehended. What has transpired shows, I think very clearly, that had I not been as explicit as I have, I should have been more grossly misrepresented, and with some degree of plausibility. I am exceedingly glad that I wrote as I did. It has removed all uncertainty on the subject. There can now be no mistake or misunderstanding. I do not think my friends have been frank with me in not telling me all that has transpired in the Conference. But it is not worth while to refer to these things now. The question is settled. I shall write to Dr. Beecham on the subject of the remarks reported to have been made in reference to me by Dr. Bunting and Mr. Methley, in the English Conference, and respecting my settled and avowed convictions and position—affording him an opportunity of stating how far he and others think such views are consistent with the relations I sustain to the Wesleyan Body. I shall also advert to the propriety of such men as Mr. Methley, or any member of the English Conference, assuming to exercise a censorship over the character of any members of the Canada Conference. After receiving Dr. Beecham's answer, I shall finally decide as to my future course. I look upon my connection with the Wesleyan body as virtually terminated. I have not been in one of their chapels, or seen one of their ministers, since I left America. On seeing, at Boston, what Mr. Spencer had written, and what was likely to occur, I thought I would keep myself entirely aloof until the final issue of the whole affair.

London, 10th October.—I wrote you on the 5th inst., under the influence of strong and indignant feelings. But I have since calmly, and with much prayer and many tears, for days considered the whole matter of Church relations. I have resolved to stand my ground in my present position, and fight out the battle with my assailants.

In a letter to me, written a few days afterwards, Dr. Ryerson thus states the conclusion which he had come to in regard to his remaining in the Methodist Church. He said:—Last Sunday I heard a very powerful sermon from Dr. Cumming on, " No man liveth to himself, and no man dieth to himself;" and I resolved, by meditation and prayer, to come to a conclusion on the subject of my Church relations, and future course. I walked, and wept, and prayed over the subject from seven till twelve o'clock last night, and the conclusion at which I have now arrived is to stand in my present position and relation, and maintain my views, and let my opponents do their worst, and thrust me out if they will or can. If I lived to myself, that is, if I consulted my taste, feelings, personal comforts, and enjoyments, I could not remain in the Methodist Church a week; I have more views and sympathies with the evangelical clergy and members of any Protestant church than I have with such men as Mr. Spencer. But still I have, in the Providence of God, been called to labour in connection with the Methodist Church, and have been prospered in it; and I think, all things considered, I can do more good to stand my ground. If I do nothing else than secure to Methodist children and youth the recognition of their rights and privileges, and the appropriate religious instruction and care, that point alone will involve more good in the end than all I could do in any other section of the Christian Church. If Methodist pulpits should be closed against me, others will be opened to me in abundance.

Paris, 18th October.—I feel very happy in my own mind since I have finally decided upon my future course, and which, I have no doubt you will think with me, is, under all the circumstances, the best that I could take. After the course which has been pursued towards me, I shall be free from all restraints on the matters respecting which they hoped to impose silence. I shall make the James Methleys, and the James Spencers, of both the English and Canadian Conferences, feel very uncomfortable, while I think I shall secure the respect and sympathies of various religious persuasions and parties in Canada, and the ultimate accomplishment of the great and divine end I have had in view. Mr. Spencer's remarks that you enclosed are very weak and flat—more so than I expected. He speaks of a difference between the Conference and me. The difference is between him and his abettors (as individuals) and me, not between the Conference and me. The Conference has avowedly based its proceedings upon my letter—which is all I care for since my letter is published. If the terms of the resolution of the Conference are not in harmony with the terms of my letter, that is of no consequence to me now—it is for the judgment or taste of those who wrote it. I am glad to hear that my remarks on Mr. Spencer are favourably received by all my friends. Mr. Malcolm Cameron has said that if I never wrote another word on the subject I had mooted, or were I even to leave the Body, the subject would not sleep—it would be taken up by others—it could not sleep—and their attacking me, and I defending myself, was, in effect, discussing the question in the most telling manner.

Paris, 8th November:—I am glad to learn that at that period when I was undecided, you entertained the views as to my relations and future course which I have at length decided to maintain and pursue. I will stand my ground and battle the affair with my adversaries, on both sides of the Atlantic, to the last. In order to exclude me from the Conference they must now bring charges against me; and, in attempting this, they will raise a difficulty such as they have never yet encountered, and will invest the whole question with an interest and importance that they little dream of. Indeed, they have done so already.

Paris, 14th November.—I am happy to learn that you also entirely concur in the course I have decided to pursue. I care not a fig for all that the parties to whom you refer may do or try to do. I have not a shadow of doubt as to the result. It is most strange that rashness should be attributed to you in the matter. It was the course best calculated to defeat the objects they wish to counteract. I do not think my letters would have appeared at all in the *Guardian* had you not pressed the matter as you did; and had I not taken the course I did at Belleville, the questions could not have been brought before the body as they can and must. I have written a reply to the *Guardian*—it contains sixteen pages of letter paper. But after your suggestion, I will keep it another week, and may, perhaps, substitute for it a note making my acknowledgements to the daily press of Toronto, and stating my position and intended course of proceedings. I think something of this kind may be best to counteract the misrepresentations which they are no doubt industriously circulating. Possibly I may not say anything at all, as you suggest.

Paris, 29th November.—I cannot but smile at the pamphlet on the Class-meeting question, after it had been declared as the determination of the Conference that the subject of my letters was not to be agitated. I could not be more effectually aided in what I would wish to see accomplished than by such a publication, as it will afford me an opportunity to re-consider the subject, and to say what I please on the general subject, and expose every petty sophism and absurdity of my opponents, and to show what are really the rights of the members of the Church in more senses than one. The strength of the opposite side of the question is silence and Conference authority; the strength of my side is discussion. For one on the opposite side to write and publish a pamphlet is to give up Conference authority, and to come upon the ground of reason and Scripture. It is also an abandonment of the pretence that the question is not a debatable or open one. There being several writers on one side and only one on the other, gives the latter an advantage. He can point out the variations and weak points of the former, illustrating the criteria of error and truth. The whole will afford me an opportunity to deal with general principles, and curiosity and enquiry will be attached to what I can say in reply to such efforts to prove me heretical. I look upon all such occurrences as the ways of Providence to open the way of truth and righteousness.

Dr. Ryerson returned to Canada in time to attend the Conference at Brockville. While there he wrote to me, on the 6th of June, 1856:—Mr. Spencer has given me notice that, as I have denied and repudiated the terms upon which I had been re-admitted into the Conference, when my name comes up in the examination of character, it will be moved that the resolution re-admitting me into the Conference be rescinded. I am glad of this. It will afford me an opportunity of exposing the conduct of my assailants, and of entering into the whole question. To-day the subject of class-meetings came up, by a philippic on the subject by one of the ministers, in connection with the return of members, and the manner of administering the Discipline. I at once accepted the challenge—reiterated my sentiments, and stated when the time came I should be prepared to show that they were founded on the Scriptures, the primitive Church, the Fathers of the Protestant Reformation, and such men as Baxter and Howe, down to the present time. What I said seemed to be favourably received by a considerable portion of the Conference. I think the Spencer clique (and it is only a clique) will be disappointed greatly when the affair comes up. I feel that I stand upon the Rock of Truth. I would that my soul were more fully baptized with the Spirit of the Truth, the principles of which I maintain.

On the 9th of June, he also wrote as follows:—This afternoon, on my name being called, Rev. J. Borland moved, seconded by Rev. W. Jeffers, the following resolution:—

Resolved, That as Dr. Ryerson has denied the authority of the verbal assurances given in his behalf at the Conference in London, and repudiated the basis upon which the resolution restoring him to his former standing in the Conference was founded; therefore, all that part of the said resolution which relates to his re-admission be, and is hereby, rescinded.

When the President came to the question as to the examination of character, he observed that that question was always considered with closed doors, and intimated to strangers to withdraw. I arose at once, and said that as far as I was concerned, notice had been given to me of a resolution to exclude me from the Conference, and that upon the ground of what had appeared in the public papers—that I had been misrepresented and maligned in the official organ of the Conference—in professed reports of what had taken place in the Conference, and I demanded, as a matter of right and equity, that the proceedings of the Conference should be public as far as I was concerned. A discussion then took place in regard to reporting. I at length moved an amendment that the proceedings of the Conference should be public as far as I was concerned. This was adopted by a large majority, though voted against by the whole clique hostile to me. Several of them made speeches against me. My brother John, Rev. E. Wood, Rev. R. Jones, Dr. Green, as well as others, stated what was said as to my pledge, just what I had supposed and intended; and my brother John made a most powerful speech, and scathed Mr. Spencer and others. His references to me were warmly cheered by an evident majority of the Conference. The cheers to the remarks maligning me seemed to be made by about fifteen or twenty—many less than I had supposed. I have no doubt they will be defeated by a very large majority. When the hour of adjournment arrived, the President asked me if I wished to make any remarks; I stated to the Conference I was willing to give my assailants the advantage of leaving their strong statements and attacks unrefuted and unnoticed until Monday morning. A large number of persons were present, and a strong popular feeling seemed to be excited in my favour. My opponents have themselves in the very position in which I have desired to get them, and I shall now have the best possible opportunity of exposing them.

At the request of the friends here, I have consented to preach to-morrow evening, notwithstanding the opposition of the preachers hostile to me. I feel as if God the Lord would help me on this occasion, notwithstanding my unfaithfulness and unworthiness; He has never failed me in such an extremity.

On the following Monday Dr. Ryerson's case was brought up for discussion. Rev. J. Borland made a strong appeal on behalf of his resolution. The *Canadian Independent*, of July 16th, in speaking of the debate said:—

Mr. Borland had not spoken long in support of this before he was interrupted by Rev. Dr. Wood, the President, who made this most important declaration, that—

He gave no verbal assurance for, or in behalf of Dr. Ryerson; that he received no such assurance from him; that the document he received from Dr. Ryerson was laid on the table, and read before the Conference, unaccompanied by any verbal statements or assurances of any kind from him.

This he afterwards repeated, when Rev. J. Spencer, the Editor of the *Guardian*, re-asserted the giving of such assurances. The co-delegate, Rev. J. Ryerson, also said that—

He never thought of pledging Dr. Ryerson to silence on any of these questions, and he was sure the Conference would not ask him to do so, as the Conference never gagged any man.

The *Independent* then proceeds:—

Dr. Ryerson has been most unfairly treated. He has not denied having made application for re-admission, but only an application with pledges of silence. The resolutions of Conference, in 1854, accepting his resignation and warmly acknowledging his past services, and, in 1855, consenting to his re-admission, were never communicated to him, and were suppressed by the *Guardian*. This was most unmanly and unjust.* The matter now before the Conference was introduced at the Toronto District Meeting in his absence, and without notice being given him.†

* Dr. Ryerson, in his speech at the Brockville Conference, referring to this omission, said:—The Conference passed a resolution complimentary and affectionate towards myself, and expressive of its high sense of my long services in defending the rights and advocating the interests of the Connexion. The copy of that resolution has never been communicated to me to this day; Mr. Spencer suppressed the publication of it in the *Guardian*, and thus defeated the noble and generous intentions of the great majority of the Conference in regard to myself.

† To this proceeding, Dr. Ryerson also referred in his speech as follows:—How did my opponents bring up their charge against me? Did they inform the defendant of the approaching ordeal, and secure his presence in an ecclesiastical court prior to his attempted execution? No, Sir; the defendant obeys the call of duty, at personal sacrifice, to attend to a meeting of the senate and annual public exercises of the students of Victoria College; and, while absent, these professed advocates of Methodistic rule, arraign him without notice, and seek to get a resolution passed against him. Is that Methodism? Is that old Methodism? If these, my assailants, believe, as they say, that the interests of the Church will be greatly promoted by my expulsion, then let them do it on Methodistic principles. Now, although I was well aware that they were opposed to me personally, yet I thought, though I was absent from the district meeting, they would treat me, at least, honourably. If I had done wrong, let them accuse me—give me a specific charge and due notice of trial, and let me prepare for my defence. This would be the manly course—this would be Methodism ; and if I had committed no offence, if no charge could be brought against me, why seek to exclude me from this body with-

He uttered some memorable things in his eloquent defence.

I believe the true foundation or test of membership in the Church of Christ is not the acute angle of a Class-meeting attendance, but the broad bases of repentance, faith, and holiness. I can have no sympathy with that narrow and exclusive spirit, the breadth of whose catholicity is that of a goat's track, and the dimensions of whose charity are those of a needle's point, whether inculcated by the Editor of *The Church* on the one hand, or by the Editor of the *Guardian* on the other. He would give no pledges, had no concessions or promises to make; would be accountable to the rules of the Church as others, and would stand in that Conference on the same footing as other members, or not at all. While he subscribed to all that had been said as to the utility of Class-meetings, and reiterated the grounds on which he had recommended and maintained them; yet, on the ground of Scripture obligation he demurred, and averred, in the language of Mr. Wesley, with whom they originated and who best knew their true position in the Church, that they are merely prudential, not essential, not of Divine institution.

The Editor of the *Independent*, in conclusion, said :—

We congratulate Dr. Ryerson on his successful defence. . . We should esteem it a dire calamity, could any dishonour be attached to his name. He is one of the most devoted, conscientious, able and successful officers in the public service. In the school system of Upper Canada, he has built for himself an enduring monument, as a benefactor of the Province. He is a brave yet courteous champion for some of our most precious rights. May those who watch for his halting be confounded and put to shame !

After a reference to some personal matters, Dr. Ryerson, in the course of his remarks, showed that he was prepared to sacrifice much for the maintenance of the truth. He said : Shortly after the occurrence to which I have just referred, an act was got through the Legislature at the end of the Session of 1849, which excluded clergymen from visiting the public schools in their official character, and which would have excluded the Bible from the schools. What was my conduct on the occasion ? Why, I forthwith placed my office at the disposal of the Head of the Government sooner than administer such a law. The result was the Government authorized the suspension of the Act, and caused its repeal at the next Session of Parliament.

The debate lasted over two days, and was finally closed by the adoption of an amendment by the Rev. A. Hurlburt, recognizing the application of the previous year as admitted by Dr. Ryerson, and as understood by the Conference. The amendment was passed by an immense majority, only 23 out of 150 members present voting against it.

out a charge and without a crime ? Is not this course opposed to all proceedings of civil and ecclesiastical tribunals, and to every principle of civil and religious liberty—to true Protestant freedom and to genuine Methodism, whether new or old ?

CHAPTER LVII.

1854–1856.

Dr. Ryerson's Third Educational Tour in Europe.

WHILE in Europe in 1854 and 1856, Dr. Ryerson, under the authority of the Government, commenced the collection of objects of art for the Educational Museum in the Education Department. While there he met Hon. Malcolm Cameron, who after Dr. Ryerson returned to Canada, wrote to him from London on the subject of his mission. In a letter, dated 3rd of January, 1857, Mr. Cameron said:—

I have myself witnessed the result of the labour and reading which you must have gone through with in order to obtain the information and cultivation of judgment necessary to get the things our young Canada can afford; things, too, of such a character and description as shall be useful, not only in elevating the taste of our youth, but of increasing their historical and mythological lore, as well as inform them of the facts of their accuracy in size and form. I was much flattered to find that my humble efforts to begin, in some degree, a Canadian gallery—by securing a few of Paul Kane's pictures in 1851—had been followed up by you in your universally-acknowledged enlightened efforts for education, which (in my bitterest moments of alienation from you, for what I esteemed a sacrifice of Canadian freedom, and right to self-government), I have ever cheerfully admitted.

Your determination to obtain a few works of art and statuary, a few paintings, prints of celebrities, and scientific instruments, has cost you much labour, anxiety and thought, which I never would have conceived of had I not met you, and gone with you, and seen your notes and correspondence.

You have passed through many trials, and in most of them I was with you. The period that presses on my mind (as Lord Elgin said of Montreal), I do not want to remember. God grant that we may see, in all matters for the rest of our few days, eye to eye, as we do now on all the subjects in which you are now engaged, publicly and privately. I think God is with you, and directing you aright in that Conference matter which is nearest to your heart, and I am confident that you will have a signal triumph.

Dr. Ryerson has written the following account of a distinguished physician whom he met at Rome:—

One of the most remarkable men with whom I became acquainted in Italy, in my tour there in 1856–7, was Dr. Pantelioni, a scholar, physician, patriot, and statesman; to whose character and banishment from Rome the London *Times'* newspaper devoted about three columns.

Prefatory to the circumstances of my acquaintance with this remarkable man, I may observe, that when in England in 1850–1, I had a good deal of correspondence with Earl Grey, who was then Secretary of State for the Colonies, and through whom I was able to procure maps, globes, and essential text-books for Canadian schools, at a discount of forty-three per cent. from the published selling prices. Earl Grey was much pleased in being the instrument of so much good to the cause of public education in Canada; wrote to the English booksellers and got their consent to the arrangement, shewed me much kindness, and invited me to dine at his residence, in company with some distinguished English statesmen, among whom was Sir Charles Wood (afterwards a peer), and the late Marquis of Lansdowne, the Nestor of English statesmen, and beside whom I was seated at dinner. The Countess of Grey shewed me many kind attentions, and the Marquis of Lansdowne invited me to call the next day at Lansdowne House, and explain to him the Canadian system of education, as he was the Chairman of the Privy Council Committee on Education, and wished to know what had been done, and what might be done for the education of the labouring classes. I called at Lansdowne House, as desired, and explained as briefly and clearly as possible the Canadian school system, its popular comprehensiveness and fairness to all parties, its Christian, yet non-sectarian, character. At the conclusion of my remarks, the noble Marquis observed, "I cannot conceive a greater blessing to England than the introduction into it of the Canadian school system; but, from our historical traditions and present state of society, all we can do is to aid by Parliamentary grants the cause of popular education through the agency of voluntary associations and religious denominations."

Five years afterwards, in another educational tour in Europe, myself and daughter spent some months at the Paris Exhibition in 1855. The Earl and Countess of Grey, seeing our names on the Canadian Book of the Exhibition, called and left their cards at our hotel. We returned the call the following day, when the Earl and Countess told us they had an aunt at Rome devoted to the fine arts, who would have great pleasure in assisting us to select copies of great masters for our Canadian Educational Museum; that they would write to her, and, if we left our cards with her on our arrival, she would gladly receive us. We did so, and, in less than an hour after, we received a most friendly letter from Lady Grey, saying that she had been expecting and waiting for us for some time, and writing us to come to her residence that evening, as she had invited a few friends.* In the course of the evening, I was introduced to Dr. Pantelioni with this remark, "Dr. Ryerson, if you should become ill, you cannot fall into better hands than those of Dr. Pantelioni." I replied that "I was glad to make his personal acquaintance, but hoped I should not need his professional services." But the very next day I was struck down in the Vatican while examining the celebrated painting of Raphael's Transfiguration and Dominichino's Last Communion of St. Jerome, with a cruel attack of lumbago and sciatica, rendering it necessary for four men to convey me down the long stairway to my carriage, and from thence to my room in the hotel, where I was confined for some three weeks, requiring three men for some days to turn me in bed. Language cannot describe the agony I experienced during that period. Dr. Pantelioni was sent for, and attended me daily for three weeks, and never charged me more than a dollar a visit. After two or three visits, finding that I was otherwise well, and had knowledge of government and civil affairs in Europe and America,

* These evening parties are conversazioni on a small scale. There were no suppers, but cups of tea and biscuits, chiefly for ladies; the gentlemen did not take off their gloves or sit down, but kept their hats in their hands or under their arms. We were introduced to, and conversed with various parties. Lady Grey seemed to be ubiquitous, and to know everybody, and to make all feel at home. She is the widow of General Grey, and is said to have been in early days a belle and bright star in the highest London society.

he entered into conversation with me on these subjects. I found him to be one of the most generally read and enlightened men that I had met with on the Continent.

He frequently remained from one to three hours conversing with me; and in the course of these frequent and lengthened visits, Dr. Pantelioni related the following facts:

1st. That he was one of the liberal party in Rome that opposed the despotism of the Papal government, and contributed to its overthrow, when Garibaldi for a time became supreme at Rome.

2nd. That he, with many other liberals, became convinced that the government which Garibaldi would inaugurate, would be little better than a mob, and would be neither stable nor safe.

(Garibaldi was a bold and skilful party leader, but no statesman. I witnessed his presence in the Italian Legislature, then held in Florence; he could declaim against government, and find fault, with individual acts; but he seemed to have no system of government in his own mind, and commanded little respect or attention after his first speech.)

3rd. Dr. Pantelioni stated, that under these circumstances, he, with several liberal friends, agreed to go confidentially to the Pope, who was then an exile at Gaeta, and offer their offices and influence to restore him to power at Rome, provided he would establish a constitutional government, and govern as a constitutional ruler. The pope agreed to their propositions, but when they reduced them to writing for his signature, and those of the gentlemen waiting upon him, he declined to sign his name; in consequence of which Dr. Pantelioni and his friends felt they had no sufficient ground upon their own individual word, without a scrap of writing from the pen of the pope, to influence their friends, and risk their lives; they, therefore, retired from the presence of his holiness, disappointed but not dishonored.

4th. On my recovery Dr. Pantelioni invited me to visit him at his residence. I did so and found him possessed of the best private library I had seen in Italy, or even on the continent. It filled three large rooms; one of which contained books (well arranged) of general history and literature, comprising the latest standard works in English (published both in England and America), French, German, Italian and Spanish. The second room was equally filled with shelves and books, beautifully arranged, on medical and scientific subjects of the latest date, and highest authority, in English, French, Italian, German, and Spanish, &c. The third room contained a fine and extensive collection of the latest standard works which had been published in England and the United States, France, Spain, Germany, and Italy, on Civil Government. I was not before aware that the Italian language was so rich in political literature. I selected the titles, and ordered several books in that language for myself.

5th. In the course of these conversations, Dr. Pantelioni related the efforts of himself and friends to establish a constitutional government, despairing, as they did, of any competence of the Garibaldi party to establish such a government. A deputation (of whom Dr. Pantelioni was one) went from Rome to Florence to consult the Right Honourable Richard Shiel, then the British Ambassador, or representative of the British Government, at Florence, as the British Government had no diplomatic relations with Rome. Mr. Shiel asked them what they wanted? They replied, nothing more than the protection of the British Government for twelve months, during which time they could establish a just and safe government, if protected from the interference of other governments. Mr. Shiel agreed to support their views, and Dr. Pantelioni and one or two others of the deputation took letters from Mr. Shiel on the subject to the late Viscount Palmerston and Lord John Russell, who encouraged their undertaking, entirely agreeing with the recommendations of Mr. Shiel, who, although a Roman Catholic, was a constitutional liberal. But it unfortunately happened that on the very day on which Dr. Pantelioni and his friends, after their mission to England, had intended to carry their plans into operation, the French army landed at Civita Vecchia, and having subdued the Garibaldi party at Rome, restored the Pope to the Vatican, with all his former pretensions and power.

6th. Some time afterwards, when the King of Italy overran the Papal territories, Dr. Pantelioni was nominated to the Italian Legislature for one of the new electoral divisions, but declined at once the acceptance of the nomination, and sent his resignation by the first post, well knowing the effect it might have upon his personal safety and interests at Rome, which was still under the rule of the Pope. But the partiality shown to Dr. Pantelioni by his newly enfranchised fellow-countrymen enraged the Court of Rome, which banished him from his city and country on a notice of only twenty-four hours! The London *Times* newspaper devoted some two articles to Dr. Pantelioni's history and banishment, eulogizing him in the strongest terms.

7th. Dr. Pantelioni then took up his abode at Nice, in the south of France, and there pursued his profession.

Some years afterward, when making my last educational tour on the Continent in 1867, I stopped a day with my son at Nice, and learned that there was an Italian physician residing there, an exile from Rome. I knew it must be my old physician and friend, and immediately called upon him. We were, of course, both delighted to see each other again; and he invited myself and son to spend the evening at his house, which we did. He had, since I saw him at Rome, married an English lady, who seemed in every respect worthy of him.

When in the course of the evening I expressed my sympathy with him in his exile, privation of his beautiful residence and fine library, he replied with energy, bringing his hand down strongly on the table, "I have such faith in the principles on which I have acted, and in the providence of God, that I shall just as surely go back to Rome, as that I am sure I am now talking to you." Some one or two years afterwards I learned from the newspapers, that Dr. Pantelioni had been recalled to Rome by the King of Italy, and appointed to the head of all the Roman Hospitals.

In a letter from Dr. Ryerson dated London, 30th October, 1857, he said: "On the 28th inst. we witnessed the consecration of Dr. Cronyn as Bishop of Huron, and were afterwards invited to lunch with the Archbishop of Canterbury. Several bishops were present. Afterwards we went with Dr. Cronyn to Woolwich, and dined with him at his son-in-law's (Col. Burrows)."

CHAPTER LVIII.

1859—1862.

Denominational Colleges and the University Controversy.

ONE of the most memorable controversies in which Dr. Ryerson was engaged was that on behalf of the Denominational Colleges of Upper Canada.

Unfortunately, at various stages of the discussion, the controversy partook largely of a personal character. This prevented that clear, calm, and dispassionate consideration of the whole of this important question to which it was entitled, and hence, in one sense, no good result accrued. Such a question as this was worthy of a better fate. For at that stage of our history it was a momentous one—worthy of a thoughtful, earnest and practical solution—a solution of which it was then capable, had it been taken up by wise, far-seeing and patriotic statesmen. But the opportunity was unfortunately lost; and in the anxiety in some cases to secure a personal triumph, a grand movement to give practical effect to somewhat like the comprehensive university scheme of the Hon. Robert Baldwin, of 1843, failed. Mr. Baldwin's proposal of that year was defeated by the defenders of King's College, as a like scheme of twenty years later was defeated by the champions of the Toronto University. The final result of the painful struggle of 1859–1863 was in effect as follows :—

1. Things were chiefly left in *statu quo ante bellum*.
2. An impetus was given to the denominational college principle; and that principle was emphasized.
3. Colleges with university powers were multiplied in the province.
4. Life and energy were infused into the denominational colleges.
5. Apathy and indifference prevailed (and, to some extent, still prevails) among the adherents of the Provincial University.

I have already stated that the issues raised in the memorable university contest of 1859–1863 were important. So they were, as after events have proved. The question, however, was unfortunately decided twenty years ago, not by an independent, impartial and disinterested tribunal, but by the parties in possession, whose judgment in the case would naturally be in their own favour. Besides, members of the Government at the time felt no real interest in the question, and were glad, under the shelter of official statements and opinions, to escape collision with such powerful bodies as the Wesleyan Methodists and the Church of Scotland.

This discussion originated in the presentation to the Legislature of a memorial from the Wesleyan Methodist Conference, prepared by Dr. Ryerson, dated November, 1859, to the following effect:—

That the Legislature in passing the Provincial University Act of 1853, clearly proposed and avowed a threefold object. First, the creation of a University for examining candidates, and conferring degrees in the Faculties of Arts, Law, and Medicine. Secondly, the establishment of an elevated curriculum of University education, conformable to that of the London University in England. Thirdly, the association with the Provincial University of the several colleges already established, and which might be established, in Upper Canada, with the Provincial University, the same as various colleges of different denominations in Great Britain and Ireland are affiliated to the London University—placed as they are upon equal footing in regard to and aid from the state, and on equal footing in regard to the composition of the Senate, and the appointment of examiners.

In the promotion of these objects the Conference and members of the Wesleyan Methodist Church cordially concurred; and at the first meeting after the passing of the University Act, the Senatorial Board of Victoria College adopted the programme of collegiate studies established by the Senate of the London University, and referred to in the Canadian Statute. But it soon appeared that the Senate of the Toronto University, instead of giving effect to the liberal intentions of the Legislature, determined to identify the University with one college, in contradistinction and to the exclusion of all others, to establish a monopoly of senatorial power and public revenue for one college alone; so much so, that a majority of the legal quorum of the Senate now consists of the professors of one college, one of whom is invariably one of the two examiners of their own students, candidates for degrees, honors, and scholarships. The curriculum of the University studies, instead of being elevated and conformed to that of the London University, has been revised and changed three times since 1853, and reduced by options and otherwise below what it was formerly, and below what it is in the British Universities, and below what it is in the best colleges in the United States. The effect of this narrow and anti-liberal course is, to build up one College at the expense of all others, and to reduce the standard of a University degree in both Arts and Medicine below what it was before the passing of the University Act in 1853.

Instead of confining the expenditure of funds to what the law prescribed—namely, the "current expenses," and such "permanent improvements or additions to the buildings" as might be necessary for the purposes of the University and University College—new buildings have been erected at an expenditure of some hundreds of thousands of dollars, and the current expenses of the College have been increased far beyond what they were in former times of complaint and investigation on this subject.

Your memorialists therefore submit, that in no respect have the liberal and enlightened intentions of the Legislature in passing the University Act been fulfilled—a splendid but unjust monopoly for the city and college of

Toronto having been created, instead of a liberal and elevated system, equally fair to all the colleges of the country.

A Provincial University should be what its name imports, and what was clearly intended by the Legislature—a body equally unconnected with, and equally impartial to every college in the country; and every college should be placed on equal footing in regard to public aid according to its works, irrespective of place, sect, or party. It is as unjust to propose, as it is unreasonable to expect, the affiliation of several colleges in one University except on equal terms. There have been ample funds to enable the Senate to submit to the Government a comprehensive and patriotic recommendation to give effect to the liberal intentions of the Legislature in the accomplishment of these objects; but the Senate has preferred to become the sole patron of one college to the exclusion of all others, and to absorb and expend the large and increasing funds of the University, instead of allowing any surplus to accumulate for the general promotion of academical education, as contemplated and specifically directed by the statute. Not only has the annual income of the University endowment been reduced some thousands of pounds per annum by vast expenditures for the erection of buildings not contemplated by the Act, but a portion of those expenditures is for the erection of lecture-rooms, &c., for the Faculties of which the Act expressly forbids the establishment!

But whilst your memorialists complain that the very intentions of this Act have thus been disregarded and defeated, we avow our desire to be the same now as it was more than ten years ago, in favour of the establishment of a Provincial University, unconnected with any one college or religious persuasion, but sustaining a relation of equal fairness and impartiality to the several religious persuasions and colleges, with power to prescribe the curriculum, to examine candidates, and confer degrees, in the Faculties of Arts, Law, and Medicine.

We also desire that the University College at Toronto should be efficiently maintained; and for that purpose we should not object that the minimum of its income from the University Endowment should be even twice that of any other college; but it is incompatible with the very idea of a national University, intended to embrace the several colleges of the nation, to lavish all the endowment and patronage of the state upon one college, to the exclusion of all others. At the present time, and for years past, the noble University Endowment is virtually expended by parties directly or indirectly connected with but one college; and the scholarships and prizes, the honors and degrees conferred, are virtually the rewards and praises bestowed by professors upon their own students, and not the doings and decisions of a body wholly unconnected with the college. Degrees and distinctions thus conferred, however much they cost the country, cannot possess any higher literary value, as they are of no more legal value, than those conferred by the *Senatus Academicus* of the other chartered colleges.

It is therefore submitted that if it is desired to have one Provincial University, the corresponding arrangement should be made to place each of the colleges on equal footing according to their works in regard to everything emanating from the state. And if it is refused to place these colleges on equal footing as colleges of one University, it is but just and reasonable that they should be placed upon equal footing in regard to aid from the state, according to their works as separate University colleges.

It is well known that it is the natural tendency, as all experience shows, that any college independent of all inspection, control, or competition in wealth—all its officers securely paid by the state, independent of exertion or success—will in a short time, as a general rule, degenerate into inactivity, indifference, and extravagance. In collegiate institutions, as well as in the higher and elementary schools, and in other public and private affairs of life, competition is an important element of efficiency and success. The best system of collegiate, as of elementary education, is that in which voluntary effort is developed by means of public aid. It is clearly both the interest and duty of the state to prompt and encourage individual effort in regard to collegiate, as in regard to elementary, education and not to discourage it by the creation of a monopoly invidious and unjust on the one side, and on the other deadening to all individual effort and enterprise, and oppressive to the state.

We submit, therefore, that justice and the best interests of liberal education require the several colleges of the country to be placed upon equal footing according to their works. We ask nothing for Victoria College which we do not ask for every collegiate institution in Upper Canada upon the same terms.

We desire also that it may be distinctly understood that we ask no aid towards the support of any theological school or theological chair in Victoria College. There is no such chair in Victoria College; and whenever one shall be established, provision will be made for its support independent of any grant from the state.* We claim support for Victoria College according to its works as a literary institution—as teaching those branches which are embraced in the curriculum of a liberal education, irrespective of denominational theology.

We also disclaim any sympathy with the motives and objects which have been attributed by the advocates of Toronto College monopoly, in relation to our National School system. The fact that a member of our own body has been permitted by the annual approbation of the Conference to devote himself to the establishment and extension of our school system, is ample proof of our approval of that system: in addition to which we have from time to time expressed our cordial support of it by formal resolutions, and by the testimony and example of our more than four hundred ministers throughout the Province. No religious community in Upper Canada has, therefore, given so direct and effective support to the National School system as the Wesleyan community, but we have ever maintained, and we submit, that the same interests of general education for all classes which require the maintenance of the elementary school system require a reform in our University system in order to place it on a foundation equally comprehensive and impartial, and not to be the patron and mouthpiece of one college alone; and the same consideration of fitness, economy and patriotism which justify the state in co-operating with each school municipality to support a day school, require it to co-operate with each religious persuasion, according to its own educational works, to support a college The experience of all Protestant countries shows that it is, and has been, as much the province of a religious persuasion to establish a college as it is for a school municipality to establish a day school; and the same experience shows that, while pastoral and parental care can be exercised for the religious instruction of children residing at home and attending a day school, that care cannot be exercised over youth residing away from home and pursuing their higher education except in a college where the pastoral and parental care can be daily combined. We hold that the highest interests of the country, as of an individual, are its religious and moral interests; and we believe there can be no heavier blow dealt out against those religious and moral interests, than for the youth of a country destined to receive the best literary education, to be placed, during the most eventful years of that educational course, without the pale of daily parental and pastoral instruction and oversight. The results of such a system must, sooner or later, sap the religious and moral

* Since established and supported, as is the one in Montreal, by contributions from the Methodist people.

foundations of society. For such is the tendency of our nature, that with all the appliances of religious instruction and ceaseless care by the parent and pastor ; they are not always successful in counteracting evil propensities and temptations ; and therefore, from a system which involves the withdrawal or absence of all such influence for years at a period when youthful passions are strongest, and youthful temptations most powerful, we cannot but entertain painful apprehensions. Many a parent would deem it his duty to leave his son without the advantages of a liberal education, rather than thus expose him to the danger of moral shipwreck in its acquirement.

This danger does not so much apply to that very considerable class of persons whose home is in Toronto ; or to those young men whose character and principles are formed, and who, for the most part, are pursuing their studies by means acquired by their own industry and economy; or to the students of theological institutions established in Toronto, and to which the University College answers the convenient purpose of a free Grammar School, in certain secular branches. But such cases form the exceptions, and not the general rule. And if one college at Toronto is liberally endowed for certain classes who have themselves contributed or done nothing to promote liberal education, we submit that in all fairness, apart from moral patriotic considerations, the state ought to aid with corresponding liberality those other classes who for years have contributed largely to erect and sustain collegiate institutions, and who while they endeavour to confer upon youth, as widely as possible, the advantages of a sound liberal education, seek to incorporate with it those moral influences, associations, and habits which give to education its highest value, which form the true basis and cement of civil institutions and national civilization, as well as of individual character and happiness.

The various statements and propositions in this memorial were fully and ably discussed on both sides at the time before a Committee of the Legislature. The discussion itself and voluminous papers and documents on either side were published in pamphlet form and in the newspapers, so that no further reference to them is necessary. The only other point raised in the discussion which is not mentioned in the memorial, is one on which Dr. Ryerson has expressed himself clearly. That is the relations of denominational colleges to the national system of public schools. On that point he says:—

The denominational collegiate system which I advocate is in harmony with the fundamental principles of our Common School system. . . The fundamental principle of the school system is two-fold. First, the right of the parent and pastor to provide religious instruction for their children ; and to have facilities for that purpose. While the law protects each pupil from compulsory attendance at any religious reading or exercise against the wish of his parent; it also provides that within that limitation "pupils shall be allowed to receive such religious instruction as their parents and guardians shall desire, according to the general regulations which shall be provided according to law." The general regulations provide that the parent may make discretionary arrangements with the teacher on the subject; and that the clergyman of any Church shall have the right to any school house being within his charge for one hour in the week between four and five, for the religious instruction of the pupils of his own Church. Be it observed, then, the supreme right of the parent, and the corresponding right of the pastor in regard to the religious instruction of youth, even in connexion with day schools, where children are with their parents more than half of each week day, and the whole of each Sunday, is a fundamental principle of the Common School system. The less or greater extent to which the right may be exercised in various places, does not affect the principles or right itself, which is fundamental in the system. The second fundamental principle in the school system is the co-operation and aid of the State with each locality or section of the community as a condition of, and in proportion to local effort. This is a vital principle of the school system, and pervades it throughout, and is a chief element of its success. No public aid is given until a school house is provided, and a legally qualified teacher is employed, when public aid is given in proportion to the work done in the school; that is, in proportion to the number of children taught, and the length of time the school is kept open; and public aid is given for the purpose of school maps and apparatus, the prize books and libraries, in proportion to the amount provided from local sources. To the application of that principle between the State and the inhabitants of localities there is no exception whatever, except in the single case of distributing a sum not exceeding £500 per annum in aid of poor school sections in new townships, and then their local effort must precede the application for a special grant.

Such are the two fundamental principles of the school system, on which I have more than once dwelt at large in official reports.

Now apply these principles to the collegiate system of the country. First, the united right and duty of the parent and pastor. Should that be suspended when the son is away from home, or should it be provided for? Let parental affection and conscience, and not blind or heartless partisanship, reply. If, then, the combined care and duty of the parent and pastor are to be provided for as far as possible when the son is pursuing the higher part of his education, for which he must leave home, can that be done best in a denominational or non-denominational College? But one answer can be given to this question. The religious and moral principles, feelings, and habits of youth are paramount. Scepticism and partisanship may sneer at them as "sectarian," but religion and conscience will hold them as supreme. If the parent has the right to secure the religious instruction and oversight of his son at home, in connection with his school education, has he not a right to do so when his son is abroad? and is not the State in duty bound to afford him the best facilities for that purpose? And how can that be done so effectually—nay, how can it be effectually done at all—except in a college which, while it gives the secular education required by the State, responds to the parent's heart and faith to secure the higher interests which are beyond all human computation, and without the cultivation of which society itself cannot exist? It is a mystery of mysteries, that men of conscience, men of religious principle and feeling, can be so far blinded by sectarian jealousy and partizanship, as to desire for one moment to withhold from youth at the most feeble, most tempted, most eventful period of their educational training, the most potent guards, helps, and influences to resist and escape the snares and seductions of vice, and to acquire and become established in those principles, feelings, and habits which will make them true Christians, at the same time that they are educated men. Even in the interests of civilization itself, what is religious and moral stands far before what is merely scholastic and refined. The Hon. Edward Everett has truly said in a late address, " It is not political nor military power, but moral sentiments, principally under the guidance and influence of religious zeal, that has in all ages civilized the world." What creates civilization can alone preserve and advance it. The great question, after all, in the present discussion, is not which system will teach the most classics, mathematics, etc. (although I shall consider the question in this light presently), but which system will best protect, develop, and establish those higher principles of action, which are vastly more important to a country itself—apart from other and immortal considerations—than any amount of intellectual attainments in certain branches of secular knowledge. Colleges under religious control may fall short of their duty and their power of religious and moral influence; but they must be, as a general rule, vastly better and safer than a College of no religious control or character at all. At all events, one class of citizens have much more valid claims to public aid for a College that will combine the advantages of both secular and religious education, than have another class of citizens to public aid for a College which confers no benefit beyond secular teaching alone. It is not the sect, it is society at large that most profits by the high religious principles and character of its educated men. An efficient religious College must confer a much greater benefit upon the State than a non-religious College can, and must be more the benefactor of the State than the State can be to it by bestowing any ordinary amount of endowment. It is, therefore, in harmony with the first fundamental principle of the Common School system, as well as with the highest interests of society at large, that the best facilities be provided for all that is affectionate in the parent and faithful in the pastor, during the away-from-home education of youth; and that is a College under religous control, whether that control be of the Church of the parent or not.

I have already given on page 344, Dr. Ryerson's opinions in regard to the provisions of Hon. Robert Baldwin's University Bill of 1843. From the extract there inserted it will be seen that the practical objection which he raised in 1859, to the administration of the University Act of 1853, was in general harmony with the views and opinions on University matters which he had expressed fifteen or sixteen years before. A fuller expression of these opinions was given in a letter which Dr. Ryerson wrote to the *British Colonist* on the 14th of February, 1846. From that letter I make the following extracts:—

The Board of Victoria College took no part in the University question until after the introduction of a Bill into the Legislature which affected the chartered rights and relations of Victoria College. On that occasion a special meeting of the Board was called, to decide whether it would, under any circumstances, acquiesce in that Bill, and upon what terms. The Board expressed a strong opinion in favour of the general terms of the Bill, but expressed an unfavourable opinion respecting some of its details, especially the project of the "Extra mural Board," and the non-recognition of Christianity. The Board also objected to the smallness of the amount proposed to be given to Victoria College. It stated that Victoria College, having been erected by public subscription, for the purpose of "teaching the various branches of science and literature upon Christian principles," could not cease to be a literary institution, as some supposed the Bill contemplated; it stated the peculiar hardships of the aspect of the Bill to the Methodist institution, under all the circumstances (which it explained), and submitted them to the honourable and generous consideration of the Government. . . Mr. Baldwin's Bill proposed to grant the sum of £500 per annum each for several years to no less than four seminaries [besides the University]. . . It was objected to on the part of both Presbyterians and Methodists, that its application to them was not liberal enough; it was objected to on the part of King's College Council that it gave even a farthing to any of them.

Afterwards King's College Council objected to the Bill, and employed counsel to oppose it, on the ground that the Legislature had no right to interfere with their charter, or to divert any portion of King's College funds in aid of other institutions. To this plea of the King's College Council an individual member of the Victoria College Board offered an argumentative reply, contending that the endowment of King's College was the property of the Province, and upon legal, constitutional, and equitable grounds, came within the limits of Provincial legislation. This principle, I believe, is now generally admitted.

From this summary of well known facts it is evident—1. That Mr. Baldwin's Bill did contemplate giving aid to other institutions than the Toronto University. 2. That the friends of Queen's, Regiopolis, Victoria and King's Colleges did expect to derive assistance from the University funds. 3. That the objections to Mr. Baldwin's Bill on the part of the Presbyterians and

Methodists were, not that any portion of the University funds should be applied in aid of their institutions, but that the portion proposed was entirely too small. 4. That those who supported Mr. Baldwin's Bill cannot consistently object to aid being given from the University funds to institutions in connection with the Church of England, Roman Catholics and Methodists. The amount and duration of such aid is a mere prudential consideration ; the principle is the same, whether the amount of aid be five hundred or five thousand pounds, whether the duration be five years or five hundred years. . . . .

That there should be a Provincial University, furnishing the highest academical and professional education, at least in respect to law and medicine; that there should be a Provincial system of common school education, commensurate with the wants of the entire population ; that both the University and the system should be established and conducted upon Christian principles, yet free from sectarian bias or ascendancy ; that there should be an intermediate class of seminaries in connection with the different religious persuasions, who have ability and enterprise to establish them, providing on the one hand a theological education for their clergy, and on the other hand a thorough English and scientific education, and elementary classical instruction for those of the youth of their congregations who might seek for more than a common school education, or who might wish to prepare for the University, and who, not having the experience and discretion of University students, required a parental and religious oversight, in their absence from their parents ; that it would be economy and patriotic on the part of the Government to grant liberal aid to such seminaries, as well as to provide for the endowment of a University or a common school system ;—these are views which I explained and argued at length when the University question was under discussion, from 1828 to 1834 ; these are the views on which the Methodists asked in establishing the Upper Canada Academy, now Victoria College ; these are views, by pressing which, a royal charter and government aid were obtained for that institution ; these are the views which received strong confirmation in the recommendation of a despatch from Lord Goderich to Sir John Colborne in 1832, and which greatly encouraged the friends of the Upper Canada Academy in their commencing exertions. That institution was not originally intended to be a University College; nor was it sought to be made so until after the establishment of a Presbyterian University College at Kingston ; when, prompted by example and emulation, and encouragement of aid, it was thought that the operations of a University might be grafted upon those of the academy, without interfering with the more extended objects of the latter. . . . .

More than a thousand youth have received more or less instruction at the Cobourg Institution ; very few of them, apart from other considerations, have gone from it without forming a high standard of education, and a deeper conviction of its importance than they had before entertained ; it has prevented hundreds of youth from going out of the country to be educated, upon whom, and upon hundreds of others, it has conferred the benefits of a good practical education. Its buildings present the most remarkable monument of religious effort and patriotic energy which was ever witnessed in any country of the age and population of Upper Canada. . . . .

The Wesleyan Methodists have not, like the Churches of England, Scotland and Rome, derived any assistance from the clergy reserve fund, or other public aid to their clergy or churches. It is much easier to figure upon a platform than to establish educational institutions, or to preach the Gospel throughout new countries. Those who have been in Canada twelve months can do the former, and sneer at the latter. The flippant allusions of certain speakers at the late Toronto meeting to the Methodists and to Victoria College . . . were as unfounded as they were unbecoming.

The discussions on the University question at Quebec in 1860 were, as I have intimated, bitter and largely personal. Dr. Ryerson, being in the fore front of the University reformers, was singled out for special attack by some of the ablest defenders of the University. I shall not enter into detail, but will give the opening and concluding parts of Dr. Ryerson's great speech, which he made before the Committee of the Legislature on the 25th and 26th of April, 1860 :—

I am quite aware of the disadvantage under which I appear before you to-day. I am not insensible of the prejudices which may have been excited in the minds of many individuals by the occurences of the last few days; . . I am not at all insensible of the fact that the attempt has been made to turn the issue, not on the great question which demands attention, but upon my merits or demerits, my standing as a man, and the course which I have pursued. This subject, of very little importance to the Committee, . . possesses a great deal of importance to myself. No man can stand in the presence of the Representatives of the people; no man can stand, as I feel myself standing this morning, not merely in the presence of a Committee, but, as it were, in the presence of my native country, the land of my birth, affections, labours, hopes, without experiencing the deepest emotion. But how much more is that the case when attempts have been made, of the most unprecedented kind, to deprive me of all that is dear to me as a man, as a parent, as a public officer, as a minister of the Christian Church. More especially do I thus feel because reading and arranging the papers on this subject, to which my attention has been called, occupied me until five o'clock this morning. . .

Sir, the position of the question which demands our consideration this day, is one altogether peculiar, and, I will venture to say, unparalleled in this or any other country. The individuals connected with myself—the party unconnected with what may be called the National University of the country, stand as the conservators of a high standard of education, and appear before you as the advocates of a thorough course of training that will discipline, in the most effectual manner, the powers of the mind, and prepare the youth of our country for those pursuits and those engagements which demand their attention as men, Christians, and patriots, while the very persons to whom has been allotted this great interest, this important trust, stand before you as the advocates of a reduction, of a puerile system which has never invigorated the mind, or raised up great men in any country; which can never lay deep and broad the foundations of intellectual grandeur and power anywhere, but which is characterized by that superficiality which marks the proceedings of the educational institutions in the new and Western States of the neighbouring Republic. Sir, I feel proud of the position I occupy; that if I have gone to an extreme, I have gone to the proper extreme; that even if I may have pressed my views to an extent beyond the present standing, the present capabilities of the Province, my views have been upward, my course has been onward, my attempt has been to invigorate Canada with an intellect and a power, a science and a literature that will stand unabashed in the presence of any other country, while the very men who should have raised our educational standard to the highest point, who should have been the leaders in adopting a high and thorough course, have confessed during the discussion of this question, that the former standard was too high, and that they have been levelling it down, incorporating with it speculations which have never elevated the institutions of any country, and adopting a course of proceedings which never advanced any nation to the position to which I hope in God my native country will attain.

The resolutions on which these proceedings have taken place, were adopted by the Wesleyan Conference in June, 1860. Now whatever other changes may have taken place, I still adhere to the people of my youth, who were the early instruments of all the religious instruction I received until I attained manhood. Whether they are a polished and learned or a despised people, I still am not ashamed of them, nor of the humblest of their advocates or professors. I stand before you without a blush, in the immediate connection, and identified with that people. The resolutions that were adopted by the Conference, in pursuance of which the Conference appointed a large Executive Committee, consisting of nearly one hundred of the most experienced members of their body, to prepare the memorial which has been presented to Parliament, are these :—

Resolved. 1st. That it is the conviction of a large proportion, if not a large majority of the inhabitants of Canada, that their sons, in pursuing the higher branches of education (which cannot be acquired in day schools, and rarely without the youth going to a distance from the paternal roof and oversight), should be placed in institutions in which their religious instruction and moral oversight, as well as their literary training, are carefully watched over and duly provided for; a conviction practically evident by the fact that not only the members of the Wesleyan Methodist Church, and other Methodists, but the members of the Churches of England, Scotland and Rome have contributed largely, and exerted themselves to establish colleges and higher seminaries of learning for the superior education of their children.

2nd. That no provision for instruction in secular learning alone, can compensate for the absence of provision, or care, for the religious and moral instruction of youth in the most exposed, critical, and eventful periods of their lives.

3rd. That it is of the highest importance to the best interests of Canada that the Legislative provision for superior education, shall be in harmony with the conscientious convictions and circumstances of the religious persuasions, which virtually constitute the Christianity of the country.

4th. That the exclusive application of the Legislative provision for superior education, to the endowment of a college for the education of the sons of that class of parents alone who wish to educate their sons in a non-denominational institution, irrespective of their religious principles and moral character, to the exclusion of those classes of parents who wish to educate their sons in colleges or seminaries where a paternal care is bestowed upon their moral and religious interests, at the same time that they are carefully and thoroughly taught in secular learning ; is grossly illiberal, partial, unjust and unpatriotic, and merits the severest reprobation of every liberal and rightminded man of every religious persuasion and party in the country.

5. That the ministers and members of the Wesleyan Methodist Church, aided by the liberal co-operation of many other friends of Christian education, have largely and long contributed to establish and maintain Victoria College, in which provision is made for the religious instruction and oversight of students, independent of any Legislative aid—in which there are fifty-nine students in the Faculty of Arts, besides more than two hundred pupils and students in preparatory and special classes—in which no religious test is permitted by the charter in the admission of any student, or pupil, and in which many hundreds of youths of different religious persuasions, have been educated and prepared for professional and other pursuits, many of whom have already honourably distinguished themselves in the clerical, legal and medical professions, as also in mercantile and other branches of business.

6th. That Victoria College is justly entitled to share in the Legislative provision for superior education, according to the number of students in the collegiate and academical courses of instruction.

7th. That we affectionately entreat the members of our Church, to use their influence to elect, as far as possible, public men who are favourable to the views expressed in the foregoing resolutions, and do equal justice to those who wish to give a superior religious education to the youth of the country, as well as those who desire for their sons a non-religious education alone.

Dr. Ryerson concluded his speech on the 26th April. Towards its close he said:—[One of the speakers] thought to amuse the Committee, by a reference to an expression of mine, used in a letter written by me several years since, that I had meditated my system of public instruction for this country—(for I contemplated the whole system from the primary school to the University)—on some of the highest mountains in Europe, and said, using a very elegant expression, it must therefore be rather "windy." . . No one can have read the history of Greece or Scotland, or the Northern and Western parts of England, without knowing that, from elevated and secluded places, some of the finest inspirations of genius have emanated which have ever been conceived by the mind of man. There are mountains in Europe where the recluse may stand and see beneath him curling clouds, and roaring tempests spending their strength, while he is in a calm untroubled atmosphere, on the summit of a mountain of which it may be said,

> "Though round his breast the rolling clouds are spread,
> Eternal sunshine settles on his head."

And I ask whether it was unphilosophical for an individual who had examined the educational systems of various countries, and who was crossing the Alps, to retire to a mountain solitude, and there, in the abode of that "eternal sunshine," and in the presence of Him who is the fountain of light, to contemplate a system which was to diffuse intellectual and moral light throughout his native country, to survey the condition of that country as a whole, apart from its political-religious dissensions, and ask what system could be devised to enable it to take its position among the civilized nations of the world ? . .

After giving expression to his views on what he conceived to be a proper and suitable University system for the Province, he concluded with these words :—It is perfectly well known to the Committee that its time, for the last four or five days, has been occupied, not in the investigation of these principles, but by attempts to destroy what is dearer to me than life, in order to crush the cause with which I am identified; and a scene has been enacted here, somewhat resembling that which took place in a certain committee room, at Toronto, in regard to a certain Inspector-General. Every single forgetfulness or omission of mine has been magnified and tortured in every possible way, to destroy my reputation for integrity, and my standing in the country. A newspaper in Toronto, whose editor-in-chief is a man of very great notoriety, has said, since the commencement of this inquiry, that, in my early days, I made mercenary approaches to another church, but was indignantly repelled, and hence my present position. I showed the other day that I might have occupied the place of Vice-Chancellor of the University which Mr. Langton now holds, had I desired (and the proposal was made to me after my return from Europe in 1856), and I have similar records to prove that in 1825, after the commencement of my Wesleyan ministry, I had the authoritative offer of admission to the ministry of the Church of England (see pages 41 and 206). My objection, and my sole objections was, that my early religious principles and feelings were wholly owing to the instrumentality of the Methodist people, and I had been providentially called to labour among them ; not that I did not love the Church of England. Those were "saddlebag days," and I used to carry in my saddlebags two books, to which I am more indebted than to any other two books in the English language, except the Holy Scriptures, namely, the Prayer Book and the Homilies of the Church of England. At this very day, Sir, though I have often opposed the exclusive assumptions of some members of the Church of England, I only love it less than the Church with which I am immediately associated.

I have been charged with being the leader of the present

movement. I am entitled to no such honour. If I have written a line it has been as the amanuensis of my ecclesiastical superiors; if I have done anything, it has been in compliance with the wishes of those whom I love and honour; and my attachment to the Wesleyan body, and the associations and doings of my early years, have been appealed to, as a ground of claim for my humble aid in connection with this movement. Sir, the Wesleyan people, plain and humble as they were, did me good in my youth, and I will not abandon them in my old age.

I have only further to add, that whatever may be my shortcomings, and even sins, I can say with truth that I love my country; that by habit of thought, by association, by every possible sympathy I could awaken in my breast, I have sought to increase my affection for my native land. I have endeavoured to invest it with a sort of personality, to place it before me as an individual, beautiful in its proportions, as well as vigorous in all the elements of its constitution, and losing sight of all distinction of classes, sects, and parties, to ask myself, in the presence of that Being, before whom I shall shortly stand, what I could do most for my country's welfare, how I could contribute most to found a system of education that would give to Canada, when I should be no more, a career of splendour which will make its people proud of it. I may adopt the words of a poet—though they may not be very poetical:—

> 'Sweet place of my kindred, blest land of my birth,
> The fairest, the purest, the dearest on earth;
> Where'er I may roam, where'er I may be,
> My spirit instinctively turns unto thee.'

Whatever may have been the course of proceeding adopted towards me in this inquiry, I bear enmity to no man; and whatever may be the result of this investigation, and the decision of the committee, I hope that during the few years I have to live, I shall act consistently with the past, and still endeavour to build up a country that will be distinguished in its religious, social, moral, educational, and even political institutions and character; to assist in erecting a structure of intellectual progress and power, on which future ages may look back with respect and gratitude, and thus to help, in some humble degree, to place our beloved Canada among the foremost nations of the earth.

The following private letters, written to me at the time from Quebec and Kingston, by Dr. Ryerson, throw additional light upon the nature of the contest in which he was engaged. They also reveal what the character of his personal feelings and the exercise of his mind during that eventful time were.

On the 20th April, Dr. Ryerson said:—I have had a very painful and laborious week; but I hope to-morrow to be able by divine help, to answer two of my principal opponents effectually. One of these gentlemen made a very plausible speech yesterday in defence of the University, and in reply chiefly to me, but full of fallacies and misquotations.

April 27th.—I finished my defence yesterday in the presence of a densely crowded room—consisting of a large number of Legislative Councillors and members of the House of Assembly —several of whom, I was told, were quite moved when I closed, and cheered me heartily when I sat down. I was congratulated on all sides by them in the afternoon, upon the manner in which I had triumphantly defended myself. I can only say, to God be all the praise. I felt myself as weak as water. I was so depressed and affected the night before, and the morning of commencing my defence, that I could not speak without emotion and tears; but I prayed and relied upon Him who had never failed me in the hour of trial, and my personal friends were also engaged in prayer in my behalf.

As soon as I commenced, I felt as if an army of such assailants were as so many pigmies, and, my friends say, I handled them as such. The remarks of members of both Houses are various, and some of them amusing—all agreeing in the completeness of the defence. All agree also as to the extravagance and defects of the system, and the unquestionable claims of denominational colleges.

I cannot review the great goodness of God to me during this mortifying week without an overflowing heart and tears of gratitude. More conscious and manifold help from above I never experienced. I hope I may never be called to pass through such another conflict. I spoke two hours and forty minutes on the day before yesterday, and one hour and three-quarters yesterday.

May 8th.—I shall be able to send you to-morrow a copy in slips of my reply to my two principal opponents. I know not what will be the result, but I trust in God, who has done better for us than all our fears or our hopes thus far. I hear that the general conviction of members is with me. One of the Senators told me that he had heard but one opinion on the subject. There are some who are satisfied that I have gained in the contest, but who are not in favour of dividing the endowment. All seem to feel that the present system is bad, and that something must be done, and that denominational colleges must be sustained. I think the House will refuse to do anything until the evidence, etc., on the subject is laid before the country. I thank you for your very kind sympathy in my conflicts.

Kingston, June 7th—The Conference met yesterday, and seems to be in a very good spirit. A Committee was appointed, named by myself, and moved by Rev. Dr. Wood—to arrange for proceedings on the University question. The Committee met last night, and agreed to have a public meeting; and myself and one or two more to draw up resolutions to be submitted to it. I am desired to address the meeting in the evening, when it is expected there will be a great gathering. I find the preachers to be very cordial and grateful.

Kingston June 8th.—The official lay members of the Church in the city of Kingston presented a congratulatory address to the Conference this forenoon, in which they referred with great feeling and force to the University question, also to the representatives of the Conference at Quebec, and especially to myself—requesting that the *Guardian* might be more and more the medium of furnishing the connexion with facts and information on the subject, and that my Defence should be inserted in it for the information of our people.

Rev. G. R. Sanderson, seconded by Rev. W. Jeffers, moved a vote of thanks to the official members of Kingston for their address. Rev. J. Spencer, Editor of the *Guardian*, regarded the address as an attack upon himself, and said the lay members had been instigated to make the attack upon him. Dr. Wood showed that the address simply made a request. Mr. Spencer was considered to have made a great mistake for himself.

The feeling of Conference in regard to myself is very cordial and very enthusiastic on the University question. The article in *The Canadian Church* is much admired. A copy of it has been sent to the Montreal *Gazette*, also to the Kingston *Daily News*. It is an able and most scholarly article.

Kingston, June 13th.—Yesterday afternoon, the Conference considered and unanimously and cordially adopted a series of resolutions on the University question—thanking those who were at Quebec, especially myself—endorsing the memorial pamphlet. My name was received with cheers, whenever mentioned in the resolutions. In the evening, a public meeting was held, and it was a perfect ovation to myself. Some of those present thought that that was the object of the meeting. Rev. W. Jeffers, the new editor, made an excellent speech. Rev. Lachlan Taylor read extracts in a most amusing and effective manner from the Hamilton *Spectator*, *Colonist*, *Echo*, and *Church Press*. The Hon. Mr. Ferrier spoke most happily on the effect of the discussion, and also of the effect of my speech on the members of both branches of the Legislature. I was cheered throughout, and sat down with four long rounds of cheers. There was much laughter, and occasional deep feeling during my criticisms on the variations, and some of the topics of the speeches of my opponents at Quebec, especially the after-dinner speeches at the Toronto University gathering.

CHAPTER LIX.

1861-1866.

PERSONAL INCIDENTS.—DR. RYERSON'S VISITS TO NORFOLK CO.

DURING the years of 1861-1866, Dr. Ryerson was chiefly engaged in his official duties, and part of the time with the University question. There is, therefore, little to record during these years except personal matters. The following letters from two of his brothers indicate how strong was their attachment to him :—

Brantford, 4th October, 1861.—Rev. John Ryerson writes : I have derived more benefit from reading Milner's History this time than I ever did before; especially the experience, writings, &c., of St. Augustine, Cyprian, Bernard, Luther and Zwingle. St. Augustine's conversion and "confessions" have been much blessed to me. I have been led to examine with more care and prayerful attention than ever before, the power, influence, and fruits of vital godliness, as experienced and manifested in the hearts and lives of both the Greek and Latin Fathers ; and also the principal instruments of the Reformation in the sixteenth century. O ! the power, wisdom, and goodness of God ; displayed in all these scenes, matters and lives !

Kingston, May 8th, 1862.—The Rev. Geo. Ryerson writes : We arrived here safely this morning. I write this by the first mail because I feel anxious concerning you. I fear that if you undertake a journey to Quebec in your present state of weakness and disease, that it will be fatal to you. You are providentially unable to bear the bodily and mental exertion. God does not send a sick man to labour in any good work, and he requires us to use ourselves tenderly, when he weakens us.

Brantford, May 9th.—Rev. John Ryerson writes : I had no idea that you had been so seriously ill. It is, however, gratifying now to learn that you are convalescent, and the loss of a little of your "fleshly substance" may prove no great calamity. Were I to lose "forty pounds," as you have, there would be very little of me left !

Brantford, December 22nd.—Rev. John Ryerson writes: During my long missionary tour I preached about ten times, always with liberty and freedom. Since I returned home I have resumed all of my domestic and private devotional exercises, and after my missionary labours realize the return of quiet peace and spiritual communion. Recently, after much prayer, I received a great blessing to my soul, the peace of God coming down upon my heart and going all over me, and I still have peace. God is my portion, my righteousness, and my salvation all the day long.

In September, 1864, Dr. Ryerson wrote the following account of visits which he made to his native county of Norfolk :—

In compliance with many requests, I have thought it would not be improper, and might be acceptable to my Norfolk friends, for me to give an account of my visits during the last two years to my native place, and to the Island within Long Point, which my father obtained from the Crown, and which now belongs to me—marked on old maps as Pottahawk Point, but designated on later maps, and more generally known, as "Ryerson's Island."

I may remark, by way of preface, that for more than thirty-five years of my public life my constitution and brain seemed to be equal to any amount of labour which I might impose on them; but of late years, the latter has been the seat of alarming attacks and severe pain, under any protracted or intense labour; and the former has been impaired by labour and disease. Change of scene and out-door exercise have proved the most effectual remedy for both. My first adoption of this course (apart from foreign travel) was two years since, when a month's daily sea-bathing, boating and walking, at Cape Elizabeth, near Portland, State of Maine, contributed greatly to the improvement of my health and strength. After again resuming my usual work for several weeks, I found that my relief, if not safety, required a further suspension of ordinary mental labour, and diversion of my thought by new objects. I determined to visit the place of my birth and the scenes of my youth. At Port Ryerse I made myself a little skiff after the model of one I had seen at the sea-side, and in which I rowed myself to and from Ryerson's Island, a distance of some thirteen miles from Port Ryerse, and about four miles from the nearest mainland—the end of Turkey Point.

Last autumn I lodged two weeks on the farm on which I was born, with the family of Mr. Joseph Duncan, where the meals were taken daily in a room the wood-work of which I, as an amateur carpenter, had finished more than forty years ago, while recovering from a long and serious illness.

When invited to meet and address the common schools of the county of Norfolk, at a county school picnic held in a grove near Simcoe, the 24th of last June, I determined to proceed thither, not by railroad and stage, as usual, but in a skiff fifteen feet and a half long, in which I had been accustomed for some months to row in Toronto Harbour, between six and eight o'clock in the morning.

Providing, as far as possible, against the double danger of swamping and capsizing, by a canvas deck, proper ballast, and fittings of the sail, I crossed Lake Ontario alone from Toronto to Port Dalhousie in nine hours; had my skiff conveyed thence to Port Colborne on a Canadian vessel, through the Welland Canal, and proceeded along the north shore of Lake Erie, rowing in one day, half-way against head wind, from the mouth of Grand River to Port Dover, a distance of forty miles, taking refreshments and rest at farm houses, and bathing three times during the day. The following day scarcely conscious of fatigue, I delivered two addresses; the one to a vast assemblage of school pupils and their friends, in a grove; the other a lecture to teachers and trustees in the evening.

After visiting my island and witnessing the productive and excellent garden of the family that occupies it, I returned to Toronto in my skiff, by the way of Niagara river, sailing in one day between sun-rise and sun-set (stopping for three hours at Port Colborne) from Grand River to Chippewa, within two miles of the Falls. I had my skiff conveyed on a waggon over the portage from Chippewa to Queenstown (ten miles), and started from Niagara to Toronto about noon of the first Friday in July. When a little more than half way across the lake, I encountered a heavy north-east storm of rain and wind, and a fog so thick as to completely obscure the Toronto light-house, which was within a mile of me. When it became so dark that I could not see my compass, I laid my course, with the sail reefed, by the wind and waves, reaching (a mile west of my due course) the east side of the Humber Bay, between ten and eleven in the evening, and making my way, by a hard pull, to the Toronto Yacht Club House a little before midnight.

About four weeks since my son and myself made the voyage in the same skiff from Toronto to Long Point, but proceeding by railroad from Port Dalhousie to Port Colborne, intending to spend a week or two on the farm, and two or three days on the Island.

I conclude this epitomised sketch with three remarks. I am satisfied of the truth of what I have long believed, that a small boat is as safe, if not safer, than a large one, if properly constructed, fitted out, trimmed, and managed. I believe that many a large open boat, if not capsized by the wind, would have been swamped by the waves over which my little craft rode in safety.

I have never experienced the benefit of out-door exertion and the comfort of retirement to the same degree as during these excursions, besides daily riding on horseback and preparing all the wood consumed at my cottage. Between two and three years ago I found it painful labour to walk one mile, I have since walked twelve miles in a day, besides attending to other duties—an improvement of my general system, which is already acting sensibly and encouragingly on the seat of thought and nervous influence. In my lonely voyage from Toronto to Port Ryerse, the scene was often enchanting, and the solitude sweet beyond expression. I have witnessed the setting sun amidst the Swiss and Tyrolese Alps, from lofty elevations, on the plains of Lombardy, from the highest eminence of the Appenines, between Bologna and Florence, and from the crater summit of Vesuvius, but I never was more delighted and impressed (owing, perhaps, in part to the susceptible state of my feelings) with the beauty, effulgence, and even sublimity of atmospheric phenomena, and the softened magnificence of surrounding objects, than in witnessing the setting sun the 23rd of June, from the unruffled bosom of Lake Erie, a few miles east of Port Dover, and about a mile from the thickly wooded shore, with its deepening and variously reflected shadows. And when the silent darkness enveloped all this beauty, and grandeur, and magnificence in undistinguishable gloom, my mind experienced that wonderful sense of freedom and relief which come from all that suggests the idea of boundlessness—the deep sky, the dark night, the endless circle, the illimitable waters. The world with its tumult of cares seemed to have retired, and God and His works appeared all in all, suggesting the enquiry which faith and experience promptly answered in the affirmative—

> With glorious clouds encompassed round
> Whom angels dimly see;
> Will the unsearchable be found;
> Will God appear to me?

My last remark is the vivifying influence and unspeakable pleasure of visiting scenes endeared to me by many tender, and comparatively few painful recollections. Amid the fields, woods, out-door exercises, and associations of the first twenty years of my life, I have seemed to forget the sorrows, labours and burdens of more than two score years, and to be transported back to what was youthful, simple, healthy, active, and happy. I can heartily symyathise with the feelings of Sir Walter Scott when, in reply to Washington Irving, who had expressed disapprobation in the scenery of the Tweed, immortalized by the genius of the Border Minstrel, he said,—

It may be partiality, but to my eyes these gray hills and all this wild border country have beauties peculiar to themselves. I like the very nakedness of the land. It has something bold, and stern, and solitary about it. When I have been for some time in the rich scenery of Edinburgh, which is ornamented garden land, I begin to wish myself back again among my honest gray hills, and if I did not see the heather at least once a year I think I should die.

Dr. Ryerson was very bold and skilful in the management of a sail boat, as may be inferred from the foregoing incidents. On one occasion, a few years ago, while sailing on the Toronto bay in his skiff, he was overtaken by a gale, during which the steeple of Zion Church was blown down, but, through God's goodness, he reached *terra firma* in safety.

He frequently sailed his little craft, as he has mentioned, from Port Ryerse and Port Rowan to his Long Point cottage—a distance of thirteen and nine miles respectively—and that, too, in all sorts of weather, and sometimes when much larger boats would not venture outside of the harbour.

For many years Dr. Ryerson was considered one of the best shots at Long Point. When over seventy years of age, he killed from seventy to eighty duck in one day in his punt and with his own gun. In the spring of 1880, when in his seventy-eighth year, he was overtaken by darkness, and, not being able to reach his cottage, was compelled to remain all night in the marsh. Rolling himself up in his blankets, in his boat, he quietly went to sleep. In the early morning he was rewarded by capturing nine wild geese.

He crossed Lake Ontario, between Toronto and Port Dalhousie, four times alone in his skiff (only sixteen feet long), and three times accompanied by his son. Fear was unknown to him, and he never lost his presence of mind, even in the most perilous circumstances.

Another favourite recreation of his was riding. He was often seen before six o'clock in the morning enjoying a canter in the suburbs of Toronto.

Writing to me from Ridgeway in August, 1866, he said:—
To-day I left Toronto in my little skiff for Port Dalhousie.

The lake was as smooth as glass the greater part of the day, and the latter part of the day there was not a breath of wind, so that I had to row. I got into Port Dalhousie in the evening. I was at the Queen's Own camp at Thorold yesterday. I visited a large number of tents, and examined the whole mode of living, and especially of cooking. It was amusing, among other cases of the same kind, to see several young gentlemen of Toronto cooking, and others assisting. I saw them cutting their meat, etc. They have the reputation of being the best cooks in the battalion. I go to Port Colborne in the rail cars, and will proceed in my skiff to Port Ryerse, or rather to Port Dover first. I hope to get there to-morrow. I went over the battle-ground here last evening.

As many people were curious to know how Dr. Ryerson spent his time at his Long Point cottage, the following letter, written to his cousin, Major Ryerse, in April, 1873, will supply the information. It relates to one day's experience, and was about the average of these experiences there:—On leaving the island cottage, I paddled and pushed my boat about six miles in the marsh, Monday forenoon. I rowed all the way to Port Ryerse against a head wind, one part of the way so strong that I shipped a good deal of water, and got wet. I was from two to eight o'clock rowing from my cottage to Port Ryerse. I was too wet and fatigued to walk to your house, but went to bed at nine, got up at five, and started for Simcoe at six. I walked eight miles out of ten on the ice, from Port Rowan over—going the other two miles by water, in a skiff which we took with us on a hand-sled. During the first eight days I did not go out in the marsh at all, but devoted myself wholly to my papers and books. The second week I went out three times, about three hours each, got a little game, but not enough to leave any on the way, except to a few friends. I am now beginning to enjoy rest more than exertion ; and am not certain when I shall come again, or whether I shall come at all again.

While on his educational tour in 1866, Dr. Ryerson wrote to me from Napanee, and said:—There was a very large meeting in Picton on Saturday and another here to-day, and both went with me in everything, with showers of compliments and almost enthusiastic feeling.

A large number of the oldest settlers and Methodists were invited to meet me last night at Mr. Dorland's, in Adolphus-town. The service in the evening was to them a feast of fat things, and some of them spoke of it as the happiest occasion of their lives. I felt very happy with them. They said it reminded them of "old times."

CHAPTER LX.

1867.

LAST EDUCATIONAL VISIT TO EUROPE.—REV. DR. PUNSHON.

IN 1867 Dr. Ryerson made his last educational tour to Europe. On his return he prepared two elaborate reports—one on Systems of Education in Europe, and the other on the Education of the Deaf and Dumb. He also went to Paris as an Honorary Commissioner to the International Exhibition held in that city in 1867. While absent he constantly wrote to me. From his letters I make the following selections:—

Paris, January 22nd, 1867.—The pretended concessions of the Emperor of France to the French nation was not much thought of in Paris, as it is regarded here of little value. His announcement of his concessions, as being final, will do him more harm, than the concessions themselves will do good.

The Attorney-General told me to-day that I had won the the heart of Mr. Adderly, M.P., Under-Secretary of State for the Colonies, who is an able man. The Attorney-General gave me a note of introduction to him (in the absence of Lord Carnarvon) in order to introduce me to Lord Stanley, which Mr. Adderly did. He asked me many questions about our school system, and told the Attorney-General I had given him an immense deal of information in a short time.

Nice, February 25.—We left Paris Wednesday evening, and reached Marseilles Thursday noon—passing Lyons, Vienne, Avignon, etc., in the valley of the Rhone, by daylight. The scenery was very beautiful, vine-yards on the hillsides, cultivated fields, trees and shrubs green, almonds in blossom. In the afternoon we "did" Marseilles, visiting the Exchange, the Palais de Justice, the ancient and modern port with its thousands of ships,—28,000 entering it per year—ascended the lofty mount, with garden walls on its sides, to the Notre Dame church which surmounts it—a small church of the sailors hung with innumerable characteristic mementoes of their escapes from shipwreck, through the intercession of their Mother-protector! The view of the city and surrounding country, all dotted with villas, is magnificent. Next morning we started for Nice.

Toulon, the Mediterranean naval station of France, is about thirty-six miles this side of Marseilles—about one-third of the way to Nice. It is strongly fortified; its port, which is admirable, contains many French ships of war. The population is about 50,000. Between Toulon and Nice lies the town of Cannes—a rival to Nice as a resort for invalids. The scenery from Marseilles to Nice is beautiful, and sometimes grand—the sea on one side, and the gardens, fields, olive and orange orchards, hillsides and mountain slopes, dotted with hamlets and villas, on the other. In the back-ground of Nice are seen the maritime Alps. Oranges are here seen on the trees; and the trees, shrubs and flowers are green, and some of them in blossom. The breezes gentle, the sun bright and warm, the sky clear, and the atmosphere soft and balmy, one seems to inhale healthful vigour with every breath, and to behold cheerful beauty on every side.

I have here met my old friend, Dr. Pantelioni, who attended me when I was ill in Rome, who was employed by Count Cavour to negotiate with Prince Napoleon and the Emperor the treaty of the 15th September, by which the French troops have evacuated Rome; but he is now an exile from Rome, but hopes soon to return thither. He has the first medical practice here, as he had at Rome.

Florence, March 19th.—Since I wrote to you from Rome, we went to Naples, in ten hours, by railway; spent three days there, and returned, the fourth, here—in 23 hours from Naples—arriving here Sunday morning, in time to dress, get breakfast, and go to church, where we heard the liturgy read evangelically, and a good evangelical sermon. The Church at Rome is High Church; that at Florence is evangelical. But I heard an excellent service from the Dean of Ely (Mr. Goodwin), at Rome. I can give you no particulars of our tour. I do not enjoy it. I have wished a good many times that you were in my place, and that I had a week's quiet on my Island. Rome was dirty, as well as almost wholly given to superstition, though there is a strong and widespread hostility among the masses to the temporal power of the Pope. Naples was dirty, but evinced much business activity. Florence is clean, industrious, and all the people cleanly and well-dressed, except some beggars—an old legacy. But the general hostility to the priesthood is remarkable, though not surprising. The Government had gained in the recent elections, but has a difficult part to play, between the Church and Anti-Church parties, and keeping up a large army, and imposing heavy taxes, of which all complain.

Venice, March 28th.—At Florence, the British Minister introduced me to Count Usedon, the Prussian Minister at Florence, formerly at Paris, a most delightful and variously learned man, who invited me to go to his villa, but I had not time, and who told me all about the working of the Prussian System of Public Instruction, in each neighbourhood—saying that the law had not been changed at all since I was in Prussia; that the Government did nothing but inspect, and see that each locality had a school of a certain kind, and that each person educated his children; but that each locality taxed itself for the support of its school. He told me I could find nothing suitable to my purpose in Prussia, in respect to the militia organization in connection with the school system, as there was no connection between the one and the other, and that the military system was expensive, and much interfered with the ordinary employments; but that Switzerland was the place for me to learn and study the blending of the school system with military training, in consequence of which every Swiss had a good education, understood the use of arms and military drill, and was yet practical, industrious, and sober, while the whole system was very inexpensive. He gave me a letter of introduction to a friend of his in Switzerland, who could give me every information I might desire, and all needful documents.

Lake Como, April 1st.—This is the first place of rest and retirement that we have had since we came to Europe. We are inhaling fresh country air every day. We are in the centre of a natural magnificence, beauty, and grandeur such as I have never witnessed—before us the little, deep, Y-shaped lake, abounding in fish, dotted with skiffs, skirted with flower gardens, walks, shrubs, and villas, and overhung on either side by snow-capped mountains—roses and plants and green flowers at the bottom of the mountains—craggy rocks and deep snow at the top, and all apparently within a mile's distance. Here where we stop is the villa of the Duke of Meiningen, and the palace-residence of the late Queen Caroline of England (now an hotel), and the villa of the King of the Belgians—a favourite place of retirement of the late King. What I have witnessed here, in the quiet Sabbath of yesterday, has given me more impressive views of the varied beauty and magnificence of the works of God than I ever had before, though I had travelled much, and finished my sixty-fourth year the Sabbath before.

London, 30th April.—I was present two hours at the anniversary of the Church Missionary Society—heard the report (a very good one) read, and heard Lord Chichester (President), the Lord Bishop of Norwich, Dean of Carlisle, and the Lord Bishop of Cork. The speaking was evangelical—Methodistically experimental, but nothing like so able and effective as that at the Wesleyan Missionary meeting yesterday.

I attended a meeting this afternoon at City Road Chapel, to hear an address from Lord Shaftesbury on Ragged Schools, and to witness the laying of the corner-stone of a chapel schoolhouse in an alley about six minutes' walk from City Road Wesleyan Chapel—one of the most wretched neighbourhoods in London. I never knew before what the ragged poor of London, in the lanes and alleys, were. I never witnessed such a sight of squalid wretchedness—the neighbourhood literally swarming with children—every window of the houses around full of heads—all indicating that lowest degradation, but many of the children had good features and bright eyes sparkling through the encrustation of dirt. We have no such class in Canada, and I hope we never may.

Lord Shaftesbury's remarks were of the highest type of Scriptural and experimental truth—eminently practical and suggestive. His address to the poor creatures, at the laying of the corner-stone of the edifice, was full of kindness and affection—adopting even the very style of address common among the class whom he addressed. As a specimen, his Lordship said:— "I just heard a boy say behind me, 'which is him?' Now, I am him; you want to see him; and I want to see you, and to talk to you, and to do you good. We have all come here to do you good, because we love you, and the poorer you are, and the more you suffer, the more we wish to help you, and to do you good." He reminded me of the Saviour going about doing good, and of the words of Job (chap. 29), "When the ear heard me, then it blessed me, and when the eye saw me it gave witness to me, because I delivered the poor that cried, and the fatherless, and him that had none to help him," etc. (verses 11, 13, 15, and 16). It was to me an impressive, affecting, and, I trust, a useful lesson.

London, 1st May.—We attended to-day the annual meeting of the British and Foreign Bible Society. The Report was admirably read, and was most gratifying and encouraging. The speeches were excellent, and some parts of them produced a wonderful effect. The Lord Bishop of Carlisle spoke nobly and scripturally; the Dean of Carlisle spoke fervently and affectingly; the Rev. Dr. Miller spoke very ably and effectively; but Mr. Calvert (of Fiji mission), spoke irresistibly to the heart; and Dr. Phillips spoke with surpassing beauty, and charming power. The latter two are both Welshmen, and Methodists—the former a Wesleyan, and the latter a Whitfield Welsh Methodist. The Rev. Mr. Nolan spoke with great excellence; Lord Shaftesbury speaks as a matter of business, naturally, simply, but with dignity, and great force.

But the speeches of clergymen to-day, as well as yesterday,

painfully impressed me with the divided, and deplorable state of the Church of England. Indeed, I thought to-day that it was hardly in good taste, or even politic, for clergymen to give such prominence to the internal heresies and divisions of the Church, at a non-denominational meeting, and before their brethren of other denominations, and before the world. But they feel that the evil and danger is so great that they should speak out, and do so on all occasions. There have been disputes and divisions among the Methodists, on personal and political quasi-ecclesiastical grounds, but never of the grave character of those which agitate the Church of England. It is the opinion of many of the clergymen and laymen of the Church, that a formal and great separation will ere long take place between the opposing parties. But, still, I think that the heart of the Church is sound—that neither the ritualists nor the neologists touch the masses of the labouring and middle classes—only some speculative minds, and imaginary spirits, seeking for excitement in religion, as they do in reading novels, and at the theatre. But, after all, I believe, as I hope, the Church will come out of this fiery trial, better, stronger, and more qualified to do good, and with a deeper baptism of the Divine Spirit for its promotion. So far as I have had opportunity to mingle with the ministers and members, and to witness services and meetings, I think I never saw the Wesleyan body in so good a state; so perfectly at peace and united, and so devoted to their one great work; and with a fervour and depth of spirituality not excelled even in Mr. Wesley's day. The personal example and influence of the most eloquent and leading men in the Connexion is highly spiritual and practical.

London, 5th May.—During my present visit to England I have been so deeply impressed with the vast benefit to my native land by a visit to it of Rev. William Morley Punshon that I have written to him on the subject, and have got others to speak to him about it. I was rejoiced, therefore, to get from him a note to-day, dated Bristol, 4th May, as follows:—The more I think about your proposition the more I am impressed that it is in the order of Providence that I should accept it. I have always hoped that I might some day see your great continent and have the opportunity of acquainting myself with the capabilities of your country, and with the work which has been done in it; and on many accounts the present seems to be the most favourable time. If, therefore, you should honour me with an invitation, and the British Conference shall see good to appoint me, I shall place no hindrance in the way, but shall endeavour to regard it as the wish of the Lord.

London, 6th May.—I have gratefully replied to Mr. Punshon, and shall now return to Canada, satisfied that I have, with God's help, accomplished a great work for her, and that we shall reap a rich reward from the services of this honoured minister of Christ.

London, 15th May.—In a kind parting note from Rev. Dr. Elijah Hoole to Dr. Ryerson, dated Mission House, May 15th, the former says: I have written to Dr. Wood to-day, and have informed him how grateful it has been to us to renew our personal intercourse with you. When you have once taken your departure we may hardly hope to meet again, but I shall always thankfully retain the impression of the ability and purity, and Christian love, and missionary zeal, which have always distinguished your personal intercourse with us.

London, 19th June.—This day I had the pleasure of writing to Rev. William Morley Punshon, inviting him to my house when he comes to Toronto. I said to him,—You have probably learned, ere this reaches you, that the Canadian Conference, (now consisting of altogether 612 ministers and preachers), has most cordially and warmly solicited your appointment as its next President, with the request that you will visit and travel through Canada the current year. I assume that you will accept this appointment, and I understood from Rev. Gervase Smith that you would probably come to Canada, in September or October next. As Toronto is the centre of Methodism in Canada, as well as the largest city, and capital of Canada West, I assume, for reasons I have stated in a letter this day addressed to your friend, Mr. Gervase Smith, that you will make Toronto your home. I shall be most happy to entertain you and yours, on your arrival there. I shall be happy to do all in my power to consult your wishes, and promote your comfort, as well as usefulness, in Canada. I pray that the Lord will direct your steps, and prosper your way, to us in this country.

London, July 17th.—In a note from Rev. Gervase Smith to Rev. Dr. Ryerson, dated July 17th, he says:—We all seemed to feel from your first call at our house, that we were adding another valuable friendship to our list, and we followed you over the water with many kind feelings and remembrances. I am very glad to hear so cheering an account of your Conference. As far as I can see, the way is opening out for Mr. Punshon's visit to Canada, as clearly as you or his friends in this country could wish. His removal from us, even for a space, will be a great loss to us; and on grounds of friendship, especially so to myself; but I hope it is all right. It is our earnest prayer that he, and the Conference in his case, may be guided rightly. I should very much like to accompany him. I do not give up the hope of seeing you and the Canadian world, during his residence

35

among you. I have formed a secret resolution to steal away for a few weeks within the next year or two. But perhaps it is wrong to anticipate. "Ye know not what shall be on the morrow."

Toronto, 24th July.—I was thankful this day to receive from Rev. Wm. Morley Punshon a letter dated Bristol, 10th July, acknowledging mine to him of the 19th June. He says :—It brought me the only intimation which I have yet received of the request of the Canadian Conference that I should be appointed to preside over its next session. I feel humbled and thankful for this mark of the confidence of my brethren over the water, and, if Providence opens my way, shall regard myself as favoured with no mean opportunity of getting and doing good. No step in this whole matter has been of my own motion. I am simply passive in the hands of God and of His Church. You have very truly interpreted my wishes and feelings in what you have said to some of my brethren. All our affairs are in higher hands than our own; and if by God's overruling providence, I shall be assured of welcome in Canada, and enabled to work for Christ upon that continent, which I have so often longed to see, I shall regard the disruption of all older ties, and the sacrifice of present position in this country, as a small price to pay—the more, if I can aid in the establishment of a grand Methodist confederacy which shall be one of the great spiritual powers of the New World.

Dr. Ryerson adds, With a grateful heart at God's goodness in this matter, I replied to the letter on the 1st of August, 1867.

While I was in England in 1867, Dr. Ryerson wrote to me (*Toronto, August 1st,*) to say that:—The Rev. W. M. Punshon, M.A., is coming out to Canada, in October, with his family. He has addressed me several inquiries, which I answer by this mail; but I wrote him to say who you were, what your address was in London, and that you could give him every needful information and suggestion as to his best mode of proceedings. I told him I would write you, and request you to write him a line—also telling him your address, and where you could see him, if he came to London, and offering him every information in your power, that he might desire. All things go on as usual in the Office.

Rev. Gervase Smith, in a letter to Dr. Ryerson, dated at the Bristol Conference, 4th August said :—We have had many important conversations and decisions. Some of which will be interesting to you, and the Canadian friends. Mr. Punshon's appointment to Canada was made by the Conference. I need not say that we are all sorely grieved at even the temporary loss of his presence and service. But the call from Canada was loud, and Providence seemed to indicate the way thither. I need not say that you will take care of him, and let us have him back again as soon as practicable. I am sure that his sojourn among you will be made a great blessing to multitudes, and I doubt not that the future of Methodism in Canada will be influenced by it. He is also heartily appointed as our Representative to the General Conference in America. I judge that the Conference now being held here will be regarded in the future as a very important one.

CHAPTER LXI.

1867.

DR. RYERSON'S ADDRESS ON THE NEW DOMINION OF CANADA.

WHILE I was in England, in 1867, Dr. Ryerson wrote to me late in July, to say:—Some of our leading public men were anxious that I should do something to assist in placing government upon the right foundation in our new civil state. But before communicating with them I determined to write boldly, an Address to the people of Upper Canada. These friends were delighted when they learned my determination, after I had written about half my address. It was printed last evening. It will, of course, draw upon me a great deal of abuse. But I have counted the cost, and thought I ought to issue it under the circumstances. I think a reaction is already beginning. I have thought it my duty to make one more special effort to save the country from future wretchedness, if not ruin, caused by the bitter party spirit of the press, whatever it might cost me. . . I am wonderfully well; but take some exercise every day, and do not work very long at a time.

The Address was issued in pamphlet form in July, 1867, and under the title of "The New Canadian Dominion: Dangers and Duties of the People in regard to their Government." From it I make the following extracts :

While I heartily unite in your rejoicings over our new birth as a nation, I beg to address you some words on our national duties and interests. I do so because my opinions and advices have been requested by many persons deeply interested in the public welfare; because I am approaching the close of a public life of more than forty years, during which I have carefully observed the hindrances and aids of our social progress, and have taken part, since 1825, in the discussion of all those constitutional questions which involved the rights and relations of religious denominations and citizens, and which have resulted in our present system of free government and of equal rights among all religious persuasions; because my heart's desire and prayer to God is, that the new Dominion of Canada may become prosperous and happy, by beginning well, by avoiding those errors which have in time past been injurious to ourselves, and which have impeded the progress and marred the peace of other peoples, and by adopting those maxims of both feeling and conduct which the best and most experienced public men of Europe and America have enjoined as essential to the strength and happiness, the advancement and grandeur of a nation. . .

We are passing from an old into a new state of political existence. The alleged evils of former civil relations have induced the creation of new ones; and the denounced evils of a former system of government have led to the establishment of a new system. . . We have been raised from a state of colonial subordination to one of affectionate alliance with the mother country. Then the first act of wisdom and duty is, to note and avoid the evils which marred our peace and prosperity in our former state, and cultivate those feelings and develop those principles of legislation and government which have contributed most to the promotion of our own happiness and interests as well as those of other nations.

If you will call up to your recollection the events of our country's history for the last twenty years, I am sure you will agree with me that personal hostilities and party strife have been the most fatal obstacles to our happiness and progress as a people—an immense loss of time and waste of public money in party debates and struggles—a most fruitful source of partiality and corruption in legislation and government. . . .
During the last two years that there has been a cessation of party hostilities and a union of able men of heretofore differing parties for the welfare of the country, there has been an economy, intelligence and impartiality in legislation, and in the whole administration of government, not equalled for many years past, a corresponding improvement in the social feelings and general progress of the country, as well as an elevation of our reputation and character abroad, in both Europe and America. . .

In no respect is the education of a people more important than in respect to the principles of their government, their rights and duties as citizens. This does not come within the range of elementary school teaching; but I have sought to introduce, as much as possible, expositions on the principles, spirit and philosophy of government, in my annual reports, and other school addresses and documents, during the last twenty years, and so to frame the whole school system as to make its local administration an instrument of practical education to the people, in the election of representatives, and the corporate management of their affairs—embracing most of the elementary principles and practice of civil government, and doing so to a greater extent than is done in the school system of any country in Europe, or of any State in America. And the strength and success of the school system in any municipality have been in proportion to the absence of party spirit, and the union of all parties for its promotion. . . What is true in school polity is true in civil polity; and what is true in the educational branch of the public service, is true in every branch of the public service.

I am aware that many good and intelligent men, of different views and associations, regard partyism as a necessity, a normal element, in the operations of free civil government. . . I think they are in error, at least in the Canadian sense of the term party; and that this error has been at the bottom of most of our civil discords and executive abuses. I think that partyism is a clog in the machinery of civil government, as in that of school or municipal government; in which there is free discussion of measures, and of the conduct of Trustees and Councillors; and there have been elections and changes of men as well as of measures. . . When party assumptions and intolerance have gone so far as to interfere with the proper functions of government, with the constitutional rights of citizens, or of the Crown, I have, at different times, in former years, being trammelled by or dependent upon no party, endeavoured to check these party excesses, and oppressions, sometimes to the offence of one party, and sometimes to the offence of another, just as one or the other might be the transgressor. I was, of course, much assailed by the parties rebuked; but no consideration of that kind should prevent the public instructor—whether educator or preacher—from . . teaching what he believes to be true and essential to the advancement of society, please or offend whom it may, or however it may affect him personally.

I have rejoiced to observe, that many who have heretofore been men of party and of party government have resolved to inaugurate the new system of government, not upon the acute angle of party, but, upon the broad base of equal and impartial justice to all parties, the only moral and patriotic principle of government, according to my convictions, and the only principle of government to make good and great men, and make a progressive and happy country. . .

Thankful to find that the new system of civil government was to be established upon the same principles as those on which our school system has been founded and developed to the satisfaction of the country, and to the admiration of all foreign visitors; and believing that the present was the juncture of time for commencing a new and brighter era in the history of

Canada—I have felt that it had a claim to the result, in epitome at least, of my fifty years reading and meditation, and more than forty years occasional discussion, respecting these first principles of government, for the freedom, unity, happiness, advancement and prosperity of a people. . .

I believe there is a judgment, a conscience, a heart in the bosom of a people, as well as in that of an individual, not wholly corrupted—at least, so I have in time past found it in the people of Upper Canada—and to that judgment, and conscience, and heart, I appeal. If what I have written is true, and if what I have suggested is wise, just, and patriotic, I am not concerned as to what any deceptive or dishonest art can do to the contrary; for, as Robert Hall beautifully said, on a similar occasion, " Wisdom and truth, the offspring of the sky, are immortal; but cunning and deception, the meteors of the earth, after glittering for a moment, must pass away."

After devoting several pages to illustrate the evils of partyism in government, Dr. Ryerson proceeds:—This partyism in government is contrary to the avowed principles and objects of reformers in the true heroic age of Canadian reform. "Equal rights and privileges among all classes, without regard to sect or party," was the motto of the reformers of those days, and was repeated and placed upon their banners in almost every variety of style and form. And what was understood and meant by that expressive motto, in the whole administration of government, will be seen from the following facts:—The reformers and reform press of Upper Canada, hailed and rejoiced in the principles of the government of Lord Durham, Lord Sydenham and Sir Charles Bagot. The Earl of Durham, in his reply to the address of the citizens of Toronto, July, 1838, said:

> On my part, I promise you an impartial administration of government. Determined not to recognize the existence of parties, provincial or imperial, classes or races, I shall hope to receive from all Her Majesty's subjects those public services, the efficiency of which must ever mainly depend upon their comprehensivenss. Extend the veil of oblivion over the past, direct to the future your best energies, and the consequences cannot be doubted.

The favourite phrase and avowed doctrine of Lord Sydenham was "equal and impartial justice to all classes of Her Majesty's subjects." After the union of the Canadas, Lord Sydenham appointed Mr. Draper Attorney-General, and the late Mr. R. Baldwin, Solicitor-General — the first "coalition" in Upper Canada. He also intimated at the time that he attached equal importance to the return of Mr. Draper and Mr. Baldwin; and that opposition to the one as well as to the other, under whatever pretence it may be got up, is equally opposition to the Governor-General's administration. Parties and party spirit have nearly ruined the country; the object of the Governor-General is to abolish parties and party feelings by uniting what is good in both parties. . .

Lord Sydenham's two years administration of the Canadian government proved the greatest boon to Upper Canada, and the principles and policy of it were highly approved by Reformers and the Reform press generally. . .

Judge Story, in his Commentaries on the Constitution of the United States, says :—

The best talents and the best virtues are driven from office by intrigue and corruption, or by the violence of the press or of party.

In harmony with the statement of the great Judge Story, the famous French writer, M. de Tocqueville, in his Democracy in America, observes :—

It is a well authenticated fact that, at the present day, the most talented men in the United States are very rarely placed at the head of affairs, and it must be acknowledged that such has been the result in proportion as democracy has outstripped its former limits. The race of American statesmen has evidently dwindled most remarkably in the course of the last fifty years.

These remarks of M. de Tocqueville apply to some extent to Canada where there has been a manifest decline in the standing and ability of our public men. There are exceptions, but what instances have we now of the representatives or equals of the Robinsons, the Macaulays, the Bidwells, the Jones', the Lafontaines, the Hagermans, the Baldwins, the Drapers, the Willsons, and many other political men of forty and twenty years ago?* To what is this decline in public men, in an otherwise advancing country, to be ascribed but to the unscrupulous partizanship of the press and politics, which blacken character instead of discussing principles, which fight for office instead of for the public good, and that by a barbarous system of moral assassination, instead of public men respecting and protecting each other's standing, and rivalling each other's deeds of greatness and usefulness. In England, the character of public men is regarded as the most precious property of the nation; and if the personal character of any member of Parliament, or other public man, is assailed by the public press or otherwise, you will see opponents as well as friends rallying round the assailed, and sustaining and shielding him by their

* It affords me pleasure to remark, and I do so without any reference to the political opinions or relations of the gentlemen concerned, that some of our rising Canadians have entered, and others are seeking an entrance into Parliamentary life upon the ground of their own avowed principles, personal character and merit, as free men, and to exercise their talents as such, and not as the articled confederates, or protegés, or joints in the tail of partizanship. Free and independant men in the Legislature, as in the country, are the best counterpoise to faction, and the mainspring to a nation's progress and greatness. Faction dreads independent men; patriotism requires them.

testimony, as a matter of common or national concern. When Sir Robert Peel, in the last great debate of his life, objected to Lord Palmerston's Grecian policy, he referred to Lord Palmerston's character and abilities—not to depreciate and calumniate his great rival, but to exclaim, amid the applause of the House of Commons, "We are proud of the man! And England is proud of the man!" But in Canada, the language of a partizan press and politician is "down with the man; execrate and execute the man as a corruptionist and traitor!"

It is with a view to the best interests of our whole country, that I have thus addressed my fellow countrymen, contributing the results of my best thoughts and experience to your beginning well, that you may do well and be well under our new Dominion, though I cannot expect long to enjoy it. My nearly half a century of public life is approaching its close. I am soon to account for both my words and my deeds. I have little to hope or fear from man. But I wish before I go hence to see my fellow citizens of all sects and parties unite in commencing a new system of government for our country and posterity,

That all things may be so ordered and settled by their endeavours, upon the best and surest foundations, that peace and happiness, truth and justice, religion and piety, may be established among us for all generations.

On the publication of this Address, Dr. Ryerson received commendatory letters from various gentlemen throughout the Province. I select three. The first is from Mr. Jasper J. Gilkinson, Brantford, dated August 10th :—

As a Canadian and British subject, permit me to thank you for the admirable pamphlet which you have had published, as it is the one thing wanted for the instruction and guidance of the people of the Dominion, aye, and for the world. It should be circulated free throughout the land. Never in the history of any country did a more favourable opportunity arise to test the fallacy that good government can alone emanate from that of party. We have, in fact, had an illustration of no-party government during the past few years productive of peace and quiet among us, and it could be continued indefinitely, were it not for bad-hearted men.

Were men actuated solely for the welfare and progress of our country, the Government could most successfully be carried on, much in the same way as a great company; the Executive and Parliament being somewhat analagous to a board of directors and shareholders.

Your pamphlet cannot fail to be productive of immense good, for it will cause reflection on a subject but little thought of by many with a vast amount of ignorance as to the true form of government calculated to confer the greatest benefits and happiness on a people, and which, I think, you have clearly pointed out. In our present position, were the Government to try the experiment, and take Parliament into its counsels, I fancy it would succeed, by all uniting for the common good.

The second was from Mr. Wm. (now Judge) Elliot, dated London, August 20th :—

Allow me to express to you a sense of gratitude, which I feel in common, I trust, with all reasonable people, on the occasion of your address on the political aspect of the Dominion of Canada.

I have had some limited connection with political contests in this part of the Province, and what I have seen and learned impels me to offer you my humble thanks for this contribution to our political treasury.

Whether we have arrived at such a condition of society as entirely to discard party political conflict may, I suppose, admit of serious doubt. But that at this juncture your admonitions are most valuable, all who reflect on the future will, I think, acknowledge. In more than one electoral contest already, I have referred, I believe with good effect, to your remarks, and I beg of you to allow me the pleasure of thus acknowledging the value of your counsel. That you may long be spared to advance the educational interests of the country, and to allay the discord and acrimony of faction, is the sincere prayer of yours faithfully,   WILLIAM ELLIOT.

The third from a gentleman in Matilda:—

Permit me to thank you for the seasonable pamphlet you have issued on the Dominion, and the sound advice it contains, addressed to the people of this country. I have read it with pleasure, and am of opinion that it should be scattered broadcast, for the consideration of electors at this very important juncture.

CHAPTER LXII.

1868–1869.

CORRESPONDENCE WITH HON. GEORGE BROWN.—DR. PUNSHON.

ON the 24th of March, Dr. Ryerson addressed the following letter to the Hon. George Brown:—

I desire, on this the 65th anniversary of my birth, to assure you of my hearty forgiveness of the personal wrongs which, I think, you have done me in past years, and of my forgetfulness of them so far, at least, as involves the least unkindness and unfriendliness of feeling.

To express free and independent opinions on the public acts of public men, to animadvert severely upon them when considered censurable, is both the right and duty of the press; nor have I ever been discourteous, or felt any animosity towards those who have censured my official acts, or denounced my opinions. Had I considered that you had done nothing more in regard to myself, I should have felt and acted differently from what I have done in regard to you—the only public man in Canada with whom I have not been on speaking and personally friendly terms. But while I wish in no way to influence your judgment and proceedings in relation to myself, I beg to say that I cherish no other than feelings of good will, with which I hope to (as I soon must) stand before the Judge of all the earth—imploring, as well as granting forgiveness for all the wrong deeds done in the body.

On the same day Mr. Brown replied as follows:—

I have received your letter of this day, and note its contents.

I am entirely unconscious of any "personal wrong" ever done you by me, and had no thought of receiving "forgiveness" at your hands.

What I have said or written of your public conduct or writings has been dictated solely by a sense of public duty, and has never, I feel confident, exceeded the bounds of legitimate criticism, in view of all attendant circumstances. What has been written of you in the columns of the *Globe* newspaper, so far as I have observed, has been always restrained within the limits of fair criticism toward one holding a position of public trust.

As to your personal attacks on myself—those who pursue the fearless course as a politican and public journalist that I have done for a quarter of a century, cannot expect to escape abuse and misrepresentation; and assuredly your assaults have never affected my course toward you in the slightest degree. Your series of letters printed in the *Leader* newspaper some years ago, were not, I am told, conceived in a very Christian spirit, but I was ill at the time they were published, and have never read them. Your dragging my name into your controversy with the Messrs. Campbell—on a matter with which I had no personal concern whatever—was one of those devices unhappily too often resorted to in political squabbles to be capable of exciting more than momentary indignation.

The following letter from Dr. Ryerson to Mr. Brown, dated Toronto, April 13th, closed the correspondence:—Your note of the 24th ult., did not reach me until Saturday evening—night before last.

I wrote my note of that date with the view of forgetting, rather than reviving, the recollection of past discussions.

I never objected to the severest criticisms of my "public conduct or writings." My remarks had sole reference to your "personal attacks" and "assaults," made over your own name, and involving all that was dear to me as a man, and a father, and a Christian—"personal attacks" and "assaults" to which my letters in the *Leader* referred to by you, and which you had engaged to insert in the *Globe*, but afterwards refused, were a reply; in the course of which I convicted you not only of many misstatements, but of seven distinct forgeries—you, by additions, professing to quote from me in seven instances the very reverse of what I had written, and your having done all this to sustain "personal attacks" and "assaults" upon me.

Besides this, on at least two subsequent occasions, you charged me with what involved an imputation of dishonesty; and when I transmitted to you copies of official correspondence relating to the subject of your allegations, and refuting them, you refused to insert it in the *Globe*, and left your false accusations unretracted to this day.

It was to such "personal attacks" and "assaults" on your part against me, and not to any legitimate criticisms upon my "public conduct or writings," that I referred in my letter of the 24th ult.

I admit the general fairness of the *Globe* towards me during the last few months; but that does not alter the character of your former "personal attacks" and "assaults" upon me, and to which alone what you call my "personal attacks" and "assaults" upon you were but defensive replies and rejoinders.

I certainly have no reason to be dissatisfied with the results of such "personal attacks" and replies, notwithstanding your great advantage in having a powerful press at your disposal; and I am prepared for the future, as I have been for the past, though I wish, if possible, to live peaceably with all men.

Dr. Ryerson having been appointed delegate (with Dr. Punshon) to the American General Conference of 1868, at Chicago, he wrote to me from that city on the 14th of May:—

On our way here we stopped at London, where Mr. Punshon lectured nobly. We reached here Tuesday evening, and were most heartily welcomed by Bishop Janes, and by our hosts.

We were introduced to the Conference to-day, and were most cordially received. Mr. Punshon was introduced by Bishop Janes, and made a touching and noble address, which won the hearts of the Conference, and vast audience, and was frequently and loudly cheered.

I was introduced heartily and eulogistically by Bishop Simpson, and addressed the Conference. The latter part of my address was warmly cheered.

Rev. Dr. Richey, President, and Representative of the Eastern Conference of British America, was introduced by Bishop Simpson, and made a very excellent address to the Conference.

Mr. Punshon preached powerfully and gloriously before the Conference and an immense crowd to-day; all were delighted, and seemed deeply affected.

On the 18th of May, Dr. Ryerson wrote again to me:—

Mr. Punshon has made a wonderful impression here by his addresses and discourses, beyond any thing they have ever heard from the pulpit and the platform. He is to lecture to-morrow evening in the Opera House—the largest room in Chicago—and there is a great rage to get tickets. He preached there yesterday afternoon to several thousand persons, a great part of whom were affected to tears several times. I trust that many sinners were awakened, while believers were greatly comforted and encouraged.

We went out on Saturday on an excursion train to Clinton, in Iowa, 145 miles west of this, crossing the Mississippi there, by railroad, and crossing the prairies. The people of Clinton—Presbyterians, etc., and Methodists—united, and prepared an excellent dinner for three hundred and six persons, after which speeches were delivered. The North-West Railroad Company prepared the excursion gratuitously for the General Conference.

Dr. Ryerson having addressed a request to the British Conference for the re-appointment of Rev. W. M. Punshon to Canada, Rev. Gervase Smith replied on the 17th of August:—

Your first request was complied with without much debate. Mr. Punshon is transferred to you for a term. The second request raised a long discussion; the result of which was that you should be left to elect your own President next year. Mr. Arthur, Drs. Waddy and Rigg, and others, pleaded for Mr. Punshon's appointment on the ground that the preceding vote placed him under Canadian jurisdiction. But there were others who were influenced by the consideration that to leave you to elect your own President, would doubtless lead to Mr. Punshon's election. I pray that you all may be guided rightly at this important juncture.

Dr. Punshon's continued residence in Canada was a source of great delight to Dr. Ryerson. Of the wonderfully beneficial effects upon Canadian Methodism of that memorable visit, it is not necessary that I should speak. The hallowed memories of those days are engraven on thousands of hearts on both sides of the lines.

Rev. Dr. R. F. Burns, of the Fort Massey Presbyterian Church, Halifax, in a letter to the *Presbyterian Witness*, gives the following graphic account of the visit of Drs. Ryerson, Punshon, and Richey to the General Conference at Chicago. The *Wesleyan*, of Halifax, speaking of Dr. Burns' letter, says :—The reminiscence is of special interest to the editor of this paper, as he was one of the party who lunched with Dr. Ryerson at Dr. Burns' on the occasion mentioned. Dr. Burns says :—

A memory of the worthy man comes up which you will excuse me for jotting down. In the summer of 1868, during my residence in Chicago, the Quadrennial Convention of the Methodist Episcopal Church was held. It was then that I first made the acquaintance of Dr. Punshon, who came out as delegate from the English Conference to that great gathering. Dr. Matthew Richey was there representing the Methodism of Eastern, and Dr. Ryerson of Western Canada. Quite a colony of Canadian Methodists came over, including my old friend Rev. A. F. Bland, to whom the celebrated Robert Collyer expressed himself more indebted than to any other living man. I invited several of the Methodist brethren to luncheon—Drs. Ryerson and Richey of the number—(Punshon had a prior engagement). Ryerson had given his speech that forenoon, and Richey too, with characteristic ability, representing the two Canadian Conferences. Dr. Richey had, a little before, met with the accident, but yet though he had aged and failed considerably since the days when I counted him the beau-ideal of elegance in manner and style in pulpit and on platform, he bore himself with much of his former stately demeanour and fine felicity of diction. Ryerson was hale and hearty as of yore, and with perhaps less of the old tendency to tremble while speaking which surprised me so much when I first witnessed it, for, under the influence of strong feeling, and a sort of constitutional timidity, linked in him with indomitable pluck, his limbs—indeed often his whole massive frame—so shook that I have felt the platform quiver. The Rev. George Goodson told me in an undertone of an unkind remark made by a distinguished member of the Conference to his neighbour as Dr. Ryerson got up to speak, and that he had rebuked him for it, not knowing at the time who he was. This gentleman, it came out in course of conversation, was closely related to Elder Henry Ryan, a well-known minister in the old Canada Methodist Church, with whom Dr. Ryerson, in his early days, carried on a keen warfare. The Ryan-Ryerson controversy is one with which the older Canadian Methodists are familiar. Without hinting at the rudeness of his relative, I alluded to Elder Ryan when conversing with Dr. Ryerson, and got from him in graphic detail, the history of that ancient controversy in which he was a principal party. It was very keen while it lasted, but there was no bitter animus in the recital—though the old war horse pricked up his ears and seemed to "hear the sound of battle from afar." I then discovered a reason for the sharp tone of the gentleman's remarks, aforesaid, which drew forth Brother Goodson's rebuke. Though but four years of age when he left Canada, he had imbibed a dislike to his old relative's chief antagonist, and to the very people amongst whom the Ryerson party had proved victorious. Hence his remark on another occasion to a lady friend of mine, with reference to his early connection with Canada, to the effect that he was "ashamed of being born there," which so roused her patriotic spirit that she promptly retorted: "Well, I am ashamed of you for saying so." The gentleman was then one of the rising hopes of that great denomination, and has since risen to a foremost rank in it. When this little incident was mentioned to Dr. Ryerson, he richly enjoyed it, and before leaving the house, with his native gallantry, he expressed a desire to use the privileges of an old man towards the fair defendress of her country's honour, saying, naively, as we all stood, before parting in the hall, "I would like to kiss you for your patriotism?" (See chapter vii.)

While at Peake's Island, near Portland, Maine, in 1869, Dr. Ryerson met with a serious accident, which nearly proved fatal. In a letter to me, he said:—

On Monday a plank from the wharf to a vessel, on the outside of which lay our boat, fell and precipitated me some feet on the deck of the vessel; I falling on my head, shoulder, and side. I was stunned and much injured, and have suffered much from my side; but I am now getting better and am able to dress myself, and to use my right arm. My head came within six inches of the band which surrounds the hatchway. There was thus but six inches between me and sudden death! I am truly thankful for my deliverance, and for my blessings.

CHAPTER LXIII.

1870—1875.

MISCELLANEOUS CLOSING EVENTS AND CORRESPONDENCE.

ON the 23rd of April, 1870, Rev. Drs. Punshon, Wood and Taylor, Chairman and Secretaries of the Central Board of Wesleyan Missions, addressed a letter to Sir George Cartier, Minister of Militia, on the subject of sending a Methodist chaplain with the Red River expedition under General Lindsay and the present Lord Wolseley. In their letter they said :—

Believing that many who will volunteer to complete this enterprize will be members of our own church, we are desirous of securing your official sanction to the appointment of a Wesleyan Minister as Chaplain to that portion of the military expedition who are professedly attached to our doctrines and ordinances, upon such terms as may be agreed upon, affecting personal rights and military operations and duties.

This letter was merely acknowledged, and no action was taken upon it. In the following June Conference, the subject was brought up, and much feeling was evoked at Sir George Cartier's apparent want of courtesy to the Missionary Board. Sir Alexander Campbell, on seeing a report of the Conference proceedings on the subject, wrote a very kind note to Dr. Ryerson, in which he expressed his opinion that some mistake must have occurred in the matter, and that he was sure no discourtesy was thought of on the part of Sir George Cartier. To this note Dr. Ryerson replied on the 18th of June :—

I yesterday received your very kind letter of the 13th inst. I think you know too well my high respect, and even affection for you, and my expectations long since formed of your success and usefulness to the country, as a public man, to doubt my implicit confidence in any statement made by you, and my desire to meet your views as far as possible.

In the matter as relating to Sir George E. Cartier, I may remark, that the President of the Wesleyan Conference stated to me the week before its annual meeting, that a communication had been addressed by himself, and the Missionary Secretaries, to Sir George Cartier respecting our sending a Wesleyan

Minister with the Red River expedition, to supply the spiritual wants of many members of our own congregations, and proposing to confer with him (Sir G. C.) as to the arrangement; that he regarded the treatment of their letter by Sir George as discourteous, and that he thought the Conference should be informed of it, and that it should take some action on the subject. The Rev. Dr. Wood, senior Missionary Secretary, read to the Conference the correspondence and the draft of four resolutions, on the subject of which he gave notice. I was not in the Conference when this took place. On reading Dr. Wood's resolutions, I suggested some modifications of them, and prepared resolutions which he preferred to his own, and which I proposed for adoption the day after giving notice of them.

As to Sir George's courtesy, I may observe that the letter addressed to him, proposed a conference with him on the subject; that his Deputy, in reply, by direction of Sir George Cartier, as he says, acknowledged the receipt of the letter addressed to him, but though that letter was dated at Toronto, and signed officially, the answer to it was addressed simply to the "Rev. Mr. Punshon, Montreal," and no further notice taken of it to this day. And it seems that Sir George did not think it worth his while even to mention, much less submit the letter, to you and your colleagues from Upper Canada.

In regard to the question of chaplain, our view is, and the proposal contemplated by our President and Missionary Secretaries was, that the Government should not pay any salary to the chaplain, but simply provide his rations and accommodations. It is our view that the Government should not pay or appoint any chaplain, but leave to each denomination the right of doing so, if it should think proper. Each chaplain thus nominated and paid, to be recognized by the military authorities, and be subject, of course, to the military regulations. In such circumstances, it is probable there would have been three Protestant chaplains—Church of England, Presbyterian, and Methodist. I infer or assume this on the ground of experience. In our Normal School of one hundred and fifty students, each is asked his religious persuasion, and the chief minister of that persuasion is furnished with a list of the names of students adhering to or professing his Church, and the day, and hour, and place where he can give them religious instruction. The result is, that by mutual consultation and agreement of ministers, all the Presbyterians, including even the Congregationalists and Baptists, meet in one class, and receive religious instruction from one minister, the ministers agreeing to take the labour in successive sessions—one minister performing all the duty one session. The arrangement voluntarily exists among the different classes of Methodists—though Wesleyan ministers do all the work. A Church of England minister attends to the instruction and religious oversight of the Church of England students, and the chief Roman Catholic priest does the same in regard to the Roman Catholic students. Nothing can be more fair, practical, and satisfactory than a similar arrangement in regard to the Red River expedition. What may be the peculiar views, habits, etc. of the Church of England chaplain appointed and salaried by the Government, I know not; but you know as well as I do that a man being a clergyman of the Church of England is no longer a guarantee that he does not entertain and teach views and practices more subversive of unsophisticated Protestant principles and feelings than could be as successfully done by a Roman Catholic priest. Besides, as a general rule, men, especially young men, do not regard, and are not controlled, as to their own worship and pastorate, except by the services and pastoral oversight to which they are accustomed and attached; and without such influence and aid to the preservation and strengthening of moral principles, habits, and feelings, more young men are liable to be demoralized and ruined in military expeditions, such as that of the Red River, than are likely to be killed in battle or die of disease.

This is the view for which the Methodist body will contend, whatever may be the result. The Secretaries of the Bible Society went among the volunteers, while at Toronto, and proffered a Bible to each one that would accept of it, and found on inquiry, that four-fifths of the volunteers, even from Lower Canada, were Protestants, and a much larger proportion of the volunteers of Upper Canada, and a large number of them not members of the Church of England but Methodists and Presbyterians. Of course, it answers the Roman Catholic purpose, and will doubtless be acceptable to many members of the Church of England, for the Government to appoint and pay chaplains of those persuasions; but I am persuaded there will be little difference of a contrary opinion on the subject among the ministers and members of the excluded persuasions. I wish I could share with you in your expressed confidence in Sir George Cartier, but I have no such confidence in him, and especially in the ecclesiastical influence under the dictation of which he acts. Wherein I may have been misinformed, and may not have stated matters correctly, I shall be prepared to correct any such errors, when I come to reply to the various attacks which have been made upon me, in vindication of myself, and the Wesleyan Conference in regard to the complaint made, and the position assumed in respect to Sir George E. Cartier, and the Red River business.

On the 30th June, Mr. James Wallace, of Whitby, addressed Dr. Ryerson a letter on the subject, in which he said :—

A stranger to you personally, although not so to your many able, pungent, and truthful letters, connected with public matters, that have from time to time appeared in the public press : I trust you will excuse this liberty, and accept my congratulations on your last effort in that connection as published in the *Globe*.

I have some knowledge of the Red River matter, having been there during the first stages of the rebellion, and had, therefore, chances of becoming acquainted with its origin and progress that few men had; and when I see one in your position come forward so bravely and lay bare the origin of that infamous revolt, I must say that I feel proud of you as a Canadian, and not only of you, but of the body with which you are connected, who so nobly sustained you.

On the 24th August, 1870, the corner stone of the Metropolitan Church, Toronto, was laid. Dr. Ryerson felt that it was a memorable day in the annals of Methodism in Toronto. I was honoured (he said) by being selected to lay the corner stone of the Metropolitan Church. Rev. Dr. Punshon, President of the Conference was present, and delivered an admirable address. He also read one which I had prepared, but which I was unable to deliver myself. The auspicious event of the day amply repaid me for the anxiety which I had so long felt in regard to the success of the enterprise, and for the responsibility which, with other devoted brethren, I had personally assumed to secure the site, and carry to a successful issue the erection of a building which would be an honour to Methodism, and a credit to the cause in Toronto.

On the 17th March, 1871, Dr. Ryerson received a letter from the venerable Rev. Dr. James Dixon, dated Bradford, Eng., 2nd inst. In it he says :—In my eighty-third year, blind, deaf, and so paralyzed as to be unable to walk without assistance, I feel that the world is fast receding. Having sense and affection remaining, I feel desirous of holding a little fellowship once more with you, my dear old friend. The world to me looks like one of your forests with the trees cut down, except here and there one a little stronger than the rest. I look upon you as one of those vigorous forest trees still remaining. And may you long remain, a blessing to your country and the Church ! After referring to his own religious life and experiences, he concludes :—As long as I live my affection for you will never vary. I also remember other Canadian friends with great interest and affection. Farewell ! my dear old friend. We shall meet again before long in a brighter world. If you can find time, I shall be most happy to receive a line from you.

Dr. Ryerson did find time to respond to the letter of his dear

and valued friend Dr. Dixon. His venerable aspect was well remembered, when, as President of the Canada Conference in 1848, he did good and valued service for the Methodist Church in Canada.

On the 29th of June, 1871, Mr. John Macdonald and Rev. Dr. Evans having asked Dr. Ryerson to enclose to Rev. W. M. Punshon a letter urging him to continue his noble work in Canada, he did so most heartily, as the letter to be enclosed expressed the real sentiments not only of the ministers and members of the Church generally, but those of the country at large. Dr. Ryerson accompanied the letter with a note from himself, in which he said to Mr. Punshon:—To have the power, as God has given you, to mould, to a large extent, the energies and labours of six hundred ministers, and developments of the Canadian Church, and to control largely the public mind in religious and benevolent enterprises—looking at the future of our country—appears to me to present a field of usefulness that Mr. Wesley himself might have coveted in his day. All that God has enabled you to do already in this country is but the foundation and beginning of what there is the prospect of your doing hereafter by the Divine blessing. You know this is the old ground on which I first proposed to you to come to this country, and which I am sure you have no reason to regret. This is the only ground on which I ought to desire your continued connection with it.

A pleasing episode in the *Globe* controversy respecting Dr. Ryerson's "First Lessons on Christian Morals," occurred in June, 1872. Bishop Bethune, in his address to the Synod of the Diocese of Toronto, spoke of the increasing spread of evil, and of the duty of the Church, under her Divine Master, to cope with it. He said:

Her work is, confessedly, to lead fallen man to the true source of pardon, and to teach him to aim at the recovery of the moral image in which he was at first created. If the passions, and prejudices, and divisions of professing Christians themselves are a distressing hindrance to the attainment of this noble and dutiful aspiration, we have much in the condition of the world around us to warn and rouse us to a vigorous and united effort to arrest the increasing tide of sin and crime. The developments of a grossly evil spirit at the present day fill us with horror and alarm; the profligacy and wanton cruelty of which we hear so many instances, make us tremble for our social peace and safety.

It is but right to enquire to what all this enormity of wickedness is traceable, that we may come, if possible, to the remedy. That is largely to be ascribed, as all must be persuaded, to the neglect of religious instruction in early life; to the contentment of peoples and governments to afford a shallow secular education, without the learning of religious truth, or the moral obligations that it teaches. The child taught and trained for this world's vocations only, without a deep inculcation of the love and fear of God, and the penalty hereafter of an irreligious and wicked life, will have but one leading idea—self-aggrandizement and self-indulgence, and will be checked by no restraint of conscience in the way and means of securing them. Gigantic frauds will be perpetrated, if riches can thus be acquired; atrocious murders will be committed, if these will remove the barrier to unholy and polluting connections, or cast out of sight the objects of jealousy and hatred.

I have no disposition to reprobate this defect in the system of education, prevailing with the authority and support of Government among ourselves. I know the difficulty, the almost impossibility, of securing the temporal boon with the addition of the spiritual; how hard it must prove in a divided religious community to introduce among the secular lessons which are meant for usefulness and advancement in this world, that lofty and holy teaching which trains the soul for heaven. The irreverent and fierce assaults recently made upon a praiseworthy effort of the Superintendent of Education in this Province to introduce a special work for moral and religious instruction amongst our common school pupils, testify too plainly the difficulty of supplying that want.

I have confidence in the good intentions and righteous efforts of that venerable gentleman to do what he can for the amelioration of the evils which the absence of systematic religious teaching of the young must induce; so that we may have a hope that, from his tried zeal and unquestionable ability, a way may be devised by which such essential instruction shall be imparted, and the terrible evils we deplore to some extent corrected.

In response to this portion of his address, Dr. Ryerson addressed the following note to the Bishop on the 1st of July.

I feel it my bounden, at the same time most pleasurable duty, to thank you with all my heart for your more than kind reference to myself in your official charge at the opening of the recent Synod of the Diocese of Toronto; and especially do I feel grateful and gratified for your formal and hearty recognition of the Christian character of our Public School System, and of the efforts which have been made to render that character a practical reality, and not a mere dead and heartless form.

It has also been peculiarly gratifying to me to learn that your Lordship's allusions to myself and the school system were very generally and cordially cheered by the members of the Synod.

My own humble efforts to invest our school system with a Christian character and spirit have been seconded from the beginning by the cordial and unanimous co-operation of the Council of Public Instruction; and without that co-operation my own individual efforts would have availed but little.

Since the settlement of the common relationship of all religious persuasions to the State, there is a common patriotic ground for the exertions of all, without the slightest reasonable pretext for political jealousy or hostility on the part of any. On such ground of comprehensiveness, and of avowed Christian principles, I have endeavoured to construct our Public School

System; such, and such only has been my aim in the teachings of my little book on Christian Morals; and such only was the aim and spirit of the Council of Public Instruction in the recommendation of it,—a recommendation to which the Council inflexibly adheres, and which it has cordially and decidedly vindicated.

The Bishop replied on the 3rd of July, thus :—I have to thank you for your letter of the 1st instant, received last evening, and to express my gratification that I had the opportunity to bear my humble testimony to your zealous and righteous efforts to promote the sound education of the youth of this Province.

I believe that in the endeavours to give this a moral and religious direction, you have done all that, in the circumstances of the country, it was in your power to accomplish. I was glad, too, to give utterance to my protest against the shameless endeavours to hold up to public scorn the valuable little work by which you desired to give a moral and religious tone to the instruction communicated in our Common Schools. If more can be done in this direction, I feel assured you would assume any allowable amount of responsibility in the endeavour to effect it.

Wishing you many years of health and usefulness, I remain, dear Dr. Ryerson, very faithfully yours, A. N. TORONTO.

This correspondence affords a striking instance of the fact that the very earnest discussions between the writers of these notes in past years, had not diminished in any way the personal respect and kindly feeling which happily existed between them. And it was so with the late venerable Bishop Strachan, with whom Dr. Ryerson more than once measured swords in days gone by. Among his very latest utterances on the Separate School Question in the Synod of 1856, he thus referred to the Head of the Education Department and his labours :—

One new feature, which I consider of great value, and for which I believe we are altogether indebted to the able Superintendent, deserves special notice: it is the introduction of daily prayers. We find that 454 schools open and close with prayer. This is an important step in the right direction, and only requires a reasonable extension to render the system in its interior, as it is already in its exterior, nearly complete. But till it receives this necessary extension, the whole system, in a religious and spiritual view, may be considered almost entirely dead.

I do not say that this is the opinion of Dr. Ryerson, who no doubt believes his system very nearly perfect; and so far as he is concerned, I am one of those who appreciate very highly his exertions, his unwearied assiduity, and his administrative capacity. I am also most willing to admit that he has carried out the meagre provisions of the several enactments that have any leaning to religion, as far as seems consistent with a just interpretation of the law.—*Charge of* 1856, *pp.* 15, 16.

In a note dated Toronto, 2nd October, 1872, Hon. W. B. Robinson sent to Dr. Ryerson an extract from the Barrie *Northern Advance* containing an obituary notice of Dr. Ryerson. In enclosing it, Mr. Robinson said:—

I send you a Barrie paper that I think will amuse you. It is not often we are permitted to "see ourselves as others see us" when once we go "hence and are no more seen,"—but you are an exception, and I congratulate you on such being the fact; and hope the Editor will be satisfied that he is in "advance" of the times, and may have cause to give you credit for much more good work in the position you have so long held, with so much benefit to the country. I observed the death of your brother William in the papers a short time ago, which I suppose accounts for the mistake.

The extract from the Barrie paper is as follows:—

Most of our readers are aware of the fact that the great champion of education in Upper Canada has gone to his rest. Coming generations, so long as time lasts, will owe a debt of gratitude to Dr. Ryerson, as the only real founder of a comprehensive school system in Ontario. Through evil report and through good report he has steadily worked on his way; neither daunted by the abuse he has received, nor unduly elated by the unmeasured tribute of praise paid to his efforts in the department to which his whole life was devoted. He kept the even tenor of his way, and we think most people, unblinded by partisan prejudice, will acknowledge that his life purpose has, more than that of most men, been accomplished. He leaves behind him a structure so nearly completed that men with a tithe of his enthusiasm, and infinitely less knowledge of the educational requirements of the Province, can lay the capstone, and declare the work complete.

Hon. Marshall S. Bidwell died in New York shortly after his visit to Canada in 1872. Hon. Judge Neilson, his friend, wrote to Dr. Ryerson for particulars of Mr. Bidwell's early life, with a view to publish it in a memorial volume. This information Dr. Ryerson obtained from Sir W. B. Richards, Clarke Gamble, Esq., Q.C., and Rev. Dr. Givens, and, with his own, embodied it in a communication to Judge Neilson. In a letter to Dr. Ryerson, dated 30th April, 1873, the late Rev. Dr. Saltern Givens said:—

A short time since, Hon. W. B. Robinson informed me that a letter of condolence was written by the late Mr. Bidwell to Lady Robinson and her family, on the death of Sir John, and that he thought it would answer your purpose. . . I am sure that you will peruse it with as much pleasure as I have done.

It ought to be a matter of devout thankfulness and congratulation with us Canadians, that two of our most distinguished statesmen and jurists have left behind them such unequivocal and delightful testimonies of their faith in Christ, and of their experience of the power of His Gospel, in extracting the sting from death and in comforting the bereaved.

I am sure that Sir John's letters to Mr. Bidwell, under his similar trial, if you could obtain them, would be read with a thrill of delight and profit by their many friends throughout Canada.

When witnessing—as we have done, some forty years ago—those fierce political contests in which our departed friends were involved, how little did we think that in the evening of their days they would have been united in the bonds of Christian love and sympathy, as this interchange of friendship evinces.

The following is Mr. Bidwell's letter to Hon. W. B. Robinson, dated 24th February, 1863:—

I thank you for your kind and friendly letter, and for the particular account of the closing scenes of the life of your honoured and lamented brother. The wound inflicted by his death can never be altogether healed. The grief which it produces is natural and rational, and is not inconsistent with any of the precepts, or with the spirit of the Gospel. It is a duty, however, to keep it within bounds, and not to allow murmurs in our heart against Divine Providence. The language of our hearts should be that of the Patriarch, "The Lord gave, and the Lord taketh away, blessed be the name of the Lord." Gratitude for the gift should be mingled with our deep sorrow for the loss of it. In my own case, a consideration of the unspeakable goodness of God in having bestowed upon me such an inestimable blessing has been continually present to my mind, and trust such feelings will abound in the bosom of Lady Robinson, her family, and yourself. He, whose removal from earthly scenes your hearts deplore, was all that you could have desired, in his public and private character, and in the homage of universal veneration and esteem. Where will you find one like him? Was there not great and peculiar goodness in God's bestowing him upon you? Was he not the joy and pride of your hearts continually? Did not his presence irradiate his home, and make it like an earthly Paradise? Every pang which you may suffer attests the value of the blessing which you have so long had. Your gratitude to God, the author of every good and perfect gift, ought to be in proportion to your grief. It is to be remembered, also, that he was not cut down prematurely in the midst of his days, but had passed the period which Moses, the man of God, in his sublime and pathetic prayer (Psalm xc.) considers as the ordinary boundary of human life, and retained all his powers and faculties to the last; and that during this long life he had not been absent from his family, at least not from Lady Robinson (if I am not mistaken) except during the transient separation when he was on the circuit. It is natural that your hearts should yearn for him, should long to see him again, and enjoy the pleasure of his company; yet death must sooner or later have separated you, and longer life might have been a scene of suffering. Would it not have been inexpressibly painful to you all to have seen his mental and bodily powers decay and fade away? Such a spectacle would have been distressing and mortifying. Now his memory is associated with no humiliating recollections; but you remember him as one always admired, respected and loved. Death has set his seal upon him, and although he is removed from you to return no more to earthly scenes, you know that it is only a removal, and that he is now in a state of exalted and perfect, though ever progressive, felicity. I trust you have the most consolatory evidence that this is now his present and unalterable state, and that you constantly think as David thought and said, "I shall go to him, but he shall not return to me." In the meantime you have the consolation of knowing that while you remember him with the tenderest affection and interest, he has not forgotten you, but has a more distinct and perfect recollection of you than you have of him. That this is literally true is the conviction of my understanding, founded not only upon reason and analogy, but upon the irrefragable testimony of divine revelation. There surely is nothing in such a thought that is improbable. We have daily experience of the revival in our minds of past events long forgotten; they lived there, though dormant. Then how many well authenticated and well known instances, where persons recovered from drowning have stated that before they lost consciousness, all the scenes and incidents of their lives flashed instantaneously, as it were, upon their minds, and appeared to be present to their view. They had been treasured up there, though latent. Death does not extinguish the mental faculties, thought does not cease, but the conscious and thinking being passes from scenes present to scenes eternal. "Mortality is swallowed up of life." There would be good ground for this conviction, if revelation gave us no higher proof; but it is explicit. "Every one of us shall give account of himself to God." This necessarily implies a perfect recollection of our lives. We are to answer for all the deeds done in the body; for every idle word, for every secret and sinful thought and feeling. This requires a perfect recollection of every event, sentiment, and emotion of our lives. The soul, therefore, must carry into the unseen world a perfect recollection of its associates and friends; and as there will be no decay then of mental powers, this will be an abiding, ever-present recollection. Every holy feeling will also continue after death—conjugal, parental, filial, fraternal affections are holy; they are expressly enjoined upon us by divine authority. Love, indeed, pure, fervent affection, is the characteristic element of Heaven. It is impossible, therefore, that the holy affections should cease at death. I have, therefore, a conviction that our departed friends, whose death we mourn, remember us distinctly and with tender affection. I have dwelt upon this subject because it has afforded me in my great affliction much consolation, and if I had time, I might expatiate more fully upon it, and adduce further evidence in support of its truth.

Yes! it is a truth, and therefore it is full of consolation. While we are thinking of our departed friends with grief, they, too, are thinking of us, with at least equal affection, and this they will continue to do until we meet. In the meantime we may comfort ourselves with the thought that, to use the language of a sober and judicious commentator on the sacred Scriptures, "The separation will be short, the re-union rapturous, and the subsequent felicity uninterrupted, unalloyed, and eternal."

I have felt peculiar sympathy for Lady Robinson. I am sure her affliction must be extreme. I hope the Son of God is with her in the furnace, and that she has a consciousness of His presence. He can give both support and consolation, and both she must greatly need. He can gently, and imperceptibly, bind up and heal her wounded and bleeding heart.

I wish that I could furnish reminiscences that would be interesting to you, for I should be glad to testify my respect for the memory of your brother, but I cannot tell you anything with which you are not familiar. I remember distinctly his appearance the first time I saw him. He had just returned to Canada, after his first visit to England. I was a student at law, and had gone from Bath to Toronto, to attend the Court of King's Bench at

Michaelmas Term. He, and Lady Robinson, came from Kingston in the steamer "Frontenac." I think that Mr. Hagerman was on board also. From another passenger, I heard that on the voyage they were overtaken at night by a storm, which stove in the dead-lights, and poured a flood of water into the cabin. It was a time of alarm, probably of danger; your brother was perfectly composed. He came into court on his arrival, and upon that occasion I saw him. His appearance was striking. His features were classically and singularly beautiful; his countenance was luminous with intelligence and animation; his whole appearance that of a man of genius and a polished gentleman, equally dignified and graceful. Altogether his features, figure and manners filled my youthful imagination with admiration, which subsequent acquaintance, and opportunities to hear him at the Bar and in Parliament, only strengthened, and which was not diminished by the difference between us in our views and opinions on public affairs. I heard him frequently at the Bar, and upon some occasions, I had the honour to be junior counsel with him.

He was a consummate advocate, as well as a profound and accurate lawyer. He had extraordinary powers for a speech *impromptu*, and needed as little time for preparation for an address to a jury, or an argument to the Court, as any one I have ever known. But he was never induced by this readiness to neglect a patient and careful attention to his client's case No one could be more faithful. He studied every case thoroughly, examined all the particular circumstances, made himself master of its details, and considered it carefully, in all its aspects and relations. I do not think he ever delivered a speech from memory. He was self-possessed in the trial, his mind was vigilant, his thoughts flowed rapidly, he had rapid association of ideas, great quickness of apprehension, as well as great sagacity, and a power of arranging anything in his mind, luminously and instantaneously; his fluency was unsurpassed.

I was present upon those occasions in Parliament which aroused him to great exertions.

He was at all times a correct, elegant, interesting speaker, but upon those occasions he spoke with great force and effect.

The fire of his eye, the animation of his countenance and the elegance of his manner, combined with dignity, cannot be appreciated by any one who did not hear him. No report of his speeches, no description of his manner and appearance, can convey to others a just and adequate idea. To report him *verbatim* was impossible. His ideas flowed so rapidly, and he had such fluency of language, that no reporter could have kept pace with his delivery. He was an admirable parliamentary leader. He never exposed himself by any incautious speech or act, and never failed to detect and expose one on the other side. He was sincere and earnest in his opinions, uncompromising, frank and fearless in the expression of them. He never attempted to make a display of himself, or indulged in useless declamation; but spoke earnestly and for the purpose of producing an immediate effect. I heard that when he was in England in 1823 (I think that was the year), the ministry had under consideration introducing him through one of their boroughs into Parliament. If it had been done, I have no doubt he would have become a distinguished member of the House of Commons, and I think it probable that he would have attained to the highest honours of the land. During two years I had the honour to be Speaker of the House of Assembly, while he was Speaker of the Legislative Council ; our official stations rendered it necessary for us to confer together concerning the business before Parliament. He was always courteous, communicative and obliging. The difference between us on political questions while I was in Parliament precluded intimate or confidential relations, but he was always pleasant and candid, and more than once did I share in that elegant hospitality which was dispensed so cordially and so gracefully by him and Lady Robinson.

I have had the honor to receive friendly letters from him occasionally since I have been here, and after my great affliction last spring he wrote to me two very kind letters for which I shall ever be grateful.

I should be sincerely glad to evince my respect for his memory. I have not space left to add anything respecting his judicial character and career, but this is unimportant. Every one in Canada knows it.

Writing to me after the Conference at London, in June, 1873, Dr. Ryerson said:—The proceedings of the Conference were very harmonious, and the discussions very able and courteous upon the whole. I received many thanks for my labours in connection with the scheme for Methodist Confederation and for union with the New Connexion Methodists. I trust I have been able, through Divine goodness, to render some service to the good cause.

In a letter to Dr. Ryerson from Rev. Dr. Punshon, dated 2nd December, the latter expressed some fears as to one or two points in the future of the General Conference arrangement. He says:—

I am looking with some solicitude to the result of the Appeal to the Quarterly Meetings on the Union question. I hope it will be carried, though your modifications of the scheme do not quite meet my approval, as one who would like to see a statesman's view taken of things. I do not see the bond of cohesion twenty years hence, when those who are now personally known to, and therefore interested in, each other, have passed off the stage. Then the General Conference will meet as perfect strangers, having hardly a common interest but that of a common name; and as there are no General Superintendents, who know all the Conferences, there will not be, as in the States, any link to bind them together. I trust some remedy will be found for this, or the lack of such link will be disastrous.

We are losing our prominent men. You will have seen that Mr. Heald has passed away—also Mr. Marshall, another Stockport "pillar." I am greatly concerned about my dear friend, Gervase Smith, the Secretary of the Conference. He has overtaxed himself, and is very ill. Absolute rest is enjoined for some time. It would be a sad day for me, if dear Gervase were to pass from my side. We have just heard of the loss of the "Ville du Havre," with 226 lives. Emile Cook, from Paris, was on board, and injured by the collision. How terrible! Now, my dear Dr. Ryerson, the good Lord be with you, and make you always as happy in His love as you desire to be, and spare you yet for many years, to counsel and to plan for His glory and the benefit of Canada.

Writing from his Long Point Cottage to me on the 12th of April, 1873, Dr. Ryerson said:—Some days I have felt quite young; but upon the whole, I doubt whether the means which have been so successful in the past in renewing my strength, can be of much use any longer to "stave off" old age. A medical gentleman here from Port Rowan said yesterday, I looked the perfection of health at my age; but my strength I feel already to be "labour and sorrow." So true are the words of inspiration to practical life.

The union question having been carried, and the General Conference established, that body met in Toronto in September, 1874. Speaking of it Dr. Ryerson said:—In 1874 I was elected the first President of the first General Conference of the Methodist Church of Canada; consisting of an equal number of ministers and laymen, and representing the several Annual Conferences of the Dominion of Canada.

On his return home from the General Conference held in Toronto in 1874, Hon. L. A. Wilmot, a former Judge, and late Lieutenant-Governor of New Brunswick, wrote to Dr. Ryerson a note, in which he said:—How can we ever repay you and your dear family for the warm-hearted hospitality and the intellectual repast we so much enjoyed while with you? To me it is much more than a sunny memory, as you have so enriched me with treasures of thought, and words of wisdom. Really, I long to see you again, and I cannot express to you the pleasure it will afford us to welcome you all to our suburban home. We have room enough for you all, and sincerly do we pray that we may all be spared to meet again. [Mr. Wilmot has since then gone home to his reward.]

CHAPTER LXIV.

1875—1876.

CORRESPONDENCE WITH REV. J. RYERSON, DR. PUNSHON, ETC.

DR. RYERSON went up to Simcoe to preach the anniversary sermons there, in December, 1874, and hoped to have gone to Brantford to see his brother John, but was prevented. He therefore wrote to him a New Year's letter, on the 3rd January, 1875: I have often prayed for you, thinking sometimes that I was even praying with you. We have spoken of you more than once during the recent holiday salutations and good wishes, and have wished you happy returns of this season of kindly greetings and renewed friendships.

I feel to bless God that during the last several weeks I have experienced, in a deeper and brighter degree than I ever experienced before, "the love of Christ which passeth all knowledge." The pages of God's book seem to shine with a brighter lustre and a more luminous, comprehensive and penetrating power than I ever beheld in them. Without care, without fear, without a shadow of doubt, I can now, through God's wonderful grace, and by His Holy Spirit, rest my all upon Christ —lay my all upon His altar, and say, "For me to live is Christ, and to die is gain."

On Sunday afternoon we had the renewal of the Covenant Service, in the Metropolitan, and the Communion. It was a good time. I think there were more than five hundred at the Communion—the largest number I ever witnessed in America, even at a camp-meeting. It took Rev. Dr. Potts and I more than an hour to distribute the elements.

I am anxious to go up to my cottage for change and retirement, so as to be quite alone for a few weeks with my books and papers.

I am at work, as hard as I can, upon my history. On New Year's Day I worked at it for fifteen hours—writing upwards of twenty pages of foolscap, besides researches, comparing authorities, etc. I am anxious to complete the two volumes of the New England Loyalists, before I go to England in May.

In reply to Dr. Ryerson's letter of 3rd January, his brother John wrote:—

My health is still precarious. . . . My attention to religious duties (reading the Scriptures, private and meditative self-examination, etc.,) I unremittingly persevere in, but my religious enjoyment is low and my faith weak. . . This winter I have read the Life of Dr. Bradshaw, an eminent clergyman of the Church of England, some time Rector of Colchester, then of Birmingham, and then of a Rectory in the suburbs of London, where he died in 1865, at the age of eighty-nine. His ministry extended over more than sixty years. He was one of the most devoted, and singularly pious ministers whose memoirs I ever read. O! into what dwarfishness the morality, and the spiritual and elevated attainments of most Christians sink in the presence of such men! Dr. Bradshaw's life was written by Miss Marsh, the authoress of the Life of Captain Vicars, and other excellent books. I have also read the Life of Miss M. Graham, a most eminently pious and devoted lady, also a member of the Church of England. She died at the early age of twenty-eight. Another memoir—of Mrs. Winslow, from the reading of which I ought to have derived much profit, one of the holiest women of whom I ever read, was a devoted member of the English Church. She was the daughter of a wealthy West India planter, and born in the West Indies. Her father died when she was quite young. She was married to a Captain in the British army, in one of the regiments stationed in the Island of Jamaica, but singular to say, not long after her marriage, was wonderfully converted, and towards the close of his life, was the means of saving her affectionate and devoted husband, who was a nephew of the once Governor of the Colony of Massachusetts. He was very wealthy, besides his West India estate—owning a large estate in England. The wonderful piety of this devoted saint, during the long years of her widowhood, ought to humble pigmy Christians, like me, in the dust. Oh, can I ever be saved, if such men and women are only saved?

I am now reading the life and labours of Rev. Dr. Shrewsbury, a Wesleyan missionary to the West Indies and South Africa—then late in life back to England, where he died in 1866, aged seventy-three years. He was a man of ability, much industry and zeal, and of more than the medium piety of Methodist preachers generally.

In reply to this letter, Dr. Ryerson wrote to his brother on the 21st of February and said:—

You speak of the want of joy in your religious experience. I do not pray for joy, I simply pray for the indwelling of Christ, for the stamp of His image upon my soul, and for the harmony of every desire, and thought, and feeling, with His holy will, and divine glory; and there comes a "peace that passeth all understanding," a rest of the soul from fear, and anxiety—a sinking into God,—and now and then greater or less ecstacies of joy. I think we mistake when we make what is usually termed joy, the end of prayer, or of desire. I believe that even heaviness, and especially when superinduced by bodily disease, is not only consistent with a high state of grace, but even instrumental in its increase—especially of faith; the faith which realizes things invisible, as visible, and things to come, as things present.

I should like to read the biographies of which you speak, especially that of Rev. Dr. Marsh, but my time is insufficient to read what I have to read for my historical purposes. After all, biographies are very much what the biographers choose to make of their heroes. The writings of the Holy Apostles are the simple and true standard of Christian experience, practice and privilege, and help us also from sinking into despondency by the illustrations they give of human imperfections and infirmities, and directing us so plainly to the source of all strength and supply, as well as to the "God of all consolation." We will talk more of these things when I see you.

Rev. John Ryerson, in his letter of February 24th, said :—

I never pray for joy in religion ; to pray or seek for such a thing would be to begin at the wrong end ; but truly pious persons might have joy as the fruit of a real experience, as growing out of a life "hid with Christ in God," joy in believing, joy in the Holy Ghost—but what I do offer my poor prayers for, is to know my sins forgiven, my acceptance with God ; that I have a lot among the sanctified, that I have peace with God, through our Lord Jesus Christ. If I had an abiding evidence of such an experience, it would produce more or less joy. Surely the Bible is the best book ; it is "The Book ;" but still he may find many blessed illustrations of its truths, of its morality, its spirituality, in the experience and lives, not only of saints of ancient days, but many of modern times. Rev. Dr. Marsh was one of these. He was a man of great learning, and extensive reading, but he loved the Bible infinitely, and above all books, read it (I was going to say) almost continually, and died with the New Testament in his hand. I try to read God's blessed Word. I am reading the Bible through by course—five or ten chapters every day in the Old Testament, and two or so in the New, besides on my knees, I read all the Psalms through every month. But what does this amount to? Nothing, so long as I am not saved from pride. irritability, selfishness, etc., within ; the workings of which, more or less, I daily feel. This greatly troubles and distresses me; besides the remembrance of my sins of unfaithfulness, wanderings, backslidings, is grievous to me, and sometimes a burthen too heavy to be borne. The temptations, trials, sorrows, of true saints sometimes shed a little light upon my dulness, and give some strength to my weak and wavering faith.

On the 28th of February, Dr. Ryerson replied :—

I thank you for your kind and interesting letter. I did not suppose you had made joy an object or subject of prayer ; but from the tone of your letter, it appeared to me that the absence of joy, or "heaviness of spirit," had led you to judge of your state too unfavourably. I quite agree with the views you express on the subject. I have not seen Rev. Dr. Marsh's life: but I can conceive him quite worthy of what is written, and of the opinion you express respecting him. During my attendance at the Wesleyan Conference in Birmingham, in 1836, my host invited Rev. Dr. (then Mr.) Marsh, Rev. John Angell James, and several other clergymen and persons of note, to meet me. I was very much struck with Mr. Marsh's appearance, and the more so from a circumstance mentioned to me by the hostess. A short time before that, a publisher there wished to get a portrait of the Apostle St. John, to have it engraved as an illustration in some book or publication he was issuing; and Mr. Marsh was solicited to sit for the artist, as his countenance was supposed to reflect more strongly the purity and loveliness of the Apostle than any ideal that could be found. In consequence of this circumstance, I was told that Mr. Marsh was often called St. John the Apostle, from his Apostolic character and truly lovely manner and countenance. His praise was then in every mouth, as I was told, among the Dissenters as well as members of the Church of England. (See page 163.)

After Dr. Ryerson became President of the General Conference in 1874, he was gratified at the many kind things said to him by his brethren and other friends. None were more kind and loving than those contained in a letter from his friend, Rev. Dr. Punshon, who speaks of his own elevation to the Presidency of the British Conference. Dr. Punshon, in his letter to Dr. Ryerson of the 19th of February, said :—

First of all, let me congratulate you most heartily upon your well-merited elevation to the Presidency of the General Conference. They did themselves honour, and you will do them honour in their choice. My elevation here was unexpected, but very grateful, although the responsibility and work which it entails make me long for July, when, if God wills, I shall doff my regalia. I hope most earnestly to have the pleasure of seeing the Canadian representatives at the next Conference in Sheffield. I have already spoken for a very sweet home for you. It will be a great gratification to see you once again, and to enjoy sweet converse with you as of old. Mr. Gervase Smith and I are to be with relatives just across the road. So please do not delay your coming for another year, as no one knows to what place the Conference will be carried. It seems almost improper to talk about it when we remember the heavy loss into which, as into an inheritance, we have all come by the death of dear Wiseman. You would, I am sure, be very grieved to hear of it. It fell on all here like a thunder-clap. But the Lord is good, and knows what is best for us all. There is a sorrowfully-occasioned vacancy at the Mission House, which the friends say I must fill, but I cannot tell how it will go, and of course, all is premature as yet. The Lord will direct us as He has always done.

By the way, I have been set seriously thinking by Mr. Wiseman's removal, whether I had sufficiently secured, by the document I gave to Rev. Dr. Rice, that the principal of the Testimonial Fund, given to me on leaving Canada, should, at my death, pass to the Canadian Conference for the benefit of the worn-out ministers and widows. I found on enquiry that it was not so secured as to be beyond doubt. I have been in consultation with my solicitor as to the best method of effecting this. I have therefore given directions for a deed of trust to be prepared, which will state that I hold this money in trust for the " Superannuated Minister's Fund of the Methodist Church of Canada." I advise you of this as the honoured President of the General Conference. I was, on the whole, satisfied with the proceedings of the General Conference. I felt a little pang at the hasty change of name. It was inevitable to do it, at the same time, but it showed rather a leaping desire of freedom, and a wish to get as far as possible from the old mother at once, which might have, perhaps, been spared. This was not, I dare say, present to all who desired the change. I admit all the force of your able reasoning for the present—but twenty years hence the General Conference will meet as strangers, with no community of interest, and I dread the result, without a visible bond of cohesion.

Writing to me from Port Rowan in September, 1875, Dr. Ryerson said :—My friends here think that I am stronger, walk better, and appear more active than when I was last in this village. This is a common remark to me, and for which I cannot feel sufficiently thankful to my Heavenly Father. He is my portion; my all is His; and I feel that He is all and in all to me—my joy as well as my strength.

Writing from his Long Point cottage to me on the 13th April, 1876, Dr. Ryerson said :—Next Sunday will be Easter

Sunday—the 51st anniversary of my ministerial life, and what a life! Much to lament over; much to humble; with many exposures and hardships; full of various labours; abounding in heavenly blessings.

Dr. Ryerson was appointed as a representative of the Conferences of British America to the General Conference of the United States in 1876. Being unable to go, he addressed a letter to Bishop Simpson, from which I take these extracts:—

I regret that I have been unable to fulfil my last public mission in behalf of our Canadian Church to the Conference of British Methodism to go to Baltimore to look upon your General Conference, and bid a last earthly farewell to brethren whom I esteem and love so much—with whom I was first brought into church membership, by whose Bishop Hedding I was ordained both deacon and elder, and with whom I feel myself as much one this day as I did half a century ago.

My first representative mission was in 1828, to visit and urge upon the late Rev. Dr. Wilbur Fisk, of Wilbraham, Conn., the request of our Conference to become our first bishop; and had he consented, or Dr. Bangs afterwards, I believe it would have been a great blessing to Methodism in Canada; but an overruling Providence ordered it otherwise, and the extension of the work of God, through our ministry and Church, down to the present time, is one of the greatest marvels to ourselves and to others.

For thirty-one years and upwards, by the annual permission of my Conference, I have administered the governmental system of public instruction in this country; but the Government and Legislature have at length acceded to my request to retire, and have done so without reducing my official allowance; and now, in the seventy-fourth year of my age, and fifty-second of my ministry, I am enabled, in the enjoyment of good health, to go in and out, as aforetime, among my brethren, with a brightening hope and increasing desire of soon being permitted to "depart and be with Christ, which is far better," and where I feel sure of joyously meeting thousands of fellow-ministers and labourers whom I have known in the flesh on both sides of the Atlantic.

In May, 1876, Dr. Ryerson went to England to consult works on the history of America in the British Museum Library. Writing to me from near Leeds, just after his arrival, he says:—
I was most cordially received by Rev. Gervase Smith, and Dr. Punshon. The latter insisted upon my being his guest first, as he had the strongest claim upon me. I was his guest for

eight days—and they were very agreeable days to me. When I came here I was enthusiastically received by the Methodist New Connexion Conference—a most cultured, gentlemanly, and respectable body of men—their whole body being not numerous, but select.

I have thus far enjoyed my visit to this country most thoroughly—free from care, and surrounded by most kind friends and agreeable associations.

Writing to me from London, on the 17th July, he says:—I experienced a great pleasure in my visit to Ireland, in becoming personally acquainted with many of the Irish preachers, and in witnessing their conferential proceedings. They are a faithful, hard-working body of men; they have hard work to do, and their success the last year has been in advance of that of preceding years.

I have seen Mr. Longman in regard to publishing my history. He was very cordial and complimentary. I explained to him in brief the origin and scope of what I had written, and of what I intended to write, and gave him the table of contents of the first fifteen chapters—to the end of the reign of Elizabeth, and the 13th chapter on the "Protestantism of Queen Elizabeth," as published in the *Canadian Methodist Magazine*.

I was at the Houses of Lords and Commons a part of one afternoon and evening. Sir Stafford Northcote, hearing that I was there, came to me under the Speaker's gallery, and conversed with me nearly half an hour. Other members also spoke to me. Earl Grey recognized me in the street, and stopped and conversed with me.

I go to the Wesleyan Conference at Nottingham next Monday, and may probably remain there ten days. I attended four services yesterday—at 8 a.m. (communion), at the parish Church of St. James, near Piccadilly, where I was lodging; at the Temple at 11 a.m., a grand service, delightful music, and an excellent sermon from Rev. C. J. Vaughan, Master of the Temple; at 3 p.m. at Westminster Abbey—prayers read by the Dean of Lichfield, and sermon by the Dean of Richmond on the words, "Where your treasure is, there will your heart be also,"—a plain, practical sermon, but the music, etc., inferior to that of the Temple. In the evening I went to one of the most fashionable and advanced Ritualistic Churches; poor singing, poorer preaching. Everything pretentious, and certainly not attractive to me. In all three churches, the hymns and tunes were old Methodist hymns and tunes, and well sung.

Dr. Ryerson did go to the British Conference as President and Representative of the General Conference of Canada. The London *Methodist Recorder*, speaking of his presence there, said:—Rev. Dr. Punshon, the President, gave a brief and discrimating introduction to Dr. Ryerson. The Doctor's personal appearance is very prepossessing; he is grey-haired; of a fine, healthy complexion; has a gentle eye; and a full, emotional voice. He dresses in the style of the "fine old English gentleman," with a refreshing display of "linen clean and white." One scarcely knows which most to admire—the simplicity of the man, his well-furnished intellect, or his practical good sense; which most to wonder at, the real progress which has been made in this one lifetime, or the boundless possibilities of the future to which that progress leads. It is something to have rocked the cradle of an empire-Church. The audience was several times deeply moved by the Doctor's allusions to the memories of the past, but most of all when, in the conclusion of his address, he said " farewell," with a tearful expression of his own rejoicing "in the hope of eternal life."

Rev. D. Savage, who was also Representative of the General Conference, in a private note, said:—It is a grand Conference. distinguished by remarkable manifestations of Divine power, The reports which will come to you through the press cannot do justice to the influence that is abroad. Dr. Ryerson's address was eloquent and impressive. The fact that Dr. Ryerson was representative to the British Conference in 1833, and that after the lapse of forty-three years, he has returned in the same capacity, is in itself a most extraordinary event. The words in which Dr. Punshon introduced Dr. Ryerson were eloquent and kindly.

The following letters were addressed to me by Dr. Ryerson while in London, at the dates mentioned:—

September 19th.—My lodgings are just opposite the British Museum, the library of which I find of great use to me. I am absorbed in revising and completing my work. Whether it will be a success or not, is one of the uncertainties of the future.

I am glad to be here, instead of being in Toronto, during the ensuing session of our Legislature, as I do not wish to be where any party can call upon me, or use my name in respect to any measure that the Government may think proper to bring forward on the subject of education.

November 14th.—The Earl of Dufferin enclosed flattering letters of introduction to the Earl of Carnarvon and the Dean of Westminster, both of whom have received me with great cordiality. The Earl of Carnarvon shook hands with me two or three times, and said how glad he was to see and shake hands with an old Canadian, whose services to his country were spoken of as Lord Dufferin has spoken of mine. His Lordship told me he would give instructions, whenever I desired, to have every possible facility and aid given me in the Record Office in referring to any documents or papers there, relating to the history or affairs of the British Colonies.

I submitted to the Dean of Westminster the last (14th), recapitulating summary chapter on the "Relations of Early English Puritanism to Protestant Unity and Religious Liberty," for his judgment. I last evening received a kind note from him (returning the manuscript), in which he says: "I have gone through the summary of the reign of Elizabeth, and find it full of just views, rendered the more attractive by the impartiality of judgment, and by the exact knowledge of the subject which pervades the chapter. The Dean kindly suggests the use of some neutral word, such as "Roman Catholics" for "Papists," and not to use the words "Ritualists" "Ritualism," as all these words are terms of reproach, and the use of them may lay me open to the charge of partizanship. I shall adopt his suggestions.

December 7th.—With your letter I received day before yesterday a long letter from my brother John—a real news letter with some sparklings of wit. He mentions that during each of two preceding Sabbaths he had attended a quarterly meeting on neighbouring circuits, and on each day he had conducted a love-feast, preached at half-past ten in the morning, administered the Lord's Supper (one to-day to 150 alone) and preached again at half-past six in the evening, riding several miles in the afternoon between each appointment, which, I think, as he says, "is pretty well for an old man in his seventy-seventh year."

I am wonderfully well—having no pain of back, or limb, or head. I am careful of my living and exercise; but during the last three years I have worked fifteen hours each day. I have every possible facility of books, retirement, and an amanuensis; and am doing what I would have to do under less favourable circumstances on my return to Canada. It is singular that your History and other books are almost the only ones which have been furnished to the British Museum, and are found on its catalogue. I have read every word of your essay on a Central University and think it admirable, exhibiting much research, acute observation, and profound thought.

December 14th.—My present purpose is to finish and publish my purely Canadian History of the United Empire Loyalists as soon as possible, and leave the other to my executors—yourself and others—to do as you please. I am assured that my two volumes on the Puritans in Old and New England will raise a storm on both sides of the Atlantic. I wish to have nothing more to do with controversy, and I do not wish to die in a storm. I am now popular with all parties. I am sure I am right and just on the character and relation of the Puritans and their opponents; but I am strongly inclined to believe what I have written in regard to them (for I am done with them) will perhaps take better if left as a legacy, than if now put forth by myself. My reputation, and the pleasure to my country, will chiefly depend upon my United Empire Canadian History, and to that my all of strength and time is now directed until I finish it.

December 26th.—I heard Dean Stanley preach in Westminster Abbey, on Christmas Day. His sermon was able and eloquent, but disappointed me by the absence of all mention of the guilt and depravity of man, and the " good tidings," including an atonement for the pardon of guilt, and the power of the Holy Spirit to regenerate and sanctify. He is a very amiable man, and looks at the good side of everything. He enumerated ten blessings brought to man by the Incarnation of Christ, as distinguished from all the advantages of science and philosophy; but I felt, if I had not received through Christ the two blessings he omitted to mention, I should never have received the blessings, to which I owe my all, of renewal, pardon, strength and comfort and hope, in the religion of our Lord Jesus Christ.

The award to the Ontario Educational Collection at the Centennial Exhibition, at Philadelphia, was made during Dr. Ryerson's absence in England. Being a government exhibit, no medal could be awarded for it. A diploma was, however, granted by the Centennial Commission, which was declared to be—

For a quite complete and admirably arranged Exhibition, illustrating the Ontario system of Education and its excellent results; also for the efficiency of an administration which has gained for the Ontario Department a most honourable distinction among Government Educational agencies.

Such was the gratifying tribute which a number of eminent American educationists paid to the Ontario system of Education, and through it to its distinguished founder, in estimating the results of his labours as illustrated at the Centennial Exhibition.

Having communicated this to Dr. Ryerson, in England, he replied :—I cannot sufficiently express my gratitude with you to our Heavenly Father, for His abounding care and goodness in connection with the Education Department, in prospering us in our past work, and in sustaining us during all these years against attacks and adversaries on all sides. It is a singular and gratifying fact, that the Centennial Exhibition at Philadelphia should afford us, at this juncture (the year of my retiring from office), the best of all possible opportunities, to exhibit the fruits (at least in miniature) of our past policy and labours. To you, with myself, equally belongs the credit, as I am sure the pleasure and gratitude, of these signal displays of the Divine goodness to us.

During his stay in England Dr. Ryerson received a note from Rev. Dr. Jobson, dated January 25th, 1877, in which he said:—

It will afford me lasting pleasure to think that I have said or done anything towards augmenting your enjoyment on what you have been pleased to term your 'last visit to England.' I remember with pleasure your former visits, and our associations together with Princes in our Israel who have passed to "the better country—even a heavenly." And, for more than a quarter of a century, I have traced your course as an acknowledged leader and counsellor for Methodism in Canada. The result of this has been to produce within me deep reverential esteem and affection towards you, which have been only slightly expressed by such attention and acts that you are pleased to acknowledge. My best wishes will accompany you on your return to Canada; and I am sure that I express the feeling of all my ministerial friends when I say that your appearance among us at our late Conference in Nottingham heightened its interests with us and that your utterances in it render it joyously memorable to us.

CHAPTER LXV.

1877-1882.

CLOSING YEARS OF DR. RYERSON'S LIFE-LABOURS.

AFTER Dr. Ryerson's return from England, he devoted some time to the final revision of his principal work, in two volumes: *The United Empire Loyalists of America*, and to two additional volumes on the Puritans of Old and New England. These works cost him a good deal of arduous labour, but their preparation was in many respects a source of pleasure to him, and of agreeable occupation. After their completion, he lived in quiet retirement at his residence, No. 171 Victoria-street, Toronto. His pen was soon again employed in writing a series of essays on Canadian Methodism for the *Canadian Methodist Magazine*, which were afterwards re-published in book form. Immediately after his return from England, his brother John addressed him the following letter on the 23rd March, 1877:—

I heartily congratulate you on your safe arrival in your native land, and also that in health and strength you are spared to see your seventy-fourth birthday. As age advances time seems to fly more and more rapidly; and however it may be with others, certainly we are to the "margin come," and how important it is that we live in readiness, and in continual preparation for our departure.

On the 7th May, 1877, Dr. Ryerson received a letter from his brother John urging him to commence a proposed series of essays on Canadian Methodism. He says:—

I am glad that you think of writing a review of Church matters, and that there are so many leading ministers who think you ought to do so. The more I think and pray about the matter, the more I am satisfied that is a path of duty opened up to you, the pursuit of which will be a great blessing to the Church and the country in coming time. The matters referred to and somewhat explained and exhibited, with other things which doubtless will occur to you, might be :—1. Missionary Society ; 2. Ryanism ; 3. Canadian Conference formed ; 4. Clergy reserve land matter; 5. *Christian Guardian* commenced, 6. Church Land and Marriage Bill; 7. Victoria College; 8. Book-Room ; 9. Centenary celebration and fund; 10. Union with the British Conference; 11. Hudson Bay mission ; 12. Disruption with British Conference; 13. Re-union ; 14. Superannuated ministers; Contingents ; Chapel Relief, and Childrens' Funds ; 15. Remarkable camp-meetings— Beaver Dams, some one hundred and fifty professed conversion ; seventy or eighty joined the Church. Ancaster Circuit: Peter Jones converted. Yonge-

Dr. Ryerson's Private Residence and Study (in the rear building), 171 Victoria St., Toronto.

street Circuit: Mrs. Taylor converted under a sermon preached by Wm. Hay. Bay Circuit: Peter Jacobs, and many other Indians saved. Hamilton, back of Cobourg, held in time of Conference—Bishop George presiding; when and where the Rice and Mud Lake bands were all converted; a nation born in a day! 16. The first protracted meeting; held at the twenty-mile camp, by Storey and E. Evans, and Ryerson, P. E.—no previous arrangement, between two hundred and three hundred professed religion, the wonderful work spreading through most of the Niagara district.

In a letter to me dated Guelph, 9th June, 1877, Dr. Ryerson said:—I came here yesterday forenoon, and was most respectfully and cordially recieved by the Conference. In the course of the day, Rev. J. A. Williams, seconded by Rev. E. B. Ryckman, moved that I be requested to prepare a history of the principal epochs of our Church, etc. The resolution, with many kind and complimentary remarks, was unanimously passed by a standing vote. I assented, and am now committed to the work, and will lose no time in commencing—dividing my time between it and my history, which I hope to complete in a few months. I hope before the next General Conference to complete what this Conference has requested, and what, from what I hear, will be repeated by other Conferences. As I am endeavouring to do some justice to the founders of our country and its institutions, I hope to do the same for the Fathers of our Church and its institutions. I spoke last night at the reception of young men, and my remarks were very favourably received.

In a letter to me from Whitby, dated 27th June, Dr. Ryerson said:—To-day I had the great pleasure of laying the foundation stone of an important addition to the Methodist Ladies' College at Whitby. Mr. Holden kindly intimated that the trustees had decided to name the new structure "Ryerson Hall." My remarks were few, and related chiefly to the importance of female education. I referred to the great attention which was now given to the education of women, on both sides of the Atlantic. There were different theories, I said, as to how it should be done, but all were agreed that women should be educated. Even the English Universities were helping in the work. I did not believe, I said, in Colleges for both ladies and gentlemen. They should be separate. It was of vital necessity that the mothers of our land should be educated. Woman made the home, and home made the man. If the daughters were educated, the sons would not remain ignorant. Both patriotism and piety should make people encourage these institutions, which would be the pride of future generations.

On the 30th July Dr. Ryerson received an affecting letter from his brother John, enclosing to him the manuscript of his

"Reminiscences of Methodism," during his long and active life. In regard to them, he said :—

What I have written is entirely from memory. In speaking about many things I had to do with, of course I had to speak a good deal about myself, but I was writing for the public, not for you ; and if any of the facts I have referred to will be of any use to you in your Essays, I shall be glad. That use, however, can be made without mentioning my name, which I have dreaded to see in print anywhere. By prayer, reading, reflection, and God's grace helping a poor worm, I have so far overcome the natural pride of my evil nature, as to be content, and sometimes happy, in my position of nothingness. My circumstances give strength to these feelings of contentment. My age and growing weakness show me that I am come very near the margin of my poor life, and unfavourable symptoms, from time to time, strongly remind me that, with me at least, "in the midst of life, we are in death." I do not, however, deprecate, nor pray deliverance from, sudden death. My prayer is that of Charles Wesley's :—

> "In age and feebleness extreme,
> Who can a sinful worm redeem?
> Jesus, my only help Thou art,
> Strength of my failing, flesh and heart ;
> Oh ! might I catch one smile from Thee
> And drop into eternity."

Several years ago I read a poem, or part of one, written in old age by the celebrated English poetess, Mrs. Barbauld, whose sweet words I very frequently repeat. She says :—

> "Life, we have been long together,
> Through pleasant and through cloudy weather.
> 'Tis hard to part when friends are dear,
> Perhaps 'twill cost a sigh, or tear.
> Then steal away, give little warning,
> Choose thine own time ;
> Say not 'good night,' but in some happier clime,
> Bid me 'good morning.'"

These words were almost prophetic, for within three months after they were written, Dr. Ryerson left Toronto for Simcoe to attend at the dying bed of his beloved brother. Immediately after his death, Dr. Ryerson wrote to me and said :—Nothing could have been more satisfactory than the last days of my dear brother ; and it was a great comfort to him and all the family that I was with him for ten days before his departure. His responses to prayer were very hearty. He seemed to dwell in a higher region. He was so nervously sensitive that he could not only not converse, but could hardly bear being talked to. On one occasion he said, "Egerton, don't talk to me, but kiss me." One day I asked him if I should unite with him in prayer ; he answered (and this was the longest sentence during the ten days I was with him) with some warmth, "Egerton, why do you ask me that ? You know I always want you to pray with me." One day I repeated, or began to repeat, the fifth verse of the thirty-first Psalm, "Into Thy hands I commit my spirit : Thou hast redeemed me, O Lord

God of truth." He said " I have uttered these words many times. I have not a doubt upon my mind." Another day he seemed to be very happy while we united in piayer, and after responding " Amen and Amen ! " he added, " Praise the Lord."

As the General Conference of September, 1878, approached, Dr. Ryerson was anxiously hoping that the Conference would be favoured with the presence of an able counsellor and friend, Rev. Dr. Punshon. Greatly to his regret. he received a note from Dr. Punshon, saying :—

You will know by this time that I am not coming to Canada this year, but that Mr. Coley is appointed Representative to your General Conference. Among other things, Dr. Punshon said :—You will see that our Conference has been a solemn one. A minister and a lay representative were smitten with death on the premises, and died before they could be removed. These shocks did not help my already shaken nerves to regain their tone. Otherwise the Conference was a memorable success. I shall have some of my heart with you in Montreal. I trust you will have a blessed Conference, and will be able to get some solution of the transfer question, and some approach to a scheme for connexional superintendency on a broad, practical basis, thus strengthening the two weak places of your present system.

On the 31st August, 1878, Rev. Dr. Wood addressed the following note to Dr. Ryerson :—

Thirty-one years ago, when appointed by the British Conference to the office of General Superintendent of Missions in the Canada Conference, I forwarded to your address some testimonials which my brethren presented to me when giving up the chair of the New Brunswick District. I now enclose to you the resignation of my office as one of the General Secretaries of the Missionary Society, which you can either present personally, or hand over to the President. I have very pleasant recollections of the past associations, especially in the early years of the Union of 1847, to which you gave invaluable assistance in the working out of its principles, which have resulted in the present wonderful enlargement of the Methodist Church.

As was his custom, Rev. Dr. Punshon sent to Dr. Ryerson a kind note at the New Year of 1879. Speaking of Methodist affairs in England he says :—

The new year has dawned gloomily enough with us in England. I never knew such protracted commercial depression. In spite of all, however, Church enterprises are projected, and we have started our Connexional Thanksgiving Fund auspiciously, both so far as spirit and money go. It is proposed to raise £200,000 at least, and some are sanguine enough to think, if times mend, that a good deal more will be raised. There never was a meeting in Methodism like the one at City Road. It was an All-day meeting. The first hour was spent in devotional exercises, and then the contributions flowed in without pressure, ostentation, or shame. We are beginning the Circuit Meetings next week. Our Brixton one is fixed for Monday evening, but the cream of our subscriptions was announced at City Road. Dr. Rigg makes a good President.

Writing to a friend in December, 1880, Dr. Ryerson said:—

You speak of being old. I feel myself to be an old man. It is more labour for me to write one page now, than it used to be to write five pages. . . We shall soon follow those who have gone before. With you I am waiting and endeavouring to be prepared for the change, and have no fear of it, but often rejoice in the bright hopes beyond.

Again, writing to the same friend on the 9th of August, 1881, he said:—

My latest attack has reduced my strength (of which I had little to spare) very much. My desire is likely soon to be accomplished—to depart hence.

Writing to another friend on the 24th of July, 1881, Dr. Ryerson said:—I have to-day written a letter of affectionate sympathy to Rev. Dr. Punshon on the decease of his son John William. I trust that his last days were his best days.

It has always been a source of thankfulness and gratification, that I was able to show him some kind attentions during his last visit to Canada.

I have been deeply concerned to read in this morning's newspaper that Dr. Punshon himself was seriously ill. I trust and pray that the Church and nation may not yet, nor for a long time to come, be deprived of his eminent services.

I cannot tell how deeply we all sympathize with Dr. and Mrs. Punshon in this great trial.

From the last (almost illegible) letter written by Dr. Ryerson, two weeks before his death and dated 6th of February, 1882, I make the following extracts. It was addressed to Rev. Hugh Johnston, B.D., of Montreal, (now of Toronto).

I am helpless myself—have lost my hearing so that I cannot converse without a tube. I have been confined to my room for five weeks by congestion of the lungs, from which I have only partially recovered. I have not been out of the house since last September, so that I can take no part in Church affairs. But God has been with me—my strength and comforter. I am beginning to revive, but have not yet been able to go down stairs, or move, only creep about with the help of a cane. I do not know whether you can read the scrawl I have written, but I cannot write any better.

Yours most affectionately,

Monday, February 6th, 1882.   E. RYERSON.

The concluding words of Dr. Ryerson's story of his life were:—

In 1878, I was elected for the third time Representative of the Canadian to the British Conference. After the fulfilment of these functions, I have retired from all active participation in public affairs, whether of Church or State. I have finished, after twenty years' labour, my "History of the Loyalists of America and their Times." I have finished the "STORY OF MY LIFE"—imperfect and fragmentary as it is—leaving to another pen anything that may be thought worthy of record of my last days on earth, as well as any essential omissions in my earlier career.

At length the end of this great Canadian drew near; and the shadows at the closing of life's eventide deepened and lengthened. I visited him frequently, and always found him interested in whatever subject or topic I might speak to him about. His congenial subject, however, was God's providential goodness and overruling care throughout his whole life. In his personal religious experience, he always spoke humbly of himself and glowingly of the long-suffering tenderness of God's dealings towards him. At no time was the character of his religious experience more practical and suggestive than when laid aside from duty. Meditation on the past was the subject of his thoughts.

To him God was a personal, living Father—a Brother born for adversity—a Friend that sticketh closer than a brother—a great and glorious Being, ever gracious, ever merciful. His trust in God was child-like in its simplicity, firm and unwavering. His conversation partook of it and was eminently realistic. He had no more doubt of God's daily, hourly, loving care and superintending providence over him and his than he had of any material fact with which he was familiar or which was self-evident to him. He entirely realized that God was his ever present friend. There seemed to be that close, intimate union—reverent and humble as it was on his part—of man with God, and this gave a living reality to religion in his life. To him the counsels, the warnings, the promises, the encouragements of the Bible, were the voice of God speaking to him personally—the very words came as living words from the lips of God, "as a man speaketh to his friend." This was the secret of his courage, whether it was in some crisis of conflict or controversy, or in his little frail craft when crossing the lake, or exposed to the storm.

To such a man death had no terrors—the heart had no fear. It was cheering and comforting to listen to him (as I often did alone) and to hear him speak of his near departure, as of one preparing for a journey—ceasing from duty, in order to be ready to be conveyed away, and then resuming it when the journey was over.

Thus he spoke of the time of his departure as at hand, and he was ready for the messenger when He should call for him. He spoke of it trustfully, hopefully, cheerfully, neither anxious nor fearful; and yet, on the other hand, neither elated nor full of joy; but he knew in whom He had trusted, and was persuaded, and was not afraid of evil tidings either of the dark valley or the river of death. He knew Him whom he believed, and was persuaded that He was able to keep that which he had committed unto Him against that day.

Thus the end drew near, and with it, as the outward man began to fail, the feeling of unwavering trust and confidence was deepened and strengthened. At length hearing failed, and the senses one by one partially ceased to perform their functions. Then to him were fully realized the inspired words of Solomon : Desire failed, and the silver cord was loosed, the golden bowl was broken, the pitcher broken at the fountain, and the wheel at the cistern. Gradually the weary wheels of life stood still, and at seven o'clock on Sunday morning, February 19th, 1882, in the presence of his loved ones and dear friends, gently and peacefully the spirit of Egerton Ryerson took its flight to be forever with the Lord !

> SERVANT of God, well done !
> Thy glorious warfare's past;
> The battle's fought, the vict'ry won,
> And thou art crowned at last;
>
> Of all thy heart's desire
> Triumphantly possessed;
> Lodged by the sweet angelic choir
> In thy Redeemer's breast.
>
> In condescending love,
> Thy ceaseless prayer He heard ;
> And bade thee suddenly remove
> To this complete reward.
>
> O happy, happy soul !
> In ecstacies of praise,
> Long as eternal ages roll,
> Thou seest thy Saviour's face.
>
> Redeemed from earth and pain,
> Ah ! when shall we ascend,
> And all in Jesus' presence reign
> With our translated friend ?

CHAPTER LXVI.
1882.

THE FUNERAL CEREMONIES, WEDNESDAY, FEB. 22ND, 1882.

AMID the tolling of bells, said the Toronto *Globe*, and the lamentations of many thousands of people, the remains of the late Rev. Dr. Ryerson were conveyed to their final earthly resting-place in Mount Pleasant Cemetery, on Wednesday, the 22nd February. During the day large numbers visited the sorrowing house, and gazed for the last time on the features of the revered dead. As was to be expected, the larger number were, like the venerable deceased, far into " the sere and yellow leaf," and many who had known him for a long time could scarce restrain the unbidden tear as a flood of recollections surged up at the sight of the still form cold in death.

No one present, probably, says the *Guardian*, ever saw so many ministers at a funeral. Among the ministers and laymen were many grey-haired veterans, who had watched with interest the whole brilliant career of the departed. . . All the Churches were well represented, both by their ministers and prominent laymen. Bishop Sweatman and most of the ministers of the Church of England were present. Nearly all the Presbyterian, Baptist, and Congregational ministers of the city were present; and even Archbishop Lynch and Father McCann, of the Roman Catholic Church, showed their respect for the dead by their presence during the day. Devotional service at the house was conducted by Rev. R. Jones, of Cobourg, and Rev. J. G. Laird, of Collingwood.

The plate on the coffin bore the inscription :—" Egerton Ryerson born 21st March, 1803: died 19th February, 1882." The floral tributes presented by sorrowing friends were from various places in Ontario, and not a few came from Detroit and other American cities. The following may be noted :—Wreath, with "Norfolk" in the centre, from Mr. E. Harris; wreath, with "Rest" in the centre, from Dr. and Mrs. Hodgins; pillow, with "Father," from Mrs. E. Harris; crown from the scholars of Ryerson school; pillow, with "Grandpapa," from the grandchildren of the deceased : wreath from Mr. C. H. Greene; cross, also scythe, with sheaf, from Mr. and Mrs. George Harris, London; crown and cross from Rev. Dr. and Mrs. Potts; anchor from W. E. and F. E. Hodgins; sheaf from George S. Hodgins; lilies and other choice flowers inside the casket from Dr. and Mrs. Hodgins.

Shortly before three o'clock the room was left to the members of the family, after which the coffin was borne to the hearse by the following pall-bearers, preceded by the Rev. Dr. Potts:— Dr. Hodgins, Rev. Dr. Nelles, Dr. Aikins, Rev. Dr. Rose, Rev. R. Jones, Mr. J. Paterson. Previous to the arrival of the hearse at the church, His Honour the Lieutenant-Governor, the Speaker of the House, members of the Legislature, which had adjourned for the occasion, and the Ministerial Association, were in the places assigned to them. The members of the City Council and Board of Education were also present in a body. The pupils of Ryerson and Dufferin Schools marched into the church in a body, wearing mourning badges on their arms. There were representatives of all conditions in society, and it might be said of all ages. The lisping schoolboy who was free from the restraint imposed by the presence of his master; and the aged man and woman tottering unsteadily on the verge of the grave—all were hushed in the presence of death. Everywhere within the building were the evidences of a great sorrow. Crape was seen wherever the eye turned—surrounding the galleries, fronting the platform, encircling the choir. But there was one spot thrown into *alto relievo* by the sombre drapery of woe. In front of the pulpit, on a small table, were the exquisitely beautiful floral tributes of friendship and affection, whispering of the beauty and glory of that spring-time of the human race, when this "mortal shall have put on immortality."

Cobourg and Victoria College were well represented; the Rev. T. W. Jeffery and Wm. Kerr, Q.C., and others, being present; also the following professors and students from Victoria College:—Rev. Dr. Nelles, Prof. Burwash, Prof. Reynar, Prof. Bain, Mr. McHenry (Collegiate Institute), and Dr. Jones. The students from the College—one from each class—were Messrs. Stacey, Horning, Eldridge, Brewster, and Crews. The Senate of Victoria University walked in a body immediately after the carriages containing the mourners. Upon entering the west aisle of the church, Rev. Dr. Potts commenced reading the burial service, the vast audience standing. The pall-bearers having deposited their charge in front of the pulpit, Rev. Mr. Cochran gave out the 733rd hymn,

" Come, let us join our friends above,
Who have obtained the prize."

Rev. Dr. Rose offered prayer, after which Rev. Wm. Scott, of

Montreal Conference, read a portion of the 1st Cor. xv., commencing at the 20th verse. The choir of fifty voices, led by the organist, Mr. Torrington, sang an anthem—

"Brother, thou art gone before us."

Rev. Mr. Telfer, from England, gave out the 42nd hymn, which was fervently sung by the congregation. The Rev. Dr. Potts then delivered the following funeral address:—

My place of choice on this deeply sorrowful occasion would be in the ranks of the mourners, for I feel like a son bereft of his father. Gladly would I sit at the feet of aged ministers before me, and listen to them speak of one they knew and loved so well. I venture to address a few words to you, in fulfilment of the dying request of my reverend and honoured father in the Gospel.

Regarding the well-known wishes of the departed, my words must be few and simple. To-day, Methodism, in her laity and ministry mourns over the death of her most illustrious minister and Church leader. To-day, many in this house, and far beyond Toronto, lament the loss of an ardent and true friend. To-day, Canada mourns the decease of one of her noblest sons. This is not the time nor the place for mere eulogy; in the presence of death and of God eulogy is unbecoming. We would glorify God in the character and in the endowments of his servant and child.

We cannot, we should not, forget the greatness of the departed. His was a many-sided greatness. Dr. Ryerson would have been great in any walk in life. In law he would have been a Chief Justice. In statesmanship he would have been a Prime Minister. He was a born leader of his fellows. He was kingly in carriage and in character. The stamp of royal manhood was impressed upon him physically, mentally, morally. We cannot forget the distinguished positions occupied so worthily and so long by our departed friend. He lived for his country, spending and being spent in the educational and moral advancement of the people.

As a servant of Methodism, he was a missionary to the Indians of this Province, an evangelist to the scattered settlers, and a pastor in this city long, long ago. He was President of Victoria College, and never ceased to love and support that institution of learning. For it he solicited money in England and in this country, and to it he gave the intellectual energy of his early manhood, as well as ranking in the front place as a personal subscriber to its funds. He was the first Editor of the *Christian Guardian*, the connexional organ of our branch of Methodism.

As a servant of Canada, he was for over thirty years Chief Superintendent of Education in this Province. His monument —more enduring than brass—is the Public School system of Ontario. When the history of this country comes to be written, the name, the imperishable name of Egerton Ryerson shall shine in radiant lustre as one of the greatest men produced in this land.

But it is not of these things Dr. Ryerson would have me speak if he could direct my thoughts to-day. Rather would have me speak of him as a sinner saved by grace, as a disciple of our Lord Jesus Christ. I knew him well in his religious life. His experience was marked by scriptural simplicity, and his conversation was eminently spiritual. Of all the ministers of my acquaintance, none spoke with me so freely and so frequently on purely religious subjects as the venerable Dr. Ryerson. He gloried in the cross of Christ. He never wearied speaking of the precious blood of the Lamb. He was one of the most helpful and sympathetic hearers in the Metropolitan Church congregation. Rarely, in my almost six years' pastorate, did he leave the church without entering the vestry and saying a kindly, encouraging word.

The doctor belonged to a class of men rapidly passing away. Most of his companions passed on before him. But few linger behind. Grand men they were in Church and State. Canada owes them a debt of gratitude that she can hardly ever pay. Let us revere the memory of those gone to their rest and reward, and let us treat with loving reverence the few pioneers who still linger to bless the land for which they have done so much. We may have a higher average in these times, but we lack the heroic men who stood out so conspiciously in the early history of Canada.

Dr. Ryerson was a Methodist, but not a narrow sectarian. He knew the struggles of our Church in this country, and shared them; he witnessed, with gratitude to God, the extension of Methodism from feeble beginnings to its present influential position. He desired above all things that our Church should retain the primitive simplicity of the olden time, and yet march abreast of the age in the elements of a Christian civilization.

At the first General Conference which met in this church, after the Union, and after that eminently providential event, the introduction of laymen into the highest Court of the Church— at that time, when the representatives of both ministry and membership desired a man to preside over the Methodist Church of Canada, to whom did they look? To the man whom Methodism delighted to honour—Egerton Ryerson.

Dr. Ryerson was regarded by the congregation belonging to

this church with peculiar respect and affection. While he belonged to all Canada, we, of the Metropolitan Church, claimed him as our own especial possession. He was a trustee of the Church, and one of its most liberal supporters; for its prosperity he ever prayed, and in its success he ever rejoiced. It is hard to realize that we shall no longer see that venerable form—that genial and intellectual countenance.

The life of Dr. Ryerson was long, whether you measure it by years or by service—service to his God, to his fellow-men, and to his native land. He was a shock of corn ripe for the heavenly garner. He was an heir, having reached his majority, and made meet for the inheritance of the saints in light, has gone to take possession of it. He was a pilgrim, who after a lengthened pilgrimage has reached home. He was a Christian, who with Paul could say, "For me to live is Christ, to die is gain." In such an hour as this, what comfort could all the honours of man give to the sorrowing family as compared with the thought that the one they loved so dearly was a man in Christ and is now a glorified spirit before the throne. Henceforth we must think of him and speak of him as the late Dr. Ryerson, and to many of us this shall be difficult and painful. We have been so accustomed to see and hear him, we have so long looked up to him as one specially gifted to lead, that a sad feeling comes over us, left as we are without the guidance of our beloved leader and father in the Church. The memory of the just is blessed, and our memory of Dr. Ryerson shall be precious, until we overtake him in the better country, that is the heavenly. Until then let us not be slothful, but followers of them who through faith and patience inherit the promises. Could he speak to us to-day from the heights of the heavenly glory to which he has just been admitted, he would say to this vast concourse of friends, "Follow Christ; seek first the kingdom of God; serve your generation; build up in your Dominion a nationality based on righteousness and truth; be strict in your judgment upon yourselves, but be charitable in your judgment of others; live that your end may be peace, and your immortality eternal blessedness."

Dr. Potts concluded by reading the following extract from a letter written by Dr. Ormiston, of New York, to Dr. Hodgins:—

Dear Dr. Ryerson, I mourn thee as a son for a father. Thou wert very dear to me. I owe thee much. I loved as I esteemed thee. I have no one left now to fill thy place in my heart and life. Through riches of Divine grace I hope soon to meet thee again. My dear Brother Hodgins—You and I knew our noble-hearted friend better than most, and to know him was to love him. You have been longer and more intimately associated with him in social life and earnest work than I was. But I scarcely think that even you loved him more, and I feel as if I was hardly even second to you in his regards. Let our tears fall together to-day, and in each of our hearts let his memory live ever fresh and fondly cherished.

Hym 624, "Rock of Ages, cleft for me," was then sung, after which prayer was offered and the benediction was pronounced by the Rev. J. G. Laird, President of the Toronto Conference. A musical voluntary and the "Dead March" concluded the impressive service.

The remains were then borne to Mount Pleasant Cemetery, where they were afterwards interred.* The concluding portion of the burial service was read by the Rev. Dr. Nelles.

On the following Sunday the funeral sermon was preached by Rev. Dr. Nelles. The *Guardian* said:—

The discourse of Dr. Nelles was a masterly and eloquent review of the salient points in Dr. Ryerson's life and character. We have rarely listened to a sermon with greater satisfaction, and never to a funeral sermon so discriminating in its statements and characterization. It was distinguished by a broad mental grasp of the great lessons and facts of history, in the light of which all personal and local events must be viewed, to be seen truly and impartially. His appreciative recognition of the privileges of religious equality which we possess in Canada, and of the prominent part taken by Dr. Ryerson in obtaining them, was very suggestive and felicitous. We rarely follow to the grave so eminent a man as Dr. Ryerson; and we seldom have heard a discourse so fully equal to a great occasion.

Tributes to Dr. Ryerson's Memory.

After Dr. Ryerson's death kind telegrams and letters of condolence were received by the family from many sympathizing friends, among which was one from the Marquis of Lorne, Governor-General. The following letter was also received by Mrs. Ryerson from the Rev. William Arthur, M.A., dated London, England, April 10th, 1882:—

The news of your great bereavement, a bereavement which, though yours in a special sense, is not yours alone, but is felt by multitudes as their own, came at a moment when a return

---

* This interment took place in May. The ceremony was a private one, attended only by immediate relatives and intimate personal friends. Among the former were the venerable doctor's aged eldest brother, Rev. George Ryerson (91 years old) and Mrs. George Ryerson; the bereaved widow, Mrs. Ryerson, Mr. Charles E. Ryerson, his two sons, and Mrs. George Duggan. Among the latter were the Rev. Dr. Potts, Mrs. Potts, Dr. Hodgins, and Mr. H. M. Wilkinson (son of Rev. H. Wilkinson), of the Education Department, and two or three others. After lowering the coffin into the grave, the Rev. Dr. Potts read a portion of the burial service, committing the body to the earth in hope of a joyful resurrection at the last day.

of an old affection of the eyes made writing difficult, and I did not like to give you a mere line. From my heart I do condole with you on the removal from your side of one who was pleasant to look upon, even for strangers, and whose presence was not only a natural delight, but a stay, and an honour. Not many women are called to sustain the loss of such a husband. But on the other hand, not many women in the day of their great loss have the legacy left to them of such a memory, such a career, and such appreciation of whole communities of the merits of that career. Very few have such a combination of true religious consolation, of full hope and unclouded faith, with the sense of comfort derived from general sympathy and universal public respect. Dr. Ryerson was the servant of God, and the Lord blessed him. He was the servant of the Church, and the Church loved and revered him. He was the servant of his country, and his country delighted to honour him, and will hold him in permanent and honourable remembrance. To many friends on this side of the Atlantic, as well as on his own, he was a rarely honoured and prized representative of long and noble services to the cause of God, and to general society, services rendered with commanding abilities and unflinching vigour. To you and to the children the loss is far different to what it is to others. To you and to them have the hearts of others turned with unaffected sympathy. You have had many praying for you; many hoping that blessings will rest upon the name of Ryerson, and that it will long be represented in every Christian work, and every branch of public usefulness. With truly affectionate regards, and condolences to Mr. and Mrs. Charles, believe me, dear Mrs. Ryerson, yours with heartfelt sympathy, WM. ARTHUR.

THE LORD BISHOP OF MANCHESTER, who was in Canada as one of the Royal Commissioners on Education, in concluding his report on our Canadian Schools, said: "Such, in all its main features, is the school system of Upper Canada. A system not perfect, but yet far in advance, as a system of national education, of anything we can show at home. It is indeed very remarkable to me that in a country, occupied in the greater part of its area by a sparse and anything but wealthy population, whose predominant characteristic is as far as possible removed from the spirit of enterprise, an educational system so complete in its theory and so capable of adaptation in practice should have been originally organized, and have maintained in what, with all allowances, must still be called successful operation for so long a period as twenty-five years. It shows what can be accomplished by the energy, determination, and devotion of a single earnest man. What national education in England owes to Sir J. K. Shuttleworth, what education in New England owes to Horace Mann, that debt education in Canada owes to Egerton Ryerson. He has been the object of bitter abuse, of not a little misrepresentation; but he has not swerved from his policy or from his fixed ideas. Through evil report and good report he has found others to support him in the resolution, that free education shall be placed within the reach of every Canadian parent for every Canadian child."

In a letter addressed to Dr. Ryerson in 1875, the Bishop says:—I take it very kindly in you that you remember an old acquaintance, and I have read with interest your last report. I am glad to observe progress in the old lines almost everywhere. I was flattered also to find that some words of mine, written in 1865, are thought worthy of being quoted. . . It is pleasant to find a public servant now in the thirty-second year of his incumbency, still so hopeful and so vigorous. Few men have lived a more useful or active life than you, and your highest reward must be to look back upon what you have been permitted to achieve.

The VERY REVEREND DEAN GRASETT, in a letter to Dr. Hodgins, dated 9th November, 1875, said:

I thank you very much for your kindness in presenting me with a complete set of the *Journal of Education* from the date of its commencement in 1848 to the present time.

You could not have given me a token of parting remembrance more acceptable to me on various accounts; but chiefly shall I value it as a memorial of the confidence and kindness I have so invariably experienced from the Rev. Dr. Ryerson from the day I first took my seat with him at a Council Board in 1846 to the time that I was released from further attendance there this year. Similar acknowledgments I owe to yourself, his coadjutor, in the great work of his life, and the editor of the record of his labours, contained in these volumes.

I shall carry with me to the end of life the liveliest feelings of respect for the public character and regard for the private worth of one who has rendered to his country services which entitle him to her lasting gratitude. My venerable friend has had from time to time many cheering recognitions of his valuable public services from the Heads of our Government, who were capable of appreciating them, as well as from other quarters; but I think that in his case, as in others that are familiar to us, it must be left to future generations adequately to appreciate their value when they shall be reaping the full benefit of them.

I esteem it an honour that I should have been associated with him in his Council for so many years (30), and a privilege if I have been of the least assistance in upholding his hands in performing a work, the credit of which is exclusively his own.

The Rev. Dr. WITHROW, in his "Memorials of Dr. Ryerson," (*Canadian Methodist Magazine,* April, 1882,) said: No man ever passed away from among us in Canada whose true greatness was so universally recognized as that of Dr. Ryerson. He lived in the hearts of his countrymen, and

"Read his history in a nation's eyes."

Even envy and detraction could not lessen his grandeur nor tarnish the lustre of his name. . . Scarce an organ of public opinion in the country, no matter what party or what interest it represented, has not laid its wreath of praise on the tomb of this great Canadian. And far beyond his own country his character was revered and his loss deplored. . . From the Roman Catholic Archbishop; from the Anglican Bishop, from many members of the Church of England and other religious bodies, as well as of his own Church; resolutions of the Board of the Bible Society, the Tract Society, School Boards and Conventions, and Collegiate Institutes, all bore witness to the fact that the sorrow for his death was not confined to any party or denominational lines, but was keenly felt in other churches as well as in that of which he was the most distinguished minister..... Almost every Methodist journal in the United States has also paid its tribute to his memory. We quote from the *North Western Christian Advocate,* of Chicago, but one such tribute of loving respect:—" We believe that Canada owes more to him than to any other man, living or dead. In all his official relations to the public he was true to his Church. Men like Wellington and Washington 'save their countries,' but men like Ryerson make their countries worth saving. The mean little soul flinches when its brethren rise in reputation and power in the Church. The more exalted soul rejoices when the Church grows rich in competent workers. The death of such a servant as Ryerson is a loss to the world greater than when the average president or king passes away. Thank God, the great Ruler lives, and He will continue the line of prophets in modern Israel!"

Dr. Ryerson possessed in a marked degree the faculty of commanding the confidence and winning the friendship of distinguished men of every rank, of every political party and religious denomination. He possessed the confidence and esteem of every Governor of Canada, from Lord Sydenham to the Marquis of Lorne. No native Canadian ever had the *entrée* to such distinguished society in Great Britain and in Europe as he. He had personal relations with several of the leading British statesmen. He enjoyed the personal friendship of the Bishop of Manchester, the Dean of Westminster, the Archbishop of Canterbury, and other distinguished divines of the Anglican and Dissenting Churches. He was one of the very few Methodist preachers who have ever shared the hospitalities of Lambeth Palace, for six hundred years the seat of the Primates of England; and when Dean Stanley passed through Toronto, he and Dean Grasett called together on Dr. Ryerson. When making his educational tour in Europe . .

Speaking of his personal worth, Dr. Withrow says:—A very good criterion of a man's character is: How does he get on with his colleagues? Does the familiarity of daily intercourse, year after year, increase or lessen their esteem? Few men will bear this test as well as Dr. Ryerson. The more one saw of him the more one loved him. Those who knew him best loved him most. Dr. Hodgins, the Deputy Minister of Education, for thirty-two years the intimate associate in educational work of Dr. Ryerson, knowing more fully than any living man the whole scope of his labours, sharing his anxieties and toils, tells us that in all those years there never was an hour's interruption of perfect mutual trust and sympathy. No son could have a stronger filial love for an honoured father than had Dr. Hodgins for his late venerated Chief. It was his privilege to minister to the latest hours of his revered friend, and it is to him a labour of love to prepare for the press the posthumous story of his life.

With all his catholicity of sentiment and charity of spirit, Dr. Ryerson was a man of strong convictions, and he always had the courage of his convictions as well. When it came to a question of principle he was as rigid as iron. Then he planted himself on the solid ground of what he believed to be right, and said, like Fitz James:

> "Come one, come all! this rock shall fly,
> From its firm base, as soon as I."

Dr. Ryerson's controversies were for great principles, not for personal interests. Hence no rancour, no bitterness disturbed his relations with his antagonists. Even his old and sturdy foe, Bishop Strachan, after his controversy was over, became his personal friend. . .

Such benefactors of his kind and of his country, as Dr. Ryerson, deserve to be held in lasting and grateful remembrance. His imperishable monument, it is true, is the school system which he devised.

To future generations of Canadian youth the career of Dr.

Ryerson shall be an inspiration and encouragement. With early educational advantages far inferior to those which he has brought within the reach of every boy and girl in the land, what a noble life he lived, what grand results he achieved! One grand secret of his success was his tireless industry. As a boy he learned to work—to work hard—the best lesson any boy can learn—and he worked to the end of his life. He could not spend an idle hour. The rule of his life was "no day without a line," without something attempted—something done. . . Over a score of times he crossed the Atlantic on official duties. He often turned night into day for purposes of work and study; and on the night before making his famous three-hours' speech on University Administration before the Committee of the Legislature in 1860, he spent the whole night long in the study of the documents and papers on the subject—to most men a poor preparation for such a task.

But again we remark his moral greatness was his noblest trait—his earnest piety, his child-like simplicity, his Christ-like charity, his fidelity to duty, his unfaltering faith. Not his intellectual greatness, not his lofty statesmanship, not his noble achievements are his truest claim upon our love and veneration —but this—

"The *Christian* is the highest style of man."

The Rev. Dr. DEWART, in the *Christian Guardian,* of February 22nd, 1882, says :—The simple announcement that Dr. Egerton Ryerson is dead, will awaken sorrow and regret in many Canadian homes. . . For several years of his early life he faithfully bore all the hardships and privations of the pioneer work of that day, being for a time missionary to the Indians of the Credit Mission—a circumstance to which he often referred with peculiar satisfaction. His keen and vigorous refutation of the misrepresentations of the Methodists and other bodies by the then dominant Church party, led by the late Bishop Strachan, revealed to his own, and other Churches, his rare gifts as a powerful controversial writer. From that time forward for many years, his pen was used with powerful effect, in defence of equal religious rights and privileges for all Churches. . . Dr. Ryerson was longer and more prominently associated with the interests of Methodism in Canada than any other minister of our Church. His life covers and embraces all but the earliest portion of the history of our Church in this country.

But it is his work as an educationist that has made him most widely known, and upon which his fame most securely rests. . . The office of Chief Superintendent of Education for Upper Canada was not a new one; but the vigorous personality of Dr. Ryerson lifted it into a prominence and importance in public estimation that had never belonged to it before. For thirty-two years he continued to discharge the duties of this high office with a broad intelligence and rare executive ability, which have for all time stamped his name and influence on the educational system of his country. He was not a mere administrator, acting under the orders of the Government of the day. He was the leader of a great educational reform. . . Changes of Government made no change in his department. Such was the estimate which the Ontario Government took of his public services that on his resignation, in 1876, his full salary was continued till the time of his death, and after his death the Legislature made a grant of $10,000 to his widow. It is not too much to say that among the gifted men whom Canada delights to honour, not one has left a more permanent impression for good on the future of our country than EGERTON RYERSON.

He was large-minded and liberal in his views on all subjects. Though strong in his attachment to Methodism he was no sectarian, but cherished the most liberal and kindly feeling toward all sincere Christians. He was an able controvertialist, and in the heat of conflict dealt heavy blows at his opponents ; but when the battle was over he retained no petty spite toward his late antagonists. His controversial pamphlets are numerous, and mostly relate to current events with which he was in some way associated. Though a man of war, from his youth engaging in many conflicts, religious and political, Dr. Ryerson's last years were eminently tranquil. He had outlived the bitterness of former times, and in a sincere and honoured old age possessed in a high degree the respect and good feeling of men of all parties. During these later years he produced his most important contributions to literature, viz., his "Loyalists of America," and "Chapters on the History of Canadian Methodism." His Educational Reports are also valuable treasuries of facts relating to public education.

During all the years of his public life he co-operated heartily with every enterprise of his Church, and was always ready to preach at the shortest notice for any of his brethren who required his help. In his later years there was an increasing spirituality and unction observable in his ministrations.

Though not exempt from the faults and failings of humanity —yet his wide range of information—his broad and statesmanlike views—his intense devotion to a great work—his patriotic interest in all public questions—his wonderful personal energy and force of character—and his long and intimate connection with Canadian Methodism—warrant us in saying :

"He was a man, take him for all in all,
We shall not look upon his like again."

Rev. Dr. Douglas, in a letter to the *Guardian*, says: A great man and a prince has fallen in our Israel! The last of the illustrious three who bore the name of Ryerson has gone to enrich the heavens. Henceforth that honoured name will be enshrined in the history of our land.

Egerton Ryerson's patriotic service to the State, in resisting the introduction of feudal distinctions and ecclesiastical monopolies will ensure to him enduring recognition, as one of Canada's noblest benefactors. No statues of marble or of bronze need be raised to perpetuate his memory. The academies and schools which his organizing genius brought into existence, lifting up successive generations to the dignity which education ever confers, will make that name immortal. For nearly six decades he laid his great powers of intellect and heart on the altar of service for Canadian Methodism—winning for her ministry equality before the law, and for her people a status which allowed no coign of vantage to a favoured class—vindicating her polity and proclaiming her distinctive truth. . .

Now, when the sepulchre has received him, will not a grateful Church arise and give a permanence to his name more lasting than marble, by the founding of a Ryerson Chair of Philosophy with whatever is required to augment the usefulness of the institution which his great manhood loved, and for which he toiled with a life-lasting endeavour? Would that every minister, who bows his head in sorrow for a fallen chieftain, might in every circuit gather the piety, intelligence, and financial strength of the Church together, and in this supreme hour of the Church's grief, decree that before the springtime shall come with its emerald robe enamelled with flowers, adorning the resting-place of our honoured dead, the name of Egerton Ryerson will be inwrought with our University, as an abiding inspiration to the student-life that shall throng her halls along the coming years.

The Methodist Ministers of Toronto, in a sketch of Dr. Ryerson's life and character, written by Rev. W. S. Blackstock, say: To most of us, from our early childhood, the name of Egerton Ryerson has been a household word, and we learned to esteem and love him even before we were capable of estimating his character, or the greatness of the service which he was rendering to his own and coming generations; and the knowledge of him which we have been permitted to acquire in our riper years, has only tended to deepen the impressions of him which we received in early days.

As the fearless and powerful champion of civil and religious liberty, and of the equal rights of all classes of his countrymen, he is associated in our memory with the patriotic and Christian struggles of a past generation, which have resulted in securing to our beloved land as large a measure of liberty as is enjoyed by any country under the sun. In respect to the incomparable system of Public Instruction, to the perfecting of which he devoted so many years of his active and laborious life, and with which his name must ever be associated, we feel that he has laboured and we have entered into his labours. We can hardly conceive how either our country or our Church could have been what they are to-day, but for his fidelity and the work which he accomplished.

The lively interest which he took in every patriotic, Christian, and philanthropic movement, especially those which tended to increase the influence and usefulness of his own Church—the zeal with which he laboured for them, and the large-hearted, generous liberality with which he contributed of his means for their support—awaken our gratitude and thankfulness, and will be a perpetual inspiration in our efforts to promote those objects which lay so near his heart, and to further the interests of that cause which he served so well.

But standing, as we are to day, with bowed heads and stricken hearts, beside the grave which has just closed upon the mortal remains of our venerable departed brother, though we would not forget what he had done for us, we prefer to think of what, by the grace of God, he was, than of what by God's good Providence he was permitted to accomplish. We delight to cherish the memory of his penitent and childlike faith in Christ—the sinner's only Saviour and hope—and of those graces of the Holy Spirit which gave so much beauty and sweetness to his character, and which were more and more conspicuous in his declining years.

Though Dr. Ryerson was a man of positive views and devotedly attached to his own Church, he was distinguished for his comprehensive charity, and his genuine appreciation of great and good men from whom he differed widely in opinion. His goodness no less than his greatness will serve to keep his memory fresh among us, and the recollections of his virtue is to us a powerful incentive to a fuller consecration to the service of God.

The General Conference at its Session of 1882, passed the following resolution :—

Whereas it has pleased Almighty God, in His divine wisdom, to call from a life of faithful service in the Church of Christ on earth to his everlasting reward in heaven our reverend and honoured father in the Gospel, the Rev. Egerton Ryerson, D.D., LL.D., the first President of the General Conference of the Methodist Church of Canada, this General Conference desires to place upon record its deep feelings of gratitude to God for His gift to the Methodist Church and to the people of this land for so many years of a man so richly endowed with native gifts and so largely adorned with the Christian graces and its profound sense of the great loss the Church and country have sustained in his death. As the devoted Christian missionary and pastor; as the faithful defender of the rights and liberties of the people of this land against ecclesiastical assumptions and civil disabilities; as the Editor for many years of the *Christian Guardian*, the official organ of our Church and the first religious journal in Canada; as the President of the University of Victoria College, the oldest institution of higher learning of Canadian Methodism; as the trusted representative of his Church in the religious councils of Methodism in the old world and the new; as the Superintendent for over thirty years of the education of his native Province—a system which he almost created, and which he developed to a state of proficiency unsurpassed by that of any country in the world; as the wise counsellor in the union movement which led to the organization of the Methodist Church of Canada; and as the President-Administrator of its highest office during the first quadrennium of its history, Dr. Ryerson has an imperishable claim upon the love and gratitude especially of his own church, and also of the entire community. We magnify the grace of God as manifested in him; we revere his memory as that of a true patriot and devoted Christian; we rejoice in his labours for the glory of God and the welfare of man; and we deeply sympathize with his bereaved family, and pray that the consolations of God may more and more abound in their souls to the end.

THE END.

INDEX.

BIOGRAPHICAL REFERENCES.

Aberdeen, Earl of, 160.
Adams, Rev. A. A., 130.
Adderley, Mr., M.P., 539.
Agnew, Sir A., 163.
Aikman, John, 32, 36.
Aikman, Miss Hannah, 86, 111, 112.
Alder, Rev. Dr. Robert, 109, 110, 114, 119, 143, 153, 155, 158, 166, 174, 206, 240, 241, 242, 243, 271, 280, 285. 320, 386, 390, 391, 392, 393, 394, 395, 397, 401, 402, 403, 404, 405.
Allan, Hon. William, 170.
Alley, Mr., 99.
Allison, Rev. C. R., 399.
Althorp, Lord, 123.
Anderson, Capt., 99.
Antonelli, Cardinal, 366, 367.
Antrobus, Colonel, 416.
Arago, M., 356, 358.
Archibald, Rev. G., 76.
Armstrong, Jas. R., 120.
Armstrong, Miss Mary, 120.
Arthur, Rev. Wm., 367, 556, 598.
Arthur, Sir George, 183, 188, 189, 193, 200, 224, 225, 230, 234, 239, 240, 241, 245, 246, 248, 249, 250, 251, 254, 260, 261, 263, 285, 320.
Atherley, Rev. Mr., 117.
Attwood, Thos., M.P., 123, 129.
Attwood, Rev. J. S., 154.
Asbury, Bishop, 408.
Ashburton, Lord, 160,
Ashley, Lord, 163.
Ashton, Michael, 272.
Atherton, Rev. Mr., 402.
Aylwin, Hon. T. C., 304.

Bagot, Sir Charles, 290, 301, 303, 304, 306, 312, 313, 324, 331, 333, 342, 345, 347, 350, 387, 389, 390, 393, 394, 398, 404, 550.
Bain, Prof., 594.
Bakewell, Rev. Mr., 117.
Baldwin, Dr. W. W., 79, 101, 310, 311.
Baldwin, Hon. Augustus, 170.
Baldwin, Hon. Robert, 127, 145, 170, 194, 264, 267, 287, 289, 303, 305, 308, 309, 313, 315, 317, 328, 332, 333, 336, 344, 346, 370, 371, 416, 417, 424, 425, 426, 433, 518, 525, 526, 550.
Bangs, Rev Dr. Nathan, 32, 78, 88, 93, 115, 269, 277, 278, 418, 577.
Baring, Thomas, M.P., 160.
Barker, Dr., 127, 150.
Bathurst, Lord, 221, 440, 445, 446.
Beadle, Dr., 348.
Beardsley, Colonel, 185.
Beatty, Rev. J., 184, 228.
Beaumont, Rev. Dr., 402.
Beecham, Rev. Dr. John, 119, 159, 228, 390, 507.

Bell, Rev. Wm., 101, 212, 221.
Belton, Rev. S., 90.
Benson, Henry, 89.
Beresford, Rev. Mr., 354.
Bethune, Donald, 102.
Bethune, Bishop A. N., 77, 216, 292, 348, 380, 564, 566.
Bettridge, Rev. Wm., D.D., 95.
Bevitt, Rev. Thomas, 277.
Bexley, Lord, 116.
Bidwell, Hon. M. S., 68, 127, 138, 145, 184, 188, 189, 190, 191, 192, 193, 194, 195, 196, 197, 198, 231, 258, 283, 308, 309, 310, 328, 414, 416, 417, 418, 561, 567, 568.
Black, Rev. John, 175, 493.
Blackstock, Rev. W. S., 605.
Blainville, M. de, 358.
Blake, Hon. Chancellor, 418.
Bland, Rev. A. F., 557.
Blockman, Dr., 363.
Blomfield, Dr. (Bishop of London), 160.
Blusse, Mr., 354.
Bond, Dr. Thomas, 396.
Borland, Rev. J., 511, 512.
Bostwick, Col. John, 24.
Boswell. G. M., M.P.P., 182, 348.
Boulton, Mr., M.P.P., 229.
Bowers, Rev. John, 158.
Bridel, M., 359.
Brock, Rev. James, 275.
Brooking, Mr., 160.
Brough, Rev. C. C., 183.
Brougham, Lord, 123, 322.
Brouse, George, 89.
Brown, Hon. George, 554, 555.
Brown, Hon. James, 453.
Brunskill, Mr., 161.
Buchanan, Hon. Isaac, 197, 286, 331, 336, 346, 347, 350.
Buller, Sir Charles, 272, 307.
Bunting, Rev. Dr. Jabez, 117, 119, 143, 154, 158, 159, 160, 162, 228, 240, 273, 279, 280, 390, 398, 401, 402, 403, 420, 506, 507.
Burchel, Mr., 89.
Burke, Edmund, 220.
Burnet, Bishop, 322.
Burns, Rev. Dr. R. F., 557.
Burrows, Colonel, 517.
Burwash, Prof., 594.
Buxton, Mrs., 163.

Calvert, Mr., 542.
Cameron, Hon. Malcolm, 370, 423, 424, 426, 509, 514.
Cameron, James W., 76, 77.
Campbell, Rev. Prof., 381.
Campbell, Sir J., 165.

INDEX.

Campbell, John, M.P.P., 184, 192.
—— Sir Alexander, 192, 559.
Canterbury, Archbishop of, 602.
Carlisle, Bishop of, 542.
Carlisle, Dean of, 541, 542.
Carnarvon, Lord, 539, 579.
Carroll, Rev. Dr. John, 214, 270.
Cartier, Sir George, 559, 560, 561.
Cartwright, M.P.P., 213, 228, 229, 245, 246.
Cartwright, Thos., 133.
Case, Rev. Elder Wm., 56, 66, 68, 74, 77, 78, 79, 81, 87, 91, 92, 93, 176, 228, 243, 270, 274, 275, 277, 378, 385.
Cassidy, Henry, 149, 191, 196.
Chalmers, Rev. Dr. Thomas, 215, 365.
Chapman, E. H., 160, 161.
Chester, Bishop of, 116.
Chichester, Lord, 541.
Clarendon, Lord, 499.
Cochran, Rev. Mr., 594.
Colborne, Sir John, 98, 102, 118, 126, 130, 155, 158, 161, 170, 171, 196, 222, 224, 232, 244, 260, 261, 263, 264, 386, 526.
Coley, Rev. Mr., 589.
Collard, Rev. Mr., 93.
Collins, F., 129.
Cook, Emile, 571.
Cork, Bishop of, 541.
Counter, John, 154.
Cowley, Lord, 360.
Crane, John, 73.
Cronyn, Bishop, 517.
Cubitt, Rev. Mr., 159.
Cull, Mr., 287.
Cumming, Rev. Dr., 508.

Daly, Sir Dominick, 333, 340, 351, 376.
Davidson, Alex., 133, 241.
—— Rev. J. C., 143, 175, 274.
Dawson, Dr. J. W., 453.
Dawson, Wm., 161.
Delille, M. Armand, 356, 358.
Delille, Mons. O., 358.
Densmore, Rev. Mr., 384.
Depretz, M. 358.
Derby, Earl of, 329, 330, 451, 452.
Derbyshire, Stewart, 307.
Dewart, Dr. E. H., 602.
Dixon, Rev. Dr. James, 400, 402, 405, 406, 562, 564.
Doolittle, Rev. Mr., 119.
Dorland, Mr., 538.
Douglas, Rev. Dr., 605.
Douse, Rev. John, 275.
Doxtadors, Mr., 75.
Draper, Hon. W. H., 50, 179, 181, 225, 228, 229, 231, 237, 261, 264, 267, 292, 301, 304, 305, 306, 313, 316, 325, 333, 334, 335, 337, 339, 342, 344, 550, 551.
Dufferin, Lord, 408, 409.
Dumas, Prof. 356.
Duncan, Mr. Joseph, 535.
Duncan, Prof. Thomas, 215.
Duncombe, Dr. Charles, 167, 168, 188, 190.
Dunjowski, 353, 365, 366, 367.
Dunkin, Christopher, 196, 197.
Dunn, Colonel, 197.
Dunn, Hon. J. H., 145, 166, 170, 180, 181, 197, 198, 325, 387.
Durbin, Dr. J. P., 115.
Durham, Lord, 196, 197, 225, 256, 257, 258, 259, 267, 272, 312, 339, 550.

Edwards, Mr. 117.
Egger, M., 358.
Elgin, Lord, 370, 405, 416, 419, 420, 451, 452, 514.
Ellice, Rt. Hon. Edward, 117, 160.
Elliott, Judge Wm., 552.
Ellis, Sir Henry, 419.
Elmsley, Hon. John, 170, 179.

Embury, Rev. Philip, 256.
Emory, Bishop, 384, 385.
Entwistle, Rev. Joseph, 116, 273.
Esten, Hon. Vice-Chancellor, 418.
Evans, Rev. Dr. Ephraim, 133, 153, 181, 237, 270, 275, 564.
Evans, Rev. James, 130, 131, 132, 153, 228, 407, 408, 409.
Exeter, Bishop of, 263.

Fallenberg, M. de, 364.
Farmer, Thomas, 159, 166, 256.
Farrar, Canon, 205.
Fawcett, Rev. Thomas 375.
Ferguson, Rev. George, 340.
Ferrier, Hon. James, 490, 533.
Fisk, Rev. Dr. Wilbur, A.M., 88, 90, 115, 162, 577.
Fitzgibbon, Colonel, 177.
Fletcher, Silas, 178.
Flint, Hon. Billa, 336.
Fox, Charles James, 220.
Fuller, Bishop (Archdeacon of Niagara), 380.

Gage, James, 78.
Gale, Rev. A., 432.
Galt, John, 221.
Gamble, John W., 268
Gamble, Clarke, Q. C., 567.
Gasparin, Count, 356, 358, 359, 360.
Geikie, Rev. Dr. Cunningham, 187.
Gibson, David, 178.
Gilchrist, Dr., 339.
Gilkison, Jasper J., 552.
Gillespie, A., Jun., 160.
Givens, Col., 44, 61, 63, 75.
—— Rev. Dr. Saltern, 77, 567.
Gladstone, Rt. Hon. W. E., 168, 272, 410, 411, 433, 452.
Glenelg, Lord, 154, 156, 158, 159, 160, 162, 165, 168, 169, 170, 178, 180, 182, 189, 190, 196, 197, 199, 224, 225, 226, 227, 228, 230, 235, 248, 250, 252, 235, 459.
Goderich, Lord, 118, 126, 155, 156, 195, 526.
Goodrich, Rev. C. B., 275.
Goodson, Rev. George, 557.
Goodwin, Dean, (of Ely), 540.
Gourley, Robt., 185.
Gowan, Ogle R. 331.
Graham, Dr. James, 28.
Grampier, Dr., 355, 356, 360.
Grasett, Very Rev. Dean, 295, 297, 600, 602.
Gray, Hon. J. H., 453.
Green, Rev. Dr. Anson, 90, 111, 129, 134, 175, 176, 181, 205, 210, 228, 270, 277, 314, 383, 401, 501, 511.
Greenfield, Mr. 79.
Greig, William, 212.
Grey, Earl, 123, 405, 419, 451, 454, 455, 456, 457, 515, 578.
Grey, Sir George, 165, 168, 169, 189, 245.
Griffin, Smith, 29.
—— Rev. W. S., 29.
Griffin, Rev. Wm., Jun., 180.
Griffis, E. C., 129, 241.
Grindrod, Rev. E., 120, 143, 147, 163.
Gurley, Rev. Mr., 279.
Guizot, M., 356.

Hagerman, Daniel, 189.
Hagerman, Mr. Justice, 119, 191, 192, 193, 194, 196, 223, 310, 551, 570.
Halkett, Capt., 177.
Hall, Francis, 78, 92, 115, 305, 417.
Hamilton, Rev. R. W., 116.
Hanet, M., 358.
Hanna, Rev. John, 158, 159.
—— Mrs. John, 159.
Harris, Dr. 79.
Harris, Rev. Mr., 102.

INDEX. 611

Harrison, Hon. S. B., 314, 315, 316, 317, 318, 337, 338, 344, 347.
Harrison, Mr. (A.D.C.), 308, 309, 310, 311.
Harvard, Rev. W. M., 181, 202, 203, 204, 228, 237, 244, 396.
Hawes, Sir Benjamin, 419, 420, 454, 456.
Hay, Mr., 160.
Head, Sir F. B., 162, 166, 170, 171, 176, 179, 180, 181, 182, 183, 189, 190, 191, 192, 196, 197, 198, 200, 201, 206, 224, 225, 228, 235, 248, 252, 253, 257, 258, 288, 309, 316, 320, 416, 417.
Head, Sir Edmund, 499.
Heald, Rev. Mr., 571.
Healy, Rev. E., 172, 173.
Hedding, Bishop, 32, 46, 97, 172, 174, 269, 385, 577.
Henings, Rev. Mr., 88.
Herkimer, Wm., 66, 72.
Hess, Mr. J., 78, 79.
Hetherington, Rev. Mr., 128, 141.
Heyland, Rev. Rowley, 40, 148.
Hickson, Mr., 339.
Higginson, Secretary, 317, 318, 319, 322, 325, 327, 331, 332, 333, 334, 335, 336, 337, 339, 340, 345, 348, 349, 350, 375, 377.
Hill, Lord, 116.
Hill, Rev. Rowland, 116, 159.
Hincks, Sir Francis, 187, 190, 290, 313, 324, 329, 330, 333, 416, 424, 451.
Holden, Mr., 587.
Holtby, Rev. Matthew, 307.
Hoole, Rev. Dr. Elijah, 390, 544.
Horne, Dr., 177.
Horton, Hon. R. W., 222.
Howard, James S., 193, 414.
Howard, Mr., 118.
Howard, Rev. I. B., 287.
Howe, Hon. Joseph, 244, 258, 331.
Howick, Lord, 118.
Hume, Joseph, M P., 118, 123, 126, 129, 134, 135, 136, 138, 167, 168, 169, 171, 175, 228.
Hurlburt, Rev. Thomas, 275, 513.
Hyland, Edward, 64.

Inglis, Sir Harry, 163.
Inglis, Sir Robert, 121.
Irvine, Rev. Mr., 154.
Irving, Rev. Edward, 116.
Izard, Miss C., 163.

Jackson, Edward, 241.
Jackson, Rev. Thos., 273.
Jacobs, Peter, 68, 78.
Jager, Abbe, 358.
James, Rev. John Angel, 162, 163.
Jameson, Vice-Chancellor, 304, 418.
—— Rev. Mr., 355.
Janes, Bishop, 556.
Jarvis, Mr., 299.
Jarvis, Sheriff, 183.
Jay, Rev. Wm., 116.
Jeffers, Rev. Dr. W., 498, 511, 533.
Jeffrey, Rev. T. W., 594.
Jenkins, Rev. Wm., 154, 159.
Jeune, Rev. Dr., 163.
Jobson, Rev. Dr., 582.
Johnston, Rev. Hugh, B.D., 590.
Jones, Dr., 594.
Jones, Jonas, 111.
—— John, 65, 66, 70.
Jones, Mr. Justice, 177, 310, 551.
Jones, Rev. R., 593, 594.
Jones, T. M., 299.
Jones, Rev. Peter, 41, 44, 45, 56, 61, 66, 69, 70, 71, 72, 73, 74, 75, 79, 83, 107, 108, 112, 223, 320, 400, 401, 413.
Junkin, S. S., 149, 150, 151, 170.

Keefer, Jacob, 348.
Kent, Duchess of, 164.

Kent, John, 97, 292, 293, 294, 296, 297.
Kenyon, Lord, 160.
Kerr, Mrs. Wm. (nee Brant), 56.
Kerr, Wm., 78, 594.

Lafontaine, Hon. L. H., 304, 315, 332, 336, 416 425, 444, 446, 551.
Laird, Rev. J. G., 593, 598.
Lane, William, 75.
Lang, Rev. Matthew, 275.
Langton, John, 530.
Lansdowne, Marquis of, 419, 425, 515.
Law, Rev. John, 28, 32, 39.
—— William, 62, 63.
Lefroy, General, 371.
Lessey, Rev. Theophilus, 116.
Lever, Rev. Mr., 493.
Lindsay, General, 559.
Lindsey, Charles, 185, 186.
Lingard, R. W., 419.
Linsey, Rev. Mr, 88.
Lloyd, Jesse, 178.
Longman, Mr. 578.
Lord, Rev. Wm., 121, 140, 148, 151, 152, 153, 164, 166, 210, 394, 401, 402.
Lorne, Marquis of, 598.
Lount, Samuel, 178, 182, 183, 184, 188.
Luckey, Rev. Dr., 68.
Lunn, Mr. Wm., 154, 169.
Lynch, Archbishop, 593.

Macaulay, Lord, 123, 205, 419.
Macaulay, Mr. Justice, 172, 173, 177, 551.
M cdonald, John, 564.
Macdonald, R., Q.C., 182.
Macdonald, Rt. Hon. Sir John A., 194, 499.
Macdonnell, Vicar-General, 106.
Macdougall, Hon. Wm., 288.
Mackenzie, W. L., 118, 124, 125, 126, 127, 128, 129, 130, 134, 135, 136, 137, 138, 144, 145, 155, 156, 157, 168, 171, 175, 178, 185, 186, 187, 188, 189, 190, 200, 207, 239, 257, 238.
Macnab, Sir Allan, 177, 229, 337.
Madden, Rev. Thomas, 29, 40, 55, 68.
Maitland, Sir Peregrine, 62, 63, 221, 440, 445.
Manchester, Bishop of, 599, 602.
Mangles, Mr., M.P., 340.
Manly, Rev. John G., 275.
Mann, Horace, 600.
Markland, Hon. George H., 170.
Marsden, Rev. G., 115, 120, 147, 163, 273, 397.
Marsh, Rev. Dr. Wm., 163.
Marshall, Rev. Mr., 571.
Matthews (see Lount and Matthews), 89, 182, 183, 184, 188.
Maule, Fox (Lord Panmure), 272.
Meredith, Mr., 163.
Merritt, Hon. W. H., 314, 315, 316, 319, 336, 337, 338, 343.
Metcalfe, Sir Charles, 193, 194, 198, 303, 308, 312, 313, 314, 315, 316, 317, 319, 323, 324, 325, 328, 329, 330, 331, 332, 333, 337, 340, 341, 342, 343, 344, 345, 347, 348, 375, 376, 377, 383, 398, 400, 404.
Methley, Rev. Mr., 507, 508.
Mitchell, Judge James, 24.
Michelet, M. 358.
Miller, Rev. Dr., 542.
Moffatt, Hon. George, 340.
Molson, Hon. Mr., 318.
Monod, M., 356, 358, 359.
Montgomery, John, 177.
Moore, Archbishop, 220.
Moore, Hugh, 211.
Morpeth, Lord, 116.
Morris, Hon. James, 337, 338.
Morris, Hon. Wm., 221, 222, 227, 228, 256, 336, 415, 455.
Morrison, Dr. T. D., 70, 118, 182.
Moseley, Rev. Mr., 163.

Moss, Mr., 163.
Mountain, Bishop, 221.
Mulkins, Rev. Hannibal, 173.
Murdoch, T. W. C., 267, 290, 312, 387.
Murray, Rev. Robt., 346, 347, 349, 350.
Murray, Sir George, 459.
Muskrat, John, 66.

McCann, Rev. Father, 593.
McCrae, Miss, 77.
McDonnell, A., 177.
McGill, Hon. Peter, 340.
McHenry, Mr., 594.
McIntyre, Rev. John, 211.
McLean, Mr. Justice, 177, 310.
McMullen, Rev. D., 210.
McMurray, Archdeacon, 77.
McOwan, 160.

Naylor, Rev. Wm., 116.
Neilson, Hon. Judge, 567.
Neilson, Mr., 257.
Nelles, Rev. Dr, 594, 598.
Newcastle, Duke of, 452, 453.
Newton, Rev. Dr. Robt., 116, 119, 162, 269, 273, 279.
Noel, Hon. and Rev. Baptist, 116, 159, 162.
Nolan, Rev. Mr., 542.
Noll, Rev. James, 212.
Normanby, Lord, 250, 251, 253.
Norris, Rev. James, 275.
Northcote, Sir Stafford, 578.
Norwich, Bishop of, 541.

Ogden, Mr. Justice, 304.
Oldham, Mr., 182.
Olin, Rev. Dr., 405.
Ormiston, Rev. Dr. 17, 597.
Osgood, Rev. Thaddeus, 75.
Ousley, Gideon, 161.

O'Callaghan, Dr., 190.
O'Connell, Daniel, 318, 323.
O'Brien, Rev. J., 77.

Packington, Sir John, 451, 452.
Palmerston, Lord, 516, 551.
Panmure, Lord (see Mr. Fox Maule).
Panteleoni, Dr,, 514, 515, 516, 517, 540.
Papineau, Hon. D. B., 337.
Papineau, Hon. L. J., 167, 168, 257, 267.
Parke, Thomas, 381.
Parsons, Rev. James, 159.
Patin, M., 358.
Patterson, Mr. James, 594.
Payer, M., 358.
Peck, Bishop Jesse T., 172.
Peel, Sir Robert, 121, 180, 291, 306, 307, 309, 311, 323, 324, 411, 551.
Perry, Peter, 156, 157, 189.
Philip, Dr., 163.
Phillips, Rev. Dr., 542.
Pitt, Rt. Hon. Wilham, 218, 219, 220, 334.
Pius IX., Pope, 361, 362, 365, 366, 367.
Playter, Rev. George, 415.
Postels, M. de, 358.
Potter, Prof., 350.
Potts, Rev. Dr., 30, 238, 573, 594, 595, 596.
Powell, Ald. J., 177.
Powell, Mr., 314.
Power, Bishop, 428.
Prince, Colonel, 338.
Prindle, Rev. Andrew, 392.
Prinsen, Mr., 354.
Punshon, Rev. Dr. W. M., 539, 543, 544, 545, 556, 557, 558, 560, 562, 564, 571, 573, 576, 577, 579, 589, 590.

Radcliffe, Mr. 127, 128, 130, 141.
Receveur, Abbe, 358.

Reece, Rev. Richard, 92, 115, 159, 162.
Reese, Rev. Dr. D. M., 279.
Reynard, Rev. Prof., 594.
Reynolds, Bishop, 383.
Rice, Rev. Dr., 576.
Richards, Sir W. B., 194, 567.
Richardson, Bishop, 40, 48, 53, 75, 78, 90, 93, 99 108, 118, 154, 183, 383.
Richey, Rev. Dr. M., 154, 209, 244, 270, 273, 387 388, 403, 404, 556, 557.
Rigg, Rev. Dr., 556, 589.
Ripon, Earl of, 118, 224, 232, 235, 386, 459.
Roads, Rev. Mr. 384.
Roaf, Rev. John, 212.
Roberts, Bishop, 269.
Robinson, Hon. Peter, 170.
—— Chief Justice, 173, 177, 200, 310, 551, 568 570.
Robinson, Hon. W. B., 567, 568.
Robinson, Mr., 162.
Roblin, John P., M.P.P., 374.
Roebuck, J. A., M.P., 167, 169, 171, 175, 228.
Rolfe, Sir R. M., 165.
Rolph, Dr. John, 127, 170, 189, 190, 288.
Rose, Rev. Dr. S., 61, 62, 594.
Routh, Sir Randolph, 340.
Rowsell, Henry, 296.
Russell, Lord John, 123, 216, 255, 260, 261, 263, 264, 267, 272, 285, 286, 378, 389, 391, 395, 435, 438, 441, 443, 451, 454, 467, 499, 516.
Ruttan, Sheriff, 348.
Ryan, Rev. Henry, 86, 87, 88, 89, 90, 131, 195, 278, 385, 557.
Ryckman, Rev. E. B., 587.
Ryerse, Major, 538.
Ryerse, Samuel, 24.
Ryerson, Rev. George, 25, 36, 37, 42, 45, 52, 53, 55, 56, 64, 67, 68, 69, 70, 79, 83, 94, 107, 108, 109, 113, 412, 534.
—— Rev. John, 25, 52, 55, 67, 86, 87, 88, 89, 109, 111, 115, 127, 128, 136, 141, 142, 147, 150, 151, 152, 154, 156, 161, 166, 171, 172, 177, 181, 183, 184, 188, 196, 199, 200, 201, 228, 239, 240, 241, 269, 270, 271, 323, 325, 328, 345, 346, 347, 348, 386, 399, 401, 402, 403, 413, 503, 507, 511, 512, 534, 573, 574, 575, 580, 585, 587.
—— Rev. William, 25, 29, 40, 52, 58, 69, 75, 78, 83, 84, 88, 111, 118, 130, 141, 142, 147, 177, 179, 228, 263, 269, 271, 272, 275, 405, 460.
Ryerson, Rev. Edwy, 69, 83, 84, 130, 133, 228, 415.
Ryerson, Mrs., Sr., 23, 25, 27, 28, 37, 42, 43, 45, 54, 55, 56, 82, 84, 139, 140, 178, 268, 358, 412.
Ryerson, Samuel, 24.
—— Colonel, 23, 24, 25, 26, 27, 28, 29, 41, 43, 44, 45, 51, 52, 55, 56, 58, 60, 61, 84, 127, 134, 178, 310, 412.
Ryerson, Lucilla Hannah, 111.
Ryland, Rev. John, 162.

Salt, Rev. Allen, 78.
Sanderson, Rev. Dr. G. R., 211, 533.
Sandon, Lord, 163, 272.
Sandwich, Dr., 159.
Saunders, Hon. J. S., 453.
Saurin, Rev. J. S., 354, 357.
Savage, Rev. D., 579.
Sawyer, Chief Joseph, 72.
Scobie, Hugh, 337, 338, 339, 341.
Scott, Rev. Jonathan, 271, 287, 294, 295.
Scott, Rev. Wm., 201, 275.
Seaton, Lord (see Sir J. Colborne).
Shaftesbury, Rt. Hon. Lord, (see Lord Ashley), 163, 542.
Sherwood, Mr. Justice, 173, 264, 304.
Sherwood Sheriff, 111.
Shiel, Rt. Hon. Richard, 516, 517.
Shuttleworth, Sir J. P. Kay, 419, 600.
Simcoe, Governor, 219, 220.
Simpson, Bishop, 556, 577.

INDEX.

Skinner, Bishop, 213.
Slater, Rev. Wm , 86.
Slight, Rev. Benjamin, 275.
Small, James E., 304.
Smart, Rev. W., 221.
Smith, Elias, 50.
Smith, Rev. Bishop Philander, 383.
Smith, Rev. Dr. Gervase, 544, 545, 571, 576, 577.
Smith, William, 336.
Snake, Wm., 77.
Sornement, M., 358.
Soule, Bishop, 269.
Spark, Dr., 216.
Spencer, Rev. James, 498, 500, 501, 502, 503, 504, 508, 509, 510, 511, 512, 513, 533.
Squire, Rev. Wm., 148.
Stanley, Right Hon. Lord, 118, 119, 123, 135, 163, 307, 331, 332, 333, 340, 381, 388, 439, 469, 539.
Stanley, Very Rev. Dean, 579.
Stanton, Mr., 311, 314.
Stead, Rev. Mr., 272.
Steer, Rev. Wm., 275.
Steinneur, Rev. Henry, 78.
Stephen, Sir James, 158, 163, 180, 228, 272.
Stewart Rev. Mr., 102, 119.
Stewart, Rt. Rev. Dr., (Bishop of Quebec), 48, 76, 103, 206, 213, 217, 222, 291, 463.
Stickney, Miss, (Mrs. Ryerson, Sen.) 23.
Stinson, Rev. Dr. Joseph, 142, 154, 174 183, 201, 204, 210, 227, 228, 237, 238, 244, 273, 337, 338, 396, 397, 401, 402.
Stoney, Rev. Edmund, 275.
Strachan, Bishop, 24, 44, 46, 47, 48, 49, 81, 83, 84, 91, 92, 95, 97, 98, 102, 103, 104, 105, 118, 125, 165, 182, 185, 195, 213, 215, 216, 217, 218, 219, 221, 222, 227, 229, 237, 239, 255, 256, 261, 262, 263, 292, 296, 299, 300, 320, 378, 379, 380, 385, 386, 389, 419, 433, 435, 436, 437, 438, 439, 441, 442, 443, 444, 445, 446, 447, 448, 449, 450, 452, 453, 455, 457, 463, 464, 566, 602, 603.
Sturge, M. P., Joseph, 154, 162, 163.
Sunday, Rev. John, 61, 77, 78, 275.
Sunegoo, Wm., 68.
Sullivan, Hon. R. B., 170, 265, 266, 289, 307, 320, 332, 333, 341, 418.
Sweatman, Bishop, 593, 580, 581, 602.
Sydenham, Lord, (C. Poulett Thompson), 193, 197, 216, 257, 258, 260, 261, 263, 264, 265, 266, 268, 282, 283, 284, 286, 287, 290, 301, 302, 303, 304, 306, 312, 313, 320, 321, 325, 331, 342, 343, 345, 346, 378, 382, 387, 388, 389, 390, 394, 395, 396, 441, 443, 550, 551.

Taylor, Rev. Dr. Lachlan, 533, 559.
Taylor, Rev. Joseph, 334.

Telfer, Rev. Mr., 595.
Thompson, C. H., 91, 195.
Thompson, Chas. Poulett (see Lord Sydenham)
Thorburn, A. B., 328.
Thyner, Father, 307.
Toase, Rev. Mr., 360.
Townley, Rev. Dr., 198.
Trevelyan, Sir Charles, 340, 376.
Turner, Rev. R. L., 153.

Usedon, Count, 540.

Vaughan, Rev. C. J., 578.
Venueil, Mons., 357.
Viger, Hon. D. B., 318, 322, 333.

Waddy, Rev. Dr., 556.
Wallace, James, 562.
Wahwahsinno, Chief, 76.
Washburn, Daniel, 188.
Waudby, John, 205.
Watson, Rev. Richard, 106, 108, 110, 280, 384, 493, 494, 495.
Waugh, Bishop, 269.
Waugh, Dr., 115.
Waugh, Rev. Mr., 119.
Wayland, Rev. Dr., 26, 431.
Wellington, Duke of, 456.
Wells, Hon. Joseph, 170.
Wenham, Dr., 79.
West, Rev. Mr., 79.
Whitehead, Rev. Thomas, 274, 276, 407, 408.
Wilkinson, Rev. Henry, 130, 214, 228.
Wilson, Mr., 176.
Wilson, Thomas, & Co., 160.
Wilmot, Lieut.-Gov., L.A., 572.
William IV., King, 118.
Williams, Rev. J. A., 587.
Willson, Hugh, 20.
Willson, Hon. John, M.P.P., 46, 195, 385, 386, 551.
Winchester, Bishop of, 116.
Wiseman, Cardinal, 420.
Wiseman, Rev. Mr., 576.
Withrow, Rev. Dr., 600.
Wolseley, Sir Garnet, 559.
Wood, Rev. Dr. Enoch, 470, 479, 480, 491, 497, 498, 503, 507, 511, 512, 533, 544, 559, 560, 589.
Wood, Rev. James, 116, 119.
Wood, Sir Charles, 515.
Wright, Rev. David, 130, 131, 228.

Yellowhead, Chief, 75, 76.
Yeomans, Rev. D., 75.
Young, Rev. E. R., 408, 409.
Young, Rev. R., 272.

INDEX TO SUBJECTS.

American General Conference of 1868, attendance at, 556.

Bagot, Government of Sir Charles, 306.
Bethune, Correspondence with Bishop, 564.
Bible, The, in Public Schools, 423, 564.
Bidwell, Defence of, 188 et seq. 306, 416, 567.
British Conference, Union with, 107 et seq. 114, 121, 141, 269.
——— Separation from, 269, 272, 277, 383.

Cartier, Sir George, Correspondence relating to, 559.
Chapel Property Cases, 172.
Christian Guardian, 93, 107, 109, 121, 131, 144, 172, 199, 201, 230, 239, et seq., 259, 269, 271.
Christian Guardian, Discussion with, 499.
Church of England, Dr. Ryerson's attitude towards, 291.
Church Property, Right of Conference to hold, 303.
Civil Rights Controversy, 81.
Class Meeting Question, 470, et seq., 491, et seq., 499.
Clergy Reserve Question, 47, 68, 81, 83, et. seq., 91, 95, et seq. 119, 155, 168, 170, 216, 218, 225, et seq., 236 et seq., 245, 250, et seq., 260 et seq., 278, 286, 300, 378, et seq., 397 et seq., 433 et seq., 454 et seq.
Confederation, Dr. Ryerson's Address on, 547.
Connecticut University, 106.
Controversy with W. L. Mackenzie, 124, 135, 145.
Controversy with Rev. W. M. Harvard, 202.
Controversies, Newspaper, 205, et seq.
Council, Legislative, 168, 170.

Denominational Colleges Controversy, 518, et seq.
Dominion, Dr. Ryerson's Address on the New, 547.
Durham, Government of Lord, 257, et seq., 312.

Early Life, Sketch of, 23.
Early Education, 24.
Education, Appointment as Chief Superintendent of, 342.
——— Retirement from Office of, 337.
Educational Administration, 352, 368, et seq.
Educational Tours, 352, 365, 371, 419, 454, 514, 539, 577.
Education, Dr. Ryerson's status in the Conference while holding Office of Chief Superintendent of, 415.
England, Visits to, 115, et seq., 121, 152, et seq., 158, 269, 272, 352, 371, 419, 454, 514, 539, 577.
Estimate of Dr. Ryerson's Character and Labours, by Rev. Dr. Ormiston, 17.
Estimates of Dr. Ryerson's Character and Work, 595, 598, 600, et seq.

Family Compact, 145.
Funeral Ceremonies, 593.

Grievance Report, 155.

Hume and Roebuck Letters, 167.

"Impressions" of England, 121, 137.
Indians, Labour among, 64, et seq.
Infant Baptism, 470, et seq., 491, et seq.

"Legion's" Letters, 341.
Loyalists, U. E., History of, 577, 585, 590.

Matrimony, Right of Methodist Ministers to Celebrate, 303.
Metcalfe, Defence of Sir Charles, 198, 312, et seq., 319, et seq., 328, et seq., 349.
Metcalfe, Administration of Sir Charles, 198, 312, et seq., 319, et seq., 328, et seq., 337, et seq., 375.
Methodist Union, 571.
Metropolitan Church, 582.
Minister, Work as, 80, 86, 149, 282, 287.
Mission to River Credit Indians, page 58, et seq.

Norfolk County, Visits to, 534.

Presidency of General Conference, 575.

Rebellion of 1837, 175, et seq., 182.
Rectories Question, 218, 225, et seq., 236, et seq., 245, 250, et seq.
Red River Expedition, 559.
Religious Experiences, 25, 30, 32, 42, 51-57, 82, 85.
Religious Instruction in Schools, 423, 564.
Responsible Government, 257, et seq.
Roebuck and Hume Letters, 167.
Ryanite Schism, 87.

School Act, 370.
Spencer, Controversy with Rev. Mr., 499.
Style, Controversial, 105.
Sydenham, Administration of Lord, 260, 284, 286, 290, 301.

Thompson, Mr. Charles Poulett, Government of, 260.

Union, Methodist, 571.
United Empire Loyalists, History of, 577, 585, 590.
University Controversy, 518, et seq.
Upper Canada Academy, 113, 152, 161, et seq., 164, et seq., 179, 301, 305, 307.

Victoria College, 113, 152, 161, et seq., 164, et seq., 179, 301, 305, 307.

OPINIONS OF THE PRESS,

OF

STATESMEN AND OTHERS,

ON

REV. DR. RYERSON'S "HISTORY OF THE LOYALISTS OF AMERICA AND THEIR TIMES, FROM 1620 TO 1816."

From the Toronto DAILY MAIL, *July 7th, 1880.*

In a lengthened review of more than two columns, the *Mail* says :

"It is with great pleasure that we introduce and commend to our readers these portly volumes, which together contain nearly a thousand pages. Dr. Ryerson deserves well of his country on account of his long and inestimable services to the cause of popular education. He is the still surviving father of our public school system, and for over thirty years directed its progress with characteristic zeal and activity. But apart from the author's public work, these volumes—the result of twenty-five years' labour—are exceedingly valuable on their own account. * * * Dr. Ryerson has performed his task with great thoroughness, inspired by a deep interest in his subject. The style is easy and flowing ; the facts stated are almost superabundantly established by reference to the authorities ; and wherever it becomes necessary to demonstrate the misrepresentations of American writers, the author's forcible way of putting the subject-matter in dispute is at once clear and cogent. In short, the narrative is interesting, whilst the arguments that crop up now and again are pointed and convincing. We had some doubts as to the venerable author's age ; but he leaves no doubt upon the point in a passage relating to the war of 1812 (Vol. II., p. 353). At the outbreak of the war, amongst the Norfolk volunteers who went with General Brock to the taking of Detroit were the elder brother and brother-in-law of the writer of these pages (he being then ten years of age). Dr. Ryerson must be consequently seventy-eight, or thereabouts ; still, as his father lived to the ripe old age of ninety-four, the author may have a long lease of life before him."

From the Hamilton EVENING TIMES, *June 12th, 1880.*

"It has been well said, that Dr. Ryerson needs no monument to perpetuate his industry, zeal, ability, and aptitude for literary work, and successful management other than the system of public and high schools of Ontario, which he may be said to have created nearly forty years ago, and nourished until 1876, when he retired from the position of Chief Superintendent of Education.

OPINIONS OF THE PRESS.

But if he do, that other monument will be found in his *History of the Loyalists of America and their Times*. This contribution to native literature is not the work of a day. It is the result of twenty-five years of more or less arduous labour and diligent inquiry. It is therefore all the more valuable and trustworthy. When one carefully examines the tersely-written pages of the two volumes comprising the History, one can, in a measure, conceive the pains taken by the venerable author to do justice to his subject. * * * The History is a mine of information. It stands alone as a voluminous authority, and will probably do so for many years. It is admirably written, thoroughly systematised, and clear and concise. It is just such a work as should adorn the shelves of every Canadian library."

From the Hamilton SPECTATOR, *June 19th, 1880.*

"No book issued in Canada in recent years is more worthy of cordial reception than the one which forms the subject of this notice. With the name of U. E. Loyalists most Canadians are familiar, but with the experience, the noble deeds, the unswerving loyalty to king and country, of those who took part in the events of the early history of America, very many are lamentably ignorant; or such knowledge as they have has been derived from unfriendly or unreliable sources. * * * The work Dr. Ryerson undertook was no light one. The time was long past when the events treated of took place, and when the actors in them could be consulted. But though the actors in the stirring scenes of our early history had passed away, there were authentic documents and records of them left behind, and these the author has searched out and consulted. The results of his researches appear as a work which must be commended for the vast amount of information it contains, its accuracy of detail, and the supplying of a want long felt and often deplored. * * * Altogether, the book is one which should be read throughout the length and breadth of Canada; and even across the sea it should, and doubtless will, find a place. The Rev. Dr. Ryerson's efforts in the cause of education have borne good fruit; it is certain that his great literary work will also accomplish high beneficial results.

"The mechanical part of the book is in every way creditable to the publishers."

From the EVANGELICAL CHURCHMAN, *Toronto, June 24th, 1880.*

"This is, without exception, the most important and elaborate historical work which has yet issued from the Canadian press. The incidents of the memorable struggle, which resulted in the separation of the colonies from the Empire, are given in nervous and graphic language, and shed a flood of light on the contest itself. The subsequent privations and sufferings of the "United Empire Loyalists" are most vividly portrayed. Their settlement in this and other Provinces are feelingly and touchingly described. Reminiscences, recollections and experiences of expatriated Loyalists are also given, and illustrations of the hardships endured by them are related in the work by many of the living descendants of these Loyalists. This portion of the history is deeply interesting and instructive, but space forbids us to enter into it. Our readers cannot do better than possess themselves of these entertaining volumes, which we most cordially commend as a most valuable addition to our colonial historical literature."

OPINIONS OF THE PRESS.

From the Toronto CHRISTIAN GUARDIAN, *July 14th, 1880.*

"This new book by the venerable Dr. Ryerson is the most important literary work of his life. It fitly crowns a career of unusual intellectual activity with a standard history of the formative period of Anglo-American civilization. The range and scope of the work are much wider than most persons would suppose from the announcement. Most people looked for a work that would be mainly made up of biographical sketches of the U. E. Loyalist pioneer in the settlement of Canada. But Dr. Ryerson goes back to the beginning, and traces the whole origin and growth of the English in America, the relation of the Colonists to the Home Government, the character and doings of the Colonial Governments, and the political causes which produced dissatisfaction, and ultimately led to rebellion and independence.

"The first thing that strikes us in examining this work is the evidence it presents of extensive research, in the examination of original documents, and consequently the extent to which it must be a valuable repertory of important historic facts for future historians of American civilization.

"One thing that invests this work with special interest to all Canadians and Britons is that nearly all the histories of the United States, as well as the popular literature of that country, glorify the deeds and character of all who took a part in the Revolutionary war, on the Republican side ; but the Loyalists who could not feel justified in fighting against their Sovereign and country, are uniformly painted in the blackest colours, as if they were cowardly and base wretches who had no redeeming qualities. All that is hateful and mean is suggested by the word 'Tory' or 'Royalist' in the annals of the United States. They have never had fair play ; because they were generally painted by those who bitterly hated them. But while the author admits fully the folly and unconstitutional despotism that goaded the colonists into rebellion, and the patriotic feeling of many on the Republican side, no one can read his work without feeling that great injustice has been done to the Loyalists, whose wrong acts were generally provoked by the relentless persecution of the other party. In the light of the real facts, it does not appear criminal or discreditable that they were unwilling to join in open war against the land of their fathers and the Government to which they owed allegiance. * * * The account of the war of 1812 will possess still greater interest for Canadians. The part played by the people of Canada at that time, in resolutely resisting an unjustifiable invasion, made by a greatly superior power, at a time when England was contending almost single-handed against the immense forces Napoleon I. had combined against her ; and the fact that eleven different attacks were repelled without loss of territory, are achievements of which Canadians have no need to be ashamed.

From the Montreal GAZETTE, *June 26th, 1880.*

In the course of an elaborate review of three columns of this work, the editor of the *Montreal Gazette*, June 26th, 1880, says :

"This most important work, whose approach to completion we had the pleasure some months ago of announcing to our readers, is now an accomplished fact, and the people of Canada will have an opportunity of gratifying their desire for a full and fair history of one of the most interesting and meritorious elements of our population. For the laborious, and in some respects perilous task of writing such a history, few, if any, of our prominent men of learning could have been so well fitted as Dr. Ryerson. Himself the son of a leading Loyalist, of a family which had given Canada many men of earnest thought and strenuous act, familiar from his childhood with the traditions of those heroic settlers who were mainly the founders of his native Province, and having himself had no small share in extending the progress and perpetuating the prosperity of which, at the cost of their fortunes and the risk of their lives, they laid the firm basis, he was indignantly conscious of the many calumnies propagated by hostile pens, from which, for nearly a century, they had suffered almost undefended. Not alone, indeed. Happily there were others also who longed to see the story of the Loyalists written by an impartial and skilful hand. And when those who represent what was best in the public life, the literature, the pulpit and the press of the two united Provinces a quarter of a century ago, looked around on each other and beyond their own circle for a person to whom they might entrust the performance of so needed a duty, they unanimously fixed upon the Superintendent of Education of Upper Canada as that person. Thus selected, and not unmoved, besides, by potent inward urgings, Dr. Ryerson accepted the honourable but difficult charge." [Then follows an analysis of the principal facts and arguments of the work.]

From the MORNING CHRONICLE, *Halifax, Nova Scotia, August 4th, 1880.*

"This is undoubtedly one of the most notable of recent works from the press of Canada. It is a work of such interest as to its subject, and, we must add, of such merit as to its execution, that no proper justice can be done to it in any such review as can be afforded within the limited eligible space of a daily newspaper."

From the MORNING HERALD, *Halifax, N. S., July 24th and August 4th, 1880.*

The *Herald* devotes two articles in review of this work, commencing with the following words :

"The author of this work is so well known to the people of this country, that any publication in which his name appears is a sufficient guarantee of its value, its accuracy, and the interesting nature of its contents. No work ever published in Canada is more worthy of a cordial reception from our people than the 'Loyalists of America and their Times,' and none will be read with more intense interest by the descendants of those noble men and women, 'who, stripped of their rights and property during the war, * * * were driven from the homes of their birth and of their forefathers,' because of their loyalty to their king, to seek new homes in the (then) wilderness of Nova Scotia and New Brunswick."

N.B.—Numerous other notices, of a similar character to the above, are said to have appeared in various provincial newspapers.

OPINIONS OF THE PRESS.

LETTER FROM SIR STAFFORD NORTHCOTE.

"79 PORTLAND PLACE, July 26th, 1880.

"MY DEAR SIR,

"I ought long ago to have thanked you for so kindly sending me your work on the 'Loyalists,' but I have been so busy since it came that I have had little time for reading. I have been much interested with it, and am very much obliged for it.

"Believe me, yours very faithfully,
(Signed)   "STAFFORD H. NORTHCOTE."

LETTER FROM LORD CARNARVON.

"HIGHCLERE CASTLE, NEWBURY, Sept. 1st, 1880.

"MY DEAR SIR,

"I have received the 'History of the Loyalists of America' which you have been good enough to send me. I have as yet only been able to turn the pages, but before long I hope to find the leisure to become acquainted with the contents of these two volumes, of which I have seen enough in my rapid glance to be sure that they embrace not only much that is most interesting, but in a historical point of view very valuable matter.

"I remain, my dear Sir, yours faithfully,
(Signed)   "CARNARVON."

LETTER FROM ALPHEUS TODD, ESQ., LIBRARIAN OF THE HOUSE OF COMMONS.

"OTTAWA, September 16th, 1880.

"MY DEAR DR. RYERSON,

"I have just returned from a visit to England, much refreshed. I found your two interesting volumes on my desk, and am very grateful for your kind remembrance of me. I shall prize them highly.

"We have all reason for congratulation that you have completed this great book, which is a noble retrospect of the loyalty of our forefathers. I earnestly hope that it may be the means of quickening and strengthening the present generation in this land in the endeavour to render themselves worthy of the noble inheritance that the zeal and devotion of our ancestors obtained for us, and that it will deepen our attachment to the British Crown and Imperial connection.

"Always with much respect and regard,
"Your sincere friend,
(Signed)   "ALPHEUS TODD."

OPINIONS OF THE PRESS.

LETTER FROM HIS EXCELLENCY THE MARQUIS OF LORNE.

"CITADEL, QUEBEC, June 10th, 1880.

" MY DEAR DR. RYERSON,

"I have to-day received your most welcome gift, and hasten to tell you my gratitude for what was to me a very pleasant surprise—a surprise, for I had not heard that you were engaged in the task you have now completed, and had I heard it, I could not have expected the kindness which has made me the recipient from the author of such a full and extremely interesting history.

" It should become a household book in Canada ; and I can well imagine the delight it will give to those who are able through the work, as you have been in its composition, to trace the actions and live again in sympathy with the thoughts of heroic ancestors.

" Believe me, with very many thanks,

"Yours very truly,
(Signed) " LORNE."

LETTER FROM LORD DUFFERIN.

" ST. PETERSBURG, September 6th, 1880.

" MY DEAR DR. RYERSON,

" I have just received your two beautiful volumes. I cannot tell you how grateful I am to you for your kind thought of me. There is no present I value more than that of a book from its author. Indeed, I have now a very interesting library composed of volumes given to me at different times by the various distinguished men of the present generation whom I have had the happiness to know, and your work will find an honoured place upon its shelves.

"You well know how fully I understand and appreciate all that you have done for education in Canada, and that there are few people in the Dominion for whom I have always entertained a greater regard or respect.

" Believe me, my dear Dr. Ryerson,

"Yours most sincerely,
(Signed) " DUFFERIN "

Canadian Methodism:

ITS

EPOCHS AND CHARACTERISTICS,

WRITTEN AT THE REQUEST OF THE

LONDON, TORONTO, AND MONTREAL CONFERENCES.

BY THE

REV. EGERTON RYERSON, D.D., LL.D.

This Volume is elegantly bound in Extra English Cloth, with ink and gold stamping, 12mo. size, containing 448 pages,

WITH STEEL PORTRAIT,

PRICE $1.25.

THIS Volume is not a mere reprint of the Essays that appeared in the Magazine from month to month, but contains a large amount of new matter which has not heretofore appeared.

It possesses also, to the many admirers of its beloved and honoured author, a melancholy interest, as being the latest production of that pen which, during a long and busy life, was ever wielded in defence of civil and religious liberty.

☞ Agents wanted to sell this important Work. ☜

Address—

WILLIAM BRIGGS, PUBLISHER,

78 & 80 King St. East, Toronto.

The Loyalists of America
AND
THEIR TIMES.
BY THE
REV. EGERTON RYERSON, D.D., LL.D.,
Chief Superintendent of Education for Upper Canada from 1844 to 1876.

THIS book is one of national importance. It is the most ample and minute account of the U. E. Loyalists and their Times which has hitherto been published. It describes very fully the early Colonial History of America, and traces the important distinction, often overlooked, between the Pilgrim Fathers and the Puritan Fathers in New England, who maintained separate Governments for seventy years. The religious persecutions of the Quakers and other dissidents from Puritan creed and civil constitution are reviewed, and the stern intolerance of the latter is shown. The fortunes of the Colonies under the Long Parliament, the Commonwealth, and the Restoration, are carefully traced. The prolonged conflict between France and England for the possession of the Continent, with its battles, sieges, and adventurous campaigns is given in detail. The growing estrangement between Great Britain and the Colonies, and the stormy events of the Revolutionary War, are recounted. This epoch is very fully discussed from a British Loyalist point of view. The author avows his sympathy with the colonists in their assertion of their rights as British subjects, and avers his belief that but for their revolutionary Declaration of Independence they would within a twelvemonth have obtained all that they desired without the shedding of blood, without the unnatural alliance with France, much less a war of seven years. But the outbreak and conduct of the war are emphatically condemned.

No portion of this history will be read with greater interest than that which describes the sufferings, in maintaining their allegiance to their King, of the U. E. Loyalist Founders and Fathers of Canada. For the first time, the full and detailed account of these sufferings is now published. The account of the early development and organization of the Government of the Maritime Provinces and of Upper Canada is full and minute. The stirring events of the War of 1812-15 are also given with much copiousness of detail. The grand patriotism of our country, struggling against tremendous odds, is amply asserted and illustrated.

To this work the venerable author has devoted several of the best years of his life. Of U. E. Loyalist stock himself, he writes with hearty sympathy with his subject. He has devoted many years to the study of historical and constitutional questions. He has made laborious and extensive research. And he furnishes in these volumes copious documentary evidence of the validity of his assertions and conclusions.

It is beautifully printed on extra calendered paper, and forms

TWO HANDSOME OCTAVO VOLUMES,
containing 1,055 pages, with Steel Portrait of the Author. Strongly bound

IN EXTRA ENGLISH CLOTH, - - - - - $5 00
IN HALF MOROCCO, - - - - - - 7 00

AGENTS WANTED.
Address for particulars,

WILLIAM BRIGGS, PUBLISHER,
78 & 80 KING STREET EAST, TORONTO.

www.ingramcontent.com/pod-product-compliance
Lightning Source LLC
Chambersburg PA
CBHW021226300426
44111CB00007B/434